THE MIRACLE OF AMSTERDAM

THE MIRACLE
OF AMSTERDAM

Biography of a Contested Devotion

CHARLES CASPERS and **PETER JAN MARGRY**

University of Notre Dame Press
Notre Dame, Indiana

Published by the University of Notre Dame Press
Notre Dame, Indiana 46556
undpress.nd.edu

Published in the United States of America

Originally published by Prometheus Amsterdam as *Het Mirakel van Amsterdam: Biografie van een Betwiste Devotie.* © 2017 Charles Caspers and Peter Jan Margry

Library of Congress Cataloging-in-Publication Data

Names: Caspers, Charles, 1953- author. | Margry, P. J. (Peter Jan), author.
Title: The miracle of Amsterdam : biography of a contested devotion /
Charles Caspers and Peter Jan Margry.
Other titles: Mirakel van Amsterdam. English
Description: Notre Dame, Indiana : University of Notre Dame Press, [2019] |
Translation of: Het mirakel van Amsterdam : biografie van een betwiste devotie. |
Includes bibliographical references and index. |
Identifiers: LCCN 2019011954 (print) | LCCN 2019017018 (ebook) |
ISBN 9780268105686 (pdf) | ISBN 9780268105679 (epub) |
ISBN 9780268105655 (hardback : alk. paper) | ISBN 0268105650
(hardback : alk. paper)
Subjects: LCSH: Processions, Religious—Catholic Church—Netherlands—
Amsterdam. | Miracles—Netherlands—Amsterdam—History.
Classification: LCC BX2324.N4 (ebook) | LCC BX2324.N4 C37313 2019 (print) |
DDC 282/.492—dc23
LC record available at https://lccn.loc.gov/2019011954

∞ This book is printed on acid-free paper.

Contents

Introduction

Each year in March, a large group of silent men and women walk through the city center of Amsterdam at night. Their walk is called the "Silent Walk." The Silent Walk is—or was—a household name for many Catholics in Amsterdam and elsewhere in the Netherlands, something they looked forward to every year. For generations, tens of thousands of men (women were only allowed to take part later) from across the country traveled to the capital to demonstrate their devotion to the Miracle of Amsterdam and their loyalty to the Dutch Catholic Church by walking in the dark, without any external display, and to the sound only of their footsteps. Their numbers and their silence impressed outsiders. A present-day uninitiated observer who encounters the Walk on the street at night will feel puzzled: what on earth are those people doing? For the participants themselves it is often a fascinating experience that stimulates the senses. In the past, it was not only the ritual of the Walk that invited contention and discord in Dutch society, but also the cult of the Miracle itself, which regularly became the subject of controversy during the almost seven centuries of its existence.

Because the Walk is not a formalized ritual—nothing is said and no one carries any attributes—every participant is left to his or her own devices. Uniquely for the Netherlands and for Western Europe, this makes the annual Silent Walk the largest collective expression of individual religiosity. The paradox is clear: a prayer and meditation walk made by individuals, but in connection with each other and with others. It was not always like this. Until after World War II, it was also a protest march against the subordination of Catholics in society. Although the position of Catholics has changed completely since then, the Walk has always retained something of its protest-march character. It has widened its scope.

When it was established in 1881, it was open to Catholic men, and from 1966 to Catholic men and women, but it is currently open to men and women of all Christian denominations, and even to all people who wish to take part discretely in this "meditative and spiritual" walk.

The Silent Walk has roots that go much further back than 1881. According to tradition, on the night of March 15 to 16, 1345, a miracle took place in a house on Kalverstraat in Amsterdam. A host that was thrown into the burning fireplace was hours later found intact. To commemorate that God had worked a miracle in this place, a chapel was erected over the spot, bearing the unambiguous name of "Holy Stead" or holy place. None of this was very remarkable for the time: reports of Eucharistic miracles came from various places during the later Middle Ages, and chapels and other shrines were built quite frequently, often to accommodate a particular cult. But the citizens of Amsterdam—not just the "ordinary faithful," but also the clergy and the city authorities—became exceptionally devoted to their Holy Stead. Together with the many pilgrims who came from outside the city, they turned the chapel into the richest church in the city. All the city's militias, craftsmen's guilds, religious, and schoolchildren participated in the processions with the miraculous host that passed through the city annually or more frequently. In addition, individual devotees would walk around the chapel a number of times praying in silence, at night or in the early morning.

In the sixteenth century, the age of the Reformation, the Holy Stead was no longer a unifying force; on the contrary, it contributed to the divisions that were occurring. The cult became a source of mental support for the Catholic part of the population, the part that remained loyal to the sovereign, Philip II. This situation continued until the so-called Alteration of 1578, when a coup brought Amsterdam into the ranks of the insurgents. The new authorities confiscated the Holy Stead from the Catholics and rebaptized it Nieuwezijds Kapel (Chapel on the New Side). But the homeless cult survived the seventeenth and eighteenth centuries, the period of the Republic of the United Netherlands. The hidden church in the Amsterdam beguinage or Begijnhof in effect became an alternative Holy Stead, and individual Catholics continued to carry out their circumambulations of the old Holy Stead. For Protestants, the cult remained an important source of irritation and an object of scorn.

During the nineteenth century, the Roman Catholics in the Netherlands successfully—though not without setbacks—claimed the status of full citizens. We would like to single out two important milestones along the road: the fifth centenary of the Miracle of Amsterdam, celebrated in

1845, and the establishment of the Silent Walk in 1881. The centenary year saw the rise of a revived historical and religious interest in the old cult. The Silent Walk was one fruit of this renewed interest, and—something its two initiators would never have been able to imagine—it developed into Dutch Catholicism's symbol and ritual of unity par excellence. It created in the end a national pilgrimage to Amsterdam, constituting at the same time a national symbol for Dutch Catholicism in its emancipation struggle.

Much has already been written about the long history of the Miracle of Amsterdam, from the miracle in 1345 to the present-day Silent Walk. This is partly because a relatively large number of sources has been preserved, making it an attractive subject for cultural and religious historians. An even more important reason is that in the past, Catholic historians especially felt the need to document and narrate the history of the Miracle cult so as to give legitimacy to its continuation. On the whole we believe there is good reason to publish the current book. The wide range of literature, its diversity, and the fact that so many leaflets, articles, sermons, books, and so on are often difficult to find calls for a new survey, with new analyses. This book then is intended to be a synthesis, based on the work of previous generations of historians and complemented with new research of the sources—especially in the last two chapters, which deal with the Silent Walk.

There is a second reason for writing this book: the historiography of Dutch Catholicism shows an important lacuna. One of the historiographical monuments in this field, a book that was awarded the Netherlands' most prestigious literary prize (the P. C. Hooft Prize), is the voluminous *In vrijheid herboren* (Reborn in freedom), published in 1953 and subsequently reworked by one of its authors, Louis Rogier († 1974) in 1956, resulting in a revised second edition published under the title of *Katholieke herleving* (Catholic revival).[1] In it, Rogier describes the social and cultural emancipation of Dutch Catholics during the nineteenth and early twentieth centuries. In our view, Rogier should have also paid attention to the nineteenth-century revival of the Amsterdam Miracle cult, and, by extension, to the wider devotional mobilization of Dutch Catholics and the national significance of the cult. This omission is all the more remarkable because he had a keen eye for new and ostensibly idiosyncratic developments in popular Catholicism.[2]

The more recent follow-up to Rogier's book, a collaborative study published in 1999 under the title of *Tot vrijheid geroepen* (Called to freedom), which deals with Dutch Catholicism since World War II, commits the same sin of omission and more generally embodies a denial of the significance of cults and popular religiosity for the church and for society. This is particularly unfortunate because the book deals with the very period in which the Silent Walk reached its quantitative peak, in the immediate postwar years. Not only are the Miracle cult and the Silent Walk frequently overlooked in histories of Catholicism, they have also been ignored in nineteenth- and twentieth-century "revival" and cultural history.[3]

The third reason for publishing this book is the place that the Miracle of Amsterdam occupies within the larger context of Western European cultural and religious history. We have thus far briefly summarized the Silent Walk's long antecedents, starting with the Amsterdam cult's foundational miracle in 1345. We will now highlight a number of aspects of this long history that are important from a comparative perspective.

In the later Middle Ages, the Miracle quickly became a pillar of civic identity in Amsterdam. This process had certain unique features, but in one form or another similar developments also occurred in other European cities in the later Middle Ages.[4] At the time, every city in the Low Countries, but also in the German Empire, England, France, and elsewhere, wanted to be able to boast of some special divine blessing, and citizens expressed this in the form of great processions on the feast days of the Virgin Mary or another saint, or, as in Amsterdam, on Corpus Christi.[5] One unique aspect is the long-lasting divergence of opinion between Amsterdam's Catholic and Protestant citizens, with the Miracle as a major bone of contention. As in other European countries, the religious conflict had turned the tide in favor of the strongest party—the Protestants in the Dutch case. But while the conflict elsewhere in Europe often led to the forced migration of large parts of the population, a certain equilibrium between the various confessions was established in the Republic.

Despite deep-seated religious differences, mutual irritations, and contrasting expectations of the future, Protestants and Catholics had an interest in developing ways of getting along with each other in everyday life. In addition to social and economic factors, the tolerant climate promoted by the urban elite played an important role in this. It was this climate that could see the Amsterdam poet Joost van den Vondel († 1679) proclaimed the "prince of poets" by the interdenominational Saint Luke's Guild of artists and writers after initial rejection by his Protestant literary friends due to his conversion to Catholicism and his publication of a panegyric on the Miracle (on the occasion of its third centenary). The example is also illustrative of the so-called multiconfessionalism and "ecumenism of everyday life" that are often averred in historiography, that is, the coexistence, desired or tolerated by the government, of various religious groups in a city or province alongside the dominant Reformed Church.[6] Thus the spiritual and religious divisions, for instance in respect of the Miracle, could persist without affecting the existing societal structures.

During the nineteenth and twentieth centuries, the various confessional groups in the Netherlands increasingly began to delineate themselves from one another socially, culturally, and politically. As this process led to the division of society as a whole into blocks or pillars, it is known in Dutch historiography as "pillarization."[7] Two phases can be distinguished in this process: proto-pillarization, from the early nineteenth century up to around 1870,[8] and classical Dutch pillarization, between approximately 1870 and 1970. During this second phase, the Netherlands witnessed social segregation along ideological and confessional lines across the full breadth of society. The specific confession or ideology professed was the foundational principle of life within these pillars, much more so than social class or regional culture.

We have used this metaphor of pillarization primarily for the Catholic community and its sometimes near-autarkic character. In their drive for equality and emancipation, Catholics closed ranks and accepted a high level of organization. The notion of pillarization took on an even sharper political dimension between 1890 and 1910 as the socialist movement emerged alongside the Protestant and Catholic groups, in addition to a fourth, smaller liberal segment.[9] Confronted with this new reality, the various groups were willing, despite their heartfelt aversion to each other, to shift alliances to achieve their political objectives. The acrimony of their exchanges sometimes took on extreme forms, leading to major and minor culture wars. The cult of the Miracle stood in the very center of the battleground, making it a showpiece of the history of multiconfessionalism. The demolition of the Holy Stead in 1908 can count as the lowest point in already icy relations between Dutch Catholics and Protestants. After the middle of the twentieth century the adversarial atmosphere rapidly dissipated, disappearing altogether as the secularization, or rather dechristianization, of Dutch society progressed.[10]

Our synthesis, which we have conceived as a cultural biography, is intended to complement the lacunae mentioned above by describing how, for nearly seven centuries, the Miracle cult and the Silent Walk were an important constituent of the identity, first of an urban society, Amsterdam, and later of a large part of the national population, the Roman Catholic community in the Netherlands. Our approach is inspired not by an institutional, church historical, or theological view of history, but by the perspective of New Cultural History and ethnology.[11] This means specifically that we have looked not only at great events, such as princely visits or papal grants of indulgence, but also at seemingly trivial facts, "ordinary" rituals, symbols, patterns of behavior, and so on. We believe that it is precisely this kind of integrated approach that can yield information on how the citizens of Amsterdam, Holland, and the Netherlands interpreted the Miracle, how they allowed their thinking and behavior to be influenced by it, and what effects this had on society at large.

The name of the Amsterdam Stille Omgang is sometimes translated into English as "Silent Procession," but this is an unfortunate choice in the religious and ecclesiastical context of the cult and therefore of this book. The collective march that emerged in the nineteenth century was intended *not* to be a church "procession," either in format or performance, nor could it legally be a procession at all. It was a "march," a "circumambulation" or "circuition" of people who walked in silence without displaying any ecclesiastical or religious signs or items. In 1881, the individual prayer walks that Catholics had long been making were transformed into a formal collective Silent Walk, which we have capitalized to highlight the change.

This cultural biography of the Netherlands' only national pilgrimage is the fruit of our long common interest in and study of the Miracle of Amsterdam.[12] We would like to thank Peter Raedts (Nijmegen), Maarten Elsenburg (Aerdenhout), and Piet Hein Hupsch (Amsterdam) for their critical reading of and comments on the manuscript, our colleagues Leonard Primiano (Radnor) and Daniel Wojcik (Eugene), who helped us with a number of substantive issues, and the former also for putting us in touch with University of Notre Dame Press, where publisher Stephen Little willingly accepted our manuscript proposal. A special word of thanks is due to Brian Heffernan (Brussels), for his exemplary English translation of the original Dutch, and to Maarten Elsenburg, for his commitment to realizing an English translation. It is now for the reader to marvel at the impact on history of the Miracle of Amsterdam—a piece of consecrated unleavened bread that failed to burn.

Amsterdam, December 6, 2018
CC & PJM

Creation and Expansion of a Cult (1345–1500)

The Rise of Amsterdam

In the Low Countries by the sea, the thirteenth century brought impressive population growth and the proliferation of cities. Many dozens of settlements, especially in the counties of Flanders and Holland and in the duchy of Brabant, rapidly transformed into what were, by the standards of the time, real cities. One of these settlements was Amsterdam, located very advantageously along the Amstel river. The rich yields of its fishing and trade activities permitted Amsterdam to distinguish itself ever more clearly from the surrounding countryside. In 1300 the de facto autonomy that it had acquired received confirmation from the count in a charter, which was official recognition of Amsterdam's status as a city. The young city prospered. Before the end of the fourteenth century, its distinctive layout was in place with the Oude Zijde (Old Side) on the east bank of the Amstel and the Nieuwe Zijde (New Side) on the west bank. While populations were contracting in large parts of Europe as a result, inter alia, of the great plague epidemic of 1347 to 1348, the citizens of Amsterdam trebled in number, from around one thousand people circa 1300 to around three thousand circa 1400. The growth did not slacken in the fifteenth century. Their number trebled again, and Amsterdam joined the other five cities of Holland—Delft, Dordrecht, Gouda, Haarlem, and Leiden—represented on the count's advisory council, the States of Holland, based in The Hague. The city experienced a veritable boom in the sixteenth century. Even before the beginning of the Dutch Revolt in 1568, the population had trebled once again, and the city managed mostly to dodge the subsequent ravages of war, despite serious "troubles." Between 1585 and 1665, during Holland's so-called Golden Age, Amsterdam's famous canal belt was built, a feature inscribed on UNESCO's list of World Heritage Sites in 2010.[1]

When Amsterdam was still a young, small city, it was the scene of a reported miracle. During Lent in the year 1345, a man fell seriously ill in a house on Kalverstraat in the south of the Nieuwe Zijde, an area called Bindwijk.[2] Fearing that the end would soon come, he summoned the parish priest, who administered last communion or viaticum—originally this meant "travel money"—at the point of transition from earthly to eternal life. Shortly afterward the sick man had to throw up, and the vomit, which contained the host, was cast into the fire that was burning in the fireplace. The following day, a radiant and intact host was found in the fire. This miracle soon attracted attention, and a chapel called the Holy Stead was built on the site. Until the Alteration of 1578, the citizens of Amsterdam cherished their Holy Stead; pilgrims came from across Holland and beyond to perform their devotions in this place.

During the course of the centuries, the founding miracle of the Holy Stead was narrated and iconographically represented countless times, and it will be discussed in greater detail in this chapter, followed by a typology of Eucharistic miracles and a history of the veneration of the Miracle up to the end of the fifteenth century. First, however, we will discuss the religious context and the symbols that were commonly used at the time. This will provide us with the instruments to interpret the miracle and its perception, and to explain why the Miracle became so important to the citizens of Amsterdam. What did communion, usually called "the Sacrament," mean to people at the time? And what value did the viaticum have to them? What was the meaning of fire, especially considering that the fireplace where the Miracle occurred has since played an important role in the history of the devotion? And from where did the oddly unspecific description "Holy Stead" come?

Religious Context

The fact that practically all inhabitants of the Low Countries were Christians in the late Middle Ages implies that religious and social life overlapped to a considerable degree. Thus, both the ecclesiastical and the civic authorities concerned themselves with enforcing the commandment to honor Sundays and feast days. In addition to the fifty-two Sundays, the diocese of Utrecht, to which Holland belonged, had some sixty holy days of obligation a year, that is, days on which the faithful were required to focus on God and his saints and to abstain from work. Because they shared the same liturgical calendar, the inhabitants of the cities and villages of the northern provinces of the Low Countries lived according to the same schedule: memorable events were usually dated by reference to the feast rather than the day of the month. This uniformity automatically also highlighted the differences. The cities of Holland, for instance, celebrated not only the feast days prescribed for the entire diocese, but also the commemoration of the consecration of their most important parish church. This was the day that "kermis" was held, an event that drew many visitors from outside.[3]

In addition, some cities observed one or more special feast days because they possessed an important relic or a miraculous statue. These feasts attracted visitors in droves, including pilgrims. Because the influx of crowds occasioned all kinds of economic and trading activities and benefited the city coffers, organizing a great celebration was as much a concern of the city authorities as of the church.[4] Every city was eager to have one or more of these feasts connected to a particular saint, although the diocese discouraged it because all these local feasts distracted from the common calendar. A successful cult contributed to the status of a city in both spiritual (the city had received special graces from God) and material (extra revenue) ways.

Feasts were marked by processions, the organization of which was usually a matter for city and church together. This was especially the case for the procession on Corpus Christi.[5] This feast will be discussed further on in this chapter, but it must be mentioned here on account of the date on which it was introduced in the different dioceses. For the diocese of Utrecht, it is certain that Corpus Christi was celebrated in the cathedral city itself before 1330, and that Eucharistic processions were held there before 1343. The rest of the diocese, including Amsterdam, would have followed suit, as parishes generally conformed to the cathedral church's liturgical calendar.[6] This means that when the Miracle of Amsterdam occurred, the faithful, or at least the clergy, would already have been acquainted with the relatively new feast of Corpus Christi and possibly also with the phenomenon of the Eucharistic procession, which was distinctive because it involved carrying around a host. But to be able to interpret the Miracle, it is also important to know whether the faithful were familiar with the Eucharistic devotion of which Corpus Christi was but one offshoot.

From about the middle of the thirteenth century, Western Christianity (priests, religious, and laypeople) had one central focus, despite—or perhaps because of—the colorful variety of religious practices that existed: the sacrament of the Eucharist. The medieval church regarded sacraments as instruments of grace that had been instituted by Christ himself. Among the Roman Catholic Church's seven sacraments—baptism, confirmation, Eucharist, confession, matrimony, holy orders, and the anointing of the sick—the sacrament of the Eucharist or of the Lord's Supper was reckoned to be the most important, because according to the church's doctrine it was the only one to contain Christ himself. The administering of this sacrament was reserved to priests, who celebrated mass, a ritual repetition of the Last Supper. During mass, the priest distributed a round, flat, white piece of unleavened bread to the faithful for consumption: the host (this word originally means "sacrificial lamb"). In this manner the faithful participated in what is called in theological language the "Mystical body of Christ," hence the terms "communion" and "the body of Christ," sometimes used to designate the host.[7]

The church used catechetic instruction, preaching, liturgy, and devout texts to explain to the faithful that communion was the manner par excellence by which they could enter eternal life once their earthly life ended. According to the religious code of the time, a believer who lived a sincere life according to the virtues of faith, hope, and charity could unite in a spiritual way with Christ by receiving communion—that is, by consuming a host. In the words of the church father Augustine, repeated innumerable times, communion was spiritual food, and there was a fundamental distinction between ordinary food and spiritual food: "You shall not change me, like the food of your flesh into yourself, but you shall be changed into my likeness," so that our spirit becomes alike to God.[8]

This concept of the Sacrament as spiritual nourishment was embraced with particular ardor among certain groups, such as the beguines, but it also posed problems for many, and perhaps most, believers. A classic formulation attributes to sacred things the power to fascinate and to terrify.[9] In this case, the faithful knew the importance of communicating, but at the same time they were reluctant to do so. According to the religious notions of the time, someone who communicated unworthily ate his own "condemnation," calling down eternal damnation (hell) upon him- or herself.[10] The faithful were so fearful that the ecclesiastical authorities felt compelled to strictly enforce the requirement that every believer should communicate at least once a year, at Easter. But the custom that everyone received last communion, viaticum, was more widespread. This gave rise to the peculiar situation that earnest believers—a famous example was Geert Grote—ardently longed for communion, but never dared to receive it until they were on their deathbed.[11] The oft-repeated reassurance given by spiritual writers that it was better to communicate out of charity than to abstain out of fear failed to persuade them. In certain Calvinist churches in the Netherlands, abstaining from communion, from partaking of the Lord's Supper, is still a common phenomenon.[12]

The chasm between God and human beings in religious experience thus risked becoming unbridgeable, and a solution was found in simplicity. Someone who prepared for communion interiorly could expect and trust that this process in itself was sufficient to partake of the sacrament or, in other words, that he or she was communicating without consuming the host. This purely interior act of faith, which was called spiritual communion, could be done at any time and in any place, but there were two favorite moments for it. The first was during the elevation at mass, when the priest repeated the words Christ had spoken at the Last Supper, "This is my body" (Hoc est corpus meum), while elevating the host to show it to the congregation (ocular communion). The second moment for spiritual communion was when the priest brought a consecrated host to the home of a sick person.

In the thirteenth and fourteenth centuries, last communion increasingly became the most important aspect of individual pastoral care, especially in the dioceses of the Low Countries. The specific procedure that was followed can be inferred from a number of synodal statutes issued by the bishop of Cambrai, Guiard de Laon, around 1240, which were subsequently adopted with minor adaptations by other dioceses. These statutes, paraphrased below, help us to better interpret the Miracle of Amsterdam:[13]

- When a sick person wishes to receive communion, the priest will first visit him without the body of Christ and, if possible, will hear his confession. He will then return to the church to ring the bell. In this way he calls on the faithful to follow him as he carries their Lord from the church to the sick person's home. On the way there and back they should pray for the sick person.
- Preceded by an acolyte, the priest enters the sick person's home; the faithful stay and wait for him. Then they return to the church together; the priest continues to carry the body of Christ so that the people can adore it. Those who intentionally disturb the procession should be punished.[14]

- If the sick person throws up after receiving communion, the remains of the host will be gathered carefully, to the extent that this is possible, and are then consumed by the priest together with some wine. The rest of the discharge is burned and buried beside the altar.
- When the body of Christ passes, the faithful along the route must kneel, beat their breasts, and pray with heads bowed and hands folded. Riders must not consider themselves above dismounting their horses; they should adore Him, who descended for them from heaven.

This last provision shows that not only the ordinary faithful but also noblemen were expected to show their respect. There was an entire genre of stories in the late Middle Ages about giving honor to the viaticum as a gauge of the veracity of someone's faith.[15] The next chapter will show how the Habsburgs even traced back the divine election of their princely house to the honor one of their predecessors had once given to a priest carrying viaticum.[16]

Receiving viaticum was considered to be so important that making sure that it would be available could be a reason for a bishop to found a new parish. More parishes meant shorter average distances for the priests, who would be able to reach the homes of their parishioners more quickly.[17] Townsmen especially became convinced of the importance of this ritual for their eternal salvation because even though they communicated at most once a year, they would regularly see how a priest and a number of the faithful walked in procession, carrying the viaticum.[18] Now that we have considered this background, it is time to look again at the Miracle, which was said to have happened in Amsterdam in 1345, only a few decades after the local church of Saint Nicholas was elevated to the status of parish church.[19]

The Miracle

Several fourteenth-century testimonies have been preserved concerning the founding miracle of the Holy Stead, either in their original form or as a fifteenth-century copy. Three copies made around 1442 contain the text of older charters (from 1346 and 1347) in which episcopal authorities confirm the miracle.[20] One original source dating from 1378, also in the form of a charter, not only confirms but also gives an account of the miracle, albeit very succinctly. A translation of this short report, not yet influenced by later legend, appears below. It is a passage from a petition sent by the acting lord of the Netherlands, Duke Albert of Bavaria († 1404), and his spouse, Margaret of Brieg († 1386), to the newly elected Avignon pope, Clement VII:[21]

> When in the city of Amsterdam in Holland, in the diocese of Utrecht, someone became seriously ill, he feared he would soon die. He therefore asked to receive the last rites from the priest. The priest went to see him and when he had heard the sick man's confession, he administered the sacrament of the Eucharist. The sick man, however, could not stop himself from throwing up; he managed to reach the fireplace and vomited into the fire. He inadvertently spewed the intact Eucharist which he had just consumed into the fire, which flared up high. But the Sacrament remained undamaged by the fire. A beautiful chapel was built on the place where the miracle took place, and in it the very same Sacrament is still reverently preserved and miracles occur daily. But the chapel requires high maintenance costs, which is why a request was made to the pope to grant ten years' indulgence to those who visit the chapel and make a donation to the church wardens.[22]

Two later literary sources, dating from around 1390, give further details about the miraculous occurrences: a poem called "Vanden Sacrament van Amsterdam" (Of the Sacrament of Amsterdam) by the Holland court poet Willem van Hildegaersberch († ca. 1408) and a passage in a chronicle known as the *Vermeerderde Beka* (Extended Beka).[23] According to Willem, the vomit, including the host, was cast into the fire not by the sick man himself, but by the faithful present, "according to what they had been taught by the priest."[24] The next morning the sick man's nurse, to her great astonishment, discovered the intact host in the fire. These two literary sources, written more than half a century after the event, understandably give rather diverging accounts, but they concur as to the essentials (which can also be found in the 1378 petition).

These two sources and the petition addressed to the pope show that a clear narrative was constructed in the decades following the "miracle of the hearth" as to what happened after the host was found in the fire. It goes as follows: (1) the miraculous host was reverently stored away by the finder or finders; (2) having been informed, the parish priest brought the host back to the church; (3) but the host miraculously returned to the place of the miracle; (4) the host was brought to the church once again, but this time in a solemn procession; (5) due in part to the miraculous cure of a child who suffered from falling sickness, the house with the hearth was recognized to be a sacred place; and (6) therefore a beautiful chapel was built there; (7) which laid the foundation for a new cult and pilgrimage.

Van Hildegaersberch's poem gives a first indication of the date of the Miracle: according to the written testimony of two men (including the sick man himself) and two women, it happened in mid-March, that is, the 15th or 16th, in the year 1345.[25] Later miracles will be discussed elsewhere in this chapter; here we will continue our attempt to interpret the miracle as it was recounted in the 1378 petition.

Thanks to Bishop Guiard's statutes we now know why the vomit was not thrown into the canal or flushed down the latrine. According to ecclesiastical statute, it had to be burned. Apparently the sick man (and his carers) were acquainted with this rule. They were then supposed to reverently bring the ashes of the vomit containing the remains of the host to the church, but it never came to that. To everyone's surprise and astonishment, the same host was found in the fireplace, untouched by the fire. Later Protestant historians have more than once expressed amazement at the unappetizing nature of the story, but it must be emphasized again that the account of the Miracle (as well as Van Hildegaersberch's later poem) simply shows that the ordinary faithful were acquainted with ecclesiastical regulations and were eager to carry them out.[26] That the place of the miracle was considered to be sacred, even though the miraculous host itself had been (temporarily) removed to the parish church, was and is a common phenomenon: the place itself was believed to be sacred or miraculous. Time and again in late-medieval legends about the origins of places of pilgrimage, a chapel was built on the place of the miracle, as a sign that God and his saints desired to be honored on that specific spot. The name "Holy Stead" was therefore initially a generic term for a place where a miracle had occurred. That the name was retained later when the cult had become well-established is intriguing, however; we will return to this issue later.[27]

We have now placed the Miracle of Amsterdam in its religious and cultural context. The miracle arose from a pastoral practice that formed part of daily life in cities and in the countryside during the late Middle Ages: the solemn carrying of viaticum to a sick person's house by a priest. The combination of communion-vomit-fire was in fact much more common that we might expect. The Miracle itself was, of course, not common, and this even at a time when people were quite used to miracles. There were, however, other instances of Eucharistic miracles and their corresponding cults. Historians have often pointed to the connections that linked these cults to each other and to the feast of Corpus Christi. We now turn, therefore, to a typology of Eucharistic feasts before returning to our account of the history of the Amsterdam cult.

Corpus Christi and Sacraments of Miracle

From circa 1210, a young religious sister called Juliana († 1258), of Cornillon Priory near Liège, received a recurring vision. After some time, Christ himself revealed to her what this vision meant. He told her the faithful must begin to celebrate an important feast that had been hidden to them up to that time: a joyous celebration to honor "the sacrament of his body and blood." He also revealed to her where this new feast should be placed in the liturgical calendar: on the second Thursday after Pentecost. In 1246, shortly before his death, the bishop of Liège, Robert of Thourotte, prescribed the celebration of Corpus Christi for his diocese. Eighteen years later, Pope Urban IV († 1264), who had been archdeacon of the Campine (which more or less covers the current Dutch provinces of Noord-Brabant and Limburg and parts of Belgium and Germany), even placed the feast on the liturgical calendar of the universal church. This decision by the bishop and the pope to introduce a completely new solemnity was inspired to a great extent by their admiration for the many exemplary women, including Juliana, in whose religious experience the spiritual union with Christ through communion took center stage.[28]

In the spirit of Juliana and other women from her circle, Corpus Christi became not only a joyful feast—with dancing, singing, and music making—but also a true feast of communion. Urban called on all the faithful to receive communion on that day. This made him the first pope in the Middle Ages to invite the faithful to do so outside of Eastertide. In addition, Corpus Christi was the feast of concord. More so than Juliana herself, the two church leaders emphasized that the feast should be celebrated with exuberance, to strengthen mutual bonds and put "heretics" to shame.[29]

Despite the bishop's and the pope's energetic introduction and propagation of Corpus Christi, the feast only really spread across Western Christendom during the fourteenth century. As has been seen, by the time of the Miracle—precisely a year after the introduction of the feast in Liège—

the people of Amsterdam were already acquainted with Corpus Christi and possibly also with the Eucharistic procession. The latter aspect is not entirely certain because neither Juliana, Robert, or Urban had mentioned anything about holding a procession on the new feast. Countless processions had been held across Western Europe up to the beginning of the fourteenth century in which crosses, statues of saints, and relics had been carried around, but never the Blessed Sacrament. This was simply too sacred to be brought out onto the streets. The Eucharistic procession—a festive procession in which a priest held a clearly visible host—could only develop, and that hesitantly and in different forms in different places, once the faithful had become familiar with the practice of communally bringing viaticum to the homes of the sick.[30]

As it turned out, the feast's message of mutual bonds suited city authorities particularly well. The organization of great processions was often a matter for both city and church in the Low Countries in the fourteenth and fifteenth centuries, especially Eucharistic processions. By influencing the way processions were composed, in particular the sequence in which the various participating groups were to appear, mayors and aldermen hoped to strengthen and sanction the urban status quo.[31] To give an example of his late-medieval practice, we turn to Kampen, a town located on the Zuiderzee almost directly across from Amsterdam, which, like Amsterdam, had strong trade links with the Baltic countries.

This town on the IJssel River had a plan or script (compiled around 1450) for the various important feasts of the year that specified exactly which urban body was responsible for what. Thus the city authorities prescribed that the clergy, the guilds (bearing candles), and members of the fraternity of the Blessed Sacrament should process through the town on Corpus Christi bearing the Blessed Sacrament and a relic of the Holy Cross. On the feast of Saint Lebuinus (June 25) there was a Eucharistic procession around the churchyard; on the feast of the Exaltation of the Cross (September 14), the Blessed Sacrament was again carried through the town in procession. Probably the most important day in Kampen when it came to emphasizing civic concord and mutual bonds was the Sunday before Epiphany (January 6). On that day, the aldermen first attended a special mass in the parish church—dedicated, as in Amsterdam, to Saint Nicholas—and then Blessed Sacrament was exposed on the main altar. After this, they went to the town hall, followed by the citizens and inhabitants of the town, where the mayor made a speech and *buurspraak* was held, that is, announcements were read out. The Blessed Sacrament remained exposed in the church for the duration of the *buurspraak*. A

similar ritual was organized on the following Sunday to conclude proceedings, including mass, exposition, and *buurspraak*.[32]

The situation in Kampen, where city authorities were involved in organizing both the Eucharistic procession and the exposition of the host, was
not much different from that in other cities, including Amsterdam. In the
fifteenth century, the Holy Stead was given its own feast (the Wednesday
after March 12) to reflect the importance of the cult; the feast was known
as "Corpus Christi in Lent." On the one hand, the citizens of Amsterdam
regarded this new feast as being on a par with the real Corpus Christi,
which they called "Corpus Christi in summer." On the other hand, they
cannot have missed the important differences between the two Corpus
Christis. Corpus Christi in summer was a universal feast; Corpus Christi
in Lent was something unique to Amsterdam.

Because of its miraculous host, the Holy Stead belongs to a category of
shrines that originated in a Eucharistic miracle—usually involving one or
more hosts, but sometimes involving sacramental wine—and were therefore known as Sacraments of Miracle.[33] Some two hundred of these cults
emerged in Europe between 1200 and 1550, twenty-three on current Dutch
territory alone.[34] These cults all arose from a peculiar game of transformation, which Austrian historian Peter Browe has subdivided into two
categories. The first category consists of miracles in which the Eucharistic
elements (host or sacramental wine) remained unchanged in a manner
that could not be explained according to the laws of nature. These miracles
were mainly "miracles of fire," where one or more hosts ended up in the
fire but remained intact. In what is currently the Netherlands, four of
these cults emerged shortly after each other in Dordrecht (1338), Amersfoort (1340), Stiphout (1342), and Amsterdam (1345).[35] The second category
of cults consists of miracles in which the Eucharistic elements changed in
a way that could not be explained according to the laws of nature. In most
cases the miracle involved hosts that appeared to bleed or change into
flesh, or white sacramental wine that suddenly assumed the color of blood.
The Netherlands had eight such shrines, erected in the following chronological order: Meerssen (founding miracle in 1222), Niervaart (c. 1300),
Middelburg (1374), Boxtel (1380), Boxmeer (c. 1400), Schraard (1410), Bergen (1421), and Alkmaar (1429).

These miraculous hosts that defied the laws of nature were regarded as
symbols of God's immutability and enduring presence. Applied specifically to the Miracle of Amsterdam, this means that the host was first
changed invisibly into the body of Christ during mass and subsequently

did not burn in the fire because God was still present and demonstrated this through his inviolability.[36]

The designation of Sacrament of Miracle can be applied fully to the Holy Stead, but the characterization of "miracle of fire" is more confusing than illuminating. The miracles in Dordrecht, Amersfoort, and Stiphout all happened during a church fire, in the first two instances during a large city fire and in the third after the building was struck by lightning. The Miracle of Amsterdam, on the contrary, took place in an ordinary fire in a domestic fireplace, not in a church but at home. The similarities with cases where one or more hosts were miraculously found somewhere outside a church—often hosts which the priest had previously lost or which had been stolen and then thrown away by thieves—are more relevant. These cases often involved viaticum, as in the Amsterdam case, and the finding place was often also turned into a holy place by the erection of a chapel. But although the Miracle of Amsterdam was essentially similar to all other Sacraments of Miracle, and although it was more similar to some Sacraments of Miracle than to others in its particulars, it still had one characteristic that especially endeared it to many generations of the city's inhabitants. This was the way in which the Holy Stead had come into being, through a fire that did not destroy but left intact, a sacred fire.[37]

The Bishop and the Count

Having situated the Miracle of Amsterdam in the wider context of Sacraments of Miracle in the Low Countries, we now return to the history of the cult up to the end of the fourteenth century. Our story continues with the three charters that preceded Albert of Bavaria's 1378 petition.[38] These charters have been discussed at inordinate length by historians, but recent research has shed new light on their content.

In the oldest charter, dated on the day following the feast of Luke the Evangelist (i.e., October 19) in 1346 and issued in Amsterdam itself, Nythardus, auxiliary bishop of Utrecht, addressed all the Christian faithful and especially the inhabitants of the city of Amsterdam.[39] To those who devoutly visited the Holy Stead, "where the miracles with the Sacrament occurred," in the evening when benediction (laus divina) was sung and gave alms to the church wardens, Nythardus granted forty days' indulgence. To those who came as pilgrims from elsewhere, at any time of the day, and gave alms, Nythardus granted the same indulgence.[40]

This is a short charter, but the information it contains is particularly relevant. The charter was not sent from the cathedral city of Utrecht to Amsterdam, but was issued in Amsterdam itself by the auxiliary bishop. Undoubtedly this was a festive occasion. It is interesting that the Latin name of the Holy Stead, *Locus Sacer*, already appears explicitly. The reference to "benediction" looked very familiar to later Catholic historians, but it was extraordinary for the mid-fourteenth century. This communal prayer service involving hymns of praise sung to the Sacrament exposed on the altar became common practice in most areas only in the late fourteenth or fifteenth century and did not become general practice in Western Europe until the Counter-Reformation. The fact that the miraculous host was exposed daily in the new Holy Stead, a place already sanctified by the Miracle, must also have been something very unusual, both to the citizens of Amsterdam and to visitors from elsewhere. The sight of the miraculous host and the possibility of earning an indulgence there would, it was hoped, inspire them to make a donation.[41] That it had exposition of the Blessed Sacrament, perhaps the first place to do this in the Low Countries, can explain to some extent why the chapel of the Holy Stead was in use so soon after the Miracle, even though it was still under construction. A sign from above—the founding miracle—had indicated that the Sacrament should be adored on that spot, and under such circumstances it was important to act without delay!

In the second charter, dated November 30, 1346, approximately a month after the first, the bishop of Utrecht himself, John of Arkel (1342–1364), addressed the priest of the parish church of Amsterdam. He referred to the "Body of the Lord" that had recently been miraculously found in the parish, as reliable witnesses had testified. Because the miraculous host—which was made of perishable matter—would begin to decay over the course of time, the bishop gave permission to replace it with a new one as often as necessary. The visible crumbling of the host would weaken the devotion of the people. In addition he permitted the host—which should always look "fresh"—to be kept in the crystal monstrance (vas sacrum cristallinum) that his vicar had blessed. He authorized the Amsterdam parish clergy to hold processions with this monstrance as often as they deemed necessary to stimulate piety, both their own and the people's. The bishop also permitted the clergy to solemnly expose the monstrance to the people who came to visit this divine place (divinus locus). Finally, he allowed the clergy to preach publicly about the miracles that had happened and would still happen in the future. All this was to honor the Blessed Sacrament.[42]

This charter was not issued on a particular solemn occasion, and, in contrast with Nythardus, the bishop did not have to come to Amsterdam to issue it. The technical instructions he gave, which were addressed exclusively to the clergy, were in full accord with the auxiliary bishop's charter. The permission to consecrate and expose a new host as often as is necessary can be found in several other Eucharistic cults. Ecclesiastical regulations prescribed that the host should have certain specific physical characteristics. It had to be radiantly white and should not be left to crumble due to age; a host that was no longer intact no longer pointed to Christ's presence. For this reason hosts consecrated during mass and reserved for the communion of the sick were never kept for more than a few weeks. Because the Miracle host was experienced as something different than ordinary communion for the sick, the episcopal instruction was intended to reassure the clergy of Amsterdam that they still were allowed to replace it when necessary. We may be certain that the miraculous host of Amsterdam was replaced on hundreds of occasions in the period up to the Alteration of 1578. Understandably, this happened without the faithful knowing about it.[43]

The explicit stipulation about a crystal monstrance that may be carried in procession and placed on the altar indicates that the "exposed" Sacrament—the host visible to all—was worshiped in Amsterdam, and this did not happen yet in other cities. It was on account of this transparent monstrance that it was important to take care of the physical condition of the host: every day, many pilgrims focused on it as they made their spiritual communion, and the clergy had to make sure it was in excellent condition. There was one particular way of doing this. Hosts were made using a host iron, which had a particular motif on the inside. This motif was then embossed onto every host. Thanks to a book of hours for the feast of the Miracle (Wednesday following March 12), which was published in 1555 and entitled *Succinta enarratio miraculorum* (Brief story of the miracles), we know that the miraculous host bore the motif of the crucified Christ at his resurrection, with one foot still in the grave and one foot outside it. It was important therefore to keep using the same host iron so as not to disturb attentive pilgrims.[44] The information about the motif on the host can only be found in this book of hours, which was intended for the clergy, and the sixteenth-century and subsequent iconography of the Miracle was clearly not acquainted with it. What is probably the oldest pilgrimage card of the Holy Stead (1518) shows a woman who takes a host out of the fireplace that bears a completely different motif: Christ on the cross with Mary and the

Apostle John standing on either side.[45] Perhaps the maker of the card, Jacob Cornelisz van Oostsanen, failed to look properly and simply chose the motif that was the most common one at the time, or perhaps the book of hours got it wrong. It is likely we will never know exactly what the miraculous host looked like.

The next important document was a third charter, again by Auxiliary Bishop Nythardus, issued on the feast of the Eleven Thousand Virgins (October 21) in 1347. This charter announced that on that day he had consecrated the chapel built in honor of the Sacrament and which bore the name of Locus Sacer. He had also consecrated four altars in the chapel.[46] He decided that the annual feast of the dedication of the chapel would be the Sunday after the feast of Saint Peter in Chains on August 1. In addition, he granted forty days' indulgence to all who visited the chapel on its new feast day, on a number of other saints' days spread across the year, on Corpus Christi and the days under the octave of that feast, or on any other special day. The same indulgence could also be earned at any time by pilgrims and those who contributed to the upkeep of the chapel, or of the street that was especially built to facilitate access and was therefore called Holy Way (quod iter sancta via vocatur). These stipulations did not exhaust Nythardus's munificence. He also granted the indulgence to those who came to pray at one of the altars or at the spot where the Blessed Sacrament had once been found in the fire, to those who circumambulated the chapel while praying an Our Father and a Hail Mary for the chapel's benefactors, and to those who performed these prayers on their knees when they heard the chapel bell ring in the evening.

The day of the dedication and the proclamation of the indulgences must have been a true feast. The consecration of a chapel was an impressive and lengthy ritual, and on top of that there was the consecration of the altars.[47] Apparently the building of the chapel had progressed far enough to be able to consecrate; moreover, the presence of the four altars indicates that considerable funds had been collected through foundations. It is remarkable that the chapel was still designated at its dedication with the general term *locus sacer*, while the charter spelled out the specific dedications of the altars. Another remarkable feature is that it mentions Corpus Christi prominently (with its octave), but that there is no reference to March 15 or 16, the day the host had been found in the fire according to later legend.

We know on the basis of this third charter that two and a half years after the founding miracle, the Holy Stead was already well provisioned as a place of worship and pilgrimage. To ensure that this would continue to be the case, Saint Nicholas's church appointed a priest to the chapel—a "chaplain"—who was responsible for the daily (early) mass, the hymns of praise mentioned above that were sung to the Blessed Sacrament in the evening, and preaching a sermon in the vernacular on Wednesdays. In addition, masses were said at the various altars on several occasions during the week, though not by the chapel's own priest, because priests were only permitted to say mass once a day. For the other sacraments—especially matrimony—the residents had to continue to go to their parish church.[48] If the chapel did not fulfil much of a role in terms of pastoral care, it was all the more innovative in devotional terms. After some time the citizens of Amsterdam no doubt grew accustomed to the permanent exposition of the host, but for visitors from outside, certainly until the end of the fourteenth century, this must have been something very strange, even spectacular.

Its special sacred significance meant that the Holy Stead also attracted religious confraternities (associations of pious laypeople) who made it their base: the Confraternity of the Holy Cross (first mentioned in 1361), the Confraternity of Our Lady (1368), the Confraternity of the Blessed Sacrament (first mentioned in 1374), and the Confraternity of Saint Laurence (1378).[49] Thus, four of the city's five religious confraternities were founded in the new chapel, which began to distinguish itself from the parish church as a kind of religious lay center. Usually confraternities had mainly or exclusively male membership, but it was the reverse for the Confraternity of the Blessed Sacrament: this organization's membership was reserved for women, and its board consisted of *overwiven*, or "mistresses."[50] This "brotherhood," consisting of women from patrician families, would become strongly involved in the religious and political history of the city in the sixteenth century.

In the last quarter of the fourteenth century, the chapel and the cult it housed gained further prestige thanks to the interest of the ruling dynasty, especially Albert of Bavaria and Margaret of Brieg. In 1367 Albert added a chapter of twelve canons and a dean to the court chapel dedicated to Mary in The Hague. This foundation was probably connected to the presence there of two important relics, one of the Holy Cross and the other of the Crown of Thorns.[51] These precious possessions ensured the success of Albert's petition in 1371 to Pope Gregory XI to grant an indulgence to the faithful who gave a donation when visiting the chapel.[52] In 1373 Albert gave the chapter another source of income by presenting it with the right of collation or appointment to the church of Amsterdam and the Holy Stead, a right he had previously exercised himself. This meant that the Hague chapter henceforth disposed of a large part of the revenues of the church and the chapel. In return it had the responsibility of making provision for pastoral care and liturgical worship.[53]

In the 1378 petition of Albert and Margaret to Pope Clement VII, the request for an indulgence for the Holy Stead was preceded by another request. The spouses pointed to the presence of the relics of the Cross and Crown in their own chapel, which many pilgrims came to visit and which the canons venerated every Friday by singing hymns of praise. They begged the pope to grant twenty years' indulgence to anyone who attended this service of prayer and hymns.[54] Their request for indulgences for the court chapel in The Hague and for the Holy Stead formed a separate section in their long petition, amid many requests for favors and privileges for members of the comital family and their protégés. By being mentioned in the same breath as the Hague cult and by being presented to the pope in Avignon together with it, the Holy Stead acquired princely allure. The indulgence that they requested, of ten years, was a considerable favor: although it was only half the time requested for the chapel in The Hague, it was still a lot more than the paltry forty days on offer from Auxiliary Bishop Nythardus in 1346 and 1347. That the matter of indulgences was dealt with to the satisfaction of all parties concerned is evident from a papal charter dated 1381, which confirmed that the right of collation to the Amsterdam church and chapel had passed to the chapter in The Hague. It is also interesting to note that this Latin charter spoke not of "locus sacer" but of "capella ter Heiligher Stede," the chapel at the Holy Stead. Apparently this title had become so familiar and accepted that it was not thought necessary to translate it.[55]

The Holy Stead had thus acquired several excellent assets and could now claim to be a bona fide place of pilgrimage. But were the pilgrims coming? A good launch does not automatically lead to enduring success, especially if we bear in mind that competition was fierce. There is sufficient evidence for the fourteenth century (i.e., the charters), but sources become scarce afterward. It is certain, however, that pilgrims continued to come. The first explicit reference to an individual pilgrimage was one imposed by a court of law. In 1370 Jan of Blois, lord of Schoonhoven and Gouda, sentenced a man found guilty of manslaughter to undertake a pilgrimage to Jerusalem. Before departing for the Holy Land, however, he first had to undertake pilgrimages to Geertruidenberg (Saint Gertrude), 's-Gravenzande (Mary), and the Holy Stead in Amsterdam.[56] Evidence of a number of other enforced pilgrimages has come to light for the period until the Reformation, especially from Leiden.[57] There is a passing reference in the accounts of the medieval female abbey of Rijnsburg to a pilgrim who came of her own accord. Two years after the papal confirmation, on July 12, 1383, the abbess went on a pilgrimage to Amsterdam, where she donated a considerable sum; she had done the same three months previously (April 21) in 's-Hertogenbosch, where a new cult of Our Lady had emerged only recently.[58] The ruling dynasty, which had close ties to the abbey of Rijnsburg, also expressed its commitment to the Holy Stead on numerous occasions by coming to visit. Albert of Bavaria visited the shrine at least three times, even on Corpus Christi in 1388. And his successor, William VI, donated a gold coin (a French crown) to the Miracle when he visited Amsterdam for his inauguration as new count in March 1405. It must be said, however, that princes traveled frequently in those days, whenever they had the opportunity, and therefore also made many pilgrimages. Moreover, the Holy Stead never succeeded in replacing the special veneration of Our Lady in 's-Gravenzande, close to the court, as the dynasty's preferred place of pilgrimage.[59]

A sobering note in relation to the Holy Stead as a place of pilgrimage can be found in a report in the miracle book of the cult of Our Lady in 's-Hertogenbosch, which attributes "failure" to Amsterdam and "success" to 's-Hertogenbosch. On May 2, 1383, two months before the abbess of Rijnsburg's pilgrimage to Amsterdam, Peter, son of Lord Wijssen, arrived with his wife and their daughter Soete in 's-Hertogenbosch. Peter's wife testified there that she had fallen off the Hoge Brug (High Bridge) in Amsterdam together with Soete on March 17, the Monday after Palm Sunday. When Soete was pulled out of the water it seemed she had drowned. Begging for a miracle, the parents brought their child to the "church of the Blessed Sacrament," but to no avail. The mother then promised that she would offer a pound of wax to Our Lady in 's-Hertogenbosch if her child would be brought back to life. This worked, and she fulfilled her vow.[60] The same miracle book contains another astonishing story, about a certain Claas Hermansz, reportedly a sacristan in Amsterdam when the Miracle took place. After his time as sacristan, Claas worked in pastoral ministry in Staveren in Friesland, but he had to stop when he became paralyzed in one leg in 1366. When in early September 1383 he heard of the miracles that were suddenly multiplying at Mary's intercession in 's-Hertogenbosch, he promised to go there as a pilgrim if he were to be healed. He was indeed cured; having walked on crutches for seventeen long years, and without visiting Amsterdam, Claas was back on his feet again. Although the Miracle of Amsterdam was well-known to the Brabant scribe who recorded the account in 1383, it is almost embarrassing for the Holy Stead that the Miracle was only mentioned to date events and not at all as a place of pilgrimage in its own right to which this former sacristan might also have gone for relief.[61] A third report in the 's-Hertogenbosch miracle book also bypasses the Holy Stead. When a certain Reiner Dey feared he might be shipwrecked during a storm on his return voyage from Prussia to Amsterdam in the spring of 1383, he promised to offer a silver ship to Mary in 's-Hertogenbosch if she would avert the danger. The wind calmed down, Reiner arrived home safely, and on February 17, 1384, he gave Mary in 's-Hertogenbosch a silver cog weighing ten lot (150 grams).[62]

Although the compilers of this miracle book were not entirely impartial, champions as they were of their own Marian shrine, it is nonetheless clear that the cult of Mary in Brabant far outshone the Holland Sacrament of Miracle as a place of pilgrimage at the end of the fourteenth century. Compared to important Marian shrines such as 's-Hertogenbosch and 's-Gravenzande, the Holy Stead was no more than an average achiever.[63] Yet the *Boec vanden mirakelen ten Bosche* (Book of miracles [wrought] in 's-Hertogenbosch) contains one indication that the Amsterdam cult may still have been a busy place of pilgrimage in its early years. The *Boec* contains no fewer than 481 miracle accounts (mainly cures), the first 461 of which reportedly took place in the period between November 1382 and April 1388, with the last twenty dated between November 1408 and October 1603. In other words, almost all recorded miracles date to the early period of the cult. The same disproportional distribution can be found in the miracle books of other cults.[64] The charters mentioned above that refer to the early years of the Holy Stead speak of the Sacrament's many, even daily miracles. This implies that there were many pilgrimages because pilgrims were the ones who made the prayers for healing or deliverance that were miraculously granted, visited the Holy Stead, and subsequently reported the answers they had received. It is quite possible that the Holy Stead also had a book with reports of miracles, mainly from its early years. If such a book ever existed, it was subsequently lost. All we have are a few of these reports, most of them dating from the fifteenth century.

To sum up, the Holy Stead made a good start as a shrine and a place of pilgrimage. The clearest indications for this are the diocesan recognition it received, with the grant of an indulgence, the statement that many miracles had occurred, the swift construction of a chapel, the erection of altars, the establishment of confraternities, and even liturgical and devotional innovations, such as the exposition of the host in a monstrance and its benediction by the faithful. A few decades later the Holy Stead was even able to claim favors from the ruling dynasty and, through the count, from the curia. The Hague continued to show its attachment to the Miracle in subsequent years as well. One proof of this is the poem, mentioned already, of Willem van Hildegaersberch, "Vanden sacramente van Aemsterdam." After speaking of the sacrament of the Eucharist as a source of grace, and of the miracle of the hearth, the poet switched confidently to the current situation: "Whenever we are burdened with illness, we should call on it in our distress." He praised the Sacrament as the best weapon against the devil's wiles. Those who visited the miraculous host with a penitent heart might be assured of God's assistance. In Holland itself, it was best to go to the chapel in Amsterdam to venerate the Sacrament in person because it sometimes happened there that someone who came supported by crutches left walking on their own two feet, and in that place sight was restored to the blind thanks to the Sacrament.[65]

Despite the accolades that William—an artist with a solid reputation—lavished on the Holy Stead, things grew quiet in the later years of the fourteenth century. No clear cause will probably ever be found for this dip, although it is possible that the turbulent history of the county of Holland in these years played a role, but to discuss this in detail would be to digress.[66] Perhaps the death of Countess Margaret of Brieg in 1386 was a factor in the decline. She was known not only for her piety and her interest in places of pilgrimage, but also as a strong personality who was always at her husband's side and who made decisions on the county together with him.[67] This would be further proof of the impact that individuals can have on the fate of any historical enterprise.

Miracles of the Miracle

After the turn of the century, the chapel of the Holy Stead was increasingly in need of repair. Economically, the city prospered, but as a place of worship the chapel had to contend with a lot of competition. More than the other cities of Holland, Amsterdam was rapidly becoming a city of monasteries. No fewer than thirteen new monasteries were founded between 1400 and 1420 in what had been a city with very few religious houses, and all of them were attracting benefactors.[68] But the chapel's biggest competitor was not a monastery, but Our Lady's Church, founded in 1409, near the city hall and Plaats ("place," later Dam). This Nieuwe Kerk (New Church), called thus to distinguish it from the Oude Kerk (Saint Nicholas's Church, the Old Church), experienced energetic growth as a parish church, favored as it was by Amsterdam's patricians and the city authorities, as well as by numerous guilds and confraternities founded in the fifteenth century. Ever more altars were erected in this church, each of them with a corresponding foundation by a benefactor to pay for the holding of liturgical services for the repose of their soul.[69]

The chapter of The Hague, more than forty miles away, proved unable to find competent subcontractors for the upkeep of the chapel. There were complaints about the state of Heiligeweg, although the chapter could not be blamed for this as responsibility for the road and its maintenance had passed from the Holy Stead to the Oude Gasthuis (Old Hospital) in 1371.[70] A number of charters show that the chapter continued to assert its rights over the chapel in the first years of the fifteenth century, but this changed in 1415.[71]

In that year, the chapter relinquished the revenue from the Holy Stead to the Amsterdam city authorities, on the condition that it would repair the chapel and Heiligeweg, which were in danger of falling into "ruins." From that moment on there was a shared right of collation: the city authorities had the right to present the priest for the Holy Stead for nomination by the chapter. To provide for his income, the city authorities undertook to pay the chapter one silver mark per year. It is clear from the charter in which the chapter announced this decision (February 24, 1415) that the miraculous host was being exposed at that time in the Oude Kerk rather than the Holy Stead for safety reasons. This had probably been the case ever since the turn of the century.[72] The intention was to return it to the Holy Stead in due course. There was a donation box in the church near the "Sacrament of the Body and Blood of Our Lord Jesus Christ found miraculously," and donations were reserved for the chapel. The material condition of the Holy Stead, built so hastily seventy years before, was clearly not good. Neither was the state of its finances, now that the new parish church was proving to be much more attractive to citizens with money to donate for the benefit of their souls. The city authorities' takeover of the chapel came just in time.[73]

The transaction shows that the mayors and aldermen regarded themselves as maintainers and promoters of religious life. But their motives were not inspired by piety alone. We have already seen from the Kampen example that cities in the late Middle Ages generally valued the sacrament of Eucharist as a symbol of unity and solidarity. Although the city of Amsterdam did not, as far as we know, have a written liturgical script, they frequently issued similar regulations about feasts—and in particular about Eucharistic processions—in the city bylaws (keuren). The city authorities issued these bylaws annually, and they had force of law both for citizens (known as *poorters*, meaning "burghers") and for temporary residents of the city (*ingezetenen*, meaning "residents"). Unfortunately, these bylaws have been preserved in substantial numbers only from circa 1470 on, so we must look to other, often incomplete sources for the public celebration of the feast of the Miracle before that period.

We have seen in the previous section that the bishop of Utrecht gave the local clergy permission to organize processions with the miraculous host displayed in a crystal monstrance as they saw fit as early as 1346. We have also seen that although the chapel had its own dedication feast, the Sunday after August 1, there was no feast to commemorate the founding miracle of the cult of the Holy Stead itself. If processions with the miraculous host—or, rather, with an ordinary host in lieu of the miraculous host—were indeed organized from that year on, they would have been held on the feast of Corpus Christi and would have commenced in the Oude Kerk. Alternatively, these processions may have been held on the Sunday after Corpus Christi, and perhaps from time to time on another feast day, but there is not the slightest indication that they were held in mid-March. We can be relatively sure that this situation lasted for the remainder of the fourteenth century.[74]

It is likely that the proper feast as it has been celebrated in later centuries, the feast of the Miracle on the Wednesday following March 12, was introduced only after 1415, the year in which the city authorities gained control over the Holy Stead.[75] The new feast must have been instituted before 1434 because on August 3 of that year the city counselors and the church wardens of the Holy Stead addressed a petition to Pope Eugene IV (1431–1447) to grant an indulgence to the benefactors and pious visitors of the chapel on its annual feast day in March.[76] They also sent the pope a report on the history of the cult. This described the founding miracle: the parish priest who came to administer the last rites; the sick man who had to throw up; the vomit (including the host) that was thrown into the fire at the time of vespers; the woman who found the host at the time of prime and managed to take it from the fire without burning her hand; and the chapel that was erected over the place where the miraculous host was found. The authors then abruptly switched to the current situation. They pointed out that the Miraculous Sacrament of the body of Christ was still being kept in this chapel and that even in these modern times (modernis temporibus) the Most High still deigned to grant many miracles to stimulate the piety of the faithful. Because of the city's important seaport, Amsterdam received many visitors, both merchants and important persons from across the world. As a result, great numbers of the faithful, visitors to and inhabitants of Amsterdam alike, came to the chapel. This involved many costs; it was necessary to increase the income of the chapel, and for this reason the councilors and church wardens asked the pope to grant a hundred days' indulgence to all believers who visited the chapel and made a donation for its upkeep on the day the Sacrament was found, that is, a Wednesday in mid-March.[77] The same request was made for the faithful who participated in the Eucharistic procession or who circumambulated the Holy Stead holding a burning wax candle on any Wednesday or Friday during the year.[78]

It is evident from this petition to the pope that the special feast of the Miracle, with its own procession, was already in existence in 1434. Its status increased considerably the following year, after the pope granted the request. The petitioners' energetic representations to the pope testify to both devotion to "their" Holy Stead and civic entrepreneurial spirit.[79] The two petitions for an indulgence in the late Middle Ages—the first sent to Clement VII and the second to Eugene IV—strikingly illustrate the societal changes that had occurred in Holland in the course of half a century. In 1378 sending a petition to the pope was a matter for the count; in 1434 it was entirely an initiative of the citizens. It was not that the count's power had diminished, but rather that his perspective had changed. From 1433 onward Holland formed part of the great Burgundian realm. The new count, Philip the Good (1433–1467), ruled many lands, many of which had places of pilgrimage that were much more famous than the Holy Stead.

That the Holy Stead managed to retain its status as a place of pilgrimage under the protection of the civil authorities is also evident from the *Succinta enarratio miraculorum* and from a miracle book entitled *Hier beghint die vindinge vant hoochweerdighe ende heylighe Sacrament* (Here begins the finding of the most excellent and blessed Sacrament) published in 1568.[80] The miracles recorded in this latter book, some of which went on to play an important role in the later narrative and iconographic tradition of the Miracle, always consisted of either a miraculous cure or a miraculous deliverance from desperate circumstances. The following examples give a brief impression.

- A blind man standing in front of the Holy Stead heard a "great noise" come from the building. When he asked what was going on, the reply was that the women of the Confraternity of the Blessed Sacrament were holding a feast there. He asked to be brought to the tabernacle. When he got there, he knelt and prayed to be cured of his blindness. When he rose, he "could see again clearly" and thanked God. The women of the guild who witnessed this miracle were astonished.[81]
- A crippled man from Gansoord (Nes) came to the Miracle to pray for a cure. God immediately answered his prayer. When he came home, his landlord asked him if he had remembered to pray first for his eternal salvation. Filled with doubt, the man returned to the Miracle, ready to accept whatever was best for his salvation, and instantly became crippled again. But he continued to pray and was cured a second time. This miracle shows that sincere faith was more important than the cure of a physical ailment.
- A priest living in sin fell seriously ill. He promised that if God were to give him back his health, he would mend his ways and visit the Holy Stead every year wearing woolen clothes and on bare feet. As soon as he uttered this promise, he was healed.
- A woman from Hoorn and her three children were in danger of drowning in a capsized tugboat. All four were saved when she promised to visit the Holy Stead, although many other passengers lost their lives.
- A skipper and his family from Oostland (near Rotterdam) had to abandon ship during a heavy storm. They promised to undertake a pilgrimage to the Miracle and make a considerable "offering" if they were to be saved. The storm calmed down, and even their ship was preserved. The family members then made good their promise.

These stories are followed in the miracle book by the account of a miracle that has a precise date and involved a pilgrim from foreign lands. In 1443 a young man from Bremen traveled to Ceuta, now a Spanish enclave in Morocco, to enlist in the king of Portugal's army. By the thousands, the soldiers marched to war, only to be routed by the Moors at Alcácer Ceguer (Ksar es Seghir). The young man was locked up in a dungeon with an iron shackle around his neck. Then he remembered that he had once been to Amsterdam, where the Sacrament had worked so many miracles.

He prayed to God and promised to give the Holy Stead a silver collar if he were to escape. The heavens answered his prayer, and he fulfilled his promise.[82] Although this is just a single example, it does confirm the city councilors' and church wardens' claim that Amsterdam attracted visitors "from across the world."

But it was a miracle that took place nine years later that ensured the Holy Stead's "definitive breakthrough." On the feast of Saint Urban (May 25) in 1452, Amsterdam was devastated by a large city fire. The Holy Stead, too, was engulfed in flames. The unanointed hands of a smith were unable to open the locks that gave access to the miraculous host, so it could not be saved. But after the chapel had burned to the ground—just as the Oude and Nieuwe Kerk, the city hall, and many monasteries had— the Sacrament was found intact, still standing in its monstrance.[83] Even the silk veil covering the monstrance had not been singed. Several pages in the miracle book were dedicated to recounting this miracle.[84] One detail is particularly important to understanding the Miracle cult, a passage describing the monstrance amid the smoldering remains: "People came from all sides to see God in His miracles. Some persons who wished to examine everything very precisely approached so closely that they had to retreat, as their shoes and feet were scorched. But when, like Moses filled with fear, they saw that the burning bush was not consumed, they removed their shoes, because the place where they were standing was holy. As once the Apostle Thomas, they saw the glorious wounds in the body of the Lord, and they praised God in astonishment and cried out: 'my Lord and my God.'" This short passage provides a theological basis for the name *Holy Stead*. The Sacrament is compared with or equated to the burning bush on Mount Horeb, as recounted in Exodus 3:1–6. To Moses's astonishment and fear, the bush burned but was not consumed because God was present. Moses thus had to remove his sandals, for the ground on which he stood was holy. This was also the place where God announced that he would not abandon his people (3:7–8).

We do not know if this theological interpretation was given to the Amsterdam cult from the start, but it does offer a convincing explanation of why the place where a host—in which God is present—was found in the fire without burning, and this not once but twice (1345 and 1452), would be called by the general name of Holy Stead, or "holy place." It also explains the custom of pious citizens of Amsterdam to circumambulate the Holy Stead barefoot, a practice that, according to a poem published in 1532, had been in existence for more than a hundred years. Incidentally, the last

sentence of the passage quoted above, on seeing Christ's wounds, is a
clear reference to the motif of the Crucified One embossed on the host.[85]

Like a phoenix, the Holy Stead arose from its ashes on the wings of
this second miracle of fire, much larger and more beautiful than before.
The new building, consisting of three naves of equal height, occupied the
space between Kalverstraat, Rokin, Wijde Kapelsteeg, and Enge Kapelsteeg. Above the entrance, on Kalverstraat, the words *Signa et mirabilia
fecit apud me Deus excelsus* ("The Most High God has done signs and wonders to me," Daniel 3:99) were written in gold letters, text that can still be
seen above the entrance to the church on the Amsterdam Begijnhof. On
the northwest side (at the corner of Kalverstraat and Wijde Kapelsteeg)
there was a special annex called the Holy Corner, which contained the
original miracle hearth.[86] Most historians have assumed that pilgrimages
to Amsterdam only really began to proliferate after the rebuilding of the
chapel, which was completed as soon as 1457.[87] Thus the Leuven professor
Joannes Molanus († 1585) mentioned, in a posthumously published book
on the feasts of the saints of the Low Countries, that God granted many
miracles in the new chapel built by the citizens of Amsterdam: "Those
who made a vow in this place were delivered from the temptations of the
devil, from heavy shipwreck, from imprisonment in Barbary, Spain and
France, from the pangs of birth, from stinging sores, and from other tor-
ments. Newly born infants who died without baptism were brought back
to life so that their souls might be saved through the life-giving sacrament.
Lost objects were found, so that the name of those wrongly accused of
theft could be cleared."[88] Molanus derived these stereotypical stories from
the *Succinta enarratio miraculorum*; his own contribution was to keep the
fame of the Holy Stead as a former place of pilgrimage alive after the Reformation through his book, which was well-known in scholarly circles. In
it he also emphasized the miraculous power of the fireplace that had been
preserved, including the ashes of the fire involved in the founding miracle
of 1345, above which an altar was reportedly erected upon which the exposed Sacrament was placed. According to Molanus, the holy ashes had
always been used to cure all kinds of disease, and the healing power and
fragrant odor of the ashes were undiminished "to the present day" (the Alteration of 1578). That the hearth became a fixture in the later historiography of the Holy Stead should not surprise us: not only the miraculous
host but also the place that had been consecrated by the fire served as an
object of veneration. It is in fact quite possible that the fireplace remained
intact despite the building of two successive chapels. If there is one part

of a building likely to survive the ravages of fire, it is surely the fireplace. The healing ashes in the hearth, which were mentioned until the Alteration of 1578, were distributed to pious visitors by successive priests attached to the Holy Stead and replenished from time to time, just as was and still is the custom with the marl sand distributed in Houthem in Limburg, an old place of pilgrimage dedicated to Saint Gerlach.[89]

The list of miracles that occurred up to the beginning of the sixteenth century is not yet complete.

- The voluminous *Speculum exemplorum* mentions a miracle that happened in 1472. In that year a man who was walking in the woods near Utrecht was attacked by the devil and left permanently injured. Hoping for a cure, he made a pilgrimage to Saint Jerome in Egmond. But on his way there, in Amsterdam, he fell seriously ill. When he had been in hospital for six or seven weeks, Mary appeared to him. She promised him that he would be fully cured if he were to allow himself to be carried around the tabernacle of the Blessed Sacrament in the Holy Stead. When this was done three times the following day, he felt his strength increase on each round, and after that he was able to complete his pilgrimage to Saint Jerome on his own.[90]

The miracle book also contains other miracle accounts from a somewhat later date.

- On May 5, 1476, the Wednesday after Pentecost, Lijsbet Franssen dochter, a religious sister from Saint Claire's convent in Amsterdam, who had been sick for six months, was carried by four sisters to the Holy Stead. She had been told in a vision that God would be merciful to her if she were to say her prayers in that place. Once she got there, she did indeed miraculously regain strength, after which she walked "around that Blessed Sacrament three times" herself, returning "to her convent on her own feet." This account was then followed by a lengthy personal testimony by Lijsbet herself.[91]
- In 1498, two skippers from Zierikzee were taken prisoner together with many other people by French soldiers. Carrying a heavy shackle on their legs, they managed to escape in a small boat, which then sank. Only one of the two, Claes Pietersoon, managed to survive. Floating on a piece of driftwood, he vowed to undertake a pilgrimage to the Blessed Sacrament on account of the many miracles that occurred there. In a

vision, he saw the host lying in the water, as if in the hands of a priest (at the elevation during mass). He reached the shore and was recaptured by the French. After a year he was able to pay a ransom and was set free. He went to the Holy Stead and there made his offering. He recounted the things that had happened to him to the priest and many others.[92]

In comparison with the 's-Hertogenbosch miracle book, it was a modest list of miracle accounts. But a miracle account from another source more than made up for this. In 1484 or 1483, Archduke Maximilian of Austria reportedly fell seriously ill during a visit to The Hague. He vowed to undertake a pilgrimage to the Holy Stead if he were to be cured, and then he was restored to health. Although it is not entirely certain that Maximilian actually visited Amsterdam at that time, this story can be regarded as the founding legend of the long and close relationship between the princes of the House of Habsburg and the city of Amsterdam, with the Holy Stead as *trait d'union*.[93]

Processions through the City

A remarkably high number of Eucharistic processions were organized during the turbulent transitional years in which the new ruling dynasty struggled to establish its hold over the Low Countries.[94] Amsterdam took the lead in this respect compared to other cities, all the more so because it already had two annual Eucharistic processions before the large fire of 1452: one on Corpus Christi, which other cities had too, and one on the feast of the Miracle, which was unique to Amsterdam and known as Corpus Christi in Lent.[95] Details about the Amsterdam processions can be gleaned from the city bylaws. Some 724 bylaws from the second half of the fifteenth century have been preserved, and 29 of these deal partly or wholly with Eucharistic processions; the first dates from 1475 and the last from 1500. The situation changed from year to year, and these bylaws therefore show continuity as well as variations and innovations.[96]

In short, three types of Eucharistic procession were organized in Amsterdam in the last quarter of the century; they are distributed equally over the bylaws. Nine bylaws mention the procession on the feast of the Miracle (Lent); seven mention the general liturgical feast of Corpus Christi (summer); three mention both feasts together.[97] In addition, ten bylaws deal with "general processions," which have not been mentioned yet: participation in these was obligatory for all citizens (both burghers and residents). This kind of procession was not held at regular intervals and sometimes occurred in different cities at the same time, usually to ask for God's blessing whenever some calamity threatened the city or the count, or to thank God when the menace had been averted.[98] Because of the difficult circumstances under which they were held, these general processions were often more subdued and always more somber than the processions on the two feasts. Nevertheless even the bylaws dealing with festive occasions betray a certain anxiety on the part of the city authorities. This can be explained on account of the military and other troubles that were taking place as power passed from Burgundian to Habsburg rulers.

Holland now belonged to the interim kingdom of Burgundy, which meant in effect that the duke of Burgundy was also the count of Holland. From the start, Amsterdam sought to establish good relations with the new counts, Philip the Good and Charles the Bold (1467–1477) successively. After Charles was killed during one of his many military exploits, sovereignty over the Low Countries passed to his daughter, Mary of Burgundy (1477–1482). When she, too, died unexpectedly after a fall from her horse, her widower, the Habsburg Maximilian of Austria, became regent of the provinces that remained loyal, including Holland. He also acted as the guardian of their son, Philip (Philip the Handsome, until 1493). In that year, most of the Low Countries passed to the House of Habsburg.

During Mary's short reign, however, an old feud flared up again, known in Holland as the Hook and Cod Wars. The Cod faction presented itself as supportive of the Burgundian and subsequently Habsburg rulers; it attracted the allegiance of many cities, including Amsterdam. Its opponent, the Hook party, was supported by many aristocrats, especially the lower aristocracy, who were reluctant to accept the hegemony of the lord.[99] This split brought threats of violence and actual fighting between Amsterdam and Utrecht. The seriousness of the situation is reflected in the bylaws issued in the 1480s that deal with processions. The three militias took center stage: all militiamen were to attend the Eucharistic procession in armor, bearing arms; a fine was imposed on those who failed to turn up. A number of bylaws give the impression that a general mobilization was imminent. The bylaw of July 1481 calling for a general procession was followed immediately by another bylaw on the expulsion of all Utrecht citizens from Amsterdam and the departure of all Amsterdam citizens from Utrecht.[100] The call for a general procession in December of that same year was followed by a strong bylaw against fearmongering: persons who treacherously said "the cause is lost, the enemy is already in the city" and similar falsehoods might be struck dead on the spot with impunity.[101]

In February or March 1483 a large-scale confrontation seemed imminent: all militiamen were ordered to be ready to go to war for lord and city and to follow the colors. All male burghers and residents aged between twenty and sixty had to obtain a clear badge and a tunic with the top dyed red and the lower part white before the feast of the Miracle, which fell on March 13 in that year; those who had not complied by this date would have to pay a fine of six Holland pounds. Everyone was expected to take part in the procession, each group bearing its own candle.[102] The red-and-white uniform was perhaps meant to be a sign of allegiance to Maximilian of Austria as the acting lord of the Netherlands. Red and white not only symbolically referred to the virtues of courage and hope, but were also the heraldic colors of the House of Habsburg.[103] The city did not count on Maximilian's support in vain. On August 31, 1483, the city of Utrecht fell to Maximilian after a siege lasting two months.[104] On October 11, the Amsterdam city authorities, in consultation with the priests of the two parish churches, decided that everyone should take part in a procession with the Blessed Sacrament on the following Saturday in gratitude at the return of peace. This procession was not held in an atmosphere of exuberance: prayers were said for the souls of those who had fallen in battle and to beseech God to deliver the city from the plague that afflicted the city at the time.[105]

The Amsterdam bylaws on Eucharistic processions show that peace was not fully restored even after the end of the Hook and Cod Wars. The militiamen's punctilious participation in the processions on the two Corpus Christi feasts remained a cause of concern to the city authorities. In the spring of 1485 they even organized an extra procession with obligatory attendance for all citizens to pray for peace, better weather, and a good harvest. The bylaw on the procession of Corpus Christi of 1487, which fell on June 16 in that year, shows how worried the city authorities were. In most bylaws, militiamen who failed to turn up for the procession had to pay a fine in money. But this time, they were to be punished with a fine of five thousand stones. Other bylaws issued during this time also mentioned fines in stones for offenders.[106] This remarkable change in currency can be explained by the fact that new city walls were being built at the time to improve the city's defenses against future threats. All burghers and residents were required to contribute in the building activities in some way or other, either through donating money or building materials, or by helping to dig, do masonry work, or other contributions.[107] The Amsterdam city authorities were always anxious about new threats, all the more so because Maximilian was fighting on many fronts at the same time. Their concerns were evident from two bylaws on general processions in 1488, which were organized to give moral support to the count, then a prisoner in rebel Bruges. The participation of militiamen in the Eucharistic processions, which must have looked much like military parades, remained an important concern for the city authorities for many years to come.

In 1492 Maximilian finally managed to set the Low Countries in order, and this had a clear impact on the processions in Amsterdam. Anxiety about how long the peace would last never completely disappeared, but in the bylaws, which increased in length from year to year, the city authorities began to think of combining Eucharistic processions with things other than the defense of the city: celebrations, the influx of visitors, and free street markets. The city was facing a new era, an era of prosperity, and this was illustrated symbolically in a bylaw of 1492 which advised parents where to bring their children to have their faces painted for Corpus Christi, which fell on May 26 that year. It is almost certain that these children were participating in theatrical performances that accompanied the Eucharistic procession. Some of them would have been playing devils. Devils were a common feature of medieval drama, and in Amsterdam they were usually played by children in blackface. Just as in subsequent carnival parades, the idea was not to frighten bystanders but to liven things up by various forms of mockery.[108]

In June 1493, Amsterdam celebrated because peace had been signed a month before in Senlis, France, between Maximilian and Philip on the one hand and their archenemy, the French king Charles VIII, on the other. The city authorities expected that prosperity, business, and trade would now flourish again. The priests of the two parish churches were instructed to carry the "venerable Blessed Sacrament" around their churches and past all monasteries. All burghers and residents of the city were to follow it to thank God for the peace that had been obtained, which they hoped would prove to be lasting. A bonfire was lit on Plaats that evening.

In early March 1495, the city authorities announced that the solemnity (March 18) was approaching on which the miraculous host would be carried through the streets to be venerated by many visitors from outside the city. In order that everything might go smoothly, they decided that visitors might not be prosecuted for any debt for the duration of fifteen days, from the Wednesday before March 12 to the second Wednesday after that date. This would enable them to both devoutly make their pilgrimage and trade their goods. Sometime in September 1494 the city had already decided to organize a similar free street market during the kermis held in the last weeks of September. This initiative was repeated a year later, and only two years later the two annual free street markets were mentioned in one breath.[109] To regulate the crowds, which grew bigger every year, the authorities banned the serving of wine and beer before the end of the procession for both Corpus Christi feasts. On Corpus Christi in Lent, when the number of pilgrims was largest, the streets and bridges that the procession would pass had to be swept and tidied up in advance. A bylaw from March 1498 shows why the distributing of cake and other food was banned: this would look "ugly and wrong" and would diminish the reverence that was due to the Sacrament of Miracle.[110] The city magistrates acted in the interests of the public purse, but they were also sticklers for doctrine![111] At the turn of the century the city organized two further general processions with the Sacrament: in September 1497 to ask God for the safe return of seafarers and for peace and a good harvest, and in July 1498 to pray for the good health of Philip the Handsome's wife, Joan of Castile, who was pregnant. In November the young couple had their first child, Eleanor.

The Amsterdam bylaws show that the city made strategic use of Eucharistic processions in two ways: to show the outside world what position it occupied in the wider political field, and to strengthen concord and solidarity within its own ranks. In the last decades of the fifteenth century the Sacrament passed through the streets of Amsterdam, followed by its burghers and residents, more often than in other cities. But what does that say about the Holy Stead and the memory of the Miracle? Did all these processions use the host of the Miracle? This question can be answered in the affirmative thanks to the bylaw of March 1498 on Corpus Christi in Lent. This bylaw contained various regulations, but it is the salutation that interests us for present purposes: "Tomorrow, if God wills it, and according to ancient custom, we will celebrate by holding a procession with the venerable Blessed Sacrament that is worshiped in the Holy Stead."[112] This made explicit what had been left implicit in previous years. At the time it was universal practice to carry only one host at a time in a Eucharistic procession. To leave the miraculous host, which was adored permanently, in the Holy Stead and instead to carry a different host in the procession would not only have made little liturgical sense, but would also have been detrimental to what these processions were supposed to achieve: unity and solidarity. There was in fact a special reason why the 1498 bylaw mentioned the miraculous host: on March 16, 1498, the Holy Stead served as the starting and end point of the Eucharistic procession through the city for the first time. It was the dawn of a new era for the Miracle of Amsterdam.

2

In the Habsburgs' Favor (1500–1600)

Royal Interest in the Holy Stead

The city authorities noted on March 13, 1498, that the Holy Stead was in excellent condition and was increasing in beauty from day to day "to the greater praise and glory of God's heavenly kingdom." They decided, therefore, that the annual procession on Corpus Christi in Lent would henceforth depart from and finish at the Holy Stead. The schoolchildren and the parishioners of the Nieuwe Kerk would first process to the Oude Kerk, where the parishioners of the two churches would join in a procession to the Holy Stead. The Blessed Sacrament would then be carried from there through the city, according to ancient custom, and would be brought back, still in joint procession, to the Holy Stead to "repose" there. The parish communities that had joined to form a single party would then go in harmony to the Plaetse (Dam square), to take leave of each other amicably before all went their separate ways.[1]

Historians have often associated the renown of the Amsterdam cult with the Habsburgs, the new lords of the Netherlands from 1482. Catholic authors in particular have pointed out that the Holy Stead functioned as a pledge of the good relationship between Amsterdam and successive rulers. This bond was said to have originated in a miraculous cure vouchsafed to Maximilian of Austria. According to the tradition, Maximilian fell critically ill during a sojourn in The Hague in 1484, when he was governor of the country as the guardian of his two-year-old son, Philip. He vowed to go as a pilgrim to the Holy Stead if his health would be restored. And that is exactly what happened, again according to the tradition, whereupon the grateful monarch donated an enormous wax candle, a chalice, and litur-gical vestments to the sanctuary.[2]

Even though the facts do not support this interpretation—Maximilian never visited Amsterdam in 1484—relations between him and the city were excellent. Like all Habsburgs, he was known for his devotion to the Eucharist and was a pious visitor to holy places. When he did visit Amsterdam in 1486, two years after the alleged "miraculous cure," he was received with great pomp and circumstance by the population.[3] Of the many Eucharistic processions held in Amsterdam around the turn of the century, several were held to pray for the well-being of Maximilian and his family.[4] Thus the city authorities decreed in February 1488 that all citizens must join in a general procession to ask God for calm and peace, but especially to secure the liberation of the king of the Romans, "our most gracious lord," who was being held prisoner in Bruges.[5] Another general procession was organized in May or June of the same year, once more with obligatory general attendance, this time to give thanks to God for having freed Maximilian from his captivity.[6] A year later, in February 1489, Maximilian thanked Amsterdam and the other allied cities for their military and financial assistance in his war against the rebel cities (including Rotterdam) by granting them permission to use the imperial crown over the city crest. The citizens of Amsterdam were extremely proud of this heraldic emblem, which enabled them to upstage other trading cities such as Lübeck.[7] At a later point in time—it is not clear exactly when—this permission to use the crown began to be seen as a unique gesture arising from Maximilian's great devotion to the Amsterdam Miraculous Sacrament.[8]

This chapter outlines first how the sacrament of the Eucharist generally, and the Sacraments of Miracle that derived from it in particular, influenced the politics of the Habsburgs.[9] It then returns to sixteenth-century Amsterdam. The vicissitudes of the Holy Stead—and its devotees and detractors—during this time can be divided into three phases: from the beginning of the sixteenth century to the Anabaptist rising of 1535; from the rising to the great Iconoclastic Fury of 1566; and from the difficult predicament in which Amsterdam thereafter found itself, as a Catholic bulwark, to the city's joining of the Protestant rebels in 1578. This century shows how the cult of the Miraculous Sacrament, which had long contributed to the city's prestige, increasingly became a source of division among its citizens.

The Habsburgs and National Consciousness

The previous chapter has shown how the counts of Holland from the House of Bavaria (1349–1433) favored the Holy Stead. By contrast, their successors from the House of Burgundy (1433–1482) had no particular interest in the Amsterdam cult. Their much larger realm was home to many other Sacraments of Miracle. The Burgundian dukes, who were also dukes of Brabant and counts of Holland, preferred the Brussels Miraculous Sacrament (1370), which was closer, as well as a new "Sacrement de Miracle" in Dijon, which they favored from 1433 onward.[10] They regarded these cults not only as forms of devotion, but also as symbolic representations of their alliance with the pope in their ideological war against the heresies that were emerging in their empire, and against the Turks who were advancing elsewhere in Europe. Places of pilgrimage could thus be used in a politico-religious strategic network.

After Mary of Burgundy's death in 1482, a large section of the Interim Kingdom of Burgundy, including the county of Holland, became part of the wider Habsburg Empire (the Northern Netherlands until 1585, the Southern Netherlands until 1794). Like their Burgundian predecessors, the Habsburgs had a particular devotion to the Brussels Sacrament de Miracle, although they also favored other Miraculous Sacraments.[11] They had two important motives. The first was that they, more so than other dynasties, felt strengthened by divine signs, which were revealed to them by means of the sacrament of the Eucharist. As early as the thirteenth century, Rudolf of Habsburg († 1291) was said to have been told by a priest after he had venerated the Blessed Sacrament that his progeny would inherit dominion over the entire world. Centuries later, it seemed that this prophecy was fulfilled when Maximilian of Austria acceded to the imperial crown, later followed in the same course by his grandsons Charles and Ferdinand.[12] Maximilian demonstrated that he fully shared his ancestor's Eucharistic sensibility. In 1471 he fell into a deep ravine near Innsbruck. As soon as the wounded monarch commended his soul to Christ, he received communion from an angel in a vision. The pious monarch was saved, and the Eucharist obtained the additional status of protective amulet of the Habsburgs. Among his admirers Maximilian acquired the honorific name of "the new Elijah," the figure from the Old Testament who had been refreshed with bread and wine by an angel (1 Kings 19:5–8), and who was seen as a precursor of Christ.[13]

The second motive was that the Habsburgs strove to bring many local devotions together under a single heading. As far as they were concerned, the various Eucharistic miracles should be used not to strengthen the identity of the "favored" local community, but rather to increase the communal bonds among their subjects. In other words, these cults were to them "subsidiary cults," all of which pointed to one and the same thing: the Eucharist in which God himself was present, as doctrine confirmed, and which was also the religious cornerstone of the Habsburg Empire. The ruler, somewhat paradoxically, favored many local devotions in order to foster a national identity.

The extent to which the descendants of Maximilian and his son Philip the Handsome were devoted to the Eucharist is very eloquently expressed in the stained-glass windows that they donated to important city churches in their empire.[14] On June 14, 1509, the octave of Corpus Christi, the governor, Maximilian's daughter Margaret of Austria, donated a stained-glass window to the Holy Stead in Amsterdam. The left half of the window showed Maximilian and his successive wives, Mary of Burgundy and Bianca Maria Sforza, kneeling in prayer. The right half showed Maximilian's son Philip the Handsome, his spouse Joanne of Castile, and their six children, among them the later emperors Charles V and Ferdinand I, all in the same posture.[15]

Another church that should be mentioned in this context is St. Gudula's in Brussels. In 1537 Charles V had a stained-glass window placed in the transept of this church, depicting himself and his wife Isabella of Portugal († 1539). Both knelt in adoration before God the Father, who held a cruciform reliquary containing three hosts, a representation of the three miraculous hosts venerated in Brussels.[16] Further donations to Brussels followed (in 1542 and 1549), but Amsterdam, too, remained clearly in the picture. As late as 1555, the year in which Charles's son Philip succeeded his father as lord of the Netherlands, a new glass window was placed in the Oude Kerk in Amsterdam, showing a representation of the miracle of the Holy Stead.[17]

The Eucharistic iconography is also strikingly obvious in another window, donated by the new King Philip to St. John's Church in Gouda in 1557. The upper part of this window, which is still in its original position in this church even though it has been a Protestant place of worship for centuries, shows Philip as a second King Solomon, praying in the temple. The middle part shows Philip together with his second wife, Mary Tudor, known to history as "Bloody Mary." The spouses kneel in adoration of the

Eucharist, which Christ institutes during the Last Supper. In this way, Philip not only illustrated the connection between the Old Covenant (in which God is present in the Holy of Holies in the temple) and the New (in which God is present in the Eucharistic sacrament, here in a monstrance placed in a church), but also his own position as the leader of Christendom.[18] A few years later, in 1561, Philip donated a further seven stained-glass windows for the recently completed choir of the Oude Kerk in Amsterdam. One of the new windows in the choir depicted Philip kneeling before the exposed Sacrament.[19] These princely donations to the Amsterdam churches, one at the beginning of the sixteenth century and two half a century later, have often been seen as visualizations of the good relationship between the city and the Habsburgs.

To sum up, we can say that in the period before the start of the Dutch Revolt (1568), Miraculous Sacraments were important for successive rulers, as they enabled them, through large-scale visits and royal donations, to foster and stimulate a national consciousness and a feeling of mutual connectedness. Amsterdam and its citizens played a comparatively important role in this game.

Eucharistic Symbolism

The success of the Holy Stead as a place of worship, which started during the new regime of the Habsburgs, continued undiminished at the beginning of the sixteenth century. In 1501, from Corpus Christi in Lent (which fell on March 16 that year) up to the second Saturday after Easter (thirteen days after April 11, i.e., April 24), the great jubilee indulgence could be obtained in the Oude Kerk and in the Holy Stead. Two centuries before, in 1300, Pope Boniface VIII had decided that the faithful should have the opportunity to obtain an indulgence in Rome at the beginning of every new century. In short, this meant that every contrite pilgrim who visited the Roman basilicas could obtain pardon of all ecclesiastical censures incurred on account of their sins, censures that they would otherwise have had to expiate either in this life or in the afterlife in purgatory. In the fifteenth and sixteenth centuries, this indulgence was offered not only in Rome, but also in other churches spread across Christian Europe during the year following the official jubilee. At these locations the pilgrims, penitent and willing to give offerings, would receive a written certificate, a so-called letter of indulgence. In the jubilee year of 1500 and the post-jubilee year of 1501, two-thirds of the financial revenues of the indulgences went toward the fight against the Turks, while a third went to the organizers of the grant.[20] In the Low Countries, faithful from Holland and Zeeland desirous of obtaining an indulgence had to go to the Oude Kerk and the Holy Stead in Amsterdam. The flood of pilgrims was enormous and did not stop after 1501. The city authorities sent word to other cities in 1502 that the pope had agreed to make the indulgence available again in Amsterdam from March 12 to April 18.[21]

The choice for Amsterdam as a Roman stand-in confirms the important symbolic function of the city as a Eucharistic place of pilgrimage, a function that would be repeatedly confirmed by high authority. Thus a large city procession with the Blessed Sacrament was held on November 19, 1503, on the occasion of the visit of the archduke of Austria, Philip the Handsome, who was also count of Holland.[22] The years that followed not only witnessed this kind of procession more often,[23] but also saw further evidence of the ruler's personal attention for Amsterdam. In August 1508, two years after Philip the Handsome's death, the city had the first opportunity in many years to greet Maximilian of Austria and pay tribute to him as the governor of his grandson Charles, who was still a minor. Perhaps this was the real beginning of the special relationship between the city and the House of Habsburg, which was sealed, as it were, a year later with Margaret of Austria's previously mentioned donation of a stained-glass window to the Holy Stead. Even more magnificent was the inauguration of Charles V as lord of the Netherlands on June 15 and 16, 1515. The citizens of Amsterdam, who had in previous decades already demonstrated their loyalty to Maximilian, enthusiastically received his grandson as their new count.[24] From 1517 to 1519 the Amsterdam printer Doen Pietersz. published a series of prints by Jacob Cornelisz van Oostsanen representing the counts and countesses of Holland, from Dirk I to Charles V.[25] This visual emphasis on the continuity between the houses of Bavaria, Burgundy, and Habsburg was an implicit expression of solidarity with the young monarch.

Despite this official display organized by the city authorities, many Amsterdam citizens proved amenable to the new religious convictions that emerged in Western Europe after the beginning of the Reformation (ca. 1517). As a trading hub and a place of pilgrimage, the city attracted many visitors from abroad. City environments afforded many opportunities for the exchange of views, and Amsterdam, with its approximately twelve thousand inhabitants, was a relatively large city in the Low Countries, which in turn were the most urbanized region in northwestern Europe.[26]

Many Amsterdam citizens were able to speak out publicly against the doctrine of the Catholic Church without the city authorities feeling the need to intervene. It was not until 1523 that the task of prosecuting "heretics" was taken seriously to hand, under pressure from the bishop of Utrecht.

The Reformation Comes to Holland

It is remarkable that the early Reformation in Holland, including in Amsterdam, was directed more so than elsewhere against the doctrine of the sacraments, particularly against the dogma of Christ's real presence in the Eucharist and the explanatory concept of transubstantiation. An important monument in the history of the Reformation in the Netherlands is a theological discourse written by Cornelis Henricxz Hoen († 1524 or 1525, a lawyer at the Court of Holland (*Hof van Holland*) in The Hague, which dealt precisely with this subject. In his *Epistola christiana admodum*, published posthumously in 1525 and better known under the title *Letter on the Lord's Supper*, Hoen argued, among other things, that there could be no such thing as transubstantiation. On the contrary, he contended that it was the devil who wished people to believe that the Eucharistic bread became God himself. If people were to give up this form of idolatry, Hoen averred, very little would remain of the church of Rome.[27] Sympathizers of Hoen, who have become known to history as Sacramentarians on account of their criticism of this Roman doctrine, would later, in the early 1530s, join the Anabaptist movement as it spread from the German lands.[28]

It was clear that some response would be forthcoming from those who remained loyal to the teachings of the church of Rome. A pilgrimage card of the Miracle printed in 1518 can be seen as a first signal to contrast the classic interpretation of the faith with that of the Sacramentarians. It depicts the hearth that could still be viewed in the Holy Stead. The card may have been printed at the behest of Pompeius Occo (1483–1537), the wealthy chapel warden of the Holy Stead.[29] Occo, who was of Frisian stock, had established himself in Amsterdam in 1511 as the agent of the Danish royal house and of the Fuggers, a banking family who were Europe's most important trading house at that time. This Maecenas endowed the Holy Stead with many gifts, "to such an extent that no one outdid him in this respect."[30] The historian Sterck lists as two of his most special gifts a beautiful church organ, whose case is still in service today in St. Nicholas's Church in the village of Jutphaas, and nine paintings by Van Oostsanen depicting the original miracle of the Holy Stead in several consecutive scenes. These large "scaffolding sheets," some of which have been preserved, were probably intended to be displayed in the open air, for the instruction of the many pilgrims who came from outside the city.[31] A lavishly executed choir book containing liturgical songs, which was given in loan to the Holy Stead by Occo shortly before his death, has also been preserved.[32]

Five years later, in April 1523, the priest and humanist Alardus of Amsterdam published a defense against the "heretics" who, he claimed, denied the Eucharist. In sharp language he pointed out that his favorite place to preach was the Holy Stead, "where once the Most Holy Eucharist was found in the flames." In this way he attempted to warn the faithful against the adherents of new religious views, such as the Lutherans. The book was illustrated with a number of woodcuts; one of them is a print of the pilgrimage card of the Holy Stead from 1518 mentioned above.[33]

The combative position that Alardus took was entirely consonant with the strict line adopted by Charles V. In his large empire, especially in the German lands, Charles was increasingly being confronted by religious convictions that he could not view in any way other than as an attack on the true faith and on the foundations of his dynasty. This is why in 1521 he regularly began to issue special decrees, the so-called placards. These were initially intended only to prohibit and punish the reading and possession of books by Luther; later they were also directed at the printing and dissemination of unauthorized translations of the Bible, the breaking of statues of the saints, and so on. The enforcement of these placards was entrusted partly to the episcopal inquisition, partly to the provincial and municipal courts, partly to the papal inquisition, and partly to the imperial inquisition established by Charles in 1521.[34] These last two institutions caused some resentment among the cities and provinces, which had for generations taken care of their own affairs in consultation with the episcopal courts. The tolerant Amsterdam city authorities, too, were not pleased with the strict measures; they did not share Alardus's concerns or Charles's strictness when it came to the fight against heretics. Thus, in 1523, the city protested to the governor, Margaret of Austria, together with the other cities of Holland, against the harsh manner in which the imperial inquisitor Frans van der Hulst was operating against Hoen and other alleged heretics. This left Margaret with no choice but to dismiss the unpopular Van der Hulst, who thereafter could not appear in public in Holland for fear of being molested.[35]

On May 21, 1524, the Amsterdam *schepenbank,* or council of magistrates, probably after consultation with the Court of Holland, nonetheless convicted nine Sacramentarians of holding assemblies and religious meetings. On the following day, Trinity Sunday (Sunday after Pentecost), all of them were required to participate in the procession to the Oude Kerk, each holding a burning wax candle—for centuries this had been the usual manner in the Western church to mark out penitents.[36] After the procession, they had to bring their candle up to the monstrance containing a host that stood in the front of the church. One of the punished men even had to go on a pilgrimage to St. Job in Brabant (Wezemaal).[37] Content with their display of decisiveness, the Amsterdam authorities reported to the court that the Lutheran sect in the city had been eradicated.[38]

But incidents continued to occur. The punishments inflicted sometimes seem farcical, such as that revealed by a city bylaw of 1527. An inebriated cooper called Jan Pauluszoon had blasphemed against the Eucharist so outrageously in the de Pot tavern that the scandalized innkeeper and his wife had decided to bring charges against him before the court. Although Jan declared to the magistrates that he could not remember any blasphemy, he was sentenced to imprisonment "on beer and bread" from May 17 to Corpus Christi (June 20 that year). On Corpus Christi he had to join in the procession, attired in a harness and holding a burning candle. The harness had to be covered with round pieces of paper displaying "figures of the Blessed Sacrament." The pieces of paper probably represented hosts, while the figures were the motifs (such as stars, crosses, and lambs) that were embossed onto altar breads during baking. Dressed in this way, Jan had to go to de Pot after the procession and ask the innkeeper and his wife for forgiveness on his knees.[39] A year later, the judges of the court were considerably stricter with a certain Hillebrant of Zwolle, who had publicly declared that the Sacrament of the Altar was just ordinary bread. Hillebrant was pilloried and, after his tongue had been pierced, he was banned from entering the city ever again.[40]

In the view of the Great Council of Mechelen, however, the Amsterdam city authorities were too lenient in prosecuting and punishing heretics.[41] The magistrates evidently attached greater importance to preventing unrest and keeping the peace than to rooting out heresy. Thus Catholics who vociferously attacked the Sacramentarians could expect to be convicted of disturbing the peace.[42] In addition, the city authorities did not fear the outbreak of violent revolution because, in the 1520s, the population of the city in large majority remained loyal to the old faith. When the Low Countries were affected in August and September 1529 by an epidemic of the feared "English sweating sickness" (a deadly infectious disease that manifested itself in summer), the citizens of Amsterdam took part in huge numbers in penitential processions, as did the citizens of other cities. The city authorities exhorted their citizens to deflect God's wrath by going to confession, by giving alms and performing other good works, and by "receiving the Blessed Sacrament worthily."[43]

When a certain Jakob Klaaszoon Backer refused to step aside on the street to let the parochial vicar of the Oude Kerk pass to bring communion (or viaticum) to the sick in the winter of 1530 to 1531, he was charged before the magistrates. The latter asked the vicar to determine the sentence: Jakob had to attend the sung mass in the Oude Kerk on Thursdays on his knees for the duration of three months.[44] The nonchalance that characterized proceedings and the relatively light sentence leave the impression that the citizens of Amsterdam did not live in fear of religious turmoil at the time. Religious turmoil was not long in coming, however.

A Women's Resistance Movement and the City's Identity

An ode published in 1532 by Alardus of Amsterdam refers to a visit to the Holy Stead by Charles V: "On account of a pious vow he made abroad, Charles, as soon as he arrived in Holland, visited the chapel as piously as he could to endow it with imperial donations." This visit is said to have taken place in March 1531, that is, around Corpus Christi in Lent. Charles did in fact visit the Low Countries in that year. It is remarkable that this visit was not recorded in the official chronicles. The theologian Albertus Kölker has suggested that Charles's visit was perhaps of a personal devotional nature.[45]

Whatever the truth about this private initiative, the fact is that Charles's Eucharistic devotion was well-known in Amsterdam and many assumed that he therefore also favored the Holy Stead. This assumption is borne out by a curious action taken by several members of the women's guild of the Holy Stead. As was seen in the first chapter, this guild had been founded shortly after the 1345 Miracle to further the glory of the Holy Stead, and on several occasions in the sixteenth century it would prove to be a particularly resilient women's movement.

In May 1531, the Amsterdam city authorities decided to build a workshop for wool processing in the narrow garden beside the Holy Stead. But after the pits for the foundations had been dug, they were filled up again by a group of approximately three hundred city women on the evening of May 31. These women apparently regarded the works as a violation of the sacred space of the sanctuary. Their action shows to what extent a large part of the population was attached to the Holy Stead as something that connected them to God and to one another. The burgomasters strongly opposed this; for them stimulating the urban economy was of overriding importance. Their response was strict: a fortnight after the pits were filled up, on June 14, three of the four women who constituted the board of the Guild of the Blessed Sacrament and who had planned the action, the so-called *overwiven*, were banished from the city for four years. The fourth escaped this fate by paying a fine of fifty guilders.

But that was not the end of the matter. Together with a number of female friends and the parish priest of the Nieuwe Kerk, Master Claes Boelen or Boelens, the three exiles went to the Low Countries' seat of residence, Brussels, where they wished to complain to Charles about the proposed desecration of land belonging to the Holy Stead. They arrived in the Brabant capital on June 23 and had ample opportunity there to express their concerns about *lutherij* and the insults given to the Blessed Sacrament. Finally, on July 14, they succeeded in gaining access in person to the emperor, who was just about to sit down to table. Master Claes asked him for grace and support, as the women were fighting a just cause. The emperor, taken aback, left the case in the hands of his chancellor, Jean Carondelet. Carondelet discussed the issue with one of the burgomasters of Amsterdam who, shrewdly, had also traveled to Brussels. The two gentlemen evidently decided to regard the case as a purely administrative issue and not to attach any significance to the *overwiven*'s imputations. The chancellor maintained the sentence by giving them the choice of banishment or paying a fine of fifty guilders. The women were no more successful with the emperor's confessor and the papal legate, who both confirmed the option the women had been given. None of this prevented them from making a truly triumphal entry into the city when they returned to Amsterdam on July 28, nearly two months after their departure. They rode through the streets in their carriage and waved to the public as if they had been entirely vindicated by the emperor's decision. The fine of fifty guilders was not much of a problem for them, for all three came from wealthy and important families. Other women from the large group of three hundred had to pay fines, but found this considerably more difficult. New pits were dug at the Holy Stead on August 7, and the wool house was built without further incident.[46] The equilibrium between sacred and commercial interests had been restored.

The whole case shows that the impulsive women's guild had overestimated its power, given that the emperor—or his chancellor—had not the slightest inclination to go against the city authorities. The latter used the case to show that they would tolerate no social unrest, regardless of the perpetrators' intentions. Nevertheless, the Amsterdam women's assertive reaction does indicate that in the 1530s a large part of the population was ready to defend the old faith and its local personification, the Holy Stead. This background makes it more significant that Alardus would, one year later, dedicate his book on communion to his friend and sympathizer Claes Boelen, the women's guild's coach and companion.

That many saw the Holy Stead as characteristic of the city and that it occupied a central place in the nascent religious struggle is evident not only from the ill-fated Brussels expedition, but even more so from a passage in Alardus's ode. Its content can be paraphrased as follows:

> The most excellent deed which Amsterdam's former church patrons wrought is that they built a beautiful temple without delay as soon as they found the Blessed Sacrament in the fiery flames, always appointed irreproachable churchwardens, appointed many virtuous and learned priests for the liturgy, and ordained that the entire clergy of the city should sing vespers and benediction to honor the Blessed Sacrament every Wednesday. Through their good example, these church patrons have also inspired the piety of the other citizens of Amsterdam, who, with the exception of a few heretics, often, particularly on Wednesdays, hold the procession at the break of dawn, with uncovered heads and bare feet, simple and without ornamentation, often holding a burning candle, with downcast eyes, without greeting anyone, with restraint and as devoutly as possible.[47] Rich and poor contributed to this sanctuary, and thus a common bond and undying friendship were forged among the citizens. All these customs, which have been practiced for more than a hundred years, have spread the fame of the Holy Stead, so that foreigners believe they have only seen Holland as soon they have set eyes upon this building, the eighth wonder of the world. Among the visitors to the sanctuary were important men, such as Maximilian and Charles V.[48]

If we are to believe Alardus, the identity of the citizens of Amsterdam, for which they were even known abroad, was constituted by their bond with the Holy Stead. This identity was characterized by a very specific, interiorized religiosity. It is an echo of the late-medieval spiritual reform movement's quest for God and the neighbor through one's own inner being. In formulating this focus on the inner life, the adherents of the Modern Devotion placed great stress on the sacrament of the Eucharist.[49] Because what happens in the inner life can only be perceived indirectly, Alardus dwells precisely on those forms of behavior that point to a pious state of mind, characterized by restraint: barefoot, without ornamentation, eyes downcast, and so on. In addition to this interiorized religious attitude, which was widespread, according to Alardus, the Holy Stead had also brought about a communal bond among the citizens of Amsterdam. Their piety kept them together and fostered mutual friendship. A militantly Catholic author, Alardus undoubtedly painted too rosy a picture of the situation in his ode: polemics always involve exaggeration. Some of his other works show that he was, in fact, concerned that the followers of Luther, Karlstadt, Oecolampadius, Zwingli, and other reformers would one day outnumber the Catholics. He wanted to avert this doom scenario by constantly dwelling on the doctrine of transubstantiation and the great graces of the Eucharist.[50] Alardus very likely wanted to exorcise his great anxiety about the future by painting an exaggerated picture of the intense ardor that the population of Amsterdam felt for the Holy Stead.

Alardus's exaggerations notwithstanding, regular processions—especially on Wednesdays, to and around the Holy Stead—must have been a familiar phenomenon in the 1520s and 1530s. Contrary to the wish that was father to Alardus's thought, however, this cult did not unite the citizens but divided them. It is remarkable to note, incidentally, that these processions already had certain characteristics of the so-called silent processions of the period after the Calvinist takeover, when the public exercise of the Catholic faith was proscribed in the Northern Netherlands.

As has been seen, Alardus's fears about the threats to religious life were not shared by the city authorities. By contrast, however, the provincial governments had strong concerns. The contrast in vision and policy came to light clearly in December 1531, when nine Anabaptists from Amsterdam were convicted and executed in The Hague, through the intervention of the Court of Holland. They escaped the stake by showing remorse and were instead decapitated, on the advice of no less an authority than Charles V.[51]

These and similar measures of the provincial government not only angered the Amsterdam sheriff and burgomasters because they infringed the rights of the city and its citizens, but also damaged the image of the Catholic Church. This is evident, for example, from the complaints of the parish priest of the Oude Kerk in 1533 that he was reluctant to bring the Blessed Sacrament to the sick for fear of negative reactions on the streets and from the homes. A notorious Sacramentarian called "One-Eyed Adriaan" declared openly and with impunity before the court that the Blessed Sacrament was just baked bread, which he would be happy to pierce with a dagger without fear of drawing blood.[52] This statement was a clear reference to the many Sacraments of Miracle, such as those in Brussels and Breda, where one or more venerated hosts were said to have bled after being pierced with a dagger or other sharp object. It had become abundantly clear by this time that the "Lutheran sect"—this was the collective designation given to anything that was not Catholic—was far from having been eradicated.

In 1534 Anabaptists from Holland were preparing to seize power in Amsterdam. As late as the beginning of 1535, the Amsterdam priest Cornelis Crocus, affiliated with the city school, published a little book about the danger that they represented.[53] Shortly afterward it became clear that Crocus's fears were well founded.

The Failed Coup of the Anabaptists in 1535

On the evening of Monday, May 10, 1535, the Amsterdam city authorities were taken completely by surprise by a coup carried out by the heretical Anabaptist movement. A group of some forty armed men occupied the Dam and the city hall.[54] There they awaited the support of other Anabaptists from the city and elsewhere and issued an appeal to all the evangelically minded—Lutherans and Sacramentarians—to join in defeating the "priests and the monks." The next day the civic militia, after heavy fighting that cost many lives on both sides, succeeded in isolating and defeating the group. The insurgents who had not been killed in the fighting were put to death a few days later, together with a number of their supporters. The total tally of the executed came to forty-six, both men and women.[55]

It was also a turbulent and disastrous year for Anabaptists outside Holland. On June 25, 1535, six weeks after the Amsterdam fiasco, the city of Münster (Germany), where Anabaptists from the Low Countries and Central Europe had established a reign of terror, was reconquered by its own bishop's troops. From that moment on, the Anabaptists relinquished their attempts to bring about the Millennium through violence and retreated from public life. They would nonetheless be oppressed for many decades on account of their religious convictions, by both Catholics and Protestants.[56] Protestants were quite as implacable in their persecution as the church of Rome because they believed the Anabaptists were trying to deprive the faithful of the sacraments.[57] It must be remarked that the views of great reformers such as Luther and Calvin on the Eucharist—for instance, on the real presence during the Lord's Supper and on the sacrament's mediation of grace—did not in fact differ very much from Catholic doctrine. The aspects that all strands of the Reformation rejected were the Eucharistic practices that had arisen during the later Middle Ages, such as exposition and processions of the Blessed Sacrament, and Sacraments of Miracle. By isolating the Eucharistic bread from the celebration of the Lord's Supper and by claiming that Christ remained really present in this bread, the papists had, in the eyes of the reformers, made themselves a "bread god."[58]

Perhaps to show their loyalty to Mother Church and to the monarch, the States of Holland donated in 1535 a stained-glass window of the Last Supper to the newly constructed St. Catherine's Church in Hoogstraten in Brabant. This church was built at the instigation of Antoine de Lalaing, count of Hoogstraten and stadtholder of Holland, and his immensely wealthy wife, Elisabeth of Culemborg. Both were close collaborators and confidants of Margaret of Austria and her successor as governor, Mary of Hungary (1531–1555), sister of Charles V.[59]

In the beginning of 1538, the hitherto tolerant city authorities of Amsterdam were replaced by new men who were very loyal to the ruler and to the church. During the following decades, up to the so-called Alteration or coup of 1578, the thirty-six members of the *vroedschap* (city council), the *schout* (sheriff), the seven *schepenen* (magistrates), and the four burgomasters belonged to an oligarchy known as the Hendrick-Dirckists. This name refers to a certain Hendrick Dirckszoon, who, as one of the pre-1535 magistrates, had been unusually hostile to heretics. In 1539 he was elected burgomaster. Some of the Hendrick-Dirckists belonged to families whose names have already featured or will soon feature in relation to the Miracle of Amsterdam, such as Boelens, Buyck, and Occo.[60]

By decree of the new city authorities, a large procession was held in Amsterdam on May 11, 1536, to commemorate the victory over the Anabaptists. The gentlemen of the court of justice and of the city council participated, as well as the guilds, followed by the parish priests of the two city churches, who together carried the Blessed Sacrament. Militiamen followed the Blessed Sacrament. All the bells of both Oude and Nieuwe Zijde (Old and New Sides) pealed during the solemnity. The city authorities decreed that this commemoration, including a procession, would from then on be held every year on May 11.[61] This meant that there were henceforth three annual feasts linked to the sacrament of the Eucharist, a situation unique in the Low Countries and which would remain in force, with a number of interruptions, until the 1578 Alteration.[62] The establishment of this new triumphal procession gave special effect, more than three centuries after the date, to Pope Urban IV's call to confound the heretics by rendering festive homage to the Blessed Sacrament.

By way of punishments, putative heretics from time to time had to acknowledge their infamy and shame to the general population. Thus on January 19, 1544, two pairs of sisters, Aef and Neel Jan Verbrughendochter and Duyff and Anna Jansdochter, were sentenced to a fine and banishment from the city for their sympathy for the Anabaptists. They were not allowed back by the Amsterdam court until May 11 of that year, when they had to follow the Blessed Sacrament in the procession as penitents, with uncovered heads and holding a burning candle. After the procession, each of them had to bring their candle to the Oude Kerk and place it before the Blessed Sacrament. A sympathizer of the four women, Diuwer Hanssen, was not banished, but also had to join in the procession holding a candle.[63]

Disciplining Faith and Cult

The 1540s appear to have passed almost without incident in Holland and Amsterdam as far as religious life is concerned. The fight against the Turks, continual flare-ups in the war with archenemy France, and the unsuccessful suppression of Protestantism in the German lands claimed most of Charles V's attention. The appearance of calm during these apprehensive years was due in large part to the policy of repression that the hated governor, Mary of Hungary, implemented on behalf of her brother. Penal restrictions in the field of religion became ever stricter. The placards mentioned earlier testify to this, as do a list of articles of the faith, drawn up by or at the behest of Charles, that bound all priests, and the introduction of the index of prohibited books.[64] On August 13, 1540, Charles, who was on a tour of Holland, publicly visited the city for the first time in twenty-five years—at least, if we discount the unconfirmed visit in 1531 mentioned by Alardus.[65] The monarch was received with much pomp and circumstance and the firing of gun salutes. Charles's tour this time was primarily for the purpose of obtaining funds: a request to the cities of Holland for a (joint) annual subsidy of one hundred thousand guilders for the duration of six years. Because of its enthusiastic cooperation, Amsterdam received a discount of 25 percent.[66]

In the years that followed, Amsterdam sheriff Willem Bardes emerged as a real hammer of heretics. He helped bring eight Anabaptists to the stake in front of the city hall on the Dam, where they were burned in the spring of 1549. Executions of Anabaptists, who always denied the real presence before the courts, would have caused much horror among the citizenry, but they did not destabilize society.[67] Previously, in April 1547, the flames had already consumed Bouwen Wybrantszoon from Bolsward at the stake, also on the Dam. Bouwen had not only stolen liturgical vessels from the Old and New Churches, but had also carelessly disposed of the hosts that were in them.[68] The churchwardens of the Oude Kerk had a new monstrance made in 1549, bigger and more ornate than the one that Bouwen melted down. This new monstrance survived the vicissitudes of the Reformation era and ultimately found its way to the parish church of the German town of Kalkar.[69]

Around the middle of the sixteenth century, the emperor and the church took two important measures to bring the population of the Low Countries to heel as far as religion was concerned: a drastic reform of church life and, more than a decade later, the erection of new dioceses. On July 9, 1548, shortly after the German Diet of Augsburg, the clergy, on Emperor Charles's instructions, adopted a long list of proposals concerning the reform and standardization of ecclesiastical and religious life. This list, known as the *Formula reformationis*, was applied more stringently in the dioceses of the Low Countries—Charles's real "hereditary lands"— than in the German Empire. In the diocese of Utrecht, the *Formula* was ratified by a specially convoked diocesan synod in February 1549.[70] It decreed that the liturgy must remain pure, that is, in accordance with age-old tradition and uncontaminated by superfluous, superstitious, and heretical elements. Thus the epistle and the gospel might only be read during mass in Latin, although they might then be explained to the faithful in the vernacular. Whenever the host was carried in procession on feasts or rogation days, all worldly games and anything that did not incite devotion had to cease. The Blessed Sacrament should only be brought out of church buildings for grave reasons. When communion was being brought to the sick, someone had to go before the priest bearing a lantern, while the bells had to be rung to alert the faithful.[71] Anxieties with respect to the current situation are most clearly visible in the chapter on the "discipline of the people." Obedience was due from the people to their secular lord and the civic authorities, as well as to the bishop. The people must honor and obey their shepherd (the parish priest) and his superiors. By consequence the faithful were forbidden to read books that were detrimental to the faith and were instead exhorted to read works that incited them to purer devotion, such as the lives of the saints. Above all, the people must reject new religious views that were not accepted by the church, and magistrates were instructed to enforce this. Secular lords and civic magistrates must not protect those who thwarted the ecclesiastical reform program. On the contrary, government bodies should assist the bishop and follow his regulations; if they refused, they would be removed from office by His Imperial Majesty's commissioners.[72]

In order to give support to the bishops, Charles issued his strictest placard so far on April 29, 1550, the so-called blood placard. All previous prohibitions remained in force, but the punishment was made more severe: henceforth, every sign of heresy was to be punished by death. Even heretics who renounced their errors had to die: men by the sword and women by drowning. People who moved house and took up residence elsewhere had to present a certificate of orthodoxy in the new parish. All of the emperor's officials were responsible for the application of the blood placard. In practice, very little was done about this; even the imperial inquisitors thought the prescribed punishments absurd. But Charles did succeed in making clear to his subjects that he was serious about the root-and-branch eradication from his territory of what he considered to be heresy.[73]

A logical follow-up of the *Formula reformationis* was the erection by Pope Paul IV ten years later, in 1559, of no fewer than fourteen new dioceses in the Low Countries. The pope had taken this decision at the prompting of Philip II, who succeeded his father as lord of the Netherlands in 1555. One of the new episcopal sees was erected in Haarlem; this meant that from then on the citizens of Amsterdam had a bishop at close quarters, in their own province.[74] Between the proclamation of the *Formula reformationis* and the foundation of the new dioceses, the Holy Stead's significance to ecclesiastical politics also increased.

In 1549, Philip II came to the Low Countries to be acclaimed there as the future heir to his father, Charles V. It made a deep impression on the Spanish prince that his future subjects repeatedly compared him to Solomon (see also the stained-glass window in Gouda mentioned above), who would complete the work of his father, King David. By analogy with the

Old Testament, the latter stood for Charles V.[75] Philip, traveling together with his father and his aunt (the governor), was received in the most important cities of the Southern Netherlands during the summer months. In late September he left for Holland, still in the company of his aunt but no longer of his father. Holland also received him with great circumstance, especially Amsterdam. During his visit to the city on October 1, the bridges under which the royal company passed were decorated and a triumphal arch was erected, adorned with feminine symbols representing Faith, Heresy, and Error. Faith bore a paten with a host in her right hand and a chain with two nooses in her left, from which were suspended Heresy and Error. According to the legend, this scene referred to the safeguarding of the true faith from the revolt of the Anabaptists and the inability of Heresy and Error to prevail against the crown prince and his invincible arms.[76] Thus were the Catholic Church's views on the Eucharist displayed in martial fashion. At the same time, Amsterdam declared its support for the policy of the Habsburgs, who had chosen the sacrament of the Eucharist as the legitimation of their ideology of power and religion.

Inspired, perhaps, by a circular letter published by the churchwardens of St. Laurence's Church in Alkmaar in 1545 to promote the local cult of the Precious Blood, the Amsterdam chapel wardens decided to publish a series of booklets to spread devotion to the Miracle of Amsterdam. The result was a Dutch-language miracle book from circa 1550 (extant only in a later edition from ca. 1568) and a Latin book of hours from circa 1555 for the feast of Corpus Christi in Lent. The title of this latter book was, in translation, "Short account of the miracles, which the Lord gloriously wrought through the venerable Sacrament in the chapel of the Holy Stead in Amsterdam."[77] Miracle books were important instruments in publicizing and legitimizing local devotions. By describing and publishing all known miracles that had ever happened to pilgrims—particularly cures of all kinds of diseases—the importance of the Holy Stead as a beneficial place of pilgrimage was reconfirmed, making it easier to compete with other places of pilgrimage, which also claimed their own miracles and cures.[78] The chapel wardens did not have to worry about the costs of publication. Due to the large flood of pilgrims, the Holy Stead was wealthier during this period than the Old and New Churches together.[79] In the meantime, the position of Catholicism as the only permitted public religion had grown stronger than it had been in the 1520s and 1530s. As has been seen, in 1555 the Oude Kerk received a new glass window representing the Miracle; this was followed in 1561 by at least one other window that also referenced the Miracle. In October and November 1556, the auxiliary bishop of Utrecht, Nicolaas van Nieuwland, came to administer confirmation to the young faithful of Amsterdam and the surrounding countryside for the first time in many years. The city authorities' request for this episcopal service was not without reason. The most important fruit of this sacrament, which the faithful might receive only once in their lifetime, was at the time considered to be an increase of the ability to persevere in the faith.[80]

The public manifestations mentioned above appear to point to a remarkable unity of purpose between the national, ecclesiastical, provincial, and city governments. In fact, however, this was a unity imposed from above. What was really taking place was that the first two of these governments were becoming more powerful—especially the national government—at the expense of the liberties of the provinces and the cities, including the city of Amsterdam. In the later Middle Ages it would hardly have been imaginable that the count's commissioners would have been able to supervise the application of ecclesiastical regulations in the cities. Nor was the establishment of a new episcopal see in nearby Haarlem welcomed by the clergy and the city authorities of Amsterdam. The city had previously had to deal with claims of the Chapter of Our Lady in The Hague, but now an entirely new relationship of dependency was looming, involving a much higher ecclesiastical authority in a different city. This relationship was far from cordial and would only improve in the 1570s, when Amsterdam and Haarlem found themselves in similar dire straits, as shall be seen.[81]

Provinces, cities, and, incidentally, also a large section of the clergy (whose large, wealthy abbeys had to finance the new dioceses) were unhappy about their loss of freedom and the spike in costs. Despite irritation at the tributes imposed, Amsterdam retained a close bond with the ruler and the church, thanks to the Holy Stead, which remained very important to the city's identity and allure. In this sense the city was unique in Holland.

1566, the "Miraculous Year"

The 1560s have gone down in history as a period of social unrest and economic decline in the Low Countries.[82] However, a number of trading cities, primarily Antwerp, but also Amsterdam, deviated from this pattern;

they experienced significant economic prosperity compared to other cities. But these two cities were not spared the great Iconoclastic Fury that visited the country's churches and monasteries in the late summer of 1566. The Low Countries were a densely populated region dependent on food imports, and the famine that occurred at this time—which naturally most affected the poor—undoubtedly contributed to the unrest that led to the iconoclastic outbreak. But this circumstance cannot fully explain the fury, which was in fact carried out by gangs consisting of no more than a few dozen members each. Led by field preachers of the Calvinists' "counter church," which had come into existence around 1550, these gangs went from city to city and from church to church.

How could such a small group inflict so much damage, while most Hollanders, including the citizens of Amsterdam, still considered themselves to be members of the Catholic Church? The passivity of law-enforcement bodies—primarily the civic militias—in acting against the vandals can in part be ascribed to the fact that they were simply taken off guard by the rapidly emerging situation. But an additional explanation is that sympathy for King Philip II had slumped across the full spectrum of the population after his departure from the Low Countries in 1559, leaving for Spain, never to return. The inhabitants of Holland, Flanders, Brabant, and the other provinces thought they were living in an empire that was much too large. They could accept the Ghent native Charles V as someone who was close to them in some respects, but not his Spanish-born son. They were being governed from a foreign country, subsidizing the wars of a foreign prince (especially wars against France), and saw how some of their neighbors and relatives were being cruelly persecuted on account of their dissenting religious convictions. This is why many experienced the Iconoclastic Fury as something directed not against their own community, but rather against a foreign king and his foreign helpers—helpers who were known for their fanaticism, an attitude quite different from the citizens' own experience of the Catholic faith.[83]

On August 23, 1566, the Oude Kerk was stormed, causing the city authorities to take the precautionary measure of closing all places of worship in the city. A second wave of iconoclasm, in late September, targeted the Franciscan priory and the Carthusian monastery outside the city. The iconoclasts also proceeded to the Holy Stead. But when they arrived there, they were outmaneuvered by an unexpected adversary. A large group of Amsterdam women, most of them from distinguished patrician families, had formed a cordon around the altar of the Sacrament of Miracle and the tabernacle. Once again, women were the first to rush to the barricades to protect the Holy Stead. They shouted that they would rather die than permit the miraculous host to be desecrated. The iconoclasts retreated upon hearing their frightful shouts and threats.[84] This heroic event made a deep impression on many contemporaries, including the governor, Margaret of Parma. In October 1566 she sent her half brother Philip II a report of the rebellion in the Netherlands and also asked for support to restore public order. Her report discussed the functioning of Philip's stadtholder William of Orange, in whom she placed a lot of trust and who she felt was the right person to calm the situation. She then recounted the plundering of the Amsterdam monasteries in late September and what she considered to be the excessive leniency of the local governments toward the "sectarians" and the rabble. Speaking of the actions of the women of Amsterdam, she wrote, "Et de la mesme fureur voulurent (certains sectaires et canailles) faire violence sur le reste des églises, voires rompre le St. Sacrement de Miracle qui'ilz ont en ladicte ville, ce que les femmes ont à force deffendu." (And with the same fury [some sectarians and scoundrels] wanted to do violence to the rest of the churches, and to break the Blessed Sacrament of Miracle that they have in the city, which [Sacrament] the women have forcibly defended.)[85]

The women's guild had indeed acted much more bravely than the city authorities, who were, it must be noted, all convinced Catholic men. Overcome with fear, the authorities granted a number of concessions to the Calvinists, such as the use of one of the monastery churches for Protestant worship. These concessions were withdrawn again in the spring of 1567 on Margaret's orders.[86] The governor was riding a favorable tide. Up until the Iconoclastic Fury, the majority of the population had some sympathy for Christians with non-Catholic beliefs, such as the Calvinists, because of their religious courage and their position as underdogs in society. But the Calvinists pushed their luck too far with their vandalism and violence in August and September 1566, resulting in a swing of public opinion against them.[87]

In March 1567, for the first time in many generations, the procession on Corpus Christi in Lent did not take place, for fear of the Calvinists.[88] But William of Orange—who took an attitude of conciliation between the various Christian confessions—soon succeeded in restoring order on behalf of the governor, which strengthened the position of the Catholic city authorities. Reform-minded citizens fled the city, while Catholic refugees from other parts flooded in. At the annual commemoration of the Anabaptist insurgence, on May 11 of that year, the procession with the Blessed Sacrament was held again, "as devout and solemn as had never been seen anywhere in the world." From then on, this procession commemorated not only the 1535 victory over the Anabaptists, but also that over the Calvinists in 1566.[89] Thus the Amsterdam processional culture continued to expand. Moreover, everywhere in northwestern Europe, at least where Catholics were in power, Eucharistic processions were regarded and used as the most effective method to demonstrate mutual solidarity and communal resilience against dissidents.[90] What did change fundamentally after 1566, however, was the composition of these Eucharistic processions in the Dutch cities. Thus, in 1567 the militias and the guilds were absent from the procession on Corpus Christi (June 8 of that year) to the chagrin of many; their members were only permitted to join on an individual basis.[91] The mutual solidarity that these processions visualized referred no longer to the civic community, but instead to the national community under the aegis of Philip.

For the king, the good collaboration between Margaret of Parma and William of Orange in checking the unrest was clearly not sufficient. In the summer of 1567, Philip sent the duke of Alva to the Low Countries to radically exterminate all heresy. A few months later, a disillusioned Margaret departed for Italy; William resigned his positions and went abroad. The severe tactics of the "iron duke" produced the opposite of what Philip intended. The number of Calvinists increased daily in the Low Countries; Calvinists soon overtook the Lutherans and Anabaptists in respect of their influence on society and level of organization.[92] In Amsterdam, too, they began to assert themselves strongly, even though the Catholic city authorities ensured that they had to restrain themselves from time to time. Just as elsewhere, the Amsterdam city authorities busied themselves with punishing the perpetrators of the iconoclastic outbreak. A total of 242 citizens were convicted, most of them in absentia as they had already fled the city; the 24 who had remained were sentenced to death.[93] The religious controversy in the Low Countries gave a strong impulse to the revolt against the king that began in 1568 under the leadership of William of Orange, who had only recently been praised for his loyalty.[94]

In 1570, the new Spanish governor Alva tried an entirely different tactic. On Sunday, July 16, a day after the closing of the provincial council at Mechelen, he ostentatiously announced a general amnesty for repentant heretics. This was his way of attempting to regain the initiative and re-Catholicize and reunite the Low Countries under the authority of Philip II. July 16 was also the feast of the Brussels Sacrement de Miracle, which celebrated its second centenary in 1570. Perhaps Alva and his counselors specifically chose this day—with its focus on the Eucharist—although the amnesty was proclaimed not in Brussels but elsewhere in Brabant. The pardon did not have the desired effect, as very few "heretics" availed of it to return to the Catholic Church.[95]

The End of Amsterdam as an International Place of Pilgrimage

When the revolt against the rule of Philip II reached Holland in the summer of 1572, Amsterdam was the only city to remain loyal to "crown and altar."[96] Just as the Blessed Sacrament more generally was a symbol of the "sacred" struggle of the Habsburgs against the heretics, the Holy Stead specifically became a symbol of Amsterdam's resistance against the advancing Beggars (or *Geuzen*). The threats and mockery that were directed from outside—and sometimes from within—against the sanctuary stiffened the citizens in their determination and courage, as the feat performed by the Amsterdam women in 1566 already demonstrated.

When the Beggars unsuccessfully attempted to take the city on November 11, 1572, by burning ships, many citizens processed barefoot to the Holy Stead to implore divine intervention through the Miraculous Sacrament. Processions were held very often during this time of crisis, sometimes up to three times a week, with the Blessed Sacrament being carried around in the presence of "innumerable" crowds.[97] When Don Fadrique de Toledo, the duke of Alva's son, stayed in Amsterdam for a short time during his campaign to regain the cities of Holland for Philip, he attended mass in the Holy Stead on December 4, 1572. He knelt devoutly on the steps of the sanctuary for the duration of the celebration.[98] We know these details thanks to the extensive diary of Brother Wouter Jacobsz, a canon regular from Emmaüs priory in Stein (near Gouda), who fled to Amsterdam in June 1572.[99] In the following pages, a number of passages from this narrative, comprising some four hundred folios, will be discussed, specifically those that deal with the intimate bond between Catholic Amsterdam and the Sacrament of the Altar, and in particular the sanctuary of the Holy Stead.

One thing that strikes the reader of this voluminous document is that Wouter and the citizens with whom he conversed on a daily basis constantly linked the fate of Amsterdam to international developments, especially the political scene, the changing fortunes of war, and the cause for which the pope and the rulers were fighting. Thus he mentions that Pope

Gregory XIII had granted an indulgence to anyone who participated three times in the procession during the first week of 1573 and received communion on the following Sunday. One condition was to pray for the restoration of religion in France, the return to the true faith of those who had lapsed in the Low Countries, and a new victory of the Christian war fleet against the Turks.[100]

The procession probably passed without incident on Corpus Christi in Lent; Wouter, in any case, does not mention it in his diary. It is certain that the Blessed Sacrament was carried in procession on Corpus Christi proper, which fell on May 21 in 1573, followed in person by the royalist stadtholder of Holland, Count Bossu.[101] Wouter was deeply impressed by the enormous crowds that attended the procession on the morning of Wednesday, June 17, answering a call the city authorities had issued the previous day. The citizens left their homes barefoot and walked in ever growing numbers as pilgrims to the Holy Stead, where they humbly offered their prayers. This large group consisted of both religious and laypeople, but, once again, mainly of women. Their collective supplications gave Wouter and other priests hope that God would avert his anger and deliver them from the threat of the "infidels" and insurgents.[102]

Even in 1651, the nonagenarian Aechtgen Hendricksdr Loen (1560–1652) could still remember that as a child she would go barefoot to the Holy Stead every Wednesday at five o'clock in the morning, come rain or shine, to participate together with her relatives in the procession held to avert the impending danger.[103] Perhaps as a young teenager she also saw the four wax candles that were offered in the chapel on July 14, 1573, by a man, his wife, and their four children, as Wouter recounts. He was told that they had come on foot from Haarlem, which had been captured by the king's soldiers the day before.[104]

On March 15, 1574, Corpus Christi in Lent, the rumor went about that the Beggars were trying to seize power in Amsterdam through treachery. A number of arrests were made, and the procession of the Miraculous Sacrament went out—as it always did around this date, Wouter added—from the Holy Stead in very tense atmosphere. According to Wouter, this was the case because it often happened that the enemies of the faith resorted to violence when the faithful were at their devotions. There was still hope that God would be merciful and spare the city and its inhabitants, now that innumerable people had sent up their ardent prayers "according to ancient custom."[105] A month later, on April 25, the Blessed Sacrament was carried around Amsterdam again in a general procession, in gratitude for the victory the Lord had granted "us" at Mookerheyde near Nijmegen (where the rebels had been resoundingly defeated). There was little reason for joy, however, because the situation remained difficult.[106] Nor could the special procession of February 6, 1575, to ask God for a favorable result of the peace negotiations with the rebels, restore courage to the citizens of Amsterdam, who remained under siege and isolated.[107] On July 11, Wouter heard from a refugee that he had seen a painting in Dordrecht odiously mocking God and the king: it showed a sacristan ringing a bell, followed by a priest bearing the Blessed Sacrament, followed in turn by the king wearing a *sotte caproen* (fool's cap) and holding a torch.[108] This small "royal" procession shows how friend and foe associated the Roman Catholic Church, the king of Spain, and the Eucharist with each other.

The citizens of Amsterdam managed to hold out, under their own steam and strengthened by their faith. Another procession was held on April 1, 1576, to thank God that the Beggars had failed to take the city by surprise, and on April 25 the citizenry implored God by means of a general procession to grant success to the peace negotiations in Breda.[109] As a result of the Pacification of Ghent (November 8, 1576), large groups of exiles, mainly Reformed, returned to Amsterdam, which exacerbated the religious and political divisions. The city authorities wrote to the other cities of Holland that despite the religious differences that existed between them, it should never come to the point where they would take up arms against each other on that account.[110] It was an unavailing call for toleration; gradually, increasing numbers of Beggars infiltrated the city. At Easter 1577, which fell on April 8 that year, a priest who brought communion to the sick was openly mocked. Two days later, a Beggar even managed to chase two religious women away from their meal by intentionally mocking the Blessed Sacrament in their presence. It was because of such incidents that the city authorities decided on April 10 that clergy must no longer bring the Blessed Sacrament to the sick after eight o'clock at night, unless they were accompanied by a number of soldiers.[111] Processions with the viaticum, which 230 years before had stood at the origins of Amsterdam's cult of the Miracle, had now become occasions to denounce the church of Rome. Even in Spain it was possible to tell whether someone was a Catholic or a dissident by observing their attitude toward the priest bearing viaticum.[112]

On Corpus Christi, which fell on June 6 in 1577, Wouter and his companions saw two warships anchored before the port of Amsterdam as they walked in the procession. The crew consisted of Beggars, who demonstrated their ridicule and contempt for the ritual of the procession from afar.[113] On September 1 the citizens felt so threatened that they decided to carry around the Blessed Sacrament every day during the following week and to celebrate special masses in all churches. On September 14, the city government again exhorted the citizens of Amsterdam to pray and fast that God might spare the city. Tension increased, and two days later it was decided to hold a procession every day, to fast three days a week, and that everyone should receive communion together every Sunday for a fortnight.[114] The situation was critical. On November 22, the rebel States of Holland and Zeeland tried to take the city by surprise. The attackers were defeated, however, and to thank God for this "glorious victory," recourse was had to the by now obvious expedient of holding a general procession with the Blessed Sacrament on November 25.[115]

Another source has been preserved for the military events of November 1577. According to the Antwerp Jesuit Martinus Delrio († 1608), appointed vice chancellor of Brabant by Philip II, the women of Amsterdam in particular were courageous and resourceful, and had even killed many enemies. Immediately after their victory, the citizens sent word to the governor, Don Juan, that they would remain loyal to the king "to their last breath." At the same time they also begged him for help, for they were badly in need of funds and provisions. It was a legitimate request, according to Delrio, given the strong loyalty that the citizens of Amsterdam had shown to both the Catholic faith and His Royal Majesty, but sadly all access routes to the city were cut off by the enemy, so it was impossible to offer assistance.[116] In January 1578, the burgomasters and the thirty-six members of the city council decided that all the silver present in the city that was not indispensable had to be used to mint emergency coins to pay the soldiers who defended the city. An important contribution came from the chapel wardens of the Holy Stead, who handed over many silver objects (in the shape of hands, eyes, feet, boats, houses, and so on) that had been donated over the course of time by pilgrims in gratitude for a cure or another intention obtained.[117]

As the prospects of successful long-term resistance to the rebels diminished, the two parish priests of Amsterdam, Jacob Buyck of the Oude Kerk and Maarten Donk of the Nieuwe Kerk, turned to a last resort: uninterrupted prayer of supplication for divine intervention. On January 26 they founded the "angelic choir of praying men and women." More than 150 people—priests, unmarried women, religious, widows, and married men and women—agreed to pray alternately for an hour before the Blessed

Sacrament as it was exposed on the high altar of the canonesses of the monastery of St. Gertrude, located on the Nieuwezijds Voorburgwal.[118] All trusted in God's protection.[119] This prayer relay gave Amsterdam a devotional world first. Historians have normally dated the beginning of "perpetual adoration" (adoration perpétuelle), a form of prayer that still exists, to 1630, when the French Compagnie du Saint-Sacrement was founded. The Amsterdam parish priests Buyck and Donk anticipated this by more than half a century.[120] The "angelic choir" was born out of necessity, but was also the logical result of a longer development. It was born out of necessity because the public space—that is, the streets of Amsterdam—was no longer safe for the participants of processions and for pilgrims, and they had to move instead to a church building that could be easily accessed. It was also a logical result of previous developments because the frequency of processions with the Blessed Sacrament had become so high that it gave rise to a permanent procession to the sanctuary of the Holy Stead.

Although the city signed a "satisfaction" with the States of Holland on February 8, 1578, that allowed many "heretical" exiles to return, the Catholic religion remained the only religion permitted by law. The Blessed Sacrament was venerated up until the last weeks before Amsterdam surrendered to the Beggars. On March 19, Corpus Christi in Lent, the customary procession was held for the last time—to commemorate "the most venerable Sacrament, how the same was miraculously found at the time in the Holy Stead." Wouter recounted with relief that the procession passed without incident and noted with amazement that the crowds, otherwise so dejected, were joyful on this occasion.[121] On May 11 a modest procession commemorated the 1535 victory over the Anabaptists for the last time.[122]

On Monday, May 26, 1578, Amsterdam was finally taken by the Beggars. On Thursday, May 29, Corpus Christi, after most Catholic dignitaries and all priests had already been chased out of the city, the tabernacle containing the Sacrament in the Holy Stead was desecrated. We are able to tell what this Sacrament—which was in fact a host—must have looked like in the 1570s because it is recounted in Molanus's posthumously published book on the veneration of the saints in the Low Countries. In accordance with ecclesiastical regulations, it was an intact, consecrated host that had taken the place of the original miraculous host of 1345. As early as 1346, the bishop of Utrecht had decided that this host should be replaced by a new one as soon as it became subject to decay, and that the replacement would be disposed of in the same way. How often the host was replaced over the course of time can no longer be established, but it is probable, on the basis of the liturgical cycle, that this happened once a year, on Corpus Christi or Corpus Christi in Lent. The host bore the motif of Jesus on the moment of resurrection, as he stepped out of the tomb. The altar upon which the miraculous host was exposed for the veneration of the pilgrims had been constructed over the preserved "hearth of the miracle" and the remaining residue of ashes. Molanus writes that the holy ashes themselves, of which there were apparently still some left after all those years, were used to cure all kinds of diseases; the medicinal power and the pleasant scent of the ashes had not diminished "until the present day"—that is up to the desecration of 1578.[123]

Wouter gives an account of the desecration itself, writing that the hearth was smashed to pieces, as were the statues of the saints in the church, and also that the perpetrators dared to relieve themselves upon the ashes that were hitherto venerated in the hearth. Obviously the Beggars thought it was appropriate to postpone this sacrilegious act until Corpus Christi.[124] This feast also inspired them to carry out violent deeds elsewhere. Thus Wouter writes that Beggars stormed into the cathedral of Haarlem as "mad wolves" on that day, just as a priest was about to hand the ciborium containing the Blessed Sacrament to the bishop. This act of violence has gone down in historiography as the Haarlem None after the time of day at which it happened, the liturgical hour recited at around 10:30 a.m.).[125]

In Amsterdam, Calvinists preached in the Holy Stead on June 1, only three days after the desecration, causing Catholics great pain.[126] On June 24, Wouter—who had since moved to Montfoort—heard from a girl from Gorcum that a "punishment miracle" had taken place in the Holy Stead. Two Calvinist preachers were said to have died unexpectedly soon after preaching their heresy in the Holy Stead. The girl also told him that the miraculous host of the Holy Stead had been concealed by a priest in a secret place in the church where the Beggars could not desecrate it. He had placed the miraculous host on the same pillow on which it had rested when it was found. When the priest came back later to bring it to a safer place, it had disappeared through no human intervention. Many virtuous people received this news with joy, but others no longer knew what to believe because it seemed that God in those days had closed his eyes to anything that was happening the world.[127] This concludes Brother Wouter's account of Amsterdam and the Holy Stead.

The Alteration of 1578 put an end to the physical cult of the Holy Stead—the cult object was destroyed, the cult place was taken from the

Catholics, and attempts to restore the cult itself were prohibited—but the memory of it remained alive among the population of Amsterdam, and pilgrims continued to visit the former chapel. This was not surprising because the Holy Stead was not simply the location where a miraculous host had been preserved and venerated—as was the case in Breda, Brussels, or Leuven. Rather, it was itself the place of the original miracle. The Holy Stead was, as the name evinces, a "holy place," a *locus sacer*, that became sacred in 1345 through a sign from God. God wished to be worshiped on this piece of ground, a hearth containing ashes.

For centuries, the connection between the Holy Stead and the Sacrament of the Altar was highlighted by means of Eucharistic processions. To be clear: these processions always carried around a recently consecrated host and not the miraculous host, which had deteriorated and decayed, and which as an object had become entirely irrelevant. That many citizens of Amsterdam, even after the demise of the old cult, continued to ascribe importance to the Holy Stead, which was at the same time a dangerous place for the enemies of the faith, is also evident from the fact that there were several versions of the "miracle" that was supposed to have taken place there, according to Wouter after the Calvinist takeover.

In addition to the version with the two preachers who soon died, there was also a story of three preachers of the Beggars who, one after the other, were struck dumb after attempting to preach a sermon in the chapel. Perhaps these rumors contributed to the fact that the followers of the new religion were in fear of this location for some time due to ghosts, so that it was used only as a storeroom.[128]

Understandably, certain Reformed voices advocated the complete demolition of the building. According to a history book published in 1642 and entitled *Op-komste der Neder-landtsche beroerten* (Emergence of the Dutch unrest), clearly written by a polemically minded Catholic, no less a personage than William of Orange strongly resisted a proposal to this effect by burgomaster Willem Bardes Jr. Whatever the truth of this, the Holy Stead was spared and from 1586 functioned again as a place of worship, albeit this time for the Protestant Walloon church.[129] William's alleged intervention would have corresponded with his policy of turning the Dutch into a confessionally mixed nation, united in the fight against Spain. Perhaps the authorities also held back from demolishing the building because the majority of the Amsterdam population at the time of the Alteration were Catholics, a situation that continued until the beginning of the seventeenth century. It was not until the Golden Age, when the number of citizens increased from around thirty thousand to more than one hundred thousand in the space of a few years, that Catholics became a minority of some 30 percent of the population.[130]

In 1624, the red-tiled fireplace (topped by a small chimney) in the chapel of the Holy Stead, which still evoked the memory of the miracle, was destroyed to put an end to visits of Catholic pilgrims.[131] But the "Papists" continued to come, in large numbers and barefoot.[132] Processions with the Blessed Sacrament were a thing of the past, and the directly visible references to the miracle had been erased, but the holy place was still there. The next chapter will demonstrate to what extent the Catholics of Amsterdam during the ancien régime continued to cherish this holy place where once the Blessed Sacrament had burned without being consumed, as Moses had once seen a bush burn without it being consumed (Exodus 3:2–5).

3

The Miracle on the Margins (1600–1795)

Hidden Devotion

Although the Holy Stead was lost forever to the Catholics of Amsterdam, they continued to cherish the memory of the Miracle. They kept the cult alive during the period of the Republic of the United Netherlands (1588–1795), albeit in a wholly different form than before. The Alteration of 1578 had been as good as bloodless, but it had nonetheless brought about a thorough change in Amsterdam society.

Like citizens in other European countries during the ancien régime, the Dutch until the advent of the Batavian Republic (1795) lived in a strongly hierarchical society in which one religion was privileged above all others. This position was given to the Reformed Church in 1579, that is, even before the establishment of the Republic of the United Netherlands. One important difference with neighboring countries was that the Republic by definition had no sovereign prince but was governed by the Estates General, which consisted of delegates from the provinces. The dominant position of the province of Holland and of the city of Amsterdam in particular also meant that the social hierarchy of Dutch society had a distinctly different composition. Whereas the aristocracy and the church held the reins of power in other countries, in the Republic these two estates were relatively weak. Instead, the business interests of the upper crust of influential trading families in the cities, the "regents," were paramount. Just as had the elite city authorities before the revolt, the regents feared unrest in society and wished to avoid conflicts. These factors—the absence of absolutist royal power and theocratic power—had a great impact on the way in which Catholics led their lives in the Republic. The government, which preferred to tolerate rather than suppress, gave them sufficient leeway to organize themselves and to preserve their identity as a religious community.[1]

Yet the difficulties they faced were not insignificant. No bishops were allowed to live anywhere in the territory, the parish system had been abolished, Catholic schools were banned, as were seminaries and monasteries, and Catholics were no longer permitted to use the churches, nor could they fulfill any public office. Because the normal ecclesiastical structures were prohibited, Rome from as early as 1592 regarded the former church province of Utrecht (which consisted more or less of the current Netherlands north of the river delta) as mission territory. The most important officials of this *Hollandse Zending,* or "Dutch Mission," were the papal nuncio, who was stationed initially in Cologne and subsequently in Brussels, and an episcopal substitute appointed by the pope, the so-called vicar apostolic, who, whenever circumstances allowed, lived (often unofficially) in the Republic.[2] Within the margins set for them, they succeeded to a certain degree in rebuilding ecclesiastical structures, and from circa 1600 onward the Republic saw the emergence of *staties,* or "stations": quasi parishes whose ministers often had to live in safe houses, relying on the offerings of their "parishioners" for sustenance.[3] In many towns these priests were tolerated, so long as they did not lay frequent or public claim to the status of pastor. Much to the chagrin of the Reformed Church, the Catholic community was soon permitted the use of its own small chapels, although these so-called domestic or clandestine churches had to be unrecognizable as such from the outside. Thanks to the work of successive new generations of priests who studied abroad at their families' expense, of regular clergy (particularly Jesuits and Franciscans) often from Flanders, and of a substantial number of "spiritual virgins," or *kloppen*— unmarried women who devoted themselves to pastoral and charitable work under the direction of a priest—the Catholic Church was able to survive in the Republic.[4]

All of this happened in circumstances that deeply influenced the experience of Catholic life. Catholics had significantly less freedom to express their faith than their coreligionists in the Spanish (later Austrian) Netherlands, for instance, but they learned to use the freedom they had in a very particular way. The first two vicars apostolic, Sasbout Vosmeer (1592–1614) and Philippus Rovenius (1614–1651), and their instructions as to how the feasts of the saints should be observed offer a striking example. This obviously could not be done in the same way as before the Alteration, but according to Vosmeer that was only for the best. It was better, he contended, to leave the celebration of most feasts to the individual piety of the faithful. The clergy should stimulate this piety by ensuring that the faithful might, through their pious prayers, obtain indulgences.[5] By arguing in this way, Vosmeer showed that he preferred the interior experience of the faith to collective religious expressions. As the latter were banned by law, this made a virtue of necessity.

Philippus Rovenius was in no better position than his predecessor to offer clergy and laity a full liturgical program.[6] He did succeed in introducing a national calendar of saints in the mission territory, a calendar that continued to observe the diocesan divisions that had existed before the Alteration. In 1623 (Leuven) and 1640 (Cologne) he published schedules of the divine office for the feasts of the saints in the "archdiocese" of Utrecht and the "dioceses" of Haarlem, Deventer, Leeuwarden, Groningen, and Middelburg.[7] These calendars distinguished between feasts to be observed in the entire church province and feasts—particularly memorials of the missionaries who had once converted the Netherlands—proper to one or several individual dioceses. This decentralization of the calendar of feasts meant that he gave more space to local communities' own initiative and responsibility. In this way, he wanted not only to strengthen the Catholics of the Republic in their faith, but also to show them that they had every reason to be proud. As venerators of the saints of their own city or region, they were treading in the footsteps of their fathers, something that could not be said of the Reformed. The diocese of Haarlem had seven proper feasts, six for early medieval missionaries—Wulfram (March 18), Engelmundus (June 21), Bavo (August 1), Jerome (August 18), Werenfridus (August 27), Remigius (October 1)—and one for the Venerabile Sacramentum Miraculosum Amstelrodami (Wednesday after March 12).[8] We will return to the special position of the feast of the Miracle in the Haarlem calendar later in this chapter.

Having described this general context, we must now turn to Amsterdam and the Miracle. Because the cult of the Miracle, like other religious expressions, had been excluded from public life and was left largely to individual piety, it continued outside the range of empirical perception. But although the history of the Miracle during the two centuries that the Republic lasted was not characterized by grand processions, princely honors, civic recognition, spectacular miracles, and hordes of pilgrims, it did not stop. With their barefoot silent walks, usually at night or at daybreak, the

Catholics of Amsterdam kept the embers of the Miracle burning, or at least smoldering. The affinity they felt for the Miracle was influenced by several factors. The following section deals with expectations of the future that emerged from time to time up to the eighteenth century, expectations that were closely related to the Sacrament's symbolic significance. The two subsequent sections deal with the way in which the Catholic community succeeded in praising, expressing, celebrating, and imagining the Miracle during the Golden Age. The Miracle repeatedly became a bone of contention between the Reformed and Catholics, although the polemics were gradually restricted to the realm of intellectual debate and sermons. This is the subject of the final section.

Catholic Hope and Reformed Fear

The climate of tolerance had to grow, and this took time. After the Alteration of 1578, the Catholics of Amsterdam initially retained the use of a number of monastery chapels and private houses as locations for worship.[9] But the city authorities soon took these meager facilities away. Every form of Catholic organization was prohibited, and all that remained was freedom of conscience.[10] These oppressive measures arose from the fear that Catholic citizens would choose the side of Philip II. Only when Frederick Henry succeeded his brother Maurice as stadtholder in 1625 did the era of religious tolerance for which the Republic has become famous really begin.

It must be said that the fears of the city authorities were not without foundation. When Amsterdam joined the revolt in May 1578, as the last city in Holland, it certainly strengthened the position of the insurgents but did not ensure immediate victory. The fortunes of war might yet change, and Reformed and Catholic alike knew it. A few months later, in the fall of 1578, Philip II appointed Alexander Farnese, the duke of Parma, as governor. Parma turned out to be an excellent general, and as it happened the tide did indeed turn.[11]

In the 1580s especially, Catholics in Amsterdam could take heart from the struggle and the fate of their coreligionists elsewhere, and their focus was on Antwerp in particular. Similarly to Amsterdam, this city on the River Scheldt had become the most successful trading city in its province during the fifteenth and especially the sixteenth centuries.[12] Both cities had in short succession experienced a Calvinist takeover. In May 1578 the

Amsterdam clergy were given their walking papers, and in May 1579 practically the same happened in Antwerp.[13] During the repressive Calvinist
rule that followed, the Catholics of Antwerp received important moral support from outside. In 1582 Pope Gregory XIII cheered them in their troubles by canonizing Norbert of Xanten. In Antwerp, in the early twelfth
century, Norbert had preached against a certain Tanchelm, according to
tradition an arch-heretic who had blasphemed the Blessed Sacrament.
From the time of his canonization, Norbert was regarded as a Eucharistic
saint or, more to the point, a holy warrior against heresy, with the Blessed
Sacrament as his weapon.[14] The Catholics of Antwerp had to be patient for
a number of years, but on August 17, 1585, Parma succeeded in conquering
their city. This happy achievement, which according to some historians
marks the definitive separation between the Northern and the Southern
Netherlands, was commemorated annually in Antwerp with a large-scale
procession of the Blessed Sacrament.[15]

For the Catholics of the Republic, or at least for those sympathetic to
King Philip, the fall of Antwerp was a great cause of hope. Parma had already set his sights on Holland, and the strict placards issued by the new
government caused many a Catholic Dutchman to long nostalgically for
Philip's rule. The insurgents' military position was distinctly perilous, all
the more so after they lost their undisputed leader, William of Orange, on
July 10, 1584, at the hand of an assassin.[16] Many Catholic citizens of Amsterdam would have pondered the similarities between recent events in
Antwerp and what had happened two generations before in their own city.
Had they not managed to overthrow the Anabaptists in 1535, and had they
not celebrated their victory with an annual Eucharistic procession?

But it all worked out differently. In 1588, the year in which the rebellious provinces chose to establish a Republic, the powerful Armada, which
had been intended to settle the conflict in one blow, perished in the waters
of the North Sea. The following year, Parma turned his attention to France,
allowing the insurgents under Maurice to recapture the previously lost territories in a lightning campaign. The arrival from Antwerp of many refugees who refused to submit to Spanish rule was one of the factors that
marked the start of Holland's Golden Age.[17]

With the enemy at safe distance, the government relaxed its repression
of the Catholics in its own territory. Nevertheless, issues connected to the
sacrament of the Eucharist continued to flare up from time to time to test
relations between Catholics and the Reformed. These issues always concerned attempts to rouse feeling: feelings of victory among Catholics, and
feelings of fear among the Reformed.

An important event that led to the association of military victory with the Blessed Sacrament was the taking of Breda by the Spaniards in 1625. On May 28, the day before Corpus Christi that year, Justin of Nassau, representing the city's insurgents, and Ambrogio Spínola, the general commanding the siege on behalf of King Philip IV and the Archduchess Isabella, began negotiations about the capitulation of the city. According to tradition, the white flag appeared over Breda at the same moment that the Eucharistic procession for Corpus Christi left St. Gudula's Church in Brussels.[18] Exactly a week later, on June 5, the octave of Corpus Christi, Justin and his garrison capitulated.[19] On June 12, a week after the capitulation, Isabella and her retinue visited the city to celebrate "the most excellent and sweetest" victory in her tenure as governor. Her joy was all the greater because Breda was known as a place of pilgrimage of a Sacrament of Miracle, the Sacrament of Niervaart. The victory was thus linked to the Eucharist in two different ways: God had granted the orthodox Spaniards victory on the feast of Corpus Christi, and this in a place hallowed by Eucharistic miracles. Isabella decreed that the victory would henceforth be commemorated every year on May 28 with a Eucharistic procession. Shortly afterward she had a series of tapestries on the theme "the triumph of the Eucharist" designed by Rubens and made in Brussels as a gift to the royal convent of the Poor Clares in Madrid.[20] As early as 1626, the Brussels Jesuit and historiographer Herman Hugo published a book in Latin on the siege of Breda; it found wide dissemination and was translated into Spanish, French, and English.[21]

Isabella and her supporters appear to have regarded the fall of Breda as a breakthrough in the war, not so much because of Spínola's military capabilities, but because they saw the hand of God in the victory as it had taken place on Corpus Christi. They were eager to spread the word about this and set off a veritable avalanche of propaganda—including Hugo's expert account of the battle, poems of praise, and works of art.[22] But their shouts of victory came too soon, as the fortunes of war changed once again. In 1626 the Republic recaptured Oldenzaal, a town that had been conquered by Spínola twenty years before and had since become known for its triumphant Eucharistic processions drawing participants from across the region of Twente. In 1637, twelve years after the glorious taking of Breda, this town, too, was reconquered, by Frederick Henry.[23] Isabella's death in late 1633 spared her from witnessing this setback. Her body was interred in a place she and her husband, the Archduke Albert, who had died in 1621, had selected long before: the chapel of the Sacrament of

Miracle in St. Gudula's Church in Brussels.[24] If the Amsterdam historian Jan Wagenaar's account of Spínola's conquest of Breda is anything to go by—it was admittedly written more than a century later—the Eucharistic symbolism failed to impress the enemy. Wagenaar contentedly remarked that the siege of this city had exhausted Spain and the Spanish Netherlands so much that it was unable to launch any further offensive during the rest of the war.[25]

In the third decade of the seventeenth century—Frederick Henry's accession to the stadtholdership has already been identified as a pivotal point above—relations between Reformed and Catholic citizens of the Republic improved. In spite of the differences that divided them, they had no choice but to tolerate each other, and for Catholics this meant resigning themselves to social inequality. This is how what Willem Frijhoff has called the "ecumenism of everyday life" emerged. Different groups of citizens who did not belong to the same group, did not attend the same church together, and did not intermarry, nevertheless were dependent on each other for services and business.[26]

Given this context, the surprisingly strict measures taken by the Amsterdam *vroedschap* on Corpus Christi in 1641 (May 30) sounded a distinctly dissonant note. On that day, the magistrates and their officers entered two Catholic clandestine churches during the celebration of a religious service attended by more than 200 worshippers. The latter were fined for the sum of no less than 6,200 guilders for their prayers, and in addition clerical vestments, liturgical vessels, and other items were confiscated.[27] This demarche was particularly unusual because the city authorities as a rule did not intervene directly, but limited themselves to imposing penalties after the fact for what they considered disruptions of public order.[28] Previously, and indeed subsequently, the mayors and magistrates did not think that Catholic worship constituted a threat to the city. So what was different in 1641?

It was most likely concern or even fear for Catholic riots that was behind this intervention. In 1641 Corpus Christi fell on June 24, the feast of Saint John the Baptist, in most Dutch provinces, which used a different calendar than Holland.[29] The convergence of these two feasts, an event that occurs only once every century and a half, had far-reaching liturgical consequences. The feast of Saint John, midsummer's day, ranked as a solemnity, but in that year it had to yield to the solemnity of Corpus Christi because the lesser (Saint John) must give way to the greater (Christ).[30] This liturgical symbolism apparently led some people to make revolutionary predictions: "the lesser must yield to the greater" might be understood to mean that those who had hitherto been in power had to yield to those who had the greater claim on power. This gave rise to the rumor that Dutch Catholics were planning a rising on this day to recover the churches and other possessions of which they had been deprived. The city council's high-handed intervention can be explained as a signal that the authorities would be closely monitoring any Catholic troublemakers when, a few weeks later, Corpus Christi would be celebrated on the feast of Saint John in the other provinces.

These other provinces also felt they had cause for concern. A few days before Corpus Christi, the deputy sheriff and his men in Utrecht disrupted a well-attended mass just outside the city's Witte-Vrouwenpoort, taking the celebrant, Herman van Honthorst, into preventive custody.[31] Naturally zealous Reformed citizens did not consider Corpus Christi or feasts of the Sacrament of Miracle as days on which God's providence was likely to manifested. But they suspected that there were Catholics who did believe this and who might perhaps, inspired by these ideas, commit subversive acts.

In 1672, the Republic's "year of disaster," and in 1673, the country's existence hung in the balance, as it was suddenly on a war footing with various neighboring powers at the same time, and French troops occupied a large part of its territory, including Utrecht. On Corpus Christi of 1673 (June 1 that year), the French King Louis XIV ordered a great Eucharistic procession through this cathedral town, with many children, no fewer than five hundred *kloppen*, religious, priests, and French occupiers in attendance.[32] The Reformed had to stay indoors and keep their shutters closed. Vicar Apostolic Johannes van Neercassel traveled from the nonoccupied city of Amsterdam for the occasion. Walking under a canopy, he carried a gold monstrance holding the Blessed Sacrament. Many participants no doubt regarded this procession for "la gloire de Dieu, et l'honneur du Roy" as the start of a new era.[33] But once again, history took a different turn. On November 13 of the same year, the French hurriedly withdrew from the Republic, and the Dom Church was restored again to Protestant worship. When Stadtholder William III arrived in Utrecht in April 1674, his supporters wrote that "the God of the Roman Catholics consists entirely of flour," which was of course a reference to the host, and that the papists, who had been quick to welcome the rule of the French on Corpus Christi, would now do well to come and profess their gratitude to the Prince of Orange.[34] But it was left at that, and the ecumenism of everyday life returned to take its course.

In view of his involvement in the cause of the French—he had clearly backed the wrong horse—Neercassel was declared persona non grata in the Republic. Surprisingly however, another incident involving the Sacrament would allow him to redeem his status. In early August 1674, an eleven-year-old citizen of Amsterdam, Robbert Hooft, the grandson of the poet and chronicler P. C. Hooft, went to communion in a church in Antwerp and then furtively took the host out of his mouth and concealed it in his hat. The sacrilege came to light, causing much commotion, and the boy was arrested. The desperate parents begged Neercassel to use his influence to secure the boy's release. Neercassel succeeded in doing this, and as a result his reputation in Amsterdam sharply improved, including among the Reformed, and he was given permission again to enter the country.[35]

Perhaps the short-lived French occupation can be seen as a turning point in the mutual understanding between Catholics and the Reformed in the Republic. The Catholics had few reasons to look back with sympathy on the depredations visited on the population by Louis XIV's soldiers. The Reformed in their turn had no cause to continue their attacks against the hatefulness of papism, especially given that it had been Catholic Spain's well-timed declaration of war against France that occasioned the occupying force's hasty withdrawal in late 1673. Furthermore, it was well known in government circles that Rome was reluctant to become involved in the war.[36] During the following decades, the Republic was on the verge of war with France on a number of occasions, and even after the Peace of Utrecht in 1713 the menace from the south continued to be felt. The authorities therefore organized a number of national days of supplication for peace, in which Dutch men and women of all persuasions, including Catholics, took part.[37]

It was a surprise, therefore, particularly for foreigners acquainted with the tolerant climate of the Republic, that sixty years after the French occupation, in 1734, panic broke out again in various towns in the provinces of Zealand, Holland, and Friesland over a rumored Catholic coup d'état on Corpus Christi. The feast again fell on the feast of Saint John on June 24 in this year, just as in 1641. Exaggerated old and new predictions were spread, both by word of mouth and through pamphlets. Many people trembled at the news that papist plotters were conspiring to massacre the Reformed. The authorities responded here and there by taking Catholics into preventive custody, often for their own protection, and by restraining the rabble that bayed for the blood of the putative conspirators.[38] Amsterdam too saw some unrest. According to city historians Jan Wagenaar and

Simon Stijl, the rumor was that the Catholics had already secretly appointed a new sheriff, mayors, and magistrates, who were ready to step out into the open to take up their offices on June 24. A number of magistrates were said to be secret papists already. As soon as the dreaded day of Corpus Christi, or St. John's Day, had passed, the superstitious hopes (of Catholics) and fears (of the Reformed) vanished, and the events only served to "ridicule the credulous and the cowardly," according to Stijl.[39]

But other witnesses testified that the atmosphere was grimmer than this suggests. The sheriff and his assistants were said to have succeeded only with great difficulty in protecting the house of one prominent Catholic from being plundered. The nuncio in Brussels, Silvio Valenti, also received disturbing information about Amsterdam. Persons from the Protestant lower classes were said to have been paid, for whatever reason, to write inflammatory notices to provoke Catholics into rebellion.[40]

For Valenti and others, the causes of this mass hysteria were unclear. Why did this happen in the tolerant Republic and not in one of the neighboring countries, where the two feasts also fell on the same day? Frijhoff has pointed out that this phenomenon was likely to occur precisely in a country where the Reformed and the Catholics did not live in separation from each other. Other countries had such a large majority of one group that any attempted takeover of power by the minority was unthinkable.[41] At any rate, the panic made clear that even in the eighteenth century, the "ecumenism of everyday life" remained something of an external varnish. The Sacrament could still incite exaggerated suspicion between the Reformed and Catholics, and this also in the city of the Miracle itself.

The Miracle Expressed

In 1604, a century after the Miracle cult had been at its peak, Amsterdam pharmacist Walich Syvaertsz, a Reformed convert from Catholicism, published a little book called *Roomsche mysterien* (Romish mysteries) in which he attacked the Catholic doctrine of transubstantiation. Syvaertsz gives many fascinating insights into all kinds of devotional practices, such as the procession on the two feasts of Corpus Christi, in which he had himself taken part as a child. He looks back with amazement on the "naiveté" of the Amsterdam citizenry of those days, but his tone becomes indignant when he discusses the miraculous host. What many Catholics of Amsterdam did not know—or at least what he did not know himself when he was a child—was that the host of the Miracle cult was regularly replaced by a fresh one. He asks how many times this must have happened, bearing in mind that as many as 233 years separated the Alteration of 1578 from the Miracle in 1345. In his view, the Catholic Church in Amsterdam had deceived its credulous flock on countless occasions, a serious case of pious fraud.[42] The argument that hosts should always be in good condition and must therefore be replaced from time to time was not valid in his eyes. His rigid counterargument was, "If [this host] was able to resist the fire, then surely it should also be able to resist decay?"[43]

The Catholics of Amsterdam had little to say in reply to books such as *Roomsche mysterien.* Syvaertsz was free to write what he wanted, and they were not. In the early seventeenth century, the Catholic Church's organization, to the extent that it was permitted to exist at all, had very little scope for self-manifestation. To the annoyance of the vicars apostolic, Catholics in the Southern Netherlands even viewed the Dutch Mission as a mine of available relics after the many cults that had existed there had been destroyed and banned.[44] It was gradually forgotten abroad that the Northern Netherlands had had its own places of pilgrimage, including the Holy Stead in Amsterdam. A number of surveys of important Sacraments of Miracle were published during the first quarter of the seventeenth century, such as that by the Augustinian Matthias Pauli († 1651) from Hasselt (Belgium). None of these publications even mentioned the Amsterdam Holy Stead.[45]

That the Catholics of Amsterdam themselves had not forgotten the Holy Stead is evident from a Latin poem, "De Patria," composed by Amsterdam lawyer Cornelis Plemp († 1638) in praise of his ancestral city. In translation, the relevant passage is as follows:

The sacred thresholds and the traces of the past,
Thank God! Are still preserved in Kalverstraat.
Each year still, on the famous feast, the footsteps
Of so many, barefoot, lead toward the temple;
They come in secret. The pious and the faithful
And salute you, O deserted shrine,
To adore the Miraculous Sacrament; to gaze
Upon the holy place, and they solemnly go round it thrice.[46]

The situation sketched here by Plemp did not last very long. In 1624, or even a few years before, many of the "traces of the past"—the red-tiled

fireplace in particular—were removed. The "footsteps of so many," however, continued to be heard. The faithful continued to come, walking
around the old chapel barefoot three times, as they had done before the
Reformation. With this ritual they sanctified the chapel time and again as
their "Holy Stead."[47]

The priests of the Dutch Mission, with their fascination for old devo-
tions of native soil, made sure that the Miracle would not be forgotten.
Thus an old class fellow of Rovenius, Joannes Stalpaert van der Wiele
(† 1630) from The Hague, composed an intriguing hymn on the Holy
Stead. In the very first stanzas, he points to the similarities between
Moses's burning bush and the miracle of 1345:

> Praised be God's strong arm:
> Which during the fire,
> Kept Moses' bush intact:
> And now preserves his Sacrament.
>
> You ask for proof! I have it.
> The Amsterdam Holy Stead
> And the pious people there
> Bear witness that my song is true.[48]

This reference to the burning bush (Exodus 3:2–5) as a prefiguration of the
Amsterdam Miracle shows Stalpart's debt to the late-medieval narrative
tradition, setting an example in his own turn for the writers, poets, and
preachers of the future. Because they found the similarities between the
burning bush and the Holy Stead as a place where God manifested himself so convincing, the burning bush became for them a kind of hallmark
of the cult. But to continue the Miracle, more was required than silent
rituals and well-turned phrases. It was necessary to create a new place that
could be the heart of the cult, and to bring the forms and message of the
cult up to date, so that it could be transmitted to posterity. These require-
ments were soon to be met.

Among the many Catholic domestic churches that existed in Amsterdam in the seventeenth and eighteenth centuries, that on the Begijnhof
occupied a special place. The beguinage enjoyed old privileges that continued to be respected by the city authorities even after the Alteration. As
the only Catholic institution in the city, it retained the right to co-opt new
residents, as well as to close its doors to the outside world at night. This
enclosure made it possible for the beguines to hold prayer services each

night, making their beguinage a favorite station for priests.[49] One pastor, Leonardus Klaasz (1588–1652), better known as Leonardus Marius ("the Zealander"), succeeded in turning the Begijnhof into a center of Eucharistic piety. The domestic church of Saints John and Ursula, which had in the early seventeenth century been located in the sacristy of the English church, and in 1682 moved to the more capacious location where it still stands, grew into a worthy successor to the Holy Stead.[50]

Marius, from Goes, was for some years president of the Holland seminary called the Hoge Heuvel (High Hill) in Cologne. He had a reputation for being a great biblical scholar as well as a dedicated pastor. He was appointed archpriest (quasi dean) of Amsterdam in 1629 and soon after elected vicar general (quasi bishop) of the Haarlem vicariate. In early 1631 he became pastor of the Begijnhof. From his earliest days, Marius had felt a connection with Amsterdam. In 1599, when he was eleven, he had started his studies for the priesthood in this city, and he had often served mass in the beguinage. In 1602 the seminary was discovered and closed, forcing Marius and his fellow students to decamp to Cologne to continue their studies.[51]

Within the relatively wide margins that the city authorities had set, despite furious protests from Reformed ministers, Marius worked tirelessly to revive the devotion to the Miracle among the Catholics of Amsterdam, as well as to have the Miracle feast included in the liturgical calendar of the Dutch Mission. He encouraged his fellow citizens to observe the feast devoutly and to receive communion on that day. He turned the domestic church of the Begijnhof into a place of adoration of the Blessed Sacrament, surrounded by female devotees who received communion on a daily basis. Marius was well aware in his endeavors that the Begijnhof church might be a worthy but not a full successor to the Holy Stead. The place that had once been hallowed by the heavenly fire could not be replaced.[52]

"Amstelredams eer ende opcomen": The Honor and Rise of Amsterdam

To further propagate devotion to the Miracle, Marius published a book at Hendrick Aertssens in Antwerp in 1639. It would become the most important literary work in the history of the cult.[53] It acquired this status because of its crystal-clear message, which is already contained in the title and which would continue to resonate for a century and a half: Amsterdam's venerable status and its rise as a city were the result of the Miracle and the Eucharistic miracles that followed in its wake. Amsterdam Catholics were keen to purchase a copy of *Amstelredams eer ende opcomen*, all the more so as they were unable to profess their faith in public. The many reprints in the seventeenth and eighteenth centuries prove that they continued to do this for several generations. Although the engravings became blurry, the contents and the title information (Antwerp 1639) long remained unchanged, which gave the book a timeless quality.[54] Until well into the nineteenth century, it took pride of place on the bookshelf of many a Catholic family, not only for spiritual edification, but also as a family book. The blank pages preceding the title page were used by successive owners to note the dates of birth and death of members of the family. Many Amsterdam Protestants inscribed these details into their family Bibles; their Catholic neighbors—at least many of them—did so in Marius's book.[55]

In his book, Marius himself made sure to display his considerable knowledge of the Scriptures and of the writings of both Catholic authors—with whom he concurred—and Protestant authors—whom he attacked. His aim was no doubt to write a clear account, but much or even most of the content would have been too difficult for many of the intended readers. The book was illustrated with sixteen engravings made some years before by the famous illustrator Boëtius à Bolswert († 1633). These images, together with accompanying Latin verses composed by Cornelis Plemp, had been published before as an independent pictorial narrative in Antwerp. Because they were indebted to older visual representations, and they themselves set a norm for later representations of the Miracle, *Amstelredams eer ende opcomen* was also a monumental work from a pictorial perspective.[56]

Most editions of the book contain a dedication by the engraver, Bolswert, to Peter Paul Rubens, hinting to this famous painter that he should create an artistic interpretation of the Miracle of his own. Bolswert then points out that, thanks to the Miracle of the Most Blessed Sacrament, Amsterdam outstripped "all neighboring cities" in both religiosity and business. It was due to this heavenly blessing that the city had been able to rise from an insignificant fishing village to a powerful seaport, the entrepôt of the world, and the granary of the Netherlands. Amsterdam owed its fame as a pious city not only to its own citizens, but also to "all manner of foreigners" who came to the city as pilgrims, according to Bolswert.[57] His words are curiously similar to those of the councilors of the city of Amsterdam, who, two centuries before, had written to Pope Eugene IV to ask for an indulgence.

Three introductory chapters, which also pointed out the significance of the burning bush,[58] were followed by a long chapter on the Miracle. Marius's account became the general view of the Miracle well into the nineteenth century.[59] In composing his reconstruction of the events, he made no use of the 1555 books of hours, *Succinta enarratio miraculorum*, or of the miracle book from 1568, entitled *Hier beghint die vindinghe vant hoochweerdighe ende heylighe Sacrament* (Beginning of the finding of the most venerable and Blessed Sacrament). He possibly considered these books, which were themselves based on John of Leiden's older Latin *Chronicle of the counts of Holland and the bishops of Utrecht*, too archaic.[60] Instead, he based his account on a more modern source, the so-called *Divisiekroniek* (Division chronicle) from 1517.[61] There are a number of differences between the miracle book in particular and *Amstelredams eer ende opcomen*; let us look more closely at three of them:[62]

- The miracle book describes the casting of the sick communicant's vomit into the fire as a communal act of piety: "The women who had been present and who had observed him, knew that he had received the Sacrament. For this reason, they collected his vomit in a clean vessel and cast it into a large fire." By contrast, Marius thought that this act resulted from ignorance.[63] In fact it was he who was ignorant of the older liturgical custom, in this case of the rule that a communicant's vomit should be burned.

- In the miracle book, the priest returned the host to the church twice; the first time without giving it much thought, and the second time "with great devotion and dignity." In Marius's book, however, the host is brought back to the church as many as three times, the last time in a triumphant procession in which all the clergy of Amsterdam participated.[64] This account of events fitted very well with the iconographic tradition of the Miracle; one of its beloved motifs was the triumphant returning of the viaticum from the house to the Oude Kerk, as if in a real Eucharistic procession.

- The miracle book's account of the Miracle was derived from a charter dated March 31, 1345, which concludes with a statement from the bailiff of Amsterdam, Floris of Boechorst, confirming the veracity of the event. Marius, however, separated the account and the declaration of authenticity. This enabled him to point out that the "noble gentlemen of Amstelland and of Amsterdam" had already confirmed the Miracle before the bishop of Utrecht even became involved. Marius knew all too well that it would please Amsterdam readers, regardless of their religious persuasion, to read that their own civic authorities had been the first to be involved in the case.[65] Marius therefore placed an illustration by Bolswert showing how seriously and harmoniously Floris and his colleagues were working on composing their charter beside his translation of the text. The following poem, in Dutch, accompanied it:

The Miracle that we adore
Is confirmed, under oath
At the city hall before the Magistrate.
Can the truth offend?
See the seal, read the letters.
It is neither dream nor children's talk.[66]

After listing a number of transcriptions or translations of documents that showed how well disposed past secular and clerical authorities had been toward the cult, Marius mentioned several miraculous rescues and cures. These had taken place either in the Holy Stead or elsewhere while following a vow to undertake a pilgrimage to the Holy Stead. It is remarkable that Marius limited himself to an abridged account of the miracles that are mentioned in the miracle book. The most recent miracle in this publication dated from 1508; were there no miracles from after this date that could be listed? There certainly were, and there is every chance that Marius was well acquainted with them. Just before the Alteration, a crippled virgin from Haarlem, Trijntgen Dircx Wy, had made the pilgrimage to Amsterdam. After praying there, she was able to leave the Holy Stead without her crutches.[67] Possibly the memory of this miracle had already faded away when Marius first came to the Begijnhof, but this cannot have been the case with the spectacular miracle of fire that occurred in 1627, shortly before his arrival in Amsterdam.

On Good Friday (April 2 that year), a burning candle fell in one of the Jesuits' hidden churches in Amsterdam, setting fire to the altar. Miraculously, the wooden pyx containing the Blessed Sacrament (the host) remained intact. All those who had been present had witnessed the miracle, according to the two Jesuits who recounted it, Augustinus van Teijlingen and Joannes Paludanus.[68] Why did Marius not include this event as a miracle? There are various possible explanations. Perhaps he felt constrained by the liturgy of the feast of the Miracle, which had been fixed long ago and which always mentioned the same old miracles. Or maybe he felt little sympathy for a new miracle, as it might distract from the inner experience of the faith or upset the ecumenism of everyday life. But closer examination shows that there was a different reason why Marius was unimpressed by this miracle. The miracles of fire that had happened in 1345 and 1452 had, by a heavenly sign—the fact that the host did not burn—hallowed the same place, the Holy Stead. This place still existed, and it was still sacred, for once and for all. Accepting the new miracle would imply that there was now a second Holy Stead, one moreover that was run by the Jesuits. This thought was simply unacceptable to Marius.

To return again to *Amstelredams eer ende opcomen*: after the fourth chapter Marius concludes his discussion of the history of the cult. Yet there are thirteen more chapters, all of which have a theological character. The reasoning behind this was that the Miracle in itself could not be venerated, but it pointed to a mystery of the faith: God's actions in the sacrament. Marius has many things to say about this. Despite the heterogeneous nature of these chapters, it is possible to identify a common thread. Time and again, Marius raises the opposing views espoused by Catholics and the Reformed with regard to the sacrament, a "realist" and a "symbolic" view, respectively. To current readers, this may seem to be a semiotic debate that need not affect the mutual relations between the Christian churches, but at the time Christians viewed matters in a decidedly different light. For Catholics, the denial of Christ's real presence in the host—the *praesentia realis*—was a form of pride and blasphemy. The Reformed did indeed deny the *praesentia realis*, and they believed Catholics worshiped a "bread god" (the host), which meant they were idolaters. Marius participated enthusiastically in this interminable debate, in the hope that the Miracle might be the trump card that would convince readers that the Catholics were right.[69]

Did *Amstelredams eer ende opcomen* contribute to strengthening the cult of the Miracle, within the limits that constrained its practice? It seems very likely that it did. The Reformed ministers of Amsterdam complained to the city authorities about Marius and what they called the "damnable effronteries of the Papists" in a strongly worded letter dated March 27, 1644: "The great superstitions and idolatries that are committed by many, especially at night at an ungodly hour, around the Great Chapel, which is called the Holy Stead, are intolerable. . . . Recently, two shameless *kloppen* stood publicly and superstitiously reciting their Our Fathers and Hail Marys in the Nieuwe Sijts Capel for the whole congregation to see. . . . Children in the streets tell us that the Papists are making barefoot pilgrimages."[70]

It is thanks to this rare reference that we know that the practice of privately walking around the chapel a number of times still existed in the middle of the seventeenth century. This still happened barefoot because the place where they walked was sacred ground.[71] Perhaps Marius had not yet given up hope that at some stage in the future the Eucharistic procession would be permitted to pass through the streets of Amsterdam once again on the feast of the Miracle. The fact that a document called "Reminiscence of the Procession of the Blessed Sacrament of Miracle from the Holy Stead in Amsterdam" was drawn up may be testimony to this hope. It recorded the memories of the ninety-one-year-old Agatha (or Aechtgen) Loen as she recounted them on December 16, 1651. As a girl she had been in the habit, together with her mother, sister, brother, and "many other devout persons," to make her devotions in the Holy Stead each Wednesday morning at five o'clock, barefoot in winter and summer, come hail, snow, or shine—that is, she attended mass and visited the Sacrament of Miracle. She also used to take part in the Eucharistic procession, of which she was still able to recount the route. Just in time, this route was recorded from oral tradition so that it could be handed down to posterity. The "Reminiscence" is still kept in the archive of the Begijnhof.[72]

The behavior of the "shameless *kloppen*" of which the Reformed ministers complained in 1644 was in fact characteristic of the attitude that Catholics in the Republic generally adopted with regard to churches that had been destined for Protestant worship, secularized, or even destroyed after the Reformation. In their eyes, the Sacred was still present there, and they viewed this as an invitation to come and pray in these places. In this they were quite different from their coreligionists in other countries such as England, who were often very reluctant to enter Protestant places of worship that had previously been Catholic churches.[73]

"Eeuwgetij der Heilige Stede t'Amsterdam" (Centenary of the Holy Stead in Amsterdam)

The year 1645 marked the third centenary of the Miracle. A commemorative card (11.3 x 8.5 inches) was distributed for the occasion, probably at Marius's behest, with allegorical texts and images that could be connected to the Blessed Sacrament in general and only partially to the Miracle itself (an image of a host in a fire, flanked by angels, and a quotation from Exodus, "The Lord appeared in the flames of the fire").[74]

The panegyric entitled *Eeuwgetij der Heilige Stede t'Amsterdam* (Centenary of the Holy Stead in Amsterdam), with which Amsterdam's most famous poet, Joost van den Vondel († 1679), surprised friend and foe in March 1645, will have caused a greater stir.[75] This singularly productive poet, an Anabaptist by birth, had become friends with his near-contemporary Marius and, under the latter's influence, became a convert to the Catholic Church in 1639.[76] With a convert's zeal, he gave ringing witness to his new faith in *Eeuwgetij*. He dedicated his poem to the "old citizenry," meaning the undividedly Catholic citizenry of pre-Reformation times, which had followed the example of Moses as he stood at the burning bush (which Vondel calls a "hedge of thorns") and would only enter the holy place barefoot. He referred explicitly to the two fifteenth-century city fires, the better to be able to follow his friend Marius in ascribing the rise of the city to the Miracle:

> Your young city, which twice into ashes fell;
> Twice also arose again from smoke;
> As if God his favor and power in flames
> displayed in Amsterdam;
> Which, grown from swamp and water,
> Now crowns the waters with tall arches,
> And carries to coasts wide and far
> The Emperor's crown, of gold and diamond.

"The Emperor's crown" is a reference to Maximilian of Austria, who had come to the Holy Stead to praise the power of God, which had once protected the three young men in the fiery furnace (Daniel 3:1–30). Can you doubt the well-documented miracles of Amsterdam, while at the same time believing the miracles of the Bible? This is Vondel's argument, and it concludes with a prayer that God might lead the citizens of Amsterdam back to the true (Catholic) faith. Like Marius, he refers to Floris of Boechorst's charter as the city's official confirmation of the Miracle in 1345.

Later in the same year, Vondel published a long didactic poem in three parts called *Altaergeheimenissen* (Altar mysteries), whose three parts are dedicated to communion, adoration of the Blessed Sacrament, and the mass respectively.[77] Any discussion of this kind of subject presupposes thorough theological knowledge, and although Vondel, as a self-taught man, had an astonishing capacity for acquiring knowledge, it is nonetheless likely that he wrote this poem in close consultation with Marius.[78] The Miracle hardly receives a mention in *Altaergeheimenissen*, possibly because Vondel considered that his readers were now sufficiently instructed on that subject. His long poem on the Sacrament of the Altar was in itself a lengthy homage to the Miracle, if only because of its year of publication.[79]

Marius's and Vondel's writings caused considerable annoyance to non-Catholics, partly because both authors had wide social networks. Marius was summoned to appear before the Court of The Hague on a few occasions in 1643 to account for himself and his conduct as a priest. When he informed the mayors of Amsterdam of this, they took umbrage at what they regarded as an unwarrantable intrusion into the affairs of their own city. They banned him from traveling to The Hague, and they told the court that they would let him go only on the court's prior undertaking that he would not be harmed and would be allowed to return unscathed to Amsterdam. Marius went to The Hague and was warmly invited for dinner by the commissary who had issued the summons. No further official measures were taken against him.[80]

Vondel, who had once sung the praises of Frederick Henry for his capture of 's-Hertogenbosch (1629), became the subject of much opprobrium for some time after publishing *Eeuwgetij*.[81] It was characteristic of the open cultural and intellectual climate of the Golden Age that the vilification gradually faded. Although Vondel remained a convinced Catholic and a close friend of Marius, whose epitaph and eulogy he composed, he was eventually restored to respectability. In October 1653 he was even honored and crowned as "the prince of poets" by members of the interdenominational artists' and writers' Guild of St. Luke. He was, after all, the man who had, more convincingly than anyone else, panegyrized the city and its magistrates.[82]

The Miracle Celebrated

With the publication of *Amstelredams eer ende opcomen* and the Begijnhof's new profile as a center of Eucharistic piety, Marius had laid solid foundations for the continuation of the cult. But it was not yet enough. The celebration of the feast of the Miracle that he found when he came to the Begijnhof was probably often more or less improvised. It was impossible to sing the Latin hymns to which the book of hours from 1555 referred because there were too few clerics and too many domestic churches in the city. To ensure that the faithful would not forget about the feast, Marius decided to give them the feast's liturgical prayers in the vernacular.

Getyden van het H. ende Hoogh-waerdigh Sacrament des Altaers
(Hours of the blessed and venerable Sacrament of the Altar)

In 1640 Marius published his translation of the liturgy of the hours for Corpus Christi, once again at Hendrick Aertssens in Antwerp.[83] He was very clear about the aim of this publication: he had translated the Latin liturgical texts into Dutch so that the "citizenry"—both "in general" and in the city of Amsterdam—would be able to pray the same prayers as the clergy and might thus be strengthened in the faith.[84] The book killed two birds with one stone: as promoter of Eucharistic piety, he recommended it to all Catholics of the Dutch Mission; as promoter of the Miracle cult, he recommended it specifically to the Catholics of Amsterdam. Particularly for this latter group, he appropriately focused on the narrative of the origins of the feast of the Miracle in his *Getyden*, which consists mainly of Psalm verses and hymns composed by Thomas Aquinas.

Thus he introduced the office with a number of fire metaphors—biblical passages about burnt offerings (1 Kings 18:38 and 2 Maccabees 2:10)—so that the prayers, "which are our burnt offering," might be acceptable to God. His translation of the office for Corpus Christi was followed by a separate chapter of readings for Morning Prayer on the feast of the Miracle and the subsequent days of the octave.[85] In addition to Psalms, the text primarily consists of passages from the history of the origins of the cult. Marius concluded his *Getydenboek* with a number of "recommendations for devoutly hearing the Mass of the Blessed Sacrament." On the whole, the *Getydenboek* contains only sparse references to the Miracle. In the introduction, he used more fire metaphors to refer to it: "Our heart is like a spiritual fire; the vanities of the world are like old ashes that hinder the fire."[86] For Marius it was important that the Miracle pointed to the Blessed Sacrament, and not the other way around. The corollary was that dwelling too long on the Miracle was to miss the point.[87]

Marius's edition must be seen in a wider context. Also in 1640, the vicar apostolic, Philippus Rovenius, published his calendar of the Dutch dioceses' feasts of the saints. An appendix containing the "specific office of special places" included Marius's readings for Morning Prayer on the feast of the Miracle, albeit in Latin. This points to coordination between the vicar apostolic and the Amsterdam archpriest. The feast of the Miracle was the only local feast to have a place on the liturgical calendar of the Dutch Mission, although there was a stipulation to say that it could not be celebrated outside Amsterdam.[88] The Catholics of Amsterdam were not obliged to celebrate the feast, but those who did so voluntarily could earn forty days' indulgence.[89] A city description from 1664 gives the impression that pious Catholics associated the Miracle more with the universal feast of Corpus Christi (in summer) than with the separate Amsterdam feast (in Lent):

> Daily still around this chapel [of the Holy Stead]
> many devout pilgrimages . . .
> are performed and particularly once a year, at night, and early in the
>   morning,
> on Corpus Christi, eleven days after Pentecost.[90]

Marius's *Getyden* made him a trendsetter in a development that was typical for Dutch Catholicism. The culture of the many hidden or domestic churches led to a narrowing of the gap between priests and people, and to a simplification of high Latin liturgy. The Dutch translations of the Latin liturgies of the hours and of the mass ensured that a liturgy-centered piety could develop, especially in female circles. Like the vicars apostolic, Marius and other pastors successfully made a virtue of necessity.[91]

Amsterdam Imaginings

Boëtius à Bolswert's series of illustrations in Marius's *Amstelredams eer ende opcomen* dominated Amsterdam Catholics' visual image of the Miracle until the mid-eighteenth century.[92] Bolswert had drawn inspiration for his composition from art objects preserved from pre-Alteration times, especially the large canvases that Jacob Cornelisz van Oostsanen painted for the Holy Stead circa 1515.[93] The series begins with the arms of Amsterdam, with Maximilian's crown atop the shield. The accompanying verse called on the citizens of Amsterdam to remain true to the faith of their fathers. The ten following prints depict the Miracle, several subsequent miracles, and the fire of 1452.[94] The last five prints represent not the Miracle but other Eucharistic subjects that Marius discusses in *Amstelredams eer ende opcomen*.[95]

The way in which Bolswert, just as Oostsanen before him and several artists after him, represents angels is particularly striking—perhaps even unique for Amsterdam. In itself there is nothing remarkable about a pair of angels; they are a classic attribute to the Sacrament. In the liturgy, one of the designations of the Eucharist is *panis angelorum*, or "bread of the angels," and in sacred art the Sacrament is often depicted flanked by angels, following the example of the cherubim atop the biblical Ark of the Covenant.[96] They are usually no more than part of the décor. But in the iconography of the Miracle—not the narrative tradition because they do not appear there at all—the angels are shown actively responding to the situation. In Oostsanen's "pilgrimage print" the two angels already appear together on one side of the fireplace so as not to hinder the woman who is taking the host from the fire with her hand on the other side.[97] Bolswert depicts the angels in moments where the miraculous host is in danger: they are there when the woman casts the host into the fire, when she takes it out of the fire again with her hand, and when her husband is bold enough to touch the host with his unconsecrated hands (the last two scenes appear in a single image). The miraculous host of Amsterdam had two real guardian angels![98]

Some eighty years after the first edition of Marius's and Bolswert's co-production, an engraving (8.3 × 11 inches) was disseminated in Amsterdam that has become known mainly because it was included in a book published by Theodorus Crajenschot containing two sermons of Joannes Nanning († 1761). This engraving, which bore the title *d'Waare afbeeldinge van het H. Sacrament van Mirakel geschiet tot Amsterdam op de H. Stede in 't jaar 1345* (The true image of the Blessed Sacrament of Miracle which happened in Amsterdam at the Holy Stead in the year 1345), offers a synthesis of the entire Miracle.[99] In the center, the sick man, lying in a comfortable canopy bed, receives communion from the parish pastor. A pious group kneels behind the priest; they had accompanied him as he brought viaticum. On the right a number of events occur successively—the vomiting, the casting into the fire, and the bringing back of the host—while a festive procession with a monstrance leaves the chapel that represents the Holy Stead. There are no angels on this "true image"; they would have been out of tune with the sober atmosphere that characterizes the image. It is striking that the casting into the fire of the host (and the vomit) is shown, but not its finding. This depiction of the Miracle does not in fact show anything miraculous![100] The engraving clearly brings us into the age of the Enlightenment, where everything had to be in accordance with the laws of nature. Even in the nineteenth and twentieth centuries, many Dutch Catholics were familiar with this "disenchanted" and therefore somewhat insipid "true image," mainly because a reproduction of it appeared as frontispiece in Pluym's book on the Holy Stead.

The Saint Caecilia Collegie

As the centenary of the Miracle (1645) approached, a number of wealthy Amsterdam Catholics decided to set up a musical society consisting of at most twenty-one "confreres"; it became known as the St. Caecilia Collegie, or Saint Cecilia's Choral Society. Its members' main activity was to sing at the weekly masses on Thursday mornings, at the liturgical celebrations on the two "holy days of Corpus Christi" (in Lent and in summer), and at mass on the feast of Saint Cecilia, the patron saint of church music (November 22). They did this in Kalverstraat, in the house of one of their members, Roelof Codde, directly across from the Holy Stead or Nieuwezijds Kapel. Due to its location, this new domestic church became known as the Miracle House. This lay initiative to found a musical society was probably welcomed by the clergy of Amsterdam because, although Marius had translated the office of Corpus Christi into Dutch, only Latin could be sung at mass. When Codde had to sell his house in 1657, the meetings of the society moved to the house of another member, Nicolaes Heijmansz Coeck, also in Kalverstraat and still close to the Holy Stead.[101]

In 1671 a Confraternity of the Blessed Sacrament was established in the Begijnhofkerk, which was being built at the time—it was probably a branch of the Archconfraternity of the Most Blessed Sacrament of the Altar that already existed. Its members could earn an indulgence by receiving communion on Corpus Christi.[102] Edified by this example, the Collegie also succeeded in obtaining a papal indulgence in 1692 for members who had devoutly received communion, had accompanied the priest as he brought viaticum to the sick, or had performed some similar act of piety. The Roman cardinal Francesco Barberini († 1723) informed the Collegie that he wished to enroll in their "confraternity" and even wished to become their protector.[103]

In 1705 the Collegie began to sing at masses in the much larger Franciscan Boomskerk, more commonly known as 't Boompje (the little tree), located between Rokin and Kalverstraat. This move was part of a general trend that began in the second half of the seventeenth century and saw Catholic worship move to ever larger "hidden" churches. In 1656 concerned Protestant ministers counted no fewer than sixty-two Catholic hidden churches in the city; in 1683 this number had fallen to twenty-six, but the churches in question were on average much larger. The ministers' protests against the presence of these "Papist meeting places" were to no avail. The city authorities replied laconically that it was indeed deplorable that "so many people were still allowing themselves to be caught in the Papacy's nets," but added that they preferred to deal with this problem themselves.[104] The number of hidden churches fell even further in the course of the eighteenth century, and eventually only eighteen remained, of which 't Boompje was the largest.[105]

The Collegie's fortunes began to deteriorate during the remainder of the eighteenth century, however, and it had to contend with declining

membership figures. The members were no longer able to engage in choral singing, although they continued—up to the present day—to stimulate
activities in the context of the Miracle cult.[106] At the same time, Amsterdam Catholics of all backgrounds were able to join an increasingly wide
range of confraternities dedicated to prayer or pilgrimage. Thus a branch
of the Confraternity of the Good Death, with headquarters in the Church
of Gesù in Rome, was founded as early as 1666 in the Jesuit hidden church
on Spui, the Krijtberg. This confraternity was quite successful in attracting the Catholics of Amsterdam, a testimony to the latter's fear of the
epidemics that were raging at the time and to their desire to earn the indulgences that were available.[107] Another confraternity that was specific
to the Northern Netherlands was the Confraternity of Kevelaer, founded
around 1690 in the Augustinian hidden church of the Posthoorn on Prin-
sengracht. From 1715 onward, this confraternity organized a pilgrimage
every summer to a shrine in Kevelaer, Germany, which at the time formed
part of the diocese of Roermond.[108] Another confraternity that succeeded
in attracting members in Amsterdam was the Confraternity of the Perpetual Adoration of the Blessed Sacrament, established in 1765 in Liège
and soon thereafter favored by papal recognition.[109] The rise and decline—
though not disappearance—of the St. Caecilia Collegie in fact reflected
the Miracle cult's own fate: having undergone a revival of interest in the
mid-seventeenth century, it faded away somewhat in the eighteenth. It
nevertheless survived the end of the ancien régime and found new vitality
thereafter in a new cultural and devotional climate.

The Miracle Weighed Up

The preceding sections—the "disenchanted" "true image" and the reduced activities of the Collegie—suggest that the Miracle cult could not
live up to its full potential in the age of the Enlightenment. Although
songs on the Holy Stead were inserted into some songbooks printed for
the Catholics in Holland, we have no indication that the Miracle appealed
to a large audience of worshippers.[110] If devotional life was kept indoors on
account of repressive government measures in the seventeenth century,
in the eighteenth this was due more to self-imposed restraint.[111] Many ra-
tionally inclined Catholics probably thought that miracles and other supernatural things no longer merited belief in their day and age, and they
preferred to speak and write about other things than the Miracle.[112] Nevertheless, a number of testimonies have been preserved that show that the

cult, in its guise of "popular piety" and particularly in the form of the ritual of the three circumambulations, did in fact continue to exist.

One hostile but reliable witness was the German Isaac le Long († 1762), who published the *Beschryvinge van de Reformatie der Stadt Amsterdam* (Account of the Reformation of the City of Amsterdam) in 1729. After a sarcastic account of the miracles of the Holy Stead, he proceeded to vent his irritation: "However disgusting these awful stories about the imaginary miracles in Amsterdam must seem to Protestants today, it is nevertheless clear that in the past, and even today, most of the Papists here in the city do not doubt these pretended miraculous deeds."[113] But even if Catholics were still convinced of the value of the Miracle, did they express this in deeds? We know of at least one person who did: a wealthy woman called Cornelia Elisabeth Occo († 1758), founder of the Occo Hofje, which still exists today. Her personal notes show that she set great store by the practice of silently walking the old, pre-Alteration processional route. She walked prayerfully around the old St. James' chapel once, around the Oude Kerk twice, and around the Holy Stead three times.[114] This personal testimony also allows us to understand why the processional route that Agatha Loen had described in 1651 was reprinted in 1737. Her "Reminiscence" was republished to meet a demand, and this implies that, even though Cornelia Occo was perhaps not typical of the majority of Amsterdam Catholics, she was not an isolated case.[115]

Testimonies of nineteenth-century Amsterdam Catholics show that their parents or grandparents had been in the habit of making the individual silent prayer walk, and this in itself is proof that the devotion survived the eighteenth century. Thus the Amsterdam priest and publicist Cornelis Broere (1803–1860) recounts in one of his poems that he accompanied his mother on a prayerful walk around the Holy Stead three times on a cold March day as a child.[116]

Having looked at this element of continuity of the old walk ritual, it is also important to keep sight of learned discourse about the Miracle during the Enlightenment. This primarily became an indirect debate between Reformed and Catholic biblical scholars. Le Long was an important participant on the Protestant side. He included long quotations about the cult in his history of the Reformation of Amsterdam and then offered brief but sharp criticism. One of his arguments to the effect that the entire Miracle was just "kitsch" (versus Marius) revolved around the suggestion that the two women who had discovered the miraculous host must have played a part at the request of the pastor. Perhaps he even bribed them, Le Long wrote, and in any case they stood to benefit much from a "pretended Miracle" such as this one.[117]

The perspective of Catholic scholars—exclusively parish clergy—on the Miracle can be deduced from sermons delivered in the Amsterdam Begijnhof and subsequently published for a wider audience, including non-Catholic readers.[118] They all deal with Catholic teaching on the real presence and proper preparation for communion; in this respect they resemble Marius's 1639 book. Remarkably, no sermon appears to have been published in 1745, which was the fourth centenary of the Miracle. Margry lists only an edited reprint of the 1645 engraving and possibly a reprint of the Bolswert illustrations from Marius's book.[119] The most famous edition contains two sermons preached in the Begijnhof by Joannes Nanning, pastor of Buitenveldert, in 1750. This edition, which also includes the "true image," begins with an engraving and a poem by Johannes Franciscus Delsing. Image and word both convey the same message: as once Moses witnessed the bush burning but not consumed, so the Amsterdam host twice burned without being consumed. The engraving shows Moses beside the burning bush on the right, the host in the fire (1345) in the center—a magnifying glass even reveals two angels—and the burning and collapsing chapel on the left, with a monstrance containing the miraculous host amid the ruins (1452).

Nanning's second sermon also discussed the triple fire. He began with an exegesis of the burning bush in Exodus 3 and then drew a comparison with the Miracle. Compared to the biblical miracle, the two Amsterdam miracles come out quite well: according to Nanning, the fire of the burning bush must have burned only for a short while, but "our sacred mystery" remained in the fire throughout the entire night, and on the second occasion for another couple of hours. After another series of similar comparisons, Nanning cheerfully concluded that the attacks against the true faith by non-Catholics had only served to increase the Catholics' unwavering adherence to it, as well as their desire to receive communion. The inference was that the Catholic faith was the one true faith, and that Protestants were in error.[120]

On Wednesday, March 17, 1773, the pastor of Vogelenzang, Wilhelmus van Wetering († 1781), preached a sermon in the Begijnhof on the occasion of the annual commemoration of the Amsterdam Miracle Sacrament.[121] He professed to be puzzled by the fact that non-Catholics were amazed at the Miracle of Amsterdam. The Bible recounts even more sensational miracles of fire, and do you ever hear Protestants complain about that? By way of example, he mentioned the burning bush and the passage from Daniel about the three young men in the fiery furnace (3:1–30), two examples that Vondel had also included in his *Eeuwgetij*. Despite his evocative style, Van Wetering had little to add to what Marius had already said before. His key argument was contained in a poem that preceded the sermon and concluded with the following line: "Thus ingenuity must yield to the word of God, far removed from all dispute and carping. Sola fides sufficit." These words, though addressed to a Catholic audience, were a clear jibe at the more enlightened among the Reformed authors. Van Wetering had succeeded in harnessing one of the Reformation's adages, *sola fide*, for a Catholic cause.

His sermon was typical of the fact that discourse about disputed religious issues—the interpretation of the Miracle, for instance—was no longer able to catch the imagination. The Reformed author Jacobus Kok, in a book significantly entitled *Amsterdams eer en opkomst* (The honor and rise of Amsterdam), published in 1778 on the second centenary of the Alteration, cocked a snook at these Catholic priests with their sermons on the Miracle. The next part of the title, *through the means of the blessed Reformation*, reveals that Kok was not only referring to Marius's book, but also rejecting his claim that Amsterdam's heyday had been due to the Miracle. Instead Kok tried to underpin Amsterdam's glory with the Reformation. The Miracle and Marius's book were mentioned only in a single footnote.[122] The conversation about the Miracle—both within the denominations and between them—had run its course. It would take a new era to reopen the debate.

4

The Battle for Public Space
(1795–1881)

A Velvet Revolution: Change and Continuity

After more than two centuries of legal restrictions, discrimination, and oppression, the nineteenth century brought Dutch Roman Catholics religious liberty and legal equality with other citizens. This new legal position laid the foundation for the slow development of social and political equality, also known in historiography as "Catholic emancipation."[1] Although the eighteenth century had already brought increasing tolerance of Dutch Catholics, a kind of "ecumenism of daily life," the "velvet" Batavian Revolution—a peaceful echo of the French Revolution—nonetheless marked the start of a wholly new, enlightened era for the Netherlands. Catholic emancipation was thus officially begun, but its realization in practice was far from complete. From that point on, however, freedom and equality were officially on the statute book of the emerging Dutch nation-state. The National Assembly, as its first parliament was called, decided to proclaim general freedom of religion, which was included in the first national constitution of 1798. This document defined the new right as follows: "Every Citizen has the freedom to serve God according to the conviction of his heart." The privileges that the Calvinist Reformed Church had enjoyed for centuries were thus formally abrogated. As a result, Catholics and other religious minorities—Mennonites, Lutherans, Remonstrants, and so on—were permitted to practice their faith again, new ecclesiastical training colleges were established, and some of the church buildings that had been taken from the Catholics after the Reformation were restored to them.[2] In those places where this did not happen and a church continued to be used for Reformed worship, the aggrieved denomination was permitted to build a new edifice. In practice this meant that hidden and house churches were abandoned, renovated, or replaced by entirely new buildings that were clearly recognizable as places of worship. The Catholic clandestine church of the Begijnhof, which had been the center of the Miracle cult since the seventeenth century, was a national first as far as its design was concerned. It was subtly restyled even before 1795, although of course it stood within the Catholic seclusion of the Begijnhof. The small sixteenth-century windows in the façade were replaced in 1793 by larger neo-Gothic church windows that recalled Catholic history, especially the Gothic windows in the erstwhile Holy Stead in Kalverstraat.

It was not always simple or even possible to return churches that had been handed over to Protestants in the sixteenth century to the Catholics. Churches with Protestant or "national" symbolic value, such as the medieval city churches of Delft and Breda, which had special links with the House of Orange, mostly remained in the hands of the Reformed Church. In Amsterdam, with its relatively spacious clandestine churches, not a single church was returned to the Catholics. Some were too important to the Reformed, while others had historical connotations that were too sensitive. The former Holy Stead, or Nieuwezijds Kapel, without a doubt belonged to the latter category, and its user at the time, the Reformed congregation, considered it out of the question that Catholics would ever be permitted to return to it to practice their "wafer cult."

Due in part to this situation, the objective of the pastors of the Begijnhof, in negotiations conducted between 1798 and 1809, was instead to regain possession of the "English church" located within the Begijnhof. As a medieval church, this would have been a small but logical alternative to the expropriated Holy Stead. A first chance to purchase this church was foregone on account of the costs involved, and during the lengthy legal procedures that followed the plan floundered on a refusal to sell by the proprietor, the English Reformed Church, whose rights were eventually vindicated in the courts.[3] It was for this reason that the Catholics of Amsterdam were forced to renovate their clandestine churches or build new edifices.

Although religious freedom had been greeted with jubilation, it came under pressure again during the post-revolutionary years between 1798 and 1813. The rapid succession of regimes, followed by occupation by the French, brought new restrictions due to the French separation of church and state. The new government structures increasingly turned the Netherlands from a country governed at the regional level into a modern unitary state. After the French finally departed in 1813, it was no surprise that calls were made for the appointment of an unaligned, supraregional head of state, preferably one of princely allure. A pretender who matched this description was quickly found in a scion of the House of Orange—a dynasty of glorious renown ever since the revolt—who ascended the Dutch throne as an authoritarian-patriarchal ruler under the name of King William I. The choice for the restoration of the House of Orange also made short shrift of the more progressive forces in the country.

William had grown up in a time in which enlightened authoritarian heads of state in Europe—for instance, Joseph II of Austria and Napoleon in France—had been accustomed to subject religion to state regulation. William too developed his own national church policy, in which he assigned to his own denomination, the Dutch Reformed Church, a continued role as the dominant, privileged religion in the new kingdom. In his view, the Reformed Church would not be a state church in the strict sense, but it would be regulated by a national church organization. The king was convinced that undogmatic Reformed Protestantism was best suited to fulfil the role of the general or national religion for Dutch citizens in society. The bourgeois liberal Protestant elite strongly supported him in this and closed ranks against the newly emerging public manifestations of strict orthodox Protestantism and ultramontane triumphalist Roman Catholicism.

The young kingdom's new constitution, drawn up in 1815 after the departure of the French, initially restored to Catholics the right to practice their faith in public. On enlightened principles, Catholics considered public expressions of the faith such as processions, pilgrimages, and devotions as a "natural right," but this view was not shared by those who came to power under William I's leadership.[4] They explicitly regarded the public space and public life as "neutral" Reformed space, where religion should never, or rarely, be visible or a factor of influence. This principle became more difficult to maintain in 1815, when in the aftermath of the Napoleonic wars, and as a result of the geopolitical rearrangement of Europe at the Congress of Vienna, the almost completely Catholic Southern Netherlands (now Belgium and Luxembourg) were added to the new kingdom.[5] To the Dutch Protestant community's consternation, this act of union in one fell swoop created a Catholic majority in the country. Protestants felt threatened by the Catholic numerical preponderance. Many saw it as a coup and whispered about papist conspiracies. They feared that the re-Catholicization of the fatherland was imminent. The idea still predominated that the Netherlands had really only emerged as a nation after the Reformation, and that the Dutch nation was therefore—and should remain—"Protestant to the bone." It was on account of these concerns that they preferred Catholicism to remain invisible to non-Catholics, despite the fact that it was permitted by law. In practice this meant that any discernible Catholic religious practices in the public space were banned. In order to keep the situation under control, the government felt obliged to take additional legal measures. Processions that had begun to be revived here and there were quickly restricted, while monasteries were forced to "die out." This last measure was intended to curb the strong influence of regular priests (religious clergy) on pastoral practice, as well as their attempts to introduce community-building devotions.[6] The Protestant establishment simply did not see any possibility in the Netherlands for public manifestations of "unenlightened" Catholics, who were "blinded" in their religious practices and guided by their clergy through "superstitious" devotions and cult.[7] It gave Catholics the feeling of living in a *dominocratie*, a country governed by *dominees*, or Protestant ministers.[8]

The acquisition of the Southern Netherlands also meant that William I gained control of the Brussels apparatus of state. Even before the French invasion, this had been oriented toward Joseph II of Austria's church policy, which focused on subjecting public expressions of devotion and the excesses of Catholicism to state supervision. The fact that William had this apparatus at his disposal made it easier for him to extend similar restrictions to the north. To facilitate this, the new government was equipped with two new departments (one for the Reformed Church and one for the Roman Catholic Church and all other persuasions) that were given the task of assisting in the organization of the denominations assigned to them. In addition to financial aid for the construction of church buildings and payment by the state of the salaries of ministers of religion, for Catholics this also meant stricter controls on the practice of their faith. This method of governing was all the more effective because Catholics in the northern part of the kingdom still lacked any formal organization. The ecclesiastical structure of dioceses and parishes in the Netherlands had been obliterated by the Reformation at the end of the fifteenth century and had never been replaced. In Roman eyes, the country was still mission territory under the supervision of a Vatican chargé d'affaires and ruled by regional "archpriests."[9] This situation remained unchanged until 1853—and the changes of that year came only with great difficulty.

Following in Napoleon's footsteps, William I had already attempted to reach an agreement with the pope about the establishment of new dioceses in the Netherlands long before 1853. In 1815 he suddenly found himself at the helm of a religiously mixed nation. He wished to ensure that "northern" Catholics in his enlarged realm would not be disadvantaged vis-à-vis their "southern" coreligionists, who had traditionally had their own ecclesiastical structure. However, the draft concordat drawn up in 1827 to remedy this situation on the basis of the Josephinist principles described above—which would have united the entire Northern Netherlands into a single archdiocese of Amsterdam—was never implemented. In practice, fears of an unduly influential Catholic bulwark in the young nation's capital city—of all places—prevailed.

In order to mitigate at least to some extent the fragmentation and limitations of the improvised regional-local ecclesiastical government through archpriests, an interim solution was found in 1832 in the form of the appointment of a titular bishop, a priest in episcopal orders without his own diocese. The man appointed, C. L. Baron van Wijckerslooth, was presumed to be wealthy enough to be able to spend time and resources on giving moral and organizational support to the Catholic community.[10]

Catholic church life had hitherto been a largely local affair, concentrated mainly in the local parish church, with strong lay involvement through devotional confraternities. This was also the case for the Amsterdam station churches that celebrated the annual feast of the Amsterdam Sacrament of Miracle, a feast that still enjoyed a measure of renown in the city and its immediate surroundings. In order to emphasize the supralocal or regional importance of the Miracle cult and its long history, Van Wijckerslooth decided to take part in the celebration of the Miracle himself two years after his episcopal consecration in 1833. He would have had the opportunity to read up on this history because, shortly beforehand, the youthful Amsterdam private tutor Jean Estré published a historical study of the Miracle: *Beknopt geschiedkundig verhaal van het beroemd Mirakel, waarmede God de Stad Amsterdam heeft vereerd en verheven* (Concise historical account of the famous Miracle, with which God honored and exalted the city of Amsterdam). This was the first such study since Marius's *Amstelredams eer ende opcomen* of 1639, and it immediately ran to several reprints.[11] It clearly met a new and growing demand for knowledge about the famous Miracle and Amsterdam's distant Catholic past.

The new titular bishop's presence at the 1835 celebrations raises the question of what influence the Netherlands' transition from provincial ancien régime to enlightened nation-state had on the annual celebration of the Miracle. Very little can be said about this, due to an almost complete lack of sources. Does this in itself perhaps point to a demise of the cult? If so, it was not a total disappearance because Miracle celebrations continued to be held in various churches in Amsterdam at the end of the eighteenth century. It does appear, however, that the cult's intensity and allure were much weaker compared to the preceding centuries, as well as the century that was to follow. The dearth of source material can perhaps also be explained because it was not felt necessary to extensively record the centuries-old practice of the celebrations because it was deeply rooted in collective memory and did not give rise to conflict. Another possibility is that the influence of the Enlightenment had made participants hesitant to give much attention to the celebration of the Miracle.[12] Perhaps it was a combination of factors.

Whatever the truth of this is, we do know that the intramural celebration of the Miracle in the station (later "parish") of St. Nicholas and in most other Amsterdam stations continued unabated in the eighteenth century.[13] The extant printed texts of a number of annual guest sermons preached by priests, described in the previous chapter, furnish additional evidence for this. These sermons generally attempted to prove to Protestants that Catholics, despite their interest in the Miracle, were in fact ordinary Christians in the context of an ecumenism of daily life, believers whose Christian faith did not perhaps even differ very much from that of their non-Catholic countrymen.[14] The sermons nevertheless attached great importance to the history of the Miracle, its tradition, and specifically its continuation. They made sure to state anew each year for what length of time the tradition had been observed. Thus in 1784 Jan Moolenaar, pastor of the Amsterdam hidden church of De Liefde, had the honor in his guest homily of lavishing praise upon the Miracle of Amsterdam for the 439th time. As such sermons were often preached by priests from outside the city, it must be assumed that the annual celebration of the Miracle was still well known beyond the immediate confines of the city and its surroundings. This homiletic tradition, or at least the custom of publishing the annual sermon, came to an end during the revolutionary period, probably, as Clemens has suggested, because the period brought fundamental changes to the legal position of Catholics. This is evident in the last sermon of the era, preached by Brouwer, the pastor of Wormerveer, in 1798, the year of the new "constitution," in which he availed of the new freedom to strongly insist on the position of the Catholic Church as the only true church.[15]

Naturally, the constant succession of changes, wars, and governments between 1795 and 1813 was a heavy burden on the population, so that there were probably no opportunities to bring about a renewed positioning of this centuries-old devotion, which had survived the eighteenth century relatively serenely.

It is certain, however, that the custom of individually walking in silence—*omgaan*—already well known in the sixteenth century—survived the revolutionary transition to the nineteenth century, although it did so only barely. As has been seen in chapter 2, the humanist scholar Alardus of Amsterdam in 1540 described the silent prayer walks early on Wednesday mornings, when large numbers of people walked prayerfully to and around the chapel, individually or in small groups, in a spirit of humility and penance—bareheaded, barefoot, and without adornment—often carrying a burning candle.[16] Alardus added that this custom was then at least a hundred years old. The previous chapter has shown Cornelia Occo and others walking the route in the eighteenth century. The next testimony to the continuation of this personal ritual of piety dates from the beginning of the nineteenth century. It comes in the form of an autobiographical note by the Amsterdam-born priest, philosopher, and church historian Cornelis Broere, who would later become one of the key figures of Catholic emancipation.[17] Broere remarked that when he was very young, around the year 1810, he used to make an annual devotional walk through the city, alone or together with his parents.[18] The uniqueness of this reference appears to indicate that such individual devotional walking had by then become something of a rarity. There is every appearance that this ritual only barely survived the Batavian-French period and was known and practiced in a very limited Catholic circle, notwithstanding the fact that Catholics in Amsterdam were an organized, major minority of some 20 percent (approximately 40,000 citizens) of the city's population.

The cult of the Miracle is not the only example of an important devotion that managed to survive the repressive ancien régime, only to lose popularity or even fall into desuetude in the years between 1795 and 1814, despite the introduction of freedom of religion.[19] Holland's famous Marian shrine of Heiloo, some forty kilometers northwest of Amsterdam, a place of pilgrimage that even experienced a new, Counter-Reformation-oriented golden age during the eighteenth century, fell out of favor in these years of Enlightenment and renewal, only to be rediscovered and successfully revived in the closing years of the nineteenth century.[20] It is quite possible that this Marian sanctuary lost its position when the various confessions achieved equal rights in 1798 precisely because of its association with the Counter-Reformation. It never quite came to this with the Miracle cult. But because the latter had functioned so emphatically as a historical and Counter-Reformation icon for seventeenth- and eighteenth-century Amsterdam Catholics, it seems likely that a similar effect, resulting in a loss of interest—excepting Broere—was the underlying reason for the relative silence that envelops the new Holy Stead in the Begijnhof at the beginning of the nineteenth century.

Incidentally, Broere's account of the walks just mentioned did not itself date from the beginning of the century; he wrote it only in 1845. At that stage he was a celebrated professor at the minor seminary of Hageveld, located at that time in Velsen, and he had been asked, together with his colleague Petrus van der Ploeg, to write a book of poetry in honor of the Miracle to mark its imminent fifth centenary.[21] This book also included Broere's poetic outpourings concerning his *bedegang* (prayer walk), his youthful experience of individual silent walking to honor the Miracle. His poem about the practice of silent walking can be viewed as a kind of prophecy of the later collective Silent Walk or Stille Omgang, as regards both its title and its content.

In romantic and sentimental tones, Broere in his *Bedegang* describes a Catholic woman he meets at the Reformed Nieuwezijds Kapel, the former Holy Stead. The tearful woman, who carries a child on her arm, stands there as night falls, asking God to cure her sick husband. This petition shows that the former Holy Stead was still a tried and tested shrine at the beginning of the century—"Famous for its work of miracles"—and continued to attract Amsterdam Catholics in dire circumstances.[22] After the woman circumambulates the edifice three times in accordance with the ritual tradition, she falls to her knees in Kalverstraat on the spot where the hearth of the Miracle had stood, makes the sign of the cross, and begins to pray. As she does this, a Protestant who has been watching her from a distance throws a stone, which grazes her, as well as some choice words.[23] This sudden, harsh expression of religious aggression shocks the child. It awakens him with one blow to the responses that Catholicism and its expressions—in this case kneeling and the sign of the cross—could still evoke, despite freedom of religion. In the opinion of Broere's biographer Gerard Brom, this story should be seen as a strictly autobiographical experience, and the child was none other than Broere himself. His mother had brought him to the chapel. By way of reparation for his mother, Broere concluded his piece with "I will now go, for you." He made the resolution to continue the practice of walking after her death. The traumatic "Protestant" casting of a stone also determined that he would feel compelled for the rest of his life to carry out a Catholic mission.[24]

As has been seen, there are very few extant sources about the Miracle cult in the decades around 1800. The annual celebration in the Begijnhof church and the meetings of the old St. Caecilia Collegie or St. Cecilia's Choral Society remained its most characteristic annual expressions. The only sermon from these years to have survived mentions the day not specifically as a feast, but as an "annual commemoration." Was this a chance exception, or does it indicate that the character of the celebration had changed into a more detached commemoration? Membership in the society, which had provided musical accompaniment to the celebrations of the Miracle since the seventeenth century, had fallen sharply, and it therefore had to give up its activities.[25] This does not mean, however, that the desire to maintain the history of the Miracle and hand on its memory also disappeared. These things happened mostly in the Begijnhof, where this history was displayed and celebrated annually, always with "much concourse," around March 12.[26] Schoolmaster and local historian Cornelis van der Vijver commented on this in his *Wandelingen in en om Amsterdam* (Perambulations in and around Amsterdam) (1829), mentioning that the material relics of the medieval Miracle cult were still being cherished in the 1820s and were displayed as "proof" of the devotion's rich devotional past and particularly of its effectiveness. The famous "narrative" Miracle paintings, with their "cartoon-like" representation of scenes from the original Eucharistic miracle and their particular emphasis on the cures that had flowed from it, were placed in good view, "to teach and to confirm."[27] The late-medieval altar cushions with embroidered Miracle logos were also displayed, as was the chasuble that Maximilian of Austria was said to have donated to the Holy Stead for his putative cure in 1484. The unique painted medieval processional banners were placed strategically in the courtyard, in front of the entrance to the Begijnhof chapel, as proud "relics" of the once glorious Eucharistic processions that had traversed Amsterdam in the Middle Ages.[28]

Despite these rich historical possessions, the Begijnhof was crippled by heavy tax debts. Falling revenue had made the complex lose much of its old glory, and at one point it was even unable to pay its own pastor's salary. The institution was forced to sell parts of its precious belongings—such as silver and gold from the treasury in 1811—and still had to ask for loans from the state to stave off bankruptcy.[29] Concern at the emerging situation was also mounting outside the Begijnhof. It led to the government recognizing the building and the historical and commemorative use of the material Miracle relicts as material heritage and *lieu de mémoire*. This is evident from the state's decision, by a royal decree of November 21, 1839, to grant the private institution of the Begijnhof, as a historical monument, a subsidy for restoration. The beguinage priest, Bernard van Kokkelink, had been trying to make up shortfalls for decades, and the Begijnhof had become seriously dilapidated. Bankruptcy loomed when he had to restore a number of houses in 1837, and he had to ask for support from the state.[30] The result was an exceptional decision for the time, motivated by the idea that the Begijnhof was one of the oldest buildings (and institutions) in the capital. An even more exceptional feature of the state's motivation was that the Begijnhof was presented as the meaningful location in which to maintain the annual celebration and commemoration of the Miracle of Amsterdam, which were almost as old.[31] This "royal consideration," remarkable for the time, escaped the attention of the Protestant community, but it does indicate that the significance of the Amsterdam Miracle tradition was recognized also by non-Catholics.

The Catholics who were closely involved with the Miracle were only too well aware of this historical significance. In addition to the annual celebrations, the Miracle had a tradition of centenary celebrations. As the nineteenth century progressed, thoughts increasingly turned to the celebration of the fifth centenary in 1845. In addition to the Begijnhof and the Andries Hofje, or inner court of St. Andrew, which had institutional bonds with the Begijnhof, the city had several other institutions that were closely associated with the Miracle. The church of 't Haantje, as the official successor to the Protestantized Oude Kerk or St. Nicholas's Church, was directly involved as the former "mother church." In this attic church, parochial pastor Michaël van Steenwijk (1789–1853) was already making preparations for the centenary by compiling a cheap popular book that ran to several editions in 1845: *Beknopt verhaal van het Mirakel te Amsterdam* (Concise narrative of the Amsterdam Miracle).[32] The house church of 't Boompje on Kalverstraat was the home of St. Cecilia's Choral Society. As it had only a few surviving members, the society had long stopped singing, but it continued its endeavors to promote the veneration of the Sacrament of Miracle. Its members were drawn from the boards of governors of the Catholic *hofjes* and from the R. C. Oude Armen Kantoor (Roman Catholic society for the indigent elderly), people from the most prominent families and institutions of Amsterdam.[33] Together, they constituted an effective elite network that supported the devotion. In addition, Amsterdam's three large Catholic charities were involved: the Jongensweeshuis (orphanage for boys) or St. Aloysius's Institution on Lauriergracht, the Maagdenhuis (orphanage for girls) on Spui, directly across from the Begijnhof, and the R. C. Oude Armen Kantoor at Keizersgracht 384.[34] The long, drawn-out warm-up for the fifth centenary resulted in a first artistic initiative. In order to involve the orphans visually in the Miracle and its celebrations, and to prepare them for a future role as bearers of the cult, the governors of the Maagdenhuis commissioned a large "new" painting. They asked painter Jan J. Berckman in 1833 to make an enlarged copy of one of the historical paintings in the Begijnhof. To show that the canvas was intended for, and the property of, the Maagdenhuis, he was asked to add a number of orphans and a commemorative text. The painting reconfirmed the old bond between the charity institution, the governors and participating orphans, and the cult of and belief in the Miracle.[35]

These kinds of confirmations or reconfirmations were important, and not only for Amsterdam and the Miracle cult. Catholic laypeople and priests across the country were busy dusting off and revitalizing their glorious pre-Reformation medieval past and using it to further the cause of Catholicism in the Netherlands. The "chain of memory," as the French religious scholar Hervieu-Léger has called this commemorative mechanism, was fully deployed to hand on the faith in its historical and "national" diversity and to stimulate its revival.[36] Heritage, both material and intangible—the latter consisting of stories, myths, liturgy, and devotions—was given a renewed place within a Catholic culture of memory designed in the first place to tighten local bonds within the Catholic community. Historical sources were traced and folk stories collected to be disseminated through new media such as magazines. In 1845 Van Steenwijk, pastor of 't Haantje, was one of the first to establish a magazine to this end, the *Zondagsblad voor Roomsch-Catholyken* (Sunday magazine for Roman Catholics). Many other initiatives followed. The Amsterdam Miracle cult was one of the first examples of this process of commemoration and revitalization.[37]

1845: The "Feast of Folly"

Despite—or perhaps because of—religious liberty, specifically Catholic things such as the Eucharist, the veneration of saints, and devotions and pilgrimages continued to feed controversy between Catholics and Protestants up to around the middle of the nineteenth century. The writer and traveler Justus Swaving listed them once again in his *Galerij van Roomsche beelden* (Gallery of Roman images), not forgetting the Miracle of Amsterdam.[38] Neither side was willing to concede much when it came to the classic points of contention, often dating from the early years of the Reformation. Protestants clung to their myth of a purely Protestant fatherland and the need to preserve it. Contemporary foreign observers also confirmed the image of the Netherlands as a Protestant country.[39] Dutch Catholics, on the contrary, regarded their devotions as important aids in bringing about the cohesion that their fragmented community needed.

As is often the case, it was a foreigner who painted a striking picture of Dutch Catholics of the time. In 1847 the French Benedictine Jean-Baptiste Pitra remarked to his abbot, Dom Prosper Guéranger, on how prosaic the Dutch Catholicism of his day appeared, especially compared to its glorious pre-Reformation past. Standing at the tomb of the Dutch "patriarch" Boniface, which he had taken the trouble to travel to the extreme north to see, Pitra asked himself where all these Catholic martyrs and saints of Holland had gone. There was very little to be found in the public space that preserved the memory of Boniface and the other medieval faith heroes.[40] For Pitra, this characterized the Catholicism of Holland, which generally kept to itself and was invisible to the outside world. The once flourishing culture of pilgrimages—to Alkmaar, Amersfoort, Bergen, Bolsward, Delft, Dokkum, Egmond, Hasselt, Renkum, Rhenen, Vrouwepolder, and others[41]—was almost totally absent north of the great river delta, and its memory had been almost completely lost. In the absence of flourishing places of pilgrimage, Dutch Catholics since the seventeenth century had sought refuge in great numbers in neighboring countries, for instance at the Marian shrines of Kevelaer (Germany) and Scherpenheuvel (Belgium).[42] There they were permitted to pray out loud and to walk in procession. There they did not have to worry about upsetting Protestants or attracting ridicule, and there they found a full devotional infrastructure with every possible sacred souvenir. These were long and expensive journeys to undertake, however, especially for pilgrims from the north and west of the country. In addition, Catholics increasingly began to experience their fear- and shame-avoiding behavior as a problem, a lack of freedom. Influenced by the new input they were receiving from the clergy about their glorious past, Dutch Catholics almost automatically began to feel the absence of their own saints and their cult.

Jubilation and Scorn: Trier and Amsterdam around 1845

Let us return to Amsterdam. The approaching celebration of the fifth centenary appeared to Catholics as an oasis in the devotional desert that the Northern Netherlands were at the time. In the poem about his mother and the *bedegang*, Broere implicitly stated that the ritual was far from outmoded or obsolete. He called on his coreligionists to honor God "even more ardently than ever before" by undertaking a silent prayer walk during the coming jubilee year of 1845. Broere concluded his poem with the urgent appeal: "Silence! silence as we go on our *bedegang*!"[43] This paternalistic imperative was an appeal to Catholics to walk in silence to venerate the Sacrament of Miracle. In doing so, Broere was the first to highlight explicitly the combination of a modern collective walk and silence. Repeated use indicates that *bedegang* (prayer walk) was the word that was used at the time for the practice of walking the old processional route at night, and not the word *omgang* (walk, circumambulation).[44] Broere's collection of poetry was typical of clerical literary production of the nineteenth century, and in its luxury edition, it is not very likely that its bombastic verbosity made it popular daily—or even occasional—reading for the ordinary Catholic. His appeal did not immediately bring about a renewed, widespread practice of walking. Perhaps the Amsterdam clergy was still hesitant and reluctant at this time of strong religious tensions; Broere gave the practice of the prayer walk a sensitive missionary connotation. His call was to undertake the walk and to venerate the Miracle in order to lead the erring Christian brethren back to the "one fold."[45] He called on Catholics to visit Amsterdam in their thousands and to resurrect the former Holy Stead on Rokin as a Catholic church.[46]

At any rate, our conclusion must be that individual walking was not a publicly known practice around 1845, in the run-up to and during the fifth centenary of the Miracle. The ritual is not mentioned as such in the many Protestant polemical and satirical pamphlets that appeared about the Miracle as an aspect of bigoted Catholic behavior, nor in the Catholic popular publications for the anniversary celebrations. The only reference to silent walking was made in a review of Pluym's study of the Miracle, and this referred not to Amsterdam, but to the practice that existed in 's-Hertogenbosch around 1840 of going on a meditative, silent prayer walk—to "go a holy way"—along the medieval processional route of Our Lady of 's-Hertogenbosch.[47] Perhaps Broere had this ritual in mind when he reflected on the future of the Amsterdam Miracle. The Dutch capital was thus not the first to have an organized silent walk. The Amsterdam practice of walking had left very few traces in the city's Catholic collective memory during the 1840s.[48]

As the fifth centenary of the Miracle approached, something in the cult began to change. In 1840, the year that William I was succeeded by his son William II (1840–1849), the Amsterdam-born Nicolaas J. A. Steins Bisschop (1802–1861) succeeded Van Kokkelink as pastor of the Begijnhof.[49] Steins Bisschop's attention was first claimed by the challenge of solving the Begijnhof's manifold financial problems. The royal restoration subsidy of 1839 had proven wholly inadequate for the Begijnhof's overdue maintenance work. Steins Bisschop therefore invented a more structural way of raising funds. He convinced a considerable number of Amsterdam Catholics to donate ten cents every week for the duration of ten years, promising in return to have a mass said in honor of the Miracle and for the souls of the donators every first Thursday of the month. This system allowed him to restore the Begijnhof's financial health, giving him leisure to concentrate more and more on the approaching centenary.[50] Steins Bisschop was not planning on letting this rare, once-a-century opportunity to boost the veneration of the Miracle pass. His preparations for the anniversary did not remain secret for long (due in part to the collections he organized) and immediately elicited negative responses from non-Catholics. Denominational tensions in society were still too strong to accommodate the organization of a religious celebration such as this one, which was controversial before it was even held. Only a few years before, in 1842, the king had canceled the planned episcopal consecration of M. J. Niewindt in the city because it was feared that the reaction to such a ceremony might get out of hand.[51]

The situation was further complicated by the controversial polemics engendered by the *heidensche tooverkap* (heathen magic cloak), the Holy Tunic or Robe of Christ, which was—for the first time in many years—going to be displayed publicly for a number of weeks in Trier, then in Prussian territory.[52] The Protestant part of the nation feared the epidemic "pollution" that might emanate from this type of large-scale, orchestrated religious manifestation. The tunic had not left the church's safe for decades and had almost become a myth that fed a kind of devotional mass psychosis. The temporary relaxation of restrictions on pilgrimages was an added stimulus to go to Trier.[53] It was estimated afterward that the exhibition had attracted a million pilgrims. The pilgrimage to Trier and the resulting "miracles" were widely reported in the press and touched a Dutch Protestant nerve.[54] Dutch Protestants were determined that nothing like Trier would happen in their own country. Although there were critical, liberal Catholics in the Netherlands, these rarely engaged in the turmoil, as if they were reluctant to question its significance within their own group. A number of individual politicians did take a public stance, including the liberal 's-Hertogenbosch lawyer and minister for Roman Catholic worship Jan Baptist van Son, who stated that he was prepared to make allowances for processions and pilgrimages in the south, but regarded them as a "profanation" for the predominantly Protestant northern part of the Netherlands, and felt that the "ill-considered enthusiasm [for processions] was a dream," but no more than that.[55]

As the Netherlands was not an isolated and uniformly Calvinist country, but instead a multicultural and multireligious mercantile nation with intense movement of people, communication and exchanges about these issues were very rapid. Protestant church circles and government circles, particularly the Departments of Worship, had strong reservations about the possible effects of "Trier." Even the establishment of a local devotional confraternity anywhere in the Netherlands was enough to set off conspiracy alarm bells at the department.[56] It is not difficult to appreciate, therefore, that the fact that Dutch Catholics were going abroad to acquire inspiration from one of the biggest international cults was regarded as a potential risk for the unity of the Calvinist fatherland. The large-scale celebration of the Holy Tunic pilgrimage ultimately caused a double controversy that would, on the one hand, divide the Catholic Church, and on the other firmly drive a wedge between Catholics and Protestants in both Germany and the Netherlands. According to public opinion in the Netherlands, the most dangerous aspect was that the exhibition was an extremely successful form of devotion organized by the church. This demonstrated for the first time the extent to which specific church policies could mobilize the Catholic population and stir emotive mass devotions.[57] The 1844 pilgrimage to Trier is therefore often characterized as an early example of a modern Catholic devotionalization strategy through mass religiosity.[58] The German Lutheran churches felt that the organization of "superstitious" devotions by the Catholic Church impeded the process of modernization in general.[59] The demonstrative use of the metaphor of the crusade—in the case of the Holy Tunic, even in the form of a symbolic "victory banner"—only served to increase the controversy, with terminology such as "conversion" and "exterminating [Lutheran] heresies" further fanning the flames.[60]

The celebration was not only a sensitive issue among Protestants in the Prussian territories, but also caused division within the Catholic community. A small section among Prussian Catholics, which was already distinguishing itself by its liberal and "national" character, decided to split off from the Roman Catholic Church as a result of the celebration and continued as *Deutschkatholizismus* under the leadership of the German Catholic dissident Johannes Ronge, who had been excommunicated in 1843.[61] In the Netherlands, it was particularly the Catholic convert J. G. Le Sage ten Broek who fulminated against Ronge,[62] while very few voices were heard of liberal or enlightened Catholics about "Trier" and "Amsterdam." A serious Rongean infection of Dutch Catholicism was not a likely prospect.

The controversy and unrest caused by Trier was stimulated even more by anti-Catholic newspapers such the *Algemeen Handelsblad*.[63] They generally characterized miracles as false, denying such wonders as the famous cure of the leg paralysis of the archbishop of Cologne's nineteen-year-old second cousin.[64] Protestants feared that the pilgrimage would have a contagious effect on other religious anniversaries. In other words, how would Dutch Catholics be influenced by it? And, especially, would the inevitable psycho-religious and emotional excitement lead to the spontaneous mobilization and activation of fanatical Catholics in the Netherlands? The media's pervasive negative stereotyping of Catholicism reached an apogee with the Trier affair. The imminent celebration of the fifth centenary of the Amsterdam Sacrament of Miracle nourished fears of a repeat of Trier, which might possibly mobilize the Catholic population en masse to literally go on the move.[65] Such ideas and fears were further fueled by the emerging pamphlet war about the Miracle celebration, a controversy in which a number of well-known voices participated. The Amsterdam religious teacher Johannes P. Heukelom had a long verse printed under the title *Feest der Dwaasheid* (Feast of folly), containing an expressive description in rhyme of the origins of the miracle:

> The Host slipped across his lips.
> Then, Oh!, his stomach indisposed
> Caused, in a violent fit,
> That Host his mouth to slip.

Heukelom concluded with a repudiation: "Despise with us this feast of folly!"[66]

A new complicating factor was that the legal ban on monasteries in the Netherlands had in the meantime been lifted. The Redemptorists were the first to obtain permission to settle in the country. They lost no time in setting up parish missions across the nation. The lengthy, emotive prayer and conversion sessions that were the trademark of this congregation, which devoted itself to the missionary offensive, were strongly mistrusted by non-Catholics as a form of indoctrination. This mistrust was further strengthened when it came to light that there was in fact a direct link between the Redemptorists' activities in the Netherlands and the celebration of Trier. The most famous and influential missionary of the age, the Amsterdam-born Redemptorist Bernard Hafkenscheid, had been asked to preach during the Holy Tunic pilgrimage in Trier. Armed with this "proof" that there was a secret direct connection, anti-Catholic opinion makers averred the existence of an international conspiracy.[67] The Protestant press suggestively speculated on how the famous procession ritual at the shrine of the "Dutch" missionary Willibrord in Echternach—near Trier— might also be introduced in Amsterdam. The "pagan" dancing procession of Echternach was thus portrayed as a "most frightful" prospect for Dutch society.[68] All this meant that the young state itself seemed to be in peril![69] This exaggerated posturing confirmed the truth of what the liberal Mennonite minister Joast Halbertsma had written to the politician Johan Thorbecke in 1842, after the foiled episcopal consecration in Amsterdam: that "only a single sensitive, I think even oversensitive, spot remains on the body of the nation as a nation: and that is religion . . ." As far as he was concerned, this was "the most irritable part of the entire human soul."[70]

When the priest-professor Broere issued his call to Catholics to come to Amsterdam in great numbers, hoping to turn the Holy Stead into a central place of pilgrimage for the young nation, tensions between the confessions were palpable.[71] It is true that, following the Trier example, the Amsterdam centenary was used to promote devotion to the Miracle at a national level and to create new momentum for it among Catholics across the country. One of the instruments used for this was the anniversary poem for the third centenary, composed two centuries earlier, in 1645, by the national poet and Catholic convert Joost van den Vondel. Vondel's verse was reprinted and disseminated. For conspiracy theorists, the use of this celebrated "national" poet meant that "everything" was now coming together: the dissemination of the Amsterdam Miracle story in large volumes, the papal grant of an indulgence, and especially ecclesiastical faculties given to priests participating in the celebration to change "faith vows."[72] Endowed with this faculty, Protestant magazines surmised, priests in Amsterdam, in those days numbering more than fifty, would actively try to persuade Protestants to abandon their religious beliefs.[73] Many

Catholics also considered the Miracle centenary as a "duty" in support of the restoration of ecclesiastical authority in the Netherlands, which strengthened the notion that vengeful and "turbulent" Jesuits were orchestrating events from behind the scenes. Or, as Halbertsma expressed it in 1842, "Not only my colleagues, but everyone I speak to, has a big Jesuit stuck in his craw at the moment." In other words, people could speak of nothing else.[74] The Jesuits, of course, had been accused of similar machinations ever since their establishment.[75] An apparent confirmation of this was found in the Jesuit order's own third centenary, celebrated in 1840.[76] Protestants not only made a connection between this and the Redemptorist Hafkenscheid's appearance in Trier, but also with Rome's "black pope," the general of the Jesuits. At the time, this position happened to be occupied by Jan Roothaan, a Dutchman from Amsterdam, of all places! Given that Roothaan had been successful in obtaining legal recognition for his order, which had been banned in large parts of Europe, it was not difficult to imagine theories about an international Catholic conspiracy against the Protestant Netherlands.[77] A Catholic coup in the Netherlands seemed only a matter of time.

Overrun by unrest and rumors such as these, the government was afraid to take any risk. Authorities across the country were instructed to monitor everything and constantly brief the king personally on any developments. The primary responsibility for this fell on the shoulders of Daniël Jacob van Ewijck van Oostbroek van de Bilt, the governor of the province of North Holland. His dispatches to the king sought to lower the temperature by reporting that he did not believe there would be much commotion in Amsterdam, as Steins Bisschop had in the meantime decided against holding manifestations in the public space such as had happened in Trier. In other words, if festivities were to be confined within the walls of the Begijnhof and the city churches, he did not expect any disturbance of the peace.

In truth, Van Ewijck did not have much of an idea what was going on in ecclesiastical circles. There was still no diocesan and parish structure in the Netherlands, and in Roman eyes the country remained a mission territory. Formal contact between the Netherlands and Rome took place via a chargé d'affaires, the internuncio. Since 1795 this had been a delegated Vatican official whose task was to consolidate bonds with Rome and strengthen the ultramontane element in the country from his base in The Hague. Innocenzo Ferrieri had held this post since 1841. More so than his predecessors, Ferrieri attempted to assume leadership of the Catholic community, and this led him to call on the Catholics of Amsterdam to support the fifth centenary en masse.[78] Apart from fanning the flames of fear of Jesuit interference, this "papal" exhortation also earned the anniversary a lot of extra attention from Dutch Catholics, all the more so as Ferrieri had personally ensured that Pope Gregory XVI granted a plenary indulgence of three hundred days to anyone who made a pious visit or pilgrimage to the Begijnhof during the eight days of the celebration. Steins Bisschop had petitioned the pope in May 1844 for a special indulgence, and Ferrieri's support had secured a positive reply within the month. In his petition, Steins Bisschop pointed out that the Catholics of Amsterdam were well aware of the approaching feast of the Miracle, and, he stated, "Their fervor for the feast of the Miracle had already become manifest in this city a long time beforehand."

The excitement continued to engender new rumors. One story claimed that the pope would come to celebrate at the Begijnhof in person, another that the Emperor Ferdinand I of Austria would visit the shrine, following in the footsteps of his ancestor Maximilian, and still another that the respective boards of churchwardens were planning to hand the Reformed Nieuwezijds Kapel and the English church on the Begijnhof back to the Catholics. This last rumor may have been caused by the negotiations that Steins Bisschop was in 1844 still conducting to obtain the original Begijnhof church for the Catholics as a "gift" for the fifth centenary. Because the chances of this happening were very slim on account of the high asking price, Steins Bisschop abandoned this plan after one attempt.

Historical Truth

The return of Catholic churches and possessions appropriated during the Reformation has proven to be a politically and legally sensitive question, leaving many blanks in modern Dutch history. In places where no restitution took place in the years following 1795, the issue was wont to flare up again from time to time. As will be seen, this was particularly the case with the former Holy Stead. But a positivist, legal-historical approach, as well as research carried out on the restitution of the built "Catholic" heritage, also occasioned a change in Catholic thinking about the Miracle that supposedly occurred in 1345. At the beginning of the nineteenth century, the Amsterdam priest Marius's 1639 book *Amstelredams eer ende opcomen* was still considered to be the standard work on the Holy Stead. Because this book was more a profession of faith than a work of historical-critical reflection, it allowed enlightened Protestant historians to characterize Catholics as naïve and superstitious.

As has been seen, a flurry of pamphlets appeared in the run-up to the centenary of 1845 in which the Catholic part of the population was portrayed in a very definite light. In order to neutralize this discourse of hatred about the "imagined miracle," at least to some extent, Steins Bisschop decided to apply the historical-critical method to the Miracle story itself for the first time. If this were successful, he considered, it would make it possible to refute the claims of all critics on the basis of "facts." This desire to know precisely what "really" happened in the past was not a preoccupation specific to Amsterdam; a new way of writing history was on the rise everywhere in Europe, an approach equipped with new methods and availing of modern source criticism.[79] Source editions were produced to make it easier to check historiographical claims. This renewal was also stimulated by a wider interest in the medieval past, driven by romanticism, in relation to both literary products of the mind and material heritage. Catholics hoped that precisely this kind of enlightened reasoning might provide greater certainty about the history of the Miracle, and that it would make short shrift of the familiar accusations of bigotry, naiveté, or superstition.

With all this in mind, Steins Bisschop personally asked Antoon Pluym, professor of church history at the seminary in Warmond, to take away the existing uncertainty about the historicity of the Miracle. This was in fact the first time that the founding miracle of the Amsterdam cult was subjected to historical research. There would be no apologetic arguments such as Marius's this time, but rather a text that would live up to the standards of scholarship, even if it was written by a Catholic professor. Pluym visited several libraries and archives in the country incognito, or at least without disclosing his subject. Steins Bisschop noted, "As a scholar and a historian, he [Pluym] was given access everywhere by the Protestants, and he did not reveal the true objective of his research."[80] In order to postpone possible suspicions for as long as possible, he visited the archives of the Holy Stead and the Burgerweeshuis (Citizens' Orphanage) last. When a non-Catholic archivist eventually began to suspect his purposes and obstructed access, Pluym was already in possession of sufficient material to be able to construct his narrative. On the basis of the historical documents he consulted, he reached the conclusion that the year that the Miracle had occurred was irrefutably 1345. He therefore ended his study with a rhetorical question: "What more could reasonably be demanded to prove that this event actually took place?"[81] From the perspective of modern science, the occurrence itself—the miracle—can of course never be proven.[82] However, a relatively high number of old and authentic documents exist that deal with the institutionalization and development of the practice of the cult in Amsterdam. The history of the Holy Stead could therefore be traced much more clearly than that of many another shrine. Pluym was therefore able to describe the development of Amsterdam as a place of pilgrimage almost from its beginnings in 1345.

The book he published in 1845 can be seen as a first attempt in the history of the Miracle to give a "scientific" account of the event. It functioned as an ideological counterweight to the arguments that the eighteenth-century Protestant city historian Isaac le Long had advanced to prove the "imaginary nature" of the Miracle cult and the "unreliability" of Marius's book.[83] Giving as precise a historical reconstruction as possible of the cult—in the form of a "historical-critical essay"—Pluym attempted to let the positivist evidence "speak for itself" to show that a miracle had taken place. Steins Bisschop wanted to be sure of his case with a large-scale celebration in view. The book could also serve to refute new accusations by Protestants about papist confabulations.[84] This proved fruitless, as the stream of pamphlets about "pagan," "ineradicable miracle belief," and papist conspiracies continued unabated.[85] Heukelom had already dubbed the anniversary the "feast of folly." All of these pamphlets caused Estré to publish an account that was "open" to both parties: *Historie van het Amsterdamsche Mirakel, voor hen die zelf willen onderzoeken en oordeelen* (History of the Miracle of Amsterdam, for those who wish to see and study it for themselves). This publication succeeded to a certain extent in calming tempers, but the Miracle's fifth centenary remained the subject of much debate.[86]

Of course, all this negative criticism was not left unanswered. The progressive liberal and writer Evert Potgieter made an unsuccessful attempt to bring both parties together. He had no difficulty in empathizing with the narrow-minded Protestant character "Jan Salie," who fearfully regarded the festivities as yet another Roman provocation and machination.[87] Catholics, for their part, tried to undermine the criticism and stifle it with new apologetic pamphlets and defenses. There were also some on the Catholic side who doubted the veracity of the Miracle. The consternation led Catholic leaders to decide that it was urgent to take a clear and univocal position, and the journal *De Katholiek*, founded in 1842 by a group of prominent Catholics, presented itself as just the right platform.

This religious and historical-literary magazine would prove to be hugely important for Catholic emancipation in general and for the evaluation and appreciation of Catholic heritage in particular. Bearing the motto "We lay claim to the heritage of our forefathers," it was oriented toward the past, but in fact its main objective was to raise consciousness about, transmit, and broadcast Catholic cultural heritage. The commotion surrounding the Miracle led to the inclusion of a mission statement in the magazine in 1845.[88] This showed that *De Katholiek* had joined the fray to vindicate Catholic heritage and the corresponding truths and rights of the church in the Netherlands, in a spirit of "civil tolerance." The publication attempted to realize a kind of cultural and enlightened self-defense against the growing stream of polemical and satirical pamphlets of those years.

The 1845 series of *De Katholiek* was dedicated in large part to the historical basis for the two controversial celebrations and the criticism leveled against them. Thus, in humorous, almost ironic fashion, the magazine attempted to put the mounting outrage about the cult of the Holy Tunic into perspective. It did so by printing an anonymous dialog between one of the editors and a Protestant acquaintance of his—the suggestion being that it could not be more trustworthy. In this conversation, the editor led his acquaintance to realize that the honor and veneration in which Protestants held the costume of stadtholder and "liberator" William the Silent of Orange († 1584), exhibited in the Mauritshuis in The Hague, showed many similarities with Catholic veneration for the garment exhibited in Trier, with the exception that the Trier cult was linked to God and the one in The Hague was not.[89] This approach helped to make *De Katholiek* a success, allowing it to give a national, cultural-political voice to the Catholics of the Netherlands. Of course, its effects on Protestants who did not read it were less profound. Le Sage ten Broek, on the other hand, was remarkably reticent when it came to the issue of the Miracle.[90] In *Catholijke Nederlandsche Stemmen* (Catholic Dutch voices) he concentrated on Trier and the "damnable sect" of Rongeanism. Perhaps the Miracle of Amsterdam failed to speak to imagination in Le Sage's hometown of Grave, near the German border.[91] It is striking that he called it a "commemorative feast," a celebration of "love for the Blessed Sacrament," but especially of "commemoration itself." He did print an extensive eyewitness account by "an Amsterdam Catholic" in the "Church Notices" section of his *Godsdienstvriend* (Friend of religion) after the event.[92]

As he awaited Pluym's results, and as he was keen to leave the adversary as little opportunity as possible to organize systematic opposition,

Steins Bisschop waited until early January 1845 before he revealed the exact program of the fifth centenary in the city—only three months before the event. Because rising excitement among Amsterdam Catholics and deepening "embitterment" among Protestants might lead to problems, Steins Bisschop left nothing to chance and canceled the programmed solemn outdoor procession in the enclosed Begijnhof.

Although normally sympathetic toward his Catholic subjects, and considerably less begrudging of their freedoms than his father, William II insisted on being informed constantly in this critical hour. Extreme circumspection was required with a view to maintaining the peace. The governor of North Holland, Van Ewijck, wrote in his fortnightly report to the king that he did not expect any disturbances of public order. But "it needs no telling that this feast has led to a great amount of talk," Van Ewijck added as he noted the general irritation of Protestants.

All commotion and the national government's constant vigilance notwithstanding, the capital's city councilors seem not to have discussed the fifth centenary at all, at least if we are to believe the Deliberatienboeken, or acts of the city council. This is where it becomes evident that Amsterdam was a large and relatively tolerant city. Insiders confirmed this and subsequently professed their gratitude to the "good Government and Police of this city" for their open-mindedness and professional attitude toward the celebration.[93] The issue of the Miracle was hard-fought primarily between the denominations and at the local-church level. The celebration itself took place entirely within the structure of the Amsterdam stations and the network of Catholic governors. For the city, as an economic metropolis that stood somewhat apart from the rest of society, the whole issue hardly mattered. The councilors paid no further attention to the event and the rising tempers that it occasioned; they trusted that the police knew how to act if necessary.

In order to receive the many pilgrims expected to travel to Amsterdam, the organization had temporarily placed a wooden "shed" (4.5 × 4.5 m) against the façade of the house church in the Begijnhof. The church's porch and windows were removed to make this possible. Steins Bisschop had purposefully omitted Catholic adornments from the outside doors of the Begijnhof because Protestants had "murmured" against them too much.[94]

The jubilee and growing interest in the past had also inspired the churchwardens of the Reformed congregation to take a closer look at the Nieuwezijds Kapel, the former Holy Stead, to see if any connections with the former cult could be found. This led to the discovery of a cabinet, hidden behind wallpaper in the churchwarden's room, containing large, colored scenes of the Miracle. Together they visualized the story of the Miracle as it had previously been depicted in "cartoon" style. In its reconstructed form, the set looks like a modern scaffolding sheet; the large, stretched-out image was used to show medieval pilgrims the miraculous story in successive scenes as they arrived at the Holy Stead or the Holy Corner. It was even established that the images were the work of the famous late-medieval Amsterdam master Jacob Cornelisz van Oostsanen.[95] The churchwardens carefully kept the discovery under wraps, but neither did they take the opportunity to dispose of these authentic relics of the "wafer cult" that they so despised. The find obviously exercised some kind of power over them, something like the reticence that held the governors of the Burgerweeshuis back from burning the famous wooden "Miracle chest" on some cold winter's day.

The Jubilee

When the moment of the celebration finally arrived, it was all something of an anticlimax, at least for the authorities. The feast passed almost without incident during the octave of the Miracle, which ran from the afternoon of March 4 up to and including March 12.[96] The opening mass had been assigned to the Roman representative in The Hague, Internuncio Ferrieri, on account of his commitment to the jubilee and the papal indulgence attached to it. He celebrated it at an altar holding an impressive set of church silver provided by the parish churches that were involved.[97] A large, gilded statue of Christ was purchased to remind the crowds in whose honor the festivities were ultimately being celebrated. The Begijnhof was brilliantly decorated for the "demi-millennial feast" with tasteful green and white velvet drapes, and in the center of the church stood an immense certificate of confirmation issued by the city authorities in 1345, on imitation parchment and bearing the arms with imperial crown of the city of Amsterdam, a reference to the presumed economic benefits of the Miracle. Signs with biblical verses were suspended from the pillars, while painted and embroidered displays with historicizing images had been placed in different parts of the church. There were pavilions with laurel branches, constantly refreshed pots of fragrant flowers placed beside the altar, a reference to the monarchy in the form of two "alluring orange trees" full of fruit, and also silver stars, wreaths, gilded ornaments, passements, festoons, lappets, tassels, and tufts of white plumes. The description of the festive decorations took up many pages.[98]

Despite an unremitting and extraordinarily severe frost, the turnout of pilgrims and their attendance at the daily masses in the churches of Amsterdam were characterized as "good."[99] Precise figures are unknown. But if we are to believe Catholic writers of the time, "none" of the forty thousand Catholics in Amsterdam stayed away from the Begijnhof that week. No one could remember such an exuberant celebration. It also attracted many to the Begijnhof who had not been to church for a long time. The jostling and pushing at the entrance was so intense that police officers— with whom Steins Bisschop had an excellent working relationship—sometimes had to restore order.[100] Those who managed to get in could attend masses, benediction, and commentaries between six o'clock in the morning and midnight daily, or see to their private devotions. Many were moved to tears.[101] The visitors were not only people from the city and its surroundings; the Miracle centenary also appealed to Catholics from much farther afield in Holland. Thus there was a delegation of members of the confraternities of the Sacred Heart and the Living Rosary from The Hague. They had been reflecting on historical relations with Amsterdam under the auspices of the rural dean of Delfsland by consulting the archives: the old rights of possession over the Holy Stead pertaining to St. Mary's chapter in The Hague.[102] They donated a Marian banner with parchments. A group of pilgrims from Den Helder made an impression with their donation of an immense twenty-pound wax candle.[103] The flower of Holland's clergy was also in attendance. The major seminary of Warmond and the minor seminary of Hageveld were represented by their professors Petrus van der Ploeg, Cornelis Broere, Antoon Pluym, and the subsequent bishop of Haarlem F. J. van Vree, who at the time was president of the major seminary. Steins Bisschop had requested their expert contributions well in advance in order to "raise interest among Catholics and Protestants."[104] Every day of the octave, one of the professors preached and Bishop Van Wijckerslooth had the honor of closing the octave. As he stood at the altar he was surrounded by no fewer than thirty-five priests in full vestments: Catholic triumphalism avant la lettre! The sermons were so well received that around a hundred prominent Catholics signed a petition afterward asking that the sermons be published, just as they had been in the eighteenth century, so that the idea and message of the Miracle could be spread among a wider public. That the celebrations remained very sensitive is clear from the fact that this proposal was not accepted. Van Vree feared

that the controversy, which had finally quietened down somewhat, might
be rekindled by such a publication, causing the sermons to "become the
target of the totality of non-Catholic scholars," thus allowing "the enemies
to concentrate their power."[105] Even so, the organization proved rather
successful in arousing the interest of Protestants. According to a tally of
Steins Bisschop, "thousands" of them came to the beguinage to satisfy
their curiosity.[106]

Among the signatories of the petition was a youthful Joseph A. Alberdingk Thijm (1820–1889).[107] This passionate young intellectual would become a pivotal figure in the Dutch Catholic emancipation movement,
especially in its Amsterdam section. As a cultural leader, he used his books
and articles to try and break through the isolated position of the Dutch
Catholic community and to teach his coreligionists national consciousness. Important instruments were his *Volksalmanak voor Nederlandsche
katholieken* (People's almanac for Dutch Catholics), which he founded and
whose contents he partly wrote himself, and the daily newspaper *De Tijd*.
For Thijm, the fifth centenary was decisive in that it led him to develop
an intimate relationship with the Amsterdam Miracle. His commitment
was enduring and even led him to write his own family into the history of
the origins of the Miracle.[108] To a large extent, he directed the cultural-
devotional revival of Dutch Catholicism through his publishing company,
C. L. van Langenhuysen, in Amsterdam. He became the most prominent
Catholic layman with a public mission.

The 1845 jubilee stimulated not only apologists, but also men of letters. They drew inspiration from a long tradition of verse composed in
honor of the Sacrament of Miracle, from Van Hildegaersberch's medieval poem, Vondel's seventeenth-century *Altaergeheimenissen,* and the
eighteenth-century rhyming sermons, to—much later, in 1945—Anton
van Duinkerken's *Het Vierenswaardig Wonder* (The Miracle worthy of celebration). The fifth centenary was marked by the writing of the "Dithyrambe op het Allerheiligste" (Dithyramb on the Blessed Sacrament), which
was mentioned above in connection with the silent prayer walk.[109] This
two-hundred-line hymn was composed by Broere at Steins Bisschop's invitation. Steins Bisschop had approached the famous poet to ensure that
Catholics would not become the subject of ridicule as literary amateurs.[110]
Within the Catholic community itself, the name of the young philosophy
professor Broere would thenceforth evoke a "magical sound." He represented an all-surpassing ideal image of the priesthood, which dominated
all fields of theology and the humanities in this early phase of the eman-

cipation. At the time of the jubilee he was the uncrowned mouthpiece of Dutch Catholic culture.[111] Well into the twentieth century, the "Dithyrambe" was regarded as a poetic masterpiece and Catholics reveled in his sacramental lodestar. Subsequently, the reception of this poem altered spectacularly. Present-day readers encounter a cryptic rhyme full of bombastic symbolism and turgid phrases. But at a time when it was common to extol the glories of the Catholic faith, this triumphant mantra of early Catholic emancipation struck exactly the right note. The hymn does not speak of the Miracle itself, but rather of God and his love in general. Only a single line specifically references the miracle: "Here the fire its flames did spray due to the Mystery Divine," while the fifth centenary is alluded to thus: "Where five times a revolving cycle turned, but who perishes not throughout the ages."[112] That was all.

The anonymous Amsterdam chronicler of the jubilee rejoiced with pride and satisfaction, "Yes, we celebrated the Jubilee," but also permitted himself a sigh: "How happy would we have been" if the old Holy Stead had been returned to the Catholics? He wrote that pilgrims would sometimes spontaneously start singing the last verses of the jubilee hymn as they left the Begijnhof.[113] In doing so, they greeted the "orphaned" Holy Stead, the Nieuwezijds Kapel, in rhyme, describing it as bereft of sanctuary, lamp, flocking pilgrims, and cloud of incense, but they ended with the loud acclamation, "Rise again, O Holy Stead." It was a beckoning prospect that would become solidly entrenched in the consciousness of Amsterdam Catholics.

How It Ended

Immediately upon the conclusion of the centenary, Governor Van Ewijck sent a report to the king. He announced with relief that the celebrations had occurred "happily without disturbance." But William wanted a clear picture of the effects of the controversies on society and therefore forwarded the report to the Department of Roman Catholic Worship for analysis. The minister in question, Jan Baptist van Son, had personally made inquiries in his own Catholic circles. These had taught him that most Amsterdam "notables," including members of the Reael, Martini, Hanlo, Kranenburg, and Everhard families, had been observed regularly in the Begijnhof. Even those not known for their piety had frequently attended services. This last point was evidence, according to Van Son, that the celebration had enhanced the "spirit of unity" among Catholics.[114] This development did not cause the king much concern. And Steins Bisschop had every reason to be gratified: the Begijnhof, Catholic Amsterdam, and its Miracle had been brought firmly to the nation's attention once again.

Not only had the jubilee and the corresponding discussion engendered a greater sense of mutual connectedness among Catholics, they had also caused the narrative of the Miracle to develop from a local into a national and even supranational, discourse. The cult and its history had become general knowledge, and the attention they attracted had ensured that the Begijnhof was now regarded as an important place of pilgrimage for Dutch Catholics. The renown that the cult had enjoyed in the later Middle Ages had been revived to some extent in the memory of society. The foundation had been laid for the large-scale revival that the cult would experience at the end of the century.

Although Van Ewijck's predictions that there would be no disturbances had proven accurate and no physical altercations had taken place, society as a whole had quite clearly suffered psychosocial injuries. Amsterdam liberal lawyer and politician Jeronimo de Bosch Kemper acknowledged this and observed with unconcealed regret that the celebrations of 1844 and 1845, and the bitter controversies they had occasioned,[115] had hastened the growing apart of the Protestant and Catholic sections of society—the seeds of later political "pillarization."[116] De Bosch Kemper's "sociological eye" noticed that the celebration of the Miracle had influence on a national scale. The celebration not only sharpened the emerging pillarization of religious relations but also divided the Catholic community.

A group of liberal Catholics was looking to a Dutch version of Ronge's Deutschkatholizismus for a solution to the difficult position of Catholics. For the Netherlands, this novel approach might mean that the Dutch church province would become independent from Rome. The Amsterdam jubilee had been a catalyst for these dissidents in their resistance against centralism and the mounting "tyranny of Rome." In this way they demonstrated their abhorrence of "ultramontane" machinations that supposedly kept the faithful dependent and stupid. They had the support of Ronge himself, who apparently personally asked permission to ordain priests in the Netherlands, and of Protestants who wrote pamphlets to encourage a split between Dutch Catholics and Rome.[117] Governor Van Ewijck saw reason to alert William II. In his report, he remarked somewhat maliciously that he regarded this development as mainly positive because it undermined the growth of Catholic power and unity in the kingdom.[118] The paradoxical final outcome—for the time being—of the many contacts between

Dutch Catholics and Trier was that the pilgrimage to the Holy Tunic, which—as the "seamless robe of Christ"—was said to symbolize the indivisible unity of Catholics, had in fact provoked schismatic developments.

It is not surprising that Ronge's "national" views found supporters among Dutch Catholics, given the relative autonomy of the Dutch Catholic community, which had lived for more than two centuries without control from Rome. Perhaps even more important in creating distance between Dutch Catholics and Rome was the fact that a certain spiritual affinity existed between Dutch Catholics and Protestants. The territory of the *missio Hollandica* was characterized by its historical legacy of an "accommodation Catholicism" (see the conclusion of this chapter) that dovetailed very nicely with the new Protestant-Catholic amalgam that Ronge was propagating for Germany. When Rome's centripetal force began to increase around the middle of the nineteenth century, and international and missionary devotions such as those of the Sacred Heart and the Holy Family consequently began to gain strength, it was no surprise that liberal enlightened Catholics distanced themselves from these religious politics.

The renown of mass religious manifestations in this time often stretched well beyond national borders. For devotees and pilgrims it was not uncommon to cross borders, especially not for the Dutch, who had a tradition of traveling to foreign sanctuaries. And just as the pilgrimage to Trier influenced the Amsterdam jubilee, the Miracle of Amsterdam was a source of inspiration for the sixth centenary of the feast of Corpus Christi, which was celebrated in Liège from June 10 to 26, 1846. Amsterdam had inspired the bishop of Liège, the Dutchman Cornelis van Bommel, to organize a celebration on a grand scale in his own diocese. To enhance festivities, Pope Gregory XVI issued the bull *Ad augendam fidelium religionem.* Operating within existing international devotional networks, Van Bommel invited to Liège not only master preacher Bernard Hafkenscheid, but also Van Wijckerslooth and a selection of prelates from surrounding countries. It was a truly international jubilee, with sermons in various languages and pilgrims of many different nationalities. In order to avoid "all semblance of evil" for non-Catholics, Van Bommel let celebrations begin with the thunder of cannons and the pealing of bells in Liège and the surrounding countryside.[119] He then had groups of delighted pilgrims from Holland process through the city bearing banners, something unthinkable at home. Steins Bisschop was in attendance with forty pilgrims from Amsterdam. The gift they brought with them was a banner with the famous Amsterdam logo of the host and the angels embroidered on it, as well as a scroll listing in calligraphy all the different miracles wrought by the Amsterdam Miracle.[120] This fraternal contact was an expression of the sacramental connection between the two cities.[121]

Perhaps the intensive efforts prior to 1845 rebounded in a subsequent period of calm in the Begijnhof, or the commotion caused by the feast had had a sobering effect on Steins Bisschop's mood. The liberal Catholic alderman Andreas A. Reael—one of the jurists of the 1848 Constitution—hinted at the latter hypothesis in his eulogy on the occasion of Steins Bisschop's twenty-fifth anniversary of ordination. He not only praised the pastor's indefatigable work and zeal for the restoration of the Begijnhof and in passing called Steins Bisschop its second "founder," but also offered the following lines:

> The Zeal for God's Honor truly consumed Thee,
> At the Jubilee of the Miracle of this City;
> For ever Thy name will be associated with the Jubilee,
> For whose glory and fame Thou wert prepared to give all.

This tribute was the last event of note in relation to the annual celebration of the Miracle for a number of decades.[122] Two episodes nevertheless merit mention. In 1851, the influential archbishop of Turin, Aloysius Fransoni, visited the Begijnhof. Partly due to the positive impression that Dutch Catholicism made on him there, he reportedly lobbied the pope for the expeditious restoration of the hierarchy.[123] Another minor achievement was that in the following year, 1852, a small-scale triduum was organized in the Begijnhof to commemorate, for the first and last time, the so-called second miracle of the Holy Stead at Kalverstraat, which had taken place four hundred years earlier. Apparently the successful celebrations of 1845 and the praise he received for it had stimulated Steins Bisschop to think about possible other Miracle jubilees. The event that was being commemorated was the city fire of 1452, which had also affected the Holy Stead, but from which the Sacrament of Miracle had once again emerged intact. This had been interpreted at the time as supernatural confirmation of the 1345 miracle of the fire.[124] Did Steins Bisschop hope to be able to achieve even more devotional success with this jubilee? The commemoration attracted very little attention. Shortly afterward, in 1857, when parishes were beginning to be established in Amsterdam, Steins Bisschop left the Begijnhof to join the new parish of St. Catharine.[125] He was succeeded by Rector Willem F. A. Mehler. The Begijnhof became a general chapel of ease, with certain facilities allowing pilgrims to visit this substitute Holy Stead without difficulty.

The Revitalization of the Medieval Past

The success and orderliness of the centenary encouraged others to call for the "rediscovery" and revitalization of the sacred character of other former medieval sanctuaries that had lain in abeyance since the Reformation.[126] This was especially strong in the Catholic diaspora in the "Protestant" Netherlands north of the country's great river delta,[127] where the desire for inspiration and the need to strengthen Catholic cohesion were strongest.[128] Whereas the celebration of the past from the national perspective focused primarily on the golden seventeenth century, the era preceding the Reformation became the main source of inspiration for Catholics. Bearing in mind Pitra's comments, quoted above, clerics and laypeople wanted to establish a Catholic spiritual and devotional program that afforded a central place to the country's homegrown saints and martyrs of the (later) Middle Ages, some of whom had perished in the struggle against the "heretics" of the sixteenth century. In this way, the revival of Dutch Catholicism could be better embedded in the faith community.[129]

First steps were taken in the diocese of Haarlem.[130] Scholarly parochial pastors and professors of the seminaries began devoting efforts to uncovering all kinds of details about former saints and their sanctuaries from historical sources. Thus Adalbert of Egmond, Willibrord, Boniface, Liduina van Schiedam, and the Martyrs of Gorcum were presented as Dutch missionary heroes of the faith and portrayed as exemplars. This approach soon spread across the country: Lebuinus, an Anglo-Saxon missionary who had worked near Deventer around 773, was rediscovered in this town and "rehabilitated" in 1865. In Nijmegen, the relics of Peter Canisius were exposed for the veneration of the faithful from 1864 onward. The cults of the Martyrs of Gorcum in Brielle and of Saint Liduina in Schiedam gained popularity after their canonizations, in 1867 and 1890 respectively.[131] Dokkum began to regain its position as the central shrine to "patriarch" Boniface from 1874.[132] The veneration of Saint Cunera of Rhenen was revitalized there in 1878, while the pilgrimage to Our Lady of Distress (Onze Lieve Vrouw ter Nood) in Heiloo and the Eucharistic procession to the St. Janskerkhof in Laren were revived in 1886. They were followed by pilgrimages to the Holy Stead of Hasselt (1891), to St. Hiero in Noordwijk (1892), and to the Precious Blood of Alkmaar (1897). These endeavors eventually paid off. In the second half of the nineteenth century, Dutch pilgrimage culture gained a new lease on life, with participation from wide layers of the Catholic population. This unprecedented process of devotionalization was successful because of the joint efforts of clergy and laity.[133] With its spectrum of cults, devotions, and corresponding confraternities, this devotionalization expanded even further during the first half of the twentieth century. Almost all sanctuaries fulfilled a regional function, some supraregional, and the Miracle of Amsterdam eventually came to fulfill a national one.

A second, material form of revitalization of the medieval past flourished in architecture and the applied arts in the neo-Gothic movement. If ever a claim was made to "cultural heritage," then it was here, in the field of architectural styles during the nineteenth century. The boom in church building was also a symbol of the revival and construction of the various religious denominations. Rijkswaterstaat, the Dutch office of public works, used a subsidized building scheme to impose the denominationally neutral classical style for public edifices and in particular for churches in places where it had not been possible to restore a church to Catholics.[134] This program was initially quite successful, but it was ultimately unable to hold out against the neo-Gothic style, which began to gain popularity under the influence of romanticism and which even William II used for his palaces.[135]

The French liberal Catholic writer Charles Forbes René de Montalembert had emphasized the importance of the "natural" bonds between Catholicism and the Gothic style as early as 1839. He and others sought new inspiration by returning to the Middle Ages, which they saw as the golden age of the Catholic Church. Dutch Catholics were open to such romantically inspired views, as they could only look to the Middle Ages as their golden age. Catholics therefore soon claimed the Gothic style for themselves: it was a style capable of expressing the ideas of Catholicism as it was in the process of being restored. Writer-publisher Thijm stimulated the adoption of this idealized medieval architectural style with a publicity campaign, trying to convince audiences across the country that architecture (not to mention neo-Gothic architecture) was in any case not something Protestants were much interested in, given that they required only the most unprepossessing spaces for their own services.[136] As a professor of art history, Thijm tried to propagate a neo-Gothic style that had been adapted to the Dutch situation as much as possible and subsequently used his social network to carry it out as effectively as possible. The country's most famous architect of these years, Pierre Cuypers—the Dutch Pugin or Viollet-le-Duc—even married Thijm's sister Antoinette. In this way the neo-Gothic style became the Catholic architectural style par excellence in the Netherlands, the style in which all required symbolic and sociocultural representations triumphantly joined together to be communicated to the outside world. Despite extensive criticism of "façade architecture" and of the not-always-felicitous interpretations of the style, the symbolism of this language of form was embraced by the Catholics of the Netherlands.[137] Gothic and Catholic henceforth belonged together, with the Gothic style viewed as directly inspired by the Holy Spirit.[138] This renewed medieval style, eminently suited to evoke sanctity and a sacred or mystical atmosphere, would later play a role in the affair of the demolition of the Holy Stead. The combination of Catholic and Gothic was symbolically expressed in 1853—the year of the April Movement, which will be discussed shortly—in the construction of the first large church in this style. The church of the Immaculate Conception on Keizersgracht in the capital was intended to be a statement—a church built by the Redemptorists, of all people, who also established a monastery there. The fact that this large church building, in "pure" Gothic style, was built in the center of Amsterdam, the national capital, and for the benefit of one of the Catholic Church's most militantly missionary congregations, made the symbolism of this architectural style even more significant.[139] There was aversion in other sections of society to the erection of these buildings, which as Catholic landmarks were said to defile the "Protestant" landscape.[140]

The extent to which the idea of an ideologically significant, subversive, and provocative architectural style had become entrenched in society became clear in the architectural competition organized for the new national monument to mark the fiftieth anniversary of the foundation of the kingdom. In 1863 the organizing committee proposed that a choice be made between two designs: one in the "traditional" neoclassical style, and one neo-Gothic design by Cuypers. During the national debate that followed, the concepts of "neo-Gothic" and "Catholic" became definitively associated with each other in collective memory. The thought alone of a possible intrusion of Catholicity into such a national monument and, a fortiori, into national identity that was still believed to be Protestant caused consternation.[141] Liberal and Protestant groups succeeded in blocking the "Catholic design."[142] As a result, The Hague saw the construction of a neutral monument in 1869, designed by the architect Willem van der Waeyen Pieterszen, showing the Dutch virgin in triumph.

The Clash of 1853

The events of 1845 had shown how complicated the manifestation of Catholicity in the public domain continued to be.[143] While Dutch Catholics' demands—the right to their own church organization—had to be resolved in the short term, it was also clear that there were enduring susceptibilities and sensitive issues in society that were regarded as a threat to the peace and unity of the country. The broad-minded liberal statesman Johan Thorbecke was well aware of this delicate situation because in 1848, the year of international revolutions, he was working on a revision of the Dutch constitution that he had prepared with the help of several advisors, including liberal Catholics. For this reason even Protestants portrayed him as a Jesuit or as an accomplice of Father Roothaan.[144]

When Thorbecke was appointed to lead a first cabinet after the introduction of the constitution in 1849, he soon noticed that the problems of the country's religious differences weighed much more heavily on the new parliamentary nation-state than any other subject. The situation was nevertheless relatively favorable to the Catholic community, as William II was sympathetic to minorities in general and Catholics in particular. His intervention gave them greater freedom and eased the burden of strict state control over the Roman Catholic Church.

The Protestant elite was essentially opposed to change, and clear aversion to and fear of one another's religion was still rife among the population. Thus the Hague antirevolutionary politician Guillaume Groen van Prinsterer attacked the weakening of Calvinism in society from the perspective of Protestant orthodoxy. In his view, the faith of the fathers was a public affair that might not be repudiated. In order to preserve order and peace in society, he somewhat rhetorically proposed to corral all Catholics in the Netherlands together and move them to a Catholic "homeland" in the south of the country.[145]

Revolutionary events abroad in 1848 strengthened Thorbecke in his intention to give all Dutch citizens equal rights through the new constitution. Alarmed by revolts in Paris and Berlin, William II hastily agreed to the drafting of a liberal and "parliamentary" constitution, which included the rigorous separation of state and church. For the first time since the Reformation, this would give the Catholic Church the freedom to organize itself as it wished. It made it possible again to restore the episcopal hierarchy in the Netherlands. Somewhat unexpectedly for those outside politics and bureaucracy who did not fully appreciate the consequences of the constitution, Pope Pius IX in 1853 announced the establishment of dioceses in the Netherlands in provocative language—he spoke of the "Calvinist heresy" that was dominant in the Netherlands.[146] This initiative was a strong challenge to repressive tolerance. As Rome and Dutch Catholics were self-consciously manifesting themselves and claiming their place in the country, the result was an intense Protestant revolt. This so-called April Movement had its core in Utrecht, the place where the archiepiscopal see was set to be established.[147] Protestant resistance against the plans of Rome spread throughout the country like wildfire. Hundreds of thousands signed a petition to the king to ban the new ecclesiastical structure. According to the typology of collective action proposed by Charles Tilly, this resistance was halfway between a traditional expression of direct action and newly emerging forms of political protest.[148] Protestant ministers protested from the pulpit, and Catholic shops were boycotted, Catholic workers dismissed, Catholic homes defaced, and Catholic clerics harassed.[149] No fewer than two hundred thousand signatures were collected for the petition within a fortnight, a clear indication of deeply rooted aversion against Catholics and of fears of a possible Catholic coup.[150] The Calvinist tradition, the power of its pulpit orators, and certainly also the power of newspapers and magazines had been thoroughly effective. Although the new constitution ensured that the Catholic hierarchy could ultimately be established as planned, the moral and social effects of the April Movement were immense.

In order to offer some solace in the face of the protesters' demands, an ad hoc bill was hastily drafted: the law on church communities. This was a mainly symbolic concession to the objections raised. Its most significant aspects were that the new bishops would not be permitted to take up residence in the provincial capitals of their dioceses, and that processions and pilgrimages were placed under somewhat more stringent restrictions than they had hitherto been. King William III (1849–1890) was not as friendly to liberals and Catholics as his father, William II, whom he had succeeded in 1849. He viewed the April Movement primarily as a confirmation of the concept of a Protestant nation and of the role of the House of Orange within it. The revolt initially seemed at risk of developing into a kind of coup, but because its politics were essentially based on the single issue of antipapism, the movement never acquired a serious political role.[151]

In the short term, the excitement led to the fall of Thorbecke's liberal cabinet, showing the existence of a gulf between the liberally oriented parliament, with its interest in constitutional law, and the majority Protestant population outside. While parliament was primarily concerned with constitutional issues and the divisions between conservatives and liberals, religious controversies—the divisions between Protestants and Catholics and the repercussions these had on daily life—were the general population's main concern. One of the few Catholic ministers of the time professed to be excessively shocked by the fact that the state paid lip service to tolerance but reduced it to zero practice.[152] Orthodox Reformed lawyer Daan Koorders—a close spectator to the April Movement—had previously made unsuccessful attempts to explain the constitution and its consequences to his coreligionists. Afterward he wrote a retrospective in which he said, "Since then, we have been led to the edge of the abyss. The passions continue to surge. The divide between Roman and non-Roman is wider than ever. The flames of religious hatred continue to flare up with uncontrolled intensity. The sons of the same fatherland carry on splitting up into two hostile army camps."[153] This passage bears out the roots of the strictness of subsequent pillarization. The mid-nineteenth century thus witnessed a form of proto-pillarization, even prior to the period of political pillarization, that by extension also drew in the liberals and, as a result of the social question, the socialists.[154]

Amsterdam's constitutional position as the capital, combined with its large number of Catholic inhabitants, ensured that the Protestant establishment would not accept the establishment of the see of a bishop, let alone an archbishop, in Amsterdam, where the Protestant head of state was formally inaugurated in the Reformed Nieuwe Kerk. Haarlem and Utrecht eventually proved to be acceptable alternatives. Across from the Nieuwe Kerk, beside the Dam Palace, a monument was erected some years after the April Movement, in the summer of 1856, in the form of a stone spire crowned with the statue of Concord. This statue was the symbol of the united "popular spirit" that had been in evidence during the 1830 Belgian revolt. Little remained of this concord a quarter of a century later. The shape of the monument was somewhat unimaginative, and as there had been little evidence of a united popular spirit since 1853, it was soon dubbed *Naaldje/Naatje op de Dam* ("Needle/Naatje [a lower-class woman's name] on Dam Square") in reference to its needle-like shape and by way of social criticism of divisions in society.[155]

If relations between Catholics and Protestants in society were troublesome, Catholics still had most to win politically from separation of church and state, and for the time being they continued to support the liberals. However, the freedom of religion gained in 1798 and the introduction of the diocesan structure in 1853 did not mean that the emancipation of

Catholics had been completed. A certain spiritual, social, cultural, and political deprivation marked Catholics until well into the twentieth century.

In 1845 a vague rumor had done the rounds that the Austrian emperor Ferdinand would follow in his fifteenth-century ancestor Maximilian's footsteps by making a spontaneous visit. In 1856 this possibility suddenly presented itself in actual fact when the emperor's son, the Archduke Ferdinand Maximilian, came to visit The Hague and Amsterdam in 1856. It inspired Steins Bisschop, in one of his last public activities as pastor of the Begijnhof church, to invite him to come and reaffirm the centuries-old connection between the Habsburgs and the Miracle. The Austrian embassy responded with a polite letter declining due to time constraints.[156] That good things come to those who persevere would only become evident a century and a half later.

Another who persevered in this time was Thijm. During the mid-1860s he became ever more closely connected with the repositioning of the Miracle cult. In early 1867 his cultural reputation earned him the privilege of being one of the first Catholics of his day to be allowed to see the actual Miracle chest.[157] Partly as a result of this, in 1869 Thijm, newly appointed professor of art history and aesthetics, edited and issued a new edition of Pluym's study of the Miracle. Hoping to enhance the historical veracity and pedagogical value of the Miracle narrative, he tried to name the unknown sick man who had supposedly vomited up the famous host in 1345. On the basis of insufficient evidence, he wrote an article in which he pointed to the Dommer family, an old patrician lineage that happened to be related to his own family, as the household where the Miracle had taken place.[158] In doing so Thijm strongly influenced Catholic historiography of Amsterdam and its Miracle, both directly and through "disciples" such as W. J. F. Nuyens, B. J. M. de Bont, Jos Winkelmeijer, and J. M. F. Sterck. His own publishing company and bookshop, C. L. van Langenhuysen, located beside the Jesuit Krijtberg church and subsequently on Spui, ensured that the message was spread far and wide.

The third quarter of the nineteenth century saw neither special manifestations nor changes to the Miracle pilgrimage. At the same time, Eucharistic devotion in general was given an immense boost at the international level through the strengthening of related devotions, such as those of the Quarant'ore and Perpetual Adoration, which spread very rapidly in the Netherlands between 1865 and 1875. In addition, an international Eucharistic movement was started in Rome; it endeavored to steer the devotional and religious life of ordinary Catholics in the direction of the sacramental core of the faith.[159] Amsterdam and its Sacrament of Miracle reaped the benefits.

After the return of the diocesan structure, the annual octave of the Miracle also gained episcopal support. It regularly brought bishops from Haarlem to the Begijnhof. In the year 1871 this was Gerard Wilmer, a Brabant native and an enthusiastic propagator not only of the Amsterdam Miracle but also of the cult of the Martyrs of Gorcum. Some fourteen thousand hosts were distributed during the octave in the churches of Amsterdam in that year, a rough indication of the number of participants. It must be borne in mind that receiving communion outside Eastertide was not a common practice for Catholics at the time. As 1871 was also the year of Pius IX's silver jubilee, Wilmer organized a prayer rally, exhorting the faithful to pray for the pope in the Begijnhof during that week.

One source for the devotional practice of this period is the reminiscences, recorded in 1930, of an older citizen of Amsterdam who could clearly remember the days of his youth sixty years earlier. As a child, he had been aware of the special dispensation in the strict laws of fasting and abstinence granted for the feast: citizens of Amsterdam and visitors from outside the city who received communion in the Begijnhof on the first Wednesday of the octave were dispensed from fasting on that day. More to the point is his memory of a custom that left no other traces in the sources since Broere. He could remember that "many good Catholic and good Amsterdam families," men, boys, women, and girls, had a tradition of walking silently, alone or in small groups. He recounted, "All members of our family, parents, children, servants, also performed the Stille Omgang, but then once in the week of the feast. We knew the way and walked it, alone or together in groups of two or three, in silence, praying the rosary which we held in our hands in the inside pockets of our overcoats. We made this journey in the morning before school, on free Saturdays and on Sunday in the afternoon."[160] Although this man stated that he had known the route at the time, there were a number of diverging interpretations of this route. More than a decade later, Lousbergh, the initiator of the collective Stille Omgang, had to go in search of the correct route so that the "official" walk could be performed accurately (see chapter 5). This citizen's clear recollection indicates that the ritual of walking had never entirely disappeared from the collective memory of Amsterdam prior to Lousbergh's initiative, as some have argued.

Antipapism and the Ban on Public Space

The year 1853 is known as a key date in Dutch Catholics' drawn-out emancipation process because it marked the restoration of the episcopal hierarchy after nearly three hundred years. In the half century that followed, a Catholic elite strove to obtain a place in national politics and gain the respect of cultural and scholarly circles. The main concession they made in return was to observe caution so as to spare Protestant sensibilities and avoid damaging relations. Politicians seldom realized, however, that ordinary Catholics had in the meantime developed a self-awareness of their own and that they had a long tradition of self-organization, which allowed them to act more assertively. As 1853 had its Protestant revolt, so 1872 saw the emergence of a broad protest of Catholics against their status as second-class citizens. It happened shortly after the First Vatican Council (1869–1870) and the promulgation of the dogma of papal infallibility. The dogma itself caused hardly a ripple in the Netherlands; the twenty-fifth anniversary of Pius IX's election in June 1871 was much more important to the self-awareness of the country's Catholics.[161] This *Piusfeest* ("feast of Pius") formed the occasion for a first public, national meeting that had a political character. Festivities were organized across the country and yellow-and-white papal street decorations were put up, leading to difficulties with non-Catholics in some places.[162] It was a prelude to many more such confrontations in 1872, when the taking of Brielle was commemorated. The capture of this city from Alva on April 1, 1572, was regarded as the turning point of the Dutch Revolt (1568–1648), and as far as nineteenth-century Dutch Protestants were concerned, this revolt had been nothing other than a struggle against Catholic Spain and Catholicism in general. They turned the commemoration into a national feast that few Catholics could appreciate. Catholic leader Thijm stayed at home on April 1, refused to fly the flag, placed his revolver on the table, closed his shutters, and asked the police to place a guard at his house.[163] This incident shows how political and cultural divisions in society were being kept alive and consolidated by means that included historiography about the "war of liberation" against Catholicism. Catholic leaders and politicians offered resistance by politely engaging in debate.[164] At the local level, the conflict offered scenes of quite a different nature in some places. Catholics who refused to fly the flag on the occasion of the feast were harassed or had their furniture destroyed or their windows broken. In areas with a large Catholic population, the roles were sometimes reversed. In the largely Catholic south of the country the population rarely participated in festivities and on occasion defaced houses that displayed the flag.[165]

These incidents made a deep impression. The liberal press increasingly turned against ultramontane Catholicism, frequently referring to Bismarck's Catholic policy as a model for the Netherlands.[166] In national politics, there had been an alliance well into the 1860s between liberals, who advocated for separation of church and state, and Catholics, who were desirous of benefiting from the freedom this gave. This changed in 1864 when Pius IX issued his so-called *Syllabus Errorum*, a list of eighty "errors" including liberalism. A few years later, in 1868, the Dutch bishops took an unconditional stand for the freedom of Catholic primary education, thus rejecting a state monopoly on neutral education as demanded by the liberals. While in 1872 orthodox Protestants and Catholics were still engaging in brawls in the streets, their interests in national politics were increasingly converging. Both groups regarded their own religion as the foundation of primary education and rejected liberal educational policies.[167] The result was a thorough transformation of the political scene in the Netherlands, one that gave rise to a pragmatic cooperation between Protestant and Catholic parliamentarians.

The divisions between the confessional politicians and the liberals came to a head during the left-liberal cabinet led by Jan Kappeyne van de Coppello (1877–1879), which introduced a liberal education bill.[168] Although there was no political appetite for direct intervention in the internal church affairs, both Catholics and orthodox Protestants called Kappeyne a Dutch Bismarck because of his views and his indirect interventions into religion in public life. It was a moderate Dutch variant of Bismarckian religious politics, of *Kulturkampf*; this variant certainly had its virulent aspects, which were particularly evident at the local level: the battle for public space and, in particular, the public manifestation of religion in processions and other rituals, a struggle only too familiar to the Catholics of Amsterdam.[169] Although the Catholic elite that was involved in national politics was keen to tread cautiously so as not to imperil its budding alliance with the orthodox Protestants and thus to avoid sliding into a weak minority position, the public manifestation of religion at a local level was an entirely different matter. This primarily involved the lower clergy and ordinary lay Catholics, who developed a new pride in their faith. It was also at this level that the sharpest confrontations occurred between the liberal and Protestant (and also antipapist) desire to have a neutral public space from which religion would be absent on the one hand, and the new Catholic self-awareness that was impatient to manifest itself on the street on the other.[170]

The difficulty lay in a direct fruit of the 1853 revolt. In order to reconcile Dutch Protestants to the advent of Catholic bishops, a peculiar concession had been made in the 1848 Constitution in the form of a ban on processions. The specific article that contained the ban stood out oddly in the text, prohibiting the public performance of certain religious rituals. In practice this prohibition affected only Catholics and was therefore known popularly as the "procession ban." It was a thorn in the side of the Catholic population and its immediate pastors, who were from then on forbidden from organizing pilgrimages. Protests from the Catholic population became louder and louder. The Brielle commemorations in 1872 deepened irritation and led Catholics to engage in provocation to see how far they could go. The example of the confrontations that were beginning to occur in Prussia, where Catholics were offering strong resistance against Bismarck's religious politics in the 1870s, was a further stimulant. In the Netherlands, participants soon found that the government was willing to disband processions at saber-point. The government—and therefore the prosecutor and the police—were determined to enforce the law. The breaking up of a procession in Roermond in 1876 by saber-wielding gendarmerie on horseback counted as a low point in this struggle, but it also led to a certain perplexity that calmed the situation.[171] At first sight, the outcome of the struggle was an unequivocal Catholic defeat. From this point on, Catholics had to hold their processions in specially designed processional parks separated from the public road. But the question soon lost some of its urgency as trains, trams, and steamships offered alternatives for journeys on foot to places of pilgrimage, so that part of collective processional pilgrimages disappeared from the public space in any case. Both sides acquiesced in the new situation, and new provocations were avoided. The new political reality forced Catholics once again to observe a certain reticence.

For the time being, the Catholic community resigned itself to the procession ban and began to brood on alternative possibilities. This was the context in which a number Catholic citizens of Amsterdam, proud of their faith and of the history of their city, realized that their dream of a revival of the Miracle procession was unrealistic. But the combination of that dream with the existing practice of individual walking, in silence and without any confessional characteristics, created a ritual with unexpected potential. Not long after the end of the relatively mild Dutch *Kulturkampf*, in 1881, they felt confident enough to put their plan into action.

The "Ultramontane Miracle Disease"

Dutch Catholics emerged from the ancien régime as a diaspora community. Although they were a numerically large minority, this did not translate into a tightly structured community, particularly not north of the river delta. The faith there had been shaped in a particularistic, local, and parochial way. Bishops in the nineteenth century had two important instruments to strengthen cohesion and create a collective identity among the faithful: the introduction and further expansion of special (i.e., Catholic) education, and devotionalization. Catholic education was eventually guaranteed by law—in the Netherlands in 1917—as a result of the so-called *schoolstrijd* (school struggle),[172] while the success of devotionalization was dependent on initiatives of the faith community itself and of priests who imposed it from above. There was strong willingness to participate in confraternity-based devotions.[173] The expressions and emotions involved in these devotions offered individual believers support for their daily lives, but also created sociability through their organizational structures. This was an important precondition that made minds receptive to forms of collective religiosity, as would later become evident with the Silent Walk.

This form of expression was particularly successful in France, where the process of nation building was accompanied by the organization of large-scale pilgrimages to national shrines. Under the guise of "modern crusades," such pilgrimages were often used for political leverage "against [liberal] evil," as one French bishop characterized the prevailing antireligious policy in Lourdes in 1872. He was in no doubt whatsoever about the utility of national pilgrimages: "La France souffre dans son âme pervertie et égarée par des utopies anti-religieuses et anti-sociales."[174] These pilgrimages were seen as the bearers of the French Catholic religious soul.[175] Mary's appeal, reported by Bernadette Soubirous near Lourdes in 1858, to organize pilgrimages and processions as a way of supporting the church was widely heeded. In 1873 Pope Pius IX confirmed this international pilgrimage movement by granting plenary indulgences to its participants. The result was that in France alone some three thousand pilgrimages were organized to larger and smaller sanctuaries, both well-known and "forgotten" ones, the latter with the purpose of effecting a revival. The intention was to strengthen the participants in their faith and religious commitment in these "furnaces" of religiosity and devotion.

This type of devotionalization was implicitly supported by a series of sensational apparitions of the Virgin Mary.[176] Mary directly intervened in the terrestrial discussion about belief and unbelief with various messages. The church followed the Marian call to prayer, penitence, and reparation for liberalism in Europe, apostasy from the faith, and the sins and crimes that were being committed around the world against Christ.[177] Christ himself had in fact already asked for reparation two centuries before, in 1675, in a vision to Margaret Mary Alacoque. The political developments since then had further heightened the urgency of reparation. This is why construction began in Paris in 1875 of a national votive church of the Sacred Heart (the Sacré Coeur) to make compensation for the collective errors of the French—for instance, the Paris Commune of 1871—and with the immediate political objective of obtaining the liberation of the Papal States. This devotional dynamic placed the religious question even more emphatically at the heart of politics. In the Netherlands, too, this movement could count on strong enthusiasm among the faithful.[178]

Mary's message to priests worldwide to organize more processions to Lourdes, transmitted through Bernadette Soubirous, fell on fertile ground in the Netherlands; the first Dutch national pilgrimage was organized in 1873. Dutch liberals may have mocked this ostentatious "lack of enlightenment," but the Dutch Catholic mind was wide open to it. The first train journey to Lourdes was, moreover, not just a Marian pilgrimage. The organizers also included a stop at Paray-le-Monial, the sanctuary that was preparing itself to celebrate the second centenary of Christ's apparitions to Alacoque. This Dutch dual pilgrimage was indicative of the growing popularity of the Christ-centered cult of the Sacred Heart in the country. This was a devotion in its own right, but it was also an ecclesiastical instrument to embed the apparently unstoppable growth of Marian apparition cult within the wider doctrinal context.[179] The significance of the Eucharistic movement ensured that the devotional role of the Blessed Sacrament was given a more central place, thus forming a kind of counterweight against the Marian onslaught. In the Netherlands this gave rise to the extraordinarily successful dual cult of Mary and the Sacred Heart, which developed into a large international shrine to Our Lady of the Sacred Heart in the Limburg town of Sittard from 1870 onward.[180]

In Protestant circles the movement was stereotyped as an "Ultramontane miracle disease," a devotional machination orchestrated from Rome to ward off modernity and keep the people stupid.[181] This miracle disease was said to have effected a mental transformation among Dutch Catholics that had "degenerated" even enlightened and "mild" Catholic spirits into ultramontanism and narrow-mindedness. This view can explain the exhortation to "Join ranks more closely than ever against the most dangerous enemy that the Netherlands has ever faced, and that has, alas! also nestled within its borders, coming from across the mountains, more threatening and presumptuous than ever. Be vigilant!"[182] Catholics and Protestants may have created a political alliance, but this did not mean that strict Protestants were minded to keep their mouths shut.

Compared to Marian devotion and the veneration of other saints, which generally appealed more to a popular constituency, Eucharistic devotions were focused on the inner experience of the faith and less on supplication (*do ut des*), more on the symbolism of "thanksgiving" and "sacrifice." The Eucharistic movement of the last quarter of the nineteenth century put the Blessed Sacrament at center stage again, separate from popular faith and healing practices. The Silent Walk strongly reflected this tendency, with its focus on the Blessed Sacrament and its minimalist ritual practice. The wider process of devotionalization was very successful in closing Catholic ranks because it led to local and regional initiatives that brought Catholics together to that end in societies or confraternities.

Catholic Self-Organization

A specifically Dutch character trait can explain why a number of ordinary citizens of Amsterdam were confident enough in 1881 to propose a grand plan for a collective devotional silent walk in the city without the knowledge of ecclesiastical authority. It can be considered a form of assertiveness deriving from the ancien régime. The absence of ecclesiastical structures, parishes, and pastors had forced Catholics before 1795 to take the initiative for the organization of their own community. Ever since the end of the seventeenth century and the beginning of the eighteenth, laypeople had been organizing pilgrimages to Germany and the Southern Netherlands through local and regional groups and organizations. During the nineteenth century, the demand for organization increased exponentially as religious segregation deepened, so that within a few decades the majority of Dutch Catholics were members of one or more (semi-)lay or religious organizations. Until the 1860s, roughly, there were relatively few official ecclesiastical organizational forms and structures; this changed only after the restoration of the hierarchy (1853). Even the preparations for the restoration began as a lay initiative. Although they did have a certain wish to have bishops of their own, it was not in the direct interests of the clergy of the *missio Hollandica* to push for such appointments too insistently, nor was it in the interests of the Roman prelates in The Hague. It was primarily younger Catholic intellectuals who fought candidly for a parliamentary democracy and for full freedom of religion, together with the liberals.[183] They were also responsible for a petition to the pope in 1847 to grant the restoration of the hierarchy. Newspapers such as *Handelsblad* and *Rotterdamsche Courant*, both founded by Catholic laymen, further worked on public opinion. At the same time, Catholic leaders such as Thijm and Judocus Smits used the daily *De Tijd* to support the new constitution adopted in 1848.

The creation of dioceses, deaneries, and parishes from 1853 on was a powerful impulse for the formalization and approval of religious and devotional organizations. This tendency was only strengthened after the first provincial council of 1865, the first Dutch bishops' conference, with the executive regulations it issued. Prior to this point, confraternities, congregations, and other organizations had functioned more or less as lay organizations. Their success was evident from their membership figures. In the 1880s, for instance, the men's congregation "for the formation of Christians" counted in excess of 110,000 members. That of the Holy Family for the promotion of Catholic families, a congregation that exercised considerable influence on daily life, was only slightly smaller with 100,000 members. Participation in this kind of congregation was nowhere higher in Europe than in the Netherlands. When Leo XIII, in an 1882 encyclical, stressed the importance of lay third orders such as those of St. Dominic and St. Francis to spread Christian virtue in society, Dutch Catholics followed up on his request on a large scale. Within only a few years the number of third-order chapters grew from four to eighty, with a total of more than 10,000 members. Several board members of the Silent Walk hailed from this background. An organization for the promotion of piety and welfare among artisans was established in Amsterdam in 1868, the so-called Josephs-Gezellen (Journeymen of St. Joseph's). In addition to large associations such as these, the Netherlands had numerous smaller confraternities that operated at local or regional level. In around 1900, 1.6 million Dutch Catholics (35 percent of the population) were organized in circa 7,000 (extrapolated) religious confraternities and associations, which together had many hundreds of thousands of members.[184] This meant that the approximately one thousand Dutch parishes had an average of seven Catholic religious associations per parish. Even from a comparative international perspective, Dutch Catholics were organized to an exceptionally high degree. The confraternities in question were generally independent religious organizations with the goal of preserving and promoting a particular devotion at the local level, or were part of an international association or international devotion, often united under the aegis of an archconfraternity. Not only did foreign visitors comment on the many associational structures with their high membership figures, they were also surprised at the serious piety displayed by the 90,000 Catholics of Amsterdam.

Seen in this light, it is remarkable that men were represented proportionally in devotional exercises, and that it could be said that they rarely neglected to go to mass, fulfilled their Easter duty, and frequently received communion.[185] One of the authors of *Neerlandia Catholica* mentioned as a noteworthy feature that "Catholics help to perfect each other in faith, virtue, and morals as if without prompting, and on their own initiative dedicate themselves together to some work of charity or other."[186] There are no specific figures for this, and the Catholic source just quoted is not neutral, but membership lists do in fact show very wide participation of men in devotional life. Men's organizations for charity, mission, or devotions with high membership figures were not uncommon. This conformed, incidentally, to the pattern of public life in the nineteenth century, with its heyday of secular associational life from which women were all but absent.[187] In the case of Catholic confraternities, it seems likely that there was a connection with the long tradition of self-organization, possibly also in combination with large-scale pilgrimages abroad, in which men were involved for all kinds of tasks. The rigid confessional segregation of the Netherlands, particularly in the predominantly Protestant north, led to strong group cohesion among diaspora Catholics, something that no doubt also caused high male participation. This evened out a path to new initiatives exclusively intended for men.

This development of self-organization provides an important explanation for the eventually very high level of pillarization among Dutch Catholics.[188] Amsterdam, with its flourishing parishes, was typical of this organizational pattern and had relatively many confraternities. The wider, typically Dutch basic structure of self-organization undeniably contributed to the start of—and subsequent success of—the twentieth-century Miracle cult and its Silent Walk. When, some years after its establishment, the Amsterdam Society was overwhelmed by large numbers of new members, its structure was simply and successfully decentralized across the country. In its heyday, the Netherlands counted more than 250 active, lay-run sister societies, which annually organized the journey to Amsterdam for tens of thousands of pilgrims.[189] The twentieth-century Miracle walk in a certain sense represents the apotheosis of Catholic self-organization in the Netherlands. Although ecclesiastical approval was eventually obtained, both the Amsterdam Society and the diocese always continued to stress the lay perspective and the separation of church and laity in the walk; in doing so, it proved possible, in a harmonious way, to mobilize large numbers of Catholics for the Dutch Catholic cause.

Diffidence and Shame

One specific aspect of Catholic historiography concerns the question of the extent to which Dutch Catholicism represents its own cultural variant, characterized by diffidence and introverted behavior. It is a question we would like to answer in the affirmative, and which we would like to connect with the phenomenon of silent walks and self-organization. Insight into this connection will allow us better to understand the rise and success of the Silent Walk in the twentieth century.

Given the *Kulturkampf* mentioned above, and given a much longer culture war between Catholic and Protestant that dates back even to the Reformation, it is not difficult to imagine that the constant coexistence "in confrontation" of the two faith communities left traces in culture. In this long-standing situation, Catholics were until 1795 formally the subordinate party, as they had limited rights and were only tolerated to a certain degree. That this situation only changed very slowly after the Batavian Revolution was because the royal house and governmental, bureaucratic, cultural, and educational structures continued to be predominantly Protestant-oriented until well into the twentieth century. Faced with this situation, the Catholic minority adopted a cautious stance, certainly at the national level, and refrained from claiming its rightful place on the basis of its numbers. This led to the strange situation in which Catholics only began to play a major role in national politics in the twentieth century and did not really begin to attain the same position as liberals or Protestants until the 1960s.[190]

For a long time Catholics resigned themselves to a culture of repressive tolerance that had begun as far back as the seventeenth century. The liberal Protestant establishment afforded them a certain degree of freedom, as long as they did not manifest themselves too conspicuously or give offense in what was supposedly a Protestant society. Their church services were tolerated as long as they kept a low profile and their churches remained hidden to the eye.

During the period of the Dutch Republic, the nation in fact consisted of two large denominations, as well as a number of smaller religious groups; these denominations had, in a certain sense, adapted to each other despite their mutual hostility. An ecumenism of daily life emerged, with Catholics as the subordinate party. Historical studies have shown that since the Reformation both Christian strands, through this ecumenism of daily life, also adapted to each other to a certain extent.[191] The resulting "accommodation Catholicism" can be defined as self-directed modifying of the expression of the Catholic faith within a society of mixed religion, by taking into account the views and opinions of the other (dominant) religion. Specifically this concerned the way in which the Catholic minority in the Netherlands took account of the Protestant majority. It did so primarily by cultivating reticence with regard to public manifestations of the faith, which ultimately led to a stricter understanding of the faith and of morality. Enlightenment thinking also introduced to the Catholic community an appreciation of a more spiritual and "puritan" approach to the practice of the faith. This created a relatively great interest in the word of God among the Catholic elite and the secular clergy, just as there was interest in mystical Catholic writing among certain groups of Protestants—for instance, the Nadere Reformatie (further Reformation) and the *bevindelijken* (Pietists).[192] Because of the enforced limitations of a "clandestine faith," day-to-day religious practice was characterized by a certain introversion, by the absence of external ostentation.[193] What happened was in fact long-standing self-censorship, fed by diffidence and shame. Thijm wrote about this at the time of the 1853 April Movement: "What did Catholics do hitherto—They kept silent—as is incumbent on those who, feeling that they undeniably have justice on their side, see no chance of being heard."[194]

Nineteenth-century Dutch Catholicism, especially that of the diaspora above the great river delta, was characterized by introversion caused by the influence of its Protestant environment. As he traveled through the Netherlands ("une terre protestante") in 1847, the Benedictine Dom Pitra concluded that if you wished to know the real Catholicism of Holland, you should go "directly to the heart of Dutch Protestantism."[195] There, in Leiden and surroundings, he saw Catholicism as it had been formed by religious cohabitation. The phenomenon that Pitra identified had been called an *infiltration calviniste* a few decades before by Vicar Apostolic Adrianus van Dongen († 1826), a Catholicism that was externally marked by "a cold and Puritan trait."[196] Van Dongen was certainly not the only one to comment on this.[197] Subsequent bishops determined that feast days should be celebrated in the Netherlands with a certain reticence, whether or not under the direction of the hierarchy, because of social or economic relations with non-Catholics.[198] Only if such celebrations took place in the seclusion of a church or a processional park could baroque registers of worship be used. Showing the Catholic faith on the public road remained out of bounds, especially north of the river delta. Where this taboo seemed under threat of being broken or was in fact broken, as happened in 1844 to 1845, 1853, or 1876, Protestant responses were undiminished in their severity.

There is an interesting paradox here: on the one hand, Catholics succeeded in emancipating themselves in a spectacularly successful fashion, partly on account of their great capacity for self-organization and a certain pugnacity, but on the other hand, the reflex of reticence they had learned throughout the centuries endured for a very long time. The explanation for this paradox lies in a widely shared feeling of inferiority and in the more general fact that centuries-old, persistent cultural practices and patterns are slow to change. Its main consequences were that Catholic pugnacity during the Dutch *Kulturkampf* received a stunning blow when the government used armed force and that the political alliance with the Protestants demanded a moderate stance by Catholics.

Compelled by legal restrictions, Catholics found new possibilities of performing saint- and shrine-related rituality in a responsible way. From the early days of the Reformation we have observed that pilgrims and worshippers displayed individual "procession-like" behavior. They walked, praying silently, perhaps carrying a rosary in their coat pocket, to or around a shrine. Silent walking as an introverted, pietistic alternative to rituals forbidden by the ban on processions can count as another consequence.[199] Archbishop Joannes Zwijsen is reported to have said to Pope Pius IX in 1853 that Catholics could do much in the Netherlands as long as they did it in silence.[200] Catholics were sometimes called "silent citizens" on account of their low religious profile. After the breaking up of processions in the 1870s, silent walking in its collective form acquired the status of a "Beggars' ritual": a forbidden practice, but one performed anyway in a form that cannot be banned. The "national" success that the Silent Walk of Amsterdam enjoyed after 1900 was therefore based, on the one hand, on the "accommodation character" of the faith and, on the other, on Catholics' sentiments of diffidence, shame, and protest. That its success was so great was possibly the result of something observed by Brom (in 1946): that introverted silent walking "was the deepest and truest form of what characterizes Catholic Holland today."[201]

5

The Silent Walk as a
National Symbol of Catholic Identity
(1881–1960)

The cult of the Amsterdam Miracle experienced unprecedented success between 1881 and 1960. Within a short period of time, the veneration grew into a cult of national proportions, and it retained this status for many years. The rise of the Silent Walk was by and large coterminous with the development of confessional "pillars" in Dutch society.[1] These pillars can be described as moral communities that encompassed not only the religious lives, but also the social and cultural lives of their constituents to a great degree. As an intensification of the previous age of confessionalization, a particular confession or ideology had become the foundational principle of life within the pillars, much more so than social class or regional culture.[2] This book uses the metaphor of pillarization primarily for the Catholic community in its sociocultural expression; it refers to the sometimes near-autarkic character of Catholic life at the time. In their drive for equality and emancipation, Catholics closed ranks and accepted a high level of organization. The notion of pillarization took on a political aspect between 1890 and 1910 as a socialist movement emerged alongside Protestant and Catholic groups, in addition to a fourth, smaller liberal segment.[3] This new political reality encouraged the various sections to be more willing to tolerate each other, even though differences continued to run deep.

The Netherlands became a country of minorities, none of which was able to dominate national politics. Thus, while in 1872 Catholics and (orthodox) Protestants were still engaging in violent altercations as their conflict over processions reached its height, by 1888 the two confessional pillars had actually joined forces to form a cabinet. The mutual interest they had discovered was that their own confessional milieus needed to be protected from encroachment by the neutral state, the liberals, and the socialists.[4] This process of pillarization would fundamentally determine the organization of, and sociopolitical conditions in, Dutch society for more than eighty years. At the same time, pillarization represented the ultimate form of identity politics.[5] In general terms, identity politics consists of strategies to emphasize the individuality of a particular community vis-à-vis the outside world and to confirm it vis-à-vis its own members. In order to achieve this, it was necessary to deploy not only religious forces, but also political, socioeconomic, and cultural forces. The result of this process was a more autonomous and equal place in society. The Catholic version of identity politics proved to be exceptionally effective, in both sociocultural and political terms.

Once fears over the survival of the monarchy had been allayed by the birth of Princess Wilhelmina (1880), politico-confessional cooperation had been established, and calm had returned to national politics on the most contentious issues of the day—education, the social question, and universal suffrage—society could turn to continuing the practical expansion of the pillars from ground level upward. The Catholic community did this by establishing a network that exercised almost totalitarian control over daily life. It consisted not only of innumerable associations and confraternities but also, as many Catholics could testify, the arm of the church that reached into the family home. Annual pastoral home calls, the practice of confession, and the "enthronization of the Sacred Heart" in the family home were all means used to establish clerical influence and control over the daily lives of Dutch Catholics.[6] Virtually nowhere else in Europe was religious practice imposed so insistently and structured so strongly with lay help, through family and associational ties. By 1900 the ground had been prepared for the large-scale mobilization of laypeople in the century that followed. Slowly but surely, a powerful collective Catholic identity was created on the basis of the themes of the medieval past described in chapter 4—saints, devotions, confraternities and associations, heritage, architectural styles—and with an appeal to the common experience of discrimination during the period of religious oppression.

This chapter proposes to show how one such lay initiative, seemingly insignificant, could lead to the successful mobilization of the Catholic community on a national scale. Never before were the emancipation and the identity politics of Dutch Catholics so intimately connected to one particular devotional cult. The cult of the Miracle—the Silent Walk and the pilgrimage to the Sacrament of Miracle—reflects a number of important developments in twentieth-century Dutch society. The growing success of the cult turned it into an increasingly significant instrument of Catholic identity politics and therefore of the country's political reality.

The Construction of the Silent Walk

Amsterdam underwent tremendous growth in the 1880s through large-scale migration. In less than a decade, the city's population increased from 317,000 to 408,000. Of those inhabitants, 22 percent were Catholics, a group that grew in the same decade from 70,000 to 90,000.[7] They had at their disposal a long-standing and well-developed network of eighteen parishes, more than twenty churches, and hundreds of associations. Although Amsterdam missed out on having its own bishop because the 1827 concordat was never implemented, the city was nonetheless the national center of Catholic life. The Dutch "lay pope," the cultural historian Joseph A. Alberdingk Thijm and his famous publishing house C. L. van Langenhuysen, played a central role in the intellectual and cultural emancipation of Catholics. The Begijnhof with its rector and the city parishes with their pastors, usually drawn from the regular clergy, formed flourishing devotional centers. Virtually every Amsterdam parish had confraternities of the Sacred Heart, the Stations of the Cross, the Immaculate Virgin, Saint Aloysius, and the Holy Family.[8] The tradition of the cult of the Miracle meant that devotion to the Blessed Sacrament, strongly stimulated across the world by Rome, found a natural habitat in Amsterdam. At the parish level, this was evident in the founding of confraternities of the Perpetual Adoration of the Blessed Sacrament. During this same period Hendrik Schlüter, pastor of the Posthoorn church on Haarlemmerstraat, took the initiative to connect the emerging Eucharistic devotion to the Miracle of Amsterdam. In 1877 he established a Guild of the Blessed Sacrament of Miracle for its female worshippers, inspired by the courageous Amsterdam women who had protected the Holy Stead from profanation in the sixteenth century, and by the Miracle chest, which was ascribed to the medieval Guild of the Miracle, a women's guild. The idea to create widespread lay support for the Miracle, even if only in the form of a "bodyguard" for the devotion, caught on, and within little more than a year the

Guild of the Blessed Sacrament had no fewer than five thousand members. Through weekly adoration and donations of money, they worked to enhance the glory of the cult.[9] As a result of this initiative, the desire soon arose to hold a monthly Eucharistic procession within the Begijnhof. The whole notion of organizing processions, or restoration of the great medieval Miracle procession, is a constant and recurring theme in the collective memory of Amsterdam Catholics. But it may be asked: what factor caused this desire? Was it the aspiration to reclaim the urban space by performing this ritual, or the effect on Catholic minds of accounts of the splendor of the medieval processions? Although the nineteenth-century processions took place within the seclusion of the Begijnhof, the possible reintroduction of a procession through the center of Amsterdam proved an emotive prospect.

The success of the women's guild inspired the founding, a year later—in September 1878—of a male equivalent. The Guild of the Procession was given the task of organizing the monthly procession ritual inside the church.[10] These signaled that interest in the Miracle was again on the upturn since the great jubilee of 1845. This time, the revival found its support base not so much among the elite, such as St. Cecilia's Choral Society and the networks of governors, which languished as far as their devotional activities were concerned. Instead, the revival found support among the petite bourgeoisie and the middle classes, who had been actively organizing themselves through a wide range of Catholic associations, such as the so-called third orders, the Archconfraternity of the Holy Family, and the St. Vincent de Paul Society. Their focus was on charity, on their own and their relatives' eternal salvation, and on social organization. They were much less interested in the apologetic causes that occupied the clergy.[11]

Unlike other Catholic countries, the young Dutch nation-state had no overarching, "national" cult or pilgrimage. This was due to its religious pluralism, the legal restrictions that were in place, and its particular political history, even if it had a plethora of religious organizations. In 1881, however, a group of Catholic young men, who knew each other through these associational networks and who were inspired by their city's Catholic past, took an initiative that would change this.

Joseph Lousbergh (1855–1914),[12] a bachelor and office clerk at the Amsterdamsche Bank who lived in Spuistraat, and Carel Elsenburg (1853–1934),[13] a married man and clerk and later a cobbler,[14] had known each other since childhood as altar boys in the Krijtberg church on Singel. Carel had spent some years in a Franciscan boarding school in Venraij in

Limburg in the southeast, but when he discovered that he had no vocation to the priesthood he returned to the family home. Both Lousbergh and Elsenburg, young men in their twenties, would have been classed at the time as "simple" Catholics, but they identified strongly with the church's social and devotional sides. Their social conscience inspired them to become involved in church charity and antipoverty work, and thus they joined the Posthoorn parish's St. Vincent de Paul conference[15] and, in the Franciscan "Moses and Aaron" church, the Third Order of St. Francis.[16] They attended mass in this church on Waterlooplein and in its chapel of ease in Kalverstraat, 't Boompje.

In their own parish they had been acquainted from early childhood with the annual celebration of, and the sermons on, the Miracle of Amsterdam. For them, the yellow vellum-bound copies of Marius's 1639 book on the Miracle, *Eer ende opcomen,* were still the main literary and visual source of inspiration on the origins and flourishing of the cult, and the presumed rise of Amsterdam as a result.[17] This devotional evergreen saw so many reprints during the ancien régime that many Catholic inhabitants of Amsterdam still possessed a copy. Inspired by Marius's legendary intervention, which had guaranteed the continuity of the Miracle cult in the seventeenth century, Lousbergh and Elsenburg, too, felt a sense of moral duty to conserve and transmit the devotion. The 1876 exhibition on six centuries of Amsterdam history, including its Miracle heritage, and the attention that the priest-journalist Bernard Klönne (1834–1921) had lavished on it in the conservative Amsterdam Catholic daily *De Tijd* only strengthened them in this sentiment.[18]

Despite the temporary revival around 1845, devotion to the Miracle, once famed among counts, emperors, the sick, the pious, and the penitent, degenerated into a limited and almost perfunctory annual celebration during the remainder of the nineteenth century. Every March, the Begijnhof saw a solemn ten-day Miracle celebration, with miniature processions held daily in the chapel, attended by associations and faithful from Amsterdam and its surroundings. A delegation from Haarlem made the pilgrimage every year on a separate day.[19] The cult was primarily a celebration observed in the city, but it had a certain regional appeal.

In hindsight, it seems as if the two men had a premonition of how far the cult might go. They realized the potential of this devotion, and its special historical roots, which could be nurtured on the one hand by the international upsurge of Eucharistic devotion in those years, and on the other by Catholics' growing interest in their own individuality, in their identity, based to an important extent on their own past and heritage.[20]

Lousbergh and Elsenburg were encouraged by initiatives to revive old devotions elsewhere in the country. The Catholic past was regarded as an
ideological foundation to spread awareness of the great significance of the
medieval past in creating the modern Netherlands. Dutch history had not,
as Protestant historiography would have its readers believe, emerged out
of nothing at the time of the Reformation and the United Provinces. The
pre-Reformation fame of the Miracle pilgrimage never ceased to fire their
imagination, especially Lousbergh's.

Although few sources have been preserved that shed light on the personal motives of the two initiators, we know that it was Lousbergh who
first suggested the idea of a devotional walk.[21] His strong interest in the
history of the city and in the phenomenon of pilgrimage led him naturally
to the Miracle. He found mention in the historical documents and publications he studied—ironically in a Protestant source—of the old custom
of walking through the city and around the Holy Stead without ostentation, in silent prayer.[22] Moreover, oral sources told Lousbergh that there
were still Catholics in his own day who performed these individual devotional walks at night.[23] The correct route was not yet very clear. As Lousbergh noted, this knowledge had been lost in the mists of time.[24] A few
inhabitants of Amsterdam were rumored to possess notes detailing the
itinerary, but there was no unanimity about the exact route. Some, inspired by the street names, walked along Heiligeweg up to what had formerly been Leidse of Heilige-wegs-poort (Leiden or Holy Street Gate),[25]
while others proceeded even further along Sloterweg until they reached
the house called Te Vraag[26] or passed through the alleyway called Klooster
near 't Boompje church, or the alleyway called 't Hol near Nieuwendijk,
and still others made a short detour to circle around Oude Kerk or St.
Olof's Chapel as they prayed.[27] It was not until 1880 that Lousbergh managed to obtain a text that marked the route much more precisely. He and
Elsenburg now had the information required to make a first joint walk in
1881. The idea of turning their individual practice into a collective one was
an explicit motive from the start.[28] In view of the legal restrictions that the
state imposed upon Catholics, Lousbergh realized very clearly that a "secret," or rather silent, walk ritual, performed without any ecclesiastical
symbols, could be a powerful one. A minimalistic walk such as this one
would not fall under the rigors of the procession ban, even if carried out
collectively.

The notion of an organized silent walk did not in fact originate with
Lousbergh. Some fifteen years previously, in 1866, during a heavy cholera

epidemic, Catholic citizens of 's-Hertogenbosch decided to make *collec-tively* the silent and unobtrusive annual walk through the city in honor of Mary that they had up to that time always made individually. They did this to strengthen the bond with their patron saint, the miraculous statue of the Sweet Mother Mary in St. John's Cathedral, and to invoke her aid. The gravity of the 1866 epidemic demanded a powerful collective invocation ritual, but one that would remain within the bounds of the law.[29] The women of 's-Hertogenbosch immediately began walking through the city, praying silently, in pairs or small groups. This form was a ritual inspired by the *individual* walking of the old processional route that had been com-mon since the taking of 's-Hertogenbosch in 1629.[30] On the feast of the Sweet Mother Mary—July 7, 1866—these women passed the house of Jan Dirks, the prefect of the 's-Hertogenbosch choral section of the Archcon-fraternity of the Holy Family, on Hoge Steenweg. They found Dirks stand-ing in the doorway talking to somebody, and when he saw them he said, "Come, let's become the first men who make the walk." Dirks proposed that his thirty choristers should hold silent walks together in a single large group during the following nine evenings to ward off the cholera epi-demic. At the end of the novena, the group had grown to more than a hun-dred participants. Inspired by this success, they spontaneously founded the Association Men's Walk.[31] Despite some negotiations with the authori-ties concerning the precise format,[32] this initiative introduced the concept of a silent *men's* walk.[33] More than a decade later, in the second half of the 1870s, when Lousbergh was developing his ideas about a similar silent walk in Amsterdam, the 's-Hertogenbosch walk was drawing more than fifteen thousand participants each year.[34]

Understandably, this striking initiative to organize a communal faith manifestation in the public space, in a manner adjusted to the Dutch situation, attracted the attention of the media. The resulting press cover-age cannot have escaped Lousbergh's attention. *De Tijd* wrote about the 's-Hertogenbosch ritual on a number of occasions. It is likely, therefore, that Lousbergh's immediate inspiration was this successful initiative of the 's-Hertogenbosch lay association. However, in the reflective *Memorandum* that Lousbergh later wrote to chronicle the emergence of the Amsterdam Silent Walk, he made no mention of his personal motives or sources of inspiration.[35]

Whatever the case may be, Lousbergh's interest in the Amsterdam Miracle was awakened at some point in the mid-1870s. In 1880 he ob-tained the historical document that detailed the route of the "Miracle way" and the attendant rituals around the Oude Kerk and the Holy Stead. The authenticity, and therefore the legitimacy, of this document proved decisive in putting into practice the plan to imitate the Amsterdam Eucharistic procession. Lousbergh discussed the historical details he had found with Elsenburg. Both reached the conclusion that the moment had come to rekindle the cult of the Sacrament of Miracle in a new way on the basis of the tradition of the old processional route. The moment was right because the church was coming under increasing pressure both in the Netherlands and elsewhere in the world. Lousbergh and Elsenburg solemnly undertook to make an unostentatious prayer walk each year on the Sunday night under the octave of the feast of the Sacrament of Miracle.[36] The day after the feast of the Miracle in 1881, Thursday, March 17, they put their resolution into effect by making the walk, starting at 11:30 p.m. It took about an hour to walk the entire route. They then repeated their walk at different times to discover which hour of the night was most suited for this devotional practice.

At the time, the old processional route traversed a notorious nightlife district, which the prim Lousbergh characterized as "Dante's inferno": "Truly, Satan is making merry there," he observed later.[37] Warmoesstraat and Nes, which were part of the route, had "red palaces" that constituted Amsterdam's nineteenth-century red-light district, and hustlers worked in Kalverstraat.[38] Following their age's notions of decency, Lousbergh and Elsenburg thought it was inadvisable for men to walk through such areas and that this was entirely "unfeasible" for women.[39] The reconnoiters that Lousbergh and Elsenburg made at different times of the night showed that the early hours of the morning, when life in the "night houses" was running to its end, was the most suitable hour for a prayer walk. The time was fixed at 5:30 a.m. on Sunday morning. In 1884, the year of their fourth walk, another acquaintance of Lousbergh's, a somewhat older man, a plumber called Adriaan Apol, joined them as fellow organizer.[40] Lousbergh had met Apol the year before, once again through the Third Order of St. Francis, which shows that the networks forged through this lay association played an important part in the Silent Walk initiative. Having made the walk, they decided that the time had come to invite more Catholics to take part the subsequent year, 1885. That year, just before making the walk, Elsenburg went to confession to P. de Hoog, associate pastor in the Begijnhof. Carel told him that he and a number of friends were performing a prayer walk each year, and De Hoog replied that although the walk was a good initiative, the route they were following was probably incorrect and needed to be reviewed critically.

In 1889 Henri de Veer, a warehouse clerk, Third Order network participant, and subsequently founder and chairman of the general Circle of Friends in Honor of the Blessed Sacrament, joined the organizers as the fourth and last board member.[41] The initiators were able to interest an ever larger group of Amsterdam Catholics through word-of-mouth advertising within their own social class, which resulted in the formation of a more or less fixed group of several dozen participants.[42] The success of this silent walk recommended itself not only to laypeople. Bernard Klönne, now the new rector of the Begijnhof, was also sympathetic to the initiators. Having served as joint editor-in-chief of De Tijd for a decade, he had left his position to take up the rectorship of the Begijnhof in 1883.[43] In 1885 his associate pastor, possibly breaking the seal of confession, told him for the first time about the new prayer walk that had been brought to his attention through Elsenburg's confession. Klönne wrote afterward in his diary that the "procession" had been held in the city that year during the early hours of the morning—he was not yet acquainted with the concept of the prayer walk. The participants had been "young gentlemen," and a number of young women had imitated their initiative around noon.[44]

Klönne informally supported the initiative from the start, but he officially sanctioned it in 1887; from then on the prayer walk concluded with mass in the Begijnhof church.[45] Klönne's dynamic involvement was important, not least because most old documents pertaining to the history of the Miracle were under his care in the Begijnhof. The archive had hardly been looked at since Pluym's research for his anniversary publication in 1845. Because doubts remained concerning the accuracy of the ritual and the exact route, Lousbergh pressed for new investigations in the Begijnhof archives. Ultimately Klönne, who had in the meantime become totally engrossed in the history of the Miracle,[46] was able to remove all doubt when he found an old parchment in the chaotic but well-provided archive in 1886. An old woman had drawn up the document in 1651 to testify that she had personally witnessed the last Eucharistic procession to pass through Amsterdam as a seventeen-year-old girl, in 1578, just before the Alteration. The founders regarded the find as the symbolic and literal confirmation of their mission to manifest themselves publicly as Catholics through a silent, toned-down version of the former ritual.

Lousbergh and his entourage were encouraged in their initiative by developments elsewhere in the Netherlands. In addition to the earlier silent walks in 's-Hertogenbosch, in 1886 an actual Eucharistic procession was reinstated on the public road in the village of Laren, not far from Amsterdam, the first place in the northern part of the country to do so. Here, too, an originally medieval ritual had been revived, but Laren had managed, through ingenious political maneuvers in The Hague, to obtain an exemption from the procession ban.[47] Moreover, the political and law-enforcement climate in general had mellowed ten years after the fierce struggle over processions during the Dutch *Kulturkampf.*

Lousbergh and Elsenburg decided to act vigorously. They sent out circular letters, managing to attract some sixty participants to "make the processional way" in 1886. This time the participants included not only Amsterdam citizens, but also faithful from Haarlem.[48] Independently from the two organizers, the walk attracted attention from the press and several Catholic newspapers published articles about the remarkable initiative. There were no critical reactions, smoothing the way for Rector Klönne to continue his support for this spontaneous lay initiative. From 1887 onward, he gave permission to use "his" Begijnhof as the starting point of the walk. An active missionary campaign among Amsterdam Catholic associations ensured that participation continued to grow, with more than five hundred men taking part in 1888. This increase in turn necessitated the assistance of more priests to celebrate mass and hear confessions.

The organizers did not at this time have a specific name for their journey. Initially they spoke of "making the processional way" or the "way of the Miracle" or "Miracle walk." Newspapers were the first to stress the "silent walk" aspect as the journey's primary characteristic in 1886.[49] Although the designation of "silent walk" was already being used popularly, the organizers continued to call it "the walk" or—in the more neutral diocesan ecclesiastical Latin of those years—*circuitus nocturnus*, nocturnal circumambulation, until 1893.[50] In that year the ritual became known as the "Silent Walk," spelled with capitals. The organizers, who had previously preserved anonymity, came forward publicly as board members of the "Society of the Silent Walk." Up to that point, Lousbergh had been the sole contact person for the church authorities and had signed all documents only as "X" in order to keep his identity hidden and avoid personal publicity. This was not an unusual practice in the nineteenth century: it was quite common to comment on delicate issues or write pamphlets under cover of anonymity. But as incorrect speculations about the identity of the organizers began to appear in the press—it was said, for instance, that the Franciscan Third Order was behind it—the organizers decided to reveal their true identity.

Despite the organizers' desire to remain anonymous, they felt at the same time that they were undertaking a historic enterprise that could no longer be halted. In zeal for the cause they came close to outdoing Rector Klönne, who had become conscious of his own important mission around 1885. The initiators began to see themselves from the long-term perspective of the Miracle's history, as bearers of a role that was not primarily personal but involved acting as catalysts, as "instruments of God."[51] This grand perspective caused them to record their activities as precisely as possible to preserve them for posterity.[52]

Even though Catholics were growing in self-confidence in this period, starting an organized devotional walk through the center of the capital without any legitimate backing or authorization remained a delicate exercise. The standpoint formulated by the initiators with regard to the walk's format remained central to the enterprise. It was included in the statutes of what was to become the Society of the Silent Walk as article 8: "The Silent Walk must never be a manifestation or a protest march, it must remain a silent prayer walk. Each participant, and therefore each member of the Society, should follow the indicated route totally absorbed in himself, praying, using no outward sign, as an individual, without imagining himself to be part of an association or a group."[53] The Silent Walk had to be as anonymous, neutral, and silent as possible because it was still not permitted in the Netherlands to pray aloud or collectively sing religious songs on the public road. Nor could any religious symbol or object be displayed in the context of a public ritual; this ruled out liturgical vestments, banners, candleholders, and any "devotional sign or badge, rosaries etc." The government was even authorized to intervene at funerals if the officiating priest wore a cassock.[54] All this was the inheritance of the 1848 Constitution and the 1853 revolt. It is misleading, therefore, to regard the Silent Walk as a silent procession: it was not, precisely because processions were banned and it therefore had to do without the signs that normally make a religious parade into a procession. When members of Catholic associations began to take part, they did so initially in small groups, so as to avoid the appearance of participating collectively and thus to give offense to *andersdenkenden,* or "those who think differently"—a term common among Dutch Catholics at the time that generally designated Protestants. It is remarkable, in view of the tumultuous procession question that so dominated the nineteenth century, that the Silent Walk, despite its minimalist execution, never attracted political controversy itself, and that there were never any serious confrontations with Protestants in these years.

Once, in 1888, one of the windows of the Begijnhof church was smashed during the mass concluding the walk.[55]

This tolerance can be explained by two factors. Toward the close of the nineteenth century, emancipation and identity politics had clearly made an impact on society by giving greater weight to Catholics as a force to be reckoned with. In addition, the Dutch *Kulturkampf* had left all parties disinclined to take a hard line. Politically, the anticlerically oriented liberal cabinets had driven the confessional political parties into each other's arms. Catholics and Protestants had been at each other's throats half a century earlier, but now they began to form a common front despite their cultural and religious differences.[56] This undoubtedly gave Catholics greater self-confidence and strengthened their nerve, and it made Protestants more tolerant or indulgent. A second explanation can be found in Amsterdam's typically urban, multicultural culture, which was characterized by openness and tolerance. Moreover, the route went through areas where inhabitants and visitors alike tended to keep to themselves. This circumstance ensured that there was an atmosphere of tolerance in the locality toward this "alien" Silent Walk that seemed so out of place there.

Clerical Takeover and Control

It was not just the lay initiative of the Silent Walk that gave a boost to the Miracle cult. The change of pastors that occurred in the Begijnhof in 1883 also added a new dynamic, one entirely its own. Rector Klönne, who assumed the position in that year, followed in the footsteps of his illustrious seventeenth-century predecessor Marius. Just as Marius before him, he fell completely under the spell of Amsterdam's Catholic history. He experienced the historical sensation in the Begijnhof presbytery of "discovering" relicts of the medieval Miracle cult that had escaped the Iconoclastic Fury. He also unearthed the medieval archive of the cult, which had never been organized or studied. Before long Klönne was spending night after night behind his writing table, going through historical documents. During these explorations he slowly but surely began to envisage a plan for the future based on Amsterdam's special devotional past, just as Lousbergh and Elsenburg had before him. Transmitting the cult and making sure that it would continue became increasingly important goals for him. A vision began to unfurl before his eyes in which the Miracle would play a central role, including magnificent processions, just as in its medieval heyday. He imagined how these processions would once again pass freely through the streets of Amsterdam as real rituals and at the same time as metaphors of Dutch Catholics' protest against their subordination. Klönne's ardor was as strong as when, as editor of *De Tijd*, he had worked to further the wider Catholic interest by demanding revision of legislation on education and popular petitions.[57]

Lousbergh's question about the precise route of the former procession had sparked a new passion that would remain Klönne's mission throughout the period of his rectorship. He did not rest until he had found the old notarial document in the archives that made it possible to determine the Silent Walk's correct itinerary.[58] He immediately informed Lousbergh. Begijnhof and Spui were the assembly point, and from there the route could be reconstructed as follows: from the Holy Stead through Kalverstraat, Dam Square,[59] Nieuwendijk, Ramskooi, Prins Hendrikkade, Nieuwebrug, Nieuwebrugsteeg, Warmoesstraat, Nes, Langebrugsteeg, Langebrug, and Taksteeg, and then back through Kalverstraat before entering the Holy Stead itself through Enge Kapelsteeg and exiting it through Wijde Kapelsteeg. Unlike in the Middle Ages, when the participants had concluded the procession by passing through the chapel—then still a Catholic place of worship—the route now passed around the chapel—now Reformed— via Rokin. From whatever direction participants were to approach the assembly point, personal devotions must begin only in Kalverstraat, at the location of the former Holy Stead.[60]

The clandestine church of 't Haantje, located on nearby Oudezijds Voorburgwal, was not part of the route. This edifice's only connection to the Miracle was that it was the successor church of the Oude Kerk or St. Nicholas's parish. Its symbolic status as expression of oppression and inequality meant, however, that it had much in common with the Silent Walk. Frequent attempts were therefore made to create some kind of link; the museum opened its doors on the Sunday morning of the Silent Walk, for instance, to allow returning participants to visit. As the museum owned nothing that had a relation to the Miracle cult, the society's board made efforts every year to acquire objects to create a permanent exhibition on the subject.[61]

In 1916, Koninklijke Hollandsche Lloyd (Royal Dutch Lloyd) built new head offices that closed off the Ramskooi alley. This meant that the historical route was blocked, forcing the Silent Walk to follow a diversion. Having failed to lodge an objection to the planning application, the board of the Silent Walk made unsuccessful attempts to persuade the management to include an archway in the plans so that practical and historical-legal continuity might be preserved for the Silent Walk.[62] The diocese of Haarlem was less concerned about a diversion via Martelaarsgracht. Bishop August J. Callier simply determined that the application that had already been made to the Vatican for an indulgence for participants would also apply to the changed route. When shortly after completion Lloyd encountered financial problems and had to abandon the new building, participants in the Silent Walk could interpret the company's difficulties as a "punishment" for its infringement of the sacred integrity of the route.[63]

The discovery of the medieval procession's itinerary and the successful reconstruction of the walk only increased Klönne's passion for the Miracle. The links to the past that he managed to pry from the historical documents continued to fire his imagination. Enthused by the positive reactions to the walk and by the resurgence of old shrines elsewhere in the country, his expectations soared ever higher. His distant predecessor Marius confidently gazed down on him from Claes Moeyaert's portrait hanging on the wall of Klönne's study. With the hand of destiny thus laying on his shoulder, the rector could imagine that he had become the custodian of the Miracle for his time. This part of Catholic heritage had to be preserved for the coming twentieth century, and, in particular, it had to be made into an instrument for the Catholic community in its emancipation struggle. The Begijnhof should become once more what it had been under Marius, the heart of Catholic Amsterdam and indeed of the Dutch Catholic community in general. Klönne gave material expression to the claim that the Catholic Begijnhof church was the new Holy Stead by placing an identical copy of the entrance portal of Nieuwezijds Kapel in front of the door to his own church as front porch. He also copied the Latin motto that had graced the old chapel (the Vulgate Bible verse Daniel 3:99), a reference to the Miracle. In this way pilgrims could be somewhat compensated for not being able to experience what it felt like to enter the old Holy Stead. Klönne recognized the symbolic potential of creating a form of national solidarity in the veneration of the Blessed Sacrament.

By pure chance he soon received a measure of foreign support. The Empress Elisabeth ("Sisi") of Austria-Hungary came to the Amsterdam Doelen Hotel in 1884 to seek treatment for her rheumatism from the famous doctor and "masseur of princes" Johann Mezger. On June 4 she came to Begijnhof church to pray for a speedy cure for her ailments, thus following in the footsteps of her ancestor Maximilian.[64] As far as can be ascertained, she left no ex-voto.

Klönne's enthusiasm soon found new outlets. In 1885 he became embroiled in an acrimonious dispute with the Jesuit Herman J. Allard, who had denied that Marius, as new pastor-missionary, had been responsible for the conversion of the Netherlands' national poet, Joost van den Vondel.[65] Although the controversy remained inconclusive at the time, Klönne was later proved to be correct.[66] Convinced of his stance, he did not hesitate to bring Marius and Vondel inseparably together by having medallions of them made by Willem Molkenboer, adding them to the new façade of his presbytery on Nieuwezijds Voorburgwal (no. 371) in 1884. In order to avoid any misunderstanding, the vain rector affixed his initials to the façade of an adjacent building (no. 381): wall clams in the shape of a *B*, an *H*, and a *K*.

It has by now become clear that Marius was the central connecting link between the past and the future of Catholic life in seventeenth-century Amsterdam. His significance for the cult lay in the fact that he salvaged the material heritage of the Miracle and especially that he succeeded in reviving and preserving the commemorative celebrations of the Miracle in a Protestant state. As Marius's "successor," Klönne openly called himself the pastor of the (new) Holy Stead and thus presented himself as the pugnacious guardian of a centuries-old tradition within a pillarized and as yet unequal society.[67] Klönne's fiery personality and many initiatives would eventually bring him the coveted epithet of "a nineteenth-century Marius."[68]

This was also the backdrop against which he created a network of friends, acquaintances, and contacts who were all committed to collecting and preserving the heritage of Catholic life in Amsterdam. He believed that he had a calling to revive the Miracle cult and give it a central role in the further development of Catholicism in the Netherlands.[69] Refashioned to suit the context of the theological and liturgical developments of his own time, Amsterdam's cult of the Blessed Sacrament might—he believed—become a fitting foundation and shining point of reference for a churchwide Eucharistic revival in the Netherlands. The sacrament of the Eucharist was being given a more central place within the liturgy in those years.[70] Klönne not only published much about the Miracle on the basis of his extensive archival research,[71] but also talked about recovering Nieuwezijds Kapel for Catholicism: a restored Holy Stead, ready for a renewed Catholic liturgy. A shrine that might once again see the old Eucharistic procession, rather than a silent walk, pass through Kalverstraat in all its traditional glory.

A Vision in Oils

That Klönne's dreams about the past and his love of creating ideals for the future on occasion got the better of him is particularly evident from what has become known as the Derkinderen Affair: the commission he gave to the young and promising artist Antoon Derkinderen. As has been seen, the medieval procession occupied center stage in Klönne's Miracle research. His archival studies had given him an ever clearer image of what this magnificent medieval ritual must have looked like. Another source that aroused his imagination was a rare and intriguing book called *Room-sche mysterien* (Popish mysteries) from 1604. The author was the Calvinist elder Walich Syvaertsz, who wrote a suggestive and almost surreal description of the exuberance of the Miracle procession as it was held before the Alteration (Reformation) of Amsterdam in 1578. Klönne considered that a visual representation of the lavish and moving ritual might be the required prelude to a modern reenactment or revival. He believed there was very strong demand for this because the procession ban meant that Dutch Catholics only knew the phenomenon of city processions from stories. At the same time, the Dutch *Kulturkampf*'s clashes over processions had generally curbed enthusiasm for them. Klönne was convinced, therefore, that an evocative, gripping representation of a procession might rekindle the ardor of Amsterdam Catholics for organizing a real procession, a belief he was not alone in professing.[72] Such a visualization would, moreover, draw on the centuries-old Amsterdam tradition of making the Miracle cult and its rituals visible to the general public.[73] The execution of this plan, a prestigious painting commission, was awarded to Derkinderen (1859–1925), a promising and passionate twenty-five-year-old 's-Hertogenbosch artist.[74]

On the occasion of the silver anniversary of Klönne's priestly ordination on August 15, 1884, the wealthy Amsterdam Catholic Piet Heseding offered to pay for a painting representing the medieval Miracle procession. Derkinderen, educated in Brussels in the academic tradition of traditionalist historical painting and a pupil of the country's leading Catholic cultural authority, Thijm, also came recommended by drawing school principal Willem Molkenboer and therefore seemed the right choice. At that moment he was already referred to, prematurely, as "the Catholic Rochussen," after the celebrated Protestant national historical painter of the early nineteenth century.[75] A mere two months later, Derkinderen showed Klönne a first sketch in watercolors. It was a historicizing and idealized representation of the Amsterdam procession, in bright colors and featuring many historical details: banners, statues, costumes, weapons, and all of the attributes and props that had been traced historically in the archives. The sketch reflected to some extent the idealized image that Klönne had in mind. Immediately taken by the design, and convinced that Derkinderen was working in the right direction, he awarded the painter the definitive commission amounting to four thousand guilders. This substantial sum in itself is proof that Amsterdam's Catholic past was a grand affair not only figuratively, but also literally. The painting was to be a canvas more than eleven meters wide and nearly two meters high, showing all of its details in "magnificence."[76] According to the rector, this kind of panoramic and vivid depiction was the best means of inspiring and motivating the faithful. Klönne made no secret of his underlying intentions: he was working toward the actual revival of the Miracle procession. The painted procession was becoming a metaphor for the Amsterdam Catholic community as well as a reflection of Klönne's personal megalomania. The rector also wanted a painting á clef: a historical scene—or better, perhaps, an image of the future—with characters who bore some resemblance to Klönne's most important Amsterdam contacts. Nearly eighty prominent Catholic friends, members of the elite, both laypeople and clergy, posed in Derkinderen's studio.[77] In this way, Klönne "bought" their support for the cause, turning them into active participants in the future Amsterdam procession, or at least into protagonists who would help to bring it about.

The initiators of the Silent Walk were not included in this painted pantheon of late nineteenth-century Catholic Amsterdam. The painting came too early for that. The walk was still in its infancy and had not yet attracted much attention. Moreover, a wide sociocultural gap divided the "common" participants of the walk,[78] people without wealth or power, and Klönne's coterie of priests, board members, and the wealthy. His powerful position among Amsterdam Catholics and his personal influence with the bishop of Haarlem at the time earned Klönne the sobriquet "Black Pope of Amsterdam," a reference to the general of the Jesuits, who owed his reputation of being his order's equivalent of the pope to his putative behind-the-scenes power.[79]

Ominously, however, the young Derkinderen seemed less than fully convinced by his own sketches and the underlying concept. Blinded by his own enthusiasm, Klönne did not notice the painter's doubts and made a serious error of judgment that he would long rue. Thinking that everything had now been settled, and that Derkinderen would complete the immense canvas, Klönne decided to indulge his penchant for travel and departed on a pilgrimage to the Holy Land in 1885. The insecure Derkinderen remained at home, out of sight of and far removed from the influence of his client. He decided to take a trip himself in search of new impressions that might provide inspiration for the definitive completion of his oil painting.[80] During his study trip, which soon turned into a kind of grand tour, Derkinderen visited Italy, where he became fascinated by fresco painting, particularly by Giotto's († 1337) innovative work. On the way back he traveled through Paris, where he immediately fell in love with the emerging French impressionist school, especially the work of his contemporary Pierre Puvis de Chavannes (1824–1898), who also used fresco painting. Puvis de Chavannes's monumental "meditations in pastels," a cycle on the life of Saint Genevieve, made a particularly strong impression. As a result, Derkinderen's view of his own painting changed radically.[81] Before his trip he had viewed the procession in historicizing-realistic fashion, as his sketches for Klönne showed, but he gradually began to dislike this arrangement—so much so that, when the painting was nearly ready in 1886, with Klönne waiting impatiently for the end result, he decided to abandon his work so far and start from scratch. Instead of using a new canvas for this, he simply painted over his previous work. Derkinderen's new experiences ensured that he no longer wished to take artistic or moral responsibility for his first painting. Meticulous historical detail and strongly contrasting colors dominated the first painting, but the second attempt showed the procession in gray and muted pastels, rendered in broad, blurry strokes. The procession, and particularly the study trip, had given Derkinderen a medieval dream of his own. He wanted to express the ideal image of that era in one "beautiful large unity of thought" in the painting. As a man of faith, he looked for the essential character of communal Christian worship to realize this. This notion was better expressed in a rough and vague way, in a kind of symbolic "cathedral," than through a historical and precise procession that included personal, contemporary scenes and other distracting historical details.[82] This artistic volte-face had important consequences, however, as regards both planning and funding. It meant another two years of work for Derkinderen, who had already used up his entire fee.

Klönne, in the meantime, was becoming increasingly vexed at the endless wait and the incessant requests for more money. He was already displeased that he had not been allowed during all those years to enter

Derkinderen's large temporary studio, the meeting hall of the St. Josephs-gezellenvereeniging (St. Joseph's Association of Journeymen) on Stad-houderskade. Finally, in 1888, more than four years after awarding the commission, Klönne was permitted to come and view the finished work. What was supposed to have been a triumphal evocative sensation in fact became a traumatic confrontation. One glance proved to Klönne that Der-kinderen had completely ruined the commission and had turned it into "a so-called impressionist imitation plaster fresco." The painter had con-cealed the actual subject, the procession, in "a peculiar haze of mist" that robbed the procession of its characteristic appearance and detail.[83] All of Klönne's ideas and directions had been systematically ignored.[84] In the place of the positivist and future-oriented Catholic triumphalism that Klönne had come to espouse and that he hoped would be depicted in a magnificent PR painting stood a vague and insipidly gray atmospheric piece. The details that he had so painstakingly researched, and the por-traits for which so many people had posed, were all "dissolved in a mist" because Derkinderen had refused to depict any "particularism of a reli-gious life image."[85] In Klönne's view, the solemn character of the proces-sion had been "mocked with rare callousness."[86] Deeply hurt, Klönne told Derkinderen that this was not the painting he had commissioned and that the artist had failed. Derkinderen, on the contrary, appealed to his artist's conscience and referred to the modernist school that was at the time beginning to dominate the scene of European painting. Presumptu-ously and pedantically, he then pointed out to Klönne that the genesis of Da Vinci's masterpiece—*The Last Supper*—had also been long and tortu-ous. This irreconcilable difference of opinion resulted in a fruitless argu-ment about the aesthetic merits of the piece. The encounter ended in a fierce row, with Derkinderen storming out in tears.[87]

Hoping to find a solution, Klönne asked Thijm to come and venture his opinion. This was a remarkable step in its own right, as Klönne had only recently launched a stinging moral attack on Thijm in the pages of *De Tijd* on account of the latter's habit of visiting the theater and of his homo-sexual son, the writer Lodewijk van Deyssel.[88] But Thijm was the unchal-lenged arbiter of all matters cultural: as the leader of the Catholic cultural community and as professor of aesthetics, his authority was unrivaled. The cause of ecclesiastical art was more or less his personal domain. As it happened, Thijm fully concurred with Klönne, a contemporary, and he disowned his former pupil. "It is regrettable," he wrote, "that such a pro-digious talent should lapse into such a character fault."[89] Fortified by this judgment, Klönne demanded that Derkinderen redo his work a third time, but to no avail. In a personal letter to Klönne, Thijm confirmed his critical judgment and stated that what he found most objectionable was the piece's "inauthenticity and affectation." This stab in the back apparently sealed Derkinderen's fate as an artist for Dutch Catholics. Thijm's slanted judgment, given shortly before he died, shows that he based his views mainly on the past and that his conservative choice was meant to please his peers. Thijm was not the only one to judge negatively. Other established Catholic leaders, such as Thijm's brother-in-law, the architect Pierre Cuypers, and the highly placed government official Victor de Stuers, were also asked to comment. Both obligingly confirmed Klönne's views.

Opposing opinions on the painting revealed the existence of a sharp division between an older Catholic elite and the younger generation of Catholic intellectuals and artists. It was a symptom of a wider Catholic conflict between dogmatism and isolation on the one hand and renewal and openness on the other.[90] Derkinderen's contemporaries rushed to his defense, albeit under cover of anonymity. The terms they used to describe the painting are indicative of their positive judgment. In their view, the work was an anonymized and mystical depiction that corresponded much more to the democratic concept of the Silent Walk—which had at this stage become more widely known—rather than a dated historical piece that gave pride of place to the Catholic lay elite.[91] They regarded the painting as an artistic expression of the "communal" and the "epic," as opposed to Klönne's "individual" and "lyrical" approach.

Klönne's negative judgment was directed at not only the aesthetic, but also the moral features of the painting, or rather its lack thereof. According to him, Derkinderen was robbing potential visitors to the shrine of a suggestive and inspiring example to revive the procession. It was out of the question that a dysfunctional canvas such as Derkinderen's would ever be displayed in Begijnhofkerk.

These strictures notwithstanding, Derkinderen had the painting exhibited in what was then the Panorama Gallery in Plantage Middenlaan in early 1889, defying Klönne's open opposition. His "capital painting" was praised in the press as a "work of art most rare for Holland."[92] Critics appreciated the fact that the procession had not been represented in a "militaristic" way, but they also questioned whether such a painting would be able to inspire religious sentiments in its viewers. The rector, whose objections pertained exactly to this point, therefore demanded that the painting not be billed at the exhibition as *Procession of the Sacrament of Miracle* because it did scant justice to that title.[93] Understandably, Derkinderen disagreed, as he thought his piece was precisely that, and this time he received support from unexpected quarters. The liberal newspaper *Algemeen Dagblad* praised the generic "piety" of his work. Klönne simply saw this as confirmation that the newspaper's liberal "freemasons" were now also out to frustrate his plans, as realizing the reality of a procession appeared increasingly illusory.

Whatever the form the painted depiction of the procession, as an image it would always have been an interpretation or a selection. Klönne refused to accept this precisely because he was no stranger to acts of forgery himself. This became evident in the preliminary study that Derkinderen and Klönne carried out together for the historical features of the image. Klönne argued that "disruptive" elements in the procession should be omitted. He had therefore forbidden Derkinderen to depict the devil characters, extras that played a role in the representation of good and evil in the medieval Amsterdam procession. Klönne regarded the "devils" mentioned in the sources around 1570 as cowardly tricks by the *geuzen* (Beggars) to desecrate the Blessed Sacrament.[94] Although he was normally very precise in his historical investigations, Klönne's decision represented a conscious lapse. There were to be no devils in his idealized procession. At the same time he stressed that Saint George, the slayer of evil or of the devil (the dragon) should have a much more prominent place.[95]

Despite this processional anticlimax—or even disaster—Klönne refused to abandon his ideal and immediately began looking for a different artist. This time he made a safe choice by opting for the older, traditionalist genre painter Carel Philippeau,[96] a sedate artist untarnished by modernism of any kind. The canvas he produced was somewhat smaller, but—wholly in line with classic academic and romantic traditions—the procession was depicted almost photographically in shining oils, and it featured the recognizable faces of Klönne's friends.[97] Saint George and his dragon were all but invisible, as if all the world's evil had been banished. Possibly Klönne's frustration had led him to commission a painting that would represent as strong a contrast as possible with Derkinderen's piece, in which Saint George and the dragon featured prominently. The following year, Klönne published a historical study called *Amstelodamensia* in which he provided a "historical" reason for this by contending that Saint George could not possibly have been represented at all in the Amsterdam procession.[98]

Philippeau completed his task shortly before the Miracle week of March 1893 and delivered his brand-new canvas to the chapel so that it could be photographed and shown on the front page of many a newspaper.[99] Klönne immediately donated this "faithful representation" to the church-wardens.[100] It was well on time for the 450th anniversary of the Miracle in 1895. Ironically, Derkinderen's rejected piece, originally intended for the jubilee, was exhibited again in the same year. It had since been purchased by a collector with a taste for modern art, who gave it on loan to the newly opened Stedelijk Museum on the Museumplein.[101]

Ultimately, the clash between these two headstrong personalities was not a generational conflict or a battle between the church and modern art.[102] This art soap opera was in fact a clash between Klönne's personal ambitions for Amsterdam and his Miracle cult, on the one hand, and the personal development of an innovative young artist on the other. What Klönne wanted was not a work of art but an inspiring naturalist visualiza-tion of the past that would entice Amsterdam and Dutch Catholics to em-brace a new devotional future. The row flared up again from time to time through letters to the editors of newspapers, dragging on until 1903.[103]

A posthumous reconciliation was effected in 1929. The Silent Walk's success had obviated any need or desire to realize Klönne's dream. The ritual, performed in silence and without any ostentatious display, turned out to be much more powerful than his procession would ever have been. The climate in Catholic Amsterdam consequently favored a retrieval of Derkinderen's fascinating painting. As the Begijnhofkerk underwent a restoration that year and was awaiting refurbishment, Klönne's successor, Rector Gerard van Noort, encountered Cees Baard, the new Catholic di-rector of the Stedelijk Museum. They spoke about having Derkinderen's painting restored; the canvas had been in storage in the Stedelijk Muse-um's depot for years and featured at the time in a temporary exhibition.[104] Van Noort, who had a fine taste in art, suggested that he would purchase the painting for 2,500 guilders so that it could finally be displayed in the place it had been intended for: Begijnhofkerk. To the surprise of many, the deal was done within a few weeks and in late October the mysterious painting with its muted colors arrived to be hung on the long north wall of the church.[105] The canvas was in place on time for the celebration of the fiftieth anniversary of the Silent Walk. It is ironic, in view of the once so acrimonious argument, that Baard and other contemporaries thought that the painting was particularly well suited to the atmosphere of the Silent Walk because of its anonymous, vague, and hazy character. For them, the atmosphere of the piece corresponded much more closely to the custom of walking in silence—by that time a generally appreciated tradition—than Klönne's thwarted plans. As the Catholic art and cultural critic Gerard Brom argued, the canvas was a "modern profession of faith."[106]

This reflected the judgment that Jan Veth gave in 1889, when he described Derkinderen's feelings as those of someone who had no taste for ostentatious display and vanity, but who wanted to depict the journeying together of people in fraternal devotion: "a beautiful, silent procession of pious, virtuous people, who, proceeding imperturbably, are animated by the same good will." Veth must have had the nascent Silent Walk in mind when he wrote these words.[107] The triumphalist pioneers of Catholic emancipation had in the meantime been overtaken by a national popular movement that was characterized by reticence and willingness to adjust, rather than ostentation and rigidity. This laid the foundation for a renewed, modern Dutch Catholic identity, inspired by the historical traditions of "accommodation Catholicism." Shortly after the painting was displayed in the Begijnhof, Brom wrote these striking words: "What is veiled here by sacred reverence is also the spirit of the Silent Walk, which has slowly become the deepest characteristic of Dutch Catholicism."[108] The organizers of the Silent Walk would have been hard pressed to think of a more beautiful anniversary gift.

Cult versus Cultural Heritage

Around the turn of the century, the Miracle cult consisted of two strands. The first was the clerically directed Miracle cult as it existed in the Begijnhof, a strand that would be increasingly marginalized, as we will see, as it became mired in endless conflicts about the Miracle heritage. Klönne, as rector of the Begijnhof, was the main protagonist of this strand, and, just as in the Derkinderen Affair, his obstinacy was ultimately fruitless. The second strand was the Silent Walk, which had begun diffidently as a lay initiative and which, as will be seen, experienced rapid growth at the start of the new century.

Klönne's comprehensive campaign to reposition the old Miracle cult consisted of a number of initiatives, of which the Derkinderen project was only one. His plan to protect, maintain, and preserve the material heritage of Catholic Amsterdam was more successful, even though it too was dogged by problems and conflict.[109] A growing sense that the country's cultural heritage was under threat of disappearing began to make itself felt in national political circles by the end of the nineteenth century. De Stuers, the government official responsible for cultural heritage, had already placed the disappearance of monuments on the national political agenda as far back as 1873.[110] His forceful and unconventional policies had considerable success in the field of heritage preservation, including as they did the restoration of medieval castles and churches.[111] For Klönne, the Catholic De Stuers was an example to follow.

Klönne wanted to transmit the same sense of the value of their own Catholic heritage to a confident group of concerned and dedicated Catholic Amsterdam citizens. They joined forces to fight for threatened former clandestine church[112] 't Haantje (currently Ons' Lieve Heer op Solder, or "Our Lord in the Attic"), a historic canalside house with a fully preserved Catholic domestic church in the (large) attic.[113] The French Benedictine and future cardinal Jean-Baptiste Pitra noted after visiting the building in 1847 that it was a monument that should be preserved for the future, all the more so because the religion practiced there reminded him of the early church in the catacombs.[114] It was not only a historical monument, on account of its shape and design, but as a religious edifice it also had strong symbolic value. Completed as a domestic church in 1663, the building represented the continuity of the Catholic faith in the city and constituted an imaginary link between the old St. Nicholas's Church, better known as the Oude Kerk (the mother church of the Holy Stead), which had become Protestant in 1578, and the new, imposing St. Nicholas's Church, consecrated in 1887, opposite Amsterdam Central Station. The attic church thus expressed both the continuity and the oppression of the Catholic religion.

In order to preserve and maintain Amsterdam's historical religious objects and art, Klönne founded the Amstelkring (Amstel circle) in 1884.[115] The neutral nomenclature was also meant to be a tribute to its founder, because—as Klönne himself insisted—the first letters could also stand for "Auctore Klönne."[116] The Amstelkring's objectives once more reflected Klönne's ambitious program. The circle described its purpose as working for the preservation of the "building blocks" of the Catholic past and actively "seeking out what otherwise might be lost to oblivion and disappear."[117] Initially, the Amstelkring's art collection was to be housed in the Begijnhof, but when plans to purchase the clandestine church on Oudezijds Voorburgwal were successful in 1887, that building became the most obvious location. Klönne, incidentally, excluded from the Amstelkring collection the old artistic artifacts—housed in the Begijnhof—that derived from the former Holy Stead, because he preferred to keep direct control over the Miracle heritage and its practical use.[118] This signaled the start of a conflict with the other directors that would not end well for him. A dispute about the possible acquisition of certain objects, such as the Miracle chest, ran so high that Klönne eventually withdrew from the Amstelkring entirely. The museum was connected to the Silent Walk from 1919 onward, when it began opening early on the morning after the event for participants.[119]

Klönne was not the only initiator of this enterprise. Together with a group of prominent Amsterdam Catholics, the initiators' aim was to use the religious patrimony as a source of new inspiration for the Catholic community in the Netherlands. Other directors shared Klönne's idolization of the Middle Ages, especially in relation to Amsterdam. Among them were historians and amateur historians, such as Klönne himself, Thijm, and younger men such as Bernard de Bont (1845–1908) and Jan Sterck (1859–1941). They were primarily interested in pre-1578 "Catholic" Amsterdam. De Bont and Sterck were well-off, and their ambitions made many things possible for the Amstelkring. A collection ultimately raised sufficient funds to purchase 't Haantje.[120] De Bont, a director at the famous distillery Wynand Fockink, became the museum's first curator. A few years later, he was also involved in buying the grounds of the former abbey of Egmond to preserve this historic location for Dutch Catholicism.[121] Sterck was a pupil of Thijm's and worked in Thijm's bookshop, C. L. van Langenhuysen. His excellent Vondel and Miracle studies earned him an honorary doctorate from the University of Amsterdam in 1919.[122]

After the Amstelkring museum had been realized and Klönne had resigned over his decision to withdraw the Miracle objects from the museum's collection, the rector decided to dedicate his energies instead to his "Miracle program": the acquisition from their Protestant owners of important items of material culture related to the Miracle cult. The so-called Miracle chest and Nieuwezijds Kapel, the former Holy Stead, were at the top of his list.

The Miracle Chest and the 1895 Anniversary

While the Silent Walk was still in its infancy, Catholic Amsterdam was celebrating a new Miracle jubilee: 1895 saw the 550th anniversary of the Miracle. As has been seen, Klönne had been preparing for the celebrations for years. It was to be his, and Catholic Amsterdam's, finest hour. Not only had he commissioned a painting of the procession, he also had a new Miracle sheet made which was hung above the main altar, giving visitors a good view of the narrative depicted in colorful scenes.[123] Then, in 1892, he decided to overhaul the languishing Adoration fraternity by transforming it into a new and independent guild of the Miracle, which was to offer fitting honor and support to the Miracle.[124] He did the rounds of *tout* Catholic Amsterdam to raise funds to realize his ideas, managing to collect some three thousand guilders. Historical studies next occupied his attention, and he wrote several articles for *De Katholiek* to give the nation a good account of the status quo of the Miracle and its cult. Klönne brought together all his material on the medieval cult of the Miracle and its procession and published it in one volume, *Amstelodamensia*, for the benefit of the jubilee. The book contained many new details that he had extracted from the sources, but the author's tendency to tweak the text from time to time to suit his missionary aims compromised its usefulness.[125] In addition to this historical edition, it was necessary to reach and inspire a wider public. To this end Klönne persuaded the popular periodical *Katholieke Illustratie* (Catholic illustration) to release a special issue devoted entirely to the Miracle cult.[126] This publication, with its print run of tens of thousands and its innovative illustrations policy, offered a first-ever opportunity to print a photograph of Jacob van Oostsanen's eight canvases, found in 1845 in the churchwardens' cabinet, depicting them as inspiring heritage objects. The whole country could now see what the Miracle of Amsterdam signified and how it had inspired the Netherlands' most important painters throughout the ages, such as—in the Middle Ages—Van Oostsanen, Van Hildegaersberch, and the Holy Stead's anonymous artist/organ builder.[127] Significantly, the issue stated that there was no need to repeat the Miracle legend itself because "we presume that all our Catholic compatriots are acquainted with it already."[128]

It was characteristic of Klönne's devotional heritage policy with regard to the Miracle cult to use certain traditions or objects for his own ends, and to place them in a context of mystification and devotion. This was the case not only with the reconstructed old entrance portal of the Holy Stead and the procession painting, but also—in 1895—with an old and worn archive chest. Throughout the nineteenth century, speculation resurfaced from time to time about the continued existence of the medieval "Miracle chest." Knowledge about the chest was sparse because the object had passed into the permanent possession of the Reformed Burgerweeshuis as far back as 1579. The chest was part of the inventory of the Holy Stead, which the orphanage had acquired at the end of the sixteenth century, with the permission of the city authorities, to be used for the care of poor orphans. In accordance with the usual visual design of the time, the outside of the chest was adorned with various painted Miracle signs or emblems: fire enveloping the intact host, flanked by two angels. The chest was forgotten after the Reformation until the eighteenth-century Amsterdam historian Jan Wagenaar noticed its existence for the first time. He had visited a number of the city's old institutions for his *Geschiedenis van Amsterdam* (History of Amsterdam), and he recounted that during his visit to the Burgerweeshuis on April 22, 1762, he had been shown, to his astonishment, a wooden chest with supernatural qualities: "This chest is held by Papists, who often come to visit it, as the chest wherein the miraculous host had been placed."

Why did Amsterdam citizens come to see this chest? Some versions of the Miracle story mention a chest or shrine in which the miraculous host was kept after it was taken from the fire in 1345. Many therefore believed that it was the original chest, and that the emblems of the cult had been painted onto it later; they regarded it as a contact relic. A contemporary of Wagenaar claimed that children suffering from fevers used to sit on the chest in the hope of a cure—even Protestant orphans did this.[129] The permissiveness that tolerated this disappeared in the nineteenth century as the new Holy Stead on the Begijnhof, very close to the Burgerweeshuis, began to become a center of a revived Miracle cult and as the devotion slowly began to grow. The governors of the orphanage decided to put a stop to these popish healing practices and around 1820 moved the chest into storage in the attic. But the ensuing oblivion was only temporary. In 1845 the bookkeeper of the orphanage found the chest again, just as the churchwardens rediscovered Van Oostsanen's drawings in that year. Perhaps the publicity surrounding the fifth centenary inspired him to go and look for it, or maybe he came across it by chance as he searched for old accounts. The board was not sure what to do with it. In view of the tensions that were flaring up on account of that year's jubilee, it even banned new and curious governors from going upstairs to look at the chest.

The sensitivity surrounding this particular cult object came to the fore again when Thijm requested access to the chest himself in the context of his genealogical studies relating to the Miracle. Although the board of the orphanage feared that it might lead to demonstrations, it gave Thijm permission to view, describe, and even touch the chest on January 24, 1867.

Thijm had the cautious mediation of Leonard M. Beels van Heemstede, a fellow member of the board of commissioners of the Rijksacademie (State Academy of Fine Arts), to thank for this. He regarded his visit as a historic event and had it officially recorded in a notarial deed.[130] The year 1876, a decade later, witnessed a breakthrough in the attitude of the board of the orphanage. It permitted the chest, together with other material "Keepsakes of the Holy Stead," to be exhibited to the public for the first time, in a neutral context: a large historical exhibition in the Oudemannenhuis (Old Men's Home) organized to commemorate the sixth centenary of Count Floris V's grant of toll exemption to Amsterdam in 1275.[131] Protestants generally thought that if the chest really had been the Miracle shrine, it would have been destroyed in 1578 just as the Miracle host itself was.[132] The orphanage's open attitude encouraged the churchwardens of the Begijnhof to make a private bid to buy the object. Formal negotiations ensued when two wealthy Catholics stated that they were willing to finance the transaction. But the Burgerweeshuis had second thoughts and ultimately proved unwilling to part with the object.[133]

Almost twenty years later, many Amsterdam Catholics, and certainly the members of the Amstelkring, still felt that acquiring the chest would be an important boost to the cult and its history in the light of the 1895 jubilee. An attempt to purchase it for the new Amstelkring museum's collection in March 1889 failed miserably. It was a delicate tripartite affair that involved Derkinderen, the Amstelkring, and the Miracle chest.[134] It turned out that Derkinderen, now in dire straits, was trying to sell his rejected procession painting for two thousand guilders. The Amsterdam alderman for culture, Bernard Driessen, had taken an interest in the artist and was trying to raise the required amount. When De Bont heard this, he made Driessen the following offer: if you give the Amstelkring the Miracle chest—which ultimately belonged to the city—then we will pay you the two thousand. Secret financial negotiations with the artist and the Burgerweeshuis followed. Eventually it was Klönne who torpedoed the offer because he objected in principle to the prospect of the Amstelkring Museum becoming the owner of the Miracle chest. Instead it should be put to active use in the devotional cult of the Begijnhof.

After this debacle, Klönne pressured the churchwardens to try to obtain the loan of the precious piece of furniture for the duration of the jubilee.[135] Although some of the governors of the orphanage were still "strongly opposed to this form of idolatry," the board decided, having consulted a legal advisor, to grant the Begijnhof's request for a temporary loan, "out of courtesy."[136] A few decades had, it appears, much improved the relations, once so hostile, between the denominations. Klönne seized the opportunity to incorporate the chest into the centenary celebrations.

The upshot was that the famous chest featured prominently in the Begijnhof from March 2 to June 1, 1895. As soon as the loan agreement was signed, Klönne completely appropriated the chest as a Catholic relic. It stood in the best spot in the sanctuary: between the high altar and the altar of the chapel's patron saint, Ursula, surrounded by draperies of blue velvet and decorated with a large bouquet of azaleas and lilacs. The two medieval processional banners stood on the other side of the altar as a counterpoint. Those unfamiliar with the miracle narrative could educate themselves by looking at the eight new elongated painted panels suspended from the balustrade, which depicted episodes from the history of the Miracle.[137]

The publicity and commotion that the chest caused attracted unusually large crowds to the church.[138] By strongly emphasizing its past healing powers, Klönne ensured that the chest, ostensibly merely a museum object, would be a self-fulfilling miracle prophecy. Newspapers wrote about the "tremendous" flood of Catholics who came to it in search of healing, while newspaper stories also guaranteed the interest of curious non-Catholic visitors.[139] Klönne received reports of no fewer than fourteen cures during these few months. The chronically open wounds of one visitor from Amsterdam suddenly healed when his wounds were dressed with cloths that had been rubbed on the chest. A crippled woman was able to walk again after sitting on the chest for an hour. Geertruide Lok, who had been bedridden for five years and suffered intense pain, returned home restored to full health after she touched the chest while praying.[140] And so it continued. This "superstitious" use of the chest led to criticism, and not only from Protestants. Catholics, too, were angered by what they believed to be Klönne's deliberate misrepresentations. How did he know that this was "the" actual Miracle chest?

The affair came to a head when Sterck made it his business to cut this devotional exuberance down to size. Sterck was a Catholic historian and the expert par excellence on the history of the Miracle, and despite the fact that he shared a common deep faith with Klönne, the two men engaged in bitter polemics about the subject. Sterck believed in the significance of the Sacrament of Miracle, but as a historian he objected to the clerical mystification of the chest. He argued that the essence of the Miracle would manifest itself all the more convincingly if it were stripped of all later fabrications. In a shrewd historical analysis, he unmasked the Miracle chest as the former archive chest of the medieval Guild of the Sacrament.[141] This chest had been made in around 1500 to store the guild's documents—nothing more, nothing less. The healing tradition of the chest, Sterck contended, went back no further than Wagenaar's eighteenth-century testimony from the Reformed orphanage. "Ignorant" Protestants had drawn incorrect conclusions about a link between the chest and the Miracle host on the basis of the painted symbols.

Catholic patriarch Thijm was asked to adjudicate on this second affair involving Rector Klönne. Thijm said it was not important whether the chest was real or not, but that the only thing that counted was belief in the Blessed Sacrament. If an object such as this one, which had special symbolic value, could help to deepen this faith, Thijm continued, then it was best to leave matters as they were.[142] This judgment put the matter to rest and more or less spared both parties.[143]

In the meantime the liberal press had a field day with the Miracle. Under the heading "We are moving forward," the humor magazine *Uilenspiegel* published ironic articles ridiculing the jubilee as a giant step backward for Catholics. Priest-politician Dr. Herman Schaepman was singled out for criticism because he had agreed to write the jubilee poem and thus demonstrated that he had renounced his political "errors" and had returned to the docile Catholic sheepfold.[144] Other articles poked fun at "Amsterdam's ancient Lourdes" as a modern ultramontane moneymaking scheme.[145] Amid this talk of Lourdes, the Catholic governors of the newly founded Onze Lieve Vrouwe Gasthuis (Our Lady's Hospital) decided to take a stand themselves. Possibly as a critique of extravagant stories of healings wrought by the chest, they planned the ceremonial driving of the hospital's first pile on the day of the jubilee itself.[146] In these doctors' minds, healing faith was better celebrated there.

As has been seen, obtaining the Miracle chest was not the only way in which Klönne intended to use the medieval past for the purposes of the jubilee.[147] Without naming the group, much less consulting it, he felt that the "Catholic community" should offer the Begijnhof a gift to thank it for the 550-year-old Miracle tradition. The gift he had in mind was a reconstruction of the original Miracle hearth that had been destroyed in the seventeenth century. Klönne regarded the building of this hearth as a synecdoche, a symbolic prelude to the "revival" of the old Holy Stead (at the time the Reformed Nieuwezijds Kapel) itself. The object would serve as an exposition throne for the Blessed Sacrament. He once again consulted Thijm's brother-in-law Pierre Cuypers for the design of this hearth. As the architect of both the national Rijksmuseum and of Catholic churches, he was an obvious and safe choice. But to the surprise and displeasure of both parties, the advisory committee judged that his design for the Miracle hearth did not match the traditional image. The tight deadline and the rather meager response to the idea of restoring the hearth eventually killed off the plan, which was deferred indefinitely.[148]

The hopes that Klönne fostered in 1895 of acquiring the original chapel of the Begijnhof—the English church—were simply unrealistic, and he soon had to abandon them.[149] He also authorized Van Waterschoot van der Gracht to make a private bid of up to five thousand guilders for the purchase of Van Oostsanen's paintings, which were still lying in Nieuwezijds Kapel, but this scheme proved fruitless too.[150] Even the relatively simple plan to publish an illustrated edition of the entire office of the Miracle could not be realized, as the printer was unable to deliver by the required date.[151] And then there was the Miracle chest. Klönne grudgingly had to hand it back, "in good condition," to the Burgerweeshuis by June 1. But he was not ready to give up yet. A few years later he concocted a devious plan to get his hands on the chest after all. He had heard in February 1901 from the city archivist, William Veder, that the archives of the Burgerweeshuis would be transferred to the City Archives. Veder also believed that the historical chest belonged in the "museum" of the Begijnhof, and thus they invented the following scheme. Veder would have the Miracle chest filled with archival documents from the Burgerweeshuis, in conformity with its original function, and then have it transported to the City Archives. In due course the documents would be repackaged, leaving the chest as packaging material. After a certain period of time, it would then be inconspicuously delivered to Klönne's doorstep.[152] This foolhardy plan had not the slightest chance of success. The chest was not released and remained in the Burgerweeshuis until well into the twentieth century. It finally ended up in the Amsterdam Historical Museum, safely turned into a museum object.[153]

The Catholic "States Bible": Neerlandia Catholica

The imminent 550th anniversary and the resulting incidents and press attention gave the veneration of the Miracle a boost that also benefited the Silent Walk. In addition, it brought the cult more expressly to the attention of the episcopal conference, which began to realize that this was not a random local devotion. The new Holy Stead and its long cult history were increasingly regarded as a characteristic expression of Dutch Catholicism, anchored in Holland's "accommodation Catholicism."

The desire to demonstrate the success of Catholic emancipation in the Netherlands to an international audience coincided with general sensitivity of the nineteenth century to the significance of history, jubilees, and commemorations. For ultramontane Dutch Catholicism, this sensitivity related to events beyond the national borders, even far beyond the Alps. The celebration in 1888 of the golden jubilee of Pope Leo XIII's ordination to the priesthood presented Catholics with an excellent opportunity to survey the state of Catholicism in the Netherlands and to publish the results in a commemorative volume. This book was to be dedicated to the "great" pope as a showpiece of Dutch Catholicism and would be offered to him as a gift on the occasion of the jubilee.

The result was truly imposing. Under the ominous title of *Neerlandia Catholica,* the impressively sized publication chronicled the phenomenal success of the emancipation of Dutch Catholics. The project cocked a snook at Dutch Protestants, and even the book's voluminous proportions—it weighed fourteen kilograms—were intended to wrestle the country's most iconic volume—the Protestant States Bible—into second place in material terms. Its contents left little to the imagination. The achievements of nineteenth-century Catholic emancipation that it listed are impressive even today: not only hundreds of newly built churches, monasteries, institutions, and hospitals,[154] but also countless organizations: hundreds of ecclesiastical and lay associations, fraternities, and societies. Everyone and everything that mattered in Dutch Catholicism was included in this "codex," or had participated in bringing it about.

When this mammoth book was nearly finished, the editors decided, at the behest of the Dutch Catholic political leader at the time, the ultramontane priest and parliamentary deputy Dr. Herman Schaepman, to add a separate supplement to underline the Catholic significance of the capital more clearly among the book's barrage of details.[155] This addendum, entitled *Amstelodamum Sacrum,* sketched the general role of Amsterdam within the revival of Dutch Catholicism, and the role of the Miracle cult in particular.[156] It had always been Schaepman's objective, he had stated previously in parliament, to "make of Catholics a political force in the Netherlands."[157] This desideratum was already being realized, but Schaepman intended to push for even more. He wanted to present the significance of Amsterdam's Catholicism, with its high level of organization, its cultural networks, and the national-devotional potential of the Eucharistic Miracle cult, even more clearly to the church and the world, urbi et orbi. The "Catholic unity" of the Netherlands had been well preserved in Amsterdam, he argued.[158] For Schaepman, Amsterdam was the true Catholic center of the country, even though it had missed out on an archiepiscopal see.

Because the Silent Walk was unknown or not widely known when the book was published in 1887 and had not yet taken on formal shape, the initiative went unmentioned in this grand compendium. There was another factor that militated against its inclusion as well: the influential Klönne was at that time still clinging tenaciously to his own ideas about the restoration of the Miracle procession. Just in time, he managed to have an image of the procession included in the book as a visionary perspective.[159] Needless to say, this image was based on Derkinderen's approved design sketch. When Klönne eventually laid eyes on the "hazy mist" painting in 1888, *Neerlandia Catholica* had already been printed and presented to Leo XIII.

The Destruction of the Holy Stead

The Netherlands' Calvinist tradition gave it the reputation of being the land of the word or, perhaps more appropriately, the Word. Of course the Bible also occupied a central place in the Dutch Catholic tradition, but for Catholics it was supplemented by "the image," or visual expressions of the faith, as another important aspect. The previous chapter has already shown how neo-Gothic buildings came to mark the public space as contested visual beacons of faith. It even led to royal protest in 1884, when King William III remarked that Cuypers's Gothic-style design for the national Rijksmuseum resembled an "archiepiscopal palace." In 1881, only a stone's throw from the Begijnhof, construction work commenced for a new, truly neo-Gothic Catholic bastion on Singel. The great demand for Catholic places of worship in the city had led to the building of the new Jesuit Church of St. Francis Xavier—also known as De Krijtberg—a church that would later function as fallback location for the small Begijnhofkerk during the Silent Walk.[160]

As the Catholic community in Amsterdam was growing in numbers, the Reformed congregation on Rokin faced a significant drop in members. This was caused by the decline of its own inner-city congregation, but even more so by the departure of members as a result of the "Doleantie" of 1886, the Protestant schism led by Abraham Kuyper. As early as 1882, when Dominee Brandt died, the decision was made not to appoint a full-time minister to replace him. The congregation, which met in the large church building that had formerly been the Holy Stead, found it increasingly difficult to maintain the upkeep of the old monument. In 1898 the building was no longer fit for use and services had to cease. When it was ascertained in that year that the chapel, which dated from 1452, showed evidence of subsidence and had cracks and pillars that were out of plumb, the time seemed ripe for new measures.[161] As Kalverstraat and Rokin had at this time become high-end shopping streets, the sale of plots of land surrounding the chapel was a financially attractive option. A second possibility was to demolish the chapel altogether and sell the entire plot. This last option sparked rumors that an offer had been made of a million guilders for the entire site, an immense sum that could only have come from Catholics because, it was said, Catholics were prepared to pay "anything" to acquire their former shrine. When the churchwardens eventually proposed demolition as a realistic option, it came as a shock to Catholics and non-Catholics alike.

At the same time—it was by now around the turn of the century—Klönne had come to grips somewhat with his procession obsession, in part because of the showdown with Derkinderen, but mainly because of the growth of the Silent Walk as an unexpectedly successful alternative to the procession. He had not yet abandoned his vision of a revival of the Miracle cult in its original location, but he thought it wiser not to say anything about his ideas and desires and to leave attempts to purchase the Holy Stead to middlemen. This expedient had been used to good effect in the past, for instance to purchase the Martyrs' Field in Brielle from Protestants.[162] The churchwardens of the Reformed congregation were fully alive to the possibility that a similar machination might be attempted in Amsterdam. They wished to prevent at all costs the return of this sacred site into Catholic hands, as that might lead to a revival of "Popish superstition" practiced in a shrine of potentially national allure, and all this right in the center of the nation's capital.[163]

The churchwardens were even more cautious because they believed that the government was not playing a neutral role in this affair, something they concluded from the prevailing "Cuypers-olatry" and his choice of new state buildings in a more or less Gothic style. Worse still, Protestants believed that a "rape of the law on the church communities" was underway, a permissive attitude on the part of the government that would lead the police to condone, and the law eventually to permit, priests and processions on the street.[164]

Most of the public attention initially focused on the debate about the important art historical value of the Gothic Nieuwezijds Kapel. Both the City of Amsterdam and the Koninklijk Oudheidkundig Genootschap (Royal Antiquarian Society) regarded it as one of the oldest and most interesting monuments of the city. But the arguments they used raised Protestant suspicions because they afforded too broad a cultural value to the building: it was important not just because of its valuable architecture, but also because of its role in the religious history of the city, or to be more precise, because of its role as a place of pilgrimage.[165] This perspective resulted from the rise of a new consciousness of the value of historic buildings for society as a whole. It all contributed to a cacophony of pros and cons on the question of demolition or restoration of the chapel. The architectural, artistic, and legal aspects ensured that the conflict dragged on for more than a decade; the "lawsuit of the century," as contemporaries called it. One of the churchwardens even argued at one point that "no lawsuit of the same import as that concerning the Nieuwezijds Kapel" had been held in the preceding centuries.[166]

The architectural advice obtained was far from unanimous. Some believed that the chapel was not in bad architectural shape at all. When Cuypers announced that the functional transfer to and restoration of the chapel by Catholics was practically possible, it caused a wave of Protestant outrage.[167] In the certainty that such a scenario would mean the restoration of the building to its use as "Holy Stead," the church's minister announced that his conscience would not allow him to hand over the building for this reason alone. The outcome of the vote taken by the churchwardens came as no surprise. On February 21, 1899, this body decided, with a thirty-two-vote majority, to demolish the chapel and replace it with a smaller Reformed church.[168] The remainder of the site would be used to build lucrative rental premises for retail use. Speedy demolition was in order because of the weak architectural construction of the building, a conclusion that appears to have been inspired primarily by strategic motives. The country's monuments supremo, Victor de Stuers, discovered during an inspection that the churchwardens had unlawfully expedited the dilapidation by failing to have it properly maintained or to repair holes and leaks. He argued that architectural investigations demonstrated that the churchwardens had wildly exaggerated the claims of dereliction and that the defects could be easily repaired. But in the eyes of the churchwardens, the Catholic De Stuers was not a neutral advisor. Had he not cooperated with Cuypers in designing the "Popish" Rijksmuseum? For them, this was more than sufficient proof. Chairman H. Harmesen of the churchwardens concluded, "Restoring in this case, where we have a Roman Catholic officer in charge, normally means: making it Roman Catholic." Cuypers's proposal simply to sell the building to the Catholic community unsurprisingly fell on deaf ears.[169]

As the case had turned into a national question, even giving rise to a pamphlet war, Klönne and his associates could not remain silent. It had become apparent from the many articles in newspapers and journals that Catholics did indeed hope fervently that the building would pass into Catholic ownership. Klönne posed the fundamental question, "To whom does the chapel belong?" and formally requested a review of the churchwardens' decision.[170] In the *Amsterdamsche Volksbode* of March 29, 1899, a Protestant professor articulated the feelings of his community in the following way: "For us Protestants it is of paramount importance to stop anything that might enhance the prestige and the self-consciousness of the Roman Catholics here. And historical considerations can't outweigh religious considerations." It seemed as if the days of the Miracle controversy of 1845 had returned. For many Protestants, handing over the church to the Catholics was akin to a symbolic reversal of the Reformation in Amsterdam. Klönne made an ultimate appeal to the City of Amsterdam to designate the chapel a cultural heritage site, aside from any religious feelings and perceptions, as it had previously done with the Begijnhof. But although the municipal authorities agreed that the monument should be preserved, they preferred to stay out of the complicated knot of legal, political, artistic, religious, and historical controversies, feelings, and claims.

A seemingly important development occurred in 1900, when a query was made to De Stuers as to how the appropriation of the Holy Stead had actually occurred in 1578—in other words, whether it was clear who was the rightful owner of the building. Was it in fact the Reformed congregation, or perhaps the City of Amsterdam, under whose authority the appropriations and transfers of ownership had taken place during the Alteration? The Holy Stead became a case for the courts.[171]

Despite these legal issues, demolition work began in February of that year. The city solicitor deemed this to be damaging of city property and demanded immediate cessation. What initially seemed to be a simple case soon gave rise to a lengthy legal battle, which required meticulous study of national and municipal history to reconstruct the transfer of ownership in the revolutionary period of the sixteenth century. It was not difficult to ascertain that, like most church spires in the Netherlands, the chapel spire and bells belonged to the city. Things were more complicated with regard to the church building itself. Eventually the city solicitor, Jan Kappeyne van de Coppello, concluded that an accord reached between the States of Holland and Amsterdam in 1581 meant that Amsterdam's church buildings could still be regarded as city property.[172] There was rejoicing in the Begijnhof when Rector Klönne heard the news.

The demolition was temporarily put on hold. In March 1900 shopkeepers returned to their stores built up against the chapel, and the trusty old commercial stalls along the Kalverstraat wall of the church reopened their shutters. After years of conflict and legal wrangling, the Amsterdam court finally pronounced its verdict on October 20, 1906: it totally rejected the city's claims and fully confirmed the Reformed congregation in its rights of ownership.

The public debates and lengthy legal proceedings had turned the Holy Stead into a "famous building" in the Netherlands, increasing the number of protests against demolition and giving the case a national dimension. The Catholic community in particular kept a close watch on proceedings on account of the Silent Walk. This successful manifestation of the faith was at the same time also the most formidable obstacle to saving the building. As the court case continued, participation in the prayer walk increased every year, and its traditional itinerary also meant that growing numbers of people circled round Nieuwezijds Kapel a number of times each year. Non-Catholics saw this as "proof" of a possible Catholic coup or conspiracy. The rumor that Catholics had succeeded in raising the immense purchase price of a million guilders did nothing to allay fears.[173] These circumambulations of the chapel, almost a modern version of the biblical siege of Jericho, forced the Reformed community into an impossible position of inflexibility. By carrying out their silent but ostentatious ritual, Catholics themselves unintentionally contributed to the downfall of their beloved shrine.

In the eyes of the Reformed congregation, the issue had degenerated into a purely political game, with the national and municipal authorities conducting proceedings solely for the benefit of the Catholic community.[174] That the government viewed the building as part of the country's "universal" heritage was not an argument likely to convince the Reformed. They ranked the city authorities among the "Popish Party." Even the liberal newspaper *Algemeen Handelsblad* was called an accomplice of Catholicism because it opposed demolition of the monument.[175] When the issue was addressed as a case in point at a linguistic conference, of all places, it proved one provocation too many, triggering an age-old conspiracy reflex among the Reformed of Amsterdam. They suspected that a plot was afoot to force them to sell the chapel. The more the case escalated, the smaller their maneuvering space became. An anonymous commentator in *Marnix, Protestantsche Stemmen,* opined that the struggle over the chapel and its demolition was an example to all heirs of the Reformation, "to encourage them in the battle against the superstitions of Rome."[176] The orthodox Reformed minister Casper Lingbeek, already appalled at Catholic participation in the coalition cabinet of the time, stated that returning the chapel would be an act of high treason to the Reformation and to the Protestant spirit of the nation.[177] The choice was now simply between "Reformation or Popish devotion." Orthodoxy prevailed.

The Leiden church historian Fredrik Pijper, a man with a reputation as an antipapist, disagreed and argued that the old church should be spared. Derkinderen, too, suddenly and unexpectedly came to Klönne's assistance by contending that demolishing it would be a cultural crime.[178] The liberal Protestant poet Albert Verwey added a poem to the chorus and lamented the "murder of old art." The debate also touched a chord in Utrecht. The Protestant minister Dr. Johannes Gunning Jr. suggested that the famous Utrecht Dom church should be sold to the Catholics because it was becoming too expensive and burdensome for the Utrecht Reformed congregation.[179] His intention was to set a pragmatic example for his Amsterdam colleague. Everyone in the country, it seemed, had an opinion on the subject.

Most members of the Reformed congregation of the chapel had advocated demolition all along, and the bitter legal battle that Klönne and his associates were waging was fast dispelling hopes of a compromise.[180] The churchwardens refused to consider sale, not even to a third party, because the chances that the building would eventually end up in Catholic hands were good. The affair came to its conclusion in 1907, when the Amsterdam city council, meeting in secret session, decided to abandon its resistance and not to lodge an appeal. A "sentence of death" had been passed.[181] A last symbolic gesture of collective resistance by antiquarians who went to the building in a "funeral procession" did not stop the destruction, which began on July 10, 1908.[182] The Dutch Catholic community had been "humiliated."[183]

The demolition literally shattered this dream of Amsterdam Catholics, who were to lick their wounds and mourn their loss. The romantic protagonists of devotion to the Miracle, Rector Klönne and historian Sterck, were completely disillusioned at this "most hurtful event."[184] On July 10, an hour before the works started, Sterck had photographs made of the interior for the record, including, for the first time, the Holy Corner.[185]

The entire episode represented a second, much more disastrous defeat for Klönne after the debacle of the Miracle painting. He had come so close to realizing his objective: linking the new mass devotion to the original sanctuary through the Silent Walk! His dream of a revitalized Holy Stead had definitively evaporated. Just before the demolition began, another opportunity presented itself to buy a property beside the Begijnhof, land that could be used to build an alternative Holy Stead. But the opportunity was lost. His many failures had drained Klönne of the energy required to switch to a new project—he was crushed.[186]

Shortly after the demolition, the Reformed congregation began building a new, much smaller Reformed Nieuwezijds Kapel. A last-ditch Catholic legal challenge was trumped up to stop rebuilding of the church. Evidence had been found that the Thijm family held property rights over the family grave in the building, but the claim was rejected by the courts.[187] The new church and a fair number of commercial premises built around it were finally ready for use in 1912.

Almost a century later, in 2007, the Reformed congregation offered the new church for sale to the Catholic community, in the person of the chairman of the Silent Walk, Maarten Elsenburg, for an asking price of fourteen million euros. This amount far exceeded the means of the local Catholic community at the time. The entire complex, church and surrounding commercial premises, eventually sold for forty million euro.[188] The church now hosts Amsterdam Dungeon, a touristic house of horrors that is, in all respects, the antithesis of everything the Miracle cult ever stood for. The dungeon offers a modern fantasy world of disbelief, darkness, death, and damnation on the same sacred site where faith, light, life, and resurrection were once celebrated.

While the demolition was in progress, it transpired that the Reformed congregation had omitted to make provision for all of the building material to be removed from the site. The state then claimed the choicest pieces. The Rijksmuseum received on loan the mysterious wooden "milkmaid," an iconic statue that was part of one of the trusses of the ceiling, as well as the "gilded" Gothic entrance portal, formerly the pilgrims' entrance to the sanctuary, and many stone elements.[189] The "municipal" bells were moved to the small tower of the former Nieuwer-Amstel town hall. Many of the columns with linking pointed arches were given in loan to the City of Amsterdam in 1926 with the unrealized aim of livening up parks as romantic follies.[190]

The government was not the only party that attempted to reap the benefits of this large demolition project.[191] Many private inhabitants of Amsterdam used their contacts with demolition men to obtain smaller objects and fragments. Within the Catholic community, these objects quickly attained the status of relics, sacred souvenirs of the great Amsterdam sanctuary. The historian Sterck personally purchased four capitals from the chancel, which were then built into a wall of the diocesan museum in Haarlem after his death. By way of an invocatory Christocentric transformation, Leonard Stolk, parish priest of St. Catharine's, symbolically carved a crucifix from one of the wooden piles that was recovered from the ground.[192]

It might have been expected after the whole sorry affair that the Reformed congregation would have kept a close watch on the demolition of the Holy Corner in the church. It would be a bad thing if its high-minded posturing were to be followed by the misappropriation of the remains of the miracle hearth, which some were convinced were still partially there. Yet Bernard de Bont succeeded in acquiring for Amstelkring a number of sandstone fragments that had "very likely" belonged to the old hearth. Similarly, the judicious offering of pecuniary inducements enabled C. A. Tel Jr. from Edam to chip off a few red stones from the old chimney.[193] They came from behind a wall that stood directly in front of where the old hearth was supposed to have been. Tel immediately gave Rector Klönne a few stones as presents: "surely very little consolation indeed," as Tel commented. The Society of the Silent Walk also received stone fragments, particles of which were from time to time presented as gifts to members at anniversaries or retirements.[194] And the Museum Amstelkring also purchased a number of sandstone fragments reputed to have originated from the hearth. These attributions were surely rather dubious, as seventeenth-century sources already mentioned that the hearth had purposely been demolished and entirely removed from the church to prevent the veneration or misappropriation of fragments.

All this gave rise to a veritable diaspora of *spolia* (scattered remains) of the Holy Stead throughout the Netherlands.[195] They still retain their significance today. After the demolition, various plans were made to rebuild the church using the remaining building material, for instance by P. Tel from Heemstede in 1935, but finding a location in the city center and funds to finance the construction always proved to be insurmountable obstacles. Of the many ideas put forward, only one was eventually realized.[196] A nine-meter-high column topped by a capital from the chapel was placed on Rokin at the corner of Wijde Kapelsteeg as a historical marker in 1988.[197] This highly symbolic reconstruction was valued on account of its cultural-historical significance, and its religious meaning—as part of the Silent Walk route—was no longer seen as a threat.

The Art Collections Department of the Amsterdam Protestant Church has been actively collecting and preserving *spolia* of the Holy Stead since 2009—a truly remarkable initiative, given that the same church community was the instigator of the demolition.[198] Is this simply a case of contemporary care for the church's own heritage, or is it also motivated by a sense of guilt? In a particularly ironic—and irenic—move, the department has indicated that it wishes to bring together parts of the collected materials in the grounds of the Begijnhof, more or less halfway between the old and the new Holy Stead.

The destruction of the Holy Stead concluded a fascinating era dominated by issues of material culture and art related to the Miracle cult. It marked the beginning of a new phase in which *intangible* expressions of the devotion came to occupy center stage, a phase in which the cult was interpreted in a radically different way. The main form of this intangible expression was the Silent Walk, a new devotional ritual, a kind of quietist pilgrimage, which proved to be an unexpected success story. The Silent Walk not only broke previous records of participation but also gained almost unassailable national status as an iconic Catholic mass ritual. Of the two devotional strands that marked the Miracle cult of this period—Klönne's clerical-ecclesiastical strand and the lay initiative of the Silent Walk—only the latter survived. The unfortunate traditionalist priest clearly lost out.

In the meantime, the Miracle cult lost its particularistic or individualistic character, as Derkinderen had already attempted to express in his procession painting, and was no longer about seeking bodily healing in a baroque devotional manner. The Silent Walk was Dutch Catholics' specific way of expressing their faith, presented collectively in a modern spiritual way. It was also a self-conscious social and political statement against inequality in society.

A National Cult

The second decade of the twentieth century saw the breakthrough of the Silent Walk on a national level as it decisively transcended its prior local-regional dimensions.[199] The Amsterdam Society suddenly found itself confronted with large organizational problems. Firstly, the board adapted the practice of the Walk to this increase and attempted to manage and consolidate the enormous increase of pilgrims in a professional way. Secondly, bowing to pressure from the diocese of Haarlem, the Society transformed itself from an informal lay group into a formally recognized association under church supervision.

The growth of, and increasing media focus on, the nocturnal but conspicuous pilgrimage served to reduce the entire Amsterdam Miracle cult to the Walk itself. Even the diocese considered reducing the feast's high liturgical status, including an eight-day Miracle octave, but this danger was averted by the ever-vigilant Rector Klönne.[200]

A crucial episode in this phase of expansion was the recruitment in 1917 of a former editor of the newspaper *De Tijd*, Leonardus van den Broeke (1882–1871), as vice chairman of the Society. Members of the board had hitherto been inexperienced ordinary Catholics, but this dynamic, dyed-in-the-wool journalist, who had worked for a newspaper of national standing, was in a different league altogether. Coming at the right hour, and endowed with charismatic verbal qualities and robust writing experience, Van den Broeke brought much-needed professionality to the board.[201] He immediately launched a public relations offensive with immense zeal, giving a tremendous boost to the Silent Walk. Van den Broeke's ambition was to enlighten all Dutch Catholics about the Silent Walk and the correct understanding of the Miracle cult and its pilgrimage. With unflagging enthusiasm, great dedication, and "glowing words" he toured the country, giving hundreds of speeches.[202] The response was not long in coming, and soon a real "Silent Walk fever" gripped the land. It seemed as if Catholics from all parts of the country began to feel the attraction. Ordinary Catholics wanted to be part of this innovative movement, drawn by its dynamic and simple, but strong, allure. This broad social basis ensured that the pilgrimage could ultimately become integral to Dutch Catholic national identity.[203]

The new dynamic became evident in a direct and concrete way in the foundation across the country of dozens of new sister societies of the

Amsterdam Society. Van den Broeke wrote a book about the history and significance of the Miracle and the new Silent Walk that proved to be an important factor in this expansion. No clerical, missionary prose this time, or disdainful Protestant or liberal criticism, but a readable and clear work of journalism. It caught on, and one edition after another rolled from the printing presses. Readers were treated to a lucid explanation of the significance of the Miracle and the Walk. This new phenomenon induced all the right emotions. Armed with tens of thousands of copies, brochures, and ubiquitous posters, Van den Broeke went from parish hall to parish hall, eloquently recruiting the thousands of Catholic men who would together form the long nightly "Walk cortège" that would wind its way through the city center of Amsterdam in the following years. At the same time he used his press contacts to ensure that the program of the Miracle celebrations appeared in the newspapers every year so that the Walk could be penciled into diaries on time.

The tremendous growth in numbers of participants demanded more intensive coordination from Amsterdam headquarters. The Society therefore held an annual general meeting with the leaders of the sister societies from 1918 onward, always some two months before the Walk. Amid the newfound success, the role of successive chairmen—and indeed of Vice Chairman Van den Broeke—in creating and expanding the Walk was not forgotten. Rector Van Noort once characteristically said of Carel Elsenburg (chairman 1914–1934), "he *is* the Silent Walk."

The Amsterdam Elsenburg family would continue to provide resolute managers who played an important role in the future history of the Silent Walk. Thus Alphons Elsenburg (chairman 1935–1957)[204] was prepared to use funds from his flourishing textile business to fill financial gaps and support the organization by making staff available.[205] The saying during his period in office was that "if you apply to Elsenburg's company, you will be hired also for the Silent Walk."[206] The premises of his textile company on Nieuwezijds Voorburgwal were known as "a reserve of nineteenth-century Amsterdam Catholicity," especially because Alphons presided over the great tradition of the Walk for half a century with "patriarchal geniality."[207] It was no coincidence that the buildings included Thijm's former residence—an almost sacred place—from which this man of letters had orchestrated the cultural emancipation of Dutch Catholics.

The growing significance of the Silent Walk for Dutch Catholicism also meant that the ritual increasingly became an object of discussion within the Catholic community. Given its success, and in view of Klönne's wild plans, which persisted in collective memory, some commentators questioned whether transforming the Walk into a formal procession should even be a desideratum at all. As a new revision of the constitution was imminent, and as hopes were rising that the end of World War I would bring a new society, the debate on maintaining the constitutional procession ban was reignited in 1917. When lawyers involved in the revision process wrote opinion pieces qualifying the procession ban as legally "improper," it inspired popular Catholic media, such as *Het Huisgezin* (The family), to propagate a revival of the procession as the Catholic ritual per excellence. The option was also discussed at the Society's annual meeting of 1918. The conclusion was that *if* the lawyers were proven right, the Walk would soon no longer be silent.[208] This apparent call to arms fell on fertile ground among a number of combative pastors in the region. By deliberately organizing processions in areas where this was not permitted, they planned to provoke test-case trials to review whether the procession ban was in conformity with existing legislation. The upshot was that Catholics received marginally wider ritual maneuvering space under the law, but no freedom to hold processions.[209] The same combative spirit was also visible in the media. Letters from zealous believers poured in to the editor of the daily *De Tijd* in 1916 and 1917, demanding the transformation of the Silent Walk into a full-blown procession.

At the same time, however, the Walk was establishing its own special position in society. Even non-Catholics generally looked kindly on the Walk. Despite its protest aspect, they regarded the humble nocturnal ritual through a romantic lens and were often sympathetic.[210] As a result Catholics increasingly began to feel that the Walk's silent character was in fact the public religious format that suited contemporary interdenominational relations. Following the views of Lousbergh, who had died in 1914, the board believed that the Walk should not become embroiled in the thorny matter of the procession ban. The journalist Van den Broeke managed to keep "pro-procession" letters out of the newspapers. Their writers received a polite personal message from him explaining on behalf of the Society that it was the founders' and the current board's intention that "the character of the Walk must never be replaced by a procession."[211]

Despite this attempt to cover up opposing views, and despite the Society's own standpoint, the possible lifting of the procession ban and the revival of a Miracle procession were raised at the 1918 annual meeting by the Nijmegen Dominican and Vondel expert Professor Bernard Molkenboer and the new rector of the Begijnhof, Theo Bosman. Catholic blood was thicker than water. Had this moment happened in earlier days, it would have given heart to Klönne, but he was now an old man and weary of his struggles after four years as an emeritus. Perhaps he had made his peace with the way things were. A regular procession of the dimensions of the Silent Walk would in any case have been unthinkable in the Netherlands.

Although tolerance of Catholics had improved a lot and the former denominational enemies cooperated well at the political level, the average Protestant's basic attitude toward typical Catholic rituals was still negative. Ideas or proposals to introduce them in the public sphere were still totally out of the question, certainly for anything to do with the capital. The time was not ripe to lift the ban. When Pieter Cort van der Linden's liberal cabinet tabled a proposal for the removal of this controversial article of the constitution, a Protestant parliamentary majority soon voted it down.[212]

One consolation that could perhaps compensate for these unfulfilled processional plans was the miniature Eucharistic procession that had been held *inside* the Begijnhof church during the Miracle octave since the ancien régime. The leaders of the Amsterdam Society and the sister societies had personally participated in it since 1907, complete with banners and votive candles.[213] The entire event took place within the small building. The secluded nature of the Begijnhof itself made it possible to hold a slightly bigger procession outside. When Bosman was appointed the new rector in 1917, he immediately decided to put this rather obvious idea into practice. On Wednesday, March 20, 1918, the procession made its way around the Begijnhof in the open air. Catholic newspapers provocatively made much of the fact that, for the first time since the Alteration of 1578, a Miracle procession had left the (new) Holy Stead to pass through Amsterdam in the open air, albeit not on the public road.[214] As the Begijnhof was private property, this procession was not affected by the procession ban. But in order to prevent discussions and problems—memories of the demolition controversy were all too fresh—Bosman had carefully consulted both Bishop Callier and Mayor Jan Willem Tellegen in advance. In addition to the mass Silent Walk, this small procession remained a supplementary, church-organized tradition within the general context of the Miracle cult until far into the twentieth century.[215]

All this gave the Silent Walk considerable national renown. But the nightly voyage retained something of its mystery for those who did not participate in it themselves. What precisely happened during the annual Walk? Who did what, and where, when, and how?

The Practice of the Walk

Until his death at fifty-nine years of age in 1914, Joseph Lousbergh remained the driving force behind the Silent Walk. He combined the functions of chairman, secretary, and treasurer in one, all this with iron discipline. He meticulously maintained all external contacts and chaired the negotiations that led up to the founding of new sister societies. He decided what happened and which developments could or could not be initiated. Strongly aware of the importance of good record keeping, he recorded all procedures, customs, and instructions on paper. Lousbergh's records were intended to make it easier to preserve the Walk's objectives, even after his own death. The *Memorandum*, a document containing his personal notes on the Silent Walk project, mentioned seven important characteristics of the Walk that Lousbergh believed should continue to be respected in the future. In short, they amount to the following:

1. The initiative for and management of the Walk must continue to rest with laypeople; priests should not become involved in the management, either directly or indirectly. Only the rector of the Begijnhof knows the names of the organizers, but he does not participate in the Walk. The anonymity of the leaders is also important because they are no more than instruments in the hand of God.
2. The participants from participating organizations must never place themselves in the forefront; all are considered to have been invited individually and not as members of an association or congregation "because this is a very sensitive point" and no offense must be given to anyone. Every participant must pray quietly and in an introverted way, without even imagining that he is part of a group.
3. A number of orphans of the Roman Catholic boys' orphanage must always participate in the Walk because "according to Holy Scripture, they are particularly pleasing in God's eye."[216]
4. Women may not take part. Lousbergh commented, "There are several reasons for this, but these are so obvious that it is unnecessary to mention them."[217]
5. The mass intention linked to the Walk must always remain the same, i.e., "For the participants of the Walk and their relations, as well as for the conversion of sinners and unbelievers, particularly those of Amsterdam."

6. Every year, a report of all activities must be drawn up "so that history will remain complete."

7. It is not enough to think of the present, but one must also work toward the future.

Things were to develop in an entirely different direction after Lousbergh died: however much he wanted to work toward the future, he could do nothing to control it. In fact, most of these points would sooner or later be abandoned.

For a start, the diocese began to interfere with the rapidly growing movement very shortly after Lousbergh's death. The anonymity of the leaders was abandoned and organizers and participants began to place themselves in the forefront, even explicitly "by way of protest." The rector of the Begijnhof, as well as a diverse range of Catholic associations and organizations, from clerics to bishops and cardinals, began to participate more or less identifiably. The orphans, on the contrary, disappeared after about a decade, while women—who were already taking part informally—were to become the mainstay of the Walk after they were allowed to participate from 1965 onward. And the intentions changed every year, precisely because the future turned out to be less predictable than Lousbergh could have imagined. The organizers increasingly felt that it was necessary to adjust the Walk's motto to address the topics of the day (World War I, Spanish influenza, etc.). Perhaps the stipulation about record keeping was the only one that was observed without change.[218]

To begin at the start of the Silent Walk practice: as has been seen, this ritual obtained its own, fixed form in the late 1880s and early 1890s. The four initiators began to designate themselves as a society, a conscious decision to adopt a certain organizational structure, but one with as little formal external status as possible. They even refrained from using the word *organizing* to describe their work, for fear that the authorities might investigate them for possibly unlawful activities. In their eyes, the Walk was a substitute for a procession that was banned by law. This meant they were uncertain of the possible legal or social consequences of their initiative, which was an activity that could in those days even have been interpreted as a conspiracy. Caution was ingrained in their minds for a long time. Initially, the leading quartet's most important tasks primarily consisted of encouraging people to participate in the Walk and ensuring that it would take place in an orderly way.

In the aftermath of the 1914 Walk, a contented Lousbergh wrote in his notebook that "the movement is increasingly gaining sympathy."[219] This was an understatement characteristic of his modesty, for at the time the Walk had already managed to win the hearts of many Catholics across the country. Because it was not easy or cheap to travel to and from Amsterdam during the night in those years, there was an even larger, untapped reservoir of potential participants, a promising prospect for the future. In retrospect, Lousbergh's comment was an unwitting personal final reflection on the success of the Walk that he had done most to bring about. Shortly after writing it, on July 27, 1914, this initiator and unrivaled leader of the Silent Walk died. Up to the time of his death, Lousbergh, as a typical representative of the nineteenth-century system of self-organization, had kept everything in his own hand. The other members of the leading quartet only gained access to the records and "historical" notes on the Walk after his death. Board member Adriaan Apol used the documents in 1916 to compile the *Memorandum*, a historical file about the origins and first years of the Walk.

For those he left behind, it was clear that Lousbergh's death was the end of an era. The board decided not to insist any longer on strict enforcement of the regulations, which had become unpractical and counterproductive. Apol proposed to the remaining leaders to change the board's policy in a number of respects. As the ecclesiastical authorities had become very conscious of the importance of the movement, they had publicly backed the Walk and were willing to cooperate in its organization in an indirect way. The opportunities that this offered made it necessary for the organizers to give up their traditional anonymity. To provide the disclosure required, and especially to effectively highlight the significance of the movement, Apol sent copies of the *Memorandum* to Bishop Callier of Haarlem and to Willem van Rossum, who had been made a cardinal of the curia in 1911. The board was seeking support and acknowledgment at the highest level.

It became easier to establish these new contacts after Rector Klönne retired from the Begijnhof in 1914. This ended the tensions that had appeared between the lay initiative of the Silent Walk and Klönne's attempts to develop the Miracle cult in a church-focused, sacramental-ritual way directed from the Begijnhofkerk. These plans had been at odds with Lousbergh's principles, so that any real rapprochement was impossible. A portrait of Klönne that appeared on the front page of the *Katholieke Illustratie* in 1903 to mark his thirtieth anniversary as pastor of the Holy Stead already showed an old and tired man.[220] The debacle surrounding Derkinderen's procession painting proved that there would be no restoration of a Eucharistic procession anytime soon. And, in any case, processions had become a nonissue in the diocese of Haarlem since the *Kulturkampf*, with the bishops preferring to commit instead to the valued and successful Silent Walk. When the Holy Stead was demolished, a disillusioned Klönne beat a retreat from the Begijnhof, never commenting publicly on the Miracle again.

From Self-Organization to Church Association

With Lousbergh's leadership gone, the remaining members of the board decided it was best to set up a formal association. As the only "initiator" still to be actively involved, Carel Elsenburg assumed the post of chairman. At the same time he asked his eldest son, Alphons Elsenburg, to join the board and his friend Henri Eijgenraam to take up the treasurership. Apol, in view of his age, designated himself a "dormant" member and handed over his duties as secretary to Jean-Baptiste Takes, whose first act was to record the board members' responsibilities and their roles in modern Amsterdam society. What had once been simply a group of friends was transformed into a formal board, which held its first official meeting on Wednesday, February 17, 1915.

Although the new board worked systematically, its message to the outside world, especially to the authorities, continued to be, "We are not organizing anything. The Walk is and remains a matter of individual devotion." Time and again the participants were urged to realize that the Walk should never become, or even look like, a demonstration or a procession. The board conveniently overlooked one historical precedent from 1911 when they had ignored this important principle. In that year an extra Walk had been organized with a clear political objective: to protest at the fiftieth anniversary of Italian unification, which had put an end to the Papal States.[221]

As more and more members of church organizations, associations, and fraternities—from the R. C. Oude Armen Kantoor to St. Cecilia's Choral Society—began to participate in the Walk, the Amsterdam Society still had no official connection to the church or approval from ecclesiastical authority.[222] This meant the growing lay Walk was an anomaly within the Roman Catholic pillar, which was otherwise strictly regulated by the church. It was in fact unthinkable that this kind of religious mass manifestation should continue to fall outside formal church supervision. Lousbergh had guarded like Cerberus the lay character of the Walk and its independent basic principles, but his death left the ground open for the ecclesiastical process of approval. The movement was simply becoming too important to Dutch Catholicism for it to remain without formal ecclesiastical supervision. The diocese of Haarlem therefore proposed that the Society should accept statutes authorized by the church. As the board members were exemplary and loyal Catholics, who moreover needed the church, for instance to have the use of the Begijnhofkerk and to have masses said, they took little convincing. Lousbergh perhaps turned in his grave when the new "ecclesiastical association" of the "Society of the Silent Walk" of Amsterdam was established in 1917: the new statutes stated clearly that the rector of the Begijnhof was the moderator of the Society and as such occupied a central position on the board. The Walk had always been a lay affair, but the statutes now placed the Society under the supervision of the bishop of Haarlem and under the comanagement of the rector of the Begijnhof. The convert Willem Wiegmans, "Ecclesiastical Decorative Artist" from the school of Derkinderen, designed a new logo for this "new" organization. The emblem, in the shape of a Gothic church window, symbolized the new situation of the Society: placed in an ecclesiastical framework, viewed through the church's neo-Gothic window.

In fact, Catholics' tradition of self-organization had generally served them well. The first group of non-Amsterdam participants who had been there from the start, Lohmann from Haarlem and the sister society that he founded in 1896—also without church supervision or control—preferred to keep things in their own hands when a second local Walk association was set up in Haarlem in 1906. This association, closely linked to the diocese, requested and received episcopal approval as a society long before the Amsterdam Society itself.[223] Writing to Lousbergh, Lohmann referred to the status of his oldest sister society in an attempt to elicit Lousbergh's disapproval for the second group, even stating that he was prepared to take police measures to prevent it from taking part. But Lousbergh refused to see the problem, replying in unequivocal terms, "Official recognition, which they have, gives them an advantage over your society which cannot be reasoned away." Even for Lousbergh, the cherished era of informal introversion appeared to be drawing to a close. He probably realized that the Walk's success made some formal link with the church inevitable and was alive to the benefits that this might bring, even though he was not ready to ask for it personally.

Interest in the new Walk ritual from surrounding towns and villages resulted in growing requests from people to be admitted to membership of the Amsterdam Society.[224] In an attempt to spread organizational responsibility for the event, the board stimulated the establishment of affiliated but fully independent "external associations" or "sister societies" that would organize the trip to the Begijnhof and the passage through the city for their own members. Nomenclature was not uniform and ranged from *society* and *company* to *association*, to the annoyance of the Amsterdam board, which preferred *Branch* of the Society of the Silent Walk. The main goal of these sister societies was to increase devotion to the Miracle by organizing a pilgrimage to join the Silent Walk.[225]

Traveling to Amsterdam at night and walking around the city was not without practical difficulties in those days. For many participants from outside Amsterdam, the practice of the Walk began far away from the capital. A nightly journey to Amsterdam and back home early in the morning demanded thorough preparation. Traveling collectively was easier, safer, and cheaper. This is how the first sister societies were established on an informal basis at the end of the nineteenth century, often in the same way as the Amsterdam Society. It first happened in places near Amsterdam with traditionally large Catholic populations, such as Haarlem, Waterland, Purmerend, Edam, and Volendam. After the Amsterdam Society received its ecclesiastical statutes, a version of these was also adopted by the sister societies, including the stipulation that the Walk must never become a manifestation or demonstration, but should remain a silent prayer walk.[226] The pastor of the place or church where the sister society was established usually acted as spiritual director, who made up the board together with a number of parishioners, and who often traveled to Amsterdam with the society. During the pilgrimage, board members led communal prayers and hymns, if the group was bold enough to recite or sing these out loud in the nocturnal emptiness of Holland's polders. They were also responsible for keeping order, determining the route, and checking their group at the gates of the churches and supervising the collection.

In the heyday of the Silent Walk, the Netherlands had hundreds of sister societies organizing the pilgrimage for their city, village, or region. At first these were founded mainly in the provinces of North and South Holland, but from the 1930s onward, the phenomenon spread to the predominantly Catholic provinces of North Brabant and Limburg. Eventually, there was barely an area in the country that did not have a sister society—with the exception of the Zeeland islands and the far northeast.

In practice the annual Walk was organized in a strongly decentralized way. In the context of the Catholic pillar, "ordinary" Catholics took charge of the practical organization—they formed the egalitarian basis for a new national movement. In Sevenum in Limburg, for instance, the local coalman, and subsequently his son, formed the core of the regional branch after the war for more than fifty years. They arranged for the group to join the pastor in the parish church for benediction before departure. Members were told to bring sandwiches, for consumption later that night in the Beurs van Berlage or some other establishment in Amsterdam. Then the participants cycled to the station; they were allowed to park their bicycles in an adjacent shed for the occasion. A specially rented train bearing a sign for Horst-Sevenum then brought the group of praying and singing men to the big city and waited there for them to return. In later years the train was exchanged for a bus that could stop in a number of other villages to pick up participants who lived outside Sevenum. After "making" the Walk in under an hour, the Limburg men attended mass in one of the city center churches before returning south on the train. Back in Sevenum, the pilgrimage concluded with a closing service before the participants could finally go home for breakfast and bed, where many of them remained until lunchtime.[227]

In Zevenhoven in South Holland it was a pious agricultural laborer, later a nurseryman, who led the sister society—founded in 1936—for many years.[228] Boys were admitted from the age of twelve as long as they were accompanied by an adult; in Zevenhoven they could be joined by the headmaster of the school. Young men were allowed to take part independently from the age of sixteen. For many people in the countryside, taking part in the Walk was a real adventure. Boys and young men looked forward to it eagerly, all the more so as life in the countryside at the time was not without monotony. It was often a formative experience for them. Once they were captivated by the special experience and atmosphere of the Walk, many participants returned every year for decades.

The 1920s saw the start of what has been characterized in Catholic historiography as the era of the "Catholic of the deed."[229] In an encyclical published in 1922, Pope Pius XI called on the world to improve morals and faith in society through "Catholic Action." Many ordinary Catholics gained greater awareness of their personal opportunities and responsibility to act in their lives and religious lives. In the Netherlands, too, Catholics became more comfortable with the idea of showing their faith in public, for instance by making the sign of the cross or praying in public, even in the presence of non-Catholics.[230] Taking part in the Walk was presented as the ultimate "Man's deed of sacrifice and prayer."[231]

The organization of Catholic life in the Netherlands became more sophisticated, and as a group, Catholics felt increasingly strong. This new self-confidence also contributed to the widespread willingness to take part in the Walk. Not only was it a ritual that individuals could participate in easily and inconspicuously, but it was also experienced as a march of protest and dissatisfaction, an implicit contestation of the fact that Catholics still had unequal rights and opportunities, exemplified by the ban on public rituals that primarily affected Catholics. Amsterdam Catholics observed that there had never been such a sense of mutual belonging since the Reformation, and they eagerly seized the opportunity to take part in the Walk to give public testimony to their faith.[232] Secrecy was increasingly felt to be counterproductive, although there must be no ostentation or provocation either that might give offense to others.

Dates and Figures

The participation figures for the Silent Walk's first decades tell their own success story. The upward trend was maintained from the start of the initiative. In 1888 organizers counted more than 500 participants, in 1892 this had increased to some 750, and it had reached 1,000 by 1895. For about a decade, the number remained stable at around 1,500. This was a period of consolidation, with a stable core of participants mainly from Amsterdam itself, while the initiative began to attract attention from the rest of the country. Mid-1905 saw the beginning of a new period of strong growth, facilitated by the increasing range of public transport on offer, including train, streetcar, bus, and boat—transport that was becoming ever cheaper. Participants from Edam, for instance, organized their own extra streetcar from 1900, while those from Volendam and Weesp on the Zuiderzee came by sailboat and motorboat respectively. In 1907 a few wagons were added to the night mail train for less agile participants from Haarlem. This example inspired others to use special trains too. Only one special pilgrims' train pulled in to Amsterdam in 1922; eleven years later there were forty-five from across the country. They were all driven by Catholic train drivers who offered their services for free, to serve the sacred cause. These special trains continued to be deployed until the end of the 1960s, when most pilgrim groups switched to buses.[233]

The procession ban applied not only to processions in the strict sense of the term, but also to any group walking on the public road while praying loudly or singing religious hymns. Jurisprudence nonetheless permitted these religious practices to be carried out in "secluded areas." The rise of closed streetcar and train wagons, buses, and cabin boats as private pilgrimage vehicles made it possible to pray and sing together during the journey without violating this contested article of the constitution. Prayers were said for the intention chosen for that year's Walk and often also for special intentions relating to the pilgrims' own city or parish. A party from Schiedam, for instance, was asked to pray "for the flourishing of the Catholic faith in Schiedam" halfway through their journey, as they were passing Leiden.

Participation figures for mass demonstrations are notoriously unreliable, certainly if the estimates are provided by the organization itself. The only year with a precise count is 1917.[234] The official count was exactly 12,205 participants. For all other years, the available figures are merely estimates, with the number of train passengers, which was recorded precisely, as their only firm basis.[235] It was more difficult to put a number to participants from Amsterdam, who often took part on an individual basis.

The figure for 1921 was more than 21,000 participating men,[236] and in 1926 this had increased to nearly 50,000. Complaints multiplied about chaos, congestion in Kalverstraat, and long waiting times. Catering capacity was very limited. Board member Frans Kristen suggested a change in the route, but Van den Broeke insisted that the existing route was sacrosanct, and so other solutions had to be found. One was to spread the Walk over two separate nights, a practice that started in 1928.[237] Three years later, during the Walk's golden jubilee in 1931, a police report recorded an exceptionally high turnout of 33,000 and 40,000 on the two nights respectively, a total of 73,000 pilgrims.[238] During the Walk's prewar heyday, at the end of the 1930s, there was an average turnout of 60,000.

Better organization, better logistics, and better propaganda stimulated participation, but the movement's success was mostly based on the proliferation of local initiatives. In 1935 the number of sister societies in villages and cities had risen to 200, a figure that would increase by the late 1950s to more than 250.[239] New groups were formed at ever-greater distances from the Amsterdam epicenter. The society of Eindhoven and the surrounding countryside grew in ten years' time from 95 members in its foundation year of 1930 to 1,800 (1,250 of whom were participants) in 1940. It made active propaganda for the Miracle in the area by giving speeches with magic lantern presentations. The results were significant. The Eindhoven society continued to grow to 3,538 members in 1961 (2,100 of whom participated in that year).[240]

Most pilgrims' societies traveled by bus, boat, or train,[241] but others preferred to come on foot or by bicycle. For instance, the statutes of St. Dominic's Bicycle Club, a Haarlem sister society, stipulated explicitly that its goal and purpose was to undertake the pilgrimage to Amsterdam *on foot*.[242] By emphatically retaining the traditional idea of a pilgrimage, and by putting it into practice, the Haarlem-Amsterdam walk acquired great renown in the area. A number of sister societies from the surrounding area that also cherished the old idea of pilgrimage on foot joined the Haarlem group. It led to the board recommending that pilgrims should not walk more than twenty-five miles, because otherwise fatigue would impede proper devotion.[243] Other sister societies first traveled to Haarlem by train and then joined the Haarlem group to walk to Amsterdam: a huge group of five thousand men could be seen walking along Haarlemmertrekvaart in the direction of Amsterdam in the 1920s.[244] Only one or two groups walked very long distances, such as participants from Egmond-Binnen and the R. K. Wandelclub Rotterdam (Rotterdam Roman Catholic walking club).

The Seminarians' Silent Walk was a separate initiative begun in 1932 by students of the Crosier College in Uden in Brabant. Student and author Bertus Aafjes took the initiative to organize a separate Silent Walk for Dutch seminarians. It was the only Walk to take place on a different date, during the Easter academic vacation. This permitted students of the 71 minor and major seminaries that were contacted to take part during their vacation.[245] It proved to be a success. A mere 33 students traveled to Amsterdam during the first year, but the average turnout was some 350 during the following years, until the war. Each year, after the Walk and mass, the participants were invited for breakfast by the sisters of the Maagdenhuis. As has been seen, this was the only Walk to be held separately from the main initiative. It is possible that the Amsterdam Society was reluctant to reject an initiative of a venerable club of future priests—the country's future clergy. The students continued this practice until 1962, when they too came under the spell of aggiornamento.

The Walk and the City

As has been seen, the organizers had their hands full with the logistical problems caused by the crowds of people who came to take part in the pilgrimage to Amsterdam and the Walk itself. During the night of the Walk, the huge flow of pilgrims ground to a halt at various points along the route. A special route had to be set out near the most troublesome "bottle-neck," a spot in Kalverstraat known as the "triple junction." According to the board's minutes, things "were often critical in Kalverstraat" due to "the virtually unbroken sequence of waves of pilgrims flowing through the narrow streets." Three different traffic flows met at this spot: those beginning the Walk, those returning from the Walk, and those who were about to begin the ritual circumambulation of the Nieuwezijds Kapel. A new system was introduced in 1919 to prevent congestion. Each group of pilgrims received a map with the new route.[246] Stewards and guides were employed to keep the participants on the right track. The increasing number of pilgrims also meant that the Walk had to start earlier in the night because otherwise the last groups would still be walking at dawn. Around 1920 the "rush hour" was still between 3:00 and 5:00 a.m. The start of this timeframe had to be pushed forward a number of times, first to 1:00 a.m., and since the 1960s even to immediately after midnight. In the twenty-first century, the Walk would begin even earlier, on the late eve of the feast (ca. 11:00 p.m.).

The huge interest also affected the availability of the surrounding parish churches and the travel schedules of trains and buses. The Amsterdam board consequently decided in 1928 to spread the Walk over two nights, the second night being the Sunday before the actual feast. The Amsterdam participants were expected to make the Walk on the second Sunday; the sister societies from outside the capital were spread over both nights, with most of them planned for the first.

Groups that began late were frequently hindered by people who had completed the Walk and got in their way. Participants from Amsterdam often caused problems because they ignored the organizers' logistical instructions, thus obstructing the smooth flow of traffic. In addition, individual participants frequently began or ended the route at random points, or deviated from the route. From time to time pilgrims ended up in a canal amid the confusion of a crowd outside a church.

The large scale of the Walk also affected the surroundings of the route. The nighttime opening of establishments was a problem, not least because it often led to rumors about pilgrims for whom the lure of a café or of the red lights proved too strong. These suspicions were probably mostly unfounded for pilgrims who came from outside Amsterdam, as their collective trips and tight schedules made it difficult to slip away from the groups without serious consequences in the form of missing a lift back home. But this is not to say that it never happened.[247] Memoirs published much later of two elderly prostitutes, veterans of the Amsterdam red-light district, support the rumors about the Walk, which they called the *geilelullenloop* (horny dicks walk) in the slang of their profession: "It was nearly midnight when we saw the whole parade start. There just was no end to the numbers of men. Whole crowds of them. I could see it well from my chair behind the window. From time to time a group left the crowd and disappeared to the girls in the red light. Suddenly we had lots of clients [from the rural province of Overijssel]. . . . The cheekiest of them did the talking. Can we join you horny girls?"[248]

Journalists were not slow to ask chairman Elsenburg about pilgrims visiting prostitutes. Elsenburg confirmed that it happened, but emphasized that it was not right to accuse all participants: "Real believers did not do such things; [but] for some the Silent Walk was an excellent alibi to come to Amsterdam for other reasons."[249] That the board was aware of the lure of the red-light district and was reluctant to lead participants into temptation is evident from the instruction it issued to lead departing pilgrims back to the Central Station along Kloveniersburgwal and the odd-numbered side of Geldersekade, "i.e., not along Zeedijk," which is part of the red-light district.[250]

This was not the only moral panic to plague the organizers. In 1920 the leader of the Uitgeest sister society complained that many participants smoked during the Walk: "Where will it end if it goes on like this? You certainly can't pray when you are smoking." Participants from outside Amsterdam often stayed standing around the route after the Walk to chat, laugh, or even drink beer. It inspired the rector to instruct all leaders to intensify their supervision, especially of young men's conversations.[251]

Each year also brought complaints about noisy cafés, illuminated advertising, intrusively curious bystanders, and "undesirable people of the night" who disturbed the silence and meditative-religious atmosphere of the Walk. For "revelers"—who were often under the influence—the unexpected and misunderstood encounter with a seemingly interminable line of silent men in traditional attire was a bizarre confrontation that could easily lead to provocation. Police officers were present to protect participants against offensive comments, provocation, or mischief. The Society attempted to close down all establishments along the route that were not required to provide catering to the pilgrims during the night of the Walk.[252] On the whole there were very few serious problems throughout the entire period.[253] The police were mainly occupied in checking cafés and drinking halls that held special permits to serve participants of the Walk. All other establishments located immediately along the route were obliged to cover their windows and doors with curtains to prevent passersby from looking in and light from shining out. This regulation was not always enforced very strictly, and in 1934 the Amsterdam police order was modified. From then on, publicans along the route were banned from serving intoxicating drink, producing loud music, or leaving their windows uncovered during the night of the Walk.[254]

Restaurants, cafés, tobacconists, and pastry shops elsewhere in the center extended their opening hours to accommodate the Catholic invasion and saw their custom rise. Vendors went onto the streets selling chocolate and books. Catholic residents along the route flew the Dutch flag from their homes, and sympathetic shopkeepers placed candles in their stores as if they were window altars. The board of the Walk once again violated its own founding principles by requesting that the municipal authorities leave the streetlights on at full strength during the night of the Walk.[255] There was obviously no further need for the cover of darkness. Was this a symbol of institutionalization and adaptation? Or was it a sign of increasing self-confidence that it was no longer necessary to remain in the dark? The city council in any case conceded the request.[256]

The frequent participation of high clerical dignitaries from across the country, bishops, deans, and abbots, was both a stimulus to the event and an informal way of endorsing it. As representatives of the Dutch church province, they gave the Walk a national dimension. Yet the Walk never became an ecclesiastical activity: it was organized by a lay society, even if it was now formally under the control of the bishop. Word of the ritual also reached Benedict XV, who showed his approval by granting the participants a plenary indulgence on January 13, 1917.[257] Politicians were not slow in participating, and Catholic members of parliament, ministers, mayors, and councilors all took part.[258] The powerful parliamentary leader of what was to become the country's main Catholic party Katholieke Volkspartij, or KVP (Catholic People's Party), Professor Carl P. M. Romme, the "sphinx of Overveen," participated a total of seventy-one times, from 1909 to 1980.[259] This broad level of participation created a growing sense of connectedness among Dutch Catholics. Participants and potential participants encouraged each other to go and were reluctant to stay behind, for the sake of the Catholic cause.

Childhood Memories

Two boys in the 1950s, W. F. (Zutphen, 1942) and H. L. (Amsterdam, 1947), both dreamed of becoming priests or missionaries. By chance both of them ended up working in Paris in the 1970s. They have since retired, but they still have lively memories of the journeys undertaken in their youth to Amsterdam and of the excitement of passing through the old city as they made the Walk, the participants' footsteps echoing off the façades of the houses. As one journalist wrote, if you have done it once, you will never forget it again.[260] What impression did the Walk leave on individual participants?

W. F.: My memories of the Silent Walk are vague in their generalness, but some details I can remember very clearly. First the context. My father and mother were traditional, but reasonably liberal-minded Catholics, my father was from a typical retailing family from Holland, and my mother's family were country people from [the provinces of] Gelderland and Overijssel. My father was a photographer and ran a camera supply store, and as such he was a member of the Catholic Retailers' Union in Zutphen. But just as my grandparents, my father was very conscious of his Catholic identity. Neither of my parents ever went on a pilgrimage as far as I know, that kind of spirituality was alien to them; it was determined socially and denominationally, not so much by religion and spirituality. But my father did always take part in the Silent Walk. As far as I know, the trip was organized by the Zutphen branch of the Catholic Retailers' Union. I think it was not so much meant to be a spiritual experience as a confirmation of Catholic group identity. I've been trying to remember when I took part: it must have been in 1954, because I was still young, and I went to the minor seminary in September 1954, and I wasn't at home anymore in March from that year on, so it can't have been after that. I remember that I felt honored that I was allowed to come along. It was undoubtedly a kind of rite of passage: I turned twelve shortly afterwards, and from then on I belonged to the adults. I knew already in March 1954 that I'd be going to the seminary; maybe that was a motive to let me come, because I really was rather young. As far as I know none of my three younger brothers ever went. I have three specific memories:

1. I still have a very lively memory of the group in the night train going to Amsterdam: I can see an open wagon with four men (including myself as an adolescent) sitting across from each other on the wooden benches that the softly lit wagons still had in those days, talking to each other. I was surely wearing my lovely plus-fours that I'm wearing in photos taken shortly afterwards. . . .

2. The mass in St. Nicholas's Church: an image of a full church, lit by candles, I can see that space as semi-dark with many nuances of light and dark, that made a huge impression on me.

3. The silent walk in a long line through the city: the place I can remember isn't a wide one like Damrak or Rokin, but much narrower, perhaps Warmoesstraat or Nieuwendijk. I don't remember anything to do with any ritual. Nor can I remember whether or not we went to the Begijnhof. Or any kind of food or meal. I suspect we went back on the train immediately after the Silent Walk.[261]

H. L.: I grew up in a very traditional Catholic family, especially my mother was very devout and went to church every day. It was still the time that women sat on the left and men on the right.[262] The women all wore scarves to cover their heads. I did the Silent Walk three times: in 1957, 1958, and 1959, after that I lost interest. All these men, in gray suits, wearing hats and their good shoes. I can still see it. I was ten years old, in the fourth year of elementary school, when my father took me to the Silent Walk for the first time. We cycled from South Amsterdam with a group from Vredeskerk church in De Pijp through Amsterdam at night; that was really exciting. I had slept beforehand and was still drowsy as I rode my bike. There were very few other boys participating in the Walk, and certainly none of my age. But it was such a special experience, the feeling that you belonged to this big group. Lots of people took part, you had to watch out not to step on people's heels. Nothing was said during the Walk, the silence was the most impressive part. All you heard was the sound of footsteps in the streets echoing off the walls. The echo even made the silence stronger. Renewed acquaintance has rekindled my interest in the Silent Walk. Who knows, I might take part again some time. You do feel this sense of connection, the serenity, and there is this meditative aspect. I experienced the enormous power of silence as a child.[263]

Women and the Walk

This chapter has described the Silent Walk as a national phenomenon. But was it also a national ritual at this stage of its history? Obviously not in the constitutional or societal sense, because it was an exclusively Catholic initiative. But not even the entire Catholic community was involved in the Walk: Lousbergh's principles barred a large group of Catholics from taking part. Not only were children younger than twelve officially banned from participating, but so were women of all ages. This rule originated from a nineteenth-century bourgeois sense of propriety, which "dictated" that a nocturnal journey through an area of doubtful morality was not suitable for women (let alone for young children). This attitude was not specifically Catholic: associations of all persuasions tended to exclude women at the time.[264]

Although women did not take part in the collective Silent Walk of the twentieth century, in the Middle Ages they had been crucial in ensuring the survival of the Miracle cult. The cult in and around the Holy Stead had relied substantially on women for its existence, the daily cult practice in the chapel as well as the confraternity of the Sacrament of Miracle and indeed the processions. It is curious therefore that the revival of the cult in the form of the Silent Walk was strictly a men's affair. As a Catholic men's prayer walk, it was the initiative of two laymen who viewed the nightlife they encountered along the route with suspicion and anxiety, and then decided that only men sixteen or older could become members. Despite this narrow masculine perspective, the Walk became and long remained a huge success, both quantitatively and qualitatively. This, too, is remarkable, as elsewhere in Europe devotion to saints and devotional rituals in general were normally the domain of women rather than men.[265] Foreigners remarked that in the Netherlands, all Catholics were involved in their religion through confraternities and associations. The French writer and convert Joris-Karl Huysmans was astonished by the high percentage of men who participated in the devotion to Saint Liduina van Schiedam, a level of participation that was extremely unusual in his own country.[266]

Seen in this light, it might be concluded that the Silent Walk came slightly "too early" because by the end of the nineteenth century women were beginning to demand their freedom and work, as volunteers or in paid positions, in all kinds of social environments, such as in the Grail Movement of the 1920s.[267] The ban on women was caused by two factors: on the one hand a generally conservative denominational culture, and on the other the fact that the Walk passed through shadowy neighborhoods at night, which was considered unseemly. This combination led the initiators to exclude women from participation on the basis of the values and bourgeois sense of decency of their time. In their eyes, the nightlife and the red-light district that the Walk traversed were not even suitable places for men, but for women they were entirely out of bounds. This was the case not only for the Walk through Amsterdam, but also for the sometimes long train and bus journeys that had to be made at night from all parts of the country. Louis Rogier averred the existence of an old system of scrupulous protection around 1900 that did not allow women to be on the street alone after dark.[268] The initiators initially planned to have the Walk in the early morning hours, even for the men, as it was the only time that the streets were practically deserted.

This policy notwithstanding, from the start women from Amsterdam demanded admittance, and they sometimes refused to be excluded. As early as 1888 Rector Klönne was angered to discover a small group of women who were participating clandestinely.[269] When a number of women again attempted to take part in 1890, it was prevented "by the energetic action of the leaders of the Walk."[270] Of course, women could not be barred from walking on the public road, but for the Society it was a rule that only men could take part in the Walk: "the circumstances do not allow any exception."

Not all women were content to leave matters at this. A few took part every year, and from a certain point in time this was tacitly tolerated. This issue was on the agenda again in 1913. A number of women wrote to Klönne, announcing that they had been participating in the Walk for as long as ten years, but that this year "gentlemen members of the fraternity and haters of women" had stopped them after the Walk as they attempted to pass through the Begijnhof.[271] They threatened to bring this act of repression to the attention of the press and of the bishop. Just as women were fighting for female suffrage—a struggle that was ultimately successful—they were also demanding the "right to the Walk."

Conceptions of decency in Dutch society played a crucial role, but so did the fact that the Walk had been the exclusive preserve of men for some thirty years already—this in itself had become a fixed custom, giving the board an extra argument to defend the "tradition" of excluding women. In the year that female suffrage was introduced in the Netherlands, 1917, the Society coincidentally also organized a precise count of the participants, and twenty-five women were found among the more than twelve thousand participants. Some of these were found to be members of the Society; they had to relinquish their membership at the behest of the rector.[272] The struggle for the right to participate in the Walk was not won yet; in fact, it would still take many years.

An exhibition dedicated to De Vrouw 1813–1913 (Woman, 1813–1913) was held in 1913, and the same year saw the foundation of the R. K. Vrouwenbond (Roman Catholic Women's Union). This union soon became an important movement in the development of women and their Catholic Action. The organization itself gave rise to the foundation of yet another union, of "Adorers" of the Blessed Sacrament, who came together in view of the diocesan Eucharistic Congress of 1922. The members of this group placed the Eucharist at the heart of the lives of women because only in this way "will she find what her woman's heart seeks."[273] The union also called on women to take part in processions, a call that was diametrically opposed to the practice in Amsterdam. The more conservative female Guard of the Blessed Sacrament was founded in 1923 in response to this call, followed a year later by a men's branch.[274]

In 1931, the fiftieth anniversary of the Walk, Nijmegen historian and priest Reinier Post attempted to resist the pressure exercised by women by providing scholarly arguments against female participation. He contended that male processions similar to the Walk represented an ancient ecclesiastical practice with roots in early Christian times.[275] This rather doubtful argument was an indication that the "problem" was exercising minds at the time. De Tijd reported with alarm in 1932 that a call to participate by the R. K. Vrouwenbond had inspired a large group of women to make the Walk during the day, led by a clergyman. The crowds in Kalverstraat had brought them to a standstill, and they had been subjected to mockery by bystanders.[276] Critics did not think this was a suitable way of reviving the seventeenth-century Amsterdam prayer walk, when Catholic women had made the Walk during the day or in the evening on an individual basis. Eventually, from 1934 onward, smaller groups of women, mainly from Amsterdam, followed the route in a more or less organized fashion on the day after the Walk, Monday night.[277] They were joined by some thirty women of the Delft Silent Walk.[278] In 1937 groups of women made the Walk every morning between 7:00 and 8:00 a.m. during the week of the Walk. They assembled at the statue of the Sacred Heart in the Begijnhof. A first gesture of recognition from the church came in the same year, when a "women's benediction" service was organized in St. Nicholas's Church, attended by some 1,800 women. They made an appeal to history to back up their demand: "We, modern women . . . want to show our love for the Blessed Sacrament of Miracle." Was it not true that they had had their own altar of the Blessed Sacrament in the Oude Kerk in the Middle Ages, and had they not protected the Miracle from desecration in 1531? They also claimed—rightly—that women had maintained the tradition of individual silent walks since the seventeenth century.[279] They concluded that there was a close and logical connection between "the event of the Miracle and women." The Vrouwenbond itself answered the rhetorical question whether the Walk was "purely a man's devotion" in this way: "No, a thousand times no!"[280]

In recognition of their difficult position, the Silent Walk for Women Committee organized a meeting to explain the issue once more, in the hope that more women would join their "truly Catholic action": "Why should we women be less forthcoming than men in honoring Christ in his Blessed Sacrament?" They received support from the progressive Franciscan Germanus Vrijmoed, who told them in 1939, "Your numbers are small, but your pilgrimage is great."[281] Of course, there were always women from Amsterdam and the surrounding area who simply made the Walk individually at a time that suited them during the Miracle week, but most wanted to take their rightful place in the fascinating train of people that wound its way through Amsterdam by night.

In his autobiographical novel *In het donkere zuiden* (In the dark south), the writer Ton van Reen included a short conversation he had with his mother just before departing on a pilgrimage to Amsterdam from his Limburg home village of Panningen at the age of fourteen in 1955. When asked why the women were not joining them, his mother replied that women could not be priests either, and when he then asked her whether she would not like to come along, she dismissed this out of hand, saying, "No, women pray at home."[282] The Silent Walk meant making a journey from the south to the "pagan" and "depraved" city of Amsterdam. But was it still self-evident that women prayed at home? Societal and ecclesiastical change was in the air, especially in Amsterdam. The participation of women was discussed again in the 1950s, but official acceptance would not come until the end of the Second Vatican Council (1965).

Offshoots of the Silent Walk

The Nijmegen cultural historian Brom wrote in 1924 that, even if the constitutional procession ban were to be dropped, he did not expect a big increase in the number of processions in the Netherlands. Given the sensitive nature of relations between the Christian denominations, he believed Catholics would in that case only sparingly invoke the right to hold processions.[283] This contention was entirely consistent with the statement of support for the Silent Walk that he had issued the year before, in which he had praised this ritual as being more in line with Christian life than the ostentation of a procession.[284]

It became clear in the 1920s just how popular the Silent Walk phenomenon was becoming in the Netherlands.[285] The idea of having an introverted collective devotional tribute in a society consisting of both Catholics and Protestants also held strong appeal for other places of pilgrimage in the country. At least thirteen Dutch shrines eventually decided to hold silent walks instead of processions. The first to copy the Amsterdam initiative were other Eucharistic places of pilgrimage. Breda began a silent walk in 1916, followed by Alkmaar in 1917 and Bergen in North Holland in 1925.[286] When Alkmaar attempted to enhance the prestige of its own walk by inviting the Amsterdam board to participate in May, board members commented that it was out of the question that they would take part in "an imitation of our Silent Walk."[287]

The ritual was later also used at Marian shrines, for instance in Delft (1929) and Amersfoort (1933), and then also for Saint Liduina in Schiedam (1933).[288] Spontaneous parades or processions of gratitude during the liberation in 1945 were transformed into silent walks in the Marian shrines of Bolsward (1946), Leeuwarden (1948), and IJsselstein (1948) after wartime ecumenism (see below) waned. The formula proved especially popular north of the river delta. During a significant part of the twentieth century, silent walks brought large groups of Catholics to the streets in a ritual way, but none of these imitation walks would survive the ecclesiastical and societal upheavals of the long 1960s.

Celebration and Goodbyes

As silent walks were being introduced here and there as a new local ritual, Amsterdam was preparing to celebrate the fiftieth anniversary of its Silent Walk in 1931. The event was celebrated on an impressive scale in the Concertgebouw (concert hall) and was broadcast live on radio so that as many participants as possible might be able to tune in from across the country.[289] For the occasion, Pope Pius XI gave his apostolic blessing to the concept and practice of the Walk. This Vatican stamp of approval crowned half a century of institutionalization. What had begun as a private initiative had obtained the highest ecclesiastical approval. Chairman and initiator Carel Elsenburg, at seventy-eight years old, was made a member of the Vatican Order of St. Gregory the Great to honor his exceptional merit for the faith and for society. He was greeted with a standing ovation that lasted several minutes. Then the Augustinian friar F. X. Duijnstee held a "masterly festive speech" on "Christ's silent passage through the world," discussing the origins of the Walk from an "accommodationist" religious perspective.[290] He noted, "Involuntarily we think of the much-discussed procession ban. Let us be honest, however, and wise in our demands. It would be unreasonable to demand the lifting of this ban even from a Christian government, if the mixed population in our Fatherland were to pose an obstacle to this."[291] Duijnstee also stated, however, that ultimately the Walk's silent format did not do justice to Christ the King, who deserved a more public tribute. He regarded the Silent Walk as a modern reflection of Christ's entry into Jerusalem, not in glory, but on a donkey: that was Christ's own silent walk through the world. His death concluded this silent walk and commenced his glorious passage, his entry into the heavenly Jerusalem.[292] Perhaps Duijnstee secretly hoped that the Catholic-Protestant coalition government under the leadership of the cautious Catholic prime minister Charles Ruijs de Beerenbrouck might nevertheless create a new opening for processions.

Three years later, in mid-December 1934, Carel Elsenburg died at the age of eighty-one. During his lengthy chairmanship, the Miracle cult in its new guise of the Silent Walk had flourished impressively. To safeguard continuity of management, as the next annual Walk was approaching in March, Bishop Johannes Aengenent quickly promoted Elsenburg's son Alphons to the position of chairman. The Catholic newspaper *De Tijd* commented that this appointment was made "on the basis of attributed hereditary succession" by the highest ecclesiastical authority, and therefore "by the grace of God." Be that as it may, Aengenent admittedly had a good eye for suitable candidates. Alphons Elsenburg was known as an enthusiastic entrepreneur, and the commercial successes of his textile wholesale company had caused him to climb to a totally different social stratum than his father, a cobbler at the time he started the Walk. The new chairman's company, including the infrastructure it provided with staff and resources, would contribute in no small part to facilitating the Walk and to maintaining its status as a lay initiative.[293] And Alphons followed in the footsteps of his father by remaining modest, very devout, and totally dedicated to the Catholic cause. This was evident especially in his deep faith in and personal commitment to the Eucharist. One relative once remembered that he "shed tears as he received communion."[294] This Eucharistic fascination nourished his strong involvement in the Amsterdam Sacrament of Miracle.

The International Eucharistic Movement

As Alphons Elsenburg's story proved, the consecrated wafer of unleavened bread, the host, was capable in those days of moving good Catholics to tears as they received it. On a totally different level, one host's "resistance to the flames" gave rise to a Miracle cult that inspired a city and a faith community for centuries. The Eucharist was and remains the most important sacrament in the liturgy of the Roman Catholic Church. By contrast, the nineteenth century especially has gone down in Catholic church history as the century of Mary, given her many apparitions and the places of pilgrimage to which they gave rise. In the devotional life of most Catholics, Mary occupied first place. Her "closeness" as a mother and her miraculous power were important causes of this devotion.[295]

To provide a fittingly theological counterweight to the often instrumental and sentimental forms of Marian devotion, the church from the last quarter of the nineteenth century onward began to emphasize the Christocentric and Eucharistic dimensions of the faith in liturgical, theological, and pastoral contexts. One expression of this tendency was the international liturgical movement, and, especially in Flanders and the Netherlands, the so-called Eucharistic Crusade, a children's movement initiated by the Flemish priest Edward Poppe that focused on self-sanctification and the struggle against materialism, naturalism, and selfishness. In addition, successive popes stimulated devotion to the Sacred Heart of Jesus. In 1875 Pope Pius IX consecrated the entire church to the Sacred Heart; in 1899 his successor, Leo XIII, did the same for the entire world. In the early twentieth century, a Chilean religious priest invented the ritual of the so-called enthronement of the Sacred Heart. This involved a priest blessing a statue of the Sacred Heart for a particular family, whereupon the statue, as the symbolic head of the family, was placed in a prominent spot in the home. The ritual was a particular success among Dutch and Flemish Catholics.[296] The pastor of the Begijnhof tried to capitalize on this new trend for the benefit of Amsterdam's own Miracle. The Nederlandsche Eucharistische Bond, or Dutch Eucharistic Union, established in Amsterdam, launched a new monthly journal in 1919 called *De Heilige Eucharistie* (The Blessed Eucharist) to spread theological and liturgical knowledge about the sacrament of the Eucharist among Catholics and to give it a more prominent place in daily life.[297] One material expression of this was the enthronement of a statue of the Sacred Heart in the middle of the Begijnhof in 1920.[298]

In 1881, the year the Silent Walk began, an international Eucharistic congress was organized in Lille at the initiative of the French religious sister Marie-Marthe Emilie Tamisier. This formula became a great success in international Catholicism; Rome set up a permanent committee charged with organizing international Eucharistic congresses on a regular basis.[299]

As the city of the miraculous host, Amsterdam was initially chosen as the venue of the 1920 congress, but this proved unfeasible. At the end of World War I, Rector Bosman, together with Stolk, pastor of St. Catharine's Church, investigated the possibilities of convening a large-scale congress, preferably using the infrastructure of the Miracle cult, that is, the Society, with its large lay network. They thought the best strategy was to proceed in two stages. They first devised a plan in 1920 to have a diocesan or "national" Eucharistic congress during the Miracle week, which could serve as a "rehearsal" for the Amsterdam Social Action Committee and the Society of the Silent Walk for a subsequent international congress.

When the diocesan congress eventually took place in October 1922, the contrast with the annual Silent Walk could not be more marked: participants from across the Netherlands came together in Amsterdam's biggest "cathedral," Willibrordus buiten de Veste (St. Willibrord's outside the ramparts, now demolished), and held a "stadium meeting." The Amsterdam Franciscan Borromeus de Greeve—the "orator of Catholic emancipation"—gave a speech and generally radiated "Catholic Glory."[300] He seized the opportunity to exhort the faithful against the modernisms of the interwar years, including naturalism, divorce, sport, fashion, and "modern love which blooms too early." At the same time he warned against Catholics' growing immunity to spiritual things and to a truly Eucharistic life. His words did not fall on deaf ears. The congress was a resounding success, thanks in large part to Van den Broeke, who had been one of the organizers. The congress gave a further boost to participation in the Silent Walk.[301]

The congress proceedings contained a futurological contribution from a seemingly visionary monk of the abbey of Egmond. In this article, he described the tenth centenary of the Miracle, in the year 2345, with countless airplanes landing in Amsterdam and the roads to the city thronged with groups of pilgrims coming from all directions. They would all participate in an enormous procession lasting for hours, including no fewer than a hundred bishops from abroad.[302] Klönne's triumphalist spirit had come to life again, if only briefly. The congress's festive displays and aspirations for the future inspired Van den Broeke to sound a sobering note by announcing that the "Silent Walk should remain a silent prayer." The only aspect of the Egmond monk's vision that turned out to be wrong, however, was its projected timeframe, as the rest of it came true—more or less—only two years later.

The ambitions of Dutch Catholics in those years were no longer as modest as they had been. The diocesan congress had been conceived as a prelude to the real event: the international congress. To help realize this aspiration, the organizers invited the bishop of Namur, Thomas L. Heylen, the chairman of the international committee. He was so inspired by the organization he encountered in the Netherlands that the international committee decided to award the hosting of the twenty-seventh Eucharistic Congress in July 1924 to Amsterdam.[303] It was the fruit of a complicated process that involved skirting around all manner of sensitivities. In the first place, organizing a manifestation such as this one was itself an affront to the Netherlands' "Protestant identity"; secondly, the nature, scale, liturgy, and international aspect of the congress posed a challenge to interdenominational and political relations in the country. For non-Catholics—for instance, Protestants—the pomp and circumstance that would accompany the congress flouted the procession ban. Even Prime Minister Ruijs de Beerenbrouck found it difficult to overcome his "innate Catholic reticence" and spoke mainly of difficulties. In an abundance of caution, Bishop Callier of Haarlem decided it would be best not to make a personal bid for the organization of the congress to the international committee. It had to seem as if the committee had spontaneously appointed Amsterdam of its own initiative. This is in fact what happened.[304]

The committee's decision was ultimately based on the strong symbolic significance of the Eucharistic miracle of 1345. Reactions to it were ecstatic. Sterck, the historian of the Miracle, saw it as "God returning home" to the city he had chosen in the past as his Holy Stead.[305] Schaepman rechristened Amsterdam as "Bread City on the IJ," while the publicist J. Scheerboom pointed out that the Catholic world would crown the capital as City of the Eucharist.

When the congress finally opened in July 1924, Pope Pius XI addressed a brief to the Catholics of the Netherlands, dated July 2, in which he visualized the Silent Walk as an "immense pageant." He interpreted this not only as a Dutch profession of faith, but also as the legitimate "desire for full freedom of Catholic worship."[306] This strongly political signal from Rome, an unmistakable reference to the procession ban, was reminiscent of the rhetoric used in the 1853 papal bull establishing the new dioceses.

Designing the layout of the pageant in question and the grand procession in the stadium was left to trusted helpers. The artistic poster was designed by the convert Jan Toorop, a symbolist artist, while the elderly Cuypers was commissioned to create the staging in the stadium.[307] To camouflage the profane character of the sports hall, he had a statue of the Sacred Heart placed over the main entrance, with angels blowing trumpets on the towers. Under their watchful gaze, a host of cardinals and an even larger host of lower-rank clergy gathered from all parts of the world, followed into the open-air temporary church by tens of thousands of laypeople, including a choir of 3,000 choirboys. The stadium attracted 120,000 Catholics. The nation's only cardinal, Willem van Rossum, officiated at the altar. He bestowed apostolic benediction, and the apotheosis of the congress was formed by the seemingly endless, solemn procession through and around the stadium.[308] The procession moved slowly, and church historian Anton Hensen exclaimed, thinking of the practice of the Silent Walk, "We Dutch have still to learn properly how to walk in a procession."[309] The whole demonstration was recorded for posterity in the four-part film *Adoro te*.[310]

Dutch Catholics in blissful complacency congratulated themselves on the congress: it had been "indescribably beautiful," even "worthy of Raphael's brush." They also saw it as a confirmation of their exemplary obedience to the hierarchy of the church.[311] It was a triumphant demonstration of the kind of Dutch Catholicism that vied to outdo all others in Catholic ardor. Given this kind of exulting by Catholics, the reactions from Dutch Protestants were remarkably subdued. It is true that a protest meeting was held in the city, and Protestant newspapers perfunctorily complained about "damnable idolatry."[312] On the whole, however, the event was of immense "profit to Catholics."[313] The massive pageant of the congress may well be regarded as the apotheosis of Dutch Catholic emancipation: it could not be outdone. Drawn by the old Miracle, which had already enthralled so many, the epicenter of world Catholicism had temporarily come to Amsterdam, propagating the faith with greater pride and glory than ever before. What more could Catholics wish for?

A visual echo of the 1924 procession came in 1933 to what had since then become the Olympic Stadium in Amsterdam. On the occasion of the Holy Year to mark the nineteenth centenary of the redemption, this stadium hosted a performance of the Eucharistic dramatic play *The Miracle of Amsterdam*. More than 3,500 people gave a "reconstructive presentation" of Derkinderen's painting of the medieval Miracle procession. It was a day "full of glorious Catholic enthusiasm," in the opinion of the *Katholieke Illustratie*.[314]

Politics and Ideology: The Interwar Years and World War II

Every year, the power of the Silent Walk could be experienced unmistakably, directly, in the streets of Amsterdam. So many people walking closely together, moving through the public space without the slightest sound and without displaying any attribute to attract attention—this was an extraordinary phenomenon. Participants were frequently accosted by puzzled outsiders; there is the story of one young woman, who, confronted suddenly by the parade, joined for a while, repeating the question, "But what are you demonstrating against?" The pilgrims, deep in prayer, gave no reply.[315]

The format of the walk was self-evidently ritual and meditative, but in its performativity it was also in a certain sense unnatural. Normally speaking, some vocal sound would come from such a large group of people. Because group marches are in fact often protest-related, it is easy to see why the Walk was often mistaken for a demonstration by those who had had no explanation or were unacquainted with it. As Father Winkel put it, "The silent nocturnal demonstration of tens of thousands of Catholics makes a much bigger impression on non-Catholic countrymen than any other Catholic demonstration would." This was not only the experience of outsiders, and the participants themselves were told to "resist the understandable, but injudicious desire to turn the Silent Walk into a kind of parade or demonstration."[316]

The "demonstration" that Winkel mentioned was linked, of course, to the constitutional ban on practicing Catholic rituals in the public domain. This procession ban, which had been part of the constitution since 1848, remained a thorn in the flesh of Dutch Catholics. The success of the Silent Walk as a substitute for a procession therefore kept drawing attention to this "injustice." That the Silent Walk was viewed in this light in Catholic circles is evident from the fact that members of the board sometimes received compliments for having made excellent "propaganda."[317] Later, in 1972, at a time of postconciliar ecumenical feeling, the then chairman of the Society, Eduard Elsenburg, addressed the fact that this function of the Silent Walk had disappeared: "The Silent Walk, which in former times may unknowingly have found its strength in the struggle for Catholic emancipation, as a way of claiming one's position, as an expression of triumphant revival, seems to have lost its meaning today."[318]

However much Lousbergh initially rejected any "political" or "demonstrative" connotation, the Walk was never entirely free from these, often implicitly and in full conformity with Lousbergh's principles. One example is the fact that attention and tacit support for the Catholic cause were a fixed aspect of the ritual practice of the Silent Walk. Every year, the participants were asked to pray for three intentions in particular on their journey. It was claimed that these prayer moments were based on "old custom," but their content primarily manifested the initiators' own nineteenth-century preoccupations. Pilgrims were asked to pray for king and country as they crossed Dam square, with its Royal Palace and its symbolic confirmation of the nation-state. A second—old—intention was linked to Nieuwenbrug on the IJ, where pilgrims were requested to pray for seamen and those who had perished at sea, reflecting Amsterdam's maritime culture. Finally, with the Holy Stead in sight on Langebrug, they were asked to pray for the Catholic Church, the pope, and the restoration of unity among Christians. The latter formula was a euphemism for the conversion of Dutch Protestants to the Catholic faith. Not only did the Walk pray for the nation-state and the royal family, but it also had a missionary—ultramontane and anti-Protestant—aspect.[319]

The Silent Walk was also used to address other concerns of the institutional church, for instance in 1906, when the dean of Amsterdam, Michael J. A. Lans, lamented the growing number of lapsed Catholics (7.2 percent at the time) and an increase in mixed marriages. He averred the existence of a "modern spirit" that was penetrating Catholic families as he heard parents complain that their older children were no longer practicing because of the "Socialist climate." Lans counseled them to make the Silent Walk for the conversion of their families, if needs be outside the Miracle week.[320]

Other religious and political groups became aware of the Silent Walk's existence when non-Catholic journals began to write about it for the first time, also in 1906. This sometimes resulted in attacks on participants.[321] When a non-Catholic paper in Haarlem published the starting time of the Walk, "several Socialists, drunkards and other rabble-rousers" posted themselves at Haarlemmerweg near Amsterdamse Poort, where they tried to obstruct and mock pilgrims entering the city and pelt them with sand.[322]

The fact that the Catholic community was growing, creating more and more societal connections, sometimes threatened the neutrality of the Walk. Although the board itself believed that the Walk had succeeded in protecting its "innocence" in this respect, this was not really true as the board itself proved willing to engage with current events from time to time. In addition to the national-political issue of the procession ban, which the Walk implicitly contested, it also became involved in other local-political or international questions. The board had previously taken a stand for king and country, and it did the same in 1911 for the protection of the church and the pope. The Walk drew greater crowds that year because a number of church associations had asked their members on behalf of the pope to offer "Eucharistic reparation" for the insults offered to Christ in Italy.[323] This turned that year's Walk into a demonstration protesting the fiftieth birthday of "supposedly United Italy," the foundation of the Kingdom of Italy under Victor Emmanuel II, which had ushered in the end of the Papal States.[324]

An extra Silent Walk was organized for the first time in the summer of 1914 for peace in Europe, and the Walk's prayer intention in 1916 was "for peace very soon," the board allowing soldiers in uniform to participate for the first time. After 1917, when the board of the "circle of friends" discarded its anonymity and became an official church society, the Walk's intentions frequently reflected national and international politics. During these years, according to secretary Takes, "some wanted to turn it into a demonstration," a development that intervention by the board managed to prevent, although its previous actions had themselves contributed to the development they were now trying to block.[325]

A few days after the end of World War I, the board again decided to organize an extra Silent Walk on account of the Spanish influenza epidemic that afflicted Amsterdam in 1918. This Walk, held on November 17, acquired the character of a public manifestation of supplication.[326] It was held at the behest of Rector Bosman, who had proposed to hold an extra Walk to bring the lethal epidemic to a halt with God's help. Although this Walk served a specific societal goal, less than a week later, on Saturday, November 23, the Society of the Walk publicly joined thousands of other Dutchmen and -women of diverse backgrounds in a political rally to protest against the communist plans of "revolutionaries" and specifically against Pieter Jelles Troelstra's failed (putative) revolution attempt.[327] The Society proudly bore aloft a procession banner with the year 1345 embroidered on it.[328] The minutes stated, "In this way the board tried to intervene actively this year." It would not be the last time it did so. The fear of communism was discussed regularly during board meetings.[329]

As a successful Catholic demonstration, the Silent Walk from time to time irritated marginal political or religious groups in society. In 1923 the board received word that the freethinkers' association De Dageraad (The dawn) was making plans on the day before the Walk to disrupt it. This was followed by a phone call intimating that the Evangelical Party from Haarlem was also planning to come and disturb the Walk under the leadership of the famous anticlerical lawyer Pieter Tideman. It turned out to be false alarm.[330] In 1931, the year of the golden jubilee, the board decided it was better to be safe than sorry and used Catholic "strong-arm boys" to protect the pilgrims from canvassers who stood along the route with insinuating anti-Catholic publications and brochures.[331] Much was made of this in the press. When the well-known anti-Catholic canvasser Miss Bon and twenty helpers took up position on Dam square the following year to hand out leaflets during the Walk, the police intervened immediately.[332] Another incident took place in 1935 involving so-called communists intent on disrupting the Walk. On the Sunday night of the Walk, some thirty men shouted slogans such as "Fascism is murder" on the corner of Martelaarsgracht and Nieuwendijk and then went in among the participants. Police officers and detectives bearing batons and sabers pursued them and were able to chase off the "reds."[333]

The godlessness of the communist and socialist worldviews frightened thoroughly Christian Dutch society. In 1937 the intention of the Walk was "That God may protect our fatherland against communism and any other new paganism." The attendance of the internuncio at the opening of the feast signaled Vatican moral support for this. The Silent Walk of this era was a far cry from what it had been in Lousbergh's time. As emancipation progressed, the members of the board increasingly regarded themselves as loyal citizens of the state, despite denominational differences in society, and they adapted their policies likewise.

The hostility between Catholics, Protestants, socialists, and communists notwithstanding—a hostility all parties fostered—on the eve of the war representatives of the different mentalities were sometimes able to discover common ground. Thus Asser B. Kleerekoper, a Jewish columnist for the socialist newspaper *Het Volk*, suddenly began to write appreciatively about the Silent Walk.[334] This "Rebellious Scribbler"—his pseudonym—saw the beauty of the "silent introversion" of the Walk amid the conflict and bewilderment in Europe, and he called for understanding for this "inaudible mass demonstration." He regarded the Walk as a moral protest against the military parades and political demonstrations that were daily occurrences in cities such as Vienna and Warsaw at the time. Kleerekoper explicitly referred to that year's intention of the Walk, against war and for peace, and praised the Walk for this. He concluded, however, by expressing the hope that the participants and supporters would show the same unyielding determination when it came to justice in the world in their daily lives. This was probably a reference to the injustices that were being perpetrated against the Jews. Several Catholic newspapers were pleasantly surprised by these positive comments from wholly unexpected quarters; others reprinted the column in whole or in part. Even the liberal *NRC* newspaper made positive reference to the Walk on the eve of war and occupation, calling it "a prayer for justice, for peace."[335] Thus outsiders gave the Walk a new ecumenical meaning, as an initiative of silence and moral reflection. It was as if wartime conditions brought a latent wider significance of the ritual to the surface, showing a glimpse of how open this ritual could in fact become.

Apart from these skirmishes with ideological adversaries—on balance they were relatively insignificant—the Walk's strongest political significance perhaps was the least obvious one: the fact that it was there at all. Its success surprised even Catholics, as they regularly testified in the press. *De Tijd* commented that "the people pray and hold their annual Walk! The Silent Walk has become a unique Dutch heritage, a totally original form and devotion."[336] In 1938 *De Tijd* evaluated the tradition for the benefit of the Catholic community under the heading "The power of silence."[337] The newspaper observed "the irresistible power of silence: more crushing than the most powerful police action." The Walk was compared to "an enormous serpent," a ceaseless silent progression of people through the city's narrow streets. This is precisely what it must have looked like. An almost unimaginable Catholic invasion of the capital dominated the center during the night of the Walk. Newspapers characterized the ritual as an "annual pilgrimage unique" in the world, both qualitatively and quantitatively. It was clear that this mass gathering of people signified so much more than just collective silent contemplation. The sociologist Herbert Marcuse has called this type of ritual a form of "subversive" commemoration. Commemorating resistance against injustice, he has argued, is itself a form of resistance, and it is therefore also directed against rulers who are guilty or are liable to become guilty of injustice.[338] Lousbergh never phrased it like this, but it more or less captures his way of thinking.

War Ecumenism

The political and social unrest of the interwar years was reflected in the phenomenal growth in numbers of participants in the Walk toward the end of the 1930s. Participation was estimated to be forty-five thousand in 1937, climbing up to sixty thousand in 1939, on the eve of the war.[339] During the lead-up to the March 1940 Silent Walk, the influence of tensions in Europe and of Germany's new military offensive was becoming ever more marked. The preparatory meeting chose a prayer intention relevant to the entire country: "That our Fatherland may be spared the disasters of war." At the Nieuwebrug, pilgrims were asked to pray particularly for seafarers because of the submarine war that the Germans were waging. An even greater number of participants was expected for that year, while Nederlandse Spoorwegen (Dutch Railways) warned that there were not enough trains available for both nights of the Walk due to the mobilization. The board therefore decided to spread the Walk across three weekends instead.[340] Chairman Alphons Elsenburg announced that "All Dutch Catholics should show their sympathy and pray together, now that peace has disappeared in Europe." Each weekend more than twenty-five thousand men took part in the Walk, nearly eighty thousand in total.[341] On March 3, 1940, the first night, soldiers also participated, including four hundred members of the Colonial Reserve. Another novelty was the portable stained-glass candle lantern, in a holder of cast-iron curls, that was placed in Kalverstraat at the point of the Holy Corner during the Walk, a custom that was continued subsequently. This made visible for passing pilgrims where the Miracle had occurred. On passing the light, some pilgrims removed their hats for a moment or genuflected.

Although numbers of participants had never been an explicit consideration for the board, on this occasion chairman Elsenburg could not resist expressing his objective for the following year: "Our motto is 100,000 participants." Elsenburg was quickly disabused of this notion. The German invasion and occupation of the Netherlands in May 1940 was followed in 1941 by a ban on all manifestations after sunset. This meant the planned national sixtieth anniversary Walk on March 15, 1941, could not take place.[342] Nederlandse Spoorwegen could no longer dispose freely of its trains, the churches could not be blacked out properly, and the authorities had in any case prohibited the holding of meetings. It was obviously an insurmountable obstacle for the Silent Walk that citizens were no longer allowed out on the streets between midnight and 4:00 a.m. The Walk had to be canceled for the first time in its history. Instead, Catholics from Amsterdam and the surrounding area were encouraged to continue the tradition by making the Walk in small groups in the early morning during the Miracle week, after 4:00 a.m., as the sun rose. In the meantime the Dutch national socialist party (Nationaal-Socialistische Beweging, NSB) had also discovered the Walk as a typically Dutch custom, and the police that year had to prevent members from spreading propaganda among pilgrims walking the route.[343]

The extent to which the Walk had been interiorized as a national ritual was evident from the fact that attempts were made across the country to ensure at all costs that the tradition of the Walk would not be broken. Sister societies organized their own Miracle celebrations in their own towns and cities, sometimes with a candlelight procession in the church as an alternative to the Silent Walk. To preserve the idea of a pilgrimage, sister societies also organized journeys or pilgrimages to alternative shrines. Thus the Ammerzoden sister society set out with three hundred pilgrims on a seven-and-a-half-mile walk to the shrine of Our Lady of 's-Hertogenbosch on March 16. There, a candlelit Eucharistic procession was held in the cathedral "to commemorate" the Amsterdam Silent Walk. In Bergen in North Holland, which itself had for centuries venerated its own miracle of the Precious Blood, a Miracle procession was organized in St. Peter Canisius's retreat house, and in Boxmeer, far away along the border, organizers were bold enough to hold a silent walk of more than one thousand participants through the streets. In cities such as Delft and Schiedam, the day of the Miracle was marked by benediction and a procession in the church. Pilgrims from across South Limburg joined in silent pilgrimage to Meerssen, which was, just like Amsterdam, a medieval shrine of a Sacrament of Miracle, albeit a regional one. In Gouda, the necessity of preserving the continuity of the Walk was felt so strongly that the local society decided to go to Amsterdam with a small group to make the Walk on behalf of all Gouda members.[344] Wartime conditions also gave the Walk a new popularity among non-Catholics. Many sought hope in the ritual or turned to it to ask for assistance "from above" for their personal problems. Tradition has it that the Jewish goldsmith Joseph Citroen made the Walk, praying for survival.[345] Relatives of prisoners of war and of forced laborers sent to Germany, people from all denominational backgrounds, made up to three personal Walks a week to pray for their well-being.

The German ban on manifestations did not stop the Amsterdam board from announcing an extra daytime Silent Walk six months later, on Sunday, November 24, for victims of the war, prisoners, and exiles, and also for peace.[346] When it became clear in early 1942 that the war was far from over and that the authorities would ban all manifestations, the Society proposed a new intention: "for a swift and just peace," although the Walk that year could only be made individually. Because Elsenburg expected that many pilgrims would attempt to make the Walk early in the morning despite the circumstances, and because organizers were not permitted to be present, he decided it was best to inform the German authorities. As a result a number of police officers were deployed to maintain order.[347] At the same time, Bishop Johannes Huijbers celebrated the feast of the Miracle as usual with pontifical benediction in the seclusion of the Begijn-hofkerk.

In those years, the Society employed the Amsterdam press agency Vaz Dias to collect press cuttings related to the Walk. The Society kept them in large scrapbooks, a stream of news that rapidly dwindled in 1942 and 1943.[348] Because conditions in the country were deteriorating, the Society again announced that there would be no organized Walk in 1944; it advised every sister society to arrange to celebrate the Miracle itself. The Society spread an information sheet in Amsterdam and the surrounding region inviting inhabitants to make the Walk once or more often, but individually or in groups of at most three or four people.[349] Thousands of Catholics heeded the call.[350] Among them was leading cultural figure and writer Anton van Duinkerken (pseudonym of Willem Asselbergs, 1903–1968), who dedicated a war poem to the many people who "were starving in body and spirit."[351] The difficult circumstances, the war, and the famine that marked the last winter of the occupation (1944–1945) led to a revival of religiosity. It inspired the Reformed historian Magdalena G. Schenk to write a book to which she gave the noteworthy title of *Amsterdam, stad van vroomheid* (Amsterdam, city of piety).

Although many years of preparation and fundraising had gone before, the grand celebration of the sixth centenary of the Miracle, planned for March 1945, had to be postponed as the country was still partially occupied. Rector Van Noort instead urged a spiritual focus, using the feast in March to promote among all who were unsettled by the war, and the thousands who would soon be returning from Germany, "a kind of spiritual renewal." For the time being, however, Amsterdam was paralyzed by the war, immobilized by hunger and cold. The church on the Begijnhof nevertheless filled up again during the Miracle week; as one commentator observed, the citizens of Amsterdam did not want to let the centenary pass unnoticed.[352]

Finally, on May 5, 1945, the country was officially liberated. On the following day, the first Catholics from Amsterdam were already making individual Silent Walks. The Society called on the Catholics of Amsterdam to make a more formal Silent Walk once or more often during the week of May 31 to June 8 to thank God that Amsterdam had been (mostly) spared.

Pastor J. Kuilman of St. Mary Magdalene's parish in Spaarndammerbuurt, a Catholic enclave in Amsterdam, even obtained permission from the police chief commissioner to hold his own Silent Walk with parishioners on June 3.[353] This initiative was also to thank God for the preservation of the city and fulfilled a collective vow taken in the parish in September 1944. Other extra Silent Walks were held in the fall of that year.[354]

The only violence that the Silent Walk encountered took place a year after the liberation, when an inebriated Canadian soldier fired a number of shots at a group of pilgrims arriving in Leidsestraat to take part in the Silent Walk, dispersing them in a panic.[355]

The Postwar Cult: Climax and Catharsis

The decades following World War II brought changes to many aspects of Dutch society, as they did elsewhere in Western Europe. Some processes had already been underway before the war and were revived with new energy in 1945, while other developments were entirely new.

During the five difficult years of the war, the Dutch had developed closer ties to each other. Party political and denominational differences were temporarily downplayed. Many felt that the end of the war signaled the start of a new era and the birth of a new, more modern society. In this new society, the growth of affluence would more or less keep pace with secularization and the modernization of daily life. The general synod of the Reformed Church, of all bodies, stated that the culture of pillarization was no longer appropriate for modern Dutch society. As far as the synod was concerned, the "unfree" public space might now be made totally free, an implicit reference to the Silent Walk as a forced alternative for a procession.[356] What had been an ideologically divided class society was slowly transforming into a strongly individualized welfare society that prized material gains above all else while the churches faded away. Christian faith communities became less concerned about what happened within the formal confines of their church organizations. These changes were evident first in the big cities. One Catholic priest spoke the following prophetic words to the *Nieuws van de Dag* (News of the day) newspaper in 1946: "We will retain the core of our people. They will remain faithful to the Church. But we will lose the rest." And he continued—in words typical of the 1950s—"They will begin to neglect their duties, will fall away and start to listen to those who promise them the most: the Communists."

This latter part of his statement proved to be less prophetic than the former, but it was characteristic of the ideological climate of the time.

Despite the innovations and the general sense of optimism that pervaded postwar reconstruction, society fell back to a certain extent on structures and processes that had been begun before the war. Exuberant Catholic religious practice, which had emerged from and was linked to the pillarized Catholicism of the interwar years, managed to continue for another decade after the war. The practice of the Silent Walk must also be seen in the light of this continuity that stretched across the war. By 1946, as soon as the Netherlands had morally and logistically recovered somewhat from the war, the Silent Walk returned in all its glory to Amsterdam's city center. The veneration of the Miracle experienced its absolute zenith in quantitative terms in these years. Although rapidly increasing secularization was strongly in evidence in Amsterdam, in the rest of the country prewar patterns of devotionalism remained strong for a while and interest in the Miracle of Amsterdam was unfaltering.[357] The system of spreading the Walk over three nights, introduced in 1940 as a one-off expedient, had to be hastily repeated in March 1946 to permit the immense throngs of pilgrims to pass through the city's narrow streets.[358]

The Sixth Centenary

The delayed liberation and the last year of the war, so dramatic for the Netherlands with its famine winter, threw plans for the celebration of the sixth centenary of the Miracle in 1945 into complete disarray. Celebrations had long been in preparation under the leadership of the dean of Amsterdam, Gerard P. J. van der Burg, and leading Catholic cultural figure Van Duinkerken.[359] A fund had been set up in 1937 under the name "1345–1945," with the intention of financing as magnificent a celebration as possible. All of the "Six Centuries" Committee's plans had to be canceled, including a centenary indulgence granted by the pope.[360]

Shortly after the liberation on May 5, it was decided to postpone the sixth centenary for a year. The new date was June 19 to 23, 1946, and the venue was the Olympic Stadium.[361] This date—later in the season than usual—was chosen, among other things, because the weather was expected to be better around Corpus Christi. It was also judged to be more fitting to hold the Miracle feast after the national celebration of the liberation on May 4, 1946, which would take place in the same Olympic

Stadium. Incidentally, as the liberation celebration was also being organized by Van Duinkerken, it was an excellent "dress rehearsal."[362]

The highlight of the sixth centenary celebrations was a performance
called "The Triumph of the Sacrament of Miracle," an exuberantly theatrical and richly iconographic pageant that was wholly in line with Catholic
celebratory traditions, and in particular with the International Eucharistic
Congress of 1924.[363] The press praised the "religious courage of Catholic
Amsterdam," which had once again transformed the stadium into an
"open-air cathedral," a giant symbolic Holy Stead.[364] This was no exaggeration. On the morning of the 23rd, mass was celebrated in the stadium for
no fewer than 43,045 participants, while the afternoon saw a performance
of *Liturgische Praeludium* (Liturgical prelude) in the presence of the entire
Dutch episcopate. This theatrical performance saw 6,000 boys and girls
from Amsterdam youth organizations depicting historical scenes from six
centuries of Miracle history. Predictably, the day concluded with a massive
Eucharistic procession on the cinder track, in which approximately 4,000
flower girls, singers, acolytes, religious, priests, abbots, and bishops took
part. At the end, Cardinal Johannes de Jong gave benediction with the
Blessed Sacrament to 53,000 attendants in the stands.[365]

Encouraged by the flawless execution of "his" celebration, Van Duinkerken spontaneously suggested that Amsterdam should now become the
country's primary place of pilgrimage and should host magnificent processions.[366] Even he temporarily succumbed to the Amsterdam "procession syndrome" in his overconfidence, forgetting the uniqueness of the
Silent Walk. But he was right about Amsterdam as a shrine: the Miracle
was still the country's most important place of pilgrimage.[367]

It was not long before fragile "war ecumenism" crumbled and society
returned to the old, pillarized structures and to anti-Catholic feeling. In
1947 the General Synod of the Dutch Reformed Church protested to the
minister for justice against infractions of the procession ban.[368] This
started a renewed legal offensive against such breaches and soon relegated
to the past the triumphalist vision of magnificent processions that had
briefly beguiled Van Duinkerken, as a latter-day Klönne.

Every Dutch Catholic knew that there was such a thing as the procession ban, and, in Rogier's evocative words of 1946, they experienced this
as "the false shame, which holds us back from manifesting publicly many
of the things that are holy, a natural result . . . of the forced position in
which our seventeenth-century fathers lived. Not to give offense, this is an
iron law, which is still passed onto Catholic children with their mother's

milk."[369] Rogier assumed that "*if* the procession ban were ever to be lifted, most pastors in Holland would still raise many objections, and great resistance would have to be overcome, which, as a hereditary trait, holds them back from anything that might draw attention to themselves."[370] In fact, it would not come to that anymore. Undoubtedly, most participants of the Silent Walk shared the feeling that Rogier described. They had been raised in a tradition of silence and were not keen on giving up their characteristic and valued ritual. The Silent Walk was a kind of ritual sublimation, one that at the same time cocked a snook at Dutch Protestantism. Van Duinkerken also realized this and somewhat pathetically and metaphorically concluded that "the glow of the solemn procession had perhaps reached its most searing intensity in the Silent Walk."[371]

The Miracle cult and the Walk flourished for about a decade before an unprecedentedly sharp decline occurred in the 1960s, as the next chapter will show.

War Symbiosis: From Silent Walk to Silent March

As has been seen, the war, the Dutch nation's humiliation, and the suffering that had been inflicted on the entire population caused existing social, denominational, political, and emotional divisions to be temporarily set aside. Certainly during the famine winter of 1944 to 1945, the main preoccupation was to survive together. Collective suffering brought about a new unity in diversity, with a certain degree of fraternization that lingered for a short while after the war.[372]

Directly after the liberation, the Dutch government set up committees to consider how the national liberation of May 5, 1945, as well as the victims of the war, could be commemorated.[373] The aim was to come "to a more profound national consciousness and to strengthen national solidarity."[374] Van Duinkerken, who had been living in Amsterdam since 1929 and who enjoyed wide national prestige as an intellectual, decided to answer the call. Immediately after the liberation, he was appointed chairman of a Committee for the Celebration of Liberation Day, part of a newly founded National Institute, a body set up to foster national consciousness and strengthen solidarity.[375] As a faithful participant in the Silent Walk, and as member of the Catholic committee for the celebration of the sixth centenary of the Miracle, he, more than anyone else, was convinced of the immanent power and dignity of collectively walking in silence.[376] The acting mayor of Amsterdam, Feike de Boer, appointed him chairman of

the Amsterdam celebration committee in May 1945. Just as the Silent
Walk was also an annual commemoration of the Miracle, Van Duinkerken
believed that it was very important that the liberation and the victims of
the war should be silently commemorated in the form of a march. Therefore, he argued that there should be silent *marches* as the national format
for the mourning and commemoration ritual that he was charged with
designing, to be held on the eve of May 5.[377] The committee's first plans
called for a static minute of silence, a stationary commemorative practice
copied from the city of London.[378]

In anticipation of a definitive format for the commemoration, Prime
Minister Pieter Sjoerds Gerbrandy designated Queen Wilhelmina's up-
coming birthday, August 31, 1945, as a one-off national day of liberation.[379]
Inspired by the various formats suggested, unofficial silent commemorative marches to former places of execution were held for the first time on
the eve of the queen's birthday.[380] These spontaneous initiatives were in
fact a form of civil disobedience because they disregarded the government's intention of organizing only one celebration of the liberation in
1945. The movement inspired former resistance fighter Jan Drop to set up
a Committee for National Commemoration 1940–1945 in The Hague. Because many people were impressed by the silent marches of August 30,
1945, the committee suggested that the evening before Liberation Day
should be designated as a National Evening of Commemoration. It proposed that from May 3 or 4, 1946, everyone should be given the opportunity to participate in a "so-called 'silent walk,'"[381] a march of approximately
thirty minutes, which in the case of The Hague would lead to Waalsdorpervlakte, which had been a place of execution during the occupation.[382]
The nomenclature used was an unequivocal reference to the organizers'
source of inspiration, the renowned Amsterdam Silent Walk, to which
they compared their own ritual.[383]

Drop managed to persuade the Vereniging Nederlandse Gemeenten,
the Dutch association of municipal authorities, to send all mayors a letter
requesting them to follow his initiative, and his plan soon received official
backing. The idea of a silent march followed by two minutes of silence was
received so positively across the country that neither the government nor
the National Institute could afford to ignore it. Thus the proposals of Van
Duinkerken's Amsterdam committee and of the Committee for National
Commemoration were combined. The result was that on May 4, 1946,
silent marches passed through each of the approximately six hundred
municipalities of the Netherlands, with hundreds of thousands of partici-

pants. The best known of these marches are still the one to Waalsdorper-vlakte in The Hague, and another one to the war cemetery in Overveen near Bloemendaal, where hundreds of executed resistance fighters are commemorated.[384]

It must have been evident to contemporaries that the new ritual was an imitation of the Silent Walk—"a national copy"—organized, moreover, at the behest of one man, among others, who was himself a celebrated participant of the Walk.[385] It is likely that the effects of the war and of "liberation ecumenism" ensured that the Catholic connotations of this new national commemoration did not seem objectionable to anyone.[386] In fact, the "neutral" format of the Walk had never caused resistance among non-Catholics even in the past. It did not appear objectionable or too Catholic. Even in the strictly Calvinist town of Putten, the many victims of the war were commemorated in what was known locally as "a silent walk," which because of its simple and introverted character was more impres-sive than "any grandiose demonstration could have been."[387]

These silent commemorative marches were a resounding success from the start. Just as the Silent Walk, their collective and minimalist ritual, serene, spiritual, and dignified, was also an implicit protest: "never again [war]." The nomenclature was soon standardized to *silent marches* to en-sure uniformity across the country and to avoid confusion with the Si-lent Walk.

Silent marches essentially were and are accessible and nonhierarchical rituals that anyone can participate in without prior conditions. The news-papers reported on the marches of May 4, 1946, by emphasizing the eu-phoria of the participants who experienced profound solidarity with each other.[388] These commemorative marches took place without external signs and without distinction of rank or position, but an exception was made for the immediate relatives of the victims, who were asked to walk at the head of the march.[389]

There is another similarity with the Silent Walk. Silent marches were not only a form of commemoration or subversive commemoration, but also a tribute. They have been called "pilgrimages" to holy places where fallen war heroes lie. A reporter of *Het Parool* expressed this as early as 1946 when he wrote, "An endless stream of people went that evening to the symbolic tomb [on Waalsdorpervlakte] as if on a pilgrimage."[390]

The Amsterdam Silent Walk served as a model for national silent com-memorative marches that still exist, but there was also reverse influence. In the late 1940s, a fourth prayer moment ("intention") was added to the three traditional ones observed during the Silent Walk. As they passed the national war monument on Dam square, the participants were asked to pray for the victims of the war. In this way, the Silent Walk in a certain sense also became a silent march.

The emergence of silent marches proves once again how strong the impact of the Silent Walk on various aspects of society has been. This post-war example of the diversification of the Walk formula was itself a direct prelude to the new mourning and commemoration rituals that emerged in the 1990s, when *the* silent march became a new ritual of mourning following trauma or crisis situations in society.

A bird's-eye view of Amsterdam. Map (116 x 159 cm) made in 1538 by Cornelis Anthonisz. Amsterdam Museum (inv. no. SA 3009).

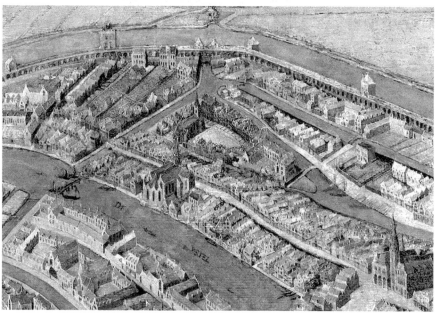

Detail of the bird's-eye view map: the Holy Stead on the Amstel; immediately behind it the Begijnhof, on the other side of Kalverstraat.

Afbeelding van 't Glas, door den Aartshertoge MAXIMILIAAN, in of omtrent den jaare 1484, vereerd, in de KAPEL der HEILIGE STEDE, nu de NIEUWE-ZYDS-KAPEL.

Schets der KISTE, waar in de MIRACULEUSE HOSTIE, te Amsterdam, allereerst zou gelegd geweest zyn.

Top: Stained-glass window (1509) from the Nieuwezijds Kapel, removed in 1832. *Left:* Maximilian of Austria, Mary of Burgundy, and Bianca Maria Sforza. *Right:* Philip the Handsome, Joanne of Castile, and their six children.

Bottom: The so-called Miracle chest recovered in the Burgerweeshuis in the eighteenth century.

Double engraving in Jan Wagenaar, *Geschiedenis van Amsterdam* (1765).

Scenes from the Miracle story: the
woman places the host in a chest
(*bottom*); the pastor places the host
in a ciborium (*center*); the host is
brought to Oude Kerk in procession
(*top*). This canvas (113 x 41.5 cm) is
part of a series on the Miracle made
by Jacob Cornelisz. van Oostsanen
ca. 1515. Amsterdam Museum
(inv. no. SB 5411).

Colored devotional print of the Miracle of Amsterdam. Wood engraving (15 x 23 cm) by Jacob Cornelisz. van Oostsanen from 1518. Rijksmuseum Amsterdam (inv. RP-P-1877-A-219).

As she warms her feet, the woman suddenly recognizes the host in the fire; two angels also appear startled. This embroidery from 1530 was applied to an older cushion (66 x 70 cm), one of a series of four. Maximilian of Austria allegedly knelt on one of these cushions during his visit to the Holy Stead in 1484. Amsterdam Museum (B 1721).

After the miracle in the fire, the Sacrament of Miracle was brought back to Oude Kerk in a ciborium, accompanied by the entire clergy of Amsterdam. Part of a banner from 1555 that was carried in Miracle processions up to the Alteration. Amsterdam Museum (B 1652).

Emblem of the Holy Stead, fastened to pilgrims' clothes after a visit to the shrine. Found during excavations on Rokin in 2006; tin-lead alloy, 1475–1525. Bureau Monumenten & Archeologie Amsterdam / Museum Ons' Lieve Heer op Solder.

The handing over of silver objects that pilgrims had presented to the Holy Stead over the centuries permitted the beleaguered city of Amsterdam to mint emergency coins in early 1578. Silver forty stiver coin, uniface (ca. 27 grams; ca. 46 x 47.5 mm), bearing the crowned city arms. Haarlem, Teylers Museum (TMNK 14981).

Host in a monstrance, being incensed by two angels. Historiated initial K (of the word Kyrie) in Hottinet Barra's *Missa de Venerabili Sacramento*. This precious hymn-book was given in permanent loan to "the chapel called the Holy Stead" in 1537 by Pompeius Occo and his son Sijbrandus. Brussels, Royal Library (ms IV.922).

✠ Hier beghint

die vindinghe van't hoochweerdighe/
ende heylighe Sacramant / in't vyer
ende vlam/ miraculeuselic ongequetst
ende gheheel geconserveert / het welcke rustende is binnen der Stadt van
Amstelredam/ende die plaetse
werdt ghenoemt der
Heyliger stede.

✠ Noch volghen hier na veel schoone
ende wonderlicke miraculē/ de welcke
ter selfder plaetsen gheschiedt zijn/ in
persoonen die haer beloften/offer-
handen ende gebeden daer
ghedaen hebben.

Title page of the Dutch-language pilgrim book *Hier beghint die vindinghe vant hooch-weerdighe ende heylighe Sacrament,* recounting the story of the Miracle and the later miracles. Printed on June 15, 1568, by Willem Jacobszoon in St. Annenstraat, Amsterdam. Amsterdam University Library (UBM PK 73-438).

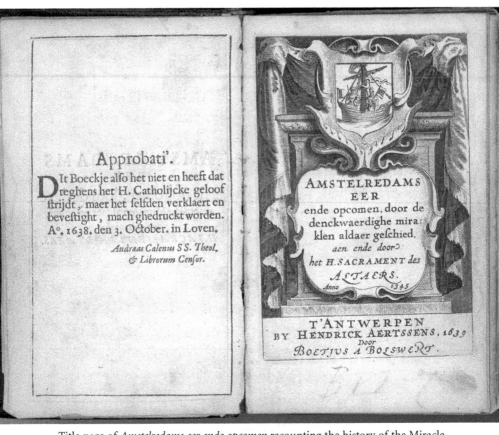

AMSTELREDAMS
EER
ende opcomen, door de
denckwaerdighe mira;
klen aldaer gefchied.
aen ende door?
het H. SACRAMENT des
ALTAERS.
Anno   1345.

T'ANTWERPEN
BY HENDRICK AERTSSENS, 1639
Door
BOETJUS A BOLSWERT.

Title page of *Amstelredams eer ende opcomen* recounting the history of the Miracle,
written by Begijnhof pastor Leonardus Marius and published in Antwerp. This edition was prepared by Marius himself. Later editions have either a mirror image of the
boat or a different publisher and place of publication.

Portrait of the learned priest Leonardus Marius in his study on the Begijnhof; painted by Claes Moeyaert in 1647, when Marius was sixty. Utrecht, Museum Catharijneconvent (StCC s24).

Entrance porch to the Nieuwezijds Kapel and the "Holy Corner," seen from Wijde Kapelsteeg. Drawing by H. P. Schouten from 1781. Part of Roelof Codde's former house can be seen behind the sweeper, the location of St. Caecilia Collegie meetings in the mid-seventeenth century. Amsterdam City Archives.

Painting (65 x 85 cm) of Rokin, with De Keyser's stock exchange in the center and the Holy Stead or Nieuwezijds Kapel on the left. Painted after 1670 in the style of Abraham Storck. Amsterdam Museum (inv. no. SA 1759).

Historical drawing (17 x 16 cm) representing the alleged written confirmation of the Sacrament of Miracle by the Amsterdam magistrates in 1346, by Jacob de Wit (1695–1754). Rijksmuseum Amsterdam (RP-T-BR-110-C).

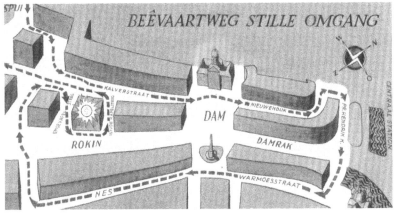

Route of the medieval Eucharistic procession and of the Silent Walk since 1881. Drawing by Jan Lammers in Amsterdam Mirakelstad from 1959.

Het *Doornebosch* ftaat gintsch in volle vlam;
't Word nochtans door de vlammen niet verflonden,
Het *Heiligdom* blinkt hier, in Amfteldam,
Tot tweemaal toe door vuur noch gloed ontbonden:
  't Zy dat het in de *Haartkolk* wierd bewaard,
En bleef in 't vuur den gantfchen nacht verfchoolen:
  't Zy daar het van de vlammen wierd gefpaard,
Die 't *Godsgebouw* veranderden in koolen.

Het *wondervuur* aan Amrams zoon vertoond,
Heeft hem gelokt om 't van naby te aanfchouwen,
  Het *Godsgeheim*, ook door het vuur verfchoond,
Noodde al het volk ook herwaarts met betrouwen.

  De Alwyze had zyn' troon in 't vuur gefticht,
't Zy toen hy vroeg aan *Mozes* zich vertoonde;
  't Zy toen hy jongst, ten blyk van 't waare licht,
Den wrevelmond toeftopte, die hem hoonde.

J. DELSING.

Engraving (9 x 11 cm) with explanatory poem by Johannes Franciscus Delsing (ca. 1745). *Top right:* Moses and the burning bush. *Center:* the miracle in the Holy Stead (with two angels). *Left:* the Holy Stead destroyed by fire while the monstrance with the Sacrament of Miracle is untouched. From Joannes Nanning, *Twee predikatiën* (1750, Nijmegen University Library).

D'WAARE AFBEELDINGE VAN HET H. SACRAMENT VAN MIRAKEL GESCHIET TOT AMSTERDAM OP DE H. STEDE in't jaar. 1345.

| Deos man die gy hier ziet, beduyt in defe prent | Maar braakte het weer uyt en meent te overlyden | Daar brant het Sacrament, gebeel en ongefchent | Sy lydt het in een kift doet het een Pryfter weten. |
| Ontfangt op't alderleft, het hylig Sacrament | Devrouw die neemt het op fmyt het in't vier ter zyden | Sy nam het in haar hant, een bier maakt fy bekent | Die haale het met triump tot glorie defer ftede. |

te Coop by Willem Meun op d hoek van t Gebedt fonder End by d ouwe Heeren Logement tot Amsterdam.

In 1729 Isaac le Long gave a satirical description of this engraving (21 x 28 cm) showing the successive stages of the Miracle narrative: "In the front, there is the sick man lying on his bed beneath a newfangled *English* pavilion, as he receives the host from the priest, whose servant and four nicely turned-out women kneel behind him. In front of the bed there is a beautiful round table, with an elegantly cut base, and which is covered with a carpet, an artfully cut crucifix, three large burning candles and a bell, and a newfangled, empty *Spanish* chair, all this on an elegant *Italian* floor."

It is striking that the Miracle itself—the host untouched by the fire—is not depicted. This engraving, which could be purchased from Willem Meun on the corner of "Gebedt sonder End bij het Ouwe Heeren Logement," is included in Nanning, *Twee predikatiën* (Nijmegen University Library).

Nine scenes from the history of the Miracle. The bottom left scene is the least known: four of her fellow sisters carry Lijsbet Franssen to the Holy Stead in 1476, where she was cured. Eighteenth-century oil painting (98 x 80 cm), hung in the Maagdenhuis. Amsterdam, Ons' Lieve Heer op Solder (AK 471).

De R. K. KERK van het BEGIJNHOF, gedurende het 5ᵈᵉ EEUWFEEST van het MIRAKEL van AMSTERDAM, gevierd van 4 tot 12 Maart 1845.

Celebration of the fifth centenary, March 4–12, 1845, in the Begijnhof chapel. Lithograph by C. G. R. Meyer. Amsterdam City Archives (no. 010097011098).

B Kühlen, Typogr Apost.__ M Gladbach

Chromolithographic print of the miracle of fire, from Winkelmeyer, *Geschiedenis van het Heilig Sacrament van Mirakel* (1886).

The alleged Miracle chest (ca. 1500–1520; height 46 cm, width 89 cm, depth 46.5 cm), with the emblem of the cult (the radiant host in the fire) painted on the side. In reality, this chest never contained the Sacrament of Miracle, but functioned as an archival repository for the Guild of the Blessed Sacrament that was attached to the Holy Stead. Amsterdam Museum (inv. no. KB 1396).

Antoon Derkinderen's controversial painting of the Amsterdam Miracle procession (c. 11 x 2 m), 1888. Begijnhof Amsterdam Collection.

The Begijnhofkerk, richly decorated on the occasion of the 550th anniversary of the Miracle. Rector Klönne proudly poses in front of the altar, 1895. Amsterdam City Archives (GSO).

Mgr. B. H. KLÖNNE. †

The "black pope" of Amsterdam: Msgr. Bernard Klönne, rector of the Begijnhof, in his official robes, depicted on the front page of *Katholieke Illustratie* after his death in 1921.

BAGIJNHOF.

20-27 MAART 1919 HOOGFEEST
VAN HET

MIRAKEL VAN AMSTERDAM.

 Dit jaar wordt, om den feestdag van St. JOSEPH, het Mirakelfeest één dag verplaatst, zoodat de eerste Vesper is op Woensdag en het Feest zelf op Donderdag; de sluiting van het Octaaf is dus ook een dag later. De dagen voor deelname aan de Processie voor de corporaties zijn allen één dag verzet.

OPENING.
WOENSDAG 19 MAART: Des morgens te 11½ uur plechtige VESPERS. 's Avonds te 7 uur plechtig LOF, PREEK en PROCESSIE.
De predikaties zullen gehouden worden door den WelEerwaarden Pater L. DANKELMAN, C.SS.R.

DE DAG.
DONDERDAG 20 MAART: Den geheelen dag Uitstelling van het Allerheiligste. Van 's morgens 6 uur af zal de H. Communie worden uitgereikt. Plechtige Hoogmis en preek te 10 uur. Plechtig Lof met Preek en Processie 's avonds te 7 uur.

Voor de bewoners van het Bagijnhof, alsmede voor allen, die in de Kerk van het Hof tot de H. Tafel naderen, is de wet van het vasten v o o r d i e n d a g o p g e h e v e n.

HET OCTAAF.
VRIJDAG 21 MAART / Uitstelling van het ALLERHEILIGSTE tot na de HOOGMIS. De H.H. MISSEN
ZATERDAG 22 MAART te 7, 8 en 9 uur. De HOOGMIS met PREEK te 10 uur. Plechtig LOF met PREEK en PROCESSIE te 7 uur.

ZONDAG 23 MAART: Den geheelen dag Uitstelling van het Allerheiligste.
(Dag van den Stillen Omgang.) De H.H. MISSEN te 6, 7 en 8 uur; de HOOGMIS MET PREEK te 10½ uur. Plechtig LOF met PREEK en PROCESSIE te 7 uur.

MAANDAG 24 MAART Uitstelling van het ALLERHEILIGSTE tot na de HOOGMIS. De H.H. MISSEN
DINSDAG 25 MAART te 7, 8 en 9 uur. De HOOGMIS met PREEK te 10 uur. Plechtig LOF
WOENSDAG 26 MAART met PREEK en PROCESSIE te 7 uur.

SLUITING.
DONDERDAG 27 MAART: Den geheelen dag Uitstelling van het Allerheiligste. De H.H. MISSEN te 7, 8 en 9 uur en de HOOGMIS met PREEK te 10 uur. Sluiting te 7 uur met plechtig LOF, PREEK, PROCESSIE en „TE DEUM".

Z.H. Paus PIUS IX heeft bij Breve van d... Mirakelfeest na gebiecht te hebben in de Bagijnenkerk tot de H. Tafel naderen en bidden voor de uitbreiding van ons H. Geloof een vollen aflaat verleend.

Corporaties die aan de Processies deelnemen:
Lees de bemerking boven bij de

WOENSDAG 19 MAART	ZONDAG 23 MAART
De Eerewacht van het Allerheiligste Sacrament onder Bescherming van den H. Jozef.	De Vereeniging der Pauselijke Zouaven. De Nederl. R.K. Volksbond onder bescherming van den H. Willibrordus.

Poster announcing the solemnity of the Miracle in 1919. Amsterdam City Archives (GSO).

Men from Volendam performing the Walk near Gedempte Begijnensteeg, March 26, 1930. Amsterdam City Archives (GSO).

Silent Walk in Kalverstraat, 1931. Amsterdam City Archives (GSO).

Poster for the 1924 Amsterdam International Eucharistic Congress, designed by Jan Toorop (105 x 65 cm). Amsterdam City Archives (GSO).

The board of the Society of the Silent Walk meets at the home of Alphons Elsenburg, 218 Amsteldijk, in 1931. Seated from left to right: Frans Kristen (treasurer), Alphons Elsenburg (librarian), Carel Elsenburg (chair), Msgr. G. C. van Noort (spiritual advisor), and J. B. Takes (secretary). Standing from left to right: Leonardus van den Broeke (vice chairman), Jacob Elsenburg, and Ed Elsenburg. Amsterdam City Archives (GSO).

From the 1930s onward, participants increasingly came by bus, for instance, with the "Splendid Car" coach company from Leiden. Amsterdam City Archives (GSO).

The triumphant culminating point of the celebration of the sixth centenary of the Miracle in the Olympic stadium, June 23, 1946. Surrounded by some 50,000 spectators and 6,000 participants in the center field, a Eucharistic procession of approximately 4,000 people passes along the cinder track. Photograph from De Triomf van het Mirakelsacrament, Herinneringsalbum.

Women's walk on Nieuwe Brug (Prins Hendrikkade), made in the early morning of March 26, 1952. Anefo, J. D. Noske. Beeldbank Nationaal Archief.

Silent Walk in Kalverstraat, at the lantern near the Holy Corner, 1964. Men reverently doff their hats as they pass. Spare candles can be seen lying at the foot of the lantern to ensure that it would be lit throughout the night. Anefo, Jac de Nijs, Beeldbank Nationaal Archief.

Painting of the Silent Walk in the late 1950s by Jan Lammers. Ons' Lieve Heer op Solder.

Plaque "Remembrance of the Holy Stead," unveiled in 2001, on the façade of the building in Kalverstraat (across from the entrance to the Amsterdam Museum) where according to tradition the Miracle took place in 1345.

STILLE OMGANG

Amsterdammers!

Het politie-geweld kan de happening om het LIEVERDJE niet stopzetten. Een happening is een magisch gebeuren waarop uniformen, sabels en knuppels geen vat hebben. DE VERSLAAFDE KONSUMENT VAN MORGEN

De anarchistische beweging provo geeft het volgende parool uit:

Laten de deelnemers aan de happening het KATHOLIEKE voorbeeld volgen en langs de imaginaire MAGIESE CIRKEL om het Lieverdje een stille INGETOGENHEID, STILTE! De deelnemers omgang houden. onderscheiden zich door het koolmonoxydegebaar met de zakdoek. BLOEMEN aan de voeten van het Lieverdje.

vrijdag 13/8 P xxx

SST! SST! SST! SSST! SSSST!

PROVO-KATIE NR:6

"Provo-Katie 6": "Silent walk, shush! shush!" Provos organize a silent protest walk on August 13, 1965, in imitation of the Catholic phenomenon. Their walk differs from its Catholic equivalent because participants walked around the Lieverdje ("darling" or "sweetheart") statue while making "the carbon monoxide gesture with a handkerchief." International Institute of Social History Collection.

The Silent Walk passes through Warmoesstraat, March 16, 1996. Photo J. Bogaerts.

"ZIEN" (SEE!), poster of the Silent Walk's youth program, 2016. BiN Collection, Meertens Instituut.

6

Revolution and the Reinvention of Tradition (1960–2015)

Reconstruction and Affluence

The end of World War II did not bring the social and cultural break-through that some had hoped for. After the worst upheavals of this catastrophe had passed, the country eagerly turned to the work of reconstruction, supported by the Marshall Plan. Despite the fact that the war had taken five long years, many customs and practices from the interwar years were simply resumed.[1] The political parties also returned to The Hague in the same old constellation. Nor did the culture of Catholic emancipation, with its devotions, rituals, liturgies, and paternalist hierarchy, prove to be a thing of the past. The need for structure and security under the all-embracing umbrella of the church continued to be felt in a large part of the country throughout the 1950s. That it was right and proper that Dutch Catholic identity should be propagated by means of large-scale collective manifestations was not in question. This included the Silent Walk, which, as steadfast as ever, had reclaimed its position on the Catholic annual calendar by the late 1940s and early 1950s. Well organized, thanks in large part to the local and regional societies, the pilgrimage very soon drew huge crowds of pilgrims to the capital. The estimate for 1946 was already forty-five thousand people, increasing to fifty-five thousand in 1948, leveling out at an average of some sixty-two thousand from 1949 to 1951, and then growing further to seventy-eight thousand in 1952.[2] The highest number of participants in the Walk ever was "counted" in 1957, when Catholic newspapers—perhaps not without denominationally inspired optimism—claimed it had been close to ninety thousand.[3] There were fifty masses each night of the Walk that year, held in some thirty churches and chapels in the city. Because of the high turnout the churches of the city's suburban parishes were also used, meaning that pilgrims also had to be brought to and from the city center by rented tramway cars at night. To assist the police, around one hundred volunteer stewards took up positions at strategic junctions to ensure that the logistical coordination would run smoothly. In addition to the special trains that were organized, circa 750 coaches also ferried pilgrims to and from Amsterdam during the three nights. Some of these came in convoys, such as the pilgrims from Waalwijk and surrounding areas, who were brought to the capital in eighteen buses accompanied by a police van.[4] Convoys were greeted at the municipal boundary by an Amsterdam police motorcade, which directed them to the right location in the city center. These were large-scale, complicated logistical operations, and police forces from across the country came to assist.

It was all rather a burden on city center residents, even at the time. Residents of Herengracht feared that their homes would be damaged by the constant reverberations of passing coaches. They hardly slept for three nights and, "with fear in their hearts," expected that their old façades would collapse any minute.[5] A number of well-to-do residents, led by J. H. de Monchi, complained to the mayor and ultimately succeeded in having the access route changed. Numerically, the Walk peaked in the 1950s; it seemed as if the interwar years had simply returned.

It seemed as if the sun would never set on the Silent Walk: there did not appear to be any important changes or problems. The board of the Society also fostered an air of continuity. Thus, in late March 1955, Hans Takes "inherited" the position of secretary of the Society, succeeding his deceased father Jean-Baptiste. Takes Sr. had collapsed and died shortly after that year's Walk, coincidentally as he was crossing the Nieuwebrug, which was part of the route.[6] The following year saw Eduard Elsenburg accede to the chairmanship, taking over from his father, Alphons. However, the board did notice certain stirrings of change among young participants. These seemed less interested in the story of the Miracle than in new cultural expressions. Their minds were full of completely different things—just before the 1956 Walk, Bill Haley's exciting hit "Rock Around the Clock" had blazed like a comet into the Dutch Top Ten. For teenagers and adolescents, this was the welcome omen of change in their seemingly static and bourgeois lives and their monotonous and lonely evenings. For them, the time when a medieval Eucharistic miracle could make hearts beat faster or moisten the eye had definitively passed.[7] The slow, collective Walk through the city was nothing in comparison to the alluring speed of your own personal scooter and the sense of freedom it provided; the product appealed to a huge market of young people. The board vainly hoped to rekindle the young generation's interest in the story of the Miracle by producing a comic strip called *Amsterdam Mirakelstad* (Amsterdam miracle city).[8]

The first cracks in the Miracle's image of strength were thus becoming evident. On yet another level, important changes and tensions were making themselves felt in the calm of postwar Dutch society. Worldwide political tensions, such as the threat of the Soviet Union in the Eastern Bloc and the Korean War, became permanent fixtures in the news. In addition, the nation was embroiled in the violent decolonization of the Dutch East Indies, causing many painful traumas. Despite this fragile security situation, under the government of Willem Drees (1886–1988), the population was determined to work hard and live respectable and frugal lives.[9] Beginning in 1953, this resulted in powerful economic growth that thoroughly changed the average Dutch citizen's consumption habits.[10] Meanwhile, the young increasingly had the opportunity to shape their own culture. Women's freedoms were still very much circumscribed, but there was a clear tendency for women to participate more actively in society. The dean of Amsterdam, Gerard van der Burg, acknowledged this trend and issued a paternalistic and unambiguous warning to circles involved in the Walk: "May God give our Catholic women the wise insight, the delicate attention, and the noble self-control required never to participate in the Silent Walk at night. Out of respect for its beautiful tradition."[11] The immediate occasion for this clerical admonition was the establishment in 1952 of a more or less formalized morning Walk for women, which also resulted in greater female participation in the nocturnal Walk. This did not escape the attention of the press, which made much of it in 1954. The deeper explanation for this trend was said to lie in the war, when the curfew had ensured that the Walk could only be held during the day, so that men, women, boys, and girls all had to make the Walk together.[12] The Society, its mind focused by Van der Burg's words, quickly backed the dean and begged God during its meeting to protect the Walk from further feminization. In accordance with the gender consciousness typical of the time, the board was convinced that there was a special form of *communitas* among men that bound the Walk together, and that would dissolve if women were to take part.[13] And yet: even though it was a tradition—even a "beautiful tradition"—many Catholics, especially the young, began to wonder by the end of the 1950s what the point of it all was. Modernity was making its presence felt.

Making the Walk during the Cold War

Before the carefree gaiety and lightness of the 1960s could burst forth, the country first had to rid itself of the ominous specter of the 1950s: the Cold War. The Western world, including the Netherlands, armed itself against the permanent menace of a nuclear attack, while the United States took on communism as it advanced in Vietnam. The Catholic Church also felt threatened and attacked by atheist ideologies, particularly by the religious persecution in communist countries, and took a strong political and ideological stance against it.

At the height of the Cold War, in the night of October 23 and 24, 1956, the Hungarian people, led by Prime Minister Imre Nagy, rose up against Soviet rule. The rising was immediately suppressed by a military invasion by the Soviet Union on November 4. The Russian forces' brutal crackdown caused a wave of indignation and hatred of communists across the globe. While the Dutch government made a formal protest, the Catholic Church in the Netherlands sharply condemned the events and took immediate action. Archbishop Bernardus Jan Alfrink called on Catholics to organize special prayer manifestations for the Hungarian people across the country, especially in its oldest shrines. Breda, a city that had been imitating Amsterdam since 1916 by having its own silent walk, took the initiative and organized a nocturnal silent walk against the Soviet intervention. The idea was copied in Amsterdam.[14] More than twenty thousand men *and* women[15] from Amsterdam, Alkmaar, Haarlem, Gooi, and Westland participated in an extra Silent Walk through the capital on that Sunday night, November 4. Many non-Catholics also joined in to demonstrate their solidarity with the oppressed Hungarian people. But this was only the beginning. In the days that followed there were spontaneous silent walks in some fifteen municipalities: from Nijmegen, where twenty-five thousand walked the old route of the Marian procession, and The Hague, where eight thousand participants walked in silence to the old shrine of Eikenduinen, to the small Brabant village of Casteren, a shrine of Elizabeth of Hungary, where a few hundred local residents made a prayer walk around the church.[16] Breda topped the list as some thirty-five thousand people, mainly from West and Mid Brabant, led by the bishop, Jos Baeten, and the mayor, Constant Kortmann, walked to the local Czestochowa chapel. This chapel was a subsidiary branch of the great Polish Marian shrine; Breda had been liberated by Polish soldiers. Czestochowa itself, in Poland, had seen a massive anticommunist prayer demonstration two months previously. Two symbols of protest against communist oppression—the walk and the chapel—thus coincided in Breda.[17] In Groningen, tens of thousands of people walked in silence through the city to protest, while in Apeldoorn a large silent march made its way to the local liberation monument.[18] The participants in these walks came from very diverse religious and political backgrounds. The formula of a silent walk as a protest and commemoration march, a formula stored in collective memory, could be easily applied across the country at this time of international crisis.

The spontaneous protest against the Soviet invasion was able to draw so much support because feelings of solidarity with the Hungarian people were widespread, as was a certain anticommunist sentiment that was further kindled by the Catholic Church. Ever since the nineteenth century, this church had been opposed to new, antireligious ideologies.[19] The Jesuits had even gone so far in 1870 as to set up a secret Black International—a counterpart to the Socialist International, named for the color of their habit—to increase the influence of the church in society and to mobilize the Catholic masses.[20] Initially, the church had engaged in an antiliberal and antisocialist crusade, but after Russia's February Revolution of 1917 and the dethroning of the tsar, this was replaced by rabid anticommunism. Mary's apparitions in the Portuguese shrine of Fatima, which directly followed the Russian Revolution, were regarded as divine confirmation of the church's rejection of this ideology. The messages received in Fatima were unambiguous in their condemnation of godless communism and its persecution of Christians. When shortly afterward the member of parliament Pieter Jelles Troelstra attempted to try out the idea of a socialist revolution in the Netherlands, it caused widespread opposition. Catholics wanted to keep the existing order of society, as the large numbers at that year's Silent Walk attest. Troelstra's botched attempt at unleashing a revolution in The Hague inspired the organizers of the Silent Walk to help to stabilize unrest in the country. For the first time in its history the intention of the Walk in 1920 openly expressed a political standpoint: "For the perfect restoration of order in society."

The Society responded to the rise of a new totalitarian ideology in Germany in the 1930s by professing a more general political creed, and the intention of the 1937 Walk was "that God may preserve our Fatherland from communism and any other form of new paganism." The use of the

Silent Walk as an instrument in political and ideological conflicts, as with the Hungarian uprising, was therefore not without precedent, even apart from the fact that the Walk itself partly originated as a form of protest.

As has been seen, anticommunist rhetoric peaked in the 1950s, in both political and ecclesiastical circles. The latter aspect became evident, for instance, in the annual meetings of the Society of the Silent Walk. In a 1951 speech, the Redemptorist Piet Wesseling demagogically portrayed Amsterdam as "the city of modern paganism, where hundreds of thousands are in the clutches of communism."[21] The popularity of the Communistische Partij Nederland (CPN; Communist Party of the Netherlands) was seen as a real danger, as was "Russia's meddling" as the Soviet Union stepped up the arms race and appeared to be infiltrating everywhere.[22] Two years later, the Jesuit Karel Vosskühler, head of the industrial chaplaincy in Amsterdam, was the guest speaker at the annual meeting. In a fiery speech, he contended that 60 percent of the workers in his city regarded themselves as unaffiliated to any denomination, and that humanism was now a much greater threat to Catholic life than communism. He was a farsighted analyst.

The historian Tijs Hakkert has argued that the restoration of the Walk and its continued growth in the 1950s can really only be explained by the transfer of the Catholic perception of the "enemy" from Protestants to communists.[23] Communism and the Soviet Union did in fact appear often on the agenda of the annual general meetings, and they perfectly matched the church's image of the enemy that Rome was propagating.[24] Fear of communism, of the Soviet Union, and of the nuclear arms race no doubt played a part in the board's and participants' existential thinking, but it seems inaccurate to ascribe the high turnout figures to this. With the exception of the extra Walk in 1956, the Cold War featured rarely or not at all in the motives of individual participants for taking part in the regular Walk, no matter how much priests used their rhetorical skills to argue that it should. In Veldkamp's later research of these motives, anticommunism did not feature at all as a reason to take part.[25] The large numbers of postwar participants testified mainly to a continuation of the prewar confidence in their own Catholicity and to the important significance of the Walk as a constituent of collective identity. It continued to be primarily a manifestation of "we Dutch Catholics" in combination with a deep attachment to the traditions of the Miracle.

Up until the late 1950s, the Walk still carried with it associations of mutual rancor between Protestants and Catholics. Ecumenism was still too much in its infancy to be able to turn this around. But the fact that people from many different denominations took part in the protest walk on the occasion of the Hungarian uprising was a first sign of change. An anonymous commentator in the Catholic daily *De Nieuwe Dag* (The new day) described the significance of the Walk for Dutch Catholics in 1959: "The Silent Walk is a national treasure, as much characteristic of us as *The Night Watch* is. This was most clearly evident on that infamous Hungarian Sunday, when all of Dutch Catholicism gave vent to its pent-up emotions by spontaneously holding silent walks everywhere. This shows how much the Amsterdam Silent Walk has become part of the customs of our people. The so-called silent marches on the commemorative eve of the fallen are also a clear reflection of this."[26] The author characterized the Silent Walk as an iconic ritual that represented a character trait of the whole of Dutch society. It appealed not only to Catholics, but also to others in society, as an anticommunist protest or as an annual commemoration of the victims of war. It would become evident later how true this observation was.

Revolution in the Long 1960s

The 1960s have gone down in history as the decade of widespread cultural and religious change, of generational conflicts and revolutions that finally brought to an end the ancien régime of the dominant bourgeois culture of the first half of the twentieth century.[27] If the necessary political decolonization of the Kingdom of the Netherlands took place in the 1950s, the 1960s brought the individual "decolonization of the citizen," as the journalist Henk Hofland once pointedly observed.[28] These fundamental changes did not fall from the sky, but had roots that went far back in history.[29]

The celebration of *100 jaar kromstaf* (100 years under the crozier), the centenary of the establishment of the Dutch dioceses, on May 16, 1953, in Galgenwaard stadium in Utrecht, turned out to be the last of a long series of large-scale "glorious" Catholic manifestations.[30] The centenary celebrations were intended to be the symbolic culmination of Dutch Catholic emancipation. The triumphalist manifestation already felt like the celebration of a bygone era. The commemorated event had, moreover, been inextricably linked with the antipapist April Movement of 1853, to which the organizers were determined to pay as little attention as possible. In fact the most important product of this almost anachronistic celebration was a new, modern history of Dutch Catholicism covering the past century (as mentioned in the introduction to this book). This monumental and innovative book was presented by its authors, the historians Louis Rogier and Nicolaas de Rooy, on the occasion of the celebration. It unintentionally represented a historiographical end to the preceding turbulent century of Catholic emancipation, with its struggles over the public domain.

This caesura did not become evident until later, as the 1950s were anything but innovative when it came to pastoral ministry. The conservative joint pastoral letter (or *mandement*) that the bishops published the following year, in 1954, was clear proof of this. Their directive, addressed to the "modern Catholic," was more a warning to steer well clear of innovation and modernity. The document attempted to halt the crumbling of what had once been a strong pillar and also to curb the growing demand for greater individual freedom. The pastoral letter proved powerless to check the advance of secularization, independent thinking, and personal development within and outside the Catholic community. The episcopate was still united in 1954, but significant cracks started to appear in their unity only a few years later. This began when the bishop of 's-Hertogenbosch, Willem Bekkers, effected a personal volte-face and became the first bishop to call for personal freedom. According to him, the life of faith required "personal conviction and responsibility" as well as ecclesiastical norms.[31] This statement let the genie out of the bottle. The involvement and deep conviction with which Dutch Catholics had professed their faith throughout the preceding centuries were quickly exchanged for feelings of shame, alienation, and aversion, a process unintentionally aggravated by Rome.[32] All the rituals and saints' cults in which they had only so recently believed so unconditionally, and in which they had participated in such huge numbers, were suddenly being dismissed by their own church leaders as "medieval," no longer suitable for a modern faith and for modern society.[33]

Dutch Catholics now embraced the renewal that the church offered in the wake of the Second Vatican Council (1962–1965) with the same rigidity and intensity with which they had lived and experienced that devotional faith in their Catholic pillar for a century.[34] For a second time, Dutch Catholics, led by their clergy, vied to outdo any other Catholic nation in zeal. They took the Council's aggiornamento, the up-to-date renewal of the church, more seriously than anyone else did, and in the process attacked their own, intensely lived past head-on. It was as if Dutch Catholics suddenly looked at themselves with astonishment through the eyes of outsiders: did we really behave like that? Their about-face was nearly to 180 degrees, and the Netherlands almost overnight became a world leader in church renewal.[35] It was an urge for renewal—for instance, through the Nieuwe Katechismus (New Catechism) or Dutch Catechism[36]—but Rome interpreted it as a form of heresy. The Vatican tried to stop other countries from being infected by this virus of renewal.[37] It was against this background that the historian Ernst Kossmann could conclude that "the cultural revolution of Catholics was less controlled than that of any other group in Dutch society."[38] The sociologist Siep Stuurman concurred and discerned traces of a "pathological rage for renewal."[39] The ferocity of the reversal was partly the result of the strictness that had for so long characterized the Catholic pillar. People experienced the cultural and religious revolutions as a liberation from the straightjacket of the hierarchical structures of the church—which had been celebrated extravagantly as recently as 1953—and of the black clericalism and almost autarkic isolation of the pillar ("an ideological ghetto"). The new era placed humans themselves at center stage, as individuals. The realization of personal expression and the reflexive self became mainstream.[40]

So much renewal could not go unchallenged. Eventually, Pope Paul VI decided to intervene. From the 1970s onward, Rome slowly attempted to maneuver Dutch Catholicism back into the traditional line that it espoused through strategic appointments of conservative bishops—for instance, of Ad Simonis in the diocese of Rotterdam in 1970, and Jo Gijsen in Roermond in 1972. This policy deepened the divisions that were already plaguing an unnerved Catholic flock, dispersing it to all sides.

The steadily growing popularity of television, motorization, and leisure time was already changing daily life drastically, but the most far-reaching social and cultural process of this period was the declining significance of institutional religion. This longer process of dechristianization and secularization gained in momentum, a phenomenon that historian Hugh McLeod has situated in the era of "the long sixties." Many individuals became less attached to church structures, with members choosing to interpret the moral frameworks of life in their own way.[41] Viewed over more than a decade, this process could be called "revolutionary" because it had far-reaching cultural implications. Your place in society was determined by the ideal and practice of your expressive-reflexive self. In fact, the Christian churches gave their blessing to this "search experiment" without realizing where it might lead them. In the Netherlands especially, with its oppressive and rigidly pillarized structure to which individuals belonged by birth, people had a strong desire to escape. The prescribed "objectivity" of values, norms, and meanings gave way to greater subjectivity regarding faith and to creative interpretations.[42] As a result, the new era, or New Age, brought with it a broad range of alternative, and mostly non-Western, forms of spirituality. Spiritual experiments attracted wide attention through a new youth culture: the Beatles' sojourn at the feet of the Maharishi Yogi in 1968 boosted the popularity of Indian spiritualities and of transcendental meditation. An era of postmaterialism emerged that focused on the ideal and nonmaterial and had its own lifestyle.[43]

In the meantime the Dutch Catholic Church fell prey to demoralization. The foundations upon which many religious truths and customs were based seemed to have crumbled. During the long 1960s, church attendance and the number of Catholic organizations dropped by half. The pillarized structure slowly disintegrated. This period of change ended sometime in the mid-1970s. New liberal and left-wing political parties, such as Democrats '66 and Politieke Partij Radikalen (PPR, Political Party of Radicals), had by then made their presence felt, but the student protests of 1968 and 1969—in Paris, Tilburg, and Amsterdam, for instance—had also become a thing of the past. The ideals of the 1960s had all but evaporated, and the romantic, utopian style of West Coast music was exchanged for the nihilism and aggression of emerging punk culture.

Decline

The societal changes that have been mentioned, and especially the changes that occurred within the churches, naturally had repercussions on the Silent Walk. Interest from Amsterdam had fallen already, as secularization arrived earlier in the city than elsewhere in the country, but it declined even more sharply in these years. That interest from the rest of the country declined as well sometimes became evident only belatedly. In absolute figures, the number of participants from certain parts of the country continued to rise until 1963, but rapid decline set in across the board after that year.[44] In 1965 the number of nights on which the Walk was held was reduced from three to two, and in 1969 it was brought down to a single night. Amsterdam's squares and streets were being used in strikingly contrasting ways at this time. While the new rebellious youth movement Provo proclaimed on Spui that all power belonged to imagination, the annual opening sermon for the Walk, which started on the same spot, was still a model of conservatism and tradition. However unbridgeable the difference may have seemed, it would become evident very soon, to both groups' mutual astonishment, that they had more in common than they could have imagined. It was an unexpected source of inspiration.

In terms of statistics, the early 1960s were a turning point for the Silent Walk. As early as March 1965, before the Council had been concluded in Rome, the number of participants dropped below fifty thousand, slipping even further to thirty-five thousand in 1966, a decline of 60 percent compared to previous years.[45] During the January meeting with the sister societies in Hotel Krasnapolsky, the Amsterdam board faced a difficult audience. "They must not get stuck in a rut, and should look critically at themselves," one assertive member from the provinces contended. Another warned that if young people could no longer be induced to participate, it would jeopardize continuity. In this case it would be better to abolish the Walk immediately, he argued. This drastic proposal gained some support, but not a majority, and instead the Society was asked to hold an inquiry to find out what its own grassroots supporters, and Dutch Catholics in general, thought about the Walk. Chairman Eduard Elsenburg promised to do his best but also indicated that it was not easy to find a solution for the central problem: a general falling away from the faith, and dechristianization. The Silent Walk was not the only initiative to experience a decline of interest. Everything associated with existing church institutions was under pressure, particularly in the Netherlands. An effective remedy seemed difficult to find, and the Amsterdam board was paralyzed, standing by idly to watch as things progressed.

At the same time, the board was receiving increasing numbers of letters from sister societies expressing their concerns. Regional newspapers were the first to notice the decline of the national ritual moment. In early 1965 a newspaper from Gouda asked whether the Gouda branch would be able to survive, and the following year the *Dagblad van het Oosten* (The Eastern daily) opened with "Days of the Silent Walk Are Numbered."[46] The Voorschoten sister society was probably the first to dissolve itself, in the turbulent year of 1966. The reason it gave was as simple as it was predictable: "It doesn't interest people anymore in this day and age." Nor did they think a silent walk as a silent form of protest against the procession ban, and therefore against the Reformation, was suitable any longer in a postconciliar society that increasingly focused on Christian unity. They refused to jeopardize their new ecumenical plans in Voorschoten by continuing to observe this hackneyed nocturnal Miracle walk.

It was to be expected that the quantitative decline would give new ammunition to women eager to participate in the Walk. It was the Hague branch that made the request, at an extra meeting in February 1964, to allow women to take part in that year's Walk. "Tradition" may have been crumbling, but the Amsterdam board was not yet for abandoning it. It did not want to "water down" the "cause" even further by allowing women to take part.[47] But there was no stopping the tide. In 1965 participants from The Hague simply announced as an accomplished fact that they would turn up with their women. Before there was any chance of conflict, Elsenburg stated that he had no objection.

Ms. Buchwald of the Katholiek Vrouwengilde (Catholic Women's Guild) made a formal request to be admitted to the Walk at a meeting held in early 1966. The eighty-three-year-old Van den Broeke, the éminence grise of the board, reiterated once more that the statutes did not permit this on account of the "men only" tradition. Representatives from Bovenkerk and Langendijk then proposed that the next annual meeting should amend the statutes.[48] Pastor Brans of the Amsterdam parish of Our Lady of the Rosary ignored the debate and simply saw off a mixed group, albeit at 6:30 a.m. as a "dawn pilgrimage." The De Tijd newspaper even told its Catholic readership that in this day and age not only women, but also Protestants, Jews, and humanists should be admitted.[49] There were to be many similar calls.[50] The participation of women was tacitly accepted, and the proportion of women participants steadily increased. No formal vote was ever taken on the subject. The controversial article "Het onbehagen van de vrouw" (The discontentment of women), published by the feminist Joke Kool-Smit in De Gids in 1967, had lost its relevance. This was not yet the case for the board, and it would take another twenty years before a woman was elected to this body.[51]

One of the younger delegates at the 1969 annual meeting argued that the Silent Walk was simply too silent for young people; after all, the new era was a time for young people to let their voices be heard, to protest or to debate. He argued that growing numbers of young Catholics consequently preferred a new, "interactive" way of walking: the Pax Christi marches that were quickly gaining in popularity at the time, organized by the international Catholic peace movement.[52] These marches killed two modernist flies with one stone: debate and peace protest. The speaker therefore proposed that debating groups should be set up at the conclusion of the Walk. It earned him the loud applause of the entire meeting, but his plan was not adopted.[53]

The quantitative decline of the Silent Walk kept pace with the decline of the Catholic pillar in general. Given the high levels of participation and its wide geographical spread, motives for nonparticipation in the Walk can also help explain the broader social and religious changes of the time.

They were the result not of a campaign by a younger generation—however quickly its members abandoned the Walk—but of the general view that suddenly emerged, both among the elite and among midlevel groups, that church structures and practices had remained unchanged for a very long time and needed to be adjusted to modernity.[54] Suddenly many felt, almost with a sense of shame, that they were participating in a phenomenon of the distant past, and they wanted to disassociate themselves from it as quickly as possible, preferably without being seen. A new urge for renewal then caused the Catholic pillar to explode. This rupture can be seen symbolically and in detail in the archives of the Society. The series of heavy, dark minute books, bound in the style of the nineteenth century and gracefully scribbled full with a fountain pen, abruptly broke off in 1965 in the middle of the last book. Minute-taking continued in a more informal way, on carelessly typed loose sheets, held together in a bright-red plastic binder.

Provo and Provocation

The creative 1960s also saw the rise of a more contemporary translation of the Silent Walk as a protest ritual. Provo, the Amsterdam-based, anti-authoritarian, anarchist, and ludic countermovement of the day, drew direct inspiration from the Silent Walk in 1965. In its publication *Provo-Katie*, number 6, entitled *Stille Omgang*, Provo wrote that their special disruptive manifestations—"happenings"—were also magic events. It called on all supporters to hold a "Walk" themselves, with participants "following the CATHOLIC example, and, following the MAGIC CIRCLE," making a silent walk around the *Lieverdje*, the famed statue of an Amsterdam urchin, a disputed gift of a cigarette company.[55] This magic happening took place only a few yards away from the Begijnhof and its Miracle.

This appropriation of the Walk ritual is remarkable because the mental difference between the two movements was immense. Writer Harry Mulisch suggestively sketched this contrast in his book *Bericht aan de Rattenkoning* (Message to the rat king) without concealing his own preferences and dislikes. In his long account of the turbulent events that occurred in Amsterdam at the time, Mulisch describes how around midnight hundreds of Provos had gathered once again in a Happening on Spui, around the *Lieverdje*. Because their previous protests against the "fascistoid regency" had earned them a hail of blows from the police, Mayor Gijs van Hall had instituted a cooling-off period with minimal police presence. The

Provos celebrated this as a triumph. Meanwhile, Mulisch writes, using analogous terminology, the "annual *happening* called the Silent Walk" was underway in the city center. A group of Provos walked from the *Lieverdje* to Dam square and stood there under the arches of the Royal Palace, the former city hall. On the other side of the square, near the liberation monument, stood Police Commissioner Hendrik Jan van der Molen with a number of other officers to preserve public order during the Silent Walk. Suddenly flames were seen under the arches. At the instigation of "miracle man" and magician Robert Jasper Grootveld, the Provos had lit a republican fire outside their "city hall." Mulisch writes,

> At that moment the Silent Walk appeared from Kalverstraat. There they went, diagonally across the square, the "happeners" from centuries ago. A drab, silent group from the provinces, an endless cortège of men of a certain age, who stared with hollow eyes at the fire at the entrance of the city hall as they passed it (without a thought of the host) and at the boys and girls clad in white who were making magic gestures. It was a metaphysical moment of great beauty, a *Sternstunde der Menschheit*, to use Stefan Zweig's words, or the encounter of a sewing machine and an umbrella on an operating table, to use Lautréamont's words.[56]

The similarities to the host in the fire are unmistakable: fire that is not always capable of destroying what it envelops. The short encounter between these two movements, one supportive of the monarchy and the other opposed to it—the *Sternstunde* (sublime moment)—did not bring any radical "change of fate." Their ways soon parted again: the walkers simply followed their traditional route, into Nieuwendijk, while the Provos moved in the direction of "Governor General" Van Hall's residence in Beethovenstraat, to shout, "Van Hall-ten val, Van Hall-ten val" (Down with Van Hall).

However unwaveringly one group kept silent and the other shouted, society could still see certain similarities between the two movements: the anomalous and the comic. It was an aspect that could produce something new. In September 1965, following other happenings near *Lieverdje* on Spui, Provo decided to organize yet another protest "Silent Walk," this time to the controversial monument to the colonial officer Joannes van Heutsz.[57] This silent Provo walk caused the liberal newspaper *Algemeen Dagblad* to argue that the languishing Catholic Silent Walk should not be abolished now that the procession ban was no longer a problem due to church renewal, but that it should be turned into a universal march of "silent protest against the advancing materialization and devaluation of humanity." These issues were similar to those against which Provo protested. The commentator tried to convince the Provos that, instead of dancing around the "cigarette monument" of the *Lieverdje* with a smokers' cough, they should walk together through Amsterdam's "magic center" in the Silent Walk as an ideological ritual counterweight against "the materialization of existence." The newspaper referred to the paradox that "everywhere the desire for reflection grows as the possibility to engage in it decreases" and therefore issued the following call: "Don't leave the privilege of walking through the nocturnal heart of Amsterdam in a silent walk to Roman Catholic men alone, or even to the ecumenism of Christians. There is a great opportunity here for those who often choose the same Spui, where the walk begins, to protest against the dulling effect of affluence."[58] It was an almost prophetic vision, for within a few decades "silent marches" as rituals of reflection and protest would in fact become a national secular ritual. Even at the time, *Handelsblad* saw the Walk as an almost ideal society-wide rite that could be used to articulate issues concerning norms and values in society in a silently reflective way.[59]

In this context of secular applications of the Walk ritual, it is fitting briefly to address the pilgrimage aspect of the Amsterdam Miracle cult since the emergence of the Silent Walk. The Begijnhof, as the successor of the Holy Stead or Nieuwezijds Kapel, is, strictly speaking, a place of pilgrimage, but the practical realization of this pilgrimage strongly diverges from that in most other Catholic places of pilgrimage. The cult of the Sacrament of Miracle lacks any concrete cult object upon which devotional practices and ritual expressions can center, such as can often be found in Marian shrines. The "actual" miraculous host, in the form of the newly consecrated hosts that took its place for centuries, had not been exposed in this capacity since the Alteration of 1578.[60] The public system of exchange between pilgrims and the saint or the sacred object, where the former seek the latter's intercession in illness or distress through votive gifts or otherwise, had not functioned for centuries, at least not in the open. There were no exuberant Catholic ceremonies: rituality was minimalist and wholly concentrated in sober church services. All this took place in a small former hidden church, without any devotional items or "religious kitsch." This means that the modern Miracle cult and the Walk were not generally experienced as a Catholic pilgrimage. This characteristic has also determined to a large extent the Silent Walk's ecumenical aspect, and has moreover made it easier for non-Catholics to relate to the Silent Walk and to its derivative, the silent march.

Suggestion: A Different Perspective

As has been seen, the general church reforms of the 1960s did not leave the Silent Walk unaffected. Several sister societies were specifically critical of parish clergy, accusing them of refusing to promote the Walk anymore or making entirely different plans for it. The progressive Catholic magazine *De Bazuin* threw oil on the fire by openly questioning the piety of the participants in the Walk and, with progressive arrogance, contending that the Walk owed its existence to the fact that it boosted the sale of alcoholic beverages and visits to the red-light district.[61] All this was strategic clerical agitation intended to hasten the disappearance of the Walk in its traditional form. The lion's share of the clergy involved had come to embrace the view that the pilgrimage should focus more on the celebration of the Eucharist—and should primarily demonstrate commitment to social justice. The cult should keep well away from "popular piety" and pilgrimage, aspects with which they obviously felt it was too strongly associated. The Amsterdam Jesuit and student chaplain Jan van Kilsdonk, the acknowledged figurehead of pastoral progressiveness at the time, was invited to speak at the 1966 annual meeting to contribute to reflection on the crisis. In the spirit of the Council, he contended that there were currently many Christians for whom a Miracle of doubtful historical veracity was clearly passé. Who could still believe in this kind of miracle? He thought the Walk had the allure of a "museum-like" ritual, and he compared the participants to "religious antiquarians."[62] Their medieval ritual, he argued, was not conducive to what he cryptically called the "theological clarification" of the Sacrament. The two initiators, Lousbergh and Elsenburg, had been too much "touched by romanticism" for Van Kilsdonk's taste. The Walk, as a relic of the past, must therefore be divested of its heritage of belief in the Miracle and its Counter-Reformation character, and should be opened up to Protestant fellow Christians.[63] A dyed-in-the-wool pilgrim from Zaandam, who had made the annual pilgrimage through Amsterdam sixty-seven times, expressed a feeling shared more widely among the audience when he told the student chaplain that a revamp along the lines suggested would resemble "currant bread without currants" and that the Walk would lose much of its attraction. The board was left wringing its hands, unable to choose between the two opposing directions. They had not yet abandoned the notion that their lay tradition meant that they should resist yielding too quickly to clerical demands. What were they to do?

As has been seen, 1966 was a turbulent year for the Silent Walk. While the clergy of Amsterdam believed that the solution lay in a thorough "transformation," the sister societies preferred further inquiry. The Eindhoven branch suggested that each sister society should report on the situation in its own region, in the hope that a summary of the findings would provide a new perspective on the Walk as a national phenomenon. They were not oblivious to the strong drop in participation every year, in the Catholic south as elsewhere. In the diocese of 's-Hertogenbosch, the decline had been talked about since 1965, and at long last it was decided to collect background information on all these silent men. A survey was posted to the members—all 11,000 of them—in the diocese, only 4,100 of whom had actually made the journey to Amsterdam in 1966.[64]

The survey showed that the "willingness to make the sacrifice" of a nocturnal pilgrimage had strongly diminished.[65] It also turned out to be true that the parish clergy was no longer interested in committing itself to the nocturnal pilgrimage or to making active propaganda for it.[66] Like Van Kilsdonk, most pastors believed it was a thing of the past. Experience also showed that once the pastor pulled out, there was no local network to take over, and local enthusiasm for the pilgrimage to Amsterdam quickly declined or stopped altogether. It was an alarming result. However much the Dutch Catholic Church had chosen to go down the path of modernism, there was still a group that remained attached to old values and rituals. They still had a common language, partly cultural and "traditional," to which they continued to relate and that they held onto.[67] These Catholics were not inclined to abandon the tested tradition of the collective Walk.

Religion, Market, and Tradition

As the Miracle was gradually being divested of its sacred and mystical dimensions, the fame of Amsterdam as a magic center increased among hippies worldwide. The appropriation of emblematic locations by long-haired Dam and Vondelpark sleepers and Provos was a symbolic public marker that times were changing. Chairman Eduard Elsenburg tried to keep spirits up for his Walk by saying that he was convinced that it would not be affected by these changes in society. The turnout figures proved him wrong.[68] Everything seemed to be eroding. Many, both within and outside the Catholic Church, called the second half of the 1960s a second Reformation. Large parts of the Netherlands even saw a "second iconoclastic fury" that stripped churches, especially in the south, of their plaster statues of saints, devotional objects, and frescos.[69] In their place came whitewashed walls, simple altars turned around, and empty niches, and the disappearance of devotional rituals and practices. The magic—and obscurantism— of the Latin, Tridentine mass disappeared and was replaced by a prosaic mass in the vernacular. Many a Catholic place of worship came to resemble a Protestant church. The speed with which this transformation took place—with regard to both material and intangible culture—caused some commentators to point out that its very irreversibility was dangerous. The Catholic radio journalist Toon Rammelt gave the following assessment: "The Netherlands has its own national pilgrimage, the Silent Walk, a precious possession. Of course the historicity of the Miracle is doubtful, but you could still have a Silent Walk that points to the Eucharist, which is not a myth. Let's not let the Silent Walk slip out of our hands because of some ill-understood craze for demythologization."[70] Rammelt acknowledged that this Dutch ritual might require some modernization, but urged that it should not be destroyed in an ultimate attack on the community's own devotional culture.[71] He argued that the idea of "folklore" that many associated with the Walk—although it was difficult to put it into words— obscured proper understanding of its intrinsic value for the Catholic community. He made a number of suggestions in the hope that the decline could still be halted and the ritual could be adapted to realistic proportions. Rammelt thought the nocturnal tradition was problematic, and he wanted the Miracle pilgrimage to shake off its "clandestine church" mentality and the "romantic" aspect of the night. This would also solve the problem of confrontations with revelers and would remove objections to the participation of women: a pilgrimage at dawn, spread out over Lent, which might also become a sporting event, a run, for young people.

Once again the Amsterdam Society stood by, unable to halt the decline or make any kind of decision. Almost in despair, it looked for inspiration from prominent persons in the Catholic world. A family friend of the Elsenburgs, Johannes Willebrands,[72] later archbishop of Utrecht, proved willing to share his ideas at the 1967 annual meeting. He knew the Walk well because he had begun his career as an associate pastor on the Begijnhof from August 1937 to late 1940. Later he became secretary (from 1969 president) of the Pontifical Council for Promoting Christian Unity in Rome, a body set up to further worldwide ecumenism. Willebrands, still inspired by the Second Vatican Council, which he had attended, had a clear message. He argued that the emphasis should shift from the Miracle to the professing of the faith. In effect, he offered the board his own—and his Council of Unity's—programmatic manifesto: the Eucharist as a unifying factor, the way par excellence to bring all Christians together around the same table. For Willebrands, the Amsterdam tradition of the Walk was ultimately a nonessential form of religious expression within the modern faith professed by the universal church. He discerned one of the Council's achievements in the Walk: because there was no hierarchy, there was no institutional church.[73] He hailed the Walk's soberness, with its penance and silent prayer, as a strongly positive aspect.

For the board, Willebrands's exegetical exercise was the final push to embrace the search for Christian unity in the context of the Walk. In his 1995 analysis of Willebrands's thinking at the time, historian Peter Raedts has described how Willebrands used a theology of the Sacrament to steer clear of the Miracle: external trappings had become obsolete after the aggiornamento.[74] Willebrands's conclusion was clear: "devotion to the Sacrament of Miracle is not an essential aspect," and neither was mass participation.[75] But viewed from this perspective, was this argument not a rear-guard battle? The Walk had always shunned external ostentation, and the Miracle had fulfilled a historical role as medieval "heritage," a source of inspiration, but not of "naïve" devotionalism. The last ones to advocate the latter had been Klönne and his Miracle chest. The nondescript Walk was already a more or less exemplary prefiguration of unity, openness, and equality.

Willebrands had other important advice concerning ecumenical participation. The question was asked whether participants should attend mass before or after the Walk. He argued that for a pilgrimage to the Holy Land, too, pilgrims had to walk before they could enter Jerusalem. This recommendation created greater openness for participation in the Walk: anyone could take part, and Catholics could then attend mass afterward.[76] Willebrands's idea was only realized in the jubilee year of 1995, when an ecumenical Walk was held, as well as a joint Protestant-Catholic vesper service in the Reformed Oude Kerk.

In addition to using the services of "internal" experts such as Willebrands, the board also took grassroots advice on what to do by using market research. What were the causes of the dramatic and, it would seem, structural decline in the numbers of pilgrims? In 1966 the board hired a reputable market research agency called Veldkamp to carry out a sociological field study. In the early hours of the Walk of March 5 and 12, 1967, the agency interviewed more than four hundred randomly selected participants. The sample provided an analysis—unique for its time—of a large-scale Catholic pilgrimage ritual.[77] On the basis of 387 usable interviews, the report painted a picture of the composition, backgrounds, and motives of normally faceless ordinary participants in the Walk.

As far as the age composition was concerned, it transpired that more than 50 percent of the participants in the mid-1960s were between twenty and forty-four years of age, and a third were between forty-five and sixty-five. Ages twenty and lower, and sixty-five and over, represented 10 and 5 percent respectively. This meant that approximately 60 percent of the participants were younger than forty-four. Even by current standards, that is still a very young group for a religious manifestation. Of the participants, 28 percent came from Amsterdam and 22 percent from elsewhere in the province of North Holland. Of the other half, 16 percent came from South Holland, 16 percent from North Brabant, 6 percent from Utrecht, 4 percent each from Limburg and Overijssel, 3 percent from Gelderland, and 1 percent from Friesland.[78] As regards socioeconomic background, the participants could be divided almost equally into workers, farmers, and the higher educated.[79] Participants from outside the capital increasingly came to dominate; they proved to be the most faithful to the tradition of the Walk. Of this group, 70 percent had been taking part for at least eight years. Many new participants made the Walk for the first time in the two years after the war as a way of showing gratitude for their survival. Younger participants who had only begun to take part recently often dropped out again very quickly. This had a strong impact, especially on participation from Amsterdam, which was the place where the tradition handed down from father to son was the strongest. A family tradition of participating in the Walk was an important factor for nearly 70 percent of Amsterdam participants, but for less than half of participants from outside the city (47 percent).[80] Because they often traveled in groups, as a parish, with friends and fellow parishioners, the Walk had an important social function for non-Amsterdam participants. The group experience and a sense of belonging were more significant factors for them. This also meant that peer pressure made structures more enduring, preventing people from breaking with tradition by dropping out.

The Veldkamp researchers explicitly asked for the participants' motives for undertaking the pilgrimage to Amsterdam and for taking part in the Walk. The motives mentioned were as follows:

Personal or general intention; to ask for grace	20%
Because of (the "manifestation of") the faith"; the Eucharist	15%
Tradition (Amsterdam 23%; others 9%)	13%
As a sacrifice; as a penitential walk	10%
Devotion; veneration of the Blessed Sacrament	8%
Personal interest; the atmosphere; the whole experience	7%
The pilgrimage; prayer	6%
Reflection or meditation	5%
The Miracle of the Blessed Sacrament	4%
Gratitude	3%
The group experience; going along with the association	3%
Sociability; going out in the city	2%
To set an example	1%
For the unity of Christians	1%
As a protest against young clerics with regard to the Eucharist and against those who don't participate	1%
No clear motive 4% (+ irrelevant 2%)	6%[81]

The research agency's general conclusion was that young participants ("teenagers") were dropping out more quickly so that the natural withdrawal of older people was no longer being compensated. According to the report, this happened because the "Silent Walk . . . offers too few possibilities to get involved in society."[82] The reasons for taking part were mainly of an individual nature, and the primary reason was normally determined by family tradition, without any contemporary motivation. As a solution, the agency proposed that "greater familiarity be given to the silent walk as a way for faithful Catholics of showing their commitment to what is going on in society and to manifest their faith in God's place in this."[83] This was easier said than done in the turbulent days of the 1960s. A medieval Eucharistic miracle was the last thing on young people's minds when they thought about getting involved in society.[84]

The Veldkamp agency already suspected as much, as some of its researchers had heard young people breaking the silence of the night of the Walk by shouting "World peace, peace in Vietnam." This was apparently a direct result of one of those spontaneous contacts described above between Provos and participants of the Walk, as both parties claimed the Spui square in Amsterdam. Spui was traditionally the pilgrims' gathering and starting place, while the Provos had more recently appropriated the *Lieverdje* as their antismoking totem and ritual place of imagining. This time, a confrontation between Catholic tradition and tongue-in-cheek disruptive rebellion seemed inevitable. Dozens of Provos tried to hold an anti–Vietnam War demonstration at the same time as the Silent Walk, thus harnessing the Walk's renown and crowds for their own political purposes. It all ended peacefully when the police managed, with some difficulty, to keep both groups away from each other.

Market research is commonly done for products or to solve commercial questions, and this was obviously not something that applied to the Silent Walk. The scope of Veldkamp's conclusions and recommendations was consequently limited. A long popular tradition cannot be adjusted on the basis of pricing mechanisms. As usual, the board was unsure as to what it should do with the results. This became painfully obvious when a special general meeting was convened in the RAI convention center on November 18, 1967. Three questions were asked from the floor: (1) Is it important to hold a Silent Walk? (2) Should it be preserved? and (3) What can we recommend? The chairman thought that the research gave good insight into the situation, so that various answers to the questions presented themselves, but also concluded that he did not want to adopt any comprehensive changes or make any rash decisions.[85] It was a disillusionment for many delegates that the board still refused to debate the status quo of the Walk. One delegate called on his fellow attendees not to sit together like funeral undertakers, but to try and inspire each other. Something else that became clear was the extent to which the clergy in the southern provinces had lost interest in the Silent Walk: "It would already be a huge improvement if they were to stop their obstruction," according to one of the Brabant board members.[86]

The report was discussed again shortly afterward, in early 1968, during the annual general meeting. This time the delegates were determined to try a different tactic, and they aired open criticism of the board's policy. The Breda branch thought the study had been a waste of money because the Amsterdam board seemed determined not to draw any conclusions from it. The Breda delegate portrayed the Society and the Walk as "an old man in old clothes, collapsing in a cold night." The board defended itself with the vintage argument that "it was quality that counted, not quantity." Still combative, it declared that it would not stop organizing the Walk, however low the turnout might become. It did make a concession to the Breda sister society by agreeing, partly on the basis of the survey, to deemphasize the Miracle story further and present the Walk more as a general manifestation of the faith, and to connect it more clearly with events in society.

While the debate in Amsterdam focused on the Walk, twenty-five miles away, in Noordwijkerhout, a much more wide-ranging discussion was taking place. The minor seminary of Leeuwenhorst there was the scene of the plenary sessions of a "schismatic" pastoral council held between early 1968 and the spring of 1970. The pastoral council held "national" discussions on the results of the Vatican Council and on how these might be translated to and implemented in the Dutch situation.[87] To give ordinary Catholics a voice, special "council mailboxes" had been placed throughout the country for individual ideas. The theological debates about the Eucharist in both Amsterdam and Noordwijkerhout were really a clerical rear-guard action that failed to interest most ordinary faithful.[88] "Inside they were busy making changes to things from which the skeptical believer had long since moved on" was the writer Godfried Bomans's comment on the council's deliberations. "They're drawing within the lines. . . . [They] never [ask]: is the whole thing actually true? People outside the hall instinctively feel this."[89] In the meantime the church of mass Catholicism had disappeared. Social Catholicism increasingly had to yield to a cultural Catholicism that involved all kinds of personal interpretations outside parish structures. This was all the more so because enthusiasm about renewal had turned to disappointment, and this had given rise to a conflict between conservatives and progressives.[90] One result of this lengthy clerical brainstorm was a liberal conception of the church within the Netherlands, and the other was much stronger awareness of what still remained of the "old-fashioned" church. For the Walk, this idea or sense of the old-fashioned would some years later serve as the foundation for a new reinvention of the ritual-religious practice.[91]

In 1969 Bomans held a number of public conversations with another well-known Catholic author, Michel van der Plas (pseudonym of Ben Brinkel), in which they looked back on and analyzed the culture of the Catholic faith since the interwar years. Their impressions confirmed the idea that had come into vogue since the Vatican Council that the Catholic faith had been something external. The two gentlemen were retrospectively amazed at the collective "play of forms" and the theater that had been so important in shaping the successful practice of the Catholic faith in the Netherlands. They asked themselves sincerely what all those Catholic men and women had actually thought or believed when they participated in those theatrical and performative situations, in performances where they were expected to be present collectively and not as individuals. Did the participants in the Silent Walk really believe in the transubstantiation of the "Most Holy Sacrament of the Altar" for which they had come officially? Did they consciously believe all that, without skepticism? The two writers assumed that there must have been a kind of "intoxication by the forms" by a church that was all about form. Was the adventurous nocturnal Silent Walk through Amsterdam really a "personal faith"? Bomans, who had himself taken part from Haarlem seven times, had experienced that pilgrims walked in a group and felt "surrounded" by others, so that "the question what I personally thought about it did not even arise," in the same way as he experienced mass itself, another example of a collective Catholic "play of forms."[92] For him, the liturgy and the practice of the faith all sent out the same message: "It's all ready for you, just jump in. No need to stop and think what it means to you personally. That was considered to be Protestant, and that is exactly what it was."[93]

According to Bomans, this meant that as a believer you ended up in a "maelstrom of religious events," "where you circled around almost unconsciously."[94] He was able to express the sensory, emotional, and performative aspects of the faith in imaginative language, and several other testimonies of the Walk show that collective ritual stimulated the senses and the emotions. Those sensory experiences and perceptions increasingly began to clash with the skeptical and critical approach that had been the fruit of both councils. The time of triumphant collectiveness had definitively passed; the Catholic flock had dispersed. Despite its unique form, both writers more or less equated the Silent Walk with all the other Catholic devotional displays. The tendency, fed by "accommodation Catholicism," to suppress ostentation, in combination with the Walk's massive scale, will have contributed to this perception.

Citykerk versus Traditions

The decline in church attendance impelled the diocese to reorganize the city's parish structure. In 1971 the parishes in the city center of Amsterdam were amalgamated under the modern name of Citykerk or "City Church," with its headquarters in the Begijnhof.[95] The pastoral leadership of the Citykerk immediately questioned whether it should continue to be involved in the Silent Walk. The priests attached to the Citykerk were eager to hand over to the Society as many tasks as possible connected with the veneration of the Miracle.[96] The future of the Walk looked bleak.

These years may count as the Silent Walk's nadir, with no more than five thousand or six thousand participants.[97] These figures finally induced the Society to ask the existential question as to whether it made sense to continue. Despite having put on a brave face before, this time it regarded the situation as desperate. In a programmatic *Manifest aan Katholiek Amsterdam* (Manifesto to Catholic Amsterdam) of February 1972, the board of the Society asked whether it would not be better to abolish "this venerable but seemingly outdated custom."[98] It called the Walk a childhood memory and stated that belief in miracles was a thing of the past. The board did not speak with total conviction—hence "seemingly." But its suggestion, when put to the annual meeting, met with "massive opposition" from the provinces. Clearly participants from the provinces, who had continued to come every year, were also the ones most attached to the tradition. An important argument they advanced was that the number of young participants was still considerable. Compared to the golden decade of the postwar years, participation may have been unimpressive, but in comparison to other contemporary religious manifestations it was not a negligible number, and the Walk had a strongly symbolic significance. Tradition notwithstanding, the *Manifest* proposed a "different point of view." Inspired partly by the success of the silent marches, and by Willebrands's recommendation, Elsenburg took the initiative toward a Walk of unity, held together with "our Protestant brothers" to confirm their common past. This Walk was also to be a penitential walk for the faults of the past.[99] At the same time, he was worried about what he regarded as Amsterdam's increasing lack of hospitality in those years. Elsenburg himself appealed to parishes and institutions to give pilgrims a warm welcome again on the night of the Walk.

The Citykerk pastors still thought the entire Walk was too fragmented and too little Eucharistic; they decided therefore to set up liturgically oriented "Eucharistic Days."[100] Despite the criticism, the remaining participants continued to feel the power of tradition and refused to give up; the sister societies, especially in rural areas, insisted strongly that the Walk should go on. The bishop of Haarlem stood aside from the debate and declined to take a position, but he said he was "glad" when the decision was made to continue. On balance, an old and established local devotional tradition can prove to be very significant for a diocese, as would become clear once more in the twenty-first century.[101]

After about a century, the Walk could claim to have become an established tradition, but groups linked to it were even more venerable. One of these was the seventeenth-century St. Caecilia Collegie, which had seen little action as a musical society for quite some time. During a meeting in March 1964, its chairman had predicted that the Collegie would soon "die a quiet death." Prosaic factors such as aging membership, lack of inner-city parking, and conflicting obligations on Thursday mornings ensured that it lost most of its membership during the 1960s and 1970s. But this society also had a tenacious sense of tradition. It acquired a new, cultural-historical role in the cult.[102]

In addition to the annual Silent Walk, the Miracle week continued to be observed on a limited scale in the Begijnhofkerk. Lack of interest caused the decline of three devotional organizations linked to the cult: the Guild of the Procession from 1878, the Guild of the Miracle from 1892, and the relatively young Guild of the Sacrament from 1950. The Guild of the Miracle was a fund for the purposes of enhancing the cult of the Sacrament of Miracle during the Miracle week and the Silent Walk. It had retained only three hundred out of formerly thousands of contributors, and most of them were in default of payment. The fund was quickly depleted. Of the members of the Guild of the Procession, half were too old and the other half too modern to attend a procession. The last procession in the Begijnhof took place on June 13, 1968. At the rector's instigation, the remaining members of the various guilds and their activities were joined together in early 1969 into a "Eucharistic Center."[103] Instead of processions, this body organized monthly catechetical courses together with a celebration of the Eucharist. The monthly sessions attracted very few people, and those who came were divided into modern and conservative factions. The center's activities were discontinued in 1971.

"It Seems Better to Me to Let It Die Out"

Despite the general predilection for modernity, it has been seen that there were still participants in the Walk who held on to tradition. They not only were dissatisfied with the Eucharistic Center, but also looked back wistfully to the Klönnite perspective of the Miracle that had been popular in the days of old. In 1975 they worked to revive the Guild of the Sacrament and to generate greater attention for the Sacrament of Miracle. A first step was to restore the devotion of the Perpetual Adoration of the Blessed Sacrament in the Begijnhofkerk. Their group was not stable, however, and the perpetual prayer had to be discontinued after a few years. In 1978 Jaap Suidgeest was appointed rector of the Begijnhof. A priest of modern, conciliar views, he was immediately skeptical of the perpetual adoration and of devotion to the Miracle.[104] The last vestiges of interest had all but disappeared among the clergy of the Amsterdam Citykerk, and reviving the Miracle cult was therefore the very last thing on Suidgeest's mind. He made it clear that the devotion was no longer suited for the time and the place. He decided that the devotion would from then on be permitted only on the official feast day of the Miracle itself, according to the rules of the church. But the conservative Guild of the Sacrament, which felt that the popular, romantic Begijnhof had been transformed from a Eucharistic center into a tourist attraction, refused to accept this. Suidgeest asked advice from the diocese. In his reply, Vicar Willem de Graaf provided him with more than enough ammunition. He wrote that the celebration "increasingly appears to me as a thing of the past that really doesn't have any meaning anymore for the church of today and tomorrow. You increasingly get the impression that this kind of devotion has passed forever. On the other hand, the group that still makes these demands is too strong to be able to abolish the whole thing without a riot. It seems better to me to let it die out. That is to say: take care of it properly without introducing too many new innovations."[105] This was plain talk. Paradoxically, De Graaf's advice not to introduce any innovations would eventually help to continue the cult of the Miracle and the Silent Walk. While many of the faithful initially went along with the rigid idea of modernization that was de rigueur at the time, many innovations quickly seemed to be outdated themselves. Aspects of church life that had seemed old-fashioned eventually began to appear meaningful again. This was all too much for the progressive priests of the Amsterdam Citykerk. Their main worry was how to change the Miracle week drastically without causing conflict, or at least how to disconnect it from the Begijnhof. One plan was to turn the Begijnhofkerk into a modern "meditative center" so that the celebration of the Miracle and the Walk could be gradually repressed. The diocese, once again in the person of Vicar de Graaf, fully supported the plan: "When something as real as a meditative center grows, you have a pragmatic motive to eventually abolish the celebration of the Miracle." But it would not come to that.

Gradually, the significance of the history and traditions of the Miracle, traditions that would later be designated as "heritage," began to be recognized again. Interest in the Walk saw a slight increase, a development that was significant in the context of a church in decline. Given the denominational fragmentation of the Netherlands, a country where many sought individual, personal forms for their spiritual feelings, the Silent Walk clearly continued to be an interesting ritual. Much of the appreciation of the power of the Walk, on account of its open, noncommittal, meditative character, and its almost neutral denominational allure, came from non-Catholic quarters.[106] Most of the participants, however, continued to stand in a family tradition of making the Walk.

The depillarization of the Netherlands had in the meantime advanced so far that the media and the public at large no longer regarded the Silent Walk only as a bigoted papist ritual, but (sometimes) also as an interesting cultural-historical phenomenon. One factor in this development was that pilgrimages were making an unexpected comeback internationally. While the old-fashioned Catholic pilgrimage had long been an object of derision, the phenomenon experienced an unexpected revival in the 1970s.[107] The popularity of making the pilgrimage to Santiago de Compostela played a huge role in bringing about this development.

The even more ancient pedigree of the medieval Miracle tradition also generated interest in the heritage surrounding the cult. The centenary of the first Silent Walk, in 1981, came at just the right moment. It drew attention once again to the phenomenon, with its medieval heritage and peculiar ritual. An exhibition organized by the Amsterdam Historical Museum in the centenary year on the history of the Miracle and the Silent Walk was a case in point.[108] The Burgerweeshuis even felt the time was ripe to "release" its old object of strife, the medieval Miracle chest, and give it in permanent loan to the museum. The Protestant daily *Trouw* reminded its readers that an orthodox attempt to prevent papist superstition had prevented the chest from being relinquished before. "The Catholics' long wait has not been in vain," the commentator wrote, forgetting that the chest had in fact been relinquished before and that it was now disappearing behind glass as a musealized object, leaving "the Catholics" with empty hands.[109] Catholic interest in the chest had in fact evaporated long ago, after Sterck had unmasked it. The chest was mainly an amusing curiosity from the long history of the Miracle. The new insights and developments caused the museum to consider that the Miracle and the Silent Walk merited a place in its history of Amsterdam, and it created a space for it in its permanent collection.

A New Chairman, a New Policy

The Walk changed little up to the early 1980s. Observers thought the structurally low turnout pointed to a trend that would see the initiative die out. The question was how long it would take. Even though the number of participants had risen by some 20 percent in the centenary year of 1981, thanks to attention in the media, the board still was unsure as to how to continue.[110] That was the situation when thirty-two-year-old Maarten Elsenburg took over from his father Eduard in 1982 and became the new chairman of the Society of the Silent Walk. He was the fourth generation of Elsenburgs to lead the movement.[111] From his own family experience he had seen personally how the Walk could occupy an important place in someone's personal religious life. As chairman, he took this experience as his point of departure for formulating policy, and he had very pronounced ideas about the significance of the Walk and its traditions. As the great-grandson of one of the two founders, Elsenburg had familiarized himself at an early stage with Lousbergh's *Memorandum*. He decided to remain neutral in the political and ecclesiastical polarization that was rampant at the time and to ensure that it would not encroach upon the Walk. Although conservative attempts were made to appropriate the Walk, it managed to steer clear of the conflicts that characterized postconciliar Catholicism until the early 1980s. This policy did occasion the departure of a number of traditionalist members, supporters of the conservative bishop Gijsen of Roermond.[112] He had criticized the Walk because the board no longer acknowledged the medieval miracle as a "fact of faith."[113] Others, by contrast, regarded the Walk as a valuable remnant of a past that had disappeared and thought this was good reason to preserve this tradition for the church. Outsiders often unreflectively viewed the ritual as suspicious and conservative because of its old pedigree and collective character. And yet others saw the practice of the Walk as an expression of conservatism: a symbol not of unity but of divisiveness.[114] This would prove to be far from the truth. At the same time, however, neither did the Walk become a vehicle for the Acht Mei Beweging (Eighth of May movement), a platform of progressive Dutch Catholics (1985–2003) that campaigned against the conservative church policy implemented in the Netherlands.[115] It was only in the twenty-first century that the diocese of Haarlem-Amsterdam would attempt to harness the Walk for an explicitly conservative strand in the church, as will be seen shortly.

Policy documents and management memos were favored instruments of management in the 1980s and 1990s, and they were churned out by the thousands. This was the heyday of the socially engineered "makeable society" that would lead to "total," or complacent, democracy, a period that has gone down in history as "the Dutch miracle" because of its economic success.[116] Policy was made in the context of the "polder model" of seeking consensus, which in politics led to the formation of a "purple" coalition (i.e., a coalition of Social Democrats and Liberals, without the Christian Democrats).

The board's enterprising new chairman ensured that the Society would not be outdone in this respect, all the more so as the board had never responded properly to the 1967 Veldkamp report. In 1985, a few years into his term, Elsenburg therefore wrote a policy document called "De Stille Omgang na het jaar 2000" (The Silent Walk after the year 2000). He worried that the persistent narrative about the Walk was that the current participants were the very last generation to take part. Time and again media reports on the Walk repeated that it was on its last legs. Elsenburg was not prepared to accept that the Walk would disappear during his term in office. But who would still be prepared, without the coercion exercised by a pillarized society, to go out at night to make the Walk, often subjected to ridicule, in good weather and bad? And yet, even though almost every public church ritual in the Netherlands had disappeared, the Walk was still continuing. Familiar as he was with its history, Elsenburg knew that popular devotions rooted in tradition are persistent. The question as to how "his" ritual would be able to survive in a widely dechristianized society remained a legitimate question.[117] On the one hand, he was reluctant to meddle with the basic principles of the Walk; on the other, he also felt that it should give greater attention to the sacrament of the Eucharist. However, as a pragmatic Catholic, and bearing in mind the advice that his family friend Willebrands had once given, he also embraced the idea that the Walk, once a crowbar for Catholic emancipation, could become an "enlightened ritual" that would be acceptable to several Christian denominations in the country. In his view, the Walk offered opportunities for wider "ecumenical emphases," something that corresponded with a newly felt need for meditation and spirituality in society. It was precisely the Walk's aspect of personal meditation that he believed was significant: he saw this as a "guarantee" that it would survive. This quality would be able to appeal to the younger generation in particular. The Walk's spiritual aspects should no longer be restricted to Catholics only, but should also be welcoming of other Christians. Elsenburg also emphasized that the Walk, as a lay initiative, transcended the institutional church, which was an important asset in a time of secularization, with its increasing shortage of priests.[118]

As it turned out, the young chairman's pragmatic vision appealed to the spirit of the age. Compared to other Western European countries, the Netherlands probably had the highest proportion of "unbelievers," at least when it came to the official religions, but also a correspondingly high number of "spirituals" who replaced them. In view of this, *Elsevier*'s religious correspondent Rex Brico wrote that the Walk would have to draw its participants from people who appreciated its meditative, mystical, spiritual character. In this view, the miracle of 1345 was simply a "symbol of the inner knowledge that there is more than what meets the eye."[119] This was indeed a perspective that many of today's "ietsists"—people who no longer believe in God, but do believe in "something"—could embrace without a problem. The question is whether this actually happened much in practice. In fact, the overwhelming majority of the participants even at this writing certainly do not belong to this nondescriptive category.[120]

In addition to reshaping the religious content of the Walk, Elsenburg acknowledged that the history of the cult was an important asset. He had been brought up from childhood with stories about the history of the Walk, and his plans for the future were based on this firm historical foundation. To be able to give a historical account of the Walk was necessary not only to inspire participants and other people involved, but also to tell outsiders, skeptical or otherwise, what the nocturnal Walk had meant throughout the ages. Exhibitions and symposiums were organized and books published at Elsenburg's behest, and he acquired historical documents and objects for the Society's own collection. This policy created new opportunities for people to relate to the Walk, either from a traditional point of view or from a heritage perspective. Elsenburg's professional skills also made an important contribution. He carried out an overhaul of the organization of the Silent Walk by ensuring that the finances were in good order and that there were funds to "work toward the future," as Lousbergh had once put it. It is doubtful whether the Silent Walk could have survived the 1980s, were it not for his interventions, not so much in terms of turnout but rather in organization and coordination. If the umbrella organization of the Society had collapsed, the pilgrimage itself would probably not have survived either.[121]

The annual number of participants during the 1980s and 1990s was around eight thousand, according to the imprecise estimates made. There was a peak in 1990, when approximately two hundred coaches ferried in the greatest part of that year's ten thousand participants. Participants henceforth generally came from clearly defined geographical areas: Limburg, North Brabant, North and South Holland, Salland, and Achterhoek (two regions in the east of the country). Very few participants came from areas that had no tradition of sending people to the Walk: Zeeland, the islands of South Holland, the west of West Brabant, Flevoland, Overijssel, and the three northern provinces (Friesland, Groningen, and Drenthe).

At the time of writing, some twenty-five years later, the number of participants had stabilized at around five thousand to six thousand, depending
on the weather. They came from almost the same areas as in 1990.[122]
There was even a slight increase for the Amsterdam region, Flevoland,
Groningen, and Friesland. The difficulty for the Walk in the twenty-first
century is not so much low turnout as the fact that it is not easy to find
successors for local leaders who organize participation in an area. If such
pivotal figures are not replaced, the pilgrimage to Amsterdam from the
area in question often disappears.

The revitalization of the Camino to Santiago has made spiritual and
ritual walking popular again, as well as the notion of going on a pilgrimage. This trend inspired a foundation called Stichting Staatsliedengreep
(Statesmen's Coup d'État Foundation) to organize a one-off historical reconstruction of the Miracle procession through the Amsterdam Staats-
liedenbuurt area in 1991 and to stage a Miracle play afterward in the
Nassaukerk.[123] Another result is that growing numbers of young participants from rural areas, such as Nibbixwoud, Volendam, and Utrecht, first
go to Amsterdam on foot before making the Silent Walk. Some of these
pilgrimages stop at other churches on the way, by way of ecumenical gesture. Every year, an interdenominational group from Heerhugowaard
makes the thirty-four-mile journey to Amsterdam on foot, visiting a Reformed church and even a Turkish mosque on the way.[124] This idea of
going on a journey together, pilgrimaging together, would become the
theme of an ecumenical celebration of the Miracle in 1995.

Ecumenical Harmony?

As has been seen, the Silent Walk appeared during and after World War II
as a ritual with a wider Christian potential. From the 1960s onward, the
idea of common Christian participation was expressed ever more emphatically. In 1967 Willebrands, then secretary of the Council for Promoting Christian Unity in Rome, made the case for using a "Reformed" Walk
(i.e., a Walk open to other Christians) as an instrument to promote Christian unity. In 1976 the bishop of 's-Hertogenbosch, Jan Bluyssen, held a
similar speech at the annual meeting, with the title "That They May All Be
One." Bluyssen saw the Eucharist—or the Lord's Supper—as a way of
bringing the Christian churches in the Netherlands closer together, and
specifically saw a role there for the Silent Walk. The Dutch Reformed

Church, which was a holding synodical discussion that year on the Lord's Supper and its relation to other churches in the Netherlands, announced, through its secretary general, Albert van den Heuvel, that it would "participate with joy in the Silent Walk."[125] The Lutheran congregation of Amsterdam had already "ecumenically" offered its church on Spui for the nocturnal provisioning of Catholic pilgrims in 1980. Not only liberal Protestants, but some orthodox Calvinists, too, were interested in the meditative Walk. One member of the Reformed church in Wageningen placed the following call to participate in the Silent Walk in his church newsletter in 1992: "Participating in the Silent Walk as a Protestant is meaningful if only because it means you are thinking about, and wondering at, what motivates other Christians. In any case, our ancestors in 1345 were still Catholics too. 'Romish' is 'roots,' right up to Luther. Why don't you join next year, it won't do your soul any harm. Will we all join the Walk next year? Walking through Amsterdam together?"[126] Non-Catholics had been taking part for a long time already on an informal basis, and Protestant ministers supported it from time to time. Following on from this, it was decided to put the ecumenical mission at center stage during the jubilee year of 1995: 650 years of the Miracle. The celebration had a specifically ecumenical purpose—its motto was "That they may all be one"—thus closing the circle of the Miracle cult, as it were. With this celebration, the board tried to symbolically bridge four hundred years of divisions within Amsterdam Christianity. The theologian and minister Sytze de Vries (*1945) of the Reformed Oude Kerk[127] insisted on hosting an "ecumenical vesper" in his church, presided over by himself and Auxiliary Bishop Joseph Lescrauwaet (1923–2013) of Haarlem. Some commentators regarded the fact that these communal vespers were held in the Oude Kerk as a greater miracle than the original Miracle itself.[128]

In 1845 Protestants had poured scorn on and rioted over the "Feast of Folly," but in 1995 Christians came together in a setting that was unique in the Dutch context, with a Protestant minister and a bishop commemorating the Miracle together. The common history and spiritual significance of the Walk, aspects that could also appeal to other denominations, were the motivating principles of the celebration. In addition, it fostered the idea that Catholics and Protestants had grown toward each other in the way they thought about the Eucharist and the Lord's Supper. As a concrete expression of the theme of the Walk ("That they may all be one"), the ecumenical vesper service was a novel ecclesiastical experiment of Catholics and Reformed who on this day transcended the boundaries of their religions. Minister De Vries and many other non-Catholics took part in the traditional Walk. It even seemed that denominational roles were reversed for a moment when De Vries talked about organizing a candlelit procession through the city. The board of the Society politely declined.[129] It did not want any adaptations, and it continued to tread carefully in view of possible reactions that might follow any change to the ritual. Not everyone was imbued with the spirit of ecumenism. For the first time in a century a counting team had been organized; despite the fact that it was a jubilee year and despite the ritual's new ecumenical departure, the turnout did not exceed 5,700.[130] However much the ecumenical initiative was propagated from above, there was very little response at the Protestant grassroots level. The Walk would continue to be something supported mainly by Catholics.

The board's apprehensions regarding religious sensitivities surrounding the cult were not entirely without foundation. This became evident at the academic symposium on the history of the Miracle that was organized on the occasion of the 650th anniversary of the Miracle.[131] Prior to the conference, an anonymous letter was received with the following message: "To whom it may concern. You really must be very retarded if you still believe in floating hosts in 1995. It's time you asked yourself if you're not floating yourself! All religions are inventions!!! Religion results from ignorance, superstition but particularly FEAR! What for???"[132] The cult was still able to provoke this kind of sentiment in society. Similarly, a number of people who took part in the panel discussion, and who themselves were among the participants in the Walk, felt that their religious feelings had been offended. Unshaken faith in miracles and a literal lack of distance were also evident during the Miracle exhibition in the Museum Ons' Lieve Heer op Solder (Amstelkring), where the illustrious Miracle chest once again basked in its fame. Visitors proved unable to resist the urge to physically touch the mythical archive chest. It was like the eighteenth-century visitors to the Burgerweeshuis who clandestinely sat on the chest in the hope of a cure for their diseases. Perhaps this was the reason why the Miracle-phobic Rector Suidgeest took steps just before his departure to demythologize his Begijnhofkerk as a place of pilgrimage even further. In 1994 Suidgeest removed the characteristic cult painting from 1891, commissioned by Rector Klönne and painted by M. C. Schenk, that represented the miraculous power of the shrine. Klönne put it in "the most important spot" in full view of the pilgrims, right above the altar.[133] It was replaced by a "neutral" canvas by Johannes Voorhout showing the Resurrection of Christ (1695).[134] From a liturgical and an artistic perspective this was perhaps an improvement, but from a cultural-historical point of view it was a great loss.

During the symposium mentioned above, the Tilburg professor Paul Post contended that the "Eucharistic fascination" that had characterized Dutch Catholicism for so long had disappeared during the last years of the twentieth century, to be replaced by a fascination for the external aspects of the ritual. He believed the Walk was becoming folklorized, musealized, and mediatized, and this, he argued, robbed the ritual of its intrinsic meaning. He contended that contemporary discourse increasingly speaks only "about" the phenomenon, while the intrinsic experience disappears behind the commentary. Media attention reduced the Walk to a ritual folly.[135] The question is, however, whether the participants in the Walk ever had the kind of Eucharistic fascination that Post ascribed to them. It is a question that Bomans previously answered in the negative. In fact, the memories and traditions handed down point primarily to a fascination for the Walk's sacred and ritual dimensions, and also to the attraction of tradition, of the night, of silence, and the collective aspect, all things that speak to the senses and leave indelible memories.

Despite limited ecumenical participation, the Walk did not relinquish the theme of unity, particularly because it is part of its essence. The experiment of 1995 was repeated at the 125th anniversary of the establishment of the Silent Walk in 2006. This time it was the Protestant minister Hans Uytenbogaardt who presided at an ecumenical vesper service together with the auxiliary bishop of Haarlem, the Sacramentine Jan van Burgsteden, in the Oude Kerk. They concluded that "it is incumbent on those who wish to bear Christ's name to foster solidarity." Uytenbogaardt hoped for a more denominationally diverse Walk of pilgrims who "together celebrate his Presence in bread and wine."[136] Because of the success of the celebration, and because the Begijnhofkapel had been entrusted to them, the Fathers of the Blessed Sacrament (S.S.S.) asked to be allowed representation on the board of the Society. The Sacramentine Fathers had a particular interest in this, given the charism of their Congregation of the Blessed Sacrament. In accordance with the directive of their founder, Pierre Julien Eymard († 1868), they prefer to exercise their ministry in places with a Sacrament of Miracle, such as Amsterdam. In 2006 they organized a lighthearted seminar on Eucharistic testimonies with a performance by the interdenominational and multicultural music group the Miracle City Singers.[137]

The jubilee of the Walk was also marked by the performance of songs from the so-called Occo Codex (1515–1517).[138] This precious hymnbook had been part of the liturgical collection of books of the Holy Stead in the Middle Ages. It was made at the behest of the powerful merchant and patron of the arts Pompeius Occo, who lived not far from the Holy Stead in Kalverstraat. Occo was also a church warden of the Holy Stead, and in this capacity he gave the book in long-term loan to the chapel. The manuscript resurfaced in 1972, when it was purchased from Occo's heirs and the Amsterdam Occo Hofje by the Royal Library of Brussels.[139]

Neutral Silent Marches

If modern Miracle anniversaries provided leads for initiatives involving other Christians, the Walk had already proven to be a source of inspiration for wider society as well. As has been seen, the silent commemorative marches held after the war were inspired by the Silent Walk. The 1960s saw the rise of another derivative of the Walk, confusingly known by the same name. This phenomenon of the silent march emerged in Dutch society as a form of protest alongside noisy demonstrations. They were incidental protest marches, organized spontaneously by citizens to protest against wars and oppressive regimes or as a show of solidarity at the death of famous people.[140] In this way, the silent march occupied a logical place in the ritual vacuum that the end of pillarization had left. It met the need for new ritual forms.[141]

To complicate things further, a slightly different kind of march developed out of these silent protest marches in the late 1990s. The kind of march that is currently known and widely accepted in Dutch society as a "silent march" is a ritual of mourning and commemoration. These silent marches are usually organized locally to commemorate victims of *zinloos geweld* (senseless violence), young road casualties, or victims of disaster. These marches of mourning also express a general sense of moral outrage vis-à-vis the Dutch government and society in general.[142] Apart from being a ritual of mourning, silent marches are also silent signals of protest against violence, insecurity, and fatal negligence. Organizers hope to generate awareness of the problem on a national level, appealing both to the government and to society at large to help prevent any further victims.[143]

Silent marches, which emerged during the individualized "ego age," with its absence of rituality, have been characterized as a new "quest for society," for togetherness in the wake of traumatic events—for instance an illogical, premature, or innocent death—in the secularized local community.[144] "Neutral" silent marches express strong moral outrage, which can spread through society if it is disseminated and amplified by the media.[145]

There was a certain degree of cross-fertilization between the silent marches and the Silent Walk.[146] The custom of formulating an annual motto for the Silent Walk referring to current issues, such as the threat of war or other ills in the world, contributed to the Amsterdam prayer walk's rise in status in society since the late 1980s. This was most clearly evident in 2003, when the intention of the Walk was against the brutalization of society and against gratuitous violence, and for a livable and loving world—a message that would have befitted a silent march.

Intra-Catholic Competition

Dutch society is one of the most secularized ("unchurched") in the world. The country does have various small religious movements that are relatively new, such as evangelical, charismatic, and Pentecostal groups, but on the whole the wider Christian community has good reason to be concerned about its future. This is even more the case as Islam has, in the meantime, gained a strong foothold in the country and is becoming an ever more visible presence, with or without the support of countries such as Turkey and Saudi Arabia. Compared to this, the traditional Christian churches in the Netherlands are only barely able to prevent the total collapse of their structures. The scenario that the archdiocese of Utrecht will have only twenty-five functioning Catholic churches left in some fifteen years' time is one dire symptom.[147] This development is not new. The highest representatives of the Dutch church province traveled to Rome in the Holy Year of 2000 to take stock: their *ad limina* visit. At the end of a national pilgrimage in St. Peter's Basilica, Pope John Paul II explicitly labeled the Netherlands a mission country and issued a warning for the future. In accordance with his missionary and pastoral strategy, the pope tried to unite the Dutch church province behind the same (conservative) policy, while at the same time rekindling the embers of faith. It has not since led to any discernible reversal of fortunes.

Despite this ecclesiastical malaise, one participant in the Walk suggested that a gesture to the city should be made in the symbolic year of

2000 by marking what was once the country's most important pilgrimage more clearly in the public space. A similar proposal had resulted in the erection of a single column on Rokin in 1988, composed of fragments of the demolished medieval shrine in commemoration of the Holy Stead.[148] The new proposal corresponded to an idea of the Amsterdam pastor G. Q. A. Meershoek to put up a permanent façade stone where the holy hearth had once stood, on the Kalverstraat side of the former chapel, on the spot where the mobile lantern was placed annually during the Walk. The owner of the commercial property at number 81, still the Reformed congregation, responded positively from a changed historical awareness: "We think it is a good idea to create a lasting remembrance of this event that has been so important for Amsterdam."[149]

The project was realized on March 11, 2001, when a rectangular stone with an empty niche was revealed in the façade of the building. The year 1345 was marked above the empty niche and the words *Gedachtenis ter Heilige Stede* (Remembrance niche for the Holy Stead) appeared below it. On the one hand, this stone fosters the memory and commemoration of the Miracle; on the other, it is an empty space that can be filled by every viewer personally.[150] In addition, the niche is a symbolic reference to the Holy Stead and the hearth of the Miracle, which have both disappeared, and to the many empty niches, stripped of their saints' statues, that were so typical of the building in later centuries. The stone also expresses the idea, as Elsenburg remarked at its unveiling, that the Walk is not just for Catholics, but is open to "everyone."[151]

This emphasis on "everyone" and on "ecumenism" had its limits. This became evident less than a week after the unveiling of the stone. On March 17, 2001, shortly before he began to systematically attack another religion, Islam, the filmmaker Theo van Gogh, who was assassinated in 2004, positioned himself along the route of the Walk under the eye of television cameras, to offer strident commentary to passersby. Near the mobile lantern, beside the former Miracle hearth, he reportedly sat behind a table with a candle under a bell jar, an alternative lantern that seemed to mark a place of enlightenment. From this strategic position, he began to harangue passing pilgrims with antireligious commentary. Inspired by a horror of Catholic bigotry, he tried to provoke participants by loudly slinging choice insults at them. None of the participants appear to have been thrown off course by this.[152]

If this incident is remarkable in retrospect because of Van Gogh's own fate a few years later, the "ecumenical" aspect of the Walk encountered an obstacle that was much more difficult to control in the form of the long-banned cult surrounding apparitions of the Lady of All Nations, a conservative and nonecumenical Marian movement.[153] This Amsterdam Marian cult arose from visions of Mary that Ida Peerdeman was said to have received between 1945 and 1959.[154] In these visions, Mary spoke of evil in the world and the need to counterbalance it. Her messages treated of war and disaster, hunger, chaos, and disbelief, all set against the background of the international politics of those days. In Cold War language, Mary warned that "the Russians will not leave things as they are," but she also worried about the deformation of the Netherlands and the growing domination of "Satan" in a modernizing world. This is why "the Lady" emphatically wanted to be the Lady "of All Nations," at least to the extent that the people of those nations were good Catholics. She had personally chosen the city of Amsterdam and stated that she wanted the largest Marian shrine in the world to be built there. Just as in the Miracle of 1345, this new Amsterdam miracle, or rather the series of miraculous apparitions, was subjected to a thorough inquiry by the diocese. Because of the strongly contemporary political and often practical and prosaic content of the messages, the diocesan commission of inquiry professed to be "profoundly shocked." It stated that Mary had never revealed herself in such a way. Moreover, the Lady appeared to contradict the Catholic Church's central teachings on redemption because she said that her son Christ had not redeemed the world *alone*, but that she herself was coredemptrix, a position that had to be recognized as a dogma.[155]

Two successive diocesan commissions of inquiry judged of Peerdeman's messages that nonsupernaturality could not be established, a conclusion that was confirmed by the Vatican's Holy Office.[156] This meant that the devotion was deemed to be inauthentic and was rejected for public veneration. But the movement's fanatical adherents placed greater trust in their "heavenly" messages than in the statements of disapproving earthly clerics: "Who do they [the diocese] think they are to criticize Mary?" The church's rejection did not appear to leave much room to maneuver, given that the dogma of Mary as coredemptrix is in contradiction with present-day church teaching and deviates from the Second Vatican Council's conclusions. The cult had little choice but to go underground in the Netherlands, but the number of the Lady's adherents increased strongly abroad, where the negative results of the diocesan investigations were either not known or simply ignored. Adherents continued to make international propaganda for the Lady as if nothing had happened.

Not everyone in the Dutch church province breathed a sigh of relief when Rome rejected the cult. Certain Catholics with a special devotion to Mary were disappointed, and some in the diocese of Haarlem also regretted it: they could not understand how the church could squander the opportunity that a sensational Marian apparition in the Netherlands, even in their own diocese, offered.

Hendrik Bomers succeeded Theo Zwartkruis, who had been skeptical of the apparitions, as bishop of Haarlem in 1983. The rigid and conservative Bomers had a particular affinity with Marian devotions. As a former missionary bishop in Africa, he had dealt with them before. He had experienced there that apparitions can be an important source of inspiration for the faith. Almost immediately, Peerdeman and her apparitions caught his interest, and he began to visit her secretly in her villa on Diepenbrockstraat, a stone's throw away from the RAI conference center.[57] She had retired there together with a few religious in an improvised shrine that was open to the public, even though it retained its "underground" character.

From this moment on, Amsterdam had two important places of pilgrimage. Curiously, almost no one in the Netherlands had heard of the devotion to the Lady, which was still clandestine and ignored, even though it was immensely popular in certain areas of the world.[58] This formed a strong contrast with the Miracle and the Silent Walk, which were reasonably well known in the Netherlands but not at all abroad. The two cults represented opposing devotional atmospheres: history, silence, meditation, ecumenism, and progressivity versus contemporary private revelations that many regard as heretical and conservative. To outsiders, these Catholic phenomena may all seem the same, but the two Amsterdam devotions are in fact polar opposites in terms of devotional culture and religious intention.

The two devotions did not really hinder each other until Bomers died suddenly in 1998 and was succeeded by his protégé, the controversial auxiliary bishop Jos Punt.[59] This bishop was a special case. Punt was a late convert. Having been an enthusiastic devotee of Gnostic sects and Eastern spiritualities, he later chose to return to the Catholic Church with the zeal of the convert. He then quickly rose through the diocesan ranks.[60]

The remarkable thing about Punt's background was that his mother had dedicated him, and named him after, the Lady of All Nations at his birth; at the time the cult was beginning to gain some adherents and had not yet come under much criticism. Punt's middle name, Marianus—

which can be translated roughly as "filled with Mary"—points to his mother's gesture. Although it was known in Rome that Punt was a devotee of the Lady, he was nevertheless allowed to succeed Bomers in 1998, albeit as "apostolic administrator." He was appointed in this capacity because it was seen as a risk to doctrinal consistency within the diocese if Punt were to act in an idiosyncratic way in the matter of the Lady. His devotional inspiration and aspiration had always been to see the cult recognized and to give it a place in the mission of the diocese.

When nothing controversial had happened after three years, Pope John Paul II, himself a devotee of Marian cults, appointed Punt bishop of Haarlem. Among his strong points was that he was an intelligent and hard worker, and he was also a conservative. He fitted perfectly into the conservative course that Rome had been following for years to bring the Dutch church province back onto the straight and narrow. Within a year of his appointment, what many in the diocese of Haarlem, in the Dutch church province, and even in Rome had feared actually happened: the "spiritual" bishop himself changed into a kind of visionary. In early 2002, on a quiet evening in his palace, Punt entered a meditative state, during which he received the inspiration that all apparitions and messages of the Lady were supernatural, that is, "real," after all, despite the previous inquiries and condemnations.[161] He possibly did this on the basis of Canon 1230 of the *Code of Canon Law*, which permits the local ordinary to approve a shrine.[162] But what if, as in the case of the Lady, previous diocesan and Vatican investigations resulted in a triple rejection of the apparitions and the statements of the Lady that form the foundation of this shrine? Nor did Punt carry out any new inquiry. Neither the *Codex* nor jurisprudence anticipated this situation. However, the rule is that a Vatican decision in issues pertaining to the doctrine of the faith remains in force as long as it has not been repealed.[163] This means that the status of the shrine, based on the private revelations of a layperson, remained unchanged. The Dutch bishops' conference, of course, conformed to the decisions of the church and kept its distance from the cult, finding the new situation perplexing.[164] But the Roman Congregation for the Doctrine of the Faith left little room for doubt, and it still unreservedly rejects Punt's point of view.[165] According to the head of the disciplinary section of the Congregation, the case is clear: the negative judgment remains in full force.[166]

With the Lady's status "changed," Punt had a second plan: awareness and appreciation of the Lady might grow in the Netherlands if her cult could be associated with that of the old, familiar, and recognized Miracle. The bishop found a number of clues for this in the Lady's messages themselves. Thus the first apparition to Peerdeman, on the feast of the Annunciation (March 25, 1945), occurred on the octave of the sixth centenary of the Miracle. Moreover, in the second apparition, on April 21, 1945, Peerdeman saw the old Miracle procession walk through the city, in the direction of her home in Uiterwaardenstraat in the modern borough of Amsterdam-Zuid, near to the place which the Lady had designated as the location of her future shrine (the current location of the RAI's Holland Complex).[167] According to Punt, the message was clear: the Lady was linked to the Miracle cult. In addition to the apparitions, Peerdeman also had a number of "Eucharistic experiences," visions, and messages in 1958 that were now presented as further confirmation of the Eucharistic connection with the Miracle.[168]

But Bishop Punt overplayed his hand shortly after his declaration that the Lady's apparitions were authentic when he tried to use the Silent Walk for his plans. The underlying idea was to associate the young and controversial cult of the Lady with the recognized and widely supported tradition of the Silent Walk. In this way, the status of the Lady cult could be strengthened in the devotional landscape as a "rehabilitated" newcomer. However cleverly devised, this plan stranded on the independence of an established lay movement that kept its distance from any other movement in the church. The Society had no wish to associate itself with the problematic Lady movement and thus to help normalize its cult.

The episcopal designs became evident on June 13, 2004, when for the first time since the Alteration of Amsterdam in 1578, a Eucharistic procession suddenly appeared on the streets of Amsterdam.[169] Punt personally carried the Blessed Sacrament in procession to the (new) Holy Stead on the Begijnhof. Catholic media from across the world reported on the historical significance. Press releases issued by the diocese stated that even the pope supported the initiative.[170] With the support of the bishop, the Dutch branch of Opus Dei had organized this procession from its church of the Blessed Virgin Mary on Keizersgracht. Was it maybe a late revenge for pastor Klönne's failure to reintroduce the Miracle procession around 1900 due to the lay Silent Walk movement?

Punt had asked for, and even received, the blessing of his Marian brother, Pope John Paul II,[171] who replied to Punt's request for support in a "personal message."[172] In this letter, John Paul invoked the assistance of the "Eucharistic Lady" for Punt's mission. This use of the title of "Eucharistic Lady" for Mary is an indication that the papal letter may even have been prompted by Punt himself. It again established a direct link between the Amsterdam Miracle and the cult of the Lady with Peerdeman's "Eucharistic experiences."

The cult of the Miracle, the new Eucharistic procession, and the Eucharistic Lady of All Nations thus became more closely associated with each other. Organizing a procession also meant contesting the tradition of the Silent Walk and the Miracle.[73] Indeed, Bishop Punt hoped that his initiative might see the existing Walk merge into a renewed tradition of Eucharistic processions in Amsterdam, hence reestablishing the pre-Reformation situation.[74] The "processionists" not only wanted to combine the Silent Walk with the Eucharistic procession, but also wanted to associate the apparitional cult of the Lady of All Nations with the Miracle. The sisters of the community of the Family of Mary, who preside over the cult in Diepenbrockstraat, naturally took part in the procession.[75] This proposition failed to convince the Society of the Silent Walk. The Society pointed out that its specifically Dutch lay initiative had its own character and value, and that the Walk should therefore not merge with a Eucharistic procession.[76]

Despite this outcome, Punt did not abandon his mission to give the cult of the Lady a central place in the diocese. He shifted his attention to the old Marian shrine of Heiloo, north of Amsterdam, and attempted instead to create a link between the Lady and the established pilgrimage there.[77] Partly on account of the strongly international dimension of the Lady devotion, the name of the diocese changed to Haarlem-Amsterdam in 2009. While the attempt to appropriate the Silent Walk was foiled, the new Eucharistic processions on Corpus Christi in summer continued to take place. The connection with the Miracle continued to be made, not only by people linked to the diocese, but also within the cult of the Lady itself. The page on [Marian] "Apparitions" on its website begins by discussing the 1345 Sacrament of Miracle. The suggestion is that the Miracle happened under the auspices of the Lady and must be seen in connection with the later apparitions.[78]

This wrangling between two Amsterdam devotions also elicited a remarkable idea from a local politician. The leader of the Christian Democrats (CDA) in Amsterdam-Centrum (Central Amsterdam), the coffee shop owner Michael Veling, proposed that a large statue of the Lady of All Nations should be erected on the square in front of the Central Station. As there are only very few recognized shrines of Marian apparitions in the world, he thought that billing Amsterdam as the new "Lourdes of the North" could be an important new source of religious tourism.[179] His proposals failed to gain much support in the city.[180]

Continuing, Broken, Restored, and New Traditions

During the last years of the twentieth century, the year 2000 was regarded as a potential caesura in world history, and more than one prophet confidently predicted the end of the world. For a long time, numerologically inclined visionaries were kabbalistic favorites of the media, which eagerly reported on the most extraordinary range of doom scenarios. Once the fireworks of December 31, 1999, faded away, it became clear that the prophets of doom were wrong: Earth continued to turn, and computers continued to compute. Although societal developments can never be linked to any single year, years can serve as a framework for historiography. The year 2000 also saw discussion about the drawbacks of Dutch multicultural society—the "multicultural disaster"—take center stage. A large part of the national public discourse was changed by a single newspaper article.[181] The position of migrants—and, correspondingly, of Islam—had already been a point of debate for some time. The growing influence of Islam on society caused concern, but the Christian churches, themselves under pressure, also realized that they should not stand idly by. In a contracting market, being reticent in promoting rituals and devotions is not a wise strategy in terms of cohesion and evangelization. For the Dutch church province, countering the large-scale erosion of its own community was the central problem. Dechristianization necessitated action, and in addition to major reorganizations, attention turned again to traditional missionary instruments. There was a marked new interest in the Catholic community's own religious roots and traditions, in an attempt to draw new inspiration from them. Dutch Catholics who had experienced the waves of church modernization in the previous decades had difficulties determining their own position with regard to the church. Against the backdrop of ecclesiastical doom and gloom, it is not surprising that the Netherlands was designated a mission territory again in the year 2000.[182]

The multicultural society debacle meant that the twenty-first century started on a melancholy note. International terrorism was approaching, and Europe seemed to drag itself from one crisis to the next. Insecurities in the existence of Europe as a political unity, and its declining plausibility, caused the return of (neo)nationalism in a more militant form. A result of this phenomenon was a greater focus on national identity, norms and values, and national traditions. Traditions were even considered so important that they widely began to be designated as (immaterial) heritage and were "canonized" by the nation.[183] Even politicians began to investigate how "national" traditions could be used to strengthen social cohesion.[184] Within the religious domain, too, traditions were reevaluated and reinvented. Revived pilgrimages became popular again, and "old-fashioned" processions received a new lease on life. Processions have been introduced in many Dutch parishes to give collective witness to the faith and to proclaim it to the outside world. The age-old metaphor of the procession as the faith community on a common journey manifested itself again. A clear example is the new Eucharistic procession through Amsterdam that has just been described. Utrecht similarly instituted a reliquary procession of the national saint, Willibrord, in 2002, under the motto "Faith does not have to hide itself."[185] In emulation of the capital, a pastor in Haarlem exclaimed, "We now have the courage to do that too."[186] His procession had an ecumenical slant and even stopped at two Protestant churches for moments of communal reflection. The procession ritual, once deemed to be old-fashioned, was reinvented as an instrument for collective religious experience and as a tangible and performative expression of Catholic or religious self-consciousness: "We're no longer afraid to show it [the sacred]." In this context of a "procession boom" and of the diocese's appropriation attempts, the Silent Walk found itself facing difficult questions: how to retain interest, how to preserve its own tradition, and, particularly, how to mobilize people at local and national levels to become involved in the organization?

Traditions exist, new traditions are created, and old traditions are revived or reinvented. They can be used for very diverse purposes. But if they can be cherished and restored, they can also be abandoned. When the board of the Society rejected the plans for a merger with the new Eucharistic procession, it safeguarded the tradition of the Silent Walk for the time being. One other tradition did come to an end around the same time: the tradition that the Elsenburg family provided the chairman of the board. Maarten Elsenburg resigned in October 2010, having earned profound esteem for his unrelenting efforts to preserve and consolidate the Silent Walk as a national pilgrimage. He was praised in particular for his ecumenical spirit, for succeeding in strengthening the Walk as a ritual for the Dutch Catholic community, and for honoring the (art) historical significance of the Miracle.[187]

He was succeeded in 2011 by Piet Hein Hupsch.[188] Elsenburg's inspiration, strongly based on the Walk's history and tradition, had been to work for an ecumenical future; Hupsch was more a theologian who focused on the faith content of the Walk, that is, the Eucharist. The Silent Walk, he said, manifested the "Eucharistic mystery" and the church as the "mystical body of Christ." Adopting a universal conceptualization of the pilgrimage, Hupsch also regarded the Walk as a metaphor for the Christian life, with Christ as food for the journey.[189] The board saw Hupsch, the former rector of a secondary school, as the right man to bridge the gap that divided it from the younger generation, and hoped he could secure the continuity of the Walk on the basis of a stronger connection between the Walk's form and content.[190]

An active youth policy was in place even before Hupsch's appointment. Observing the success of the World Youth Day in Cologne in 2005, the previous chairman became conscious of the necessity of having a specific youth program, and he set out to devise one. As a result, youth services have been held prior to the Walk since 2006 in the context of a specific program in the St. Nicholas Basilica or in the Moses and Aaron Church. These services attract an average turnout of some five hundred young people, who come from far and wide, from Brabant to the north of the country. These new participants are a "pure" gain for the Walk because they were not mobilized through a long-standing family tradition.[191] The evening programs, which have trendy English titles such as "iBelieve!," "Friends?!," and "Where to go," offer a variety of gospel music, dance, theater, video clips, and liturgy, all presented in a dazzling format. The board has also tried to interest young people in the Miracle through sports by facilitating pilgrimages on foot from surrounding towns and villages. Research has shown that younger participants valued the Eucharistic adoration that is part of the evening program, but were primarily fascinated by the large-scale collective walk in the silence of the night. They experienced this as enthralling and beautiful, and they appreciated the collective aspect and the chance to encounter other young people. Once again, what convinced them most were the Walk's traditions.[192] "Something really religious happens, to be present to yourself in silence," one of them said.[193] But the sense of a faith connection—no longer a common experience in a secularized country—was also a valuable aspect. The board applied this new target group approach not only to the younger but also to an older generation. A morning Walk for older people has been organized on the Sunday after the Walk since 2014.[194]

It is not easy to conclude the "biography" of a devotion that has lasted for nearly seven centuries with sufficient distance from the present. It may help to quote comments made by the previous chairman of the Walk, Maarten Elsenburg. On the basis of his religious concern, he characterized the Silent Walk at the end of the twentieth century in the following words:

> They are private demonstrations supported by the group. The allure is very special. I have to say, I never really think much about the Miracle itself, but when I stand on Dam square and see all these groups walk past, the worn farmers' faces, and the hands that suggest they just stepped off the land . . . , then I know how deeply rooted the faith is for these people. If you were to ask these people what they are experiencing, they wouldn't be able to answer, but their involvement testifies to a simple religious conviction that was passed on to them from generation to generation.[195]

Elsenburg's ethnographic observation encapsulates the extent to which mystery, mysticism, and romanticism are still important in modern perceptions of the Walk. How deeply rooted is the faith of the people? Bomans had his doubts. But the people keep coming, belying all predictions and demographic extrapolations. This shows that, just as Veldkamp was unable to give a precise sociological explanation in 1967, it remains difficult to account for the attraction that the Silent Walk exerts. Even in modern times, when religion is deconstructed and subjectivized, the phenomenon shows that religion manifests itself as an individual combination of cognitive reflection and emotion, which human beings, as social animals, can experience in a neutral, collective, and social way in the ritual of the Walk.[196] The traditions surrounding the Miracle have played a decisive role in this. They offer the lifeline of a ritual to those who make the Walk; they offer a supportive structure in which they can mirror themselves. In the words of Hervieu-Léger, this represents a "chain of memory and tradition" that forms the participants into a community. For her, the ritual is a symbolic, ideological, and social device that creates and controls the collective and individual consciousness of belonging to the same group and lineage of believers.[197] In this process, the relevant cultural dimensions of the Miracle cult are continually unearthed from history. A religious phenomenon based on culture and tradition can be closely attuned to the needs of a society, particularly in an era in which Catholics self-identity as "cultural Catholics" and that sets great store by "heritage."

Having undergone a process of extensive retraditionalization—a consequence of the Second Vatican Council—the Catholic Church is no longer inclined to abandon anything that might count as tradition. The diocese of Haarlem-Amsterdam, for instance, is always looking for ways of linking up with traditions, especially if they involve devotions or pilgrimages, or of confirming existing practices. This was the case with the Lady of All Nations, and in 2005 the Marian shrine of Heiloo was designated a diocesan missionary center.[198] The same attitude is also evident on a smaller scale. In view of Maximilian of Austria's miraculous cure and his (reputed) visit to the Holy Stead in 1484, several futile attempts were made over the centuries to bring a male Habsburg—therefore leaving Sisi aside—back to the Begijnhof. Once again, it was Bishop Punt who became a champion for the restoration of this international and "royal" tradition of the Miracle cult. At Punt's invitation, the Archduke Karl, grandson of the last Austrian Emperor Charles I, and a direct descendant of Maximilian I, visited the Begijnhof in 2012.[199] This distant descendant, a successful businessman, received a princely welcome from the bishop on March 15. Together they walked parts of the route of the Walk and inspected the material relics of the cult.[200] It was above all a symbolic encounter that permitted the diocese to strengthen its association with the Amsterdam Miracle and its Silent Walk after the recent difficulties.

This may seem an insignificant genealogical incident, but it does show how, over the past two centuries, "incidents" have led to the emphasizing or de-emphasizing of certain strands in the long history of the Miracle. Miracle chests and processions played an important role, but ultimately proved unsuccessful. By contrast, walking in silence was a success. It is tempting therefore to ascribe to the phenomenon of the Walk a charismatic and neutral ("ecumenical") character, an allure that has the power to captivate and attract. The Walk is still a relevant, current religious expression in society that provides inspiration to many people and with which they are willing to identify, be it as participants, clergy, organizers, or indeed as descendants of a royal family.

It is fitting, therefore, to conclude this long history of the Miracle modestly with the year 2015, when Pope Francis announced amid an international refugee crisis that the church would hold an extra Holy Year of Mercy.[201] This initiative inspired the board of the Society to organize an extra Silent Walk related to this theme. A shortened Walk was held, starting from Spui, around the former Holy Stead, and back again on December 12, 2015, on the eve of the Holy Year of 2016.[202] This "little Walk" was intended as a gesture of solidarity with refugees and with the victims of war and terrorism, the dramatic topics that dominated world attention in 2015. Just as in Rome itself, the turnout in Amsterdam was not high; a mere forty people participated.[203] The figure did not detract from the ritual's idealistic intentions, but it did make one thing clear: this was not the "real" Walk. Only the Silent Walk as defined by tradition can be both *tremendum*, terrifying and fear-inducing, and *fascinans*, endowed with an attractive allure, just as the medieval Miracle itself once was.[204] For more than seven centuries, and especially so in the past century, this fascination has drawn crowds of religiously or spiritually motivated people to Amsterdam.

7

Conflict or Consensus?

We have described this book—metaphorically—as a "biography of a devotion." Our investigations have resulted in an extensive study of a cult that emerged from what might at first sight seem a trivial event involving a host, an occurrence that was regarded in the Middle Ages as something supernatural—a miracle. Throughout the centuries, however, this cult has left deep traces, first in Amsterdam's urban society, then regionally, and eventually nationally.

Our intention was to describe this phenomenon and to interpret it from a cultural-historical perspective, primarily because the story of the Miracle of Amsterdam is little known, among both scholars and the general public. Our study connects a rather unknown but eminent and intriguing example of long-term confession building and pillarization to modern confessionalization studies. An added stimulus was the fact that this devotion is by no means a relic of the past, even though its history extends back for seven centuries. Although it nearly disappeared only relatively recently—in the 1960s—the long-contested devotion managed to draw from its own history the strength and the flexibility to reinvent itself and, ironically and irenically, to bring Catholics and Protestants closer to each other and build new bridges to the future. In fact, in the last decades of the twentieth century, it became an unexpected source of inspiration for ecumenical spirituality and for collective manifestations in Dutch society.

Matters could not have been more different during the preceding centuries. Veneration, honor, unity, and triumphalism have appeared often in this book, but so have revilement, mockery, discord, repression, contention, and struggle. In fact, the two largest Christian denominations in the Netherlands, Protestantism and Catholicism, used the contentious Miracle cult as a device to bolster their own group identities, thus smoothing the way for later political pillarization. Having arrived at the conclusion of the book, we would like to describe once more in broad brushstrokes what struck us most in this turbulent and fascinating history, and what new insights this history has yielded.

What makes the Miracle of Amsterdam unique in comparison to other "Sacraments of Miracle" was the manner in which the Holy Stead (Locus Sacer) came to be what it was: through a fire that did not destroy but rather left intact. From the start, the chapel that was soon built on this location bore this elementary name, which it would keep. For citizens of Amsterdam as well as for foreigners, the ground, that specific location, had been hallowed by this sign from God. They expressed this by walking around the chapel as they prayed. As early as 1347, two years after the founding miracle, an indulgence was granted to the faithful who performed this practice. This circumambulation ritual gained yet another rationale after the Holy Stead fire of 1452. The miracle that reportedly happened on that occasion was in fact much more spectacular than that of 1345: this time the entire chapel went up in flames, except for the monstrance containing the host, which remained intact. The event was interpreted in biblical terms. Just as Moses had once seen the bush burn without being consumed by the fire, thus the citizens of Amsterdam had seen that the miraculous host, for a second time, remained intact amid the flames, and they regarded this miracle as a sign that God would not abandon them. Just as Moses, they removed their shoes when they entered the holy place.[1] Since that time, many pilgrims from Amsterdam and abroad made their prayer walk on bare feet.

This "naturalization" of the ancient ritual marked the Amsterdam cult, as did a strong Eucharistic focus, which it shared with all other Sacraments of Miracle. The first half of the fifteenth century even saw the introduction of a separate feast of the Amsterdam Miracle, including a large-scale procession through the city each year on the first Wednesday after March 12. The citizens celebrated this feast, "Corpus Christi in Lent," in a fashion almost indistinguishable from the universal feast, which in Amsterdam was called "Corpus Christi in summer." One consequence was that the clergy encouraged the faithful to receive communion more frequently. The main bearers of the cult, however, were "ordinary faithful," such as the women of the Guild of the Blessed Sacrament and the city authorities. The latter, in their 1434 request to Pope Eugene IV for an indulgence, pointed to the link between the pilgrimage to the Holy Stead and the city's economy. Pilgrimage and prosperity stimulated each other.

From the end of the fifteenth century to the Alteration of 1578, there was a clear affinity between the city on the Amstel and successive Habsburg rulers. The privilege of having the imperial crown over the city arms, donations of stained-glass windows in Amsterdam churches, and several princely visits to the city strengthened the bond.[2] The Holy Stead played a crucial role in this. More than other cities in Holland, Amsterdam and its Miracle suited the Habsburgs in their pursuit of a great, prosperous empire that, thanks to its many Sacraments of Miracle, could trust in divine protection.

An unintended effect of the Holy Stead and its Miracle was that it served to widen the gulf that was inexorably opening up between various diverging opinions at the advent of the Reformation. In the eyes of the Sacramentarians, the Anabaptists, the Lutherans, and the Calvinists, the cult symbolized the "idolatry" of the Catholic Church. The Amsterdam city authorities initially favored an accommodating approach to these dissidents, but they gradually began to adopt the policy pursued by the ecclesiastical and national governments, which exercised fanatical repression of anything found lacking in Catholicity.

But repression was unable to turn the tide. During the Iconoclastic Fury of 1566, the Holy Stead was stalwartly defended by a group of Amsterdam women. Their heroic involvement even attracted the interest and admiration of the governor. In the turbulent years that followed, Amsterdam Catholics desperately clung to their shrine. All their prayers and processions, and even the world's first invention of the ritual of Perpetual Adoration of the Blessed Sacrament, were to no avail. After a bloodless coup in 1578, Amsterdam finally went over to the side of the Calvinist insurgents, who turned the tables on the Catholics and began to suppress Catholicism. They dismissed the royalist magistrates and the entire clergy, desecrated the Holy Stead, and destroyed the miraculous host. The cult, it seemed, had been eradicated in one fell swoop.

But it continued, away from the public view. To the great annoyance particularly of Reformed ministers, Amsterdam Catholics continued the old ritual of walking barefoot around the Holy Stead—now called Nieuwezijds Kapel—in silent prayer. They passed this practice on to following generations. Thanks in part to the tolerance that prevailed in the cities of Holland, the Catholic Church was able to recover and create a new home for the cult during the seventeenth century. Although it no longer had the means to shape society according to its own designs, church leaders were nonetheless able to build up the morale and strengthen the identity of the Catholic faithful, primarily by reminding them of the faith of their fathers. In Amsterdam, this propaganda strategy was aggressively pursued by two learned friends, the biblical scholar Leonardus Marius, pastor of the Begijnhof, and the convert Joost van den Vondel, the Netherlands' national poet. In well-timed interventions around the time of the third centenary of the Miracle in 1645, they pointed out to their fellow citizens that Amsterdam's greatness was entirely due to the devotion of the earlier generations of its inhabitants; for both men this devotion implied faithfulness to Catholic doctrine on the Eucharist. These two Catholic leaders, and of course many others, including Vicar Apostolic Philippus Rovenius and his fighting spirit, as well as the countless Catholic "spiritual virgins" or *kloppen*, who more than the small number of priests kept the Catholic community together, ensured that the Catholic Church in Holland, and not least in Amsterdam, experienced a remarkable revival. Under Marius's leadership, the Amsterdam Begijnhof emerged as a veritable new Holy Stead.

An "ecumenism of everyday life" developed in Holland and other provinces—though not everywhere in the Republic—during the seventeenth century. It did not quite amount to mutual religious interest and appreciation, but involved willingness on the part of both Protestants and Catholics to make the best of it together. For a long time, this ecumenism of everyday life went hand in hand with mistrust, all the more so because, after all, Catholics belonged to the church of Rome, whose religious practices Protestants decried as "diabolical idolatry." The sacrament of the Eucharist played an important role in the mutual suspicion, as became evident in 1734 when, to the amazement of the uninitiated, serious unrest arose in the tolerant Republic over fears that Catholics were plotting to seize power on Corpus Christi, which fell on the feast of St. John the Baptist, June 24, that year.

Once this historical farce had been cleared up, it seemed as if the edge had come off the ecumenism of everyday life. Even though Dutch Catholics belonged to a worldwide church, during the eighteenth century they were very different from their coreligionists elsewhere. They resigned themselves to leading their lives within the margins that had been set for them. This habitus has been described in this book as "accommodation Catholicism": the adaptation of Catholics' own expression of their faith through constant conscious or subconscious awareness that no provocation must be given to the dominant Protestant denomination.[3] Catholics did not want to impose on non-Catholics, and the implicit corollary was their acceptance of a subordinate place in cultural, academic, and political life.[4] The same attitude can also be seen in the Miracle cult. Thus the fourth centenary in 1745 passed without any special celebration, a stark contrast from Marius's and Vondel's high drama of a century before. The Miracle became an object of reflection for priests who, wishing to meet the Enlightenment head-on, had submerged themselves in biblical studies and philosophical musings. In long, contrived sermons—perorations that were intended more for colleagues, or for Protestant ministers with an interest in this kind of subject, than for the faithful—they legitimized the Miracle devotion. Attempting to gloss over its "dark," medieval, and "superstitious" origins, they frequently pointed out the resemblance— even the substantial similarity—between the two miracles of the host in the fire (1345 and 1452) and Moses's burning bush.

While scholar-priests exerted themselves at their desks and from their pulpits to defend the legitimacy of the cult, the actual devotional practice was carried out by other groups of people. The scarce but unambiguous testimonies that have been preserved permit us to conclude that the archaic ritual of the walk had survived into the eighteenth century and was being continued there by citizens of Amsterdam, mainly women, and probably also by pilgrims from outside the city. Under the cover of darkness, or at first light in the morning, they walked around the Holy Stead or Nieuwezijds Kapel a number of times and sometimes walked part of the old processional route. Their numbers were substantially lower than in previous centuries. This was inevitable, given the repression and the fact that all visible traces of the old cult had been erased; even the name of the Holy Stead fell into oblivion. At one stage there even was uncertainty among the Catholic community in Amsterdam as to where exactly in Kalverstraat the Miracle of 1345 had supposedly taken place.[5]

The final years of the eighteenth century brought the end of the ancien régime in many parts of Europe; in the Netherlands, the "French era" and the Batavian Revolution brought fundamental changes to the constitution and consequently also to the country's religious position. Henceforth, all denominations of the "Protestant" Netherlands had to coexist in openness and equality. This did not happen overnight, and the transition occasioned intense antipathies and fierce clashes. All of this also affected the Miracle cult, which initially found it difficult to shed its "hidden church mentality." But the growth of a new, transnational Catholicism in Western Europe in the 1840s brought in its wake large-scale jubilee celebrations and mass pilgrimages. The unrest that this caused in the Netherlands meant that the fifth centenary of the Miracle in 1845 was placed under direct supervision by the Protestant government system. The celebration led to heated debates between the government and the Protestant section of society, which was not yet habituated to Catholic equality and which feared a further Catholic takeover of power. Protestants worried that the Protestant character of the nation would be compromised or even destroyed by the "false community" of Catholics in the country.[6] The old Miracle cult, which had lain almost dormant during the eighteenth century, now turned out to have political dimensions of national scope. Many a Protestant perceived the Miracle pilgrimage as an archetypal instrument of the ultramontane lust for power, its only purpose to undermine the nation. The controversy of this era, primarily a pamphlet war, breathed new life into an antipapism that made virulent use of the "classic" bones of contention: superstition, processions, pilgrimages, Jesuitical conspiracies. It put interdenominational relations on edge.

At the same time, Protestants also had a covert fascination for papist "smells and bells." The Miracle jubilee was a novelty, and many of them wanted to see it with their own eyes. The whole discussion about the celebration of the jubilee—the "feast of Folly," according to its opponents—not only proved that the devotion had far outgrown its previously local and regional scope, but also served to strengthen the identities of the denominations involved in the dispute, identities that were more clearly defined precisely because each was constructed in opposition to the prevailing hostile image of the other. In retrospect, the political and social unrest caused by the gradual success of the mass mobilization of national and international Catholic devotionalism, first through the pilgrimage to Trier in 1844 and subsequently through the Amsterdam Miracle jubilee in 1845, turned out to be the prelude to a "national" anti-Catholicism that manifested itself in the April Movement of 1853. The protagonists of this movement wanted to avoid further contamination of the Netherlands by Catholicism, as if it were cholera—a contagious disease, the spread of which other conspiracy theorists had held the Jesuits responsible.[7] The Miracle cult, which had reclaimed its place in national consciousness due to this societal, political, and religious turbulence, proved to contain an unexpectedly large mobilizing potential. To master the forces that had been unleashed, and to reassure and appease the Protestants, the government introduced a ban on processions and pilgrimages in 1848 and 1853. The conflict never really took a grim or violent turn, with the exception of a number of skirmishes and police interventions. Fittingly for a country of the Word, fear and aggression were experienced mentally and expressed in vituperative journal articles, brochures, and pamphlets.

Pilgrimages in the Netherlands, especially in its southern parts, were traditionally linked to Marian cults and the veneration of healing saints and involved traditional, instrumental devotional practices. The Catholic shrines created or revived north of the river delta in the nineteenth century, such as Amsterdam, Brielle, and Dokkum, were different. In practice, these "emancipatory" shrines functioned primarily as cohesion-enhancing, moral-religious points of reference that pointed both to the past and to the future of the Catholic community. Thus the pilgrimages to Brielle embodied the notion of catechetical "formation voyages."[8] They took place under the close supervision of the clergy and were executed in the seclusion of a geographically isolated and architecturally introverted shrine. The Amsterdam lay initiative, by contrast, was eager to avoid strong clerical control and focused on the capital's city center as an open, "interactive" podium for its annual Silent Walk. Thus the Amsterdam pilgrimage consciously developed into a nationwide Catholic unity movement, which implicitly strove for societal emancipation and recognition.

With their initiative of the Silent Walk, these lay Catholics chose to perform the old "basic ritual" in a collective and minimalist fashion. A silent walk was a perfect expression of the "modest" accommodation Catholicism of the Netherlands. This ritual enhanced self-confidence and created visibility, even if it was performed at night and in silence. In doing so, it automatically raised the contentious issue of Catholic presence in the public space. This made the Walk both a devotional ritual and a protest movement: a self-confident manifestation that at once created cohesion and visualized the growing influence of the country's large Catholic minority. It was a "ritual of appropriation," which on balance helped Catholics to improve their situation. The "shutters" that they had previously kept closed to protect them in a pillarized society were now opened a little.[9] The constant growth of the Silent Walk, with ever larger numbers of participants every year, occurred more or less at the same time that the role of Catholics in politics expanded. The faithful participation in the Silent Walk by a politician such as the KVP leader Carl Romme throughout most of his life is a fitting symbol of this.

The success of the Walk, and the concomitant Protestant fears, led to one last expression of institutional aggression: the destruction of the original shrine, the Holy Stead or Nieuwezijds Kapel. But Catholic revenge proved sweet. Every year, huge crowds of Catholics walked three times around the holy place, even though a new Reformed church now stood on the spot. This annual manifestation ensured that Amsterdam was the unofficial capital of Dutch Catholicism.[10] It was the largest annual public ritual in the Netherlands. The Silent Walk was also one of a kind in the context of the universal Catholic Church, and this did not go unobserved.[11]

The Walk's immense success during the fifty years between 1910 and 1960 also surprised Catholics themselves. The significance of the Silent Walk is therefore much wider than statistics about participants and members of the numerous sister societies can attest. Although there was guidance from a central organization, the movement could only grow to the extent that it did thanks to the grassroots dynamics set in motion by ordinary Catholics in hundreds of places across the country. The organization was deliberately in the hands of laypeople, both in Amsterdam and elsewhere. Thus all layers of Dutch Catholicism were democratically mobilized to participate in the movement, from the elite to laborers and farmers, in a true national pilgrimage. Its fundamental principle was that all participants, even if they traveled to Amsterdam and back in groups, took part as individuals, in accordance with the old silent prayer walk. The high turnout in fact represented only half of the potential turnout, because women, though not permitted to join in the nocturnal walk, were very much emotionally involved in the movement. Their husbands and sons represented the whole Catholic family. That a movement borne by men and boys was in fact possible at all was something difficult to imagine, and impossible to realize, outside the Dutch setting.[12] Mainstream Catholic or devotional culture across the globe was characterized by the dominance of female participation and low levels of male involvement, or even by the absence of men. The historically determined necessity of self-organization of devotional practices to a large extent explains the stronger and often proportional male involvement in devotion and ritual in the Netherlands.

It has been pointed out before that the initiators of the Silent Walk very consciously chose the Amsterdam city center for their project. This proved an excellent decision because Amsterdam's unique nature contributed strongly to making the Silent Walk a success. The fact that the topographical pattern of medieval Amsterdam on both sides of the Amstel has been preserved more or less intact made it possible to walk almost the exact same route taken by the old procession on Corpus Christi in Lent. This route alone, which passes several intrinsically sacred places—such as the Oude and Nieuwe Kerk—as well as the Holy Stead, immediately implicates the participants in the tradition and the Miracle of 1345.[13]

Not only the topography, but also the spiritual climate of the capital proved conducive to the Walk. Although the nineteenth century was dominated by the culture war between Catholics and Protestants, with its flareups of 1845 and 1853, and the Dutch *Kulturkampf* of the 1870s, toward the end of this century, the city of Amsterdam proved the right setting for the lay initiative of the Silent Walk. The city authorities' open attitude and the urban citizenry's unconventionality and nonchalance literally created space to come together and hold a demonstration without fear of giving offense or of causing problems. Even when participation took on very large proportions and came to reflect the Walk's new functions, this particular ritual of pilgrimage encountered surprisingly little resistance. The Silent Walk, defined as a ritual of prayer, soon acquired significance as a commemoration of the glorious Catholic past—the Miracle had never totally disappeared from view—and especially as a subversive protest against society's failure to give the Catholic community its due. This critical aspect of walking in silence—the power of silence—also pertained, in various guises, to other protests or commemorative demonstrations that were inspired by the Silent Walk in the period after the Second World War: from commemorative marches relating to the war (May 4), to disruptive Provo marches, to the silent marches that are organized to mark a traumatic fatality.

The Walk, performed in its "neutral" form, even proved able to play a mediating role in the tense relations that dominated Dutch society for so long. In 1966, Ben Kroon, a journalist for *De Tijd*, made an insightful comment on the Silent Walk in this context. He praised its nonclerical aspect, as well as the laypeople who had resisted "the neo-Gothic trumpetblowers of the Roman restoration of power" in 1881. Kroon thought that they had created something valuable for the whole of Dutch society: "It is really all very un-Catholic, not even Protestant or ecumenical. It's just brilliantly Dutch."[4] Kroon suspected that the Walk would not disappear and contended that if it had not existed, it would have been invented in the 1960s. This proved to be very true: the Walk not only continued to exist but, as has been seen, was also reproduced and reinvented in the form of silent commemorative marches.

Despite the Silent Walk's exemplary function in the postwar years, the Walk itself, after record participation figures in the 1950s, went into steep decline in the 1960s. This change was simultaneous with secularization and dechristianization, processes that took place much more rapidly in the Netherlands than elsewhere. Traditionally, Dutch lay Catholics had relied on self-organization when it came to their religion. Even when the number of priests rose and remained high in the nineteenth and twentieth centuries, laypeople continued to undertake initiatives independently, and the Silent Walk is perhaps the most important example of this. They did this in a spirit of evident loyalty to their bishops and to the pope in Rome. But when the institutional Catholic Church began to doubt itself in the 1960s and dropped its pretension to be the sole vessel of salvation, Dutch Catholics regarded it as confirmation and an encouragement of their self-reliance. The result was that many of them decided to go their own way, and the ecclesiastical structures that they had helped to support collapsed.

The two jubilee celebrations that were organized over the recent decades (1995 and 2006) in collaboration with the Protestant community focused specifically on wider ecumenical representation in the Silent Walk. However, the effect of this on participation figures has so far been limited. Perhaps the lengthy tradition of the Walk that is enshrined in the cultural chain of memory is still too strongly linked to a specific Catholic past. It is therefore all the more remarkable that the Protestant Church in Amsterdam recently decided to collect as many of the scattered remains of the former Holy Stead as it could find—the remains of the very monument whose demolition it once forced through, and which stands at the beginning of this long history in 1345. It is the irony of history that, of all organizations, it was the Protestant Church that took this initiative. Today, the Walk as a ritual of silence represents togetherness and consensus. None of us knows what the future holds in store for the Silent Walk that emerged from the Miracle of Amsterdam. What we do know is that it will depend on the wisdom and power of the organizers and the involvement of the participants, but also on external factors. Its turbulent history shows that this is no guarantee that it will not once again be contested. The story continues, and we must now conclude our research of its history.

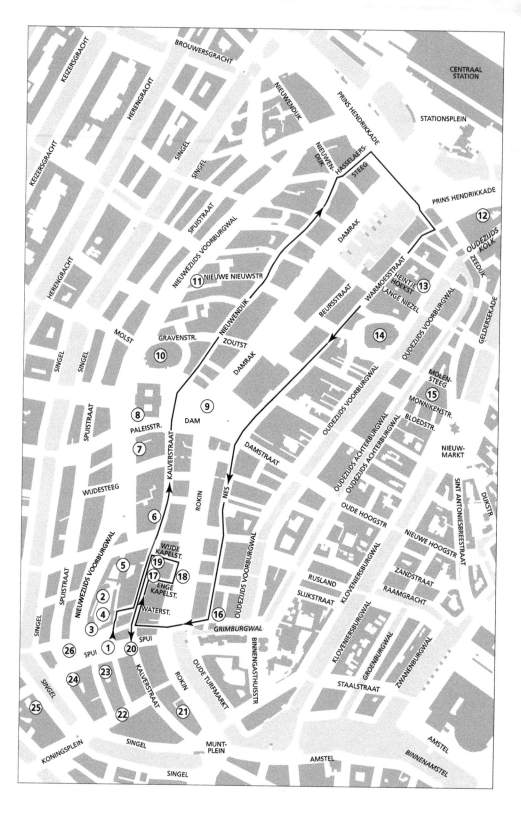

Route of the Silent Walk

During the decades before the Alteration (1578), the Holy Stead (17) was the starting point and end point of the procession with the miraculous host; the participants would then part ways on Plaats, currently Dam square (9). The current Silent Walk is held annually on the night of Saturday to Sunday closest to March 15. The Walk begins and ends on Spui (1 and 20) and follows the route indicated on the map.

1. Spui, starting point of the Silent Walk
2. Begijnhof
3. Begijnhofkerk
4. English Church
5. Amsterdam Museum, previously Burgerweeshuis
6. Church of SS. Peter and Paul, "de Papegaai"
7. former textiles company Alph. Elsenburg, previously home of J. Alberdingk Thijm
8. formerly Oude Gasthuis
9. Dam, previously Plaats
10. Nieuwe Kerk
11. formerly Monastery of St. Gertrude
12. Church of St. Nicholas
13. Ons' Lieve Heer op Solder
14. Oude Kerk
15. former Franciscan Monastery
16. formerly St. Clare's Monastery
17. formerly Holy Stead and Nieuwezijds Kapel
18. Miracle column
19. formerly Holy Corner, commemorative plaque
20. Spui, end point of the Silent Walk
21. formerly hidden church 't Boompje
22. Heiligeweg
23. Maagdenhuis
24. Old Lutheran Church
25. Church of St. Francis Xavier, "de Krijtberg"
26. *Het Lieverdje* statue

Timeline

Year	Europe / Rome / World	Low Countries / Amsterdam	Miracle / Silent Walk
1246	Corpus Christi Liège instituted		
1264	Corpus Christi Rome instituted		
1300		Amsterdam granted city charter	
1306		Oude Kerk consecrated	
1337–1453	Hundred Years' War		
1345			The Miracle
1346			Episcopal indulgence; permission to replace the miraculous host
1347–1348	The Black Death		
1347			Consecration of the Holy Stead; episcopal indulgence for participation in procession
1358–1404		Albert (governor/ count Holland)	
1374			First mention Guild of Blessed Sacrament
1378			Request for papal indulgence
1384		Geert Grote dies	
1388			Albert visits Amsterdam on Corpus Christi
1404–1417		William VI (count Holland)	
1413		Nieuwe Kerk consecrated	
1415			City responsible for Holy Stead

Year	Europe / Rome / World	Low Countries / Amsterdam	Miracle / Silent Walk
1415–1434			Corpus Christi in Lent instituted
1421		City fire	Holy Stead damaged
1433–1465		Philip the Good (sovereign)	
1434			Request for papal indulgence
1450	Invention of printing		
1452		City fire	Holy Stead completely destroyed; miraculous host found intact
1453	Fall of Constantinople		
1465–1477		Charles the Bold (sovereign)	
1477–1482		Mary of Burgundy (governor)	
1481–1483		City walls erected	
1484			(Legendary) visit of Maximilian
1486–1519		Maximilian, king and later emperor of the Romans	He is welcomed in Amsterdam
1489		Imperial crown in city arms	
1492	Discovery of America		
1494–1506		Philip the Handsome (sovereign)	
1498			Procession on Corpus Christi in Lent henceforth begins and ends at Holy Stead
1501		Jubilee celebrated in Amsterdam	Indulgence to be earned in Holy Stead
1506	Building of Saint Peter's church starts		
1506–1530		Margaret of Austria (regent)	
1508		Maximilian welcomed in Amsterdam	

Year	Europe / Rome / World	Low Countries / Amsterdam	Miracle / Silent Walk
1509			Margaret donates stained-glass window
1515–1555		Charles V (sovereign)	
1515		Charles V welcomed in Amsterdam	
1517	Luther criticizes indulgences		
1518			Oldest pilgrimage print
1521		Beginning of imperial inquisition	
1523		First martyrs, Antwerp	
1525		Cornelis Hoen's *Letter on the Lord's Supper*	
1529	Turkish siege of Vienna		
1530	Charles V crowned emperor; Imperial Diet at Augsburg		
1531			Women of Guild of Blessed Sacrament protest to Charles V in Brussels
1531–1555		Mary of Hungary (regent)	
1532			Alardus of Amsterdam's ode
1534	Beginning of Anglican Church		
1534–1535	Anabaptist kingdom of Münster		
1535, May 10–11		Anabaptist coup Amsterdam	
1536, May 11			Extra annual feast of Corpus Christi to celebrate victory over Anabaptists
1540	Society of Jesus recognized by the pope	Charles V received in Amsterdam	
1548		*Formula reformationis* issued	
1549		Philip inaugurated in Amsterdam	

Year	Europe / Rome / World	Low Countries / Amsterdam	Miracle / Silent Walk
1550		"Blood placard" issued	
1555	Peace of Augsburg		Book of hours published
1555–1598		Philip II (sovereign)	
1559		Erection of new dioceses	
1559–1567		Margaret of Parma (regent)	
1566, April 5		Petition addressed to Margaret	
1566, Aug/Sept		Iconoclastic Fury	Holy Stead spared
1567–1573		Alva (regent)	
1568			Miracle book published
1568–1648		Eighty Years' War	
1571	Battle of Lepanto		
1572–1584		William I (stadtholder Holland)	
1572, Dec 4			Don Fadrique visits Holy Stead
1573			Papal indulgence
1576		Pacification of Ghent	
1577, Nov 22–23		Failed attack on Amsterdam	
1578, Jan 26			Angelic Choir of Praying Men and Women
1578, late May		Alteration of Amsterdam	Holy Stead desecrated
1578–1592		Alexander Farnese (regent)	
1579		Union of Utrecht	
1582	Gregorian calendar introduced		
1584, July 10		William I assassinated in Delft	
1585–1625		Maurice, stadtholder Holland	
1585		Fall of Antwerp	
1588	Destruction of Spanish Armada	Republic of the United Netherlands	
1592–1853		Dutch Mission	
1592–1614		Sasbout Vosmeer, vicar apostolic	

Year	Europe / Rome / World	Low Countries / Amsterdam	Miracle / Silent Walk
1598–1633		Reign of Albert and Isabella	
1602	Dutch East India Company (VOC) founded		
1604		Book *Roomsche mysterien*	
1609–1621		Twelve Years' Truce	
1614–1651		Philippus Rovenius, vicar apostolic	
1624			Holy Hearth demolished
1625–1647		Frederick Henry (stadtholder Holland)	
1625	New Amsterdam founded	Spínola captures Breda	
1627			Miracle in Jesuit hidden church
1631–1652		Marius, pastor Begijnhof	Begijnhof becomes second Holy Stead
1637		Frederick Henry recaptures Breda	
1639			*Amstelredams eer ende opcomen*
1640			*Getyden van het . . . Sacrament*
1640, ca.			St. Caecilia Collegie founded
1641, May 30		Disruption of mass in Amsterdam	
1644			Reformed ministers complain about walk
1645			Third centenary of Miracle; Vondel's *Eeuwgetij*
1651			Agatha Loen on the route of the procession
1663–1686		Joh. van Neercassel, vicar apostolic	
1664	New Amsterdam becomes New York		
1666		Guild of Good Death in Krijtberg	

Year	Europe / Rome / World	Low Countries / Amsterdam	Miracle / Silent Walk
1671			Guild of Blessed Sacrament in Begijnhofkerk
1672–1673		Year of Disaster	
1672–1702		William III (stadt-holder Holland)	
1683	Turkish siege of Vienna	Amsterdam has 26 hidden churches	
1690		Confraternity of Kevelaer in Post-hoorn	
1713		Peace of Utrecht	
1720, ca.			*Waare afbeeldinge van het Sacrament van Mirakel*
1723		Schism of Utrecht	
1734, June 24		Saint John's Day panic	
1737			Agatha Loen's *Memorie* published
1745			Fourth centenary of Miracle
1750–1765	Didérot's *Ency-clopédie*		
1750			J. Nanning's Miracle sermon
1758			Cornelia Occo dies; she was accustomed to making the walk
1773			W. van Wetering's Miracle sermon
1776	American indepen-dence		
1780–1787		Patriot era	
1784			Last printed Miracle sermon
1789	French Revolution; end of ancien régime		
1793	Louvre Museum opened		
1795		Batavian Revo-lution/Batavian Republic	
1798		Freedom of religion	
1804	Napoleon crowns himself emperor		

Year	Europe / Rome / World	Low Countries / Amsterdam	Miracle / Silent Walk
1806		Louis Napoleon, King of Holland; start of "French era"	
1810		The Netherlands annexed by France	
1813	Napoleon defeated; Treaty of Vienna	Kingdom of the Netherlands	
1814–1840		William I (king of the Netherlands)	
1815		The Netherlands and Belgium joined in one kingdom	
1816		General Regulation of Reformed Church	
1820		J. A. Alberdingk Thijm born	
1827		Failed concordat with Rome	
1829	Jan Roothaan, Jesuit General, Rome		
1830–1831		Belgian Revolution	
1832			Publication of Estré, *Beknopt geschied-kundig verhaal van het beroemd Mirakel*
1839		Secession of Belgium becomes final	Begijnhof receives state subsidy
1840–1849		William II (king of the Netherlands)	Steins Bisschop, rector of Begijnhof (until 1856)
1841		Internuncio Innocenzo Ferrieri	
1842		Journal *De Katholiek* founded	
1843	J. Ronge excommunicated (Prussia)		
1844	Pilgrimage to Holy Tunic, Trier		
1845		Daily *De Tijd* founded	Fifth centenary of Miracle
1846	Sixth centenary Corpus Christi, Liège		
1847		Benedictine J. B. Pitra visits the Netherlands	

Year	Europe / Rome / World	Low Countries / Amsterdam	Miracle / Silent Walk
1848		New constitution, incl. "procession ban"; the Netherlands become parliamentary democracy	
1849–1890		William III (king)	
1853		Restoration of episcopal hierarchy / April Movement	
1854		Our Lady's Church (Redemptorists)	
1858	Marian apparitions, Lourdes		
1863		Abolition of slavery	
1864	Antiliberal *Syllabus Errorum*		
1866		First collective silent walk, 's-Hertogenbosch	
1867		Canonization Martyrs of Gorcum; *Katholieke Illustratie* founded	Thijm examines Miracle chest
1869–1870	First Vatican Council	Stamp Act abolished	
1871	Paris Commune		
1871, June	Pope Pius IX's Silver Jubilee		
1872, April 1		Commemoration 300 years Brielle	
1876	Telephone invented	"Kermis riot"	
1877			Guild of Blessed Sacrament of Miracle founded
1878			Guild of Procession founded
1879		ARP party founded	
1881		Krijtberg church built	First Silent Walk in Amsterdam
1883		World Exhibition	Klönne rector of the Begijnhof (until 1914)
1884		Rijksmuseum opened	Museum Amstelkring founded
1886		Eucharistic processions in Laren begin; "Eel riot"; Kuyper's "Doleantie"	

Year	Europe / Rome / World	Low Countries / Amsterdam	Miracle / Silent Walk
1887			Our Lord in the Attic purchased
1888	Pope Leo XIII's golden jubilee	*Neerlandia Catholica* published; first confessional cabinet	Procession painting A. Derkinderen finished
1889		J. A. Alberdingk Thijm dies	
1890		Emma (regent); Liduina canonized	
1892			Guild of the Miracle founded
1894		SDAP founded	
1893			Procession painting Phlippeau
1895			550th anniversary of Miracle
1898–1948		Wilhelmina (queen)	Nieuwezijds Kapel (Holy Stead) closed
1906			25th Silent Walk
1908			Nieuwezijds Kapel (Holy Stead) demolished
1914	World War I begins		Extra Silent Walk for peace; Klönne retires
1916			Route of Walk blocked due to new development
1917	February Revolution in Russia	Constitutional reform	Silent Walk R. C. Society; L. van den Broeke joins board of Society; plenary indulgence for participants in Silent Walk
1918	World War I ends	Troelstra "Putsch"; new constitution; male suffrage	First open-air procession in seclusion of Begijnhof
1919		Female suffrage	
1922	Encyclical on Catholic Action	National Eucharistic Congress	
1924, July 22–27		27th International Eucharistic Congress	
1926		R. K. Staatspartij Catholic party founded	
1928			Silent Walk spread over 2 nights
1931		NSB founded	50th jubilee Silent Walk celebrated

Year	Europe / Rome / World	Low Countries / Amsterdam	Miracle / Silent Walk
1932–1962			Separate Silent Walk for seminarians
1939–1940	World War II begins		Silent Walk spread over 3 nights
1944	Benelux founded		
1945	World War II ends; Indonesian independence	Apparitions Lady of All Nations begin	Sixth centenary of Miracle
1946		Extra Silent Marches on May 4	First postwar Silent Walk; celebration sixth centenary of Miracle
1948–1980		Juliana (queen)	
1949	NATO founded		
1950			Guild of the Blessed Sacrament founded
1952		Unemployment Insurance Act (WW)	Formalized morning Walk for women begins
1953	North Sea flood	Celebration of centenary of restoration of hierarchy	
1954		Episcopal mandement to Dutch Catholics	
1956	Russian invasion of Hungary		75th anniversary of Silent Walk; extra silent walks for Hungary
1957	European Economic Community	State pension (AOW) introduced	Highest turnout Silent Walk: "90,000"
1962	Second Vatican Council opens		
1965	Second Vatican Council	National social assistance law introduced (ABW) Provo "happenings"	Number of Walk nights reduced from 3 to 2
1966		Disability stipend (WAO) introduced	Women allowed to take part in Walk; first sister society disbands
1967			J. Willebrands addresses Society; Veldkamp report Silent Walk

Year	Europe / Rome / World	Low Countries / Amsterdam	Miracle / Silent Walk
1968	Student protests		Grassroots criticism of board; last Eucharistic procession in Begijnhof
1968–1970		Pastoral Council Noordwijkerhout	
1969			Eucharistic Center founded in Begijnhof
1970		Ad. Simonis bishop of Rotterdam	
1971		City center parishes: Citykerk Amsterdam	
1972		Occo Codex found	Lowest turnout Silent Walk (ca. 5,000); "crisis memorandum" "Manifesto to Catholics of Amsterdam" by board
1973	Oil crisis		
1975	Surinamese independence		
1978–1997			Jaap Suidgeest rector Begijnhof
1980–2013		Beatrix (queen)	Lutheran church at disposal of pilgrims
1981			Celebration of centenary of Silent Walk; Miracle chest to Amsterdam Museum
1982			Maarten Elsenburg, chairman Silent Walk
1985, May 11–14	Papal visit to the Netherlands	Memorandum "Silent Walk after the year 2000"	
1988			Miracle column erected on Rokin
1993		European Union established	
1994			Miracle painting (Schenck) removed from above main altar Begijnhofkerk

Year	Europe / Rome / World	Low Countries / Amsterdam	Miracle / Silent Walk
1995	Srebrenica, July 11		Ecumenical celebration of 650th anniversary of Miracle
2000	Holy Year, Rome	"The multicultural disaster" (article Scheffer); Recalibration Dutch Catholicism: mission territory	
2001	WTC attacks New York, 9/11	Jos Punt, bishop of Haarlem	Remembrance niche Kalverstraat unveiled
2002	Euro introduced	Pim Fortuijn assassinated; apparitions of Lady of All Nations recognized	
2004		Theo van Gogh assassinated; first Eucharistic procession in Amsterdam since 1578; United Protestant PKN church formed	
2006			Ecumenical celebration 125th anniversary of Silent Walk; sung Occo Codex performed
2009		New name of diocese: Haarlem-Amsterdam	
2010	Arab Spring		End of "chairmen's dynasty" Elsenburg
2012, March 15		Karl von Habsburg visits Begijnhofkapel	
2012, December 8		Saint Nicholas's church made Basilica Minor	
2013		William-Alexander (king)	
2015	Holy Year; refugee crisis	Refugee crisis	Extra Silent Walk for refugees

Notes

Introduction

1. Rogier received the P. C. Hooft Prize in 1954 for his own three chapters in the book, not for the entire work; the other three chapters were authored by the priest Nicolaas de Rooy. Not content with the hybrid setup of the book, Rogier reworked the entire text and published *Katholieke herleving* three years later. For more on this handbook, see Bornewasser, "Ontstaan, ontvangst en heruitgave van een geruchtmakend geschiedwerk."

2. The first edition contained lengthy passages about piety, confraternities, and lay initiatives (207–52); only half a page (217) remained of this in the revised edition of 1956. Neither edition mentions the Miracle cult or the Silent Walk.

3. See, for instance, Mathijsen, *Historiezucht*; Kesteren, *Het verlangen naar de middeleeuwen*. By contrast, Raedts does discuss it in his book *De ontdekking van de middeleeuwen*, 259–61.

4. Cf. Trio and Smet, "Processions in Town"; Bijsterveld and Caspers, "Origines de l'archidiocèse de Malines," 39–47.

5. As chapter 1 explains, Amsterdam even had two separate feasts of Corpus Christi in the later Middle Ages.

6. Rooden, "Kerk en religie in het confessionele tijdperk"; Safley, "Multiconfessionalism"; Headley, Hillerbrand, and Papalas, *Confessionalization in Europe*, 1–49 (historical definitions); Boettcher, "Confessionalization."

7. It must be noted that the concept of a pillar or block structure is not as firm as the metaphor itself suggests; cf. Van Dam's deconstructionist synthesis of "pillarization" in Dam, *Staat van verzuiling*, 101–20. Van Dam questions the concept itself and the prevailing static model of pillars and demonstrates that society was more multiform and more dynamic than this mythical concept allows. The confessional groups were nevertheless more or less separated from each other, something that made a considerable impact on society during this period.

8. Margry, *Teedere Quaesties*, 380–83.

9. The socialist and liberal pillars were hegemonic communities to a much lesser degree than the Catholic and Protestant pillars.

10. Eijnatten and Lieburg, *Nederlandse religiegeschiedenis*, 328–73.

11. For this perspective, see Burke, *What is Cultural History*; Kaschuba, *Einführung in die Europäische Ethnologie*.

12. The basic text of chapters 1, 2, and 3 was written by Caspers and that of chapters 4, 5, and 6 by Margry.

Chapter 1. Creation and Expansion of a Cult (1345–1500)

1. For the first two centuries of the historical development of Amsterdam, see the first volume of *Geschiedenis van Amsterdam*, published in 2004, especially Speet, "Een kleine nederzetting in het veen," 1:21–61; Dijkhof, "Op weg naar autonomie," 1:63–73; Speet, "Verstening, verdichting en vergroting," 1:75–107; Kaptein, "Poort van Holland," 1:109–73. For the later development of the city, see Bakker, "De zichtbare stad, 1578–1813," 2-1:17–101.

2. On Bindwijk, see Breen, "De Heilige Stede te Amsterdam," 71–73.

3. On compulsory holy days and the like, see Caspers, "The Role of the People in the Liturgy"; Verhoeven, "Kerkelijke feestdagen in de late middeleeuwen."

4. Nijsten, *Volkscultuur in de late middeleeuwen*.

5. On processional culture in Oudenaarde, cf. Ramakers, *Spelen en figuren*.

6. Caspers, *De eucharistische vroomheid*, 66.

7. Cf. Bossy, "The Mass as a Social Institution, 1200–1700"; Lubac, *Corpus mysticum*.

8. Augustinus, *Confessionum libri XIII*, 103–4 (VII, x, 16); Caspers, *De eucharistische vroomheid*, 24.

9. See especially the classic study by Otto, *Das Heilige*.

10. This religious conviction was based on the Apostle Paul's first letter to the Corinthians, especially 1 Corinthians 11:29. See Caspers, "*Magister consensus*: Wessel Gansfort."

11. Caspers, *De eucharistische vroomheid*, 41; Caspers, "The Sacrament of the Eucharist and the Conversion of Geert Grote."

12. Cf. Beelen, *Doet dit tot mijn gedachtenis*. One literary work in which the protagonist struggles with his unworthiness to receive communion is Jan Siebelink, *Knielen op een bed violen: Roman* (Amsterdam: Bezige Bij, 2005). This book ran to many editions and is available in English as *In My Father's Garden: A Novel*, trans. Liz Waters (Amsterdam: De Bezige Bij, 2013).

13. Avril, *Reims*, 41–43 (nos. 71, 72, 74, 76, 77). These statutes were adopted by the diocese of Tournai ca. 1300 (ibid., 330) and by the diocese of Liège as early as 1288; see Avril, *Liège*, 115. Other dioceses of the church provinces of Rheims and Cologne adopted the ritual regulations regarding viaticum, but the bishops of Utrecht never succeeded in updating their statutes; see, for instance, the rather rudimentary statutes in Joosting and Muller, *Bronnen voor de geschiedenis der kerkelijke rechtspraak*, 5:62 (no. 13, statute from 1293), 82 (no. 18, statute from 1310).

14. The faithful could obtain an indulgence by following the priest as he brought viaticum to the sick; see Avril, *Reims*, 178 (Cambrai 1300, no. 179); Caspers, "Indulgences in the Low Countries," 93–97.

15. Cf. Caspers, "Heilig Aduard," section. 1.1. There are many examples of riders who dismounted to show their respect for the Blessed Sacrament; see, for instance, Caesarius Heisterbacensis, *Dialogus miraculorum*, 2:206; Pauli, *Vier historien van het H. Sacrament van Mirakel*, 186–88. For one of the many examples of the indispensability of viaticum, see Thomas a Kempis, *Orationes et meditationes de Vita Christi*, 187: "You should beg Jesus to be purified from sin and to be strengthened by the viaticum of his precious body, so that you can die in happiness."

16. Cf. Andlau, "Die heilige Eucharistie und das Haus Habsburg."

17. Avril, "La pastorale des malades," 93–95. The author gives examples of parish foundations, but also of hospitals that had to have a chaplain to hear last confession and bring viaticum.

18. In a city with two thousand inhabitants, the procession with viaticum must have been a weekly occurrence, and one that did not go unnoticed, accompanied as it was by the ringing of church bells, a lantern, a bell, and loudly recited prayers.

19. In the historiography of Amsterdam, 1334 is usually regarded as the foundation year of the Amsterdam parish; see Melker, "Burgers en devotie," 254. But see also Joosting and Muller, *Bronnen voor de geschiedenis der kerkelijke rechtspraak*, 2:338, who point out that Saint Nicholas's Church was separated from Oude Kerk as early as 1306 and therefore reject 1334 as the year of foundation.

20. Regnerus Post, "Het Sacrament van Mirakel te Amsterdam," 245.

21. Riemsdijk, *De tresorie en kanselarij van de graven van Holland en Zeeland*, 406–7; Gisbert Brom, *Archivalia in Italië*, I-2:479 (no. 1322); Nolet, "Historische zekerheid," 34 (Dutch translation); Regnerus Post, "Het Sacrament van Mirakel te Amsterdam," 251–52; Laan, *Oorkondenboek van Amsterdam*, 234–235 (no. 352). Cf. Browe, *Die eucharistischen Wunder*, 146–47. Clement VII († 1394) had been bishop of Cambrai before his pontificate. His election as pope caused the so-called Western Schism (1378–1417), with popes in Rome and Avignon. Albert of Bavaria gave allegiance initially to Avignon but later to Rome; see Gisbert Brom, "De tegenpaus Clemens VII en het bisdom Utrecht"; Asseldonk, *De Nederlanden en het Westers Schisma*, 110–13. Albert of Bavaria acted as lord of Holland and Zeeland on behalf of his brother, Count William V, who had been declared insane in early 1358. Albert succeeded to the title of count of these two provinces after William's death in 1389. He was also duke of Bavaria-Straubing and count of Hainault.

22. An indulgence was a partial or full remission of the temporal punishment due for sin after confession. This punishment was expressed in days, weeks, or even years that had to be spent doing penance, or in purgatory after death.

23. Regnerus Post, "Het Sacrament van Mirakel te Amsterdam," 252–60; Carasso-Kok, *Repertorium*, 46–47 (no. 40); Meder, *Sprookspreker in Holland*, 329–30.

24. For an edition of Hildegaersberch's poem, see Nolet, "Historische zekerheid," 23–32. Lines 114–15 mention that the bystanders were familiar with the canonical instruction to cast the discharge into the fire: "But they followed the priest's teaching / And quickly threw it into the fire." For the *Vermeerderde Beka* edition (the Middle Dutch Beke continuation), see Lautenschütz, "Het Mirakel in de historische literatuur," 46–48; Bruch, *Johannes de Beke*, 186–87.

25. Nolet, "Historische zekerheid," 30 (lines 301–6). According to the *Vermeerderde Beka*, the miracle happened in 1342. Apart from the year, the various narrative traditions give two different indications of the date: "Mid March" (Van Hildegaersberch) and the Tuesday before Palm Sunday (Johannes of Leiden's *Hollandse Kroniek*). Tuesday before Palm Sunday fell on March 19 in 1342 and on March 15 in 1345, which concurs with Hildegaersberch's indication. At the time a day was normally reckoned to begin after sunset. According to tradition, the sick man received viaticum before sunset and the miracle occurred after sunset. This has given rise to the tradition of celebrating Wednesday as the feast, leading some authors (including Molanus) to regard Wednesday, March 16, 1345, as the day of the Miracle. Cf. Regnerus Post, "Het Sacrament van Mirakel te Amsterdam," 253; Meder, *Sprookspreker in Holland*, 101. See also Carasso-Kok, *Repertorium*, 224 (no. 203-2).

26. Moll, *Kerkgeschiedenis van Nederland vóór de hervorming*, 32; Pijper, *Middeleeuwsch christendom*.

27. Usually it applied to the returning of miraculous statues of Mary to the place where they had been found; see, for instance, for the province of North Brabant, Margry and Caspers, *Bedevaartplaatsen in Nederland*, 2:351–68 (Handel), 585–98 (Meerveldhoven), 659–68 (Oirschot), 682–94 (Ommel).

28. Rubin, *Corpus Christi*, 164–81; Caspers, *De eucharistische vroomheid*, 36–56; Delville, *Fête-Dieu (1246–1996)*; Gy, "Office liégeois et office romain de la Fête-Dieu"; Walters, Corrigan, and Ricketts, *The Feast of Corpus Christi*; Newman, "The Life of Juliana of Cornillon"; Caspers, "The Original Place and Meaning of Corpus Christi."

29. Cottiaux, "I precedenti liegesi della festa del Corpus Domini"; Baldassarri, "Il pontificato di Urbano IV"; Franceschini, "Origine e stile della bolla *Transiturus*"; Walters, "The Feast of Corpus Christi as a Site of Struggle."

30. Caspers, "How the Sacrament Left the Church Building."

31. Hermesdorf, *Rechtsspiegel*, 53–63.

32. Jappe Alberts, *De ordinarii van Kampen*, 9–11; and cf. 28–29: in the younger version of the *liber ordinarius* the references to the exposition of the Sacrament have been struck through and replaced with the indication "when the sermon is finished."

33. The term *Sacrament of Miracle* was probably translated directly from Latin or French, *Sacramentum Miraculi* and *Sacrement de Miracle* respectively. The *Internationaal Eucharistisch Congresboek: Officieel programma* (Amsterdam, 1924) on the congress of July 22 to 27, 1924, points out that the term was adopted in various languages. In addition to the three already mentioned, the book also quotes "Sacramento del Miraculo," "Sacramento del Milagro," "Sacramente af Miraklet," "Sacrament of Miracle," and "Sacrament des Mirakels." The term has since gone out of use, and we have chosen to speak simply of "the Miracle" for the Amsterdam cult.

34. The following miracles gave rise to cults in what is now the Netherlands (listed in chronological order): Meerssen (c. 1222); Binderen (thirteenth century); Hasselt Overijssel (thirteenth century); Niervaart-Breda (c. 1300); Dordrecht (1338); Amersfoort (1340); Stiphout (1341); Amsterdam (1345); Middelburg (1374); Boxtel

(1380); Boxmeer (c. 1400); Haarlem (fifteenth century); Schraard (c. 1410); Staveren (before 1418); Bergen North Holland (1421); Alkmaar (1429); Woudrichem (1442); Helpman (1483); Ypecolsga (c. 1496); Enkhuizen (1515); Uden (1517); Solwerd (c. 1520); Standdaarbuiten (before 1530). For a characterization of these shrines, see Regnerus Post, *Kerkgeschiedenis van Nederland in de middeleeuwen*, 2:294–99; Caspers, *De eucharistische vroomheid*, 232–35. For Standdaarbuiten, see Margry and Caspers, *Bedevaartplaatsen in Nederland*, 2:806–7. For Woudrichem, see http://www.meertens.knaw.nl/bedevaart/bol/plaats/1468. For a complete overview of Eucharistic shrines in Europe, see Browe, *Die eucharistischen Wunder*, 139–46. For a recent popularizing book on Eucharistic miracles, see Meloni, *I Miracoli Eucaristici*.

35. For the miracles of fire of Dordrecht and Amersfoort, see Margry and Caspers, *Bedevaartplaatsen in Nederland*, 1:308–210 (Dordrecht) and 130–31 (Amersfoort). For Stiphout, see ibid., 2:815–19. Cf. Browe, *Die eucharistischen Wunder*, 74.

36. Cf. Bynum, "Seeing and Seeing Beyond."

37. It is interesting to note that there were three other Sacraments of Miracle known as the "Holy Stead" in the late Middle Ages in what is now the Netherlands: in Hasselt (in Overijssel), and in Helpman and Solwerd (both in Groningen). In all three cases theft or desecration of hosts prompted a miracle. See Margry and Caspers, *Bedevaartplaatsen in Nederland*, 1:421–31 (Hasselt), 460–62 (Helpman), 721–23 (Solwerd); Frijhoff, *Embodied Belief*, 235–73 (Hasselt).

38. Many historians of the Holy Stead have mentioned a letter written in Latin by Florentius of Boechorst, bailiff of Amstelland, on March 31, 1345, which questions the veracity of the miracles, in this case the miracle of fire, the repeated bringing back of the host to the church, and the cure of the child suffering from epilepsy. The historians Sterck and Post have characterized this document as a misleading later construction; see Regnerus Post, "Het Sacrament van Mirakel te Amsterdam," 243–45.

39. In the late Middle Ages, bishops were often too busy dealing with administrative affairs to be able to carry out their pastoral duties. For this reason they left a number of these to a special assistant, who held appointment as bishop of a diocese in a country currently ruled by "infidels." The Dominican Nythardus was bishop of the Greek town of Thermopylae i.p.i. (in partibus infidelium), and occupied the position of auxiliary bishop of Utrecht from 1344 to his death in 1356. See Weijling, *Bijdrage tot de geschiedenis van de wijbisschoppen van Utrecht*, 154–57.

40. Nolet, "Historische zekerheid," 35–36; Regnerus Post, "Het Sacrament van Mirakel te Amsterdam," 248–249; Laan, *Oorkondenboek van Amsterdam*, 75–76 (no. 78).

41. On benediction, see Browe, *Die Verehrung der Eucharistie*, 161–66; Caspers, *De eucharistische vroomheid*, 118.

42. For a more literal Dutch translation of John of Arkel's charter, see Nolet, "Historische zekerheid," 36. For Bishop John of Arkel's dealings with the Holy Stead, see Rutgers, *Jan van Arkel*, 243. For an overview of the many new chapels and altars that were erected in the diocese of Utrecht during his tenure, see ibid., 200–206.

43. Caspers, *De eucharistische vroomheid*, 252–57 (Alkmaar, Amsterdam); Bynum, *Wonderful Blood*, 85–111. Cf. Marten Micron, *Een claer bewijs van het recht gebruyck des Nachtmaels Christi, ende wat men van de Misse houden sal*, in Cramer and Pijper, *Bibliotheca Reformatoria Neerlandica*, 423–563, at 428 and 485 (on the Leuven Sacrament of Miracle); Browe, *Die eucharistischen Wunder*, 163 (Pulkau). See also Nußbaum, *Die Aufbewahrung der Eucharistie*, 243–59. After being replaced by a new host, the old host was consumed by a priest. If a miraculous host had changed color or composition to such a degree that it could barely pass for a host anymore—which was the case in Alkmaar—it was not exposed or consumed but stored together with the relics.

44. *Succinta enarratio miraculorum*: "Erat autem hostia resurgentis Domini imagine consignata, pedem alterum super sepulchrum alterum in crorsum defigentis" (Reading for morning prayer on Friday under the octave of the feast of the Miracle). See also Molanus, *Natales sanctorum Belgii*, 50vo–51vo. On host irons, see Corblet, *Histoire*, 188–90. Cf. Caspers, "Heilig Aduard," 83–85 (on hosts with a star).

45. See Meuwissen, *Jacob Cornelisz van Oostsanen*, 236. An interesting detail is that this image was also included in the book of hours, but because the text and the image did not correspond, the host has been removed!

46. The altars were dedicated to (1) the Sacrament, (2) Michael and the Blessed Virgin Mary, (3) Peter, Paul, and all the other apostles, (4) John the Baptist, John the Evangelist, and the martyrs Laurence and Catharine.

47. See, for instance, *Pontificale Romanum*, 280–396.

48. The first evidence of this priest's position comes from a charter from 1415, which refers to the situation as "has been the custom in the aforementioned chapel for ten, twenty, thirty, forty, fifty years before the previous years"; see Sterck, *De Heilige Stede in de geschiedenis van Amsterdam*, 176 (appendix 6). Cf. De Melker, *Metamorfose van stad en devotie*, 58–62. Of course, it is not certain whether this charter portrays the original situation correctly; the mention of a sermon in the vernacular looks like a later addition, because the city authorities were particularly keen on "popular education." On the ban on priests in the diocese of Utrecht celebrating mass more than once a day (other than in certain exceptional circumstances), see Joosting and Muller, *Bronnen voor de geschiedenis der kerkelijke rechtspraak*, 5:81 (no. 15, statute 1310).

49. Sterck, *De Heilige Stede in de geschiedenis van Amsterdam*, 169 (appendix 1, Confraternity of the Holy Cross), 169–70 (appendix 2, Confraternity of Our Lady), 187 (appendix 20, Confraternity of the Blessed Sacrament); Laan, *Oorkondenboek van Amsterdam*, 151–52 (no. 214, Confraternity of the Holy Cross), 155 (no. 222, Confraternity of the Blessed Sacrament), 206 (no. 308, Confraternity of the Blessed Sacrament), 233–34 (no. 351, Guild of Saint Laurence); Melker, *Oorkondenboek*, 32 (no. 408a, Confraternity of the Blessed Sacrament).

50. Melker, *Metamorfose*, 58–62.

51. Kuys, *Repertorium van collegiale kapittels*, 135–47. The relics were reportedly donated to the chapel by the French King Charles V. See Janse and Veen, "Kerk en vroomheid," 223. Cf. Jongen and Kan, "Amersfoort en de doornenkroon," 22. On

the superior value of relics of Christ compared to relics of "ordinary saints," see Caspers, *Een bovenaardse vrouw*, 32–33.

52. Kuys, *Repertorium van collegiale kapittels*, 139, mentions an additional indulgence for attendance at certain services held in the court chapel, granted in 1381 by Cardinal Pilaeus de Prata.

53. Laan, *Oorkondenboek van Amsterdam*, 206 (no. 307); Meder, *Sprookspreker in Holland*, 461. This transfer was confirmed in 1375 by the Utrecht bishop Arnold of Hoorn; see ibid., 209–10 (no. 313). Cf. Kuys, *Kerkelijke organisatie*, 50–57.

54. Riemsdijk, *De tresorie en kanselarij*, 406.

55. Laan, *Oorkondenboek van Amsterdam*, 249–50 (no. 370).

56. Herwaarden, *Opgelegde bedevaarten*, 54.

57. Ibid., 728.

58. Hüffer, *Bronnen voor de geschiedenis der abdij Rijnsburg*, 754–55. The abbess spent 22 pounds and 8 groats, significantly more than what was needed simply for accommodation in those days. She spent 19 pounds and 2 groats in 's-Hertogenbosch.

59. Margry and Caspers, *Bedevaartplaatsen in Nederland*, 1:378–83 ('s- Gravenzande); Smit, *Vorst en onderdaan*, 54–61. Albert's spouse, Margaret of Cleves, also visited the Holy Stead. But 's-Gravenzande was the favorite place of pilgrimage of the counts of Holland and was later also much favored by the Burgundian dukes; see Jongkees, *Staat en kerk in Holland en Zeeland*, 245.

60. Hens, *Mirakelen van Onze Lieve Vrouw*, 239–40 (no. 59).

61. Ibid., 416–18 (no. 236). See also Sterck, *De Heilige Stede in de geschiedenis van Amsterdam*, 33–35.

62. Hens, *Mirakelen van Onze Lieve Vrouw*, 528–29 (no. 313).

63. Amsterdam also ranked low in numbers of pilgrimages imposed by courts in the cities of Holland, with the Marian shrines of 's-Hertogenbosch, 's-Gravenzande, and Amersfoort topping the list as far as Dutch places of pilgrimage are concerned; see overviews in Herwaarden, *Opgelegde bedevaarten*, 724–34.

64. An extensive miracle book has also been preserved for Our Lady of Amersfoort, with no fewer than 542 reports. More than 400 of these (but by contrast with the reports from 's-Hertogenbosch, the Amersfoort reports were usually not dated) related to the first eight years after the founding miracle in December 1444; the other miracles were from the 1453–1545 period. In 1491 a man with paralyzed legs from Oosterbeek undertook a pilgrimage to Amersfoort via Amsterdam, and he was cured in Amersfoort. The editors of this miracle book have suggested that he made this detour to pray at the Holy Stead; see De Boer and Jongen, *In het water gevonden*, 257 (no. 503). Miracle books shorter than those of 's-Hertogenbosch and Amersfoort also show that the early phase of a cult was often marked by a reasonable number of miracles, but that this number then declined, sometimes to zero. Thus the chronicle of the miracles of the Niervaart/Breda Sacrament of Miracle reports twelve miracles from 1449 (when the miraculous host was translated to Breda) to 1456, and none after that year; see Asselbergs and Huysmans, *Het spel vanden Heiligen Sacramente*, 79–95. See also Margry and Caspers, *Bedevaartplaatsen in Nederland*, 2:173–85.

65. Nolet, "Historische zekerheid," 30–31 (lines 306–42). It is remarkable that William in the following verses stressed the veracity of all this again and rebuked those who doubted the graces that the Sacrament bestowed. See also Meder, *Sprookspreker in Holland*, 128.

66. For an extensive study of church-state relations up to 1477, see Jongkees, *Staat en kerk in Holland en Zeeland*.

67. Smit, *Vorst en onderdaan*, 60, 79.

68. Eeghen, *Vrouwenkloosters en Begijnhof*, 2–6, with special focus on Gysbert Douwe or Dou († 1420), who is reckoned to have belonged to Modern Devotion circles.

69. Melker, "Burgers en devotie," 293–304.

70. This means that the change in ownership of Heiligeweg preceded by two years the Hague chapter's acquisition of the right of collation; see Sterck, *De Heilige Stede in de geschiedenis van Amsterdam*, 170 (no. 3); Laan, *Oorkondenboek van Amsterdam*, 299 (no. 299). See also Gouw, *Geschiedenis van Amsterdam*, 2:316–17 (Holy Stead and Oude Gasthuis).

71. Sterck, *De Heilige Stede in de geschiedenis van Amsterdam*, 41–43 (seven charters between 1410 and 1414).

72. Cf. Regnerus Post, "Het Sacrament van Mirakel te Amsterdam," 254: according to the author of the *Vermeerderde Beka*, the miraculous host had been in Saint Nicholas's Church from the start. This is wrong, but it is an indication that the host was no longer in the Holy Stead at the time that this chronicle was compiled, ca. 1390.

73. Sterck, *De Heilige Stede in de geschiedenis van Amsterdam*, 43, 174–78, appendix 6 (charter The Hague chapter, 2-24-1415), appendix 7 (charter confirming transfer by bishop of Utrecht, 6-6-1515), appendix 8 (sixteenth-century copy of city charter confirming the transfer, 6-28-1415).

74. According to Pluym, *Het H. Sacrament van Mirakel*, 19, referring to Long, *Historische beschryvinge van de Reformatie der stadt Amsterdam*, 211, there had been two Eucharistic processions from as early as 1360, and he assumed that these would have been held with particular ceremony in Amsterdam on account of the Miracle. But Le Long clearly states that the procession on Corpus Christi was first introduced in the cities of Holland around the date mentioned. A letter from the city authorities to the militias from 1394 does mention "the day of the Blessed Sacrament in summer," but this is to distinguish it not from another Corpus Christi, in Lent, but from Saint Martin's feast (November 11), "in winter"), see Breen, *Rechtsbronnen*, 537–39.

75. Cf. Smit, *Vorst en onderdaan*, 147. Smit points out that William VI (1404–1417) concluded his inaugural visit to the cities of Holland with a special visit to Amsterdam. He left The Hague for Amsterdam on March 11 and was inaugurated there two days later. Smit assumes that this visit had been planned in such a way that William could take part in the Eucharistic procession on the feast day of the Holy Stead in March. On the one hand, it is unlikely that this feast already existed at the time. When Corpus Christi in Lent eventually did emerge, it was held on the Wednesday after the feast of Saint Gregory: March 12. In 1405 this feast fell on a

Wednesday, so that if a Eucharistic procession was held at all, it must have been on March 19. On the other hand, it is possible that a special procession was held for the occasion of the inauguration, and William honored the miraculous host during his visit by giving a donation; see Meder, *Sprookspreker in Holland*, 461.

76. Gisbert Brom, *Archivalia in Italië*, 489 (no. 1359, August 3, 1434, Vatican Archives, registrum supplicationum, vol. 290, f. 126r–126v.): request by the city councilors and the church wardens of the Holy Stead for indulgences on the annual feast day in March. It must be added that this request was part of a wave of indulgence requests sent to the pope. Many other "Dutch" requests for indulgences can be found for the 1340s in the *Registrum Supplicationum* and the *Regesta Lateranensia* of the Vatican Archives, and all of these were granted by the pope: for the church of Saint Magnus in Anloo (no. 1346); for the church of Woerden (no. 1349); for the church of Rhenen (no. 1357); for the church of the Holy Sepulcher near the Augustinian convent outside Utrecht (no. 1358); for the benefactors of the Holy Stead (no. 1359); for a chapel of the Holy Sepulcher in Veere (no. 1363, see also nos. 1345 and 1405); for the church of Bergen (no. 1370 and 1585); for the chapel of Mariënwijngaard near Utrecht (no. 1371); for the parish church of Kampen (no. 1590); for the church of Westkerke (no. 1591); for the hospital of Saint George in Delft (no. 1595).

77. Thus the citizens of Amsterdam insisted on a Wednesday in mid-March and not on a fixed date on the calendar. It is understandable that they did not retain the original indication of the date of the Miracle: the Wednesday (or Tuesday) before Palm Sunday. In that case, the feast of the Miracle would have depended on the date of Easter and would have moved considerably from year to year, from early March to somewhere in mid-April. The provision of a Wednesday in mid-March was later narrowed down to the Wednesday after March 12, the feast of Saint Gregory. This means that Corpus Christi in Lent was a moveable feast, falling between March 13 and 19.

78. On the significance of holding a burning candle, often indicating penitents who had been reconciled with God, see Caspers, "Über die Schwelle."

79. It is not clear for every petition addressed to Pope Eugene IV who the petitioners were; often they were clerics, but sometimes (for instance, in the case of the petitions from Rhenen [no. 1357] and Amsterdam [no. 1359]) they were clearly laypeople. The Amsterdam petition is unique in one particular aspect: all the other petitions requested indulgences of several years, but theirs only of a hundred days, albeit, absurdly, with the same number of quadragenes (four thousand days). It was probably a mistake, especially if we bear in mind that Albert requested an indulgence of ten years in 1378.

80. On the relation between the Latin book of hours and the Middle Dutch miracle book, see Regnerus Post, "Het Sacrament van Mirakel te Amsterdam," 258–59; Eeghen, "Willem Jacobsz in Engelenburgh," 174–76; Fontaine Verwey, "Herinneringen van een bibliothecaris." A number of the Amsterdam miracles are also characterized briefly in Sterck, *De Heilige Stede in de geschiedenis van Amsterdam*, 52–53. Also reproduced in Long, *Historische beschryvinge van de Reformatie der stadt Amsterdam*, 325–27, 430–34.

81. See also Sterck, *De Heilige Stede in de geschiedenis van Amsterdam*, 110–11.

82. Sterck, *De Heilige Stede in de geschiedenis van Amsterdam*, 45–46 (abridged); Pluym, *Het H. Sacrament van Mirakel*, 38–40.

83. According to a nineteenth-century certificate, a wooden sculpture group representing Mary and the apostles at Pentecost, currently owned by the Rijksmuseum in Amsterdam (inv. no. BK-2007-7), originated in the Holy Stead that was destroyed by fire in 1452. If this is true, this would be the only object from the old chapel known to have survived.

84. Reproduced in Sterck, *De Heilige Stede in de geschiedenis van Amsterdam*, 47–49 (abridged); Pluym, *Het H. Sacrament van Mirakel*, 40–44 (including Latin text). See also Long, *Historische beschryvinge van de Reformatie der stadt Amsterdam*, 327–30. In the chronicle of his monastery of Agnietenberg (near Zwolle), Thomas a Kempis († 1471) recounted that the fire in Amsterdam showed that God's anger was particularly directed at the houses of the brothers and sisters of the common life, as no fewer than fourteen monasteries were destroyed. "Many virgins that had taken the veil, putting aside their maiden modesty, wandered about the city lamenting and begging for hospitality, whereby the hearts of many were moved to tears"; see Thomas a Kempis, *The Chronicle of the Canons Regular*, 103–4; Thomas a Kempis, *Chronica Montis S. Agnetis*, 428–29. Amsterdam had already experienced a large city fire in 1421, but on that occasion the Holy Stead was spared, even though it was damaged; see Sterck, *De Heilige Stede in de geschiedenis van Amsterdam*, 44.

85. See also Molanus, *De Historia SS. Imaginum et picturarum*, 423 (liber IV, cap. 17); Molanus, *Traité des saintes images*, 524. Molanus pointed out that the custom of having motifs on hosts already existed among their ancestors. He mentions the example of the host of the Holy Stead, which he discusses in his book on the Dutch feasts, under March 16.

86. Breen, "De Heilige Stede te Amsterdam"; Gawronski and Veerkamp, *Zerken en graven in de Nieuwezijds Kapel*, 7–10.

87. See for instance Gouw, *Geschiedenis van Amsterdam*, 5:167. Cf. Pluym, *Het H. Sacrament van Mirakel*, 48–49; quoted by Sterck, *De Heilige Stede in de geschiedenis van Amsterdam*, 51.

88. Molanus, *Natales sanctorum Belgii*, 50vo–51vo. This book was published posthumously, ten years after Molanus's death.

89. Margry and Caspers, *Bedevaartplaatsen in Nederland*, 3:324–50.

90. This miracle is mentioned in a collection of examples that was (probably) compiled by the Carthusian Aegidius Aurifaber (Giles the Goldsmith) and was frequently reprinted. For a later edition, see Kruitwagen, "Het *Speculum exemplorum*," 382–84. See also Carasso-Kok, *Repertorium*, 225 (no. 203–26); Matuszak, *Das Speculum exemplorum*, 36. On the pilgrimage to Saint Jerome, see Margry and Caspers, *Bedevaartplaatsen in Nederland*, 1:572–78 (Noordwijk, with reference to Egmond).

91. Cf. Long, *Historische beschryvinge van de Reformatie der stadt Amsterdam*, 430–33, who has serious doubts as to whether this miraculous cure must be dated to 1414 or 1514, and has characterized it as an ordinary cure, i.e., not a miracle. His

dating is wrong, however: it should be 1476; see Bont, "De voormalige Amsterdam-sche vrouwen-kloosters," 38–39.

92. The miracle book ends with a miracle from 1508. A man from Weesp, Martijn Willemsoon Hollaer, had been taken prisoner by soldiers from Gelre. He vowed to go on a pilgrimage to the Holy Stead if he were to be set free. He was, and Martijn had a notarial deed drafted in the presence of two honorable men to attest to the miracle. Marius, in his *Amstelredams eer ende opcomen*, situates this miracle in Weesp (Holland), but later, in his *Getyden van het H. ende Hoogh-waerdigh Sacrament des Altaers*, locates it in Wezep in Gelderland. Cf. Gouw, *Geschiedenis van Amsterdam*, 3:342–44.

93. Sterck, *De Heilige Stede in de geschiedenis van Amsterdam*, 53. Historians have invariably mentioned 1484 as the year of Maximilian's cure. Smit points out, however, that it is quite possible that this happened in 1483, but that Maximilian did not visit the surroundings of Amsterdam again after that year; see Smit, *Vorst en onderdaan*, 56 and 81.

94. On this transitional period, see for instance Jongh, *Margaretha van Oost-enrijk*, which is still worth reading.

95. Other places that had a Sacrament of Miracle, such as Brussels, often also had a special feast with a procession, but this was not called a "second Corpus Christi"; see Bijsterveld and Caspers, "Origines de l'archidiocèse de Malines," 46–47.

96. For an overview, showing the date on which the bylaw was issued, spe-cifics of the procession, the target group, and the number of the bylaw in question, see Caspers and Margry, *Het Mirakel van Amsterdam*, 380–81.

97. The bylaws concerning the two feasts provide clues as to the nomencla-ture: in 1480 they still referred to the "Corpus Christis," in 1498 to "the two Corpus Christis, i.e., Corpus Christi in summer and Corpus Christi in Lent," and in 1500 to "the two Corpus Christis, i.e., in summer and in Lent."

98. General processions were held in cities across the Low Countries from the 1430s onwards, but more frequently in the south than in the north. They can be characterized as a form of "religious propaganda" of the Burgundian and later the Habsburg rulers, who attempted to use the church to unify their empire; see Regnerus Post, *Kerkgeschiedenis van Nederland in de middeleeuwen*, 2:297; Jongkees, *Staat en kerk in Holland en Zeeland*, 263–69; Caspers, *De eucharistische vroomheid*, 121–24.

99. Carasso-Kok and Verkerk, "Eenheid en verdeeldheid," 227–28.

100. Breen, *Rechtsbronnen*, 164 (A CCLXXXII).

101. Ibid., 171–72 (A CCC).

102. Ibid., 186 (A CCCLVII, 1–2).

103. On the symbolic meaning of the combination of white and red, see Smit, *Vorst en onderdaan*, 342: "Red was the color of chivalry, and was used for deco-ration to welcome the ruler's entry; combined with white, these colors expressed ideal splendor and beauty." Red and white are still the colors of the flag of Austria (red-white-red).

104. A more important reason for Maximilian to conquer Utrecht was perhaps to help the bishop of Utrecht, David of Burgundy (a half brother of Charles the Bold) to restore his authority after he had been chased out by the Hook factions. On the Hook and Cod Wars in Utrecht (1481–1483), see Tenhaeff, *Bisschop David van Bourgondië*.

105. Breen, *Rechtsbronnen*, 192–93 (A CCCLXXIX). On the plague epidemic that raged in Amsterdam at the time, see Noordegraaf and Valk, *De Gave Gods*, 230.

106. See for instance Breen, *Rechtsbronnen*, 224 (A CCCCXLIX and CCCCL): a fine of one thousand stones for driving overloaded carts through the streets and a fine of three thousand stones for blocking bridges.

107. The walls of the city were completed in the late 1480s; Speet, "Verstening, verdichting en vergroting," in *Geschiedenis van Amsterdam*, 1:91–92.

108. Devils featured frequently in late-medieval Eucharistic processions and plays that included scenes from salvation history, such as the Fall. They often played a comic role, constantly fighting with each other. In some cases, devils were played primarily by barbers, smiths, cobblers, and tanners on Corpus Christi: "It was easiest for them to obtain the required accoutrements such as paint, soot, coal, and animal hides," Haslinghuis, *De duivel in het drama der Middeleeuwen*, 184. On the costumes of the Amsterdam devils in the sixteenth century, described by Walich Syvaertsz, see ibid., 192. See also Roodenburg, *Onder censuur*, 63.

109. Breen, *Rechtsbronnen*, 297 (B XIV, September 1494 bylaw), 309 (B XXXII, September 1495 bylaw), 316–17 (B L, September 1496 bylaw).

110. Breen, *Rechtsbronnen*, 343 (B C-3). This ban had been issued before, in 1480, but then without any explanation; see ibid., 146 (A CCXXXV).

111. The judges of the court thus had the times of the sermon and mass on Sundays and holy days changed for both parish churches because too many parishioners attempted to leave the church prematurely. In addition, they ordered that it was only permitted to sell food after high mass had ended; see Breen, *Rechtsbronnen*, 356–57 (B CXVIII).

112. Breen, *Rechtsbronnen*, 342 (B C): "Alzoe op morgen, oft God wil, na ouden hercomen ende gebruykinge men alhier houden ende doen zal de feeste en processie van twairde Heylige Sacrament, dat men verzouckt te Heyliger Stede."

Chapter 2.   In the Habsburgs' Favor (1500–1600)

1. Breen, *Rechtsbronnen der stad Amsterdam*, 614; Sterck, *De Heilige Stede in de geschiedenis van Amsterdam*, 55–57.

2. Sterck, *De Heilige Stede in de geschiedenis van Amsterdam*, 53–54.

3. Ibid., 53–55; Breen, *Rechtsbronnen der stad Amsterdam*, 217–18 (bylaw 430). According to Teylingen, *Op-komste der Neder-landtsche Beroerten*, 139, Maximilian's visit to Amsterdam took place in 1484, on which occasion he ennobled the Amsterdam coat of arms, "viz. the three crosses, with the imperial crown."

4. Caspers, *De eucharistische vroomheid*, 121–22.

5. Breen, *Rechtsbronnen der stad Amsterdam*, 235 (art. 465).

6. Breen, *Rechtsbronnen der stad Amsterdam*, 236 (art. 467).

7. Gouw, *Geschiedenis van Amsterdam*, 3:189–91. For the symbolic significance of the "crown," see Kempers, "Loyalty and Identity in the Low Countries"; Kempers, "Assemblage van de Nederlandse leeuw"; Kempers, "Het enigma van de kroon."

8. Sterck, *De Heilige Stede in de geschiedenis van Amsterdam*, 55.

9. Cf. Geoffrey Parker, *The Grand Strategy of Philip II*, 94–99.

10. Lefèvre, "A propos d'une bulle d'indulgence d'Eugène IV"; Damen, "Vorstelijke vensters," 171–72. For the miraculous host of Dijon, see Rubin, *Gentile Tales*, 162–69; Wieck, "The Sacred Bleeding Host of Dijon."

11. For the Brussels Sacrement de Miracle, see Dequeker, *Het Sacrament van Mirakel*.

12. Duerloo and Thomas, *Albrecht & Isabella*, 233–35. Cf. Knipping, *Iconography of the Counter Reformation*, 2:305–6; Martin, "Das Bild Rudolfs von Habsburg als 'Bürgerkönig,'" 213; Tanner, *The Last Descendant of Aeneas*, 207–22, 301–5; Krieger, *Rudolf von Habsburg*, 237.

13. Corblet, *Histoire*, 1:491; Tanner, *The Last Descendant of Aeneas*, 211–12.

14. For an impression of the Habsburgs' many donations of stained-glass windows, see Damme, "The Donation of the Seventh Window," 133–36 (Margaret of Austria, Charles V, Philip II). Cf. Damen, "Vorstelijke vensters." Cf. Helbig, "L'iconographie eucharistique," 370–72 (Antwerp, St. James's Church and Church of Our Lady).

15. Damen, "Vorstelijke vensters," 172; Smit, *Vorst en onderdaan*, 172. The donation of this stained-glass window, or of part of it, was traditionally dated much earlier and was associated with Maximilian's "miraculous" cure in 1484; see Sterck, *De Heilige Stede in de geschiedenis van Amsterdam*, 142–44; Margry, *Amsterdam en het Mirakel van het Heilig Sacrament*, 30–31.

16. Helbig, "L'iconographie eucharistique," 374; Aristodemo and Brugman, "The *joyeuses entrées* of 1549," 33 and fig. 48.

17. Janse, *De Oude Kerk*, 359 (figs. 666, 667, 679).

18. Helbig, "L'iconographie eucharistique," 374; Snoep, *Praal en propaganda*, 160; Aristodemo and Brugman, "The *joyeuses entrées* of 1549," 33–34; Cuadra Blanco, "King Philip of Spain as Solomon the Second."

19. Wim de Groot, "Habsburg Patronage," 164–65.

20. Breen, *Rechtsbronnen der stad Amsterdam*, 376–77 (CLIX); Sterck, *De Heilige Stede in de geschiedenis van Amsterdam*, 93. Cf. Caspers, "Indulgences in the Low Countries," 83–84.

21. Fredericq, *Codex documentorum sacratissimarum indulgentiarum*, 412–13 (no. 285).

22. Breen, *Rechtsbronnen der stad Amsterdam*, 408 (bylaw 229-3). In the meantime the new pope, Julius II, had already been elected.

23. Breen, *Rechtsbronnen der stad Amsterdam*, 422 (bylaw 276).

24. On the travels of the young Charles, see Gachard, *Collections des voyages des souverains des Pays Bas*, 3:3–490.

25. Carasso-Kok, "Ter ere van God en tot aanzien van de stad," 416; Kempers, "Loyalty and Identity in the Low Countries," 43.

26. In the later Middle Ages, the Low Countries saw much more rapid urbanization than other parts of Europe. In Holland, approximately half of the population lived in a city. There were more than two hundred cities in the Low Countries in around 1550, nineteen of which had ten thousand inhabitants or more (by contrast, England at that time had only three cities with a population of that size); see Geoffrey Parker, *The Grand Strategy of Philip II*, 115. Cf. Nübel, *Pompejus Occo*, 5.

27. Pijper, *Middeleeuwsch christendom*, 80–81; Spruyt, *Cornelis Henrici Hoen*.

28. Gouw, *Geschiedenis van Amsterdam*, 4:128–66.

29. Sterck, "Het boekje *Amstelredams eer ende opcomen*," 126–30; Eeghen, "Willem Jacobsz in Engelenburgh," 174 (Occo).

30. Kölker, *Alardus Aemstelredamus*, 29–31. Occo was a chapel warden from 1513 to 1518.

31. Sterck, *De Heilige Stede in de geschiedenis van Amsterdam*, 123–42; Nübel, *Pompejus Occo*, 245–48. The sixteenth-century organ functioned until 1870, when it was purchased by the founding parish priest of Jutfaas, Gerard van Heukelum. The Amsterdam organ case was positioned in the new parish church, with a new interior mechanism. See Dekker, "De lotgevallen van het orgel van de H. Stede"; Dirkse, *Begijnen, pastoors en predikanten*, 55–64. The views of experts on the function of the nine canvases diverge; see Kruijf, "'Gods mirakel machmen sien,'" 70–78.

32. Huys, *Occo Codex*.

33. Sterck, *Onder Amsterdamsche humanisten*, 38–46; Kölker, *Alardus Aemstelredamus*, 60–64.

34. Regnerus Post, *Kerkelijke verhoudingen*, 540–46; Gielis and Soen, "The Inquisitional Office." Contrary to what is often assumed, the ecclesiastical authorities did permit the reading of the Bible in the vernacular. Strictly forbidden, however, was the reading of translations with Lutheran introductions, marginal notes, etc.; see François, "Die Ketzerplakate Kaiser Karls."

35. Fredericq, *Corpus documentorum inquisitionis*, 4:218–19 (no. 153). Cf. ibid., 229–35, 254–57.

36. Caspers, "Über die Schwelle," 67–70.

37. Gouw, *Geschiedenis van Amsterdam*, 4:139–40. See Fredericq, *Corpus documentorum inquisitionis*, 4:271–73. Cf. ibid., 255–56, 267, 284, 298, 300–2, 331. See also Fredericq, *Corpus documentorum inquisitionis*, 5:328–32, 345–46.

38. Gouw, *Geschiedenis van Amsterdam*, 4:144.

39. Gouw, *Geschiedenis van Amsterdam*, 4:144–45 (note 5); Fredericq, *Corpus documentorum inquisitionis*, 5:229. Cf. Corblet, *Histoire*, 1:188–90 (on motifs on altar breads).

40. Fredericq, *Corpus documentorum inquisitionis*, 5:366. Cf. Mellink, *Amsterdam en de wederdopers*, 17.

41. Fredericq, *Corpus documentorum inquisitionis*, 5:205–8, 219–20, 331, 343–44; Fühner, *Die Kirchen- und die antireformatorische Religionspolitik Kaiser Karls V.*, 249 (no. 297).

42. Gouw, *Geschiedenis van Amsterdam*, 4:145. See also Fredericq, *Corpus documentorum inquisitionis*, 5:32.

43. Gouw, *Geschiedenis van Amsterdam*, 4:100–4.

44. Ibid., 4:163–64.

45. On Alardus Aemstelredamus, *Parasceve*, see Kölker, *Alardus Aemstelredamus*, 100–7. Kölker has noted that Alardus might also have been referring to Charles's visit of 1515, but the young prince was not an emperor yet at that time and could therefore not have given imperial gifts. The *Parasceve* repeats many passages from the writings of authoritative authors, such as Origen, Gregory of Nazianzus, Cyprian, and Augustine. Authors from the Low Countries were also consulted, especially Dionysius the Carthusian and Thomas a Kempis. Alardus included three of the latter's chapters from *Devota exhortatio ad sacram communionem*, one of the four books that make up the *Imitation of Christ*; see Alardus Aemstelredamus, *Parasceve*, fol. Qvvo–Qviivo, Xviiro–Xviivo. Cf. Gouw, *Geschiedenis van Amsterdam*, 4:184–96.

46. Gouw, *Geschiedenis van Amsterdam*, 4:197–203; Sterck, *De Heilige Stede in de geschiedenis van Amsterdam*, 103–13; Sterck, *Onder Amsterdamsche humanisten*, 95.

47. The Latin text is as follows, from "particularly on Wednesdays": "praecipue quarta quacumque feria ab ipso statim lucis exortu, aperto capite, nudis pedibus, vestitu honesto quidem sed parum tamen splendido ardentem faculam plerumque circumferens, vultu in terram deiecto, nemineque inter eundem salutato, singulari quadam animi summissione, quampotest reverentissime, iterum atque iterum obambulando adorabundus suscipiat, veneratur, adoret."

48. Sterck, *De Heilige Stede in de geschiedenis van Amsterdam*, 119–23; 189–90; Kölker, *Alardus Aemstelredamus*, 101–2; Alardus Aemstelredamus, *Parasceve*, fol. Ziv–Zv.

49. Caspers, "Thomas von Kempen und die Kommunion."

50. Kölker, *Alardus Aemstelredamus*, 241–42. Alardus published two more books in 1539, *Baptismus christianus* and *Haeretici descriptio*, in which he asks, among other things, whether Anabaptists should be killed; see ibid., 131–42.

51. Mellink, *Amsterdam en de wederdopers*, 20–21; Jochen A. Fühner, *Die Kirchen- und antireformatorische Religionspolitik Kaiser Karls V.*, 267; Dudok van Heel, *Van Amsterdamse burgers tot Europese aristocraten*, 52.

52. Mellink, *Amsterdam en de wederdopers*, 9–26, esp. 22–24.

53. Kölker, *Alardus Aemstelredamus*, 203–5.

54. According to Reynier Brunt, the procurator-general of the Court of Holland, Amsterdam in 1535 numbered only a hundred Anabaptists among its citizens; see Fühner, *Die Kirchen- und antireformatorische Religionspolitik Kaiser Karls V.*, 281.

55. Grosheide, *Verhooren en vonnissen der wederdoopers*; Mellink, *Amsterdam en de wederdopers*, 63–75; Mellink, *Documenta Anabaptistica Neerlandica*, vol. 5; Mellink, "Anabaptism at Amsterdam after Munster"; Burgers and Knevel, *Nieuwe Maren*. For later persecutions of the Anabaptists, see Mellink, *Documenta Anabaptistica Neerlandica*, vol. 2.

56. Rogier, *Geschiedenis van het katholicisme*, 1:139–57. Among the many polemical publications against the Anabaptists, it is relevant to mention one, *Tumul-*

tus anabaptistorum (. . .) descriptio, which the rector of the Latin School (Latijnse School), Johannes Nivenius, had printed by Willem Jacobsz circa 1552; see Eeghen, "Willem Jacobsz in Engelenburgh," 172; Heesakkers and Kamerbeek, *Carmina Scholastica Amstelodamensia,* 25–51. In 1631 this poem was translated into Dutch by C. G. Plemp.

57. Cramer and Pijper, *Bibliotheca Reformatoria Neerlandica,* 1:434–35, 452–54.

58. For the similarities between the Catholic and Protestant views of the Eucharist, see, for instance, Brink, "Thomas en Calvijn tezamen ter communie"; Lurz, *Die Feier des Abendmahls.* For the Reformers' aversion to certain Catholic customs, see, for instance, Luther, *Am tag des heiligen warleichnams Christi,* 748: "Es ist das aller schedlichst fest, als es durch das ganze jar ist. An Kainem fest wird got und sein Christus serer gelestert dann an disem tag, und sonderlichen mit der Procession, die man vor allen dingen sol abstellen." See also Pijper, *Middeleeuwsch Christendom,* 74–100; Dankbaar, *Communiegebruiken in de eeuw der Reformatie;* Maag and Witvliet, *Worship in Medieval and Early Modern Europe.*

59. Helbig, "L'iconographie eucharistique," 370–71; Helbig and Bemden, *Les vitraux de la première moitié du XVIe siècle.* The church of Hoogstraten also has a series of stained-glass windows that represent the seven sacraments. Their donator, Isabella of Portugal, Charles V's wife, is depicted on the window representing the Eucharist, together with her patron saint; see Helbig, "L'iconographie eucharistique," 373. Cf. Kempers, "Assemblage van de Nederlandse leeuw," 66–67.

60. Elias, *Geschiedenis van het Amsterdamsche regentenpatriciaat,* 1–18; Tracy, "A Premature Counter-Reformation"; Lesger, *Handel in Amsterdam ten tijde van de Opstand,* 142–44; Dudok van Heel, *Van Amsterdamse burgers tot Europese aristocraten,* 59–104.

61. Gouw, *Geschiedenis van Amsterdam,* 4:278; Mellink, *Amsterdam en de wederdopers,* 79–80.

62. After a citizens' rebellion in February 1567 was suppressed, the city authorities even instituted a fourth procession, which was to be held annually on February 25. This procession did not have enough time to become a tradition. Cf. Deen, *Moorddam,* 85.

63. Mellink, *Documenta Anabaptistica Neerlandica,* 2:48–50 (nos. 45–46).

64. Fühner, *Die Kirchen- und die antireformatorische Religionspolitik Kaiser Karls V.,* 287–312.

65. Smit, *Vorst en onderdaan,* 251.

66. Gouw, *Geschiedenis van Amsterdam,* 4:302–4.

67. Ibid., 4:397.

68. Ibid., 4:409–411; Mellink, *Documenta Anabaptistica Neerlandica,* 2:69–72 (nos. 59–60a).

69. Gouw, *Geschiedenis van Amsterdam,* 4:333–39; Klönne, *Amstelodamensia,* 242–49; Cremer, "'Die Amsterdamer Monstranz.'"

70. Regnerus Post, "Karel V' Formula Reformationis."

71. *Statutorum synodalium ecclesiae Cameracensis,* 1:189–91: Titulus duodecimus: "De missae caeremoniis."

72. *Statutorum synodalium ecclesiae Cameracensis*, 1:202–4. Titulus decimus nonus: "De disciplina populi."

73. Regnerus Post, *Kerkelijke verhoudingen*, 546; Fühner, *Die Kirchen- und die antireformatorische Religionspolitik Kaiser Karls V.*, 315–26.

74. Haarlem came to the fore as the best candidate in the search for a new diocese in Holland: a city more than twice the size and population of Trent. The second serious candidate was Alkmaar, and there was no mention of Amsterdam; see Dierickx, *Documents inédits sur l'érection des nouveaux diocèses aux Pays-bas*, 1:115.

75. Cuadra Blanco, "King Philip of Spain as Solomon the Second," 170–71.

76. Snoep, *Praal en propaganda*, 18–21; Carasso-Kok, "Ter ere van God en tot aanzien van de stad," 440–42; Aristodemo and Brugman, "The *joyeuses entrées* of 1549," 31. Cf. Gouw, *Geschiedenis van Amsterdam*, 4:328–41.

77. Eeghen, "Willem Jacobsz in Engelenburgh," 174–76. In 1668 a new edition of the booklet from 1568 was published; see *Beschryvinge van het H. Sacrament van Mirakel*. For the cult of the Precious Blood in Alkmaar, see Margry and Caspers, *Bedevaartplaatsen in Nederland*, 1:109–115.

78. For the many miraculous cures in miracle books, see Broek, *Wonderen in het zonlicht*.

79. Gouw, *Geschiedenis van Amsterdam*, 5:167.

80. Weijling, *Bijdrage tot de geschiedenis van de wijbisschoppen van Utrecht*, 305–6; Gouw, *Geschiedenis van Amsterdam*, 4:405; Caspers, "Het sacrament dat moed geeft."

81. Voets, *De schittering*, 25–26.

82. In the historiography of the city of Amsterdam, the year 1566 started in spectacular fashion with an episode of mass hysteria among the children of the Burgerweeshuis, which upset the entire city for some time and provided the moniker of "miracle year." See Wagenaar, *Amsterdam in zyne opkomst, aanwas, geschiedenissen*, 1:274–75; Gouw, *Geschiedenis van Amsterdam*, 6:77–80 (the orphanage crisis); Nierop, "Van wonderjaar tot Alteratie," 451.

83. Woltjer, *Tussen vrijheidsstrijd en burgeroorlog*, 9–63; Kempers, "Assemblage van de Nederlandse leeuw," 69–77.

84. *Geschiedenis van het H. Sacrament van Mirakel*, 29–30; Sterck, *De Heilige Stede in de geschiedenis van Amsterdam*, 158; with reference to Famianus Strada S.J., *De Neder-landtsche Oorloge* (1655).

85. Bakhuizen van den Brink and Theissen, *Correspondance française de Marguerite d'Autriche*, 1:186; Sterck, *De Heilige Stede in de geschiedenis van Amsterdam*, 159.

86. Nierop, "Van wonderjaar tot Alteratie," 451–69.

87. Woltjer, *Tussen vrijheidsstrijd en burgeroorlog*, 36–37.

88. Klönne, *Amstelodamensia*, 90; Sterck, *De Heilige Stede in de geschiedenis van Amsterdam*, 158–59.

89. Nierop, "Van wonderjaar tot Alteratie," 465; Roodenburg, "'Splendeur et magnificence,'" 532.

90. Trio and De Smet, "Processions in Town," 75–81.

91. Deen, *Moorddam*, 84.

92. Regnerus Post, *Kerkelijke verhoudingen*, 533–39.

93. Five sentences were handed down by the so-called Council of Troubles, nineteen by the Amsterdam magistrates; see Deen, *Moorddam*, 87.

94. The Battle of Heiligerlee, the resounding victory of the insurgents under the command of Louis of Nassau on May 23, 1568, is usually considered to mark the beginning of the revolt against Spain, the so-called Eighty Years' War (1568–1648). In fact this revolt did not start until 1572, when the province of Holland defied the will of the king by electing William as stadtholder, and when the Sea Beggars took Den Briel (on April 1).

95. Diercxsens, *Antverpia Christo nascens et crescens*, 5:136–39; Toorenenbergen, "Alva's amnestie"; Janssens, *Brabant in het verweer*, 89; Janssens, "*Superexcellat autem misericordia iudicium*"; Schepper, "Repressie of clementie," 358–59 (Philip II had issued this general amnesty on November 16, 1569, but Alva deferred the promulgation until July 16 and had to extend it in February 1570 on the king's orders); Soen, "De reconciliatie van 'ketters.'"

96. Nierop, "Van wonderjaar tot Alteratie," 469–75. William of Orange converted to Calvinism in 1573. According to Teylingen, *Op-komste der Neder-landtsche beroerten*, 54, Willem Jacobsz in the Engelenburgh (St.-Annastraat) published a number of encouraging lines composed by Hendrick van Bisten, O.F.M.: "Amsterdam die 't al te boven gaet / Als een lely onder de doornen staet / Is sy onbesmet ghebleven / Al lagh sy in haer Vyanden quaet / Die moet heeft haer niet begeven. (Amsterdam, rising above all / Standing as a lily among thorns / Remained unsullied / Even though she was in her enemies' evil power / She never lost courage.)

97. Eeghen, *Dagboek van Broeder Wouter Jacobsz*, 1:57.

98. Ibid., 1:90.

99. Ibid., 1:v–xvi.

100. Ibid., 1:118. The victory over the Turks was the Battle of Lepanto in 1571. Cf. Fredericq, *Codex documentorum sacratissimarum indulgentiarum*, 622–23.

101. Eeghen, *Dagboek van Broeder Wouter Jacobsz*, 1:253.

102. Ibid., 1:263–64.

103. Dudok van Heel, *Van Amsterdamse burgers tot Europese aristocraten*, 16.

104. Eeghen, *Dagboek van Broeder Wouter Jacobsz*, 1:276.

105. Ibid., 1:382.

106. Ibid., 1:397.

107. Ibid., 2:472.

108. Ibid., 1:510. Cf. also 172, about the silver medal that shows the pope's countenance merging into that of the devil.

109. Ibid., 2:566 and 570. Fruitless attempts were made in April 1576 to resume the peace negotiations conducted in Breda in 1575; see Baelde and Van Peteghem, "De Pacificatie van Gent," 10–18.

110. Teylingen, *Op-komste der Neder-landtsche beroerten*, 56.

111. Eeghen, *Dagboek van Broeder Wouter Jacobsz*, 2:655–56; Nierop, "Van wonderjaar tot Alteratie," 477–81. Cf. Noordeloos, *Pastoor Maarten Donk*, 2:59; Deen, *Moorddam*, 86–87 (protective measures in 1568).

112. Thomas, *In de klauwen van de Inquisitie*, 345.

113. Eeghen, *Dagboek van Broeder Wouter Jacobsz*, 2:668.

114. Ibid., 2:681–83.

115. Ibid., 2:688; Noordeloos, *Pastoor Maarten Donk*, 2:60–63.

116. Delvigne, *Mémoires de Martin Antoine Del Rio*, 2:371.

117. Klönne, *Amstelodamensia*, 268–82; Eeghen, *Dagboek van Broeder Wouter Jacobsz*, 2:697, 701. Brother Wouter emphatically added that this emergency money was minted only on one side. Gelder was not aware of this and gave an erroneous description of the 1578 emergency money; see Enno van Gelder, *De noodmunten van de Tachtigjarige Oorlog*, 36–39.

118. For this monastery, see Eeghen, *Vrouwenkloosters en begijnhof*, 115–26. See also www2.let.vu.nl/oz/monasticon (Gertrudis Amsterdam).

119. Eeghen, *Dagboek van Broeder Wouter Jacobsz*, 2:698–99 (the parish priest of the Nieuwe Kerk is mentioned as the first initiator); Noordeloos, *Pastoor Maarten Donk*, 2:63. Little is known about the monastery of St. Gertrude; see Eeghen, *Vrouwenkloosters en begijnhof*, 115–26; Melker, *Metamorfose van stad en devotie*, 184–85. Relations between the two parish priests deteriorated considerably during the weeks before the capture of Amsterdam on May 26 due to a fundamental disagreement about the oath on the "satisfaction" (Noordeloos, *Pastoor Maarten Donk*, 2:90–111; Dudok van Heel, *Van Amsterdamse burgers tot Europese aristocraten*, 85–86). Donk, who argued in favor of taking the oath, had already published an apologetic book called *Vant rechte Evangelische Avontmaal Christi Jesu* in Utrecht in 1558 (later editions in 1567 and 1583), in which he defended Catholic religious convictions against a certain Steven Mierdman (Noordeloos, *Pastoor Maarten Donk*, 1:46–47; 2:115–16). Just before the capture of the city in 1578, Donk published another book in Amsterdam called *Corte confutatie ende wederlegginghe van een feneynich Boeck des Byencorf der H. Roomscher Kercken*, to refute Marnix of St. Aldegonde's understanding of the Eucharist (Noordeloos, *Pastoor Maarten Donk*, 2:48–49, 96–98, 119). In 1580 he published a three-volume book on the Sacrifice of the Mass, which strongly emphasized the real presence, the sacrificial character of the mass, and frequent communion (Noordeloos, *Pastoor Maarten Donk*, 2:78–80; Nouwens, *De veelvuldige H. Communie*, 41–44).

120. Descamps, "L'adoration du Saint-Sacrement à Port-Royal." Cf. Caspers, "De betekenis van de Moderne Devotie," 28–31.

121. Eeghen, *Dagboek van Broeder Wouter Jacobsz*, 2:710–11.

122. Ibid., 2:721.

123. Molanus, *Natales sanctorum Belgii*, 50vo–51vo: "Memoria venerab. Sacramenti Amstelredami. Ex officio impresso cleri Amsterodamensis."

124. Eeghen, *Dagboek van Broeder Wouter Jacobsz*, 2:727. Committing sacrilege by soiling the sacred object with excrement occurs more frequently in historical reports. Cf. Hous, *Leuvense Kroniek*, 248 (on the desecration in 1816 of the altar of the church of Our Lady in Leuven).

125. Teylingen, *Op-komste der Neder-landtsche beroerten*, 148; Vregt, "De Haarlemsche Noon"; Hoogland, "Nog een ooggetuige der Haarlemsche Noon"; Hensen, *De twee eerste bisschoppen van Haarlem*, 235. See Delvigne, *Mémoires de Martin Antoine Del Rio*, 3:219; Torre, "Relatio seu descriptio."

126. Eeghen, *Dagboek van Broeder Wouter Jacobsz*, 2:728.

127. Ibid., 2:733–34.

128. Even in 1625 it was still rumored in the city that ghosts haunted the Holy Place; see Klönne, *Amstelodamensia*, 38.

129. Teylingen, *Op-komste der Neder-landtsche beroerten*, 142–43. In addition to Augustijn van Teylingen († 1665), Antonius van Schellingwou († 1651) has also been mentioned as author; see Vermaseren, *De katholieke Nederlandse geschiedschrijving*, 276–80. See also Sterck, *De Heilige Stede in de geschiedenis van Amsterdam*, 162–64. Cf. Brom and Hensen, *Romeinsche bronnen*, 254–55 (no. 223): the third minister was the renegade abbot of St. Bernard's Abbey near Antwerp. The Holy Stead's possessions were transferred to the orphanage as early as 1579; see Eeghen, "Willem Jacobsz in Engelenburgh," 170.

130. The number of Catholics in the Republic of the United Netherlands steadily increased again during the first half of the seventeenth century, and around 1650 Catholics were more numerous than Calvinists; see Charles Parker, *Faith on the Margins*, 17–18.

131. According to Teylingen (or Schellingwou), the hearth was demolished in 1624 at the behest of chapel warden Gerrit Geurtzen Doodtshoofd. But as this person died in 1622, the hearth was either demolished before 1624 or in 1624, but at someone else's command; see Gawronski and Veerkamp, *Zerken en graven in de Nieuwezijds Kapel*, 9 (n2), 64.

132. Long, *Historische beschryvinge*, 569; Dudok van Heel, *Van Amsterdamse burgers tot Europese aristocraten*, 16, 112. For the small chimney, see Teylingen, *Op-komste der Neder-landtsche beroerten*, 140.

Chapter 3.   The Miracle on the Margins (1600–1795)

1. See for this especially Rogier, *Geschiedenis van het katholicisme in Noord-Nederland*; Israel, *The Dutch Republic*; Charles Parker, *Faith on the Margins*; Spohnholz, "Confessional Coexistence," 49.

2. See Rogier, *Geschiedenis van het katholicisme in Noord-Nederland*, 2:53 ("Hollandse Zending" and "Missio Hollandica"), 76–85. The Haarlem chapter occupied a special place in the Dutch Mission as it was permitted to continue, albeit with only a fraction of its previous possessions; see ibid., 85–100. On the successive vicars apostolic, see Spiertz, "De katholieke geestelijke leiders."

3. Rogier, *Geschiedenis van het katholicisme in Noord-Nederland*, 2:102.

4. Both secular and regular priests were subject to the jurisdiction of the vicar apostolic. His relations with the secular clergy were much better than with the regular clergy, however, because the latter's first concern was to report to the superiors of their religious institutes; see Rogier, *Geschiedenis van het katholicisme in Noord-Nederland*, 2:114–64 (on the relations between secular and regular clergy). See also Charles Parker, *Faith on the Margins*, 69–111 (training for the priesthood), 112–48 (pastoral ministry), 149–89 (the contribution of laypeople, especially women).

5. Heussen, *Batavia Sacra*, 3:195–96; Visser, *Rovenius und seine Werke*, 76–78.

6. Frijhoff and Spies, *1650: Bevochten eendracht*, 376; Israel, *The Dutch Republic*, 378, calls Rovenius the real organizer of the Catholic Church.

7. Rovenius, *Officia Sanctorum Archiepiscopatus Ultrajectensis*. The 1640 (Cologne) edition is an extended version of the 1623 (Leuven) one. On the diocesan structure of the Low Countries, which was introduced in 1559 but had ceased to exist in Rovenius's time, see Dierickx, *De oprichting der nieuwe bisdommen in de Nederlanden onder Filips II*.

8. Caspers and Tongeren, "Body and Feast," 226–31.

9. Around 1600, approximately half of the population of Amsterdam were Catholics, meaning that Protestants were in the minority. Only 10 percent of the population adhered to the Nederduits Gereformeerde Kerk (Dutch Reformed Church), the public church. Around 1650 (i.e., two generations later), the Reformed were in the majority and Catholics made up approximately 30 percent of the city's population, later stabilizing at circa 20 percent. This shifting balance was caused to a certain extent by the arrival of Protestant and, to a lesser degree, Jewish immigrants from abroad, and also because it was attractive socially for Catholics to convert to the Reformed Church. See Spaans, "Stad van vele geloven," 401, 405; Frijhoff and Spies, *1650: Bevochten eendracht*, 376; Israel, *The Dutch Republic*, 380.

10. Spaans, "Stad van vele geloven," 387–88. See also Bakker, "De zichtbare stad," in *Geschiedenis van Amsterdam*, 2:24–27.

11. Soen, "Reconquista and Reconciliation in the Dutch Revolt."

12. Frijhoff and Spies, *1650: Bevochten eendracht*, 18.

13. Eeghen, *Dagboek van Broeder Wouter Jacobsz*, 769: "Op den IIen [juni] hoorden wij, hoe op den XXVIIen Mey laetsleden binnen Antwerpen die geestelickheyt met schepen wuyt die stadt gesonden waeren. . . ." (On the second [of June] we heard how on May 28 in Antwerp the clergy was expelled from the city in boats. . . .") Cf. Marnef, "Le Brabant dans la tourmente"; Diercxsens, *Antverpia Christo nascens et crescens*, 5:356, 362.

14. Diercxsens, *Antverpia Christo nascens et crescens*, 5:95–97, 7:182 (on Norbert's relics); 1:151–52 (canonization); Caspers, "Norbertus (non?) eucharisticus."

15. Diercxsens, *Antverpia Christo nascens et crescens*, 6:211–25; Essen, *Alexandre Farnèse*, 4:148.

16. The suspicion that fell on a number of Catholics of being pro-Spanish was justified for the first decades of the Revolt, but not thereafter; see Polman, *Godsdienst in de Gouden Eeuw*, 47–48.

17. Frijhoff and Spies, *1650: Bevochten eendracht*, 20.

18. Vosters, *Het beleg en de overgave van Breda*, 1:147–52.

19. Spínola's magnanimous conduct and that of his party were linked so often to the noble character of the Spanish people by writers and artists that Breda is still a cause célèbre in Spain.

20. Vergara and Woollett, *Spectacular Rubens: The Triumph of the Eucharist*.

21. Hugo, *Obsidio Bredana*. Translations in Spanish (Antwerp 1627), English (two separate translations, London 1627), and French (Antwerp 1631).

22. Thus Pedro Calderón de la Barca wrote a play about Breda, *El Sitio de Bredá*, and Velázquez painted a large canvas of the surrender, known as *Las Lanzas* (Prado).

23. On Oldenzaal, see Jong and Knuif, *Philippus Rovenius en zijn bestuur der Hollandsche zending*, 7, 17, 46. On Breda, see Hugo, *The Siege of Breda*, 142–52; Vosters, *Het beleg en de overgave van Breda*, 1:149–51; Margry and Caspers, *Bedevaartplaatsen in Nederland*, 2:173–85.

24. Schoutens, *Geschiedenis van den Eerdienst van het Allerheiligste Sacrament*, 293–95.

25. Wagenaar, *Vaderlandsche historie*, 11.

26. Frijhoff, *Embodied Belief*, 39–65; Kaplan, "Integration vs Segregation," 50–51.

27. Klönne, *Amstelodamensia*, 138–50; Knuttel, *De toestand der Nederlandsche katholieken*, 1:168–69; Voets, "Een leider van het Haarlemse bisdom," 281; Spaans, "Stad van vele geloven," 404.

28. Cf. Frijhoff, *Embodied Belief*, 23. The Amsterdam city authorities' strict intervention also caused amazement elsewhere. Thus the Franciscan Joannes Boener, in a report of his activities for 1640–1641, wrote that the persecutions were multiplying every day: "Even in Amsterdam on the day before yesterday, on the feast of Corpus Christi, the priests, who are used to more freedom than we are, fell victim to large-scale raids"; see *Epistolae missionariorum ordinis S. Francisci ex Frisia et Hollandia*, 43.

29. The Julian calendar was used in most provinces of the Republic up to 1700–1701. This calendar was ten days behind the Gregorian calendar that was used in Holland, Zeeland, and the Generality Lands.

30. On the Julian and Gregorian calendars, see Caspers, "Het Sint Jansfeest in kerk- en volksgebruik."

31. Hofman, "Het kerspel buiten de Witte-Vrouwenpoort te Utrecht," 92–93. Frijhoff, in "De paniek van juni 1734," 193 (note 124), thinks that Hofman's dating is mistaken, but he does not appear to realize himself that the Julian calendar was still in use in Utrecht at this time.

32. Thursday, June 1, was Corpus Christi according to the Gregorian calendar, which the French observed. For citizens of Utrecht who still observed the Julian calendar, this was an ordinary Thursday that fell on May 22. The confusion about the two calendars has caused historiographers to give different dates for the procession.

33. Cf. Frijhoff, "Shifting Identities in Hostile Settings," 11; Kaplan, "In Equality and Enjoying the Same Favor," 117–18.

34. The Utrecht Dom church was used for Catholic worship from July 1672 to November 1673. On the Eucharistic procession, see Rogier, *Beschouwing en onderzoek*, 156–57; Margry, *Teedere quaesties*, 183–85; Vanhaelen, "Utrecht's Transformations," 264–374. In 1670 Neercassel was one of the guests of honor at the third centenary of the Brussels Sacrament of Miracle; see Heussen, *Batavia Sacra*, 3:434.

35. Rogier, *Geschiedenis van het katholicisme in Noord-Nederland*, 2:213–14; Rogier, *Beschouwing en onderzoek*, 177–78; Voorvelt, "Enkele minder bekende facetten."

36. Rogier, *Geschiedenis van het katholicisme in Noord-Nederland*, 2:203–9.

37. See, for instance, Haks, *Vaderland en vrede 1672–1713*, 111.

38. Frijhoff, "De paniek van juni 1734"; Frijhoff, *Embodied Belief*, 181–213.

39. Stijl, *Amsterdam in zyne geschiedenissen*, 1:61.

40. Frijhoff, "De paniek van juni 1734," 174.

41. Frijhoff, *Embodied Belief*, 188–93.

42. Syvaertsz, *Roomsche mysterien*, 33v.

43. Ibid., 32.

44. Caspers and Hofman, *Een bovenaardse vrouw*, 29–48.

45. Pauli, *Vier historien van het H. Sacrament van Mirakel* (with a more extensive list including more places than the four mentioned in the title). The surveys published by Petrus Biverus, Tilman Bredenbach, and Guilielmus van Gent do not mention the Holy Stead either. Places that are frequently mentioned are Brussels (1370) and Boxtel (1400). Remarkably, Jean Bertholet, the eighteenth-century historian of the feast of Corpus Christi, does pay some attention to the Amsterdam Sacrament of Miracle; see Bertholet, *Histoire de l'institution de la Fête-Dieu*, 153–54.

46. Sterck, *De Heilige Stede*, 166, 194 (appendix 24): "Limina sacra manent hodie, et vestigia perstant, / Nobiles a vitulis qua via nomen habet. / Servaturque dies fastis celeberrima nostris, / Et videt haec nudos annua mane pedes. Clam veniunt multi memores, valvasque salutant, / Sacrum et adorant ter, circumeuntque locum."

47. Frijhoff, *Embodied Belief*, 115.

48. Wiele, *Gulde-Iaers Feest-daghen*, 287–88. On this songwriter, see Knipping, *Iconography of the Counter Reformation*, 2:299; Leeuwen, *Hemelse voorbeelden*, 11–20; Porteman and Smits-Veldt, *Een nieuw vaderland voor de muzen*, 476–79.

49. Eeghen, "Het begijnhof te Amsterdam"; Dijk, *Van "Der Beghinenlande" tot Begijnhof*.

50. Dijk, *Van "Der Beghinenlande" tot Begijnhof*, 27–29 (English church), 45–53 (current church). On the amazement of a French priest-visitor to Amsterdam at the privileges of the Begijnhof in a Calvinist city in 1719, see Eeghen, "Het Begijnhof te Amsterdam," 213–14.

51. Voets, "Een leider van het Haarlemse bisdom"; Ceyssens, "Leonardus Marius in de Nederlanden."

52. Voets, "Een leider van het Haarlemse bisdom," 276–78. In 1630, when Marius became pastor of the Begijnhof, there were 160 women living in the beguinage, including 54 beguines. This balance gradually shifted. When the current Begijnhofkerk was built in 1682, there were 150 beguines and only 12 widows and single women; see Dijk, *Van "Der Beghinenlande" tot Begijnhof*, 22, 46.

53. Some authors believe that Marius had this book printed in Amsterdam rather than Antwerp. But Sterck, "Het boekje *Amstelredams eer ende opcomen*," 155–56, contends that Antwerp was in fact the place of publication.

54. Sterck, "Het boekje *Amstelredams eer ende opcomen*," 184–86, distinguishes eight different editions, the last two of which were published by Gerardus van Bloemen in Amsterdam in the eighteenth century; see also Leuven, *De boekhandel te Amsterdam*, 65. Cf. Sterck, "De dichter van de versjes in Marius' Amstelredams eer ende opcomen"; Sterck, "De opkomst van Aemstelredam."

55. Sterck, "Het boekje *Amstelredams eer ende opcomen*," 183.

56. Ibid., 138–46 (Jacob Cornelisz van Oostsanen's paintings as an example for Bolswert), 146–48 (on Cornelis Plemp), 149–50, 161–72 (on the separate edition of the prints by the Antwerp printer Hieronymus Verdussen). See also Porteman and Smits-Veldt, *Een nieuw vaderland voor de muzen*, 486–88. See also Jong et al., *Van Bolswert naar Antwerpen*, 138–39.

57. Sterck, "Het boekje *Amstelredams eer ende opcomen*," 133–37 (on Boëtius à Bolswert).

58. Marius, *Amstelredams eer ende opcomen*, 35.

59. Ibid., 57–61. Thanks to Marius's book, the citizens of Amsterdam under the Republic were better acquainted with the precise details of the Miracle than their fourteenth- and fifteenth-century ancestors.

60. The *Chronicon Comitum Hollandiae et episcoporum Ultrajectensium* dates from 1468; cf. Regnerus Post, "Het Sacrament van Mirakel te Amsterdam," 256.

61. Cf. Regnerus Post, "Het Sacrament van Mirakel te Amsterdam," 257. The Division Chronicle was first published in Leiden in 1517 and a second time in Amsterdam in 1595. For a synopsis of the Miracle account in Holland chronicles, the book of hours, and the miracle book, see Lautenschütz, "Het Mirakel in de historische literatuur," 46–49.

62. The minor differences in the content between the miracle book and Marius's book are less relevant. One striking difference of detail is that Marius has the host jump up and down on the man's hand, where the miracle book and the *Chronicon* say that the host quivered "like a pike's heart."

63. *Hier beghint die vindinghe vant hoochweerdighe ende heylige Sacrament*, line 3: "Ende die vrouwen de daer by waren ende sijns waer namen, aendenckende vanden heyligen Sacrament dat hi ontfangen hadde, namen dat hi over gaf in een reyn vat ende gotent in een groot vuer" ("The women who had been present and who had observed him, knew that he had received the Sacrament. For this reason, they collected his vomit in a clean vessel and cast it into a large fire"). Marius, *Amstelredams eer ende opcomen*, 58: "Dit, alsoo het onder de fluymen, ende andere materie was vermengt, is van die Vrouwe, die den siecken man diende (trouwens uyt onwetendheit, overmidts sy het niet ghesien en hadde) in het vier geworpen" ("This, that is what was mixed in with the vomit and other matter, was cast by the women who served the sick man into the fire [through ignorance as it happens, because they had not seen it]").

64. *Hier beghint die vindinghe vant hoochweerdighe ende heylige Sacrament*, 4v: "ende hi is gecomen ende heeftet heylige Sacrament met groter devotie ende waerdicheyt weder gebrocht in die kerck" ("and he came and brought the Blessed Sacrament back to the church with great devotion and dignity"). Marius, *Amstelredams eer ende opcomen*, 60–61: "Als die Priester dat hoorde; docht hy dat God dit Mirakel verkondight ende openbaer ghemaeckt woude hebben; dede dit te verstaen alle Priesteren gheestelijck en weerlijck binnen Amsterdamme ende sy quamen in haer religie met kruysen ende vanen ter heyliger Stede daer dat H. Sacrament gevonden was ende brochtent met love ende met sanghe met grooter eeren ende waerdigheidt in de Parochi-kercke" ("When the priest heard that; he thought that God wished this miracle to be proclaimed and made public; he told all priests both

spiritual and secular in Amsterdam, and they came with their crosses and banners to the Holy Stead where the Blessed Sacrament had been found and brought it with praise, singing, and great honor and dignity to the parish church").

65. Cf. Frijhoff, *Embodied Belief,* 26–27, 35–36 (*concordia* of the city).

66. Marius, *Amstelredams eer ende opcomen,* 63. For a later edition and translation of Floris of Boechorst's charter, see Pluym, *Het H. Sacrament van Mirakel,* 12–13. See also Sterck, *De Heilige Stede,* 10–14.

67. Graaf, "Uit de Levens der 'Maechden van den Hoeck' te Haarlem," 255. On this Trijntgen, who was highly regarded for her exemplary piety, see also Graaf, "De 'Vergaederinghe der Maechden van den Hoeck' te Haarlem," 405–7, 412, 427–29; Theissing, *Over klopjes en kwezels,* 69, 119; Spaans, *De Levens der Maechden,* passim.

68. Barten, "Een herhaling van het Sacramentswonder van Amsterdam in 1627."

69. Any readers who were still unconvinced after reading all these chapters were directed by Marius to three non-Catholic but sincere historians who had studied the history of the Christianization of the Northern Netherlands: Janus Dousa († 1604), Bernardus Furmerius († 1616), and Ubbo Emmius († 1625); see Marius, *Amstelredams eer ende opcomen,* 284–94.

70. Klönne, *Amstelodamensia,* 169–82 (quotation on 178–79); Voets, "Een leider van het Haarlemse bisdom," 284. Cf. Spaans, "Stad van vele geloven," 402.

71. Cf. Klönne, *Amstelodamensia,* 177, on the rare information contained in this letter of complaint: "a particularity that I have not been able to find a trace of anywhere else."

72. Klönne, *Amstelodamensia,* 81–83. See also GAA, Westerholt Archive 713, inv. no. 17–12 (copy of the Reminiscence). The route that Loen indicated was in fact the route of Corpus Christi in summer, which deviated slightly from that of Corpus Christi in Lent. See also Roodenburg, "Het verleden opgepoetst."

73. Pollmann, "Burying the Dead," 93–94.

74. Pluym, *Het H. Sacrament van Mirakel,* 132–34; Schillemans, "De Begijnhofkerk als nieuwe Heilige Stede," 50.

75. Sterck et al., *De werken van Vondel,* 5:133–38; Zeij, *Vondel's Altaargeheimenissen,* 161–66.

76. Sterck et al., *De werken van Vondel,* 4:5–37; Brom, *Vondels geloof,* 195–211. Cf. ibid., 151: Brom suggests that Vondel and Marius were also on good terms because of their mutual affinity with Cologne, the former having been born there and the latter having studied and worked there.

77. Sterck et al., *De werken van Vondel,* 4:641–826. The poem was supposedly published in Cologne at the "Nieuwe druckerije" (New printer), but in fact it was published in Amsterdam; see Leuven, *De boekhandel te Amsterdam,* 24.

78. Molkenboer, *Altaergeheimenissen;* Molkenboer, "Het Vierenswaerdigh Wonder."

79. Zeij, *Vondel's Altaargeheimenissen,* 142.

80. Klönne, *Amstelodamensia,* 151–68; Knuttel, *De toestand der Nederlandsche katholieken,* 1:154; Dijk, *Van "Der Beghinenlande" tot Begijnhof,* 24–25.

81. Margry, *Amsterdam en het Mirakel van het Heilig Sacrament*, 46; Margry, "In Memoriam Miraculi," 22.

82. Porteman and Smits-Veldt, *Een nieuw vaderland*, 562–64. Cf. Molkenboer, who points out, in "Het Vierenswaerdigh Wonder," 144, that Vondel made no further reference to the Miracle in any of his works after 1645.

83. Marius, *Getyden van het H. ende Hoogh-waerdigh Sacrament des Altaers*. In his preface, Marius refers to *Amstelredams eer ende opcomen*, also an anonymous work, which he states was written by an "obliging soul and pen," a modest if transparent reference to himself. In one of the blank pages in the front of the copy of the *Getyden* preserved in the Nijmegen University Library (641 C54), there is a dedication by Marius to a beguine of the Amsterdam Begijnhof: "Eer ende deughdrijcke Maeghd / Machthildis Lubberti / Gods suijver lof / dient ons op 't Hof. / Geeft seghen Heer / dat ick U eer. / L. Marius" ("Honorable and virtuous maid / Machthildis Lubberti / God's pure praises / we serve in the beguinage. / Bestow your blessing, Lord / that I may honor you. / L. Marius"). On this copy, see Sterck, "Het boekje *Amstelredams eer ende opcomen*," 151n2. A new edition of the *Getyden* was published in Amsterdam at Gerardus van Bloemen in 1717; a revised edition was published by Gebr. J. & H. Langenhuysen in The Hague in 1869.

84. To stimulate liturgical piety, Marius also published his own translation of the office of the Blessed Virgin Mary in 1651; see Marius, *Kerkelijke getyden van de hoogwaerdige Moeder Gods*.

85. Marius, *Getyden van het H. ende Hoogh-waerdigh Sacrament des Altaers*, 147–78; quoted in Long, *Historische beschryvinge van de reformatie der stadt Amsterdam*, 434–43.

86. Marius, *Getyden van het H. ende Hoogh-waerdigh Sacrament des Altaers*, 185–87.

87. Cf. Clemens, "Het Mirakel van Amsterdam tussen zijn opgang in vuur en omgang in stilte," 36–38.

88. Rovenius, *Officia Sanctorum Archiepiscopatus Ultrajectensis*, x–xxiiii (*In festo Venerabilis Sacramenti miraculosi*). See also Clemens, "Het Mirakel van Amsterdam tussen zijn opgang in vuur en omgang in stilte," 33–36.

89. "Lyste van alle gheboden vier-daghent," 266.

90. Broeke, *Stille Omgang Herdenking 1881–1931*, 40; Schillemans, "De Begijnhofkerk als nieuwe Heilige Stede," 48.

91. Polman, *Godsdienst in de Gouden Eeuw*, 65–66 (mentions "liturgically hearing mass" among other things). For an extensive treatment of translations of liturgical prayers in church books, see Clemens, *De godsdienstigheid in de Nederlanden in de spiegel van de katholieke kerkboeken 1680–1840*.

92. For extensive surveys of the Miracle in visual art, see Schillemans, "De Begijnhofkerk als nieuwe Heilige Stede"; Dijk, *Van "Der Beghinenlande" tot Begijnhof*, 80–82; Kruijf, "Gods mirakel machmen sien."

93. Four embroidered cushions and two painted processional banners are also important for the iconography of the Miracle; see the previous footnote and Sterck, "Het boekje *Amstelredams eer ende opcomen*," 139–45. Cf. Meuwissen, *Jacob Cornelisz van Oostsanen*, 209–12.

94. The administering of viaticum to the sick man (2); the casting of the vomit into the fire (3); two plump angels flanking the host in the fire (4); the finding of the host in the fire (5); the procession with the host back to St. Nicholas's Church (6); a child falls off his father's lap near the fire (7); Floris of Boechorst and his party confirming the veracity of the Miracle (8); the fire in the chapel in 1452 (9); Maximilian of Austria praying in front of a monstrance containing the miraculous host (10); the cure of a blind man at the Holy Stead (11), respectively.

95. A pelican feeding its young with her own blood (12); two angels holding a monstrance containing a host (13); a man who comes for confession (14); the administering of communion (15); the freeing of a soul from purgatory at the moment of the elevation of the host during mass (16), respectively.

96. Molanus, *Traité des saintes images*, 151, 525. See also Knipping, *Iconography of the Counter Reformation*, 2:300; Huys, *Occo codex*, xi.

97. Oostsanen also exuberantly used the motif of "angels making music" in some of his works; see Meuwissen, *Jacob Cornelisz van Oostsanen*, 214–17.

98. The series by Boëtius à Bolswert does contain a number of images of "static" angels, but these prints were clearly made in a different style and do not match the iconographic tradition of the Miracle that he had studied; see Sterck, "Het boekje *Amstelredams eer ende opcomen*," 138–39.

99. The engraving was already mentioned and satirized in Long, *Historische beschryvinge van de reformatie der stadt Amsterdam*, 208–9.

100. The caption underneath the image does refer to the miracle. The full text is "Dees man die gij hier ziet, beduyt in dese prent / Ontfangt op 't alderlest, het hylig Sacrament / Maar braakte het weer uyt en meent te overlyden / De vrouw die neemt het op smyt het in't vier ter zyden / Daar brant het Sacrament, geheel en ongeschent / Sy nam het in haar hant, een buer maakt syt bekent / Sy lydt het in een kist doet het een Prister weten / Die haalt het met triump tot glorie deser stede" ("This man that you see here, depicted in this print / Is, at the end [of his life], receiving the Blessed Sacrament / But he vomited it out and thought he would die / The woman who picked it up flung it into the fire at the side / There the Sacrament burned, whole and intact / She took it in her hand, and told a neighbor / She put it in a chest and notified a priest / He came to get it in triumph, to the glory of this place"). There is a painted panel in the Museum Catharijneconvent in Utrecht with this scene (inv. no. BHM s. 9578) which was probably made on the basis of the engraving; see Beijne, "Mirakel van Amsterdam," 16–17.

101. On the Collegie, see Bont, *Het H. Cecilia Collegie*; Margry and Joor, *St. Caecilia Collegie*. See also Wagenaar, *Amsterdam in zyne opkomst, aanwas, geschiedenissen*, 3:407 (Miracle House).

102. Schillemans, "De Begijnhofkerk als nieuwe Heilige Stede," 51–52 (confraternity 1671, with an indulgence granted by Pope Clement X); Margry and Joor, *St. Caecilia Collegie*, 14; Beringer, *Die Ablässe, ihr Wesen und Gebrauch*, 2:71–74 (Archconfraternity of the Most Blessed Sacrament of the Altar).

103. Bont, *Het H. Cecilia Collegie*, 30–32; Polman, *Romeinse bronnen voor de kerkelijke toestand*, 3:277 (no. 350); Margry and Joor, *St. Caecilia Collegie*, 15. In the late seventeenth century, during the pontificate of Pope Innocent XII, the Catholic

faithful were exhorted particularly to receive communion; see, for instance, Godeau, *Meditatien over 't allerheiligsten Sacrament des Altaers*.

104. Bont, "Naemen van de paepsche vergaderplaetsen"; Polman, *Godsdienst in de Gouden Eeuw*, 54. Israel, in *The Dutch Republic*, 390, mentions that the Catholics of Amsterdam had the use of around eighty hidden churches in the late seventeenth century.

105. Margry and Joor, *St. Caecilia Collegie*, 13.

106. Bont, *Het H. Cecilia Collegie*; Margry and Joor, *St. Caecilia Collegie*; Spaans, "Stad van vele geloven," 452.

107. *De Zalige Dood*, 4–16; Wingens, *Over de grens*, 222–23.

108. Kronenburg, *Maria's Heerlijkheid in Nederland*, 8:269–76; Wingens, *Over de grens*, 221–58, especially 221, 227, 233.

109. Polman, *Katholiek Nederland*, 2:317; 3:254.

110. Stichter, *Oude en nieuwe geestelyke liedekens*, 15–16; *Het Evangelische Visnet*, 126–28.

111. In 1730 the government permitted Roman Catholic priests to take up official residence in the Republic, albeit subject to all manner of restrictions; see Polman, *Katholiek Nederland*, 2:6–11.

112. Margry, *Amsterdam en het Mirakel van het Heilig Sacrament*, 48–51. Cf. Clemens, "Het Mirakel van Amsterdam tussen zijn opgang in vuur en omgang in stilte," 38–39.

113. Long, *Historische beschryvinge van de reformatie der stadt Amsterdam*, 210.

114. Caspers and Margry, *Identiteit en spiritualiteit van de Amsterdamse Stille Omgang*, 44–45. Cornelia Occo was a distant descendent of Pompeius Occo († 1537), who was famous as a patron of the Holy Stead.

115. *Memorie volgens het origineel*. Cf. Clemens, "Het Mirakel van Amsterdam tussen zijn opgang in vuur en omgang in stilte," 32.

116. Brom, *Cornelis Broere*, 14. Cf. Klönne, *Amstelodamensia*, 83 (about himself when he was a young boy).

117. Long, *Historische beschryvinge van de reformatie der stadt Amsterdam*, 203. For the passages on the Miracle, see ibid., 196–211 (the history of the Miracle), 324–35 (later miracles and the fire of 1452); 390–417 (more criticism of the miracles, such as the cure of Maximilian of Austria, etc.), 427–49 (more criticism of the miracles, etc.; on 447–48 support for Wallich Syvaertsz's view of the pious fraud by constantly renewing the miraculous host); 493–95 (Charles V and Philip II); 558–69 (the Holy Stead after the Alteration); and passim.

118. Spaans, "Stad van vele geloven," 426. Clemens, "Het Mirakel van Amsterdam tussen zijn opgang in vuur en zijn omgang in stilte," 42–49.

119. Margry, "In Memoriam Miraculi," 23–24. Cf. Sterck, "Het boekje *Amstelredams eer ende opcomen*," 159.

120. Nanning, *Twee predikatiën*, 38–60. Nanning's first sermon is about the correct (Catholic) interpretation of John 6.

121. Wetering, *Leer- en lofrede tot bevestiging van de waare, weezenlyke, en eigenlyk gezegde tegenwoordigheid van Jesus Christus in het Hoogwaardigste Sacrament des Autaers*.

122. Kok, *Amsterdams eer en opkomst*, 2:105–6. A century later the rejection was repeated; see Stieler, *Amsterdam's eer en opkomen*.

Chapter 4.   The Battle for Public Space (1795–1881)

1. Cf. Marinus van der Heijden, *De dageraad van de emancipatie der katho-lieken*; Versluis, *Geschiedenis van de emancipatie der katholieken*; Homan, "Catholic Emancipation in the Netherlands."

2. Noordeloos, *De restitutie der kerken*; Bornewasser, *Kerkelijk verleden*, 98–113 ("The Authority of the Dutch State over the Churches, 1795–1853"). See also Witlox, *De Katholieke Staatspartij*.

3. Begijnhof Archives, *Registri Memorialis*, October 26, 1798; Akker, "Ge-schiedenis," 50:203–224; Voets, *De schittering*, 134–35; Roon and Rutgerink, "Be-gijnhof Amsterdam," 11–15.

4. Margry, *Teedere Quaesties*, 212–27.

5. This "United Kingdom" only existed for fifteen years. In 1830 the part that is currently Belgium rose in revolt and continued independently as a new king-dom. The Dutch king was also the grand duke of Luxembourg until the death of King William III in 1890.

6. See Margry, *Teedere Quaesties*, 222–38.

7. Thijm, in *De Katholieke kerkregeling*, 13, wrote, "So often talk has been of the Protestant Netherlands, of exclusive bonds that supposedly exist between Prot-estantism and the Netherlands; so often it has been made to seem as if there were no Catholics in the Netherlands."

8. This concept was frequently used, for instance, in the *Catholijke Neder-landsche Stemmen* magazine.

9. These archpriests held appointments roughly for the areas north of the river delta; two vicars apostolic were appointed for the southern parts, especially for the province of North Brabant.

10. As titular bishop, Van Wijckerslooth was appointed bishop of Curium i.p.i. in Cyprus.

11. Estré, *Beknopt geschiedkundig verhaal*.

12. Cf. Bornewasser, *Kerkelijk verleden*, 251–61.

13. Clemens, "Het Mirakel van Amsterdam," 32–36.

14. Ibid., 42–44.

15. Ibid., 44.

16. Sterck, *De Heilige Stede in de geschiedenis van Amsterdam*, 119–20.

17. Brom, *Cornelis Broere*; *Katholieke Encyclopedie*, 6:286.

18. Brom, *Cornelis Broere*, 14.

19. In addition this period also saw new devotional initiatives in other re-gions; cf. Margry, "Bedevaartrevival?"

20. The pilgrimages came to an involuntary end in 1808–1809. The sup-posed "revival" of 1815 concerned Saint Willibrord; see Margry, *Teedere Quaesties*, 186–219.

21. Broere and Ploeg, *Gedichten bij het vijfde eeuwgetij*, 26, 29.

22. Ibid., 25.

23. Ibid., 26, 29, 31.

24. Brom, *Cornelis Broere*, 14.

25. Margry and Joor, *St. Caecilia Collegie*, 18–23.

26. GAA, Begijnhof Archive, inv. no. 853, 3, from a note of pastor Steins Bisschop of 1845.

27. It is unclear whether these paintings were hanging in the chapel at this time or whether they were only displayed for the celebration of the Miracle; an engraving of the interior of the Holy Stead from 1792 shows no sign of any Miracle painting or related object on the walls of the chapel; see Schillemans, "De Begijnhofkerk," 53–55.

28. Vijver, *Wandelingen*, 211–12.

29. Clemens, "Het Mirakel van Amsterdam," 45; Akker, "Geschiedenis," 50:230–31.

30. Ibid., 50:232–33.

31. Ibid., 50:s233.

32. Steenwijk, *Beknopt verhaal van het Mirakel te Amsterdam*.

33. Bont, *Het H. Cecilia Collegie*. Thus the governors of the Occo Hofje erected a tabernacle with a silver mounting bearing the image of the Miracle in their private oratory. This tabernacle was placed in the Begijnhof church during the jubilee (Amsterdamsch Catholijk, "Het Mirakel van Amsterdam," 197); it is unclear whether the governors commissioned this work themselves.

34. For the networks within these institutions, see Vis, *Liefde het fundament*; Wolf, *De kerk en het Maagdenhuis*; Jager, "Het R C Jongensweeshuis."

35. The painting was probably purchased by the pastor of St. Cornelius's parish in Wanroij when the building was abandoned in 1953 (after being sold to Nationale Handelsbank). The canvas was traced there by Suzette van 't Hof in 2014.

36. Hervieu-Léger, *Religion as a Chain of Memory*.

37. For an overview of important Catholic *lieux de mémoire*, see Jacobs et al., *Aan plaatsen gehecht*.

38. Swaving, *Galerij van Roomsche beelden*, 40–45. In an ironic sentence (45) he called the Nederlandsche Handel-Maatschappij (Dutch Trading Society), established in that year, the result of the favors of the Amsterdam "wafer-god."

39. See, for instance, Schutte, *Het Calvinistisch Nederland*.

40. Pitra, *La Hollande catholique*, 306.

41. See Margry and Caspers, *Bedevaartplaatsen in Nederland*, passim, or *Bedevaart en Bedevaartplaatsen in Nederland*, Meertens Instituut (2018), www.meertens.knaw.nl/bedevaart/bol/.

42. For this cross-border pilgrimage, see Wingens, *Over de grens*; Caspers and Gielis, "Scherpenheuvelbedevaarten."

43. Broere and Ploeg, *Gedichten bij het vijfde eeuwgetij*, 31.

44. *De Katholiek* 4 (1845), 7:198 confirms this usage of the word when the author mentions the practice of performing the silent prayer walk "in an introverted way," and also "to go a holy way." Others also used this concept for individual silent walking; cf. Leesberg, "Herinnering," 217–20.

45. Broere and Ploeg, *Gedichten bij het vijfde eeuwgetij*, 31–32.

46. Ibid., 63–64.

47. See the anonymous review of Pluym's book by a 's-Hertogenbosch cleric in *De Katholiek* 4 (1945), 7:198.

48. Akker, in "Geschiedenis," 58:305–7, mentions that the written *Memorie* of the walk and the version of it that was printed in the eighteenth century were deposited in the Begijnhof archives long after 1845. This means that neither Steins Bisschop nor Pluym would have been able at the time to ascertain the course of that route or how it might have been followed.

49. Steins Bisschop had been an associate pastor in the Begijnhof before, between 1828 and 1838.

50. Akker, "Geschiedenis," 58:303–4; Brom, *Cornelis Broere*, 287.

51. Heel and Knipping, *Van schuilkerk tot zuilkerk*, 221–23.

52. On this celebration, see Aretz, *Der Heilige Rock zu Trier*; Vaissier, "Mirakel-verzen," 153–54.

53. Schneider, "Wallfahrt, Ultramontanismus und Politik," 246.

54. For the Netherlands, see, for instance, *Catholijke Nederlandsche Stemmen*, September 21, 1844, 303. Cf. H. van Lottom in *Catholijke Nederlandsche Stemmen*, December 7, 1844, 390–93; Schneider, "Presse und Wallfahrt."

55. Albers, *Geschiedenis van het herstel*, 2:78–79.

56. Margry, *Teedere Quaesties*, 151.

57. Schieder, *Religion und Revolution*, 60–62, 66.

58. Cf. Ebertz, "Die Organisierung von Massenreligiosität."

59. See, for instance, "De Heilige Rok te Trier en te Argenteuil," in *De Protestant* 3 (1845): 252–56.

60. Schneider, "Presse und Wallfahrt, 291–96."

61. Steinruck, "Die Heilig-Rock-Wallfahrt von 1844"; Detzler, "Protest and Schism."

62. See the 1844–1845 editions of *Catholijke Nederlandsche Stemmen*, with many articles that took a stand against him and his "sect." Cf. also *De Godsdienst-vriend* 54 (1845): 123–40.

63. Rüter, *Rapporten van de gouverneurs*, 3:227.

64. Ibid., 3:125; "Wonderbare genezing in Trier," in *Catholijke Nederlandsche Stemmen*, September 21, 1844, 303.

65. "De H. Rok te Trier en het Amsterdamsch mirakel," in *De Protestant* 3 (1845): 372–82; "Wat moet gedaan worden bij de tegenwoordige godsdienstige be-wegingen in Europa," in *De Tijdgenoot* 5 (1845): 580–87.

66. H[eukelom], *Het feest der dwaasheid*, 11. On Heukelom, see *Nieuw Neder-landsch Biografisch Woordenboek*, 5:228–29. The anonymous publication has been ascribed wrongly to the poet Jan Pieter Heije.

67. Lans, *Het leven van pater Bernard*, 239.

68. This is what the anonymous author of *Wonderdoeners en aflaatkramers in de 19de eeuw*, 122–28, suggested.

69. B., *De roomsch-katholijke godsdienst*.

70. Quoted in Jong, "Godsdienst," 138–39, letter to Thorbecke, September 17, 1842.

71. Broere and Ploeg, *Gedichten bij het vijfde eeuwgetij*, 64.

72. Bosch Kemper, *Geschiedenis van Nederland*, 5:64–66; Rüter, *Rapporten van de gouverneurs*, 3:311–12. For Ferrieri's published text, see *De Godsdienstvriend* 54 (1845): 151–54.

73. This turned out to be an erroneous interpretation of Ferrieri's pastoral letter; see *Catholijke Nederlandsche Stemmen*, February 22, 1845, 64, and Lottom's reaction to the articles in *De Kerkbode* and *De Tijdgenoot* in *Catholijke Nederlandsche Stemmen*, March 15, 1845, 85. Amount of priests: GAA, Begijnhof Archive, inv. no. 853, 6.

74. Quoted in Jong, "Godsdienst," 139.

75. For this kind of conspiracy theory, see Cubitt, *The Jesuit Myth*; Margry, "Jezuïetenstreken"; Laurens van der Heijden, *De schaduw van de jezuïet*, 43–46. For the extent and impact of specific transnational cult, see Busch, *Katholische Frömmigkeit und Moderne*. Cf. Bornewasser, *Kerkelijk verleden*, 362–75 ("Mythical Aspects of Dutch Anti-Catholicism in the Nineteenth Century").

76. See Roothaan's circular letter of December 27, 1839, on the subject, published in *Catholijke Nederlandsche Stemmen*, September 21, 1844, 241–44, 249–52, 257–60.

77. Margry, "Jezuïetenstreken," 39–64.

78. Letter of February 8, 1845; for the Dutch translation, see Steenwijk, *Beknopt verhaal van het Mirakel te Amsterdam*; also included in Rüter, *Rapporten van de gouverneurs*, 3:332–36. Cf. Valk, *Romeinse bescheiden*, 132, a previous dispatch from Ferrieri to Propaganda Fide on the intended jubilee, June 3, 1844.

79. These endeavors were indebted to the criticism used previously by the Bollandists for their editions of the lives of the saints.

80. GAA, Archive Begijnhof 853, 9 (report Pastor Steins Bisschop).

81. Pluym, *Het H. Sacrament van Mirakel*, 185. It would later transpire that he had missed many sources and that his text contained inaccuracies. Thijm edited a new and revised edition in 1869; cf. Lautenschütz, "Het Mirakel in de historische lieratuur," 66–67. For Pluym's methodology and significance, see Raedts, "Vier pleidooien voor het Mirakel," 56–58.

82. Nor did Pluym think it could be, as his Protestant critics presumed he did. On p. 135 of his book he states that he has left the supernatural aspect aside in his investigations.

83. Long, *Historische beschryvinghe*, 196–210, 327–35, 391–97, 569; S.r., *Wat moet ik gelooven*. Cf. Dudok van Heel, "Uit Goethe-Dante-Vondelen gaan," 108–9.

84. See the announcement of the book in *De Katholiek* 7 (1845): 180–207, esp. 206–7.

85. Most editions from this period can be found in the Begijnhof collection in the University Library of Amsterdam. See, for instance, Buddingh, *Mirakel-geloof en mirakelen in de Nederlanden*; Margry, "Jezuïetenstreken," 39–64. Governor Van Ewijck reported on the notion, still lingering, of the influence of Trier on Amsterdam; see Vaissier, "Mirakel-verzen," 153–54.

86. For an example of how this discussion arose in daily life, see *De Katholiek* 4 (1845), 7:251.

87. Brom, "Broere's preek," 245.

88. "Een woord van den Katholiek aan zijne lezers," in *De Katholiek* 4 (1845), 7:1–11.

89. "Ronge, Czerski en de Duitsch-Katholieke Kerk," in *De Katholiek* 4 (1845), 7:244–64.

90. One factual article was devoted to it, consisting mainly of Ferrieri's pastoral letter about the celebration of February 6, 1845, *Catholijke Nederlandsche Stemmen*, February 22, 1845, 63–64; this letter, with an introduction, also appeared in *De Godsdienstvriend* 54 (1845): 149–54. The pastoral letter was especially sent to Le Sage ten Broek by Steins Bisschop (cf. GAA, Archive Begijnhof 853, 7). The Miracle is not discussed in Gorris's biography.

91. He wrote that the annual celebration was "too little known" in "our days of lukewarmness and disbelief" and he hoped that the indulgence granted would change this.

92. Amsterdamsch Catholijk, "Het Mirakel van Amsterdam," 190–209.

93. Amsterdamsch Catholijk, "Het Mirakel van Amsterdam," 209.

94. GAA, Archive Begijnhof 853, 11 (report Pastor Steins Bisschop).

95. Meuwissen, *Jacob Cornelisz van Oostsanen*, 209–12.

96. Only once did a—probably Protestant—visitor have to be removed from the chapel, where he was taking notes, because he obstinately refused to take off his hat; see *De Godsdienstvriend* 54 (1845): 208.

97. In those years the following churches also observed the prescribed Miracle feast: Krijtberg, Zaaijer, Pool, Duif, Maagdenhuis, "Pothuis," "Stadhuis van Hoorn" (St. Dominic), Mozes en Aäron, and De Ster.

98. See Amsterdamsch Catholijk, "Het Mirakel van Amsterdam," 196–204.

99. The jubilee was announced and/or discussed in the press throughout the country, from the *Leydsche Courant* of March 5, 1845, and the *Drentsche Courant* of March 7, 1845, to the *Kamper Courant* of March 3 and 10, 1845.

100. Amsterdamsch Catholijk, "Het Mirakel van Amsterdam," 208.

101. GAA, Archive Begijnhof 853, 13 (report Pastor Steins Bisschop).

102. Akker, "Geschiedenis," 58:314–15.

103. Amsterdamsch Catholijk, "Het Mirakel van Amsterdam," 196; [Klönne], *Het Mirakel van Amsterdam*, 29.

104. Quoted in Akker, "Geschiedenis," 58:310.

105. Brom, "Broere's preek," 245.

106. GAA, Archive Begijnhof 853, 13 (report Pastor Steins Bisschop).

107. See on Thijm, Plas, *Vader Thijm*.

108. Nolet, "Historische zekerheid."

109. See edition with commentary, *Broere's Dithyrambe*. Cf. also Derksen, *Critisch-analytische toelichting*; Vaissier, "Mirakel-verzen," 155–73; Brom, *Cornelis Broere*, 287–95.

110. Broere and Ploeg, *Gedichten bij het vijfde eeuwgetij*.

111. Vaissier, "Mirakel-verzen," 156–59.

112. Broere and Ploeg, *Gedichten bij het vijfde eeuwgetij*, 15.

113. Amsterdamsch Catholijk, "Het Mirakel van Amsterdam," 190, 206. For Ploeg's jubilee hymn, see Broere and Ploeg, *Gedichten bij het vijfde eeuwgetij*, 59–64.

114. Vaissier, "Mirakel-verzen," 154.

115. Bosch Kemper, *Geschiedenis van Nederland*, 5:66.

116. Designated as a phase of "proto-pillarization" by Margry, *Teedere Quaesties*, 380–83. Dutch pillarization, the rigid political and sociocultural segregation of Dutch society according to ideological-confessional divisions between ca. 1870 and 1970, is also discussed in chapter 5.

117. Valk, *Romeinse bescheiden*, 141–45.

118. Rüter, *Rapporten van de gouverneurs*, 3:341; cf. Akker, "Geschiedenis," 58:316–17.

119. "Feest te Luik," in *De Godsdienstvriend* 57 (1846): 294–95.

120. Akker, "Geschiedenis," 58:319.

121. Brom, *Cornelis Broere*, 294; Brom, "De schilderij op het Begijnhof," 190.

122. Akker, in "Geschiedenis," 58:321, explicitly mentions that this was a quiet period in the Begijnhof.

123. Akker, "Geschiedenis," 58:321.

124. "Heilig Sacrament van Amsterdam," in *De Godsdienstvriend* 68 (1852): 291–300.

125. There is a portrait of Steins Bisschop in the meeting room of the presbytery of the Begijnhof ("knee-length portrait," 57 x 42 cm) with the cartouche *Hostia in Flammis* in the top corner.

126. For this theme in general, see Raedts, *De ontdekking van de middeleeuwen*; Kesteren, *Het verlangen naar de middeleeuwen*.

127. Many cults had remained active without interruption in North Brabant and Limburg, even though there was no direct missionary necessity. Certain important cults had been interrupted, such as that of the Zoete Lieve Moeder or Our Lady of 's-Hertogenbosch, which was revived in 1853, or the Sacrament of Miracle of Breda, which followed in the footsteps of Amsterdam when the celebration of its fourth centenary in 1863 marked a new start of the cult there.

128. For the functional deployment of cults in a wider societal-political context, see, more generally, Korff, "Politischer 'heiligenkult,'" and for the Netherlands, Raedts, "Katholieken op zoek naar een Nederlandse identiteit 1814–1898," 713–25.

129. This specific spirituality has long been regarded as a special trait of the *missio Hollandica*; see Rogier, *Geschiedenis van het katholicisme*, 2:769; Bank, *Het roemrijk Vaderland*, 36–37.

130. See Rogier and Rooy, *In vrijheid herboren*, 228–35.

131. The cult of the Martyrs of Gorcum was partly orchestrated from Rome; see Valk, *Roomser dan de paus?*, 157–72; Margry, "Het Martelveld te Brielle"; Caspers and Hofman, *Een bovenaardse vrouw*, 65–70.

132. *Neerlandia Catholica*, 456.

133. Margry, *Teedere Queasties*, 383–91; Margry, "Dutch Devotionalisation."

134. Landheer, *Kerkbouw op krediet*.

135. Kesteren, *Het verlangen naar de middeleeuwen*, 320, 501.

136. Plas, *Vader Thijm*, 157 and passim; Kesteren, *Het verlangen naar de middeleeuwen*, 315–31.

137. Cf. Brom, *Herleving van de kerkelike kunst*, 82–97. *De Katholiek* 3 (1843): 192–201 is an early example of the explicit suggestion that Catholic and Gothic were linked.

138. Brom, *Herleving van de kerkelike kunst*, 103.

139. Rosenberg, *De 19de-eeuwse kerkelijke bouwkunst*, 29–31.

140. As late as forty years after 1853, reference was still being made to the continuing aversion to the "high spires" of Catholic churches, which were supposedly proof of Catholics' provocative public stance; see Kerkhoff, *Na veertig jaren*, 110; Alkemade, *Vrouwen XIX*, 246–48; Margry, "Imago en identiteit"; Hoogewoud, "Katholiek en protestantse kerkgebouwen." Cf. Alkemade, *Vrouwen XIX*, 75–104, on the political decision-making process concerning monasteries in the first half of the nineteenth century; on the monastery question, see also Raedts, "Katholieken op zoek naar een Nederlandse identiteit 1814–1898," 717–19.

141. Maas, *De literaire wereld van Carel Vosmaer*, 108–10.

142. A new competition was organized nearly twenty years later, this time for the building of a new national monument. Architects from various architectural schools and sociopolitical backgrounds submitted designs, including Pierre Cuypers. His designs for the Rijksmuseum again gave rise to a nationwide avalanche of criticism, but this time he won, with a design that Protestants called a "bishop's palace." Cuypers's victory can be regarded as the epitome of a successful process of appropriation of an architectural style; see also Margry, *Teedere Quaesties*, 152–54; and the section "Het Rijksmuseum en de stijlenkwestie" in Bank and Buuren, *1900: Hoogtij van burgerlijke cultuur*, 170–76.

143. Margry, "Imago en identiteit."

144. Quoted in Jong, "Godsdienst," 139.

145. Rooy, *Openbaring en openbaarheid*, 26–27; Bornewasser, *Kerkelijk verleden*, 357–61.

146. For all related details and for the preceding events, see Albers, *Geschiedenis van het herstel*.

147. See, for this, Rogier, *Schrikbeeld*; Vis and Janse, *Staf en Storm*. For the intervention of the Utrecht professor Mulder, see also Raak, *In naam van het volmaakte*.

148. Cf. Tilly, *The Contentious French*, 386–98; Tilly, *Popular Contention in Great Britain*, 41–48.

149. Bronkhorst, *Rondom 1853*, 67–68. Generally speaking, violence was only a minor aspect of the "revolt"; see Houkes, "Het succes van 1848," 87–104.

150. Cf. Rogier, *Schrikbeeld*.

151. See, for this period, Rooy, *Republiek van rivaliteiten*, 46–76.

152. Witlox, *Studien over het herstel der hiërarchie*, 35.

153. Quoted in Rooy, *Openbaring en openbaarheid*, 28.

154. For the notion of proto-pillarization, see Margry, *Teedere Quaesties*, 380–83. The most recent historical survey of pillarization that focuses on the nineteenth

century and also takes the culture of daily life into account is Blom and Talsma, *De verzuiling voorbij*. For a comparative perspective on the Catholic "pillar" in a number of smaller European countries, see Righart, *De katholieke zuil in Europa*.

155. The provenance of this monument's epithet was hitherto unexplained and gave rise to all kinds of speculation. Contemporary sources make it possible to conclude that this name derived from the word for the shape of the monument, "needle"; cf. *Bredasche Courant*, September 4, 1856. Naatje was a lower-class woman's name in Amsterdam.

156. Begijnhof Archives, *Registri Memorialis*, 14 (1856).

157. Thijm, "Het Amsterdamsch geslacht der Dommers," 321–22, offers a description of the chest on the basis of his visit. See also Dudok van Heel, "Uit Goethe-Dante-Vondelen gaan," 110–11.

158. Thijm, "Het Amsterdamsch geslacht der Dommers," 313, 323; Dudok van Heel, "Uit Goethe-Dante-Vondelen gaan," 110.

159. Voets, *Bewaar het toevertrouwde pand*, 86–87; Sluijter, "Rooms-katholieke broederschappen"; Caspers, "Een verre spiegel"; Caspers, "Eerherstel."

160. Ws., "Het Mirakelfeest en de Stille Omgang zestig jaar geleden," in *De Tijd*, March 30, 1930, morning paper, p. 2, 7. The term *Stille Omgang* (with capitals) that is used here was only coined around 1890 and is therefore used anachronistically in this article.

161. Willemsen, *Het zilveren jubelfeest van Zijne Heiligheid Paus Pius IX*, appeared to commemorate the Maastricht celebration.

162. Valk, *Roomser dan de paus?*, 145; Margry, *Teedere Quaesties*, 369.

163. Plas, *Vader Thijm*, 411–17.

164. A flurry of mostly utterly inadequate books on the Dutch Revolt (e.g., Motley) appeared at the time, further clouding the debate.

165. Frans Groot, "Papists and Beggars," 161–77; Frans Groot, "De strijd rond Alva's bril," 161–81. Cf. other controversial celebrations: Zeijden, *Katholieke identiteit en historisch bewustzijn*, 234–96.

166. Coninck, "De natie in pacht," has developed this comparison further.

167. Velde and Verhage, *De eenheid & de delen*.

168. Velde, *Gemeenschapszin en plichtsbesef*.

169. The school struggle is mentioned in the standard history of the Netherlands, Kossmann, *The Low Countries 1780–1940*, but not, however, the procession question; see, for this, Margry, *Teedere Quaesties*, and Margry and Te Velde, "Contested Rituals."

170. See Margry, "Imago en Identiteit," 64–86; Zuthem, "*Heelen en halven.*"

171. Margry, *Teedere Quaesties*, 317–30.

172. This is the struggle between Catholics and Protestants on the one hand and liberals on the other concerning the right to denominational schools (in addition to public schools), fought in the Netherlands from the early nineteenth century until 1917, when this right was enshrined in the constitution.

173. Sluijter, "Rooms-katholieke broederschappen"; Margry, "Dutch Devotionalisation."

174. A. Tilloy, "Le pèlerinage national," in *Le Pèlerin: Organe du Conseil Général des Pèlerinages* 1 (1873): 4–5. Cf. Caspers, "Van 'groot mirakel' tot 'wonder van ontmoeting.'"

175. Chélini and Branthomme, *Les chemins de Dieu*, 321.

176. Well-known apparitions at the time took place in Pontmain (1871), in Pompeii (1872), in Marpingen ("the Prussian Lourdes," 1876), in Pellevoisin (1876), and in Knock in Ireland (1879). Cf. Harris, *Lourdes*, 343–45; Blackbourn, *Marpingen*, 134. It also reached the Netherlands, and a book was published in 1877 under the title *De verschijningen der Moeder Gods en de wonderbare genezingen te Marpingen* (The apparitions of the Mother of God and the miraculous cures at Marpingen).

177. On this subject, see Caspers, "Eerherstel."

178. See "De kerk van het H. Hart te Parijs," in *De Katholieke Illustratie* 20 (1886–1887): 139–42, 144; 24, (1890–1891): 374–75.

179. Harris, *Lourdes*, 279–83.

180. Margry and Caspers, *Bedevaartplaatsen in Nederland*, 3:903–22; Caspers, Cortjaens, and Jacobs, *De basiliek van Onze Lieve Vrouw van het Heilig Hart*.

181. Merz, *Ultramontaansche wonderziekte*, 1, 6. Dutch ultramontanism has not yet been thoroughly studied; cf. Zeijden, *Katholieke identiteit en historisch bewustzijn*, 165–71.

182. Merz, *Ultramontaansche wonderziekte*, last page.

183. Rogier and Rooij, *In vrijheid herboren*, 71–73.

184. Knippenberg, *De religieuze kaart*, 273; Margry, "Dutch Devotionalisation," 145–48; Sluijter, "Rooms-katholieke broederschappen." Cf. the database of Dutch associations in the nineteenth century at http://www.historici.nl/Onderzoek/Projecten/Broederschappen.

185. L. C. L. Eijgenraam in *Neerlandia Catholica* [pars Amstelodamum Sacrum], 44–45.

186. *Neerlandia Catholica*, 582, written by the secretary of the book project, I. A. H. G. Jansen.

187. Boudien de Vries, "Van deftigheid," 49, 87.

188. Boudien de Vries, "Van deftigheid," 97–98, 102, concludes that associations also began to develop more strongly along denominational lines between 1830 and 1870.

189. See the list of sister societies in Margry, *Inventaris*, 40–47.

190. Cf. Rogier, *Het verschijnsel der culturele inertie*.

191. Frijhoff, *Embodied Belief*, 39–65, chapter on "interconfessional conviviality." On the theory of pillarization during the ancien régime, see Groenveld, *Huisgenoten des geloofs*. Cf. also the contrasting Calvinist indulgence toward Catholic rituality *outside* the Netherlands: Verhoeven, "Calvinist Pilgrimages and Popish Encounters"; Hoppenbrouwers, *Oefening in volmaaktheid*, 95–98; Schutte, *Het Calvinistisch Nederland*, 202–10; Eijnatten and Lieburg, *Nederlandse religiegeschiedenis*, 188–207.

192. The folklorist Meertens not only observed a specifically Dutch Catholicism, but also concluded that there were specific national traits within Dutch Protestantism. This not only because of the relatively wide distribution of liberal

views and biblical humanism, but also precisely because of lengthy sociocultural interaction with Catholics; see Meertens, "Geloof en volksleven," 169–70. The enduring appreciation in Protestant circles for *The Imitation of Christ*, written by the "Catholic" Thomas a Kempis, is a remarkable feature; see Bange, *De doorwerking van de Moderne Devotie*.

193. Eijnatten and Lieburg, *Nederlandse religiegeschiedenis*, 221–25; Rogier, *Geschiedenis van het katholicisme*, 795.

194. Thijm, *De Katholieke kerkregeling*, 11.

195. Pitra, *La Hollande catholique*, 2 and 316–17.

196. Rogier, *Katholieke herleving*, 186–87; on pp. 197–98 Rogier ascribes a Calvinist Puritanism to Vicar Van Dongen.

197. The Dutch folklorist Pieter Meertens observed that Dutch Catholicism deviated from coreligionists in other European countries. Dutch Catholics are "more temperate, more introverted, stricter, more Calvinist" than their Flemish counterparts; see Meertens, "Geloof en volksleven," 169–70. The psychologist Alfons Chorus contended that Calvinism had given rise to a headstrong "frontier mentality" among Dutch Catholics and at the same time observed "all kinds of characteristics that distinguish them from non-Dutch Catholics, and in particular these are characteristics that make them more severe, more serious, more moralizing, in short more in line with Calvinism"; see Chorus, *De Nederlander uiterlijk en innerlijk*, 135–36.

198. This reticence was, for instance, stimulated as best practice by the diocese of Haarlem; see Noord-Hollands Archief, Archief Bisdom Haarlem, inv. no. 322.1–2, December 19–20, 1854.

199. Margry, *Teedere Quaesties*, 306–7.

200. Peijnenburg, *Joannes Zwijsen*, 142.

201. Brom, "De schilderij op het Begijnhof," 199. Cf. also the comment in "Traditie van kerk en vaderland," in *De Tijd* of March 6, 1937: "but the people . . . pray and hold their annual walk! Thus the Silent Walk became a unique Dutch possession, its very own way of form and devotion." Cf. also Brom, *Areopaag*, 145–58 ("*Stille Omgang*," consisting of an apology of the Silent Walk).

Chapter 5.   The Silent Walk as a National Symbol of Identity (1881–1960)

1. It must be noted that the concept of a pillar or block structure is not as firm as the metaphor itself suggests; cf. the recent deconstructionist synthesis of "pillarization" in Dam, *Staat van verzuiling*, 101–20. Van Dam questions the concept itself and the prevailing static model of pillars and demonstrates that society was more multiform and more dynamic than this mythical concept allows. See also Blom and Talsma, *De verzuiling voorbij*; Righart, *De katholieke zuil in Europa*.

2. Cf. Headley, Hillerbrand, and Papalas, *Confessionalization in Europe*, 1–35.

3. The socialist and liberal pillars were hegemonic communities to a much lesser degree than the Catholic and Protestant pillars.

4. On politics and culture at the turn of the century, see Velde, *Gemeenschaps-zin en plichtsbesef.*

5. On identity politics, see the entry in Edward N. Zalta, ed., *Stanford Encyclopedia of Philosophy*: https://plato.stanford.edu/; in Frijhoff's words, identity is a combination of self-image and image imposed from outside, and their mutual interaction; see Frijhoff and Van der Vlies, *De Nederlandse identiteit.*

6. Caspers, "Het jaarlijks algemeen huisbezoek," 129; Bastiaanse, *Onkuisheid.*

7. More than 90 percent of the inhabitants in most municipalities in the south of the Netherlands were Catholics, but these municipalities each had fewer inhabitants than Amsterdam.

8. *Neerlandia Catholica* [pars Amstelodamum Sacrum], 44–46.

9. *Neerlandia Catholica*, 451, [pars Amstelodamum Sacrum], 54.

10. GAA, Begijnhof Archive, inv. no. 854; the guild consisted of at most fifty single men. A certain P. J. A. Elsenburg joined this guild in 1878.

11. Rogier and Rooy, *In vrijheid herboren*, 404–6.

12. Very few details about Josephus Johannes Lousbergh (January 4, 1855–July 27, 1914) and his background have come to light. He was the only son of the office clerk Bernardus Josephus Lousbergh and his wife, Agatha Maria Doornbosch, who lived at Nieuwendijk 36. Joseph briefly moved to Dordrecht in 1870, before returning to Amsterdam in 1877, to Roomolenstraat 3. In 1880 he moved to Spuistraat 285 and in 1891 to Spuistraat 318. See GAA, Bevolkingsregisters 1874–1893.

13. Carolus Augustinus Johannes Elsenburg (August 28, 1853–December 15, 1934) was the son of billiard maker Jacobus Elsenburg (1816–1882) and Maria Margaretha van Lingen (1814–1891), who lived at Nieuwezijds Voorburgwal 151. As a child he was sent to the Franciscan "gymnasium" or preparatory high school in Venraij, from which he returned in 1869 just before his sixteenth birthday. After having lived in the family home again for a short period, he left for unknown reasons for Utrecht in early 1878 and married Anna M. J. Buekers in Amsterdam on February 6, 1879. They lived at Utrechtsestraat 16. He worked briefly as a clerk for his uncle Jacobus Wilhelmus Elsenburg (*March 30, 1847) in his billiard factory on Nieuwezijds, where Jacobus had established himself as a billiard maker in 1878 at no. 175 and at no. 151 between 1882 and 1885, after his older namesake, Carel's father, also a billiard maker, died and the premises there became available. The company moved to 177 in 1885, where it stayed for many years; see GAA, Bevolkingsregisters 1874–1893.

14. Carel started his own business as a cobbler around 1881, at the time that he made his first prayer walk with Lousbergh. His wife served as shopkeeper in one of the buildings built up against Nieuwe Kerk. They lived in an apartment at Bloemstraat 4 with their seven children from 1888 on; see GAA, Bevolkingsregisters 1874–1893. The entry "cobbler" under profession was struck through on his personal file in 1894 and replaced by "None."

15. Established in that church since 1848; *Neerlandia Catholica*, 474.

16. A new or renewed congregation was founded in the Moses and Aaron (St. Anthony's) church in 1882; cf. *Neerlandia Catholica*, 421–22. It is likely that Lous-

bergh and Elsenburg joined this third order before 1882. Many years later, after 1893, Lousbergh, in his capacity of prefect of this third order, was to found both St. Francis's Charitable Society (St. Franciscus-Liefdewerk) for religiously and socially "backward and neglected" boys, and the Friends of the Blessed Sacrament devotional association. Celibate, he devoted the best part of his life to the church and to social care. Lousbergh was also a *broedermeester* (master of the brothers) in the annual Amsterdam pilgrimage to Our Lady "in 't Zand" in Roermond, and for many years he wrote stories in braille for the Grave institute for the blind. See also his obituary in *De Tijd*, July 30, 1914. On St. Francis's Charitable Society, see *De Tijd*, September 4, 1904, and Driedonkx, *Het Sint Franciscus Liefdewerk*.

17. During the third centenary of the reformation of Amsterdam in 1878 a new—as in 1778—protestant publication saw the light which rejected the claim that Amsterdam's heyday had been due to the Miracle but should be seen instead as a result of the reformation of the town in 1578. A service was held in de Nieuwezijds Kapel to commemorate not the fire miracle, but God's intervention in 1578, the Amsterdam Alteration; see Stieler, *Amsterdam's eer en opkomen*, 77–78.

18. B. H. Klönne, "De Heilige Stede," in *De Tijd*, August 24 and 25, 1876. Cf. the editorial "In het Middelpunt der Tentoonstelling," which he authored, on August 11 and 12 in the same newspaper.

19. *Neerlandia Catholica*, 451, states that approximately five hundred Haarlem pilgrims used to visit around 1885; this can explain why participation from Haarlem in the Silent Walk would later grow so quickly.

20. GAA, GSO, inv. no. 2, *Memorandum*, 54–55, has a study of Lousbergh's pious and fiery character and his life's motto "To serve God is to rule," which points to how he viewed his mission and followed it, incidentally in self-chosen anonymity.

21. Ibid., 54: "Joseph Lousberg, the man who formed the plan to renew the walk" [the beginning of the public, collective walk].

22. Ibid., 3. The typescript version of the manuscript has been used here and references in this book refer to it. Lousbergh is referring to an anonymous Protestant description of Amsterdam from 1644.

23. Lousbergh probably also knew the route described in the article that Klönne had written about it before: Klönne, "De Heilige Stede"; the second part of this text contains a simplified route of the procession.

24. GAA, GSO, inv. no. 2, Memorandum, 4.

25. Cf. *De Godsdienstvriend* 54 (1845): 150: "a number of streets in Amsterdam are currently called 'Holy Street' because of the Miracle and the transferring of the Blessed Sacrament."

26. According to an uncertain tradition, Maximilian of Austria, on a pilgrimage to the Holy Stead, asked for directions in this inn, thus giving the house its peculiar name.

27. Broeke, *Stille Omgang Herdenking*, 1–2.; GAA, GSO, inv. no. 2, *Memorandum*, 3. In the first half of the nineteenth century, the route passed along Heiligeweg; see Brom, *Cornelis Broere*, 14; Leesberg, "Herinnering," 217–20.

28. GAA, GSO, inv. no. 2, *Memorandum*, 6; both evaluated in 1881 how the route might be followed collectively by men and women in the future.

29. Because of Limburg's divergent constitutional history, the procession ban did not apply there: for this reason a real procession of supplication could be held in Roermond during the epidemic, and thousands of participants were allowed to pray and sing aloud in Maastricht.

30. One author, probably the regent of the Gestel seminary, H. J. Smits, or T. Spierings, writing in *De Katholiek*, called the walk a "silent prayer walk" or "Our Lady's way"; see *De Katholiek* 4 (1845), 7:198. See also 's-Hertogenbosch, City Archive, Archive of the Fraternity of the Sweet Mother, inv. no. 14b, sub dd. 1889, with reference to past individual walks.

31. Kronenburg, *Maria's Heerlijkheid in Nederland*, 6:265–66.

32. The 's-Hertogenbosch public prosecutor tried to proscribe the walk on the basis of the procession ban. However, as it was performed in silence and without any external display, it was deemed not to fall under the procession ban. This did not allay Bishop Godschalk's fears that the authorities might nevertheless intervene because the walk was gradually beginning to take on the aspect of a public procession. He therefore ordered that the walk should no longer be made in one long cortege, but in separate groups.

33. The 's-Hertogenbosch walk began as a men's walk but after some years turned into a mixed walk. The Amsterdam walk (as well as a number of subsidiary walks elsewhere in the Netherlands) would remain a men's affair until far into the twentieth century.

34. According to the *De Tijd* of July 15, 1889.

35. The *Memorandum* (GAA, GSO, no. 2) drawn up by Lousbergh and his successors is an important source for the origins of the Silent Walk; the transcribed typescript version has been used for this book. Van den Broeke's overview *Stille Omgang Herdenking* offers an additional factual summary.

36. A privilege granted by the Holy See meant that this feast could be celebrated in Amsterdam as a double of the first class with octave.

37. GAA, GSO, inv. no. 2, *Memorandum*, 6.

38. Amsterdammer, *Physiologie van Amsterdam*, 18–25.

39. In fact it was uncommon in those years for women to leave the home alone at night; the perpetual adoration of the Blessed Sacrament held in the Sacré Coeur in Paris at that time was also carried out exclusively by men during the night hours.

40. Adrianus Godefridus Apol (*June 5, 1844) was the oldest son of Eduard Apol, a soldier from Breda, and Alida Elisabeth Schmitkamp from Amsterdam. Together with his brother Adriaan he took over his father's zinc foundry and plumbing company. The family moved to a basement apartment at Bloemstraat 4 in 1869, in the same building where Carel Elsenburg came to live from 1888; see GAA, Bevolkingsregisters 1874–1893.

41. For more on De Veer, see GAA, GSO, inv. no. 2, *Memorandum*, 46–47. Henricus Johannes Petrus de Veer (July 19, 1857–June 25, 1906) was the son of Franciscus Gerardus de Veer, commission agent, and Maria Theresia Velthuijse, who lived at Staalstraat 9. He married his sister-in-law's sister, Geertruida Petro-

nella van Ravensteijn, from Gorinchem; see GAA, Bevolkingsregisters 1874–1893 and personal file.

42. Boys from the Lauriergracht orphanage—through the network of governors—also participated for a number of years to make young people acquainted with the custom; see Broeke, *Stille Omgang Herdenking*, 3. The governors of the orphanage stopped this practice around 1910.

43. GAA, Begijnhof Archive, inv. no. 563, January 24, 1883 (appointment). On his editorship, see Rogier, *Katholieke herleving*, 268–71. In addition to his post as editor, he was also chaplain of St. Bernard's Institute.

44. GAA, Begijnhof Archive, inv. no. 40, March 18, 1885, 42. This is the only source from this period for a separate afternoon walk for women; it was probably a one-off initiative.

45. Because of this official involvement, Klönne regarded this as the first year of the walk; see his diary, GAA, Begijnhof Archive, inv. no. 41, sub 1912: 25th Silent Walk. Later, 1881 was always regarded as the first year.

46. Klönne wrote two articles about the Miracle in *De Tijd* as early as 1876 on the occasion of the Historical Exhibition on Amsterdam's sixth centenary: "De Heilige Stede."

47. On the claimed uniqueness and the origins of the Laren procession, see Margry, "Transformatie," 33–57.

48. GAA, Begijnhof Archive, inv. no. 40, March 1886.

49. See *De Maasbode*, March 24, 1886. Klönne did mention "the silent walk" already in that year in a note; see Voets and Noord, "Het verhaal van een honderdjarige," 34.

50. A literal Latin translation was found later: *taciturnus circuitus*, as used in the title of a brochure published by Van den Broeke in 1934.

51. See GAA, GSO, inv. no. 2, *Memorandum*, 54, "naschrift," where Lousbergh is called "the instrument in God's hand for the revival of the Silent Walk" shortly after his death.

52. Lousbergh also had a codicil drawn up on April 9, 1888, to secure the material heritage for the community; see GAA, GSO, inv. no. 48.

53. For the statutes, see Margry, *Inventaris*, 39.

54. Margry, *Teedere Quaesties*, 302, 360–61, 430–31.

55. GAA, Begijnhof Archive, inv. no. 40, 81; Voets and Noord, "Het verhaal van een honderdjarige," 35–36.

56. Valk, "Caught between Modernism, Pillarization and Nationalism," 102–15.

57. On this period, see Peijnenburg, *Jodocus Smits en zijn Tijd*, 129; "Bij Mgr. B. H. Klönne," in *De Tijd*, February 20, 1914.

58. GAA, GSO, inv. no. 70.

59. Klönne found details a few years later that shed further light on the issue: it transpired that the "loop" that the procession had supposedly made along Middeldam/Markt and the medieval weigh house, a loop followed for a number of years by the Silent Walk, was not part of the Miracle procession, but only of the "second" medieval Eucharistic procession on Corpus Christi. It was subsequently omitted from the route.

60. GAA, GSO, inv. no. 3, August 13, 1918; cf. *De Tijd*, March 17, 1918.

61. GAA, GSO, inv. no. 4, April 11, 1923; hundreds of pilgrims visited the clandestine church, showing a desire for a Miracle exhibition. Only when the fund for the sixth centenary provided five hundred guilders to this end in 1939 did it become possible to set up a small exhibition, March 28, 1939; see also the annual report for 1938–1939.

62. GAA, GSO, inv. no. 3, July 16, 1916–February 4, 1917.

63. Eighty years later, in 1996, the extension and renovation of the adjacent Victoria Hotel caused the reopening of an underpass, so that the historical route through Ramskooi could be restored.

64. GAA, Begijnhof Archive, inv. no. 40, June 4, 1884.

65. See Allard, *Laurens en Vondel,* and Klönne's reply, *Marius gehandhaafd.* Cf. Dudok van Heel, "Uit Goethe-Dante-Vondelen gaan," 127–29.

66. Marius was in fact responsible; see Brom, *Vondels geloof,* 196–97.

67. "Mgr. B. H. Klönne," in *Katholieke Illustratie* 47 (1903): 293

68. [In Memoriam] "Mgr. B. H. Klönne," in *De Tijd,* August 8, 1921.

69. "Mgr. B. H. Klönne," in *Katholieke Illustratie* 47 (1903): 293.

70. This was evident, for instance, in the international Eucharistic congress movement since 1881, the foundation of the Eucharistic Crusade in 1914 and, in the Netherlands, the Eucharistische Bond (Eucharistic union) in 1916.

71. Published together in Klönne, *Amstelodamensia.*

72. In mid-1917, the daily *De Tijd* received many letters it did not publish asking that the silent walk be turned into a procession; see GAA, GSO, *Memorandum,* meeting March 24, 1917.

73. Cf. Meuwissen, *Jacob Cornelisz van Oostsanen;* Schillemans, "De Begijnhofkerk."

74. GAA, Begijnhof Archive, inv. no. 847, contract, October 10, 1884. On Derkinderen, see the catalog edited by Trappeniers, *Antoon Derkinderen;* B. H. Molkenboer, "Het ontstaan van Der Kinderens Mirakel-Processie," in *De Tijd,* October 30, 1929, 2nd part, 5, with an addition by Cuypers in *De Tijd,* November 4, 1929.

75. Brom, "De schilderij op het begijnhof," 193–95; Plas, *Vader Thijm,* 573.

76. Trappeniers, *Antoon Derkinderen,* 29–31, 66–70; Brom, "De schilderij op het begijnhof"; Brom, *Herleving van de kerkelike kunst,* 368–71; Roodenburg, "Het verleden opgepoetst," 17–29.

77. Rogier and Rooy, *In vrijheid herboren,* 416, describes this image as a "jolly procession."

78. Characterization from GAA, GSO, inv. no. 2, *Memorandum,* 46.

79. This nickname comes from an oral tradition within the Society of the Silent Walk.

80. In a letter to the editor written by Klönne, edited afterward and published in *De Tijd* on December 23, 1903, he described their successive departures abroad as the start of the problems, in GAA, Begijnhof Archive, inv. no. 852.

81. Voets and Noord, "Het verhaal van een honderdjarige," 37–38.

82. Certain details that did not correspond to Tridentine regulations had already been erased by Klönne himself; see Roodenburg, "Het verleden opgepoetst," 28–29.

83. Brom, "Het treurspel van Derkinderens processie."

84. On Klönne's ideas about the exact execution and features of the painting and the changes to which these were subject over time, see Roodenburg, "Het verleden opgepoetst." Cf. Klönne's descriptions of the procession in Klönne, *Amstelodamensia*, 49–118.

85. Voets and Noord, "Het verhaal van een honderdjarige," 38.

86. GAA, Begijnhof Archive, inv. no. 849, letter by Klönne, October 17, 1888, in which he forbids *Katholieke Illustratie* from depicting the painting in its pages.

87. GAA, Begijnhof Archive, inv. no. 849.

88. Plas, *Vader Thijm*, 533–37.

89. Brom, "De schilderij op het begijnhof," 204.

90. Rogier and Rooy, *In vrijheid herboren*, 414–16.

91. See the articles by J. Staphorst (pseudonym of Jan Veth) and of Willem du Tour (pseudonym of R. N. Roland Holst) in *De Nieuwe Gids* 4 (1889): 461–67 and in *De Amsterdammer*, January 6, 1889. Cf. Trappeniers, *Antoon Derkinderen*, 20–22. Brom, "De schilderij op het begijnhof," 199, also pointed to the spirit of the Silent Walk captured in this painting.

92. As in *De Portefeuille, Kunst- en Letterbode*, January 26, 1889, 464–65. Cf. GAA, Begijnhof Archive, inv. no. 849, letter Derkinderen to Klönne, November 11, 1888.

93. Brom, "De schilderij op het begijnhof," 203.

94. Roodenburg, "Het verleden opgepoetst," 20.

95. This is why it is no surprise that it has been represented in the painting; cf. Roodenburg, "Het verleden opgepoetst," 19–20.

96. The painter Philippeau (1825–1897) also used the abbreviated signature "C.F. Phlippeau," for instance on the Amsterdam procession piece.

97. GAA, Begijnhof Archive, inv. no. 852, contains the new portraits of the persons depicted on the painting.

98. Klönne, *Amstelodamensia*, 105–6. On the historian Robert Fruin's critical judgment of the canvas, see Dudok van Heel, "Uit Goethe-Dante-Vondelen gaan," 123–24.

99. GAA, Begijnhof Archive, inv. no. 852, e.g., in the *Nieuwe Haarlemsche Courant*, March 26, 1893.

100. GAA, Begijnhof Archive, inv. no. 563, March 12, 1893, 84–92. The painting was described in great detail in *De Tijd* of March 14, 1893.

101. *Dagblad De Tijd*, July 11, 1895; *Algemeen Handelsblad*, May 31, 1896, evening edition.

102. Brom, "De schilderij op het begijnhof," 208–9; Voets and Noord, "Het verhaal van een honderdjarige," 38.

103. GAA, Begijnhof Archive, inv. no. 852; *De Tijd*, December 23, 1903.

104. Brom, "De schilderij op het begijnhof," 209; *Algemeen Handelsblad*, October 19, 1929, evening edition.

105. Begijnhof Archive, Liber memorialis 1929–1945, 3–5. The formal sale was contracted on July 16, 1930. As a result Philippeau's painting was taken out and moved to the St. Jozefsgezellen building, until it too was demolished in 1960. The painting then moved back to Begijnhof and was hung just above Derkinderen's

painting, although it is almost invisible in the gallery above it. Cf. "Der Kinderen's mirakelprocessie in het bagijnhof," in *Geïllustreerd Zondagsblad*, no. 45, November 10, 1929: 353–60.

106. Brom, "De schilderij op het begijnhof," 199; Brom, *Herleving van de kerkelike kunst*, 369–70. The Catholic historian Hensen also interpreted the painting in this way; see Hensen, *In den Hollandschen tuin*, 106.

107. Veth, "Derkinderen's Processie," 4, 10.

108. Brom, *Herleving van de kerkelike kunst*, 370.

109. Klönne, *Amstelodamensia*, 291.

110. Stuers, *Holland op zijn smalst* (published originally in *De Gids* 37 [1873]: 320–403); Perry, *Ons Fatsoen als Natie*, 65–95.

111. Perry, *Ons Fatsoen als Natie*.

112. Much has been written about whether the Dutch designation of *schuilkerken* ("hidden churches" or "clandestine churches") is correct, and about the contrast between the descriptions used by Catholics and by the Protestant authorities (with the latter preferring "Papist churches" or "public meeting places and conventicles"). This last designation implied that it was no secret that Catholics were becoming institutionalized (cf. Schillemans, "De Begijnhofkerk als de nieuwe Heilige Stede," 54–56; Dudok van Heel, "Amsterdamse schuil- of huiskerken"). The controversial nineteenth-century concept of *schuilkerk* is not necessarily incorrect. It is incorrect if it is used to suggest that people had to hide to avoid a hunt for Catholics or that the church's existence was a secret. It is not, however, if it is used to stress that the church building as a Catholic building occupied a "hidden" position in the urban public space and was not easily recognizable from outside.

113. Previously named Museum Amstelkring (now Our Lord in the Attic), at Oudezijds Voorburgwal 38. For this church and its history, see Blokhuis et al., *Vroomheid op de Oudezijds*, 37–99.

114. Quoted in Cuypers and Kalf, *De Katholieke kerken*, 242–43. Cf. Dudok van Heel, "Amsterdamse schuil- of huiskerken," 10, which discusses the later reception of Pitra's comment by Camus and others.

115. Cf. "De Stichting van den Amstelkring," in Klönne, *Amstelodamensia*, 290–94; *Neerlandia Catholica*, 545; Hout, "Een Rooms-Katholiek Museum."

116. Klönne, *Amstelodamensia*, 290–94 ("The foundation of the Amstelkring"). This appropriation of the name was his way of settling the score after his "forced" resignation from the board of Amstelkring after repeated clashes with De Bont about the Miracle chest; see Hout, "Een Rooms-Katholiek Museum," 92–93.

117. Amstelkring focused exclusively on Amsterdam, and heritage affairs not relating to Amsterdam belonged to the remit of the diocesan museum in Haarlem.

118. Hout, "Een Rooms-Katholiek Museum," 80.

119. GAA, GSO, inv. no. 2, *Memorandum*, sub June 5, 1919. It is not certain how long this special opening existed.

120. Hout, "Een Rooms-Katholiek Museum," 84–85.

121. Inspired by the significance of St. Denis's Church for France, De Bont wanted to give the mortal remains of the counts of Holland in Egmond an honorable "mausoleum," as well as to revive the former Benedictine abbey as a spiritual

center of Catholicism; see Sterck, "Levensbericht van Bernardus Joannes Maria de Bont," 286–87.

122. Sterck-Proot, "Dr. Johannes Franciscus Maria Sterck."

123. This was a canvas by M. C. Schenk that hung there from 1891 to 1994; it replaced Moeyaert's *Assumption of the Blessed Virgin*; see Schillemans, "De Begijnhofkerk," 59–61.

124. GAA, Begijnhof Archive, inv. no. 789–90.

125. The historical world, in the person of the Leiden professor Robert Fruin, criticized the reliability of the research carried out for this book; see Dudok van Heel, "Uit Goethe-Dante-Vondelen gaan," 123–25; and Dudok van Heel, "Amsterdamse schuil- of huiskerken," 6–9. Klönne also published a liturgical book, *Het Mirakel van Amsterdam: Jubel- en processieliederen.*

126. Jentjens, *Van strijdorgaan tot familieblad,* 37. The print run in those years was between thirty thousand and fifty thousand copies. In addition, a number of special editions was published on the occasion of the jubilee: "Overzicht van geschriften en afbeeldingen, uitgegeven bij gelegenheid van het Zesdehalve Eeuwfeest van het mirakel van Amsterdam MDCCCXCV," in *Het jaarboekje van Alberdingk Thijm. Almanak voor Nederlandsche Katholieken* 45 (1896): 39–42.

127. Sterck, "Uit de geschiedenis der H. Stede"; Sterck, "Jacob Cornelisz."; Meuwissen, *Jacob Cornelisz van Oostsanen,* 209–12; Dekker, "De lotgevallen van het orgel."

128. "Een hulde aan het H. Sacrament van Mirakel te Amsterdam," in *Katholieke Illustratie* 27 (1893–1894): 387.

129. The "fever" tradition is however mentioned for the first time in 1866, by Thijm; see Sterck, *De "Mirakelkist,"* 59.

130. Thijm, "Een getuigenis omtrent de Mirakelkist"; Dudok van Heel, "Uit Goethe-Dante-Vondelen gaan," 110–15.

131. *De Tijd,* May 16, 1876. Meijer, *Wandeling door de zalen,* 128–31, commented that Catholic visitors would appreciate the inclusion of the Miracle chest in the exhibition. Cf. *Historische Tentoonstelling van Amsterdam,* 101–2.

132. See Meijer, *Wandeling door de zalen,* 128–31.

133. GAA, Begijnhof Archive, inv. no. 563, 17–28; a board member, the public notary W. S. J. van Waterschoot van der Gracht, had conducted these negotiations.

134. For this question see GAA, Begijnhof Archive, inv. no. 41, March 18–April 2, 1889.

135. GAA, Begijnhof Archive, inv. no. 563, 93–103 (in 1893).

136. GAA, Begijnhof Archive, inv. no. 792, document of March 1, 1995.

137. The Amsterdam decorator A. H. Trautwein was asked to decorate the church for the jubilee. He delegated the painting of the panels to the painter Leo Arentzen (who would make a number of other Miracle paintings in 1897).

138. Articles that encouraged pilgrims to visit Amsterdam appeared not only in the Netherlands, as in *De Morgenpost: Dagblad voor het Katholieken Volk* or *Het Centrum,* but also in Germany, e.g., in *Der Arbeiter-Freund* in the Crefeld region on March 6, 13, 16, 24, and 30, 1895 and in "Il Miracolo d'Amsterdam" in *l'Osservatore Romano,* March 13–14, 1895, 2.

139. GAA, GSO, inv. no. 2, *Memorandum*, 26–28.

140. GAA, Begijnhof Archive, inv. no. 1219. Klönne also clashed with his "own" Catholic historians—e.g., with Bernard de Bont—on the issue of cures; see GAA, Begijnhof Archive, inv. no. 1218.

141. Sterck, *De "Mirakelkist."*

142. Thus Thijm contended in an article in *De Tijd* in March 1895; see Voets, *Blijf, Meester,* 14–15.

143. The chest was exhibited a second time in the same year in the Old Amsterdam exhibition in the Panorama Building, and again in historical exhibitions in 1925 and 1946. When the Burgerweeshuis moved to a new location outside the city, it took the chest with it. J. J. M. Takes, secretary of the Silent Walk between 1955 and 1989, remembered that people continued to visit the new building to touch the chest for cures.

144. *Uilenspiegel: Humoristisch-satirisch weekblad,* March 23 and 30, 1895, 1. Schaepman first visited Klönne together with G. van Heukelum to read the poem to him; Begijnhof Archive, inv. no. 41, February 11, 1895.

145. C. N. Wybrands, "Hoe een melkgevende koe tevens een varken was, of het Amsterdamsche Mirakel van 16 maart 1345," in *De Nederlandsche Spectator,* March 16, 1895, 89.

146. "De eerste heipaal," in *De Telegraaf,* March 13, 1995.

147. New Miracle iconography was also placed in the new St. Nicholas's Church, in the form of bronze bas-reliefs; see "Een hulde aan het H. Sacrament van Mirakel te Amsterdam," in *Katholieke Illustratie* 27 (1893–1894): 387–90.

148. GAA, Begijnhof Archive, inv. no. 41, 26–36; inv. no. 563, 99–100.

149. GAA, Begijnhof Archive, inv. no. 563, 99, June 29, 1894.

150. Ibid., 102, January 28 and May 27, 1895.

151. Ibid., 100–2.

152. GAA, Begijnhof Archive, inv. no. 41, February 7, 1901.

153. The chest has been on loan from the Burgerweeshuis since 1985 as part of a permanent exhibition on the Sacrament of Miracle in the Amsterdam [Historical] Museum.

154. A similar tome contains a very extensive visual and written record of the Catholic church-building boom of the nineteenth century, although it is slightly smaller and lighter (nine kilograms); see Cuypers and Kalf, *De Katholieke kerken,* published in 1906.

155. *Neerlandia Catholica* [pars Historia libri], 62.

156. Included at the back of the book with its own page numbers. The author was L. C. L. Eijgenraam, chief editor of *De Tijd,* later rector of the Maagdenhuis. It begins with the history of the Miracle and the procession; *Neerlandia Catholica* [pars Amstelodamum Sacrum], 3, 5–12, 19–20.

157. See Meertens et al., *Biografisch woordenboek van het socialisme,* 2:141–44.

158. *Neerlandia Catholica* [pars Amstelodamum Sacrum], 4.

159. *Neerlandia Catholica,* [586].

160. On this building, see Lansink and Dael, *De Nieuwe Krijtberg.*

161. Sterck, *De Heilige Stede: De slooping,* 23–24.

162. Margry, "Het Martelveld te Brielle," 22–26.

163. There had been a plan to demolish the building at the end of the sixteenth century to make way, according to Commelin, for a new market square on Rokin; Commelin, *Beschryvinge van Amsterdam,* 470.

164. [Vos], "Paganistische Ouwel-cultus," 115.

165. See, for instance, Weissman, *De Nieuwe Zijds Kapel,* 18–19.

166. [Vos], "Paganistische Ouwel-cultus," 63.

167. Sterck, *De Heilige Stede: De slooping,* 25.

168. GAA, Begijnhof Archive, inv. no. 1222.

169. *Algemeen Handelsblad,* March 1, 1900.

170. GAA, Begijnhof Archive, inv. no. 1222, petition Dutch Catholics, 1899.

171. For details of the process, see Sterck, *De Heilige Stede: De slooping,* 30–43.

172. Kappeyne, *Aan wien is de eigendom?* Cf. *Processtukken.*

173. The costs of the proceedings briefly caused the Reformed congregation to consider selling the building "to Rome" after all, for the offer of a million guilders, which would have been a much more profitable course of action; cf. [Vos], "Paganistische Ouwel-cultus," 113.

174. [Vos], "Paganistische Ouwel-cultus," 71, 112.

175. Article in *Algemeen Handelsblad,* June 11, 1908.

176. [Vos], "Paganistische Ouwel-cultus," 63.

177. Sterck, *De Heilige Stede: De slooping,* 46.

178. Letters to the editor in *Algemeen Handelsblad* of February 22, 24, and 26, 1908.

179. "De Utrechtsche Dom," in *Leeuwarder Courant,* February 19, 1907.

180. A vote taken by the congregation resulted in 100 votes for and 20 against demolition; [Vos], "Paganistische Ouwel-cultus," 119.

181. "Doodvonnis van de N.Z. Kapel," March 5, 1908, see Museum Amstelkring, "Mirakel-Collectie," MS *Proces betreffende de H. Sacramentskapel* gebouwd 1345 tusschen de Gemeente Amsterdam, en de Hervormde Gemeente 1898–1907; cf. *Processtukken.*

182. [Vos], "Paganistische Ouwel-cultus," 119.

183. According to Sterck-Proot, "Een wachter bij de H. Stede," 222.

184. Klönne wrote one last piece, "N. Z. Kapel. Een klaagtoon," in the newspaper; see Museum Amstelkring, "Mirakel-Collectie," *Proces betreffende de H. Sacramentskapel.* He started it as follows: "Poor me, I have suffered a death blow."

185. Sterck, "Bij de slooping," 353, 355–57, 423. He discussed the ideological differences in art that existed between Catholics and Calvinists in this text, and quoted Abraham Kuyper, who had said that Calvinism "must liberate art from [Catholic] domination." This led Sterck to refer to a "liberation that destroys everything."

186. [Vos], "Paganistische Ouwel-cultus," 110.

187. Sterck, *De Heilige Stede: De slooping,* 75–84; in order not to delay reconstruction—which had already begun—on account of possible claims, the architect Posthumus Meyes left a space above the tomb open and accessible in one of the commercial buildings; this space still exists.

188. "Kerk levert 40 miljoen op," in *Het Parool*, November 9, 2007; a private monuments foundation purchased the site.

189. Koomen, "Een lamantatio," sums up all the chapel elements that were deposited at the Rijksmuseum and what happened with them. See also Breen, "De Heilige Stede te Amsterdam."

190. All building elements and fragments were inventoried in 1943. Much later the journal *Amstelodamum* asked what should be done with them. A number of pillar follies were meant to be erected in the Amerbos en Elpermeer park in North Nieuwendam, and the rest ended up in an almost forgotten corner of Frankendael building site. The suggestion was made that they should be built into Begijnhofkerk, this being the successor to the Holy Stead, to realize a tangible connection with the demolished building, but this was not implemented.

191. The upside of the demolition of the chapel was that it yielded new information on the building's construction history and the relation of the chapel to the mother church, St. Nicholas's, on Oude Zijde; see the results presented by Glaudemans and Smit, "Een andere kijk."

192. In the Museum Ons' Lieve Heer op Solder collection, AK164, 1918, height 23 inches.

193. Sterck, *De Heilige Stede: De slooping*, 66. C. A. Tel Jr., chairman of the sister society in Edam, acquired these "relics" and gave them to the Begijnhof, among other beneficiaries; see *De Tijd*, March 13, 1922; on Tel, see also GAA, GSO, inv. no. 4, annual report for 1928–1929.

194. For example, Mr. and Mrs. N. L. Borst at their twenty-fifth wedding anniversary on October 4, 1931. GAA, GSO, inv. no. 177.

195. Sterck, *De Heilige Stede: De slooping*, 66–69. For a list of the larger fragments of greater artistic value, see Breen, "De Heilige Stede te Amsterdam," 123–24.

196. On the history of this column, see GAA, GSO, inv. no. 179. Much of the remaining material of the chapel was lost when it was used for the strengthening of dykes, and a large collection ended up in the hands of Amsterdam antique dealers through neglect on the part of the municipality and through illegal sale; see Frank van Kolfschooten, "Heilige Zwerfstenen," in *NRC-Handelsblad*, February 1, 1988. Fragments were spotted again in the antiques trade in the twenty-first century; they were sold to (un)known buyers. Cf. Koomen, "Een lamantatio," 324–25.

197. The column was temporarily removed in 2001 to facilitate construction work on a new North–South metro line. It was returned to its original location in mid-2017.

198. Cf. Ingmar Sillius, "Mirakels Amsterdam: Opkomst en ondergang van de Heilige Stede en haar bouwfragmenten," unpublished text. Sillius has been working for the Amsterdam Protestant Church since 2009 and is actively collecting Holy Stead *spolia*.

199. The cult never had a formal (Catholic) national status, but it gained a national dimension as it became the only pilgrimage site that attracted pilgrims from all over the country and was hence implicitly and symbolically perceived as national.

200. GAA, Begijnhof Archive, inv. no. 796, letter, December 31, 1901, Klönne to A. J. Callier, in which he demonstrates that the celebration had always had an octave and that the new directory for the diocese was wrong to omit it. Incidentally, on March 2, 1862, Pius IX had granted a plenary indulgence to anyone participating in the octave (see inv. no. 575). Klönne's protest was successful; see also inv. no. 791: B. Kruitwagen complained to Klönne about the "Italianization" of the directory, a process that threatened the feast's octave, which was a "part of the national glory" of this old feast.

201. See Broeke, "De Stille Omgang en het H. H. Sacrament van Mirakel," 148, containing the Amsterdam city councilor F. Wierdels's characterization of Van den Broeke.

202. Broeke, *Stille Omgang Herdenking*, 13. GAA, GSO, inv. no. 4, February 1, 1920 (quotation).

203. Raedts, "Le Saint Sacrement," 242, points to the prior absence of a single communal place of pilgrimage. It is clear from a number of facts that the Society was not immune to a certain degree of "national feeling." Thus the board donated a tile for the decoration of the tomb of Pope Pius IX around 1900; see Muskens, *Wees niet bang*, 295, on the small political gesture for the pope and the defense of the Papal States.

204. Alphons G. P. M. Elsenburg (January 28, 1882–November 1, 1960) first worked as a clerk, then received commercial training in the Manchester Trading Company, a British colonial trading firm, and subsequently set up his own company in 1910, a textile wholesaler (drapery products and fashion).

205. The N. V. Textielhandel Alph. Elsenburg (Alph. Elsenburg's Ltd. Textile Company) was based at number 167 in 1910, later expanding as far as number 161, previously J. Alberdingk Thijm's residence. The façade bears a plaque commemorating Thijm; cf. the corporate publication *Van Thijm-huis tot textiel palazzo* (Amsterdam: N. V. Textielhandel Elsenburg, 1955). The company moved to Joan Muyskenweg 24a in 1971. The entire company and its staff were sometimes placed at the disposal of the Society, for instance during the 1924 International Eucharistic Congress, when it closed its doors for the duration of a week; see *De Tijd*, July 18, 1924. The company's chief clerk, F. Kristen, looked after the Silent Walk's financial administration for decades. Similarly, when C. Bieckmann succeeded him in 1936 as treasurer, there was talk of an "in-crowd"; GAA, GSO, inv. no. 4, annual report 1936; cf. *De Tijd*, April 11, 1940. The families of the later Elsenburg chairmen were also heavily involved in the organization.

206. Brenninkmeijer, *Stilte in de stad*, 25.

207. Ben Kroon, "Gordijnen dicht aan de Nieuwe Zijde," in *De Tijd*, February 11, 1972.

208. GAA, GSO, *Memorandum*, board meeting, January 20, 1918.

209. The Hoge Raad (Dutch supreme court) determined on November 29, 1918 (W10346), that processions were not banned a priori, but that the public prosecutor would henceforth have to prove that a contested procession did not have a basis in history.

210. The connection with the Begijnhof often only strengthened this romantic perspective; see, for instance, J. F., "Het Mirakel van Amsterdam," in the liberal newspaper *Algemeen Handelsblad*, March 19, 1906, evening edition, 2.

211. The absolute terms *never* and *intention* were qualified somewhat by the conditional statement that "the time is not ripe yet for a public procession bearing the Blessed Sacrament through the streets of Amsterdam"; see GAA, GSO, inv. no. 2, minutes following *Memorandum*, March 24, 1917.

212. Margry, *Teedere Quaesties*, 410–11.

213. GAA, GSO, inv. no. 2, *Memorandum*, 49.

214. GAA, GSO, inv. no. 2, minutes following *Memorandum*, March 17, 1918; GAA, Begijnhof Archive, inv. no. 859; *Geïllustreerd Zondagsblad*, March 30, 1918, and *Geïllustreerd Zondagsblad voor Katholieken*, March 31, 1917–1918, 313–19.

215. Two processions were initially held in the grounds of the Begijnhof, just as in the Middle Ages, one on the feast of the Miracle and the other on Corpus Christi, but because the weather in March was often inclement, the first procession was eventually discontinued. The processions and the attending rules were carefully recorded; see GAA, Begijnhof Archive, inv. no. 575, with a chronicle for 1918–1944.

216. It is not clear why Lousbergh included this specific group, orphans of the Lauriergracht orphanage, in his regulations; he was not an orphan himself, but perhaps he had some personal involvement in the board or otherwise in the orphanage. In any case, he insisted on the importance of involving this old Catholic institution in the Walk project (cf. GAA, GSO, inv. no. 31). Possibly there was a historical connection with the Holy Stead: in 1532, Pompeius Occo earmarked a bequest for the "poor orphans next the Holy Stead"; see Sterck, "Aanteekeningen over 16e eeuwsche Amsterdamsche portretten," 263–65.

217. More on this subject in the section Women and the Walk.

218. The archive has generally been well preserved for the entire existence of the Society (not of the sister societies), until approximately the year 2000, and is currently in the Amsterdam City Archives; see Margry, *Inventaris*, and the archives online at https://stadsarchief.amsterdam.nl/archieven/archiefbank/over zicht/30382.nl.html.

219. GAA, GSO, inv. no. 2, *Memorandum*, 52.

220. "Mgr. B. H. Klönne," in *Katholieke Illustratie* 47 (1903): 289, 293. On Klönne, see also "80 jaar," in *De Tijd*, February 20, 1914; "Zestig jaar priester," in *De Tijd*, August 14, 1919; *Katholieke Illustratie* 55 (1920–1921): 553, 556. Klönne died in Huize Duinrust in Overveen on August 7, 1920, at the age of eighty-seven; see Sterck-Poot, "Wachter der Heilige Stede."

221. GAA, GSO, inv. no. 2, *Memorandum*, 50–51: "het 50-jarig bestaan van het zogenaamde eene Italië" (the fiftieth anniversary of the supposedly united Italy).

222. Vis, *Liefde het fundament*, 50.

223. On its foundation and history, see *Gedenkschrift van het 25-jarig bestaan*.

224. The Amsterdam society became a coordinating umbrella organization that increasingly left the work of looking after pilgrims and participants of the Silent Walk to the sister societies; for this reason, the Amsterdam Society itself did not experience any large increase in membership.

225. Statutes of the Society of the Silent Walk, art. 1: "It is the objective [of the Society] to further devotion to the Most Holy Sacrament of Miracle"; see Margry, *Inventaris*, 38.

226. Article 1 of the statutes mentions that the Society was founded in the Begijnhofkerk in 1881, but this is a post ex facto construction; see Margry, *Inventaris*, 38. The Society adopted new statutes in 1999 due to newly arising liability issues. These statutes changed its status from an ecclesiastical association into a "private-law organization with an ecclesiastical link."

227. See Jeanne Raedts, "Stille Omgang," in *Jaarboek Sevenum* (2009): 80–81. Cf. other experiences: Jan Vriend, "Bidden na en om een wonder," in *Alkmaarse Courant*, March 20, 1995. Breakfast was often taken collectively after the return home, and after World War II increasingly in Amsterdam itself after completing the Walk; see GAA, GSOA, inv. no. 60.

228. "Piet van Veen over kracht van Stille Omgang," in *Rijn en Gouwe*, March 11, 1995.

229. "De katholiek van de daad in het openbaar godsdienstig leven," in *Officieel Verslag van de 6en Bredaschen Katholiekendag te Roosendaal, op Dinsdag 15 augustus 1916*, 89. This concept originated in the international Catholic Action movement.

230. The Silent Walk also had links to Catholic Social Action; see Broeke, *Stille Omgang Herdenking*, 13.

231. GAA, GSO, inv. no. 4, annual report 1925.

232. In those years Amsterdam had ca. 135,000 Catholic inhabitants, around 23 percent of the total population of the city.

233. *Stille Omgang Amsterdam 1930–1980*, 9. There were no extra trains in 1956 on account of a scarcity of coal.

234. GAA, GSO, inv. no. 3, March 24, 1917. The count was carried out by tertiaries, but it is not as precise as has often been presumed because the count stopped at 6:00 a.m. even though hundreds of pilgrims passed after that time; see *De Tijd*, March 19, 1917.

235. The society itself remained wary of providing statistics: as the board commented, "What do they mean anyway?" Also the number of participants from Amsterdam, who were not organized, was even more difficult to estimate; see Broeke, *Stille Omgang Herdenking*, 15.

236. The newspapers *De Maasbode* and *Het Centrum* counted fifty thousand and sixty thousand participants, respectively, on March 21, 1922; this doubling in the space of one year must probably be regarded as a form of Catholic wishful thinking.

237. GAA, GSO, inv. no. 4, annual reports 1926, 1927, and 1928.

238. See the report on the two nights during the golden jubilee: S. E. S., "Een halve eeuw gebedsnacht," in *Katholieke Illustratie*, March 11, 1931, 564–65.

239. For a (nonexhaustive) list of sister societies, see Margry, *Inventaris*, 40–46.

240. *Stille Omgang Amsterdam 1930–1980*, 8–10. The number of participants declined after 1961 to level out at a stable 1,500 (some 450 of whom were annual participants) in the 1970s.

241. From the 1930s onward, the railways experienced increasing competition from bus companies. Nevertheless, extra trains carried between twenty-three thousand and twenty-seven thousand people in those years.

242. *Gedenkschrift van het 25–jarig bestaan*, 18.

243. GAA, GSO, inv. no. 4, annual report 1938–1939.

244. *Gedenkschrift van het 25–jarig bestaan*, 21.

245. See, for instance, a report in the daily newspaper *De Maasbode* of April 4, 1940. Jan van den Bosch wrote about the group in 2007 in "Uden inspirator van Stille Omgang voor priesterstudenten."

246. GAA, GSO, inv. no. 4, January 16, 1918.

247. The annual meeting of 1923 heard, for instance, that many participants from Utrecht and surrounding areas had not traveled back with the group at night: GAA, GSO, inv. no. 4, February 4, 1923.

248. Fokkens and Fokkens, *Ouwehoeren*, 83–86.

249. Jan Repko and Rob Stallinga, "Amsterdam mirakelt voort," in *De Groene Amsterdammer*, March 15, 1995.

250. GAA, GSO, inv. no. 4, annual report 1938.

251. Ibid.

252. Broeke, *Stille Omgang Herdenking*, 14–15.

253. Only very few incidents were reported, for instance in 1935, when a group of agitating "Communists" was dispersed at saber-point; in 1938 the same happened to a group of rowdy persons on Nieuwendijk; in 1939 there was a baton charge against noisy persons on Martelaarsgracht; and in 1940 a saber charge against noisy persons on Martelaarsgracht; see GAA, Police 1814–1956, inv. no. 4702.

254. GAA, Municipal police (Gemeentepolitie), inv. no. 3003; the order was confirmed in 1972.

255. GAA, GSO, inv. no. 4, annual report 1922.

256. GAA, GSO, inv. no. 2, minutes following *Memorandum*, December 22, 1918.

257. New indulgences were granted to participants of the Walk on January 5, 1937: a plenary indulgence for completing the Walk and saying a prayer for the pope, and seven years' indulgence for completing the Walk without the prayer.

258. The former prime minister Charles Ruijs de Beerenbrouck also took part; GAA, GSO, inv. no. 4, January 15, 1936.

259. GAA, GSO, inv. no. 7, annual report 1980.

260. Kroon, "Stille Omgang."

261. Willem Th. M. Frijhoff, in an e-mail to P. J. Margry, September 14, 2015, Meertens Institute, BiN documentation, sub Amsterdam, Miracle.

262. The interviewee mistakenly reported that the women sat on the right and the men on the left.

263. Interview with Hans Lurvink, taken from Brenninkmeijer, *Stilte in de stad*, 22–23.

264. Boudien de Vries, "Van deftigheid," 85, 91; Boudien de Vries, "Voluntary Societies in the Netherlands."

265. In his study of the Holy Stead of Hasselt in Overijssel, Frijhoff observed a different variant. The confraternity Association of "The Holy Stead" had a wider recruitment field than the shrine's registers of visitors: i.e., the entire archdiocese. Female members strongly predominated for areas that were outside walking distance of Hasselt (a circle of about twelve miles), although it appears that the actual pilgrimage was made mainly by men.

266. Huysmans, *Sainte-Lydwine de Schiedam*, 322–23.

267. Derks, *Heilig moeten*, 236–32.

268. Rogier and Rooy, *In vrijheid herboren*, 481.

269. GAA, Begijnhof Archive, inv. no. 40, March 18, 1888, 81.

270. GAA, GSO, inv. no. 2, *Memorandum*, 19.

271. GAA, GSO, inv. no. 78.

272. GAA, GSO, inv. no. 4, annual report 1921; the decision to admit women to the annual meeting was made on December 19, 1920.

273. *Gedenkboek van het eerste Diocesane Eucharistisch Congres*, 107.

274. GAA, Begijnhof Archive, inv. no. 795.

275. R. R. Post, "Nachtelijke ommegangen in de oude kerk," in *De Maasbode*, March 23, 1931.

276. "Vrouwen-Ommegang. Geen optocht van vrouwen door de stad!" in *De Tijd*, March 15, 1932, morning edition.

277. It inspired a Women's and Mothers' Silent Walk in The Hague to mark League of Nations Day (Goodwill Day) on May 18, 1934.

278. Women were also normally barred from participating in other Silent Walks inspired by the Amsterdam Walk (see below), such as the silent walk in honor of Our Lady of Jesse in Delft. Women in Delft organized their own walk from 1949 onward, with the men's and women's walk held together for the first time in 1964. The Schiedam walk was initially only for men, just as the Vrouwevaart in Amersfoort held from 1933 onward.

279. Report of the meeting in *De Tijd*, March 10, 1937.

280. "De Stille Omgang. Hoe vrouwen er aan deel kunnen nemen," in *De Maasbode*, March 11, 1938.

281. GAA, GSO, Scrapbook 1938–1939; on the priest in question, Pater Vrijmoed, see http://verhalenwiki.nl/index.php?title=Vrijmoed%2C_Pater.

282. Reen, *In het donkere zuiden*, 139.

283. Gerard Brom, "Kroniek en kritiek," in *De Beiaard* 9 (1924): 218–20.

284. Brom, *Areopaag*, "Stille Omgang" chapter; Caspers and Margry, *Identiteit en spiritualiteit*, 32–35. The year before, at the Dutch Catholics' Day of 1922 in Nijmegen, Brom had said, "a procession is good, a silent walk is better, a retreat is best!"; see Broeke, "De Stille Omgang en het H.H. Sacrament van Mirakel," 155.

285. There are only a few references to silent marches outside the Netherlands: in 1929 there was one in London to celebrate the centenary of Catholic emancipation (1829), which attracted around thirty thousand participants. A second march was held in London on September 18, 1938, from St. George's Cathedral to Westminster Cathedral. Cardinal Hinsley had written a letter calling for a march to offer reparation for the public insults given to God in the context of an

international congress of freethinkers in the city that month. It is not clear whether the London march served as an example for Amsterdam; this is not unlikely.

286. On these Eucharistic places of pilgrimage, see Margry and Caspers, *Bedevaartplaatsen in Nederland*, vols. 1 and 2.

287. GAA, GSO, inv. no. 4, May 20 and December 19, 1920. But an Alkmaar invitation was accepted for the fifth centenary of the Precious Blood in 1929.

288. Catholics in the predominantly Catholic south also began to form walks with a more explicitly religious character, such as the Marian procession of 's-Hertogenbosch since 1927 or the 1932 mass processions in Nijmegen, which had experienced cautious revival a few years previously as a "Marian procession"; see "De Maria-omdracht," in *Gedenkboek van het nationaal Maria-Congres*, 115–36.

289. S. E. S., "Een halve eeuw gebedsnacht," in *Katholieke Illustratie*, March 18, 1931, 575, 606.

290. "Gouden Jubelfeest van den Stillen Omgang," in *De Zeeuwsche Koerier*, March 20, 1931, no. 3745; *De Echo van het Zuiden, Waalwijksche en Langstraatsche Courant*, March 18, 1931, 2; *Leidsch Dagblad*, March 16, 1931.

291. "Het gouden feest van den Stillen Omgang," in *De Tijd*, evening edition, March 16, 1931.

292. Duijnstee, *Jubelend Nederland rondom het H. Sacrament van Mirakel*.

293. Alphons Elsenburg was an agent of the Manchester Trading Company until 1910 and then set up his own company as an agent for a number of foreign textile companies.

294. See [Maarten Elsenburg], "Vier generaties Elsenburg: Bestuurlijke ruggengraat Stille Omgang," in Brenninckmeijer, *Stilte in de stad*, 24.

295. See, for instance, Caspers, Cortjaens, and Jacobs, *De basiliek van Onze Lieve Vrouw van het Heilig Hart*, 53–109.

296. Caspers, "Eerherstel," 99–112.

297. On this organization, see *Gedenkboek van het eerste Diocesane Eucharistisch Congres*, 140–46.

298. GAA, Begijnhof Archive, inv. no. 575, on June 11, 1920.

299. Moreau, *Zur Geschichte der Eucharistische Kongresse*.

300. Borromaeus de Greeve, "De Roomsche weelde der aanbiddelijke Eucharistie in haare beteekenis voor de moderne tijden," in *Gedenkboek van het eerste Diocesane Eucharistisch Congres*, 21–32.

301. Broeke, *Stille Omgang Herdenking*, 13.

302. W. Nieuwenhuis, "De stad van het Mirakel A.D. 2345," in *Eucharistisch congresboek*, 38–40.

303. *Gedenkboek van het eerste Diocesane Eucharistisch Congres*, 20. In his speech, Heylen said, "May this congress be the harbinger of a World Congress, to be held here in Amsterdam." Cf. Slijpen et al., *Congresboek*.

304. On this question, see the paper given by Vefie Poels, "Volksgeloof of provocatie? De Eucharistische congressen in Amsterdam (1922) and (1924)," 6–9, which I was kindly allowed to consult.

305. Jan Sterck, in *De Maasbode*, July 24, 1924.

306. The full text was printed across the entire front page of *De Tijd*, July 24, 1924.

307. Cuypers, "Het stadion te Amsterdam."

308. See the description of the procession in *Gedenkboek van het XXVIIe Internationaal Eucharistisch Congres*, 784–88.

309. Hensen, *In den Hollandschen tuin*, 108.

310. Preserved in GAA, GSO, 1320.AV.

311. *Gedenkboek van het XXVIIe Internationaal Eucharistisch Congres*, 789.

312. Active anti-Catholicism was becoming less pronounced in Amsterdam. A celebration held on May 24, 1928, to commemorate the 1578 Alteration of Amsterdam as a victory over Catholics hardly managed to attract any Protestants; see Rooy in *Geschiedenis van Amsterdam*, 4:136.

313. Poels, "Volksgeloof of provocatie?" 9–10.

314. "Anno Sancto," in *Katholieke Illustratie* 67 (June 21, 1933): 830; Derks, "Manifestaties van katholieke fierheid," 621.

315. Jan Leechburch Auwers's memories of the Silent Walk, in an e-mail to P. J. Margry, May 8, 2013.

316. GAA, GSO, inv. no. 3, sub February 24, 1918.

317. Broeke, "De Stille Omgang en het H. H. Sacrament van Mirakel," 153.

318. GAA, GSOA, inv. no. 19.

319. This had been an explicit feature even in the early phase of the Walk, in 1889. In a letter to Klönne, Lousbergh requested him to say the masses after the Walk not only for the participants themselves, but also "for the conversion of all non-Catholics, especially those of our country and our city"; see GAA, GSO, inv. no. 28, March 10, 1889.

320. Voets, *Blijf, Meester*, 42–43.

321. Handelsblad, March 19, 1906; cf. GAA, GSOA, inv. no. 2, *Memorandum*, 38–45.

322. GAA, GSO, *Memorandum*, 45.

323. GAA, GSO, inv. no. 2, *Memorandum*, 47.

324. Ibid., 50–51.

325. GAA, GSO, inv. no. 4, annual report 1925.

326. GAA, GSO, inv. no. 2, *Memorandum*, board meeting June 5, 1919; inv. no. 4, annual report 1918–1919.

327. Broeke, "De Stille Omgang en het H. H. Sacrament van Mirakel," 153, appears to be referring to this episode when he says that the board decided "for one moment to break the silence amidst the noise of the street" in 1917. In fact this did not happen until 1918, while both activities have been erroneously recorded for the year 1919 in the *Memorandum*; cf. inv. no. 4, annual report 1918–1919.

328. GAA, GSO, inv. no. 2, *Memorandum*, board meeting, February 16, 1918.

329. At the time these meetings were appropriately held in the Cornelis Broere House, St. Catharine's boys' group, later the Leidseplein Theater.

330. GAA, GSO, inv. no. 4, annual report 1923; cf. "Een polemiek," in *Leidsche Courant*, May 11, 1918.

331. GAA, GSO, inv. no. 4, annual report 1925, brochures spread by the Evangelische Maatschappij (Evangelical society).

332. See *De Maasbode*, March 14, 1932.

333. GAA, Police 1814–1956, inv. no. 4702, report March 16/17, 1935.

334. A. B. Kleerekoper, "Oproerige krabbels. Nacht en dag," in *Het Volk*, March 9, 1940.

335. "Wekelijkse Spiegel," in *Nieuwe Rotterdamsche Courant*, March 10, 1940.

336. "Traditie van kerk en vaderland," in *De Tijd*, March 6, 1937.

337. For instance as a header in *De Tijd*, March 17/18, 1938.

338. Barnard and Post, *Ritueel bestek*, 183–84 ("Gedenken").

339. GAA, Police 1814–1956, inv. no. 4702; see estimates in the police reports of these years.

340. GAA, GSO, inv. no. 4, November 15, 1939, February 4, 1940.

341. See report in *De Tijd*, March 17, 1940, which mentions eighty thousand participants, a figure that is probably too high, like most unilateral estimates; cf. GAA, Police 1814–1956, inv. no. 4702, with eighty-five thousand.

342. The annual general meeting with the board members of the sister societies, held in Amsterdam, was subsequently also canceled due to limited travel possibilities.

343. GAA, Municipal Police Archive (5225) 1814–1956, inv. no. 4702, telegram dated March 16, 1941.

344. See GSOA for the different reports.

345. It is not entirely certain that it was Joseph Citroen, as the report was of a *sculptor* Citroen, but no such person could be traced in Amsterdam during those years.

346. *De Tijd*, November 22, 1940. The Breda branch of the Silent Walk preceded Amsterdam in this. As an alternative for the pilgrimage of June 23, it had participated that year in the Silent Walk of Breda, held every year in Breda to honor another medieval Eucharistic miracle (Niervaart). As this was always held during the day, it did not at this time fall under the ban.

347. GAA, Municipal Police Archive (5225) 1814–1956, inv. no. 4702.

348. Only the Vlijmen branch still came to 's-Hertogenbosch that year, and only four silent pilgrimages to Meerssen took place.

349. Begijnhof, Liber memorialis 1929–1945, 27–29.

350. Voets, *Bewaar het toevertrouwde pand*, 295, in a letter from Noort to the bishop.

351. Plas, *Daarom, mijnheer*, 346–48.

352. On the day itself, March 17, the program "Nederland Herrijst" (Resurgent Netherlands) also broadcast six commemorative speeches on the Miracle in the Netherlands; they have been preserved on six gramophone records; see GAA, GSO, 1320.AV. Catholic antiquarian Leo Bisterbosch made a Miracle exhibition in his shop at Nieuwezijds Voorburgwal 349.

353. GAA, Municipal Police Archive (5225) 1814–1956, inv. no. 4604, letter dated May 26, 1945.

354. GAA, Municipal Police Archive (5225) 1814–1956, inv.no. 4702; a Eucharistic Week was held from October 22 to 28, during which both individual and group walks took place; inv. no. 4604, letter dated May 26, 1945.

355. GAA, Police 1814–1956, inv. no. 4703, report March 9–10, 1946.

356. Rooy, *Openbaring en openbaarheid*, 44.

357. In *Geschiedenis van Amsterdam*, 4:59–60, Rooy argues that pillarization was less dominant in the city than it was elsewhere.

358. Begijnhof, Liber memorialis 1929–1945, 1945–1978, p. 36: seventy thousand participants, fourteen special trains, one hundred buses, and nine hundred by boat.

359. Plas, *Daarom, mijnheer*, 366.

360. Archive Archdiocese of Utrecht, minutes bishops' conference meeting, May 10, 1944, under no. 3 and July 9/10, 1945, agenda no. 30.

361. On the celebration, see Begijnhof, Liber memorialis, 1945–1978, 40–67; Plas, *Daarom, mijnheer*, 366–67.

362. He was chairman of the Uitvoerend Comité Nederland Herdenkt 1940–1945 (Executive committee of the Netherlands commemoration 1940–1945); Plas, *Daarom, mijnheer*, 365.

363. See a report in *De Tijd*, June 24, 1946; Derks, "Manifestaties van katholieke fierheid," 621–22.

364. GAA, Begijnhof Archive, inv. no. 864; *De Maasbode*, June 24, 1946; "Het zesde eeuwfeest van het Mirakel," in *Maandblad Amstelodamum* 33 (1946): 44.

365. In addition to this celebration there was an exhibition called Zes eeuwen katholiek Amsterdam (Six centuries of Catholic Amsterdam) and a commemorative volume, *Het Vierenswaardig Wonder* (The Miracle worthy of celebration), which made yet another attempt to prove that the Miracle had taken place with "absolute historical certainty."

366. Duinkerken, "De plechtige processie met het Allerheiligste." Van Duinkerken, echoing Klönne, referred to the practice of medieval Eucharistic processions in Amsterdam. He wrote that "an insatiable desire for the glory of Jesus . . . awakens" in those who contemplate the beauty of the Eucharistic procession. Cf. Van Duinkerken's reflections in *Het Vrije Volk*, June 26, 1946.

367. The actual shrine remained the church of the Begijnhof. The suggestion made in 1946 of using the building elements of the former Holy Stead in a newly build chapel was never executed; see Breen, "De Heilige Stede te Amsterdam," 123.

368. Margry, *Teedere Quaesties*, 416.

369. Rogier, *Geschiedenis van het katholicisme*, 2:795.

370. Ibid.

371. Duinkerken, "De plechtige processie met het Allerheiligste," 215.

372. Almost no Protestant took offense at the "processions of thanks and liberation" that Catholics held in several places in 1945 and 1946, despite these being prohibited by law; see Margry, *Teedere quaesties*, 414–15.

373. On the history of the various commemorations, see Ginkel, *Rondom de stilte*, esp. 173–86.

374. GAA, Police Archive 1814–1956, inv. no. 3157, brochure Foundation The National Institute.

375. Plas, *Daarom, mijnheer*, 351, 365.

376. Cf. "De macht van het zwijgen," in *De Tijd*, March 17/18, 1938: "unique prayer walk."

377. Plas, *Daarom, mijnheer*, 351, contends (although without referencing any sources) that Van Duinkerken did indeed advocate silent marches by way of analogy with the Silent Walk.

378. GAA, Police Archive 1814–1956, inv. no. 3157, draft directive on celebration of day of commemoration and liberation of the National Institute. The adoption of the practice of having a minute's silence from the London example is mentioned in "Nederland herdenkt zijn dooden," in *Het Parool*, May 6, 1946, 5. The tradition of holding two minutes' silence to commemorate World War I had existed in Great Britain and the Commonwealth since 1919; it had been instituted by King George V, who commented that "All locomotion should cease, so that, in perfect stillness, the thoughts of everyone may be concentrated on reverent remembrance of the glorious dead." After 1945, this commemoration on November 11 became a combined ritual for both world wars; see www.veteransagency.mod.uk. It must be mentioned that the Walk had inspired a silent peace ritual before: the Women's and Mothers' Silent Walk held in The Hague on May 18, 1934, by five thousand women, to mark League of Nations Day and the disarmament conference; see *Leeuwarder Nieuwsblad*, May 4, 1934.

379. For a report of the celebration, see *Algemeen Handelsblad*, September 1, 1945.

380. Reports of this cannot be found in the national newspapers consulted. It is mentioned in Jolanda Keesom, "Op 4 mei herdenken we, op 5 mei vieren we onze vrijheid," accessed at https://www.herdenkenenvieren.nl/hev/geschiedenis, April 15, 2014 (no longer available). She based her statement on a letter in the National Archives that these former resistance leaders had written to the prime minister in early 1946 about the possible format of a commemoration.

381. GAA, Police Archive 1814–1956, inv. no. 3157, circular letter National Commemoration Committee, dated March 16, 1946. From 1947 the designation *silent march* was used in most municipalities, with the exception of a few places in Catholic areas, for instance, in the *Graafschapsbode* of May 2, 1974, which still spoke of "silent walk," or in the *Nieuw Haagse Courant* of September 19, 1974.

382. There was some coverage of the National Program in the press, mainly of the commemorations and the minute's silence at the graves and places of execution, but no mention yet of the marches themselves; cf. *Algemeen Handelsblad*, May 3, 1946, May 6, 1946.

383. The assistant pastor, Dominican friar, and resistance leader Nicolaas Apeldoorn (resistance pseudonym "Victor"), who was acquainted with the Silent Walk, was also involved in formulating this proposal.

384. See also Keesom, "Op 4 mei herdenken we, op 5 mei vieren we onze vrijheid"; Marina de Vries, "Twee minuten," 15–26; Barnard and Post, *Ritueel bestek*, 187–93; Boom, "Den Haag. De Waalsdorpervlakte"; Ginkel, *Rondom de stilte*, 187–205.

385. Plas, *Daarom, Mijnheer*, 351. Several authors later also pointed to this imitation, including Kroon, in "Stille Omgang": "The silent march of May 4 is a national copy of the Silent Walk." Ginkel, *Rondom de stilte*, 184, thinks it is "highly unlikely" that the example of the Silent Walk was copied, as Drop was a Calvinist.

But he underestimates Van Duinkerken's role and the "war ecumenism" still current at the time, as well as the "ecumenical" character of the Silent Walk; the sources clearly point to imitation.

386. On the emergence of war piety and "war ecumenism," see Schenk, *Amsterdam, stad der vroomheid*.

387. "Nederland herdenkt zijn dooden," in *Het Parool*, May 6, 1946, 1 and 5.

388. Marina de Vries, "Twee minuten," 17. The *Algemeen Handelsblad* of May 3, 1946, expressed a similar expectation in respect of the observance of a minute's silence: "We will be one again for that one minute, exactly as we were during last year's May days."

389. Municipal Archive Amsterdam, Police Archive, no. 3157, circular letter National Commemoration Committee, dated March 16, 1946. Despite this official principle, one newspaper reported that the invited civil and military authorities in The Hague did in fact walk directly behind the relatives of the victims, which undermined the nonhierarchical aspect of the march in respect of the other participants; see *Het Parool*, May 6, 1946, 5.

390. "Nederland herdenkt zijn dooden," in *Het Parool*, May 6, 1946, 5; Ginkel, *Rondom de stilte*, 187–205.

Chapter 6.   Revolution and the Reinvention of Tradition (1960–2015)

1. Righart, *De eindeloze jaren zestig*, 12–17, 44–45; moreover, 62 percent of the people stated that their lives had not been really changed by the war.

2. *De Maasbode*, March 21, 1946; GAA, Police 1814–1956, inv. no. 4703.

3. The Society's reasonably reliable extrapolation on the basis of the numbers of special trains and coaches came to more than eighty thousand; more than eighty thousand men took part again in 1959, see GAA, GSO, inv. no. 5.

4. GAA, Municipal police, inv. no. 3304, letter dated March 9, 1955.

5. GAA, Municipal police appendix, inv. no. 3304, complaints from De Monchi concerning 1952–1954.

6. GAA, GSO, inv. no. 5, January 25, 1955.

7. Righart, *De eindeloze jaren zestig*, 114–65.

8. Verkerke and Lammers, *Amsterdam Mirakelstad*; the book was not a success, and only a few hundred of the print run of seven thousand were sold.

9. Righart, *De eindeloze jaren zestig*, 38–40, 79–100.

10. Ibid., 26.

11. Voets and Noord, "Het verhaal van een honderdjarige," 36.

12. GAA, GSO, inv. no. 5, annual report 1954–1955.

13. GAA, GSO, inv. no. 6, sub 1956.

14. "Tienduizenden bij de Stille Omgang in Amsterdam," in *De Tijd*, November 5, 1956, 7.

15. "Zo reageerden de kerken op Hongarije," in *Het Parool*, November 10, 1956.

16. GAA, GSO, newspaper cuttings 1956; *Algemeen Handelsblad* of November 5, 1956.

17. On August 26, 1956, hundreds of thousands of people prayed at Poland's national shrine for the liberation of the captive Cardinal Stefan Wyszyński.

18. *Algemeen Handelsblad* of November 6, 1956, 4 and 9.

19. Perry and Echeverría, *Under the Heel of Mary*.

20. Lamberts, *The Black International*. This movement had very little support in the Netherlands due to its radicalism.

21. The title of his speech was "The Return of Those Who Have Strayed, and the Conversion of Those Who Are in Error, Especially the City of the Miracle"; see KDC Nijmegen, P. H. J. Wesseling Papers, inv. no. 57; Margry, *Amsterdam en het mirakel*, 102.

22. See, for instance, the report by Greeve, *Zó werkt en wroet Rusland*.

23. Hakkert, "Het geluid van een omgang," 138–41. His argument is that the Walk's growth can be explained by the transformation of a Counter-Reformation image of the enemy into an anticommunist one. He contends that such a transformation was necessary because participants would not otherwise have had a motive to take part in what he calls an already "strongly depillarized society" in the 1950s; society was not depillarized yet, however, and the Silent Walk could continue for so long to attract large crowds precisely because the old motives (which were not in themselves "Counter-Reformation" motives either) retained their validity until into the 1960s.

24. Christian, "Religious Apparitions and the Cold War in Southern Europe."

25. See Veldkamp, *Stille Omgang*, 13. Nor was this motive mentioned often or at all by participants in the many newspaper articles from this period.

26. "Amsterdam Mirakelstad," in *De Nieuwe Dag*, March 10, 1959 (this was a publication of *De Tijd*).

27. Cf. Bank and Buuren, *1900. Hoogtij van burgerlijke cultuur*.

28. Quoted in Righart, *De eindeloze jaren zestig*, 14

29. Righart, *De eindeloze jaren zestig*, 74–114.

30. In a public circular letter, the bishops emphasized the celebration of spiritual values and not external display; see *Eeuwfeest van het Herstel*, 7. Rogier mentioned the Miracle and its intimate piety during the celebration; see *Eeuwfeest van het Herstel*, 37–38. Cf. Bos, *Verlangen naar vernieuwing*, 23–26.

31. See W. J. M. Dings, "Wilhelmus Marinus Bekkers (1908–1966): (televisie) bisschop," at https://www.brabantserfgoed.nl/personen/b/bekkers-wilhelmus -marinus. Cf. Bos, *Verlangen naar vernieuwing*, 138–43. At the level of the international church, this view was only proclaimed in 2016 by Pope Francis in *Amoris Laetitia* (March 19, 2016).

32. Cf. Palm, *Moederkerk*, 217–19. Their aversion drove many young Catholics into the arms of other ideologies (cf. ibid., 200–23).

33. Voets and Noord, "Het verhaal van een honderdjarige," 43; at the board meeting: "Are you still interested in going to Amsterdam, if your pastor or associate pastor tells you that the whole affair is medieval?"

34. On the period of change, see Goddijn, Jacobs, and Tillo, *Tot vrijheid geroepen*.

35. Goddijn, Jacobs, and Tillo, *Tot vrijheid geroepen*, 493–95; Bos, *Verlangen naar vernieuwing*, 221–31.

36. This catechism became an international bestseller; see Chiaruttini, *Het dossier van de Nederlandse Katechismus*.

37. Goddijn, Jacobs, and Tillo, *Tot vrijheid geroepen*, 493–95.

38. Kossmann, *De Lage Landen*, 2:331.

39. Quoted in Bos, "De jaren zestig," 138.

40. Brown, "What Was the Religious Crisis"; Rooden, "Secularization"; Rooden, "*Oral history* en het vreemde sterven," 547–48 (see this article also for the ideological ghetto concept).

41. McLeod, *The Religious Crisis*, 262.

42. McLeod, *The Religious Crisis*; Brown, "What Was the Religious Crisis."

43. Righart, *De eindeloze jaren zestig*, 19.

44. Up to the early 1960s, the minutes of the Society recorded with some amazement that the proportion of young participants remained stable; cf. GAA, GSO, inv. no. 5.

45. In addition to decrease in the provinces, there was a strong decline among Amsterdam Catholics as the younger generation dropped out en masse, breaking with the father-to-son tradition.

46. In *Nieuwe Dagblad van Gouda*, October 27, 1965, and *Dagblad van het Oosten*, March 5, 1966.

47. Articles in *De Tijd-Maasbode*, February 22, 1964, and *Twentse Courant*, March 16, 1964; cf. GAA, GSO, inv. no. 6, February 7, 1964.

48. GAA, GSO, inv. no. 92. This amendment was not adopted; the participation of women was—somewhat less than wholeheartedly—discouraged one last time on practical grounds at the annual meeting of January 21, 1968; see GAA, GSO, inv. no. 7, January 21, 1968.

49. Kroon, "Stille Omgang, echt Hollands."

50. Toon Rammelt, "Gedachten bij de Stille Omgang. De bedevaart in de stroom van de ontmythologisering," in *De Tijd-Maasbode*, March 11, 1967.

51. The woman in question was Marijke L. A. E. Elsenburg, the sister of the then chairman, on March 16, 1987. She has so far been the only one.

52. Cf. Nadorp, "Een lopende geschiedenis."

53. GAA, GSO, inv. no. 7, January 19, 1969, November 24, 1969.

54. Cf. Bos, *Verlangen naar vernieuwing*, 12–15.

55. *Provo-Katie*, no. 6, August 13, 1965; on the Provo movement, see Pas, *Imaazje*.

56. Mulisch, *Bericht aan de Rattenkoning*, 140–45, quotation 143–44.

57. Photos of this happening can be found in GAA, Cor Jaring Papers (30883), inv. no. 94.

58. [Editorial], "Omgang der provo's," in *Algemeen Handelsblad*, March 17, 1966.

59. Not only the *Handelsblad* made this argument; see Kroon, "Stille Omgang, echt Hollands."

60. The Eucharist (host) was in fact regularly exposed for the adoration of pilgrims and visitors, but it was not presented as the host of the Miracle. There is

no indication to suggest that this was the case. The Miracle host was said to have been destroyed in 1578.

61. Quoted in "De Stille Omgang, weg er mee?" in *Sursum Corda*, April 9, 1965.

62. The antiquarians metaphor was derived from Kroon, "Stille Omgang, echt Hollands."

63. GAA, GSO, inv. no. 92.

64. Of the 4,100, 20 percent were younger than 25, 51 percent were between 25 and 50, and 29 percent were older than 50.

65. The results of the inquiry were announced on February 4, 1967, in a circular letter. Of the respondents, 25 percent were less willing to make the sacrifice, 15 percent dropped out due to old age or because they had moved house, 15 percent were no longer interested, 15 percent preferred to participate in other activities such as carnival or mid-Lent, and 10 percent dropped out because of the ecclesiastical renewal. These categories are not exclusive because, for instance, the reduction in willingness to make the sacrifice, etc. also partly flowed from ecclesiastical renewal.

66. GAA, GSO, inv. no. 93. Of the pastors in the diocese, 45 percent made good, 20 percent moderate, 25 percent little, and 10 percent no propaganda for the Walk.

67. McLeod, *The Religious Crisis*, 264.

68. Interview in *De Volkskrant*, February 27, 1967.

69. North of the great river delta, the area of "diaspora Catholicism" in mainly Protestant territory, Catholics were less inclined to get rid of all kinds of typically Catholic things immediately. Old, often neo-Gothic, decorations and elements have therefore been preserved to a greater degree there than in the south. For an example of the stripping that was done, see Palm, *Moederkerk*, 182–88.

70. Toon Rammelt, "Gedachten bij de Stille Omgang. De bedevaart in de stroom van de ontmythologisering," in *De Tijd-Maasbodem*, March 11, 1967. Rammelt had in the meantime become director of the Geïllustreerde Pers (VNU).

71. This is comparable to what Thierry Baudet would later call "oikophobia": Baudet, "Oikofobie: de angst voor het eigene," *The Post Online*, September 8, 2013, retrieved from http://politiek.tpo.nl/2013/09/08/oikofobie-de-angst-voor-het -eigene/.

72. Through the Walk, the Society chairmen Alphons and Eduard Elsenburg had become friendly with Rector Van Noort, and it was through this connection that they became friendly with Willebrands during the years that he worked in the Begijnhof.

73. Willebrands, *Rede*, 18.

74. Raedts, "Vier pleidooien voor het Mirakel," 58–61.

75. Willebrands, *Rede*, 18–19.

76. Oral communication from Maarten Elsenburg, March 9, 2016.

77. Some months previously, the sister societies in 's-Hertogenbosch had also carried out a limited survey of participants' declining interest and willingness to make sacrifices. The society believed it could halt the decline by providing more information about the Miracle and the Walk and by getting the clergy to be more cooperative and set a better example; see Veldkamp, *Stille Omgang*, 1.

78. Veldkamp, *Stille Omgang*, 4; Groningen, Drenthe, and Zeeland were not mentioned.

79. Ibid., 5: industrial and agricultural workers 47 percent; higher, midlevel, or lower administrative staff or intellectual workers 42 percent; students and schoolboys 7 percent; clergy 2 percent. These are results that are consonant with a less traditional or instrumental pilgrimage.

80. Ibid., 16.

81. Ibid., 13.

82. Ibid., I [= 28].

83. Ibid., II [= 29].

84. Faith in the Miracle was still remarkably strong that year: among citizens of Amsterdam 74 percent and among others 85 percent, with a strong differentiation per age category, with a figure approaching 100 percent for older people and a figure approaching 50 percent for younger respondents; Veldkamp, *Stille Omgang*, 25.

85. GAA, GSO, inv. no. 118, file on this special meeting.

86. GAA, GSO, inv. no. 118, meeting November 18, 1967, the speaker was A. H. C. W. Vermeeren from Eindhoven.

87. Houtepen, "Rome of Noordwijkerhout?" 184–205; Righart, *De eindeloze jaren zestig*, 61–62.

88. Bos, "De jaren zestig," 139; Goddijn, Jacobs, and Tillo, *Tot vrijheid geroepen*, 489–90.

89. Bomans and Plas, *In de kou*, 10–11.

90. Goddijn, Jacobs, and Tillo, *Tot vrijheid geroepen*, 265–75.

91. Peter Jan Margry, "De processie is terug—katholieke emancipatie voltooid," in *De Volkskrant*, June 21, 2005.

92. Bomans and Plas, *In de kou*, 8–9.

93. Bomans and Plas, *In de kou*, 10. Cf. Rooden, "*Oral history* en het vreemde sterven," 537–38.

94. Bomans and Plas, *In de kou*, 10.

95. This Catholic Citykerk was abolished again on July 1, 2001. In its place came one large city parish under the patronage of Saint Nicholas, with the eponymous church as parish church and the entire city center as its territory. Within this parish, the other Catholic churches continue to function with a certain degree of independence. A new online Citykerk was established in 2015 (run by "Dominee [Reverend] Tim"), but this has no links with the former Catholic Citykerk.

96. Begijnhof Archives, archives of the rector, binder 1968–1973.

97. *De Tijd* of March 15, 1971, mentions seven thousand participants for 1971, five thousand of whom came in a hundred coaches and two special trains, and two thousand of whom came on their own, mainly from Amsterdam and the surrounding area; ten churches and chapels held celebrations of the Eucharist preceding the Walk; *De Telegraaf* incidentally estimated the number of participants at ten thousand.

98. GAA, GSOA, inv. no. 19; cf. Voets and Noord, "Het verhaal van een honderdjarige," 43.

99. GAA, GSOA, inv. no. 19.

100. See, for instance, the report dated May 12, 1973, *Begijnhofkerk en Citypastoraat* by M. A. J. Duindam, which can be found in the Begijnhof Archives.

101. Voets and Noord, "Het verhaal van een honderdjarige," 43.

102. In order to safeguard continuity, the Collegie was placed under the protection of the Amsterdam Society of the Silent Walk in 1988. It has had an adapted function since 2014—"acquiring and managing the cultural heritage of the Miracle and the Walk, and stimulating cultural-historical and musical activities"—and meets annually in the Ignatiushuis in Amsterdam during the Miracle week. The Collegie's membership currently consists of managers of charitable foundations; see Margry and Joor, *St. Caecilia Collegie*, 28–29.

103. Begijnhof Archive, Eucharistic Center file, 1959–1971.

104. Begijnhof Archive, Guild of the Sacrament file, letter from Suidgeest dated December 19, 1978.

105. Episcopal Vicar W. J. de Graaf, in a letter to Suidgeest, April 2, 1979; the end of the Guild of the Sacrament came in 1978, when daily adoration abruptly stopped.

106. Yvonne Laudy, "Stille Omgang, een bijna mystieke ervaring," in *De Telegraaf*, March 14, 1981, T23.

107. This was the case both within and outside the Catholic Church. The realization that previously despised forms of "popular devotion" were still important finally also came to the church; see, for instance, the special edition on "Popular Religiosity" of *Concilium, Internationaal tijdschrift voor theologie* 22, no. 4 (1986).

108. GAA, Municipal Museums Service (30103), inv. no. 73 (100 years Silent Walk).

109. During the night of the Walk in 1985, and for the duration of this night only, the chest was placed on a spot where it could be accessed openly, in a part of the museum located directly along the route of the Walk, so that pilgrims could drop by to visit it. The line between religious practice and museum visits was briefly blurred. VPRO television crews were there in the hope of recording a miracle.

110. Estimated at eight thousand to nine thousand in 1981. The deanery of Terborg, for instance, recorded a doubling of the numbers of participants, including more young people; "Belangstelling voor Stille Omgang Stijgt," in *Geldersche Post*, 51 (1984): 2, March 21.

111. Born April 15, 1950, in Amsterdam (economist; organization consultant) and married to Annette Herkenhoff. See also J. van Burgsteden, *Laudatio voor Maarten Elsenburg bij gelegenheid van de opname van Maarten Elsenburg in de Orde van St. Gregorius met de rang van Commandeur* (Haarlem: n.p., 2011; copy in Meertens Instituut, Collection BiN, sub Amsterdam, Miracle).

112. Calls were made for Gijsen to speak at the annual meeting of 1973, at which point moderator J. van der Hoogte would have resigned had he not been stopped by Zwartkruis; GAA, GSO, inv. no. 7, February 6, 1973.

113. GAA, GSO, inv. no. 107; Yvonne Laudy, "Stille Omgang, een bijna mystieke ervaring," in *De Telegraaf*, March 14, 1981, T23; Maurits Schmidt, "Het Mirakel verliest zijn roomse stigma," in *Het Parool*, March 11, 1995.

114. Raedts, "Le Saint Sacrement," 250–51.

115. See the interviews with Maarten Elsenburg by Pieter van der Ven, "Stille Omgang is een echt mirakel," in *Trouw*, March 10, 1995, and Maurits Schmidt, "Het Mirakel verliest zijn roomse stigma," in *Het Parool*, March 11, 1995.

116. Rooy, *Republiek van rivaliteiten*, 276–87.

117. My own estimation in 1988 was that it was impossible to predict how the Walk would develop after 2000, and that there was no clear trend either way; see Margry, *Amsterdam en het mirakel*, 118. The latter was still the case in 2018: participation continues to be relatively stable.

118. GAA, GSOA, management memo "De stille omgang na het jaar 2000" (1985).

119. Rex Brico, "Het Mirakel van Amsterdam," in *Algemeen Dagblad*, March 13, 1995.

120. Newspaper articles often feature older participants who began making the Walk in imitation of their fathers, and also people who take part after having been cured of an illness or to pray for a sick person; see, for instance, Jan Vriend, "Bidden na en om een wonder," in *Alkmaarse Courant*, March 20, 1995.

121. His merits were acknowledged by the Catholic Church in 2011 when he was made a member of the Order of St. Gregory the Great; see the Laudatio of November 25, 2011, by Bishop J. van Burgsteden.

122. Most participants in 2015 came from six areas: Amsterdam and the surrounding area; West Friesland–Haarlem Kennemerland; the Utrecht region, Gooi, and Amersfoort; Rotterdam and Westland; East Brabant (especially around 's-Hertogenbosch and Eindhoven); and Limburg. There were sixty-seven groups in total and twenty masses in ten churches. E-mail dated February 9, 2016, from M. Elsenburg to P. J. Margry.

123. GAA, GSOA, inv. no. 37: Miracle play on Sunday August 25, 1991, an initiative of the publicist and satirist Mohamed el-Fers.

124. Ed Dekker, "Chocolademelk voor pelgrims in Amsterdamse schuilkerk," in *Alkmaarsche Courant*, March 20, 1995.

125. Rex Brico, "Dr. Albert v.d. Heuvel over de Stille Omgang," in *Elseviers Magazine*, March 27, 1976, 44–47.

126. Reinier A. R. Elders, "Het Sacrament van Mirakel," in *Kerkwijzer: Gemeenteblad van de Gereformeerde kerk te Wageningen*, March 1992.

127. The Oude Kerk was a logical location for this service because the Miracle was said to have occurred within the jurisdiction of the oldest parish of Amsterdam in 1345. In addition, the Miracle host was kept there for some time.

128. Maurits Schmidt, "Het Mirakel verliest zijn roomse stigma," in *Het Parool*, March 11, 1995; Verdonck, "Une procession silencieuse."

129. See Schmidt's interview with Maarten Elsenburg in *Het Parool* of March 11, 1995.

130. Participants who perhaps began the Walk before midnight were not included. The trend has been to start the Walk earlier than in the past. The lantern is now placed in Kalverstraat as early as 11:00 p.m.

131. Margry, *Goede en slechte tijden*. In addition to this symposium, the anniversary was marked by an exhibition in Museum Amstelkring that portrayed the

dissemination of the emblem of the Miracle on flags, church plate, drawings, and paintings in the Netherlands; see Hout, Margry, and Schillemans, *Het Mirakel: 650 jaar*. Furthermore, the archive of the Silent Walk was inventoried, described, and given in loan to the City Archives for research; Margry, *Inventaris*.

132. Anonymous letter, Meertens Institute, BiN Collection.

133. Schenk's canvas was moved to the side chapel (originally intended for beguines), which thus became a kind of new Miracle chapel, where most of the objects from the Miracle cult were placed together.

134. Schillemans, "De Begijnhofkerk," 59–61; Dijk, *Van "Der Beghinenlande" tot Begijnhof*, 47–50.

135. Paul Post, "Goede tijden, slechte tijden," 79–80.

136. "De Stille Omgang van een protestant," in Brenninkmeijer et al., *Stilte in de stad*, 20–21.

137. Heyst, *Ik ben met jullie alle dagen*.

138. On the Occo Codex, see "The Occo Codex," edited by Jaap van Benthem, Marnix van Berchum, Anna Dieleman, Theodor Dumitrescu, and Frans Wiering, at the Computerized Mensural Music Editing Project, http://www.cmme.org/data base/projects/4. Valkestijn's edition, *Gezangen uit de Occo Codex*, was used for the service.

139. The manuscript was acquired from the estate of Baron Charles Gillès de Pélichy. It is strange that this special piece of Dutch or Amsterdam cultural heritage was not offered to a Dutch cultural institution, all the more so because the family still owns the Occo Hofje and the manuscript came from the estate of the last Amsterdam Occos. A facsimile of the manuscript was published in 1979: Bernard, *Occo Codex (Brussels, Royal Library Albert I, MS. IV. 922)*.

140. For instance, on June 18, 1966, in The Hague, against the Vietnam War; on March 24, 1967, in Amsterdam, against the Vietnam War; on April 6, 1968, in Amsterdam, after the assassination of Martin Luther King Jr.; on September 10, 1969, in Amsterdam, after the death of Ho Chi Minh; February 18, 1978, in The Hague, against apartheid in South Africa; on June 16, 1978, in Amsterdam, and in the early 1980s in various cities, as "Mothers of the Plaza de Mayo" against the Argentine regime, etc.

141. Cf. Lukken, *Rituals in Abundance*.

142. For the most extensive study of this new ritual, see Post et al., *Disaster Ritual*, 79–186.

143. Caspers and Margry, *Identiteit en spiritualiteit*, 41–90; Margry, "Civil Religion in Europe."

144. Jansen, "Stille Omgang," 79.

145. Silent marches appear to be a uniquely Dutch phenomenon; however, they have begun to occur elsewhere recently. The phenomenon seems to have spread internationally since the beginning of the 21st century, for instance, in the form of the silent marches organized by Americans Against Handgun Violence since 1996; the silent march against poverty across Westminster Bridge in London in 1996; and silent marches of UN staff after the killing of colleagues, such as for instance in New York (Baghdad victims) in 2003; and the 2004 silent march in

Birkenau to commemorate the Holocaust. In 2005 the United World Federation launched the idea of Silent Marches for the Innocent Victims of War, which were to be held simultaneously on January 20 in cities across the world.

146. This must be compared with the cross-fertilization between the Silent Walk and the silent war commemoration marches through the introduction of a fourth prayer moment during the Silent Walk when passing the monument on Dam square.

147. The archdiocese of Utrecht counted previously three hundred parishes; in 2014 only forty-nine parishes remained, and the bishop estimates that this figure would drop further to twenty to thirty parishes and churches during a period of fifteen years; see Robin de Wever, "Aartsbisdom Utrecht vreest massale sluiting rk kerken," in *Trouw*, December 12, 2014.

148. The column was temporarily removed around 2003 on account of the construction of the North-South metro line and returned to its location in 2018.

149. GSO Aerdenhout, letter dated January 24, 2000. The stone was a joint initiative of the Society and of the Vrienden van de Amsterdamse Gevelstenen (Friends of Amsterdam Façade Stones).

150. See the brochure "1345 GedachteNis Ter Heilige Stede," published in 2001, Meertens Institute, BiN-Collection; Jos Otten, "'GedachteNis' ter Heilige Stede 1345," in *Binnenstad* 35 (March 2001): 21–23.

151. Meertens Institute, BiN-Collection, text of speech by Maarten Elsenburg at the unveiling of the stone, March 11, 2001.

152. Information from the Nijmegen historian Joost Rosendaal, who carried out a participatory observation Walk together with Jan Roes and a number of Nijmegen students and witnessed this episode, in an e-mail to P. J. Margry, December 11, 2015. Van Gogh was the director of the ironic television series *De Bovenwereld* for the Humanistische Omroep (Humanist Broadcasting Corporation). In an episode called "De uitdaging van het lijden" (The challenge of suffering) (published on DVD by Column Productions in 2006), journalist Max Pam and artist Jeroen Henneman went in search of healing for Pam, who became wheelchair bound after a car accident. From a nodding and weeping statue of Mary, via the Silent Walk, they ended up in Heiloo, where Pam appeared to be reborn as a young god. Van Gogh's own performance was not filmed, or at least the AT5 archive does not contain any footage.

153. The cult was banned by both the diocese of Haarlem and the Vatican, until Bishop Bomers of Haarlem declared on June 20, 1997, that he would permit the veneration of Mary under the title of "Lady of All Nations," and his successor Punt declared on May 31, 2002, that the messages were authentic. As the apparitions and messages that remain banned constitute the shrine's raison d'être, the cult must still be regarded as banned (by the Vatican).

154. On the cult, see Margry and Caspers, *Bedevaartplaatsen in Nederland,* 1:161–70; Margry, "Paradoxes of Marian Apparitional Contestation," 182–99.

155. See on this the movement's own statement at http://www.devrouwevanal levolkeren.nl/en/the-dogma/ and a critical assessment, Munsterman, *Marie corédemptrice?*

156. The Amsterdam apparitions were assessed as "non-constat de supernaturalitate" ("it is not evident to be of supernatural origin"), which leaves some doubt, and not a "constat-not," which excludes supernaturality. As further investigations stopped after the second diocesan commission, the Vatican takes in practice the "constat-not" position. Cf. Alles, *De Vrouwe van Alle Volkeren*; Margry and Caspers, *Bedevaartplaatsen in Nederland*, 1:166–68.

157. These visits were well known in circles around the Lady and in the diocese; oral sources included the former archivist of the diocese, Anton van Veldhoven, and Jan Leechburch Auwers. For the latter, see also *Interviews met Jan Leechburch Auwers inzake de Vrouwe van Alle Volkeren* (Meertens Instituut, 2014), 31.

158. The devotion has spread far and wide across the world. It is very popular especially in the United States and the Philippines, but also in Africa and Asia. A copy of the statue of the Lady of All Nations began to weep in Akita in Japan in 1973, and it was recognized by the local bishop even before recognition was forthcoming in the Netherlands. In Canada there is a "separatist movement" (since excommunicated) that claims to represent the authentic continuation of the Lady in Amsterdam; see on this Margry, "Mary's Reincarnation and the Banality of Salvation."

159. Punt succeeded Bomers, whose powers over his diocese had been curtailed after a conflict. This led to criticism in the diocese: the vicar general, G. Geukers, thought that Punt should have declined, while the auxiliary bishop of Utrecht characterized the appointment as "a big step back to something that really isn't on anymore"; see "Mgr. Punt had voor benoeming moeten bedanken," in *Trouw*, April 4, 1995.

160. Steven Derix and Nelleke van der Heiden, "Een Mariavereerder als hoeder van de sacrale kerk," in *NRC-Handelsblad*, August 6, 2001.

161. See Alles, *De Vrouwe van Alle Volkeren*, 69–71, which includes Punt's declaration and how "all this [came to him] in prayer and theological reflection." Punt later also stated that he reviewed the case together with two confidants. This "inquiry" was partly responsible for occasioning his new insight. No public account has ever been given of this review of the existing question.

162. The Code of 1983 states in Canon 1230 that the local bishop may approve a shrine that many of the faithful visit as pilgrims for a special cause of piety. The special cause in this case is the apparitions and messages that are contrary to church teaching and that have therefore been rejected by the Vatican. The Congregation for the Doctrine of the Faith has stated, in an e-mail by P. M. Funes Diaz dated May 7, 2016, that approval of the Lady on the basis of this canon is not possible.

163. It is strange therefore that Punt declared in July 2005 that he had received an order from the Congregation for the Doctrine of the Faith to remove the controversial passage "who was once Mary" from the prayer to the Lady. No document concerning such an order can be found either in Rome or in Haarlem. The diocese (B. Putter) itself has stated, "It seems that the case was discussed and decided orally"; e-mail dated April 16, 2016. But the Congregation follows proper procedure in cases such as this one. My impression is that this was a unilateral and spontaneous initiative of Punt's in order to make the case of the Lady less contro-

versial, thus increasing the chances of a long-term toleration of the cult; cf. the ambiguous text on the diocesan website, http://www.bisdomhaarlem-amsterdam .nl/?p=oud&ids=2005/vvav_discussie (August 9, 2005).

164. The Dutch bishops' conference has always judged the case of the Lady negatively. After Punt's declaration that the Lady was authentic, there was always "an elephant in the meeting room": no one spoke about it anymore, and the subject did not appear on the agenda, nor did any colleague dare to confront Punt about it; oral communication from Bishop Tiny Muskens to P. J. Margry, April 25, 2007.

165. Communication from P. M. Funes Diaz, head of the "Disciplinare" section, in a conversation with P. J. Margry, February 2, 2016, in the offices of the Congregazione per la Dottrina della Fede. Funes said that Punt should not have issued the approval in 2002. Professor Peter Gumpel, relator of the Congregatio de Causis Sanctorum, added to this in a conversation on February 29, 2016: "What the bishop does locally is his own concern, but the Congregation is responsible for the church in general and Punt will have to conform to that. The issue of 'co-redemptrix' in the message is essential and no concession whatsoever can be made on this point."

166. The Holy Office wrote to the Bishop of Haarlem on August 25, 1961, following a request to review the case, that (in translation) it "had no reason whatsoever to review what was decided after thorough and conscientious consultations; it considers the entire question [the putative authenticity of the apparitions and messages of the Lady] resolved to the extent that there is no room for any further action." See *Analecta voor het Bisdom Haarlem* 8, no. 10 (1961): 156. A new inquiry by Zwartkruis in the 1970s was presented to the Congregation for the Doctrine of the Faith, which confirmed on May 25, 1974, that there was no question of anything supernatural. For the document in question, see Alles, *De Vrouwe*, 116–17.

167. For the texts, see Stichting Vrouwe van alle Volkeren, *De boodschappen van de Vrouwe van Alle Volkeren* (Amsterdam: Stg. VvAV, 2002), 19–21.

168. Peerdeman, *Eucharistic Experiences.*

169. The procession was organized on the somewhat contrived occasion of the fifth centenary of the granting of permission to sing the office of Corpus Christi on the feast of the Miracle in the Holy Stead, in 1504. Cf. Sterck, *De Heilige Stede*, 58–60. See also "Processie, de eerste na 1578," in *Het Parool*, March 26, 2004; "Grote opkomst bij eerste sacramentsprocessie," in *Katholiek Nieuwsblad*, June 18, 2004.

170. See the papal letter of March 22, 2004, at http://www.bisdomhaarlem -amsterdam.nl/?p=oud&ids=2004/stilleomgang4; cf. "Paus blij met sacramentsprocessie Amsterdam," in *Katholiek Nieuwsblad*, November 26, 2004.

171. In the letter of March 10, 2004, just before the Silent Walk, Pope John Paul II pointed to Mary as the supporter of the Amsterdam Eucharistic cult and ascribed to her the ominous title of "Eucharistic Lady," thus making an unambiguous link with the cult of the apparitions. The text can be found under "Documents" at https://www.rkdocumenten.nl/rkdocs/index.php?mi=600&doc=247. In relation to the Miracle of Amsterdam, the pope also confirmed that Eucharistic

processions formed the authentic testimony of the faith; there was no mention of the Silent Walk. In *Katholiek Nieuwsblad* of June 25, 2004, one of the propagandists of the Lady, the writer Robert Lemm, once again recalled Punt's inspired idea to construct a link in this way between the controversial Lady and the official cult of the Miracle.

172. Joseph Punt, "Brief van de paus over de Stille Omgang," March 22, 2004, retrieved from http://www.bisdomhaarlem-amsterdam.nl/?p=oud&ids=2004/stil leomgang.

173. The significance was further expressed by photo exhibitions and a book by M. van Ham and C. Montón Lecumberri, *God tussen ons Amsterdammers: Een terugblik op de eerste Amsterdamse Sacramentsprocessie sinds 1578* (Valkenswaard: Ho LaPress Communicatie, 2004). "Foto-expositie sacramentsprocessie," in *Katholiek Nieuwsblad*, October 21, 2005. See also photos and texts concerning the procession on the Opus Dei website at https://opusdei.org/nl-nl/article/eerste-sacramentspro cessie-in-amster dam-sinds-1578/ and https://opusdei.org/nl-nl/gallery/fotoreport age-sacraments processie-amsterdam-2018/.

174. Punt made this request to the Society. This "threat" led in 2005 to consultations between the diocese and the Society of the Silent Walk. The outcome was that both parties would respect each other's traditions as much as possible, and that both rituals would continue to exist alongside each other.

175. On this community, which was recognized in 1995, see "Work of Jesus the High Priest," *Pro Deo et Fratribus—Family of Mary* (PDF-FM), http://www .familiemariens.org/html/en/gemeinschaft.html.

176. This happened in early 2005 during a dinner at the home of chairman Elsenburg, together with a number of members of the board of the Society. The Society argued that "the Silent Walk has acquired such a unique form and significance that it would be wrong to interrupt this kind of tradition"; e-mail from Elsenburg to P. J. Margry, February 11, 2016. Punt informed Elsenburg, in a letter of January 31, 2005, that he supported Elsenburg's rejection of a merger.

177. The first Lady retreat took place there in 2013 and the first pilgrimage to the Lady on the occasion of the seventieth anniversary of the first message in 2015; see Stichting Vaak, "Vrouwe van alle Volkeren nu ook naar Heiloo?," August 26, 2013, http://stichtingvaak.blogspot.nl/2013/08/vrouwe-van-alle-volkeren-nu-ook -naar.html, and Stichting Vrouwe van alle Volkeren, "Fotoverslag van 24 mei 2015," https://www.devrouwevanallevolkeren.nl/fotoverslag-van-24-mei-2015/.

178. Family of Mary, "Het Mirakel: Het Eucharistisch wonder van Amsterdam," http://www.de-vrouwe.info/nl/het-mirakel.

179. "CDA wil religieus toerisme," in *Het Parool*, February 28, 2006; Tom Kreling, "Coffeeshophouder (CDA) tegen coffeeshops," in *NRC-Handelsblad*, February 9, 2006.

180. A similar issue occurred in 2014, when it was suggested to ask Pope Francis to confirm or recognize the apparitions in order to realize the building of a great Marian shrine. The lay initiative Stichting Lourdes aan de Amstel (Lourdes on the Amstel Foundation) (http://hetvijfdemarialedogma.nl) was established for this purpose. Cf. Alexander Bakker, "Lourdes aan de Amstel nabij," in *De Telegraaf,* December 27, 2014.

181. Paul Scheffer, "Het multiculturele drama," in *NRC-Handelsblad*, January 29, 2000, retrieved from http://retro.nrc.nl/W2/Lab/Multicultureel/scheffer .html.

182. Margry, "Nederland en het Heilig Jaar 2000," 333–52.

183. See Kenniscentrum Immaterieel Erfgoed Nederland (Dutch Centre for Intangible Cultural Heritage), http://immaterieelerfgoed.nl.

184. Parliament and the permanent parliamentary committee on education, culture, and science held debates on this topic; cf. Roodenburg, "De 'Nederlandsheid' van Nederland." Government policy in this field is implemented by the Nederlands Centrum voor Volkscultuur (Dutch Center for Popular Culture, later KIEM) and the Fonds voor Cultuurparticipatie (Cultural Participation Fund).

185. "Met geloof de straat op," in *Katholiek Nieuwsblad*, September 23, 2005.

186. Birgit Kooijman, "Maria na 427 jaar weer straat op," in *Haarlems Dagblad*, April 30, 2005.

187. Elsenburg was awarded a high papal honor, Commander in the Order of St. Gregory the Great, on the basis of his exceptional merits for church and society, for the city of Amsterdam, and especially for the significance of the Walk on a national level. See also "Vier generaties Elsenburg: Bestuurlijke ruggengraat Stille Omgang," in Brenninkmeijer et al., *Stilte in de stad*, 24–27.

188. Elsenburg was succeeded by the classicist and theologian Piet Hein Hupsch (*1949).

189. Piet Hein Hupsch, *Verkenning toekomst Stille Omgang*, memorandum dated January 4, 2011.

190. Hupsch's plan to reach out to both younger and older participants through the Walk's unique character was founded on three principles: (1) the absence of external display; (2) the twofold aspect of silent devotion amid noisy nightlife; (3) the "non-dogmatic" character of the Walk, as opposed to the theological disputes and the various factions within the Catholic Church: joint silence as a form of unifying, communal adoration.

191. Haan-Zijlstra, *Jongeren en de Stille Omgang*, 13–14.

192. Ibid., 15–19.

193. Hettie van der Ven, "Het is uitgaan met God," in *Katholiek Nieuwsblad*, February 13, 2009.

194. Another shortened Walk was held for people with a disability in 1995, but this was not repeated due to lack of interest. In the 1960s a similar Walk was held in a convoy of cars, organized by St. Liduina's Union of the Disabled; see GAA, GSO, inv. no. 6, annual report 1961, inv. no. 7, January 16, 1966, and annual report for 1966 and 1967.

195. Interviewed in Jan Repko and Rob Stallinga, "Amsterdam mirakelt voort," in *De Groene Amsterdammer*, March 15, 1995.

196. Margry, *Bloed kruipt!*, 9–10.

197. Hervieu-Léger, *Religion as a Chain of Memory*: "Religion is the ideological, symbolic and social device by which individual and collective awareness of belonging to a lineage of believers is created and controlled" (back cover).

198. Punt, "'Heiloo' krijgt missionaire taak,'" February 18, 2005, http://www .bisdomhaarlem-amsterdam.nl/?p=oud&ids=2005/heiloo.

199. Corrie Verkerk, "Deze man is zelf historie," in *Het Parool*, March 16, 2012.

200. The church located on this spot was closed for worship, and the Reformed Church sold the entire complex, including the stores, in 2007. Eventually the Amsterdam Dungeon moved into the church. Despite that fact that the Walk and the Dungeon represent more or less polar opposites—a celebration of light and hope versus a celebration of death and darkness—it did not affect the practice of the Walk; there is no evidence here of "dissonant heritage"; cf. Jildou Feenstra, *Van het Mirakel van Amsterdam tot de Amsterdam Dungeon. Een onderzoek naar de botsing tussen cultuurhistorische en commerciële belangen* (BA Thesis ACW, UvA, 2015).

201. The 2016 Silent Walk focused on the Holy Year of 2016; its intention was "Jesus—face of God's mercy—bread of grace for you." Almost all Dutch bishops made the pilgrimage to Amsterdam on March 12 to take part in the Silent Walk.

202. Announced at http://www.stille-omgang.nl/nieuws.html (no longer available), accessed January 15, 2016.

203. Despite high expectations, the Holy Year of Mercy saw a disappointing turnout of pilgrims. The number of participants is mentioned in an e-mail from P. H. Hupsch to P. J. Margry, February 10, 2016.

204. These terms come from Rudolf Otto's book *Das Heilige* (1917), which uses the terms *tremendum ac fascinosum*. The concept of "fascinans et tremendum" is therefore a misquotation, but it has gained wide currency through use in the Anglo-Saxon world.

Chapter 7.   Conflict or Consensus?

1. Reference is often made in the history of the Miracle to the burning bush featured at the beginning of the account of the calling of Moses; see Exodus 3:1–8.

2. The privilege of the imperial crown was granted to Amsterdam in return for financial support that the city gave to Maximilian. Its spurious association with the Holy Stead was a subsequent invention.

3. See chapter 4.

4. Cf. Rogier, *Het verschijnsel der culturele inertie.*

5. Bont, *Het H. Cecilia Collegie,* 5–8.

6. Rooden, *Religieuze Regimes,* 200.

7. *Hoogstbelangrijke bewijsgronden, dat de Cholera Morbus door de jezuïten in Europa gebragt is, door hen geleid, en tot hunne oogmerken aangewend wordt* (Amsterdam: no name, 1832), and published immediately after the April Movement: *Cholera-Morbus door de Jezuiten naar Europa overgebragt en tot bereiking van hun doel in de XIX eeuw aangewend* (Amsterdam: Brinkman, 1854).

8. For this term, see Bank and Buuren, *1900: Hoogtij van burgerlijke cultuur,* 419.

9. *Geschiedenis van Amsterdam,* 3:413; the Catholics' "closed shutters" are a metaphor for the tendency of Catholics to shut themselves up in their own parallel world.

10. Voets and Noord, "Het verhaal van een honderdjarige," 40; amazement at the strong love of Catholics across the Netherlands for Amsterdam and its Miracle was widespread.

11. In 1934, at the Eucharistic congress in Buenos Aires, the later Pope Pius XII, then papal legate, told Leonardus van den Broeke that the Walk was well known in the Vatican, adding, "It is the pride of Amsterdam, may this devotion remain your future"; see GAA, GSO, inv. no. 5, annual report 1955–1956.

12. As an outsider, Huysmans mentioned the great religious involvement of men in his book *Sainte-Lydwine de Schiedam*. The Society of the Walk also realized this later: "the whole country looks at this pilgrimage" because nowhere else in the world do so many men take part in a pilgrimage; see GAA, GSO, inv. no. 5, February 4, 1951. Incidentally, Flanders also had high levels of male participation.

13. Walk Chairman Van den Broeke even spoke of a "providential tradition"; he contended that thanks to this route, the Walk had, according to God's will, been permanently engraved in "the memory of the citizens of Amsterdam"; see Broeke, "De Stille Omgang en het H. H. Sacrament van Mirakel," 153.

14. Kroon, "Stille Omgang, echt Hollands."

Bibliography

Abbreviations

GAA   Amsterdam City Archives
GSO   Archives of the Society of the Silent Walk
GSOA   Archives of the Society of the Silent Walk—Addendum
KDC   Katholiek Documentatiecentrum (Catholic Documentation Centre)

Archival Sources

Amsterdam

Begijnhof Archives, archives of the rector, 1869–1990
GAA, Archives of the Begijnhof, 1389–1955
GAA, Archives of the Chapel of the Holy Stead, 1361–1578
GAA, Archives of the Society of the Silent Walk (+ addendum), 1881–1990
GAA, Archives of the St. Caecilia Collegie (no. 767), 1651, 1675–1978
GSO, addendum archives interwar years and World War II period (kept by R. C. Maagdenhuis)
Meertens Institute, BiN-Collectie, Amsterdam-Miracle of Sacrament Papers
Museum Amstelkring, "Mirakel-Collectie"
University of Amsterdam Library, Begijnhof collection

Haarlem

Noord-Hollands Archief, archives of the diocese of Haarlem, code no. 333, Amsterdam, 1915–1981

Nijmegen

KDC   Katholiek Documentatiecentrum (Catholic Documentation Centre), Radboud University

Utrecht

Archive Archdiocese of Utrecht
Museum Catharijneconvent, collections

Published Sources and Literature

Akker, J. A. van den. "Geschiedenis van het Beggijnhof te Amsterdam." *De Katholiek* 49 (1866): 281–308; 50 (1866): 89–144, 196–233; 58 (1870): 203–338.

Alardus Aemstelredamus. *Parasceve ad Sacrosanctam Synaxin, seu preparatio ad augustissimi Eucharistiae sacramenti perceptionem.* Cologne: P. Quentell, 1532.

Albers, Petrus H. *Geschiedenis van het herstel der Hiërarchie in de Nederlanden.* 2 vols. Nijmegen: Malmberg, 1903–1904.

Alkemade, Allegonda J. M. *Vrouwen XIX: Geschiedenis van negentien religieuze congregaties 1800–1850.* 's-Hertogenbosch: Malmberg, 1966.

Allard, H. J. *Laurens en Vondel, bekeerder en bekeerling.* Utrecht: Van de Weijer, 1885.

Alles, Hildegard. *De Vrouwe van alle Volkeren: De verschijning van Amsterdam: Bovennatuurlijk . . . ?* Hilversum: Stichting Vaak, 2008.

Amstelodamum Sacrum: [Bibliografie van] Het Mirakel 1345: Kerkelijke geschiedenis vóór 1578 en later. Amsterdam: C. L. van Langenhuysen, 1895.

Amsterdammer, Een. *Physiologie van Amsterdam.* Amsterdam: Leepel & Brat, 1844.

Amsterdamsch Catholijk. "Het Mirakel van Amsterdam en de viering van het vijfde eeuwgetij." *De Godsdienstvriend* 54 (1845): 190–209.

Andlau, P. K. "Die heilige Eucharistie und das Haus Habsburg." In *Bericht über den XXIII. Internationalen Eucharistischen Kongreß: Wien 12. bis 15. September 1912,* edited by Karl Kammel, 355–61. Vienna: St. Norbertus-Druckerei, 1913.

Aretz, Erich, Michael Embach, Martin Persch, and Franz Ronig, eds. *Der Heilige Rock zu Trier: Studien zur Geschichte und Verehrung der Tunika Christi.* Trier: Paulinus-Verlag, 1995.

Aristodemo, Dina, and Fernando Brugman. "The *joyeuses entrées* of 1549: The Staging of Royal Power and Civic Prestige." In *The Seventh Window,* edited by Wim de Groot, 29–37.

Asselbergs, Willem J. M. A., and Anton P. Huysmans. *Het Spel vanden Heilighen Sacramente vander Nyeuwervaert.* Zwolle: Tjeenk Willink, 1955.

Asseldonk, Gerardus A. van. *De Nederlanden en het Westers Schisma (tot 1398).* Utrecht: Dekker en Van de Vegt, 1955.

Augustinus, Aurelius. *Confessionum libri XIII.* Edited by Lucas Verheijen. Turnhout: Brepols, 1981.

Avril, Joseph. "La pastorale des malades et des mourants aux XIIe et XIIIe siècles." In *Death in the Middle Ages,* edited by Herman Braet and Werner Verbeke, 88–106. Leuven: Leuven University Press, 1983.

———. *Les statuts synodaux de Jean de Flandre, évêque de Liège (1288).* Liège: Bulletin de la Société d'art et d'histoire du diocèse de Liège, 1996.

———. *Les statuts synodaux de l'ancienne province de Reims (Cambrai, Arras, Noyon, Soissons et Tournai)*. Paris: Comité des Travaux Historiques et Scientifiques, 1995.

B., A. F. *De roomsch-katholijke godsdienst gevaarlijk voor den staat*. Amsterdam: Joh. van der Hey en Zoon, 1844.

Baelde, Michel, and Paul van Peteghem. "De Pacificatie van Gent." In *Opstand en pacificatie in de Lage Landen: Bijdrage tot de studie van de Pacificatie van Gent*, edited by Michel Baelde, and Paul van Peteghem, 1–62. Ghent: Snoeck-Ducaju / Nijgh & Van Ditmar, 1976.

Bakhuizen van den Brink, Reinier, and Johann S. Theissen. *Correspondance française de Marguerite d'Autriche, duchesse de Parme, avec Philippe II*. Vol. 1. Utrecht: Kemink, 1925.

Baldassarri, Salvatore. "Il pontificato di Urbano IV." In *Studi eucaristici: Atti della settimana internazionale di alti studi teologici e storici. Orvieto, 21–26 Settembre 1964*, edited by the Settimana Internazionale di Alti Studi Teologici e Storici, 271–84. Torino: Scaravaglio, 1966.

Bange, Petty, ed. *De doorwerking van de Moderne Devotie: Windesheim 1387–1987*. Hilversum: Verloren, 1988.

Bank, Jan. *Het roemrijk Vaderland: Cultureel nationalisme in Nederland in de negentiende eeuw*. The Hague: SDU, 1990.

Bank, Jan, and Maarten van Buuren. *1900: Hoogtij van burgerlijke cultuur*. The Hague: Sdu, 2000.

Barnard, Marcel, and Paul Post. *Ritueel bestek: Antropologische kernwoorden van de liturgie*. Zoetermeer: Meinema, 2001.

Barten, J. "Een herhaling van het Sacramentswonder van Amsterdam in 1627." *Haarlemse bijdragen* 63 (1955): 253–54.

Bastiaanse, René. *Onkuisheid: De Nederlandse biechtpraktijk 1900–1965*. Zwolle: WBooks, 2013.

Beelen, Jacob van. *Doet dit tot mijn gedachtenis: Een onderzoek naar de relaties tussen avondmaal en ambt: Over avondmaalmijding van ambtsdragers en het probleem van de bediening*. Leiden: Groen, 1996.

Beijne, Gina. "Mirakel van Amsterdam: 650 jaar traditie en verbeelding." In *Het Mirakel: 650 jaar*, edited by Guus van den Hout, Peter Jan Margry, and Robert Schillemans, 6–19.

Beringer, Franz. *Die Ablässe, ihr Wesen und Gebrauch*. 2 vols. 14th ed. Paderborn: Schöningh, 1915–16.

Bertholet, Jean. *Histoire de l'institution de la Fête-Dieu, avec la vie des bienheureuses Julienne et Eve, qui en furent les premieres promulgatrices*. Liège: Jacques-Antoine Gerlach, 1781.

Beschryvinge van het H. Sacrament van Mirakel . . . : Als mede seer veele ander schoone ende wonderlijcke mirakelen. . . . Na de kopye t'Amsterdam, by Willem Jacobssoon (1568). Rotterdam: Joannes Stichter, 1668.

Bijsterveld, Arnoud-Jan, and Charles Caspers. "Origines de l'archidiocèse de Malines." In *L'archidiocèse de Malines-Bruxelles, 450 ans d'histoire*. Vol. 1, *L'archidiocèse de Malines de la réforme catholique à la période révolutionnaire, 1559–1802*, edited by Jan De Maeyer, Eddy Put, Jan Roegiers, André Tihon, and Gerrit Vanden Bosch, 14–61. Antwerp: Halewijn, 2009.

Blackbourn, David. *Marpingen: Apparitions of the Virgin Mary in Nineteenth-Century Germany.* New York: Knopf, 1994.

Blokhuis, Marco, and A. H. P. J. van den Hout., eds. *Vroomheid op de Oudezijds: Drie Nicolaaskerken in Amsterdam: De Oude Kerk, Ons' Lieve Heer op Solder, de Sint Nicolaaskerk.* Amsterdam: De Bataafsche Leeuw, 1988.

Blom, Johan C. H., and Jacobus Talsma, eds. *De verzuiling voorbij: Godsdienst, stand en natie in de lange negentiende eeuw.* Amsterdam: Spinhuis, 2000.

Boer, Dick E. H. de, and Ludo Jongen, eds. *In het water gevonden: Het Amersfoortse Mirakelboek.* Hilversum: Verloren, 2015.

Boettcher, Susan R. "Confessionalization: Reformation, Religion, Absolutism, and Modernity." *History Compass* 2, no. 1 (2004): 1–10.

Bomans, Godfried, and Michel van der Plas. *In de kou: Over hun roomse jeugd en hoe het hen verder ging.* Bilthoven: Ambo, 1969.

Bont, Bernard J. M. de. *Het H. Caecilia Collegie, zijnde de Broederschap van het Allerheiligste Sacrament ter eere van het H. Sacrament van Mirakel van Amsterdam, met den aankleve van dien.* Amsterdam: Van Langenhuysen, 1895.

———. "Naemen van de paepsche vergaderplaetsen (te Amsterdam) soo als deselve syn opgegeven door predicanten in den'jaere 1683." *Bijdragen Haarlem* 15 (1888): 215–17.

———. "De voormalige Amsterdamsche vrouwen-kloosters." *Bijdragen Haarlem* 23 (1898): 18–50.

Boom, Bart van der. "Den Haag: De Waalsdorpervlakte: Verzet en repressie in de Tweede Wereldoorlog." In *Nederland in de twintigste eeuw,* edited by Wim van den Doel, 122–33. Amsterdam: Bert Bakker, 2005.

Boomgaard, Jan E. A. *Misdaad en Straf in Amsterdam: Een onderzoek naar de strafrechtpleging van de Amsterdamse schepenbank 1490–1552.* Zwolle: Waanders, 1992.

Bornewasser, Hans. *Kerkelijk verleden in een wereldlijke context.* Amsterdam: Van Soeren & Co. / De Bataafsche Leeuw, 1989.

———. "Ontstaan, ontvangst en heruitgave van een geruchtmakend geschiedwerk." In *Boeken als Bron,* edited by Jan Jacobs, 105–22. Tilburg: TFT, 2001.

Bos, Maarten van den. "De jaren zestig als culturele revolutie." *Tijdschrift voor Nederlandse Kerkgeschiedenis* 15, no. 4 (2012): 136–41.

———. *Verlangen naar vernieuwing: Nederlands katholicisme 1953–2003.* Amsterdam: Wereldbibliotheek, 2012.

Bosch Kemper, Jeronimo de. *Geschiedenis van Nederland na 1830.* 5 vols. Amsterdam: Witkamp/Müller, 1875–1882.

Bossy, John. "The Mass as a Social Institution, 1200–1700." *Past and Present* 100 (1983): 29–61.

Breen, J. van. "De Heilige Stede te Amsterdam." In *Het Vierenswaardig Wonder,* 71–124.

Breen, Johannes C. *Rechtsbronnen der stad Amsterdam.* The Hague: Nijhoff, 1902.

Brenninkmeijer, Jeroen, ed. *Stilte in de stad: Beleving van de Stille Omgang in Amsterdam.* Amsterdam: Gezelschap Stille Omgang, 2014.

Brink, L. "Thomas en Calvijn tezamen ter communie." *Tijdschrift voor theologie* 29 (1989): 232–49.

Broek, Hans van den. *Wonderen in het zonlicht: De medische kant van mirakelverhalen*. Deurne: Koorts en Honger, 2013.

Broeke, Leonardus van den. "De Stille Omgang en het H.H. Sacrament van Mirakel." In *Gedenkboek van het eerste Diocesane Eucharistisch Congres*, 147–57.

———. *Stille Omgang Herdenking 1881–1931*. 25th rev. ed. Amsterdam: Gezelschap Stille Omgang, 1931.

Broere, Cornelis, and Petrus van der Ploeg. *Gedichten bij het vijfde eeuwgetij van het Mirakel van Amsterdam*. Amsterdam: J. H. Laarman, 1845.

Broere's Dithyrambe op het Allerheiligste, toegelicht door J. C. Alberdingk Thijm. Amsterdam: C. L. van Langenhuysen, 1892.

Brom, Gerard. *Areopaag*. Hilversum: Paul Brand, 1923.

———. "Broere's preek in het Bagijnhof." *Bijdragen Haarlem* 61 (1946): 245–57.

———. *Cornelis Broere en de Katholieke Emancipatie*. Utrecht: Spectrum, 1955.

———. *Herleving van de kerkelike kunst in katholiek Nederland*. Leiden: Ars Catholica, 1933.

———. *Herleving van de wetenschap in katholiek Nederland*. The Hague: Ten Hagen, 1930.

———. "De schilderij op het Begijnhof." In *Het Vierenswaardig Wonder*, 193–209.

———. "Het treurspel van Derkinderens processie." *Studia Catholica* 7 (1930–1931): 102–20.

———. *Vondels geloof*. Amsterdam/Mechelen: De Spieghel/Het Kompas, 1935.

Brom, Gisbert. *Archivalia in Italië*. Vol. I-2, *Rome Vat. Archief*. The Hague: Nijhoff, 1909.

———. "De tegenpaus Clemens VII en het bisdom Utrecht." *Bijdragen en mededeelingen van het Historisch Genootschap* 28 (1907): 1–102.

Brom, Gisbert, and Antonius H. Hensen. *Romeinsche bronnen voor den kerkelijkstaatkundigen toestand der Nederlanden in de 16de eeuw*. The Hague: Nijhoff, 1922.

Bronkhorst, Alexander J. *Rondom 1853: De invoering der Rooms-Katholieke hiërarchie: De April-Beweging*. The Hague: Boekencentrum, 1953.

Browe, Peter. *Die eucharistischen Wunder des Mittelalters*. Breslau: Müller & Seiffert, 1938.

———. *Die Verehrung der Eucharistie im Mittelalter*. München: Hueber, 1933.

Brown, Callum G. "What Was the Religious Crisis of the 1960's?" *Journal of Religious History* 34, no. 4 (2010): 468–79.

Bruch, Hettel, ed. *Johannes de Beke, Croniken van den Stichte van Utrecht ende van Holland*. The Hague: Nijhoff, 1982.

Buddingh, Derk. *Mirakel-geloof en mirakelen in de Nederlanden: Historisch-letterkundige proeve, naar aanleiding van het vijfde eeuwfeest van het H. Sacrament van Mirakel*. The Hague: H. C. Susan C.Hz., 1845.

Burgers, J. W. J., and P. Knevel. *Nieuwe Maren: Een ooggetuigenverslag van de opkomst en ondergang van de wederdopers te Amsterdam 1534–1535*. Hilversum: Verloren, 2016.

Burke, Peter. *What Is Cultural History?* Malden: Polity, 2004.

Busch, Norbert. *Katholische Frömmigkeit und Moderne: Die Sozial- und Mentalitätsgeschichte des Herz-Jesu-Kultes in Deutschland zwischen Kulturkampf und Erstem Weltkrieg*. Gütersloh: Kaiser, 1997.

Bynum, Caroline Walker. "Seeing and Seeing Beyond: The Mass of St. Gregory in the Fifteenth Century." In *The Mind's Eye: Art and Theological Argument in the Middle Ages,* edited by Jeffrey F. Hamburger and Anne-Marie Bouché, 208–40. Princeton, NJ: Princeton University Press, 2006.

———. *Wonderful Blood: Theology and Practice in Late Medieval Northern Germany and Beyond.* Philadelphia: University of Pennsylvania Press, 2007.

Caesarius Heisterbacensis. *Dialogus miraculorum.* 2 vols. Edited by Joseph Strange. Cologne: Heberle, 1851.

Carasso-Kok, Marijke. *Repertorium van verhalende historische bronnen uit de middeleeuwen.* The Hague: Nijhoff, 1980.

———. "Ter ere van God en tot aanzien van de stad." In *Geschiedenis van Amsterdam,* 1:393–449.

Carasso-Kok, Marijke, and Cornelis Verkerk. "Eenheid en verdeeldheid: Politieke en sociale geschiedenis tot in de zestiende eeuw." In *Geschiedenis van Amsterdam,* 1:205–49.

Caspers, Charles. "De betekenis van de Moderne Devotie voor de Heilige Stede." In *Identiteit en spiritualiteit,* edited by Charles Caspers and Peter Jan Margry, 11–40. Hilversum: Verloren, 2006.

———. "Een verre spiegel: Juliana van Cornillon en Zuster Rosa als strijdsters voor Eerherstel." In *Een soort onschuldige hobby? Een eeuw liturgisch werk van de Norbertijnen in Nederland,* edited by Piet Al and Marc Schneiders, 45–53. Heeswijk-Dinther: Abdij van Berne, 1992.

———. "Eerherstel: De belediging van God en de ervaring van tegenslag bij rooms-katholieken, van de twaalfde tot in de twintigste eeuw." In *Of bidden helpt? Tegenslag en cultuur in West-Europa, circa 1500–2000,* Amsterdam: Amsterdam University Press, 1997.

———. *De eucharistische vroomheid en het feest van Sacramentsdag in de Nederlanden tijdens de late middeleeuwen.* Leuven: Peeters, 1992.

———. "Heilig Aduard: De Sint-Bernardusabdij als godsdienstig centrum en cultusoord." In *De abtenkroniek van Aduard,* edited by Jaap van Moolenbroek and Hans Mol, 81–106. Hilversum: Verloren, 2010.

———. "How the Sacrament Left the Church Building: Theophoric Processions as a Constituent of the Feast of Corpus Christi." In *Christian Feast and Festival: The Dynamics of Western Liturgy and Culture,* edited by Paul Post, Gerard Rouwhorst, Louis van Tongeren, and Anton Scheer, 383–403. Leuven: Peeters, 2001.

———. "Indulgences in the Low Countries, c. 1300–c. 1520." In *Promissory Notes on the Treasury of Merits: Indulgences in Late Medieval Europe,* edited by Robert N. Swanson, 65–99. Leiden: Brill, 2006.

———. "Het jaarlijks algemeen huisbezoek in katholiek Nederland rond de eeuwwisseling." *Trajecta* 4 (1995): 122–40.

———. "*Magister consensus*: Wessel Gansfort (1419–1489) und die geistliche Kommunion." In *Northern Humanism in European Context, 1469–1625: From the "Adwert Academy" to Ubbo Emmius,* edited by Fokke Akkerman, Arie J. Vanderjagt, and Adri H. van der Laan, 82–98. Leiden: Brill, 1999.

———. "Norbertus (non?) eucharisticus: Beschouwingen over Norbertus van Gennep als eucharistische heilige." In *Omgang met norbertijner heiligen:*

Achtergronden en vormgeving van de heiligenverering in de orde van Prémontré, edited by Stijn Van de Perre, 9–20. Brussels: Werkgroep Norbertijner Geschiedenis in de Nederlanden, 1998.

———. "The Original Place and Meaning of 'Corpus Christi' in the Liturgical Year." In *Il "Corpus Domini": Teologia, antropologia e politica*, edited by Laura Andreani and Agostino Paravicini Bagliani, 171–85. Firenze: SISMEL / Galluzzo, 2015.

———. "The Role of the People in the Liturgy According to the Synodal Statutes of the Ancient Dioceses of Cambrai, Liège and Utrecht (c. 1300–c. 1500)." In *Omnes circumadstantes: Contributions towards a History of the Role of the People in the Liturgy*, edited by Charles Caspers and Marc Schneiders, 155–76. Kampen: Kok, 1990,

———. "Het sacrament dat moed geeft: Grepen uit de geschiedenis van het vormsel." In *Over moed: De deugd van grenservaring en grensoverschrijding*, edited by Herman Beck and Karl-Wilhelm Merks, 115–49. Budel: Damon, 2001.

———. "The Sacrament of the Eucharist and the Conversion of Geert Grote." In *Diligens scrutator sacri eloquii: Beiträge zur Exegese- und Theologiegeschichte des Mittelalters: Festschrift Rainer Berndt*, edited by Hanns Peter Neuheuser et al., 523–36. Münster: Aschendorff, 2016.

———. "Het Sint Jansfeest in kerk- en volksgebruik." In *Getuigenis op straat: De Larense Sint Janstraditie*, edited by Leo Janssen and Karel Loeff, 121–35. Laren: Noord-Holland, 2005.

———. "Thomas von Kempen und die Kommunion: Die Stellung des vierten (dritten) Buches der Imitatio innerhalb der spätmittelalterlichen und späteren eucharistischen Frömmigkeit." In *Aus dem Winkel in die Welt: Die Bücher des Thomas von Kempen und ihre Schicksale*, edited by Ulrike Bodemann and Nikolaus Staubach, 158–72. Münster: Aschendorff, 2006.

———. "Über die Schwelle: Mittelalterliche Liturgie am Kirchenportal." *Liturgisches Jahrbuch* 63 (2013): 63–80.

———. "Van 'groot mirakel' tot 'wonder van ontmoeting': Een bijdrage tot de geschiedenis van de mariale bedevaart, in het bijzonder die van Lourdes." In *Wonderlijke ontmoetingen: Lourdes als moderne bedevaartplaats*, edited by Charles Caspers and Paul Post, 53–84. Heeswijk: Uitgeverij Abdij van Berne, 2008.

Caspers, Charles, Wolfgang Cortjaens, and Antoine Jacobs, eds. *De basiliek van Onze Lieve Vrouw van het Heilig Hart te Sittard: Architectuur—devotie—iconografie*, Sittard: Aartsbroederschap O. L. V. v.h. H. Hart, 2010.

Caspers, Charles, and Marcel Gielis. "Scherpenheuvelbedevaarten uit Noord-Brabant, in het bijzonder de (doods)kistprocessie van Breda." In *Van tweeën één: Kerk en West-Brabant door de eeuwen heen*, edited by P. H. A. M. Abels, E. H. Bary, A. J. A. Bijsterveld, and O. Thiers, 115–48. Delft: Eburon, 2001.

Caspers, Charles, and Rijcklof Hofman. *Een bovenaardse vrouw: Zes eeuwen verering van Liduina van Schiedam*. Hilversum: Verloren, 2014.

Caspers, Charles, and Peter Jan Margry. "Cults and Pilgrimage Sites in the Netherlands." In *Saints of Europe: Studies towards a Survey of Cults and Culture*, edited by Graham Jones, 29–42. Donington: Shaun Tyas Publishing, 2003.

———. *Identiteit en spiritualiteit van de Amsterdamse Stille Omgang.* Hilversum: Verloren, 2006.

———. *Het Mirakel van Amsterdam: Biografie van een betwiste devotie.* Amsterdam: Prometheus, 2017.

Caspers, Charles, and Louis van Tongeren. "Body and Feast: The Liturgical Calendar of the Old Diocese of Utrecht." In *Sanctifying Texts, Transforming Rituals: Encounters in Liturgical Studies,* edited by Paul van Geest, Marcel Poorthuis, and Els Rose, 206–37. Leiden: Brill, 2017.

Catalogus van het bruikleen van de Stichting Het Begijnhof te Amsterdam 1981. Amsterdam: Universiteit van Amsterdam, 1984.

Catalogus van Zeldzame Boeken: Bevattende werken over het Mirakel van Amsterdam, Brussel en Brugge, voorafgegaan van eenige bemerkingen op de "Bibliographische aanteekeningen over L. Marius, Amstelredams Eer ende Opcomen" van den heer J. M. F. Sterck etc. Leiden: J. W. van Leeuwen, 1900.

Ceyssens, Lucien. "Leonardus Marius in de Nederlanden (april 1633 en februari 1635)." *Bijdragen tot de geschiedenis inzonderheid van het oud hertogdom Brabant* 49 (1966): 85–94.

Chélini, Jean, and Henry Branthomme. *Les chemins de Dieu: Histoire des pèlerinages chrétiens des origines à nos jours.* Paris: Hachette, 1982.

Chiaruttini, Aldo, ed. *Het dossier van de Nederlandse Katechismus.* Amsterdam: Bruna & Zoon, 1969.

Chorus, Alfons. *De Nederlander uiterlijk en innerlijk.* Leiden: Sijthoff, 1965.

Christian, William A., Jr. "Religious Apparitions and the Cold War in Southern Europe." In *Religion, Power and Protest in Local Communities: The Northern Shore of the Mediterranean,* edited by Eric R. Wolf, 239–66. Berlin: Mouton, 1984.

Clark, Christopher, and Wolfram Kaiser, eds. *Culture Wars: Secular-Clerical Conflict in Nineteenth-Century Europe.* Cambridge: Cambridge University Press, 2003.

Clemens, Theo. *De godsdienstigheid in de Nederlanden in de spiegel van de katholieke kerkboeken 1680–1840.* 2 vols. Tilburg: Tilburg University Press, 1988.

———. "Het Mirakel van Amsterdam tussen zijn opgang in vuur en omgang in stilte: De verering in de achttiende eeuw." In *Goede en slechte tijden,* edited by Peter Jan Margry, 30–49.

Commelin, Casper. *Beschryvinge van Amsterdam.* Amsterdam: A. Wolfgang, 1693.

Coninck, Pieter de. "De natie in pacht: Katholieke minderheid, liberale onderwijspolitiek en natievorming in Duitsland en Nederland tijdens de jaren 1870." In *De eenheid en de delen: Zuilvorming, onderwijs en natievorming in Nederland 1850–1900,* edited by Henk te Velde and Hans Verhage, 57–83. Amsterdam: Het Spinhuis, 1996.

Corblet, Jules. *Histoire dogmatique, liturgique et archéologique du sacrement de l'Eucharistie.* Vol. 1. Paris: Société Générale de Librairie Catholique, 1885.

Cottiaux, Jean. "I precedenti liegesi della festa del Corpus Domini." In *Studi eucaristici: Atti della settimana internazionale di alti studi teologici e storici. Orvieto, 21–26 Settembre 1964,* edited by the Settimana Internazionale di Alti Studi Teologici e Storici, 249–70. Torino: Scaravaglio, 1966.

Cramer, Samuel, and Fredrik Pijper. *Bibliotheca Reformatoria Neerlandica: Geschriften uit den tijd der Hervorming in de Nederlanden.* Vol. 1, *Polemische geschriften der Hervormingsgezinden.* The Hague: Nijhoff, 1903.

Cremer, Marina. "Die 'Amsterdamer Monstranz' in der St. Nikolaikirche in Kalkar: Ein Goldschmiedewerk erzählt Geschichte." In *Vorträge zum Karl-Heinz-Tekath-Förderpreis 2010*, 14–45. Geldern: Historischer Verein für Geldern und Umgegend, 2010.

Cuadra Blanco, Juan Rafael de la. "King Philip of Spain as Solomon the Second: The Origins of Solomonism of the Escorial in the Netherlands." In *The Seventh Window*, edited by Wim de Groot, 169–80.

Cubitt, Geoffrey. *The Jesuit Myth: Conspiracy Theory and Politics in Nineteenth-Century France*. Oxford: Oxford University Press, 1993.

Cuypers, Pierre. "Het stadion te Amsterdam bij gelegenheid van het Euch. Congres." *Het Gildeboek: Orgaan van het St. Bernulphus-Gilde* 7 (1924): 75–77.

Cuypers, Pierre J. H., and Jan Kalf. *De Katholieke kerken in Nederland: Dat is de tegenwoordige staat der kerken met hunne meubeling en versiering beschreven en afgebeeld*. Amsterdam: Van Holkema & Warendorf, 1906.

Dam, Peter van. *Staat van verzuiling: Over een Nederlandse mythe*. Amsterdam: Wereldbibliotheek, 2011.

Damen, Mario J. M. "Vorstelijke vensters: Glasraamschenkingen als instrument van devotie, memorie en representatie (1419–1519)." *Jaarboek voor middeleeuwse geschiedenis* 8 (2005): 140–200.

Damme, Jan van. "The Donation of the Seventh Window: A Burgundian-Habsburg Tradition and the Role of Viglius van Aytta." In *The Seventh Window*, edited by Wim de Groot, 131–44.

Dankbaar, Willem F. *Communiegebruiken in de eeuw der Reformatie*. Groningen: Instituut voor Liturgiewetenschap, 1986.

Deen, Femke A. *Moorddam: Publiek debat en propaganda in Amsterdam tijdens de Nederlandse Opstand (1566–1578)*. Amsterdam: Instituut voor Cultuur en Geschiedenis, 2012.

Dekker, Alfred. "De lotgevallen van het orgel van de H. Stede te Amsterdam." *Mens en Melodie* 25 (1970): 247–50, 318.

Delvigne, Ad., ed. *Mémoires de Martin Antoine Del Rio sur les troubles des Pays-Bas durant l'administration de Don Juan d'Autriche, 1576–1578*. 3 vols. Brussels: Société de l'Histoire de Belgique, 1869–1871.

Delville, Jean-Pierre. *Fête-Dieu (1246–1996)*. Vol. 2, *Vie de Sainte Julienne de Cornillon*. Louvain-la-Neuve: Institut d'Études Médiévales de l'Université Catholique de Louvain, 1999.

Dequeker, Luc. *Het Sacrament van Mirakel: Jodenhaat in de Middeleeuwen*. Leuven: Davidsfonds, 2000.

Derks, Marjet. *Heilig moeten: Radicaal-katholiek en retro-modern in de jaren twintig en dertig*. Hilversum: Verloren, 2007.

———. "Manifestaties van katholieke fierheid: Het Olympisch Stadion in Amsterdam." In *Aan plaatsen gehecht*, edited by Jan Jacobs, Lodewijk Winkeler, and Albert van der Zeijden, 609–25.

Derksen, Hyacinthus. *Critisch-analytische toelichting van Prof. Broere's Dithyrambe op het Allerheiligste Sacrament van Mirakel*. Amsterdam: C. L. van Langenhuysen, 1874.

Descamps, Geneviève. "L'adoration du Saint-Sacrement à Port-Royal." *Chroniques de Port-Royal* 43 (1994): 25–39.

Detzler, Wayne. "Protest and Schism in Nineteenth Century German Catholicism: The Ronge-Czerski Movement 1844–5." In *Schism, Heresy and Religious Protest*, edited by Derek Baker, 341–50. Cambridge: Cambridge University Press, 1972; repr. 2008.

Diercxsens, Joannes Carolus. *Antverpia Christo nascens et crescens*. Vol. 5, 1567–1579. Antwerp: Joannes Henricus van Soest, 1773.

Dierickx, Mich. *Documents inédits sur l'érection des nouveaux diocèses aux Pays-bas (1521–1570)*. Vol. 1, *Des premiers projets sous Charles-Quints à la promulgation des bulles de circonscription et de dotation (1521-août 1561)*. Brussels: Palais des Académies, 1960.

———. *De oprichting der nieuwe bisdommen in de Nederlanden onder Filips II, 1559–1570*. Antwerp: Spectrum, 1950.

Dijk, Ger van. *Van "Der Beghinenlande" tot Begijnhof: De geschiedenis van het Begijnhof van 1307 tot heden*. Amsterdam: Begijnhof, 2004.

Dirkse, Paul. *Begijnen, pastoors en predikanten: Religie en kunst in de Gouden Eeuw*. Leiden: Primavera, 2001.

Driedonkx, Guus. *Het Sint Franciscus Liefdewerk (S.F.L.) te Amsterdam: Ontstaan en geschiedenis, 1894–1974*. Nijmegen: printed privately, 2013.

Dudok van Heel, Sebastien A. C. "Amsterdamse schuil- of huiskerken." *Holland* 25 (1993): 1–10.

———. "Uit Goethe-Dante-Vondelen gaan: Opkomst van de katholieke Amsterdamse geschiedschrijving in de negentiende eeuw." *Jaarboek Amstelodamum* 79 (1986): 100–34.

———. *Van Amsterdamse burgers tot Europese aristocraten: Hun geschiedenis en hun portretten: De Heijnen-maagschap 1400–1800*. The Hague: Koninklijk Nederlandsch Genootschap voor Geslacht- en Wapenkunde, 2008.

Duerloo, Luc, and Werner Thomas. *Albrecht & Isabella 1598–1621*. Turnhout: Brepols, 1998.

Duijnstee, Franciscus-Xaverius P. D. *Jubelend Nederland rondom het H. Sacrament van Mirakel*. Amsterdam: 't Kasteel van Aemstel, 1935.

Duinkerken, Anton van. "De plechtige processie met het Allerheiligste." In *Het Vierenswaardig Wonder*, 210–15.

Ebertz, Michael N. "Die Organisierung von Massenreligiosität im 19. Jahrhundert; Soziologische Aspekte zur Frömmigkeitsforschung." *Jahrbuch für Volkskunde* 2 (1979): 38–72.

Eeghen, Isabella H. van. "Het begijnhof te Amsterdam." *Haarlemse bijdragen* 62 (1953): 203–14.

———. *Dagboek van Broeder Wouter Jacobsz (Gualtherus Jacobi Masius), prior van Stein*. 2 vols. Groningen: Wolters, 1959–1960.

———. *Vrouwenkloosters en begijnhof in Amsterdam van de 14e tot het eind der 16e eeuw*. Amsterdam: H. J. Paris, 1941.

———. "Willem Jacobsz in Engelenburgh en de mirakelboekjes." In *Festschrift Hellinga: Forty-three Studies in Bibliography Presented to Prof. Dr. Wytze Hellinga*, edited by Anthonie Croiset van Uchelen, 169–78. Amsterdam: Israel, 1980.

Eeuwfeest van het Herstel der bisschoppelijke hiërarchie in Nederland: Toespraken bij de nationale viering in Utrecht en Nijmegen gehouden. Utrecht: Spectrum, 1953.

Eijnatten, Joris van, and Fred van Lieburg. *Nederlandse religiegeschiedenis.* Hilversum: Verloren, 2005.

Elias, Johan E. *Geschiedenis van het Amsterdamsche regentenpatriciaat.* The Hague: Nijhoff, 1923.

Enno van Gelder, Hendrik. *De noodmunten van de Tachtigjarige Oorlog.* The Hague: Staatsdrukkerij, 1955.

Epistolae missionariorum ordinis S. Francisci ex Frisia et Hollandia. Quaracchi: Collegium S. Bonaventurae, 1888.

Essen, Léon van der. *Alexandre Farnèse: Prince de Parme, gouverneur général des Pays-Bas (1545–1592).* 5 vols. Brussels: Nouvelle Société d'Éditions, 1933–1937.

[Estré, Jean G.F.]. *Beknopt geschiedkundig verhaal van het beroemd Mirakel, waarmede God de Stad Amsterdam heeft vereerd en verheven.* 's-Hertogenbosch: Gebr. Van Langenhuysen, 1832.

————. *Historie van het Amsterdamsche Mirakel, voor hen die zelf willen onderzoeken en oordeelen.* Amsterdam: C. L. van Langenhuysen, 1845.

Eucharistisch congresboek: Eerste Eucharistisch Congres voor het bisdom Haarlem, Amsterdam 19, 20, 21 en 22 October 1922. Amsterdam: 't Kasteel van Aemstel, 1922.

Het Evangelische Visnet, bevattende sommige veranderde liedjes uit het zelve, andere uit de Evangelische Triumph-Wagen, Zingende zwaan, en anderen. Amsterdam: F. J. van Tetroode, 1794.

Fokkens, Martine, and Louise Fokkens. *Ouwehoeren: Verhalen uit de peeskamer.* Amsterdam: Bertram & De Leeuw, 2011.

Fontaine Verwey, H. de la. "Herinneringen van een bibliothecaris, 4. Het Mirakelboekje." *De boekenwereld* 2 (1985–1986): 74–79.

Franceschini, Ezio. "Origine e stile della bolla *Transiturus.*" In *Studi eucaristici: Atti della settimana internazionale di alti studi teologici e storici. Orvieto, 21–26 Settembre 1964,* edited by the Settimana Internazionale di Alti Studi Teologici e Storici, 285–317. Torino: Scaravaglio, 1966.

François, Wim. "Die 'Ketzerplakate' Kaiser Karls in den Niederlanden und ihre Bedeutung für Bibelübersetzungen in der Volkssprache: Der 'Proto-Index' von 1529 als vorläufiger Endpunkt." *Dutch Review of Church History* 84 (2004): 198–247.

Fredericq, Paul, *Codex documentorum sacratissimarum indulgentiarum neerlandicarum: Verzameling van stukken betreffende de pauselijke aflaten in de Nederlanden (1300–1600).* The Hague: Nijhoff, 1922.

————. *Corpus documentorum inquisitionis haereticae pravitatis Neerlandicae: Verzameling van stukken betreffende de pauselijke en bisschoppelijke inquisitie in de Nederlanden.* 5 vols. Ghent: Vuylsteke / The Hague: Nijhoff, 1889–1902.

Frijhoff, Willem. *Embodied Belief: Ten Essays on Religious Culture in Dutch History.* Hilversum: Verloren, 2002.

————. "De paniek van juni 1734." *Archief voor de geschiedenis van de katholieke kerk in Nederland* 19 (1977): 170–233.

————. "Shifting Identities in Hostile Settings: Towards a Comparison of the Catholic Communities in Early Modern Britain and the Northern Netherlands." In *Catholic Communities in Protestant States,* edited by Kaplan et al., 1–17.

Frijhoff, Willem, and Marijke Spies. *1650: Bevochten eendracht*. The Hague: Sdu Uitgevers, 1999.

Frijhoff, Willem, and Bas van der Vlies. *De Nederlandse identiteit: Feit of fictie? Tekst van de Johan de Witt-lezing, gegeven op donderdag 9 oktober 2008 in de Augustijnenkerk te Dordrecht*. Dordrecht: Stichting Dordtse Academie, 2008.

Fühner, Jochen A. *Die Kirchen- und antireformatorische Religionspolitik Kaiser Karls V. in den siebzehn Provinzen der Niederlande 1515–1555*. Leiden: Brill, 2004.

Gachard, Louis Prosper. *Collections des voyages des souverains des Pays Bas*. 4 vols. Brussels: Hayez, 1876–1881.

Gawronski, Jerzy, and Jørgen Veerkamp. *Zerken en graven in de Nieuwezijds Kapel: Inventariserend veldonderzoek Rokin (2005)*. Amsterdam: Bureau Monumenten & Archeologie, 2007.

Gedenk-Album: Herinnering aan het XXVIIste Internationaal Eucharistisch Congres gehouden te Amsterdam, 22–27 Juli 1924. Haarlem-Leiden: Spaarnestad/Ars Catholica, 1924.

Gedenkboek van het eerste Diocesane Eucharistisch Congres in het Bisdom Haarlem, Amsterdam, 19, 20, 21 en 22 October 1922. Amsterdam: 't Kasteel van Aemstel, 1922.

Gedenkboek van het nationaal Maria-Congres gehouden te Nijmegen 6, 7 en 8 augustus 1932. Den Bosch: G. Mosmans, 1934.

Gedenkboek van het XXVIIe Internationaal Eucharistisch Congres gehouden te Amsterdam van 22 tot 27 juli 1924, edited by Henry D'Yanville and W. van Dijk. Amsterdam: 't Kasteel van Aemstel, 1925.

Gedenkschrift van het 25-jarig bestaan van het Genootschap "De Stille Omgang" te Haarlem. Haarlem: n.p., 1932.

Geschiedenis van Amsterdam. 4 parts in 5 vols. Edited by Marijke Carasso-Kok, Maarten Prak, Willem Frijhoff, Remieg A. M. Aerts, Piet de Rooy, Barend J. van Benthem, Doeko Bosscher, and Salvador Bloemgarten. Amsterdam: SUN, 2004–2007.

Geschiedenis van het H. Sacrament van Mirakel en van de Kapel de H. Stede: benevens het verhaal van de merkwaardige wonderen geschied tot Ao 1578. Amsterdam: Borg, 1887.

Gielis, Gert, and Violet Soen. "The Inquisitorial office in the Sixteenth-Century Habsburg Low Countries: A Dynamic Perspective." *Journal of Ecclesiastical History* 66 (2015): 47–66.

Ginkel, Rob van. *Rondom de stilte: Herdenkingscultuur in Nederland*. Amsterdam: Bert Bakker, 2011.

Glaudemans, Ronald, and Jos Smit. "Een andere kijk op de architectuur- en bouwgeschiedenis van de Kapel ter Heilige Stede." *Jaarboek Amstelodamum* 94, no. 6 (2007): 19–31.

Goddijn, Walter, Jan Jacobs, and Gerard van Tillo. *Tot vrijheid geroepen: Katholieken in Nederland 1945–2000*. Baarn: Ten Have, 1999.

Godeau, Antoine. *Meditatien over 't allerheiligsten Sacrament des Altaers, om voor de geduurige aenbidders van dit mysterie alle uuren van den dag en nacht te gebruiken: Ook heel dienstig om zich tot de H. Communie te bereiden*. Antwerp: Voor Hendrik van Rhyn te Delft, 1692.

Gorris, Gerardus. *J. G. Le Sage ten Broek en de eerste faze van de emancipatie der katholieken*. 2 vols. Amsterdam: Urbi & Orbi, 1947–1949.

Gouw, Johannes ter. *Geschiedenis van Amsterdam*. 8 vols. Amsterdam: Scheltema & Holkema, 1879–1893.

Graaf, Jacobus J. "Uit de Levens der 'Maechden van den Hoeck' te Haarlem." *Bijdragen Haarlem* 18 (1893): 197–258.

———. "De 'Vergaderinghe der Maechden van den Hoeck' te Haarlem." *Bijdragen Haarlem* 35 (1913): 383–463.

Greeve, H. T. M. de. *Zó werkt en wroet Rusland: Rapport samengesteld naar aanleiding van de Russische spionnage in Canada in 1946*. Amsterdam: ENUM, 1948.

Groenveld, Simon. *Huisgenoten des geloofs: Was de samenleving in de Republiek der Verenigde Nederlanden verzuild?* Hilversum: Verloren, 1995.

Groot, Frans. "Papists and Beggars: National Festivals and Nation Building in the Netherlands during the Nineteenth Century." In *Nation and Religion: Perspectives on Europe and Asia*, edited by Peter van der Veer and Hartmut Lehmann, 161–77. Princeton: Princeton University Press, 1999.

———. "De strijd rond Alva's bril: Papen en geuzen bij de herdenking van de inname van Den Briel, 1572–1872." *Bijdragen en Mededelingen betreffende de Geschiedenis der Nederlanden* 110 (1995): 161–81.

Groot, Wim de. "Habsburg Patronage and the Particular Situation of the Emperor's and King's Windows during the Dutch Revolt." In *The Seventh Window*, edited by Wim de Groot, 153–68.

———, ed. *The Seventh Window: The King's Window Donated by Philip II and Mary Tudor to Sint Janskerk in Gouda (1557)*. Hilversum: Verloren, 2005.

Grosheide, Greta. *Verhooren en vonnissen der wederdoopers betrokken bij de aanslagen op Amsterdam in 1534 en 1535*. Amsterdam: Johannes Müller, 1920.

Gy, Pierre-Marie. "Office liégeois et office romain de la Fête-Dieu." In *Fête-Dieu (1246–1996)*, vol. 1, *Actes du colloque de Liège, 12–14 septembre 1996*, edited by André Haquin, 117–26. Louvain-la-Neuve: Institut d'Études Médiévales, 1999.

Haan-Zijlstra, Evalien de. "Jongeren en de Stille Omgang Amsterdam, 2006–2012." Master's thesis. Leiden: Geschiedenis RU Leiden, 2013.

Hakkert, Tijs. "Het geluid van een omgang: Een beschouwing over de Stille Omgang in de periode 1945–1988." *Skript, historisch tijdschrift* 10 (1988): 131–42.

Haks, Donald. *Vaderland en vrede 1672–1713: Publiciteit over de Nederlandse Republiek in oorlog*. Hilversum: Verloren, 2013.

Harris, Ruth. *Lourdes: Body and Spirit in the Secular Age*. London: Penguin, 1999.

Haslinghuis, Edward J. *De duivel in het drama der middeleeuwen*. Leiden: Van der Hoek, 1912.

Headley, John M., Hans J. Hillerbrand, and Anthony J. Papalas, eds. *Confessionalization in Europe, 1555–1700: Essays in Honor and Memory of Bodo Nischan*. Aldershot: Ashgate, 2004.

Heel, Dalmatius van, and Bonfilius Knipping. *Van schuilkerk tot zuilkerk: Geschiedenis van de Mozes en Aäronkerk te Amsterdam*. Amsterdam: Urbi et Orbi, 1941.

Heesakkers, Chris L., and Wilhelmina G. Kamerbeek, eds. *Carmina Scholastica Amstelodamensia: A Selection of Sixteenth Century School Songs from Amsterdam*. Leiden: Brill, 1984.

Heijden, Laurens van der. *De schaduw van de jezuïet: Een pathologie van de Franse publieke opinie tijdens de schoolstrijd van 1841–1845.* Amsterdam: n.p., 2004.

Heijden, Marinus J. M. van der. *De dageraad van de emancipatie der katholieken: De Nederlandsche katholieken en de staatkundige verwikkelingen uit het laatste kwart van de achttiende eeuw.* Nijmegen: De Koepel, 1947.

Helbig, Jean. "L'iconographie eucharistique dans le vitrail belge." In *Studia eucharistica DCCi anni a condito festo Sanctissimi Corporis Christi 1246–1946,* edited by Stephanus Axters, 369–78. Bussum: Paul Brand / Antwerp: De Nederlandsche Boekhandel, 1946.

Helbig, Jean, and Yvette Vanden Bemden. *Les vitraux de la première moitié du XVIe siècle conservés en Belgique: Brabant et Limbourg.* Ghent: Erasmus, 1974.

Hens, Harrie, H. van Bavel, G. C. M. van Dijck, and J. H. M. Frantzen, eds. *Mirakelen van Onze Lieve Vrouw te 's-Hertogenbosch 1381–1603.* Tilburg: Zuidelijk Historisch Contact, 1978.

Hensen, Antonius H. L. *In den Hollandschen tuin.* Utrecht: Van Rossum, 1930.

———. *De twee eerste bisschoppen van Haarlem.* Hilversum: Paul Brand, 1927.

Hermesdorf, Bernard H. D. *Rechtsspiegel: Een rechtshistorische terugblik in de Lage Landen van het herfsttij.* Nijmegen: Dekker & Van de Vegt, 1980.

Hervieu-Léger, Danièle. *Religion as a Chain of Memory.* Cambridge: Polity, 2000.

Herwaarden, Jan van. *Opgelegde bedevaarten: Een studie over de praktijk van opleggen van bedevaarten (met name in de stedelijke rechtspraak) in de Nederlanden gedurende de late middeleeuwen (ca. 1300–ca. 1550).* Amsterdam: Van Gorcum, 1978.

Hesseveld, Petrus J. *Overwegingen bij het H. Sakrament des Altaars, gedurende het Octaaf van het Vijfde Eeuwfeest van het Mirakel van Amsterdam, mede geschikt voor het jaarlijksche Feest van Mirakel en andere Uren van Aanbidding.* Amsterdam: J. J. van Spanje en J. S. de Haas, 1845.

H[eukelom], J. P. *Het feest der dwaasheid gevierd op het vijfde eeuwgetijde van het mirakel te Amsterdam van 5 tot 12 Maart 1845: Dichterlijke uitboezeming.* Amsterdam: J. Tak, 1845.

Heussen, Hugo Franciscus van. *Batavia Sacra, of Kerkelyke Historie en Oudheden van Batavia . . . .* 3 vols. Antwerp: Christianus Vermey, 1715–1716.

Heyst, Eugène van, ed. *Ik ben met jullie alle dagen: Opstellen over de Eucharistie.* Nijmegen: Centrum voor Parochiespiritualiteit, 2006.

Hier beghint die vindinghe vant hoochweerdighe ende heylighe Sacrament, int vier ende vlam miraculoselijck ongequest ende geheel geconserveert, het welke rustende is binnen der stadt van Aemstelredam ende die plaetse wert ghenoemt der Heyliger stede. Amsterdam: Willem Jacobszoon, 1568.

Historische Tentoonstelling van Amsterdam, gehouden in den Zomer van 1876 [catalog]. Amsterdam: C. L. van Langenhuysen, 1876.

Hofman, J. H. "Het kerspel buiten de Witte-Vrouwenpoort te Utrecht bij zijn ontkiemen." *Archief voor de geschiedenis van het aartsbisdom Utrecht* 26 (1900): 91–96.

Homan, Gerlof D. "Catholic Emancipation in the Netherlands." *The Catholic Historical Review* 52, no. 2 (1966): 201–11.

Hoogewoud, Guido. "Katholiek en protestantse kerkgebouwen als merktekens van het verleden: Geel en Oranje, geel versus oranje." *Jaarboek Amstelodamum* 90 (1998): 39–60.

Hoogland, A. J. J. "Nog een ooggetuige der Haarlemsche Noon." *Bijdragen Haarlem* 8 (1880): 128–33.

Hoppenbrouwers, Frans J. M. *Oefening in volmaaktheid: De zeventiende-eeuwse rooms-katholieke spiritualiteit in de Republiek.* The Hague: Sdu, 1996.

Houkes, Annemarie. "Het succes van 1848: Politiek in de aprilbeweging." In *Staf en Storm,* edited by Jurjen Vis and Wim Janse, 87–104.

Hous, Jan-Baptist. *Leuvense Kroniek (1780–1829).* Heverlee: Abdij van Park, 1964.

Hout, Guus van den. "Museum Amstelkring, de mirakelkist en de Nieuwezijds Kapel." In *Het Mirakel: 650 jaar,* edited by Guus van den Hout, Peter Jan Margry, and Robert Schillemans, 35–45.

———. "Een Rooms-Katholiek Museum voor Amsterdam: De geschiedenis van museum Amstelkring." In *Vroomheid op de Oudezijds: Drie Nicolaaskerken in Amsterdam: De Oude Kerk, Ons' Lieve Heer op Solder, de Sint Nicolaaskerk,* edited by Marco Blokhuis, Peter van Dael, Guus van den Hout, and Jos Sterk, 75–99. Amsterdam: De Bataafsche Leeuw, 1988.

Hout, Guus van den, Peter Jan Margry, and Robert Schillemans, eds. *Het Mirakel: 650 jaar Mirakel van Amsterdam 1345–1995.* Aerdenhout: Gezelschap Stille Omgang, 1995.

Houtepen, Anton. "Rome of Noordwijkerhout? De conflicten in rooms-katholiek Nederland na 1950." In *Kerk en conflict: Identiteitskwesties in de geschiedenis van het Christendom,* edited by Willemien Otten and W. J. van Asselt, 184–205. Zoetermeer: Meinema, 2002.

Hüffer, Maria. *Bronnen voor de geschiedenis der abdij Rijnsburg.* The Hague: Nijhoff, 1951.

Hugo, Hermannus. *Obsidio Bredana, armis Philippi IIII auspiciis Isabelaae ductu Ambr. Spinolae perfecta.* Antwerp: Officina Plantiniana, 1626.

———. *The Siege of Breda.* London: Iudocus Dooms, 1627.

Huys, Bernard, ed. *Occo Codex (Brussels, Royal Library Albert I, Ms. IV.922).* Utrecht: Vereniging voor Nederlandse Muziekgeschiedenis, 1979.

Huysmans, Joris-Karl. *Sainte-Lydwine de Schiedam.* Paris: P.-V. Stock, 1901.

Israel, Jonathan Irvine. *The Dutch Republic: Its Rise, Greatness, and Fall, 1477–1806.* Oxford: Clarendon Press, 1995.

Jacobs, Jan, Lodewijk Winkeler, and Albert van der Zeijden, eds. *Aan plaatsen gehecht: Katholieke herinneringscultuur in Nederland.* Nijmegen: Valkhof Pers, 2012.

Jager, Jozef L. de. "Het R C Jongensweeshuis tussen 1780 en 1820." *Jaarboek Amstelodamum* 75 (1983): 106–38.

Janse, Antheun, and Mirjam van Veen. "Kerk en vroomheid." In *Den Haag: Geschiedenis van de stad,* vol. 1, *Vroegste tijd tot 1574,* edited by Johannes G. Smit, 215–70, 338–39. Zwolle: Waanders, 2004.

Janse, Herman. *De Oude Kerk te Amsterdam: Bouwgeschiedenis en restauratie.* Zwolle: Waanders, 2004.

Jansen, Jacques. "Stille Omgang: Een zoeken naar samenleving. Plechtigheden en morele verontwaardiging rondom 'zinloos geweld.'" In *Zinloos geweld herdacht,* edited by E. D'Hondt, 65–79. Baarn: Gooi & Sticht, 2000.

Janssens, Gustaaf. *Brabant in het verweer: Loyale oppositie tegen Spanje's bewind in de Nederlanden van Alva tot Farnese, 1567–1578.* Kortrijk: UGA, 1989.

———. *"Superexcellat autem misericordia iudicium:* The Homily of François Richardot on the Occasion of the Solemn Announcement of the General Pardon in the Netherlands (Antwerp, 16 July 1570)." In *Public Opinion and Changing Identities in the Early Modern Netherlands: Essays in Honour of Alastair Duke,* edited by Judith Pollmann and Andrew Spicer, 107–24. Leiden: Brill, 2007.

Jappe Alberts, Wybe. *De ordinarii van Kampen uit de 15de en 16de eeuw.* Groningen: Wolters, 1961.

Jentjens, Leonard. *Van strijdorgaan tot familieblad: De tijdschriftjournalistiek van de Katholieke Illustratie 1867–1968.* Amsterdam: Otto Cramwinckel, 1995.

Jong, Alpita de. "Godsdienst als 'kittelig plek' aan het lichaam der natie: Joast Halbertsma (1789–1869) en het religieus gevoel in de vroege negentiende eeuw." *De negentiende eeuw* 34, no. 2 (2010): 125, 138–39.

Jong, Jan de, and Wilhelmus L. S. Knuif. *Philippus Rovenius en zijn bestuur der Hollandsche zending.* Utrecht: Aartsbisdom, 1925.

Jong, Tjebbe de, and Anique de Kruijf, eds. *Van Bolswert naar Antwerpen: Gouden Eeuwgravures naar Bloemaert, Rubens en Van Dijck.* Bolsward: Titus Brandsma Museum, 2013.

Jongen, Ludo, and Fred van Kan. "Amersfoort en de doornenkroon: Over een bijzondere relikwie in laat-middeleeuws Amersfoort." *Flehite: Historisch jaarboek voor Amersfoort en omstreken* 4 (2003): 10–33.

Jongh, Jane de. *Margaretha van Oostenrijk.* Amsterdam: Querido, 1946.

Jongkees, Adriaan Gerard. *Staat en kerk in Holland en Zeeland onder de Bourgondische hertogen, 1425–1477.* Groningen: Wolters, 1942.

Joosting, Jan G. C., and Samuel Muller, eds. *Bronnen voor de geschiedenis der kerkelijke rechtspraak in het bisdom Utrecht in de Middeleeuwen.* Vol. 2, *De indeeling van het bisdom.* The Hague: Nijhoff, 1915.

———, eds. *Bronnen voor de geschiedenis der kerkelijke rechtspraak in het bisdom Utrecht in de Middeleeuwen.* Vol. 5, *Provinciale en synodale statuten / Seendrechten.* The Hague: Nijhoff, 1914.

Kannegieter, Jan Z. "De weg der oude Mirakelprocessie en de jaarlijkse stille omgang." *Amstelodamum, maandblad voor de kennis van Amsterdam* 21 (1934): 34–37.

Kaplan, Benjamin. "In Equality and Enjoying the Same Favor: Biconfessionalism in the Low Countries." In *A Companion to Multiconfessionalism in the Early Modern World,* edited by Thomas Max Safley, 99–126. Leiden: Brill, 2011.

———. "Integration vs Segregation: Religiously Mixed Marriage and the 'verzuiling' Model of Dutch Society." In *Catholic Communities in Protestant States,* edited by Kaplan et al., 48–66.

Kaplan, Benjamin J., Bob Moore, Henk van Nierop, and Judith Pollmann, eds. *Catholic Communities in Protestant States: Britain and the Netherlands c. 1570–1720.* Manchester: Manchester University Press, 2009.

[Kappeyne van de Coppello, Johannes]. *Aan wien is de eigendom der N. Z. Kapel? Aan de . . . wethouder voor de Publieke Werken*. Amsterdam: n.p., 1899.

Kaschuba, Wolfgang. *Einführung in die Europäische Ethnologie*. München: C. H. Beck, 2006.

De Katholieke Encyclopedie. 25 vols. Amsterdam: Joost van den Vondel / Antwerp: Standaard-Boekhandel, 1949–1955.

Kempers, Bram. "Assemblage van de Nederlandse leeuw: Politieke symboliek in heraldiek en verhalende prenten uit de zestiende eeuw." In *Openbaring en bedrog: De afbeelding als historische bron in de Lage Landen*, edited by Bram Kempers, 60–100. Amsterdam: Amsterdam University Press, 1995.

———. "Het enigma van de kroon." In *Representatie: Kunsthistorische bijdragen over vorst, staatsmacht, en beeldende kunst, opgedragen aan Robert W. Scheller*, edited by Johann-Christian Klamt and Kees Veelenturf, 125–35. Nijmegen: Valkhof Pers, 2004.

———. "Loyalty and Identity in the Low Countries: Regional, National and Global Imagery in the Sixteenth Century." In *The Power of Imagery: Essays on Rome, Italy and Imagination*, edited by Peter van Kessel, 31–47. Rome: Apeiron, 1992.

Kerkhoff, Antonius van. *Na veertig jaren: Een terugblik op het herstel der bisschoppelijke hiërarchie en zijne gevolgen in Nederland*. Vlaardingen: Coebergh, 1893.

Kesteren, Ronald van. *Het verlangen naar de middeleeuwen: De verbeelding van een historische passie*. Amsterdam: Wereldbibliotheek, 2004.

Klönne, Bernhard H. *Amstelodamensia*. Amsterdam: F. H. J. Bekker, 1894.

———. *Marius gehandhaafd*. Leiden: J. W. van Leeuwen, 1885.

[———]. *Het mirakel van Amsterdam: Met gebeden en litanieën, benevens 10 afbeeldingen naar aloude voorstellingen van het mirakel*. Amsterdam: C. L. van Langenhuysen, 1895.

Knippenberg, Hans. *De religieuze kaart van Nederland: Omvang en verspreiding van de godsdienstige gezindten vanaf de Reformatie tot heden*. Assen: Van Gorcum, 1992.

Knipping, John B. *Iconography of the Counter Reformation in the Netherlands: Heaven on Earth*. 2 vols. Nieuwkoop: De Graaf, 1974.

Knuttel, Willem P. C. *De toestand der Nederlandsche katholieken ten tijde der Republiek*. 2 vols. The Hague: Nijhoff, 1892–1894.

Kölker, Albertus J. *Alardus Aemstelredamus en Cornelius Crocus, twee Amsterdamse priester-humanisten: Hun leven, werken en theologische opvattingen: Bijdrage tot de kennis van het humanisme in Noord-Nederland in de eerste helft van de zestiende eeuw*. Nijmegen: Dekker & Van de Vegt, 1963.

Kok, Jacobus. *Amsterdams eer en opkomst, door middel der gezegende Hervorming, geschied in den jaare MDLXXVIII. . . .* Amsterdam: Jacobus Kok, 1778.

Koomen, Arjan de. "Een lamentatio over een lapidarium: De Nieuwezijds Kapel in de Rijksmuseumtuin." *Bulletin van het Rijksmuseum* 55 (2007): 299–331.

Korff, Gottfried. "Politischer 'Heiligenkult' im 19. und 20. Jahrhundert." *Zeitschrift für Volkskunde* 71 (1975): 202–20.

Kossmann, Ernst H. *De Lage Landen 1780–1980: Twee eeuwen Nederland en België*. 2 vols. Amsterdam: Elsevier, 1986.

Krieger, Karl-Friedrich. *Rudolf von Habsburg*. Darmstadt: Wissenschaftliche Buchgesellschaft, 2003.

Kronenburg, Joannes A. F. *Maria's Heerlijkheid in Nederland*. 8 vols. Amsterdam: Bekker, 1904–31.

Kroon, Ben. "Stille Omgang, echt Hollands." *De Tijd*, March 21, 1966.

Kruijf, Anique C. de. "'Gods mirakel machmen sien': Het mirakel van Amsterdam in woord en beeld in de veertiende, vijftiende en zestiende eeuw." *Jaarboek Amstelodamum* 97 (2005): 49–83.

Kruitwagen, Bonaventura. "Het *Speculum exemplorum*." *Bijdragen Haarlem* 29 (1905): 329–453.

Kuys, Jan. *Kerkelijke organisatie in het middeleeuwse bisdom Utrecht*. Nijmegen: Valkhof Pers, 2004.

———. *Repertorium van collegiale kapittels in het middeleeuwse bisdom Utrecht*. Hilversum: Verloren, 2014.

Laan, P. H. J. van der, ed. *Oorkondenboek van Amsterdam tot 1400*. Amsterdam: Israel, 1975.

Lamberts, Emiel, ed. *The Black International 1870–1878: The Holy See and Militant Catholicism in Europe*. Leuven: Leuven University Press, 2002.

Landheer, Hugo A. *Kerkbouw op krediet: De financiering van de kerkbouw in het aartspriesterschap Holland en Zeeland en de bisdommen Haarlem en Rotterdam tussen 1795 en 1965*. Amsterdam: Aksant, 2004.

Lans, Michael J. A. *Het leven van pater Bernard: Priester van den congregatie des Allerheiligsten Verlossers, doctor in de godgeleerdheid*. 4th ed. Amsterdam: C. L. van Langenhuysen, 1905.

Lansink, Lydia, and Peter van Dael. *De Nieuwe Krijtberg: Een neogotische droom*. Amsterdam: Stichting Frans Dubois Fonds, 1993.

Lautenschütz, Karel J. H. "Het Mirakel in de historische literatuur." In *Het Vierenswaardig Wonder*, 39–70.

Leesberg, Joannes F. A. "Herinnering bij het vijfde eeuwgetij van het Mirakel van Amsterdam." *De Katholiek* 7 (1845): 217–20.

Leeuwen, Charles van. *Hemelse voorbeelden: De heiligenliederen van Joannes Stalpart van der Wiele, 1579–1630*. Nijmegen: SUN, 2001.

Lefèvre, Placide. "A propos d'une bulle d'indulgence d'Eugène IV en faveur du culte eucharistique à Bruxelles." In *Recueil des travaux de l'Institut historique belge de Rome*, 163–68. Brussels: Lamertin, 1931.

Lesger, Clé. *Handel in Amsterdam ten tijde van de Opstand: Kooplieden, commerciële expansie en verandering in de ruimtelijke economie van de Nederlanden, ca. 1550–ca. 1630*. Hilversum: Verloren, 2001.

Leuven, Liendke Paulina. *De boekhandel te Amsterdam door katholieken gedreven tijdens de Republiek*. Epe: Hooiberg, 1951.

Long, Isaac le. *Historische beschryvinghe van de Reformatie der Stadt Amsterdam*. Amsterdam: Johannes van Septeren, 1729.

Lubac, Henri de. *Corpus mysticum: The Eucharist and the Church in the Middle Ages*. Notre Dame, IN: University of Notre Dame Press, 2013.

Lukken, Gerard. *Rituals in Abundance: Critical Reflections on the Place, Form and Identity of Christian Ritual in Our Culture*. Leuven: Leuven University Press, 2005.

Lurz, Friedrich. *Die Feier des Abendmahls nach der Kurpfälzischen Kirchenordnung von 1563: Ein Beitrag zu einer ökumenischen Liturgiewissenschaft*. Stuttgart: Kohlhammer, 1998.

Luther, Martin. *Am tag des heiligen warleichnams Christi, Euangelion Johannis: VI.* In *D. Martin Luthers Werke, Kritische Gesamtausgabe*, 17: 742–58. Weimar: Böhlau, 1927.

"Lyste van alle gheboden vier-daghen, abstinentie-daghen ende vasten-daghen, in het bisdom van Haerlem, mitsgaders van alle daghen van veertich daghen aflaet." *Bijdragen Haarlem* 10 (1882): 266–72.

Maag, Karin, and John Witvliet, eds. *Worship in Medieval and Early Modern Europe.* Notre Dame, IN: University of Notre Dame Press, 2004.

Maas, Nop. *De literaire wereld van Carel Vosmaer: Een documentaire.* The Hague: Sdu, 1989.

Margry, Peter Jan. *Amsterdam en het mirakel van het heilig sacrament: Van middeleeuwse devotie tot 20e-eeuwse stille omgang.* Amsterdam: Polis, 1988.

———. "Bedevaartrevival? Bedevaartcultuur in het Bataafs-Franse Nederland (1795–1814)." *Trajecta* 3 (1994): 209–32.

———. *Bloed kruipt! Over de culturele hemoglobine van de samenleving.* Amsterdam: Universiteit van Amsterdam, 2014.

———. "Civil Religion in Europe: Silent Marches, Pilgrim Treks and Processes of Mediatization." *Ethnologia Europaea* 41, no. 2 (2011): 5–23.

———. "Dutch Devotionalisation: Reforming Piety: Grassroots Initiative or Clerical Strategy?" In *The Dynamics of Religious Reform in Northern Europe, 1780–1920*, vol. 3, *Piety and Modernity*, edited by Anders Jarlert, 125–56, 187–90. Leuven: Leuven University Press, 2012.

———, ed. *Goede en slechte tijden: Het Amsterdamse Mirakel van Sacrament in historisch perspectief.* Aerdenhout: Gezelschap Stille Omgang, 1995.

———. "Imago en Identiteit: De problematische manifestatie van 'het katholieke' in de Nederlandse samenleving rond het midden van de negentiende eeuw." In *Staf en Storm*, edited by Jurjen Vis and Wim Janse, 64–86.

———. "In Memoriam Miraculi: Jubelfeesten rond het Amsterdamse sacramentsmirakel." In *Het Mirakel: 650 jaar*, edited by Guus van den Hout, Peter Jan Margry, and Robert Schillemans, 20–34.

———. *Inventaris van het archief van het Gezelschap van de Stille Omgang te Amsterdam, 1881–1990.* Aerdenhout: Gezelschap Stille Omgang, 1995.

———. "Jezuïetenstreken: De attributie van bedrog en de constructie van mythen in het Nederland van de 19e eeuw." *De Negentiende Eeuw* 28 (2004): 39–64.

———. "Het Martelveld te Brielle: De creatie van een sacraal katholiek baken in het 'protestants' Hollandse landschap." In *Tot stantvastighijt in haer gelooff: De Martelaren van Gorcum: geestelijken in Gorinchem—slachtoffers in Den Briel—heiligen in Rome*, edited by Lies van Aelst, Viorica van der Roest and Aron de Vries, 13–43. Gorinchem: Historische Vereniging Oud Gorcum, 2014.

———. "Mary's Reincarnation and the Banality of Salvation: The Millennialist Cultus of the Lady of All Nations/Peoples." *Numen, International Review for the History of Religions* 59 (2012): 486–508.

———. "Nederland en het Heilig Jaar 2000: Verslag en evaluatie." *Trajecta* 10 (2001): 333–52.

———. "Paradoxes of Marian Apparitional Contestation: Networks, Ideology, Gender, and the Lady of All Nations." In *Moved by Mary: The Power of Pilgrim-*

age in the Modern World, edited by Anna-Karina Hermkens, Willy Jansen, and Catrien Notermans, 182–99. Aldershot: Ashgate, 2009.

———. *Teedere Quaesties: Religieuze rituelen in conflict: Confrontaties tussen katholieken en protestanten rond de processiecultuur in 19e-eeuws Nederland.* Hilversum: Verloren, 2000.

———. "Transformatie van Bedevaart naar Processie: De Larense Sint Jansverering in de negentiende en twintigste eeuw." In *Getuigenis op straat: De Larense Sint Janstraditie,* edited by Leo Janssen and Karel Loeff, 33–57. Wormer: Noord-Holland, 2005.

Margry, Peter Jan, and Charles Caspers, eds. *Bedevaartplaatsen in Nederland.* 4 vols. Amsterdam: Meertens Instituut / Hilversum: Verloren, 1997–2004.

Margry, Peter Jan, and Johan Joor. *St. Caecilia Collegie: Muziek en Mirakel in Amsterdam.* Aerdenhout: Gezelschap Stille Omgang, 2006.

Margry, Peter Jan, and Henk te Velde. "Contested Rituals and the Battle for Public Space: The Netherlands." In *Culture Wars: Secular-Clerical Conflict in Nineteenth-Century Europe,* edited by Christopher Clark and Wolfram Kaiser, 129–51, 347–50. Cambridge: Cambridge University Press, 2003.

Marius, Leonardus. *Amstelredams eer ende opcomen, door de denckwaerdighe miraklen aldaer geschied, aen ende door het H. Sacrament des Altaers: Anno 1345.* Antwerp: Hendrick Aertssens, 1639.

———. *Getijden van het Allerheiligste Sakrament des Altaars: Met het eigen feestoctaaf voor het Hoogwaardig Sakrament van Mirakel te Amsterdam.* The Hague: Van Langenhuysen, 1869.

———. *Getyden van het H. ende Hoogh-waerdigh Sacrament des Altaers: Soo in 't gemeijn, als voor de stadt van Amsterdam: Met een aenwijsingh om met devoti de H. Misse te horen.* Antwerp: Hendrick Aertssens, 1640.

———. *Getyden van het Heylig ende Hoogh-waerdigh Sacrament des Altaers, Soo in 't gemeyn, als voor de Stadt van Amsterdam: Met een aenwysingh om met Devotie de H. Misse te hooren.* Amsterdam: Gerardus van Bloemen, 1717.

———. *Kerkelijke getyden van de hoogwaerdige Moeder Gods, zo als die in de Roomse Kerk in 't gebruik zyn.* Antwerp: Hendrick Aertssens, 1651.

Marnef, Guido. "Le Brabant dans la tourmente." In *Histoire du Brabant du duché à nos jours,* edited by Raoul Van Uytven et al., 291–307. Zwolle: Waanders, 2004.

Martin, Thomas M. "Das Bild Rudolfs von Habsburg als 'Bürgerkönig' in Chronistik, Dichtung und moderner Historiographie." *Blätter für deutsche Landesgeschichte* 112 (1976): 203–28.

Mathijsen, Marita. *Historiezucht: De obsessie met het verleden in de negentiende eeuw.* Nijmegen: Vantilt, 2013.

Matuszak, Juliane. *Das Speculum exemplorum als Quelle volkstümlicher Glaubensvorstellungen des Spätmittelalters.* Siegburg: Schmitt, 1967.

McLeod, Hugh. *The Religious Crisis of the 1960s.* Oxford: Oxford University Press, 2007.

Meder, Theo. *Sprookspreker in Holland: Leven en werk van Willem van Hildegaersberch (circa 1400).* Amsterdam: Prometheus, 1991.

Meertens, Pieter Jacobus. "Geloof en volksleven." In *Meertens over de Zeeuwen: Zeeuwse studies uitgegeven naar aanleiding van zijn tachtigste verjaardag,* edited by Marinus P. de Bruin, 169–81. Middelburg: Fanoy, 1979.

Meertens, Pieter Jacobus, et al., eds. *Biografisch woordenboek van het socialisme en de arbeidersbeweging in Nederland.* Amsterdam: IISG, Aksant, 1986–2003.

Meijer, D. C., Jr. *Wandeling door de zalen van de Historische Tentoonstelling van Amsterdam.* Amsterdam: J. M. E. Meijer & G. H. Meijer, 1876.

Melker, Bas de. "Burgers en devotie 1340–1520." In *Geschiedenis van Amsterdam,* 1:251–311.

———. *Metamorfose van stad en devotie: Ontstaan en conjunctuur van kerkelijke, religieuze en charitatieve instellingen in Amsterdam in het licht van de stedelijke ontwikkeling, 1385–1435.* Amsterdam: Universiteit van Amsterdam, 2002.

———, ed. *Oorkondenboek van Amsterdam tot 1400: Supplement.* Hilversum: Verloren, 1995.

Mellink, Albert F. *Amsterdam en de wederdopers in de zestiende eeuw.* Nijmegen: SUN, 1978.

———. "Anabaptism at Amsterdam after Munster." In *The Dutch Dissenters: A Critical Companion to Their History and Ideas,* edited by Irvin B. Horst, 127–42. Leiden: Brill, 1986.

———. *Documenta Anabaptistica Neerlandica.* Vol. 2, *Amsterdam (1536–1578).* Leiden: Brill, 1980.

———. *Documenta Anabaptistica Neerlandica.* Vol. 5, *Amsterdam (1531–1536).* Leiden: Brill, 1985.

Meloni, Sergio. *I Miracoli Eucaristici e le radici cristiane dell'Europa.* Bologna: Studia Domenicano, 2005.

Memorie volgens het origineel van de Processie van 't H. Sacrament van Mirakel uyt de H. Stede tot Amsterdam. Amsterdam: Gerardus van Bloemen, 1737.

Merz, G. *Ultramontaansche wonderziekte in de tweede helft der negentiende eeuw.* Purmerend: J. Schuitemaker, 1873.

Meuwissen, Daantje, ed. *Jacob Cornelisz van Oostsanen (ca. 1475–1533): De Renaissance in Amsterdam en Alkmaar.* Zwolle: Waanders, 2014.

Molanus, Joannes. *De historia SS. imaginum et picturarum pro vero earum usus contra abusus.* Antwerp: Gaspar Bellerus, 1617.

———. *Natales sanctorum Belgii et eorundem chronica recapitulatio.* Leuven: Ioannes Masius & Philippus Zangrius, 1595.

———. *Traité des saintes images.* Edited by François Boespflug, Olivier Christin, and Benoît Tassel. Paris: Cerf, 1996.

Molkenboer, Bernardus H., ed. *Altaergeheimenissen: Ontvouwen in drie boeken door J. V. V.* Utrecht: Dekker & Van de Vegt, 1942.

———. "Het Vierenswaerdigh Wonder in Vondels Poëzie 1345–1645–1945." In *Het Vierenswaardig Wonder,* 125–46.

Moll, Willem. *Kerkgeschiedenis van Nederland vóór de Hervorming.* Vol. 2, part 4. Utrecht: Kemink, 1869.

Moreau, Rudolf von. *Zur Geschichte der Eucharistischen Kongresse.* München: n.p., 1959.

Mulisch, Harry. *Bericht aan de Rattenkoning.* Amsterdam: Bezige Bij, 1966.

Munsterman, Hendro. *Marie corédemptrice? Débat sur un titre marial controversé.* Paris: Cerf, 2006.

Muskens, Tiny. *Wees niet bang: Het levensverhaal van bisschop Tiny Muskens verteld aan Arjan Broers.* Nijmegen: Valkhof Pers, 2004.

Nadorp, Paul. "Een lopende geschiedenis: Over de religieuze betekenis van pelgrimstochten, in casu de Pax Christi-voettochten Den Bosch: 1958–1983." *Jaarboek van het Katholiek Documentatie Centrum* 22 (1992): 129–47.

Nanning, Joannes. *Twee predikatiën op den jaarlykschen gedenkdag van het wonder der Heilige Stede, gedaan binnen Amsteldam.* Amsterdam: Theodorus Crajenschot, 1750.

Neerlandia Catholica of Het Katholieke Nederland: Ter herinnering aan het gouden priesterfeest van Z. D. Paus Leo XIIII. Utrecht: P. W. van de Weijer, 1888.

Newman, Barbara. "The Life of Juliana of Cornillon." In *Living Saints of the Thirteenth Century,* edited by Anneke B. Mulder-Bakker, 143–302. Turnhout: Brepols, 2011.

Nierop, Henk van. "Van wonderjaar tot Alteratie, 1566–1578." In *Geschiedenis van Amsterdam,* 1:451–81.

Nieuwenhuis, Willibrord. "De stad van het mirakel A.D. 2345." In *Eucharistisch congresboek,* 38–40.

Nijsten, Gerard J. M. *Volkscultuur in de late middeleeuwen: Feesten, processies en (bij) geloof.* Utrecht: Kosmos, 1994.

Nolet, Willem. "Historische zekerheid." In *Het Vierenswaardig Wonder,* 20–38.

Noordegraaf, Leo, and Gerrit Valk. *De Gave Gods: De pest in Holland vanaf de late middeleeuwen.* Bergen: Octavo, 1988.

Noordeloos, Pieter. *Pastoor Maarten Donk.* Vol. 2, *1567–1590.* Utrecht: Spectrum, 1948.

———. *De restitutie der kerken in den Franschen tijd.* Nijmegen: Dekker & Van der Vegt, 1937.

Nouwens, Jac. *De veelvuldige H. Communie in de geestelijke literatuur der Nederlanden vanaf het midden van de 16e eeuw tot in de eerste helft van de 18e eeuw.* Bilthoven: Nelissen / Antwerpen: 't Groeit, 1952.

Nübel, Otto. *Pompejus Occo, 1483 bis 1537: Fuggerfaktor in Amsterdam.* Tübingen: Mohr, 1972.

Nußbaum, Otto. *Die Aufbewahrung der Eucharistie.* Bonn: Hanstein, 1979.

Otto, Rudolf. *Das Heilige: Über dat Irrationale in der Idee des Göttlichen und sein Verhältnis zum Rationalen.* Gotha: Klotz, 1917.

Palm, Jos. *Moederkerk: De ondergang van rooms Nederland.* Amsterdam: Contact, 2012.

Parker, Charles H. *Faith on the Margins: Catholics and Catholicism in the Dutch Golden Age.* Cambridge, MA: Harvard University Press, 2008.

Parker, Geoffrey. *The Grand Strategy of Philip II.* New Haven, CT: Yale University Press, 1998.

Pas, Niek. *Imaazje! De verbeelding van Provo (1965–1967).* Amsterdam: Wereldbibliotheek, 2003.

Pauli, Matthias. *Vier historien van het H. Sacrament van Mirakel: 1. In de Abdije van Hercken-rode in t'landt van Luyck. 2. Ten Augustijnen tot Gendt. 3. S. Goedelen tot Brussel. 4. Ten Augustijnen tot Loven. Verciert met veel schoon leeringe, bevestight met veelderhande exempelen ende historien van 't H. Sacrament des Autaers.* Antwerp: Geeraerdt van Wolfschaten, 1620.

Peerdeman, Ida. *Eucharistic Experiences.* Edited by Josef Künzli. Jestetten: Miriam-Verlag, 1987.

Peijnenburg, Jan W. M. *Joannes Zwijsen, bisschop, 1794–1877.* Tilburg: Stichting Zuidelijk Historisch Contact, 1996.

———. *Judocus Smits en zijn Tijd.* Nijmegen: KDC, 1976.

Perry, Jos. *Ons Fatsoen als Natie: Victor de Stuers 1843–1916.* Amsterdam: SUN, 2004.

Perry, Nicholas, and Loreto Echeverría. *Under the Heel of Mary.* London: Routledge 1988.

Pijper, Fredrik. *Middeleeuwsch Christendom: De vereering der H. Hostie: De godsoordeelen.* The Hague: Nijhoff, 1907.

Pitra, Jean-Baptiste. *La Hollande catholique.* Paris: Bibliothèque Nouvelle, 1850.

Plas, Michel van der. *Daarom, mijnheer, noem ik mij katholiek: Biografie van Anton van Duinkerken (1903–1968).* Amsterdam: Anthos, 2000.

———. *Vader Thijm: Biografie van een koopman-schrijver.* Amsterdam: Anthos, 1995.

Pluym, Antonius. J. *Het H. Sacrament van Mirakel en de H. Stede te Amsterdam: Historisch-kritische proeve, ter gelegenheid van het vijfde eeuwfeest.* Amsterdam: H. A. Zweers, 1845.

Pluym, Antonius J., and Josephus A. Alberdingk Thijm. *Het H. Sacrament van Mirakel en de H. Stede te Amsterdam: Historisch kritische proeve.* Amsterdam: Van Langenhuysen, 1869.

Pollmann, Judith. "Burying the Dead; Reliving the Past: Ritual, Resentment and Sacred Space in the Dutch Republic." In *Catholic Communities in Protestant States,* edited by Kaplan et al., 84–102.

Polman, Pontianus. *Godsdienst in de Gouden Eeuw.* Utrecht: Spectrum, 1947.

———. *Katholiek Nederland in de achttiende eeuw.* 3 vols. Hilversum: Paul Brand, 1968.

———. *Romeinse bronnen voor de kerkelijke toestand der Nederlanden onder de apostolische vicarissen 1592–1727.* Vol. 3, *1686–1705.* The Hague: Nijhoff, 1952.

Pontificale Romanum. Brussels: Le Charlier, 1741.

Porteman, Karel, and Mieke B. Smits-Veldt. *Een nieuw vaderland voor de muzen: Geschiedenis van de Nederlandse literatuur 1560–1700.* Amsterdam: Bert Bakker, 2008.

Post, Paul. "Goede tijden, slechte tijden: Devotionele rituelen tussen traditie en moderniteit." In *Goede en slechte tijden,* edited by Peter Jan Margry, 62–80.

Post, Paul, R. L. Grimes, A. Nugteren, P. Pettersson, and H. Zondag, eds. *Disaster Ritual: Explorations of an Emerging Ritual Repertoire.* Leuven: Peeters, 2003.

Post, Regnerus R. "Karel V' Formula Reformationis en haar toepassing in Nederland 1548–1549." *Mededeelingen der Koninklijke Nederlandsche Akademie van Wetenschappen, afd. Letterkunde,* new series, 10 (1947): 173–97.

———. *Kerkelijke verhoudingen in Nederland vóór de Reformatie.* Utrecht: Spectrum, 1954.

———. *Kerkgeschiedenis van Nederland in de Middeleeuwen.* 2 vols. Utrecht: Spectrum, 1957.

———. "Het Sacrament van Mirakel te Amsterdam." *Studia Catholica* 30 (1955): 241–61.

Processtukken inzake de Nederduitsch Hervormde Gemeente te Amsterdam contra de Gemeente Amsterdam. Amsterdam, n.p., 1900.

Raak, Ronald van. *In naam van het volmaakte: Conservatisme in Nederland in de negentiende eeuw van Gerrit Jan Mulder tot Jan Heemskerk Azn.* Amsterdam: Wereldbibliotheek, 2001.

Raedts, Peter. "Amsterdam: de Heilige Stede, 1345. Ommegangen en mirakelen." In *Plaatsen van Herinnering: Nederland van prehistorie tot Beeldenstorm,* edited by Wim Blockmans and Herman Pleij, 291–301. Amsterdam: Bert Bakker, 2007.

———. "Katholieken op zoek naar een Nederlandse identiteit, 1814–1898." *Bijdragen en Mededelingen betreffende de Geschiedenis der Nederlanden* 107 (1992): 713–25.

———. *De ontdekking van de middeleeuwen: Geschiedenis van een illusie.* Amsterdam: Wereldbibliotheek, 2011.

———. "Le Saint Sacrement du Miracle d'Amsterdam: Lieu de mémoire de l'identité catholique." In *Lieux de mémoire et identités nationales,* edited by Pim den Boer and Willem Frijhoff, 237–51. Amsterdam: Amsterdam University Press, 1993.

———. "Vier pleidooien voor het Mirakel." In *Goede en slechte tijden,* edited by Peter Jan Margry, 50–61.

Ramakers, Bart A. M. *Spelen en figuren: Toneelkunst en processiecultuur in Oudenaarde tussen Middeleeuwen en Moderne Tijd.* Amsterdam: Amsterdam University Press, 1996.

Reen, Ton van. *In het donkere zuiden.* Amsterdam: Contact, 1988.

Ridder, Barend de. "De mirakelkist." *Jaarboek Amstelodamum* 50 (1963) 54–61.

Riemsdijk, Thedorus van. *De tresorie en kanselarij van de graven van Holland en Zeeland uit het Henegouwsche en Beyersche Huis.* The Hague: Nijhoff, 1908.

Righart, Hans. *De eindeloze jaren zestig: Geschiedenis van een generatieconflict.* Amsterdam: Arbeiderspers, 1995.

———. *De katholieke zuil in Europa: Het ontstaan van verzuiling onder katholieken in Oostenrijk, Zwitserland, België en Nederland.* Amsterdam: Boom, 1986.

Rogier, Louis J. *Beschouwing en onderzoek: Historische studies.* Utrecht: Spectrum, 1954.

———. *Geschiedenis van het katholicisme in Noord-Nederland in de 16e en de 17e eeuw.* 3 vols. 2nd ed. Amsterdam: Urbi & Orbi, 1947.

———. *Katholieke herleving: Geschiedenis van Katholiek Nederland.* The Hague: Pax, 1956.

———. *Schrikbeeld van een staatsgreep in 1853.* Amsterdam: Noord-Hollandsche Uitgevers Maatschappij, 1959.

———. *Het verschijnsel der culturele inertie bij de Nederlandse katholieken.* Amsterdam: Urbi & Orbi, 1958.

Rogier, Louis J., and Nicolaas de Rooy. *In vrijheid herboren: Katholiek Nederland 1853–1953.* The Hague: Uitgeversmij Pax, 1953.

Rooden, Peter van. "Kerk en religie in het confessionele tijdperk." In *Veelvromige dynamiek: Europa in het ancien régime, 1450–1800,* edited by Willem Frijhoff and Leo Wessels, 374–402. Amsterdam: SUN, 2006.

———. "*Oral history* en het vreemde sterven van het Nederlandse Christendom." *Bijdragen en Mededelingen betreffende de Geschiedenis der Nederlanden* 119 (2004): 524–51.

————. *Religieuze Regimes: Over godsdienst en maatschappij in Nederland, 1570–1990*. Amsterdam: Bert Bakker, 1996.

————. "Secularization, Dechristianization and Rechristianization in the Netherlands." In *Säkularisierung, Dechristianisierung, Rechristianisierung im neuzeitlichen Europa: Bilanz und Perspektiven der Forschung*, edited by Hartmut Lehmann, 131–53. Göttingen: Vandenhoeck & Ruprecht, 1997.

Roodenburg, Herman. "De 'Nederlandsheid' van Nederland: Een nieuw project aan het Meertens Instituut." *Volkskunde: Tijdschrift over de cultuur van het dagelijkse leven* 113 (2012): 203–12.

————. *Onder censuur: De kerkelijke tucht in de gereformeerde gemeente van Amsterdam, 1578–1700*. Hilversum: Verloren, 1990.

————. "'Splendeur et magnificence': Processions et autres célébrations à Amsterdam au XVIe siècle." *Revue du Nord* 69 (1987): 515–33.

————. "Het verleden opgepoetst. Pastoor Klönne, het 'folklore' en de zestiende-eeuwse sacramentsprocessies." In *Goede en slechte tijden*, edited by Peter Jan Margry, 17–29.

Roon, Marije van, and Bas Rutgerink. "Begijnhof Amsterdam: Eigendom van de paden." Master's thesis, Amsterdam University, 2001.

Rooy, Piet de. *Openbaring en openbaarheid*. Amsterdam: Wereldbibliotheek, 2009.

————. *Republiek van rivaliteiten: Nederlands sinds 1813*. Amsterdam: Mets & Schilt, 2002.

Rosenberg, H. P. R. *De 19de-eeuwse kerkelijke bouwkunst in Nederland*. The Hague: Staatsuitgeverij, 1972.

Rovenius, Philippus. *Officia Sanctorum Archiepscopatus Ultraiectensis, digesta iuxta normam Breviarii Romani*. Leuven: Bernardinus Masius, 1623.

————. *Officia Sanctorum Archiepiscopatus Ultrajectensis et Episcopatuum Suffraganeorum, Harlemensis, Daventriensis, Leovardiensis, Groeningensis et Middelburgensis, digesta ad normam breviarii Romani*. Cologne: Johannes Kinckius, 1640.

Rubin, Miri. *Corpus Christi: The Eucharist in Late Medieval Culture*. Cambridge: Cambridge University Press, 1991.

————. *Gentile Tales: The Narrative Assault on Late Medieval Jews*. New Haven, CT: Yale University Press, 1999.

Rüter, A. J. C. *Rapporten van de gouverneurs in de provinciën 1840–1849*. Vol. 3. Utrecht: Kemink en zoon, 1950.

Rutgers, Carel A. *Jan van Arkel: Bisschop van Utrecht*. Groningen: Wolters-Noordhof, 1970.

S.r. *Wat moet ik gelooven van het Mirakel van Amsterdam? Eene vraag van een Roomsch Katholieke aan Roomschen en Onroomschen, na het lezen van hetgeen over dat Mirakel door Isaak le Long in zijne Historische Beschrijvinge van de Reformatie der Stadt Amsterdam, beschreven is*. Amsterdam: G. J. D'Ancona, [ca. 1845].

Safley, Thomas Max, ed. *A Companion to Multiconfessionalism in the Early Modern World*. Leiden: Brill, 2011.

Schenk, Magdalena G. *Amsterdam, stad der vroomheid*. Bussum: Kroonder, 1948.

Schepper, Hugo de. "Repressie of clementie in de Nederlanden onder Karel V en Filips II." In *Een rijk gerecht: Opstellen aangeboden aan P. L. Nève*, edited by Beatrix C. M. Jacobs and E. C. Coppens, 341–64. Nijmegen: Gerard Noodt Instituut, 1998.

Schieder, Wolfgang. *Religion und Revolution: Die Trierer Wallfahrt von 1844*. Vierow: SH-Verlag, 1996.

Schillemans, Robert. "De Begijnhofkerk als de nieuwe Heilige Stede: Uitbeeldingen van het Mirakelwonder in de H. H. Joannes en Ursulakerk te Amsterdam." In *Het Mirakel: 650 jaar*, edited by Guus van den Hout, Peter Jan Margry, and Robert Schillemans, 46–63.

Schneider, Bernhard. "Presse und Wallfahrt: Die publizistische Verarbeitung der Trierer Hl.-Rock-Wallfahrt von 1844." In *Der Heilige Rock zu Trier*, edited by Erich Aretz et al., 291–96.

———. "Wallfahrt, Ultramontanismus und Politik: Studien zu Vorgeschichte und Verlauf der Trierer Hl.-Rock-Wallfahrt von 1844." In *Der Heilige Rock zu Trier*, edited by Erich Aretz et al., 237–80.

Schoutens, Stephanus. *Geschiedenis van den Eerdienst van het Allerheiligste Sacrament des Altaars in België*. 3rd ed. Antwerp: Van Os–De Wolf, 1902.

Schutte, Gerrit Jan. *Het Calvinistisch Nederland: Mythe en werkelijkheid*. Hilversum: Verloren, 2000.

Slijpen, Aloysius, Reinier Welschen, Eduard Brom, and Leonardus van den Broeke, eds. *Congresboek officieel programma*. Amsterdam: De Tijd, 1924.

Sluijter, Ronald. "Rooms-katholieke broederschappen in Nederland in de negentiende eeuw: Betekenis, omvang en verspreiding van een onderschat fenomeen." *Trajecta* 22 (2013): 349–75.

Smit, Johannes G. *Vorst en onderdaan: Studies over Holland en Zeeland in de late middeleeuwen*. Leuven: Peeters, 1995.

Snoep, Derk P. *Praal en propaganda: Triumfalia in de Noordelijke Nederlanden in de 16de en 17de eeuw*. Alphen aan de Rijn: Visdruck, 1975.

Soen, Violet. "De reconciliatie van 'ketters' in de zestiende-eeuwse Nederlanden (1520–1590)." *Trajecta* 14 (2005): 337–62.

———. "Reconquista and Reconciliation in the Dutch Revolt: The Campaign of Governor-General Alexander Farnese (1578–1592)." *Journal of Early Modern History* 16 (2012): 1–22.

Spaans, Joke. *De Levens der Maechden: Het verhaal van een religieuze vrouwengemeenschap in de eerste helft van de zeventiende eeuw*. Hilversum: Verloren, 2012.

———. "Stad van vele geloven, 1578–1795." In *Geschiedenis van Amsterdam*, 2-1:385–467.

Spiertz, Mathieu. "De katholieke geestelijke leiders en de wereldlijke overheid in de Republiek der Zeven Provinciën." *Trajecta* 2 (1993): 3–20.

Spohnholz, Jesse. "Confessional Coexistence in the Early Modern Low Countries." In *A Companion to Multiconfessionalism in the Early Modern World*, edited by Thomas Max Safley, 47–73. Leiden: Brill, 2011.

Spruyt, Bart Jan. *Cornelis Henrici Hoen (Honius) and His Epistle on the Eucharist (1525): Medieval Heresy, Erasmian Humanism and Reform in the Early Sixteenth-Century Low Countries*. Leiden: Brill, 2006.

Statutorum synodalium ecclesiae Cameracensis. Pars prima. Paris: Marc Bordelet, 1739.

Steenwijk, Michaël A. van. *Beknopt verhaal van het Mirakel te Amsterdam, met bijlage van den brief ter uitschrijving van het jubilé*. Amsterdam: A. Zweesaardt en zn., 1845.

Steinruck, Josef. "Die Heilig-Rock-Wallfahrt von 1844 und die Entstehung des Deutschkatholizismus." In *Der Heilige Rock zu Trier*, edited by Erich Aretz et al., 307–24.

Sterck, Jan F. M. "Aanteekeningen over 16e-eeuwsche Amsterdamsche portretten." *Oud-Holland* 43 (1926): 249–66.

———. "Bij de slooping der Heilige Stede." *Katholieke Illustratie*, July 18, 1918: 353, 355–57.

———. "Het boekje *Amstelredams eer ende opcomen, door de gedenkwaardighe mirakelen aldaer geschied A°. 1345* en zijn schrijver." *Bijdragen Haarlem* 43 (1925): 122–86.

———. "De dichter van de versjes in Marius' Amstelredams eer ende opcomen." *De Katholiek*, 165 (1924): 329–34.

———. *De Heilige Stede: De slooping van een middeleeuwsch Amsterdamsch heiligdom in de twintigste eeuw: Geschiedkundige herinneringen.* Hilversum: Gooi & Sticht, 1939.

———. *De Heilige Stede in de geschiedenis van Amsterdam.* 2nd ed. Hilversum: Gooi & Sticht, 1938.

———. "Jacob Cornelisz. en zijne schilderijen in de Kapel ter Heilige Stede." *Oud-Holland* 13 (1895): 193–208.

———. "Kunst van de oude H. Stede te Amsterdam." *Het Gildeboek*, July 1924: 24–32.

———. "Levensbericht van Bernardus Joannes Maria de Bont." *Jaarboek van de Maatschappij der Nederlandse letteren* (1909): 273–91.

———. *De "Mirakelkist" en de traditie: Een bijdrage tot de geschiedenis van het kerkelijk Oud-Amsterdam.* Amsterdam: C. L. van Langenhuysen, 1896.

———. *Onder Amsterdamsche humanisten: Hun opkomst en bloei in de 16e eeuwsche stad.* Hilversum: Paul Brand, 1934.

———. "De opkomst van Aemstelredam, godsdienstig en economisch." *Tijdschrift voor Geschiedenis* 41 (1926): 156–69.

———. "Uit de geschiedenis der H. Stede." *Katholieke Illustratie* 28 (1894–1895): 321–31.

———. *Uit de geschiedenis der Heilige Stede te Amsterdam (De "Nieuwe-Zijds-Kapel"): Mededeelingen over hare kunstschatten, dienst en inrichting.* Amsterdam: C. L. van Langenhuysen, 1898.

Sterck, Jan F. M., H. W. E. Moller, C. R. de Klerk, and R. N. Roland Holst, eds. *De werken van Vondel.* 10 vols. Amsterdam: Maatschappij voor goede en goedkoope lectuur, 1927–1937.

Sterck-Proot, Jo M. "Dr. Johannes Franciscus Maria Sterck." In *Jaarboek van de Maatschappij der Nederlandsche Letterkunde te Leiden, 1940–1941,* 48–56. Leiden: Brill, 1941.

———. "Een wachter bij de H. Stede." In *Het Vierenswaardig Wonder,* 216–23.

Stichter, Johannes. *Oude en nieuwe geestelyke liedekens, op de heylige dagen van het geheele jaer.* Amsterdam: Gerardus van Bloemen, 1724.

Stieler, Joh. F. *Amsterdam's eer en opkomen door de Hervorming: Ter gedachtenis van het 300-jarig eeuwfeest der Hervorming van Amsterdam, 1578–26 Mei–1878.* Amsterdam: J. M. E. & G. H. Meijer, 1878.

Stijl, Simon. *Amsterdam in zyne geschiedenissen, voorregten, koophandel, gebouwen, kerkenstaat, schoolen, schutterye, gilden en regeeringe beschreeven.* Vol. 1. Amsterdam: P. Conradie en V. van der Plaats, 1788.

Stille Omgang Amsterdam 1930–1980, 50 jaar Kring Eindhoven en omstreken. Eindhoven: afd. Stille Omgang Eindhoven, 1980.

"Stille Omgang in Amsterdam." *Catholic World: A Monthly Magazine of General Literature and Science*, no. 835 (1934): 728.

Stuers, Victor de. *Holland op zijn smalst.* Bussum: De Haan, 1975.

Succinta enarratio miraculorum quae gloriose operatus est dominus per venerabile Sacramentum in Sacello sacri loci in Amstelredam, excerpta ex libris et literis per notarios et sigilla confirmatis, in quibus miracula ipsa plenius declarantur. Amsterdam: Guielmus Jacobi, 1555.

Swaving, Justus G. *Galerij van Roomsche beelden of beeldendienst der XIX eeuw.* Dordrecht: Blussé & Van Braam, 1824.

Syvaertsz, Walich (W. S.). *Roomsche mysterien: Ondeckt in een cleyn tractaetgen: alwaer bewesen wert, dat over de leere vande transsubstantiatie by vele doctoren ende gheleerden der Roomsche kercke seer wonderbaerlijc gedisputeert: ende van sommighe wederghesproocken, ende by andere in twijfel ghetrocken is gheweest.* Amsterdam: A. Ianszoon, 1604.

Tanner, Marie. *The Last Descendant of Aeneas: The Hapsburgs and the Mythic Image of the Emperor.* New Haven, CT: Yale University Press, 1993.

Tenhaeff, Nicolaas B. *Bisschop David van Bourgondië en zijn stad: Utrechts-Hollandsche jaarboeken 1481–1483 van de hand van een onbekende, gelijktijdige schrijver.* Utrecht: Oosthoek, 1920.

Teylingen, Augustijn van. *Op-komste der Neder-landtsche Beroerten: Invoeringhe der ketteryen, kerck-schenderyen, ende grouwelycke moorden.* Keulen: Wed. Gasper de Kremer, 1666.

Theissing, Eugenie. *Over klopjes en kwezels.* Utrecht: Dekker & Van de Vegt, 1935.

Thijm, Joseph A. Alberdingk "Het Amsterdamsch geslacht der Dommers." *De Dietsche Warande* 8 (1869): 201–28, 313–35.

———. "Een getuigenis omtrent de Mirakelkist der H. Stede te Amsterdam." *Jaarboekje van Alberdingk Thijm* 41 (1892): LVII.

———. *De Katholieke kerkregeling in ons Vaderland.* Amsterdam: C. L. van Langenhuysen, 1853.

Thomas a Kempis. *Chronica Montis S. Agnetis.* In *Thomae Hemerken a Kempis, Opera omnia*, edited by Michael Joseph Pohl, 7: 331–478. Freiburg: Herder, 1922.

———. *The Chronicle of the Canons Regular of Mount St. Agnes.* Translated by J. P. Arthur. London: Kegan Paul, 1906.

———. *Orationes et meditationes de Vita Christi.* In *Thomae Hemerken a Kempis, Opera Omnia*, edited by Michael Joseph Pohl, 5: 1–463. Freiburg: Herder, 1902

Thomas, Werner. *In de klauwen van de Inquisitie: Protestanten in Spanje, 1517–1648.* Amsterdam: Amsterdam University Press, 2003.

Tilly, Charles. *The Contentious French.* Cambridge, MA: Harvard University Press, 1995.

———. *Popular Contention in Great Britain 1758–1834.* Cambridge, MA: Routledge, 1995.

Toorenenbergen, Albertus van. "Alva's amnestie." In *Voor drie-honderd jaren: Volks-bladen ter herinnering aan de schoonste bladzijden uit onze geschiedenis, 1570*, 63–78. Utrecht: Van Bentum, 1870.

Torre, Jacobus de la. "Relatio seu descriptio status religionis Catholicae in Hollandia." *Archief voor de geschiedenis van het aartsbisdom Utrecht* 10 (1883): 95–240.

Tracy, James D. "A Premature Counter-Reformation: The Dirkist Government of Amsterdam, 1538–1578." *Journal of Religious History* 13 (1984): 150–67.

Trappeniers, Maureen, ed. *Antoon der Kinderen 1859–1925* [catalog]. 's-Hertogenbosch: Noordbrabants Museum, 1980.

Trio, Paul, and Marjan De Smet. "Processions in Town: The Intervention of the Urban Authorities in the Late Medieval Urban Processions of the Low Countries." In *Processions and Church Fabrics in the Low Countries during the Late Middle Ages*, edited by Marjan De Smet, Jan Kuys, and Paul Trio, 5–82. Kortrijk: Subfaculteit Letteren, K.U. Leuven Campus Kortrijk, 2006.

De Triomf van het Mirakelsacrament 1345–1945: Herinneringsalbum 19–23 juni 1946. Amsterdam: Van Munster's uitgevers, 1946.

Vaissier, J. M. "Mirakel-verzen van den Nieuwen Tijd." In *Het Vierenswaardig wonder*, 147–80.

Valk, Hans de. "Caught between Modernism, Pillarization and Nationalism: Dutch Liberals and Religion in the Nineteenth Century." In *Under the Sign of Liberalism: Varieties of Liberalism in Past and Present*, edited by Michael Wintle and Simon Groenveld, 102–15. Zutphen: Walburg Pers, 1997.

———., ed. *Romeinse bescheiden voor de geschiedenis der Rooms-katholieke kerk in Nederland 1832–1914*. Vol. 1. The Hague: ING, 1996.

———. *Roomser dan de paus? Studies over de betrekkingen tussen de Heilige Stoel en het Nederlands katholicisme, 1815–1940*. Nijmegen: Valkhof Pers, 1998.

Valkestijn, Johannes W. N., ed. *Gezangen uit de Occo Codex*. Haarlem: Stg. Ondersteuning Stille Omgang, 2005.

Vanhaelen, Angela. "Utrecht's Transformations: Claiming the Dom through Representation, Iconoclasm and Ritual." *De zeventiende eeuw* 21 (2005): 354–74.

Velde, Henk te. *Gemeenschapszin en plichtsbesef: Liberalisme en nationalisme in Nederland, 1870–1918*. The Hague: Sdu, 1992.

Velde, Henk te, and Hans Verhage, eds. *De eenheid & de delen: Zuilvorming, onderijs en natievorming in Nederland, 1850–1900*. Amsterdam: Het Spinhuis, 1996.

[Veldkamp]. *Stille Omgang, een onderzoek naar de beweegredenen en achtergronden van deelnemers aan een bedevaart*. Amsterdam: Veldkamp/marktonderzoek, 1967.

Verdonck, Jan. "Une procession silencieuse sous la bannière oecuménique." *Septentrion* 24 (1995) 83–85.

Vergara, Alejandro, and Anne T. Woollett, eds. *Spectacular Rubens: The Triumph of the Eucharist*. Los Angeles: J. Paul Getty Museum, 2014.

Verhoeven, Gerrit. "Calvinist Pilgrimages and Popish Encounters: Religious Identity and Sacred Space on the Dutch Grand Tour (1598–1685)." *Journal of Social History* 43, no. 3 (2010): 615–34.

———. "Kerkelijke feestdagen in de late middeleeuwen: Utrechtse en Delftse kalenders." *Holland* 25 (1993): 156–73.

Verkerke, Evert, and Frans Lammers. *Amsterdam Mirakelstad: Van Heilige Stede en Stille Omgang*. Amsterdam: Gezelschap van de Stille Omgang, 1959.

Vermaseren, Bernard A. *De katholieke Nederlandse geschiedschrijving in de 16e en 17e eeuw over de opstand*. Leeuwarden: Gerben Dykstra, 1981.

De verschijningen der Moeder Gods en de wonderbare genezingen te Marpingen aan het katholieke volk verhaald door een pelgrim uit het diocees Paderborn. With a foreword by Bernhard H. Klönne. Amsterdam: Bekker, 1877.

Versluis, Willem G. *Geschiedenis van de emancipatie der katholieken in Nederland van 1795–heden*. Utrecht: Dekker & Van de Vegt, 1948.

Veth, Jan. "Derkinderen's Processie van het H. Sacrament van Mirakel." *Nieuwe Gids*, February 1, 1889.

Het Vierenswaardig Wonder: Gedenkboek uitgegeven ter gelegenheid van het zesde eeuwfeest van het H. Sacrament van Mirakel 1345–1945. Amsterdam: Urbi & Orbi, 1946.

Vijver, Cornelis van der. *Wandelingen in en om Amsterdam*. Amsterdam: J. C. van Kesteren, 1829.

Vis, Jurjen. *Liefde het fundament: 400 jaar Roomsch Catholijk Oude Armen Kantoor in Amsterdam*. Amsterdam: Boom, 2008.

Vis, Jurjen, and Wim Janse, eds. *Staf en Storm: Het herstel van de bisschoppelijke hiërarchie in Nederland in 1853: actie en reactie*. Hilversum: Verloren, 2002.

Visser, Jan. *Rovenius und seine Werke: Beitrag zur Geschichte der nordniederländischen katholischen Frömmigkeit in der ersten Hälfte des 17. Jahrhunderts*. Assen: Van Gorcum, 1966.

Voets, Bert. *Bewaar het toevertrouwde pand: Het verhaal van het bisdom Haarlem*. Hilversum: Gooi & Sticht, 1981.

———. *Blijf, Meester, blijf ons bij: Predikaties gehouden in de mirakelweek 1960*. Amsterdam: Gezelschap van de Stille Omgang, 1960.

———. "Een leider van het Haarlemse bisdom uit de vervolgingstijd: Levensschets van Leonardus Marius." *Haarlemse bijdragen* 62 (1953): 225–305.

———. *De schittering van de kroon: De opbouw van het kerkelijk leven in Amsterdam*. Hilversum: Gooi & Sticht, 1958.

Voets, Bert, and H. van Noord. "Het verhaal van een honderdjarige: De stille omgang begon in 1881." *Ons Amsterdam* 33 (1981): 34–45.

Voorvelt, Cornelius P. "Enkele minder bekende facetten van het leven van de apostolisch vicaris Johannes van Neercassel (1663–1686)." *Trajecta* 5 (1996): 44–55.

[Vos, G. J.]. "Paganistische Ouwel-cultus of Godewaardig gebruik (de Nieuwezijdskapel-historie)." *Marnix, Protestantsche Stemmen* 11 (July/August 1909): 63–125.

Vosters, Simon A. *Het beleg en de overgave van Breda in geschiedenis, litteratuur en kunst*. 3 vols. Breda: Gemeentelijke Archiefdienst, 1993.

Vregt, Johannes F. "De Haarlemsche Noon." *Bijdragen Haarlem* 6 (1878): 405–27.

Vries, Boudien de. "Van deftigheid en volksopvoeding naar massacultuur: Het Amsterdamse verenigingsleven in de negentiende eeuw." *Jaarboek Amstelodamum* 98 (2006): 83–105.

———. "Voluntary Societies in the Netherlands, 1750–1900." In *Civil Society, Associations and Urban Places: Class, Nation and Culture in Nineteenth-Century*

Europe, edited by Graeme Morton, Boudien de Vries, and Robert John Morris, 179–93. Aldershot: Ashgate, 2006.

Vries, Marina de. "Twee minuten lang stilstaan bij de doden: De betekenis van de Overveense Stille Tocht in de jaren '80." In *Feestelijke vernieuwing in Nederland?*, edited by Jeremy Boissevain, 15–26. Amsterdam: Meertens Instituut, 1991.

Wagenaar, Jan. *Amsterdam in zyne opkomst, aanwas, geschiedenissen* etc. 3 vols. Amsterdam: I. Tirion, 1760–1767.

————. *Vaderlandsche historie vervattende de geschiedenissen der Vereenigde Nederlanden, inzonderheid die van Holland.* . . . Vol. 11. Amsterdam: Isaak Tirion, 1754.

Walters, Barbara R. "The Feast of 'Corpus Christi' as a Site of Struggle." In *Il "Corpus Domini": Teologia, antropologia e politica*, edited by Laura Andreani and Agostino Paravicini Bagliani, 139–54. Firenze: SISMEL/Galluzzo, 2015.

Walters, Barbara R., Vincent Corrigan, and Peter Ricketts. *The Feast of Corpus Christi*. University Park, PA: Penn State University Press, 2006.

Weijling, Johannes F. A. N. *Bijdrage tot de geschiedenis van de wijbisschoppen van Utrecht tot 1580*. Utrecht: Van Rossum, 1951.

Weissman, Adriaan W. *De Nieuwe Zijds Kapel*. Amsterdam: L. J. Veen, 1908.

Wetering, Wilhelmus van. *Leer- en lofrede tot bevestiging van de waare, weezenlyke, en eigenlyk gezegde tegenwoordigheid van Jesus Christus in het Hoogwaardigste Sacrament des Autaers, uit de woorden der instelling: Dit is mijn ligchaam. Gepredikt op het beggynhof te Amsterdam, op den 17 maart des jaars 1773. Ter gelegenheid van de jaarlyksche gedachtenisse, en plechtige feestvieringe van het Hoogwaardig, heilig, en aanbidlyk Amsterdamsche Wonder-Sacrament*. Amsterdam: Theodorus Crajenschot, 1773.

Wieck, Roger S. "The Sacred Bleeding Host of Dijon in Choir Books and on Posters." In *Manuscripten en miniaturen: Studies aangeboden aan Anne S. Korteweg bij haar afscheid van de Koninklijke Bibliotheek*, edited by Jos Biemans, Klaas van der Hoek, Kathryn M. Rudy, and Ed van der Vlist, 385–96. Zutphen: Walburg Pers, 2007.

Wiele, Stalpart van der. *Gulde-Iaers Feest-daghen of Den Schat der geestlycke Lof-Sanghen Gemaeckt op Elcken Feest dagh van 'tgeheele Iaer*. Antwerp: Cnobbaert, 1635.

Willebrands, Jan, *Rede ["De Eucharistie, Sacrament der Eenheid"] gehouden door z.n. Exc. Mgr. J. G. M. Willebrands op de jaarvergadering van het Gezelschap van de Stille Omgang te Amsterdam, op Zondag 15 januari 1967*. Amsterdam: Gezelschap Stille Omgang, reprint 2006.

Willemsen, Michaël A. H. *Het zilveren jubelfeest van Zijne Heiligheid Paus Pius IX, gevierd te Maastricht van 16 tot 21 juni 1871*. Maastricht: Henri Bogaerts, 1873.

Wingens, Marc. *Over de grens: De bedevaart van katholieke Nederlanders in de zeventiende en achttiende eeuw*. Nijmegen: SUN, 1994.

Winkelmeyer, Jos. *Geschiedenis van het H. Sacrament van Mirakel en van de Kapel de H. Stede, benevens het verhaal van de merkwaardige Wonderen geschied tot ao. 1578*. Amsterdam: G. Borg, 1886.

Witlox, Joannes H. J. M. *De Katholieke Staatspartij in haar oorsprong en ontwikkeling geschetst*. 3 vols. Den Bosch: Teulings / Bussum: Brands, 1919–1969.

————. *Studien over het herstel der hiërarchie in 1853.* Tilburg: Henri Bergmans, 1928.

Wolf, Henderikus C. de. *De kerk en het Maagdenhuis: Vier episoden uit de geschiedenis van katholiek Amsterdam.* Utrecht: Spectrum, 1970.

Woltjer, Jan Juliaan. *Tussen vrijheidsstrijd en burgeroorlog: Over de Nederlandse Opstand, 1555–1580.* Amsterdam: Balans, 1994.

Wonderdoeners en aflaatkramers in de 19de eeuw: Eene parallel der 16de en 19de eeuw, als een teeken des tijds, uitgelokt door de bedevaart naar Trier, derzelver bevorderaars en bestrijders, en inzonderheid door het geschrift: Johannes Ronge, de katholieke priester en de slechte drukpers. Amsterdam: Weijtingh & Van der Haart, 1845.

Xanten, Harry J. van. *"Katholieken, wat zijt Gij toch een wonderlijk volk!" De Katholiekendagen in Nederland 1899–1940.* Nijmegen: Valkhof Pers, 2007.

De Zalige Dood: Handboekje voor de leden van de Broederschap van den Zaligen Dood. Opgericht 30 oct. 1666 in de kerk van den H. Franciscus Xaverius (Krijtberg) Amsterdam. 2nd ed. Amsterdam: H. J. Koersen, 1915.

Zeij, Jac. J. *Vondel's Altaargeheimenissen in dertien lezingen uitgelegd.* 's-Hertogenbosch: Teulings, 1924.

Zeijden, Albert van der. *Katholieke identiteit en historisch bewustzijn: W. J. F. Nuyens (1823–1894) en zijn "nationale" geschiedenis.* Hilversum: Verloren, 2002.

Zuidema, Willem. *Het wonder der Heilige Stede van Amsterdam.* 2nd ed. Amsterdam: Protestantsche Boek- en Brochurehandel, 1925.

Zuthem, Jonn van. *"Heelen en halven": Orthodox-protestantse voormannen en het "politiek" antipapisme en in de periode 1872–1925.* Hilversum: Verloren, 2001.

Index of Names

Index of Places

Charles Caspers is an expert in the field of popular devotions, spirituality, liturgy, and mission history. Together with Peter Jan Margry he published a four-volume study on pilgrimage sites in the Netherlands. He is a senior fellow of the Titus Brandsma Institute in Nijmegen.

Peter Jan Margry is professor of European ethnology at the University of Amsterdam and a senior fellow at the Meertens Institute. He is the editor of *Shrines and Pilgrimage in the Modern World: New Itineraries into the Sacred*.

9 780268 105655